TWIN POPULIST REFORM WARRIORS 500 YEARS APART

TWIN POPULIST REFORM WARRIORS 500 YEARS APART

Martin Luther & Donald Trump — Astonishing Similarities

PASTOR PAUL F. SWARTZ

gatekeeper press™
Tampa, Florida

The views and opinions expressed in this book are solely those of the author and do not reflect the views or opinions of Gatekeeper Press. Gatekeeper Press is not to be held responsible for and expressly disclaims responsibility of the content herein.

The author does not take responsibility for editing inconsistencies that appear in the text nor in the footnote citations regarding form, capitalization, and punctuation other than those the author has specifically noted with asterisks indicating personal preferences.

Twin Populist Reform Warriors 500 Years Apart: Martin Luther & Donald Trump -- Astonishing Similarities

Published by Gatekeeper Press
7853 Gunn Hwy, Suite 209
Tampa, FL 33626
www.GatekeeperPress.com

Library of Congress Control Number: 2022938510

ISBN (hardcover): 9781662923821
ISBN (paperback): 9781662923838
eISBN: 9781662923845

Dedication

To those I have been privileged to journey alongside, through pleasant green pastures of nurturing and under the beautiful blue skies of encouragement:

> My wife and children,
> parents and family,
> teachers and pastors,
> friends and critics.

I thank God for all these people He sent into my life who gave their best so that I could experience more fully His love embracing me and the hand of Christ and His Spirit leading me!

Table of Contents

Illustrations

Abbreviations for Footnote Citations

The following abbreviations are used in this book's footnotes as sources for direct quotations from the works of Martin Luther and from the various translations of The Bible, and Hymnals referenced.

LUTHER'S WORKS

WA	*D. Martin Luthers Werke: kritische Gesamtausgabe* (Weimar: Hermann Böhlau, 1883). 61 vols. (Also known as *Weimarer Ausgabe* or the Weimar Edition)
Web	*D. Martin Luthers Werke: Briefwechsel* (Weimar: Hermann Böhlau, 1930-). 18 vols.
WATr	*D. Martin Luthers Werke: Tischreden* (Weimar: Hermann Böhlau, 1912-1921). 6 vols.
WT	*D. Martin Luthers Werke: Kritische Gesamtausgabe,* Tischreden, 6 vols.
LW or AE	*[American Edition of] Luther's Works,* eds. J. Pelikan and H. Lehmann (St. Louis and Philadelphia: Concordia and Fortress, 1955ff). 56 vols.
St. L.	*Dr. Martin Luthers Sammtliche Schriften,* ed. Johann Georg Walch (St. Louis and Philadelphia: Concordia and Fortress, 1881-1910). 23 vols.

BIBLES

NRSV	*The Holy Bible,* New Revised Standard Version, eds. Bruce M. Metzger and Roland Murphy (New York: Oxford University Press, 1991)
KJV	*The Holy Bible,* King James Version
RSV	*The Holy Bible,* Revised Standard Version

PME *The Holy Bible,* Phillips Modern English

NIV *The Holy Bible,* New International Version

WEB *The Holy Bible,* World English Bible

NEB *The Holy Bible,* New English Bible

HYMNALS

LBW *Lutheran Book of Worship,* Inter-Lutheran Commission on Worship, (Minneapolis: Augsburg Publishing House, and Philadelphia: Board of Publication, Lutheran Church in America, 1978).

ELW *Evangelical Lutheran Worship,* (Minneapolis: Augsburg Fortress Publishers, 2006).

LW *Lutheran Worship,* Commission on Worship of the Lutheran Church—Missouri Synod, (St. Louis: Concordia Publishing House, 1982).

LSB *Lutheran Service Book,* Commission on Worship of The Lutheran Church—Missouri Synod. (St Louis: Concordia Publishing House, 2006).

Prologue

It all started back when I was seven or maybe eight years old. Intrigued by the offer on a cereal box for free stamps, my parents not only permitted me to send for them but assisted me in completing the "coupon" on the box top, and even provided the three-cent stamp to mail it. Perhaps part of the rationale was that it would occupy me and keep me out of Mom's hair for a while, since I had a twin brother and three older siblings who obviously kept our mother quite occupied.

Collecting U.S. stamps became my hobby at an early age, going through all the mail and tearing off the stamps, and seeking out other "free offers." Then a couple of women who were philatelists, members of our church, living less than a block away, took an interest in me. They happily mentored me with their stamp collecting expertise, providing me with every new stamp the U.S. Postal Service (USPS) issued, plus lots of cancelled stamps they saved for me. I was and still am fascinated with the individuals portrayed, the background behind the buildings and objects depicted, as well as the scenery pictured on a stamp. My wife cannot understand my appreciation for "those little pieces of paper" which I consider works of art, that present windows into the world in which I live. My U.S. collection has expanded throughout the years, and today it is quite extensive.

Then, in 1983, the USPS issued a stamp commemorating Martin Luther—showing him wearing his academic cap as an educator, not a Church* reformer—to celebrate his 500th birthday. Being a Lutheran pastor, I decided it would be interesting to see what the rest of the world did philatelically with honoring the Great Reformer, thus combining my vocation with my avocation. Today, my specialized collection of Reformation/Martin Luther philatelic material fills over 50 albums. It then occurred to me that perhaps the best way to preserve the collection would be to write a history of the life and times of Luther. In a book underway, entitled *A Life Stamped, Cancelled and Delivered—Illustrated Philatelically*, my research led me to some fascinating and uncanny observations.

* I use the capitalized "Church" to signify the world-wide Church, the Body of Christ, inclusive of all believers, as opposed to localized congregations which I will refer to as "churches" or "church buildings."

Those discoveries revealed similarities between Martin Luther and someone else with whom I was familiar: Donald Trump. I began making notations for an article I intended to write, but soon found myself immersed in writing an entire book, the one you're now holding.

Who "has an orangish complexion and an oddly coiffed hairstyle?" Who "is an outsider?" Who "has taken on the establishment…?" Who "has embraced new media platforms to communicate directly to the population?" Who uses "language that cuts against political correctness and resonates with ordinary people?"[1] To these questions which Paul Hender asks in a blog, I add: Whose rhetoric, foul language, and methods of communicating have been deemed inappropriate for the position held? Who has acted contrary to long-accepted norms and practices for the roles they play? Whose positions attacked injustices perceived in the existing state of affairs, leading to deep divisions? For Hender, it is Martin Luther. For me it is both **Martin Luther and Donald Trump—Twin Populist Reform Warriors…500 Years Apart!**

When I suggest similarities between Donald Trump and Martin Luther, I am not making a comparative assessment based on their faithfulness to God, nor on the level of their Biblical knowledge or depth of theological understanding, nor even their devotion and passion to purity in ecclesiastical matters. They are not identical twins, but there are enough similarities (which we will explore throughout this book) that the longer you view the ways they resemble each other, even in comparing the context and events of the times in which they lived, the more closely they begin to look alike too!

[1] Hender, Paul, "A New Media Reformation?" <https://www.gorkana.com/2017/11/paul-hender-opinion-a-new-media-reformation>.

1

Populism: Disrupting The Privileged Elite Establishment

It will be helpful in this analysis to be clear on what we mean by "populism." A dictionary definition reads: "Support for the concerns of ordinary people, or the quality of appealing to or being aimed at ordinary people." Politically, that appeal has had reference to those who feel exploited, or who have had their concerns disregarded by the established privileged elite. Populists can be leftist, rightist or centrist. No identifiable economic or social set of conditions give rise to it, nor is it confined to any particular social class.[2] As we will discover in the similarities I note, we will detect both Donald Trump and Martin Luther wooing alienated publics and taking their side against an elitist establishment to restore and reform, not overthrow, the established order.

In our present time, it is popular to contrast "populism" with "democracy" when in fact the two are more alike than different. Like the Reformation of 500 years ago, populist movements aim to wrest power from the elites and give it back to the people as we have witnessed in Trump's candidacy and presidency. As a matter of fact, both "*demos*" and "*populus*" derive from the words for people in Greek and Latin. Populism is really a democratic phenomenon which aims to bring power back to the people. In a real sense "populism" is the authentic voice of democracy but, as with all forms of politics, it can become toxic. Through propaganda, manipulation in "fake news" and censorship of social media, truth is not only sacrificed, but often becomes its casualty.

The word "Protestant" born out of the Reformation was an appropriate description of the people who protested because they wanted their sacred status returned to them. The real story of populism is an account of enlightenment and liberation. It is the story we have claimed living in a democracy striving toward a "more perfect union" with its ever-widening promise of a decent life for all. Yet while claiming to champion the common good and especially empowering the disenfranchised, the behavior and interests of entrenched autocrats, politicians, and the "privileged" elite who feel they need to tell the people what and how to think starts to collide with the hopes they have fostered and the values they had

[2] <http://evangelicalfocus.com/blogs/2241/Was_Luther_a_populist_Jeff_Fountain>.

symbolized. Such elitist groups of "experts" have reliably detested true populism which, at its core, is the language of promise and optimism.

Appealing to the Populace

The Church Times

Adweek

One of the remarkable things about researching an iconic, historic individual as complex, perplexing, charismatic, bruising, paradoxical, appalling, appealing, and intriguing as Martin Luther is the discovery of new insights. One can pick almost any adjective, good or bad, and invariably apply it to the German Reformer at one time or another in his turbulent life. These revelations often impart deeper significance to the person than mere hero status ascribed or portrayed in a saintly bronze statuary figure over which a halo or other sign of divine favor has been suspended. Often portrayed as otherworldly, religious personages are easily elevated to canonization in our minds with the allurement of making these "saints" more spiritual than God. "Luther cuts a perplexing historical figure," Elizabeth Bruening notes in a 2017 article in *The Nation*. "In various depictions, [Luther] is by turns fiery or meek, bombastic or shy, licentious or pious, revolutionary or reactionary, cunning or naively bewildered by what his high-minded remonstrance unleashed in the world."[3]

Pulling back the hagiographic* legends that have shielded Luther's flaws and failings reveals a human who struggled as we all do with the challenges of life, one's own identity and purpose, as well as one's destiny here and now, and for eternity.

---

[3] Bruenig, Elizabeth, "Luther's Revolution," *The Nation*, July 12, 2017. <https://www.thenation.com/article/martin-luthers-revolution>.

*The idolizing or idealization of an individual or event in language that is excessively flattering , such as with saints or other past historical figures or occurrences.

2

Comfortable Living in One's Own Skin

In all my years of studying and preaching the "Reformation faith," I have never fully made the connection between the Reformation Gospel text of John 8:31-36 with the Ninety-Five Theses Luther is credited with posting on the Wittenberg Castle church's door 500 years ago: *"If you continue in My Word*,"* Jesus says in verse 31 (NRSV), *"you are truly My disciples and you will know the Truth, and the Truth will make you free!"* Obviously, by offering His questioners freedom, Jesus implies that they (and we) are not free.

Luther prefaced the Ninety-Five Theses with these words, revealing his motivation: "Out of love for the Truth and the desire to bring it to light."[4] Immediately, his attention is to the idea of penance being those outward acts of going to Confession and completing the tasks prescribed by the priest for having sinned. Alternatively, in his day, one could skip all the "to-dos" through the simple purchase of an indulgence. An important distinction became clear when Luther examined the original Greek text of Matthew 4:17, which had been mistranslated as "*do penance*" instead of "*Repent.*" Repentance is a whole-souled heart change that results in outward acts of obedience. The mistranslation had set up a domino effect that tragically led Church practice in the wrong direction. The enslaving question which Luther personally found haunting was whether he had ever "done" enough to cancel out his sin and merit salvation. In Luther's time, Rev. V. H. H. Green[†] affirms succinctly that there "was a widespread 'salvation anxiety' …manifested in an intense hyperactive, performance of piety."[5] People were concerned about how to assure their place in heaven.

---

* I use the capitalized "Word" throughout this book as an intentional reference to Christ, who was the summation and content of Scripture for Luther, and when it specifically is referencing God in the Scriptures as the Word of God. Likewise, I capitalize personal pronouns referring to Jesus or Christ.

[4] LW 31:25. *Career of the Reformer I*, "Ninety-Five Theses."

[†] Rev. Vivian H.H. Green was a Fellow and Rector of Lincoln College, Oxford, an Anglican priest, author, teacher and historian.

[5] Green, V.H.H., *Renaissance and Reformation: A Survey of European History between 1450 and 1660* (London: Arnold, 1982 [reprinted]), p.43.

David Lose—author, former President of Luther Seminary in Philadelphia, PA, and now Senior Pastor of Mount Olivet Lutheran Church in Minneapolis, MN—provided meaningful understanding of this in his weekly column, "In the Meantime," for Reformation Sunday in 2017. He was struck by the fact that "the first of Luther's Ninety-Five Theses is about repentance: 'When our Lord and Master Jesus Christ said, "*Repent*" (Mt. 4:17), He willed the entire life of believers to be one of repentance.'" Dr. Lose goes on to explain that:

> We're not all that big on repentance these days, but some of that might be our confusion about what it actually means. And that's not new. Luther goes on to say that by repentance he's actually not talking simply about confession and penance as administered by the clergy (2nd Thesis), or an inward, cathartic kind of feeling-really-bad moment (3rd Thesis). Rather, true repentance for Luther is a kind of truth-telling that allows you to be honest about how you are deceiving yourself or letting yourself be deceived by the world (or both!), that gives you an opportunity to think and speak and act differently. Or, to put it another way, to live in freedom.
>
> Jesus' invitation to freedom however, demands an act of repentance as truth-telling before it hits home and does its saving work because it demands that we come clean about our need, which isn't easy for self-made men and women to admit…. The truth of which Jesus speaks is actually two truths, first about us and then about God's response to us. Which means that His promise of freedom will sound more like bad news before it's good news.[6]

Alcoholic recovery literature of the '70s rings true with the similar saying, "The truth will set you free, but first it will make you feel miserable."[7]

Luther was one who indeed hated the word "righteous" when it referenced God, because he knew that, by himself, he was not able to obtain that status to qualify his standing before such a holy God, and that no amount of indulgences, good works, good intentions, status updates, or social media "likes" can redeem any of us. His penitential exercises only intensified his sense of unworthiness. He became a virtuoso self-examiner, boring his confessor Johann von Staupitz with lengthy soul searching, by trying to remember every sin

---

[6] Lose, David J.; "Reformation Sunday: The Truth About the Truth," *In the Meantime*, October 25, 2017. <http://www.davidlose.net/2017/10/reformation-sunday-the-truth-about-the-truth>.

[7] <https://quoteinvestigator.com/2014/09/04/truth-free>.

his mind would try to cover up. Martin Marty, Lutheran scholar, pastor, author and professor at the University of Chicago Divinity School, reports that Staupitz, an ordained listener, once "had to sit for six hours, listening to Luther being hyper-scrupulous and searching and gabby, [when] his patience wore out, and in one remembered counsel made the real point of Christian confession by negative reference: 'Martin, you don't have to confess every fart.'"[8] His father-confessor could not understand Luther's obsessive brooding over faults which were trivial, too slight to be taken seriously. Whenever Luther did feel satisfied that he had finally done enough and confessed enough, he would hear a voice saying, "Well done, brother Martin! Soon you will not need God at all."[9]

The Father Confessor Who Loved Luther

Luther in Monastery

Johann von Staupitz

Images: LutheranFormation.org, TimeToast.com

Luther dreaded every mention of the "righteousness of God" in Scripture, even in the passage that affirms "the righteous shall live by faith" (Romans 1:17 [KJV]), stating, "I did not love, yes I hated the righteous God who punishes sinners, and secretly, if not blasphemously, certainly murmuring greatly, I was angry with God.... Thus I raged with a fierce and troubled conscience."[10] He had a burning desire to understand what St. Paul meant, but his eyes were drawn not to the word "*faith*" but to the word "*righteous*." He

---

[8] Marty, Martin, "Inconclusive Conclusion," *Mentoring for Ministry: The Grace of Growing Pastors*, eds. Craig T. Kocher, Jason Byassee, and James C. Howell (Eugene, OR: Cascade Books, 2001), p.119.

[9] Pelikan, Jaroslav, "The Enduring Relevance of ML 500 Years after His Birth," *New York Times Magazine*, September 18, 1983.

[10] LW 34:336-37. *Career of the Reformer IV*, "Preface to the Complete Edition of Luther's Latin Writings."

understood, as he was taught "according to the custom" of the teachers, that God Himself is righteous, and He not only judges but punishes the unrighteous sinners. As a result, young Luther was internally and mentally terrorized, understanding clearly that Biblical teaching of his wretchedness before a holy God proved he could not live by faith. He knew all too well that he was not righteous, and therefore could never be accepted. Luther was an individual tangled up in the nets of his certainty and uncertainty, bluster and fear, trust and doubts about God—all at one and the same time, each bubbling up in startling and often confusing mixtures. He is obviously a real person struggling to find his way forward as he seeks to discover the reassuring message of the Christian faith. All Scripture stood like a wall, until he was enlivened by the words *"the righteous shall live by faith."*

Luther recalls what is often referred to as his "Tower Experience" when the Scripture's meaning of "*righteous*" and "*righteousness*" was graciously unveiled to him by the Holy Spirit, who opened his eyes and enlightened his heart and mind:

> The words '*righteous*' and '*righteousness of God*' struck my conscience like lightning. When I heard them, I was exceedingly terrified. If God is righteous [I thought], He must punish. But when by God's grace, I pondered, in the tower and heated room of this building, over the words, *that 'He who through faith is righteous shall live'* [Romans 1:17, RSV] and '*the righteousness of God*' [Romans 3:21 RSV] soon came to the conclusion that if we, as righteous men, ought to live from faith and if the righteousness of God should contribute to the salvation of all who believe, then salvation won't be our merit but God's mercy. My spirit was thereby cheered. For it's by the righteousness of God that we're justified and saved through Christ. These words [which had before terrified me] now became more pleasing to me. The Holy Spirit unveiled the Scriptures for me in this tower.[11]

Luther had been thinking of "*righteousness*" as a quantity of goodness he needed to accumulate and offer to God; but now viewing Scripture in a different light, he discovered that "*righteousness*" was indeed a quality that God gave freely on account of Christ. The peace of heart and mind that he so desperately craved came through the words of the Apostle Paul, as he experienced the "embrace of Grace." Justification by grace implied for Luther

---

[11] LW 54:193-94. *Table Talk*, "Description of Luther's Tower Experience, No.3232*e*."
See also *Table Talk*, Smith and Gallinger edition [Pilgrim Press, Boston, 1915; modern paperback editing by Keats, USA, 1979], p.131.

that he was liberated from the constant need to justify himself not only in his own eyes or in the eyes of his neighbor, but most critically in the eyes of God. Instead, he discovered he was now totally at liberty to fully love God and his neighbor!

The relevance of that Reformation insight has not faded over the last five hundred years. Michael Reeves, President and Professor of Theology at Union School of Theology in England, writes:

> The answers to the same key questions still make all the difference between human hopelessness and happiness. What will happen to me when I die? How can I know? Is justification the gift of a righteous status (as the Reformers argued), or a process of becoming more holy (as Rome asserts)? Can I confidently rely for my salvation on Christ alone, or does my salvation also rest on my own efforts toward success in achieving holiness? [Reeves emphasizes that the Reformation was not just a reaction to some problem of the day]—not principally a negative movement about moving away from Rome and its corruption [but] it was a positive movement, about moving toward the Gospel. And that is precisely what preserves the validity of the Reformation for today.[12]

The truth Luther re-discovered for the Church through his study of God's Word, and from his personal experience, is that we are broken human beings. We encounter the reality of our human condition as we are confronted with our mortality, finitude, and vulnerability. Pastor Lose reminds us that the problem is not sins, as in the quantity, but that "we *are* sinners—God's fallen, at times flailing, regularly confused, and always imperfect children—from birth to death."[13] I am a sinner and God is holy. This is why Luther sometimes declared that he hated God, and incidentally why we are prone to despise or hate those who succeed where we have failed, or when others rise above those we have favored:

> But, [Lose continues,] "here's the second truth-bearing Good News—we are also those sinners, who are simultaneously God's beloved children, those sinners who God calls blessed, and holy and perfect, those sinners for whom Christ died, those sinners whose futures are not determined by their regrets

[12] Reeves, Michael, "Reformation Still Matters," *Table Talk*, 2017. <https://tabletalkmagazine.com/article/2017/10/reformation-still-matters>.

[13] Lose, David J., "Reformation Sunday: The Truth About the Truth."

> and mistakes, but rather by the possibility created by resurrection, those sinners whom God loves above all else. We are not perfect…and we don't have to be in order to be loved. But it's hard to trust that we're really loved—let alone the experience of freedom that comes from knowing we are loved and accepted—if we're not honest first.[14]

Luther writes in the preface to the first volume of his collected works another remembrance of that "Tower Experience," or incandescent moment of profound religious insight that came to him while sitting on the toilet. As a result of

> meditating day and night, I gave heed to the context of the words…and began to understand that the righteousness of God is that by which the righteous lives by a gift of God, namely by faith…. Here I felt that I was altogether born again and had entered paradise itself through open gates. There a totally other face of the entire Scripture showed itself to me…I extolled my sweetest word with a love as great as the hatred with which I had before hated the word, "righteousness of God."[15]

This theological epiphany led Luther to understand that the "merciful God justifies us by faith." God did not demand, God gave! The "*righteousness of God*" was not the justice which God required of us sinners—a performance in accordance with the absolute standards of the law—but rather was the free and unmerited gift by which God made us sinners acceptable through Christ, so that all we needed to do was to accept our acceptance. The idea of "Justification by Faith Alone," he famously claimed, "struck him like a thunderbolt."[16]

This is none other than remembering both halves of St. Paul's mighty words: first the difficult truth that "*all have sinned and fall short,*" and then the blessed news that "*they are now justified by His grace as a gift…*" (Romans 3:23-24 [NRSV]). For Luther, this understanding was succinctly immortalized in his theological concept "*Simul Justus et Peccator,*" which means we are "simultaneously righteous and sinners." Here, Luther discovered the truth that sets one free…free to be who one is without pretense, or to be comfortable in one's own skin. Luther was honest enough with himself to acknowledge that that truth should inform

---

[14] Ibid.

[15] LW 34:337. *Career of the Reformer, IV*; "Preface to Luther's Latin Writings."

[16] Crane, David, "The Man Who Changed the World," review of *Martin Luther: Renegade and Prophet*, by Lyndal Roper, *The Spectator*; <https://www.spectator.co.uk/article/the-man-who-changed-the-world>.

and inspire behavior, but recognized honestly how human failure always intervenes. That enlightening truth still has the capacity to change lives, the Church, politics, and indeed the whole world...if we're honest!

The Freed One

Luther, or rather Luder, was born to Hans and Margarete Luder on November 10, 1483, and was baptized the following day, the feast day of Martin of Tours. The proud parents followed a well-established practice by naming their child after the saint on whose day he was baptized. As Luder became aware of the breakthrough he had experienced, Heinz Schilling* notes:

> He developed a different sense of self as he grasped the life's task that had fallen to him. (Luther never doubted that God had called him to be His prophet.) His newly recognized relationship with God had made him a new person, a man who felt himself emphatically free. He gave expression to this new self-consciousness in a new name. Between November 1517 and January 1519, he signed letters to close friends...with the designation *'Eleutherios.'* Ostensibly Luder had adopted a Greek form of his existing name, as was common amongst humanists, to produce a scholarly pseudonym. But the new name carried a distinct message, for it expressed the mission of its bearer: *'Eleutherios,'* the free one—the one who had been liberated, and, at the same time, the one who would liberate. As it became clear that Luder would not remain simply a scholar or a man of the Church, but had been sent, as it were, for the salvation of all mankind...[17]

He later abandoned the name which he had taken as an emblem of his rebirth as an evangelical, as it was incomprehensible to most people. However, he preserved a reminder of the freedom that was at the heart and kernel of his theology, the central "*th*" in the Greek, as in "Theos" for God who freed him. Martin Luder then became Martin Luther,

---

* Heinz Schilling was Professor of Early Modern History at Humboldt University, Berlin until his retirement in 2010.

[17] Schilling, Heinz, *Martin Luther: Rebel in an Age of Upheaval* (Oxford, UK: Oxford University Press, 2017), p.139.

as we now know the Reformer, who believed he was called to lead a movement we call the Reformation, that would lead others into the freedom he now enjoyed.

And that got me to thinking about Donald Trump. Here was someone who "made it," as the world so often renders its judgment. He didn't need the perks, money, stature and power that a role in politics affords so many. He already had "it" all. He was at the top. He wasn't in the pocket of anyone. He didn't owe anyone anything. And most of all, he was free from being the puppet of elite patrons. He was free to be himself, obviously comfortable with himself, and not afraid to have his failures and shortcomings exposed, unlike so many others who work so hard to hide the image of who they actually are, getting elected by projecting a spurious persona. Perhaps because of all of that, he just might be a different kind of leader and head a movement to "Make America Great Again."

Throughout the campaign, I began seeing similarities emerge between Donald Trump and Martin Luther who I was researching,* and began appreciating the new and more honest—and indeed, insightful—scholarship being given *The Man Who Rediscovered God and Changed the World*, the subtitle of Eric Metaxas' 2017 book on Martin Luther.

Looking back at that historic time in our observance of the 500th anniversary of the Reformation in 2017, Professor and Historian Peter Marshall at Warwick University, England, offered a timely caution in a *TIME* magazine article: "I suppose the danger with anniversaries is that they can serve to reinforce myths and entrenched narratives of the past, rather than..."[18] encourage us to look afresh at historical events and processes. Many well-known scenes and famous stories in Luther's life appear now to be urban legends while other newly revealed events and circumstances expand and enrich our understanding and perception of the individual being studied.

It is my experience within the Church that we are particularly adept at treating the Biblical narrative in much the same manner as we do anniversaries. We know the story, especially of heroes who are bigger than life, because that's what we were taught; but we're not as clear as to the story's meaning or significance of how God chose to use those individuals or events in the furtherance of His mission. Memorials and narratives are meant

---

* U.S. stamp collecting is a hobby of mine, and with the 500th commemoration of Luther's birth in 1983, I began collecting world-wide Luther/Reformation philatelic material from which I intend to illustrate the coming book *A Life Stamped, Cancelled and Delivered*, thus combining my vocation as a Lutheran pastor with my avocation.

[18] Marshall, Peter, quoted in "Martin Luther's 95 Theses Are 500 Years Old. Here's Why They're Still Causing Controversy" by Billy Perrigo, TIME, October 31, 2017; <http://time.com/4997128/martin-luther-95-theses-controversy>.

to hold far more meaning than simply commemorating an anniversary or noting an event that may be remembered far differently from the way it happened in reality.

We know, too, how easy it is to lose the individual as a human being with frailties when we look back from a historical distance, and thus forget that God chooses to work through sinners—always has and always will! That's a spiritual benefit we reap when we recognize the faults of our heroes: If God can work through such sinners, surely He can work through us too!

3

Attacking the Past to Control the Present

It is just as tempting to interpret past events through the lens of modern values and concepts, and thus divorce them from their unique historical context. We are currently witnessing the cultural bias of "presentism" as an attractive tendency that gives uncritical adherence to present-day attitudes, while applying fragile sensitivities when interpreting past events. As past events are evaluated in terms of modern values and concepts in presentism, we risk having a distorted understanding of the subject or event in its time and place. For example, the accomplishments of George Washington, the commander-in-chief of the Colonial armies and the first President of the United States, and Thomas Jefferson, draftsman of the U.S. Declaration of Independence and the third American President, have been disregarded in modern times and their legacies reduced to one fact only: they owned slaves. Former Arlington, Virginia, Mayor Richard Greene reminds us that twelve U.S. presidents owned slaves, eight of them while they were in office.[19]

James C. Robbins examines the current cultural effects of the widespread Orwellian attempt to expunge our ancestors' contributions and history in *Erasing America: Losing our Future by Destroying Our Past.* Sounding a lot like a party slogan from George Orwell's *1984* nearly 70 years ago ("He who controls the past controls the future; he who controls the present controls the past") is a quote often misattributed to him: "The most effective way to destroy people is to deny and obliterate their own understanding of their history." Along with that same thought, George MacDonald Fraser, author of the "Flashman" novels, "thinks little of people who will deny [or destroy] their history because it doesn't present the picture they would like."[20]

As Robbins insightfully contemplates the recent removal of various Confederate markers and memorials, and now stained-glass windows in the National Cathedral, he reveals a movement attempting to demean, demolish, and relentlessly attack America's past to control the present. Bill Martinez, reviewing this book on his nationally syndicated talk radio show

---

[19] <https://www.star-telegram.com/opinion/opn-columns-blogs/richard-greene/article27547456.html>.

[20] Fraser, George MacDonald, "The Last Testament of Flashman's Creator: How Britain has Destroyed Itself," *Daily Mail*, UK, January 5, 2008; <https://www.dailymail.co.uk/news/article-506219/The-testament-Flashmans-creator-How-Britain-destroyed-itself.html>.

on October 1, 2018, declared: "This toxic movement has already brainwashed an entire generation and is rapidly changing the cultural, historical, and spiritual bonds of our nation. American exceptionalism, history, and patriotism are a magnificent legacy, Robbins warns, but to pass it on to our children, we must view the past with understanding, the present with gratitude, and the future with hope."[21] However, Robbins sadly observes:

> The United States is divided between factions of people who may as well be living in different countries. In some respects, they already do. They have separate histories, cultures, and visions for the future. They are two distinct nationalities, divided by mutual distrust.... Politics has become a chaotic mud pit where old norms of compromise and respect for the law have been discarded in the unrestrained pursuit of power. And the time-honored tradition of American exceptionalism is being replaced with a dreary story of a misbegotten country founded on slavery and oppression by deeply flawed men who have been falsely elevated as heroes.[22]

Robbins goes on to contrast what he sees as the maturity of the past with the shallowness of our times. There is a prevalent belief operative in our society that we should feel embarrassment instead of pride for our country's history and

> do penance before the gods of political correctness for their national sins. The assault on the past is based not so much on the facts of history as on its supposed meaning. Those who take pride in America emphasize stories that reflect the best about our country and inspire hope for the future. Progressives seek to demean and demolish, elevating the victims of the past as an indictment of the present. They wield history as a weapon on behalf of the aggrieved, never gratified by the progress made. Indeed, as one supposed injustice after another is rectified, their attacks become fiercer, their complaints more numerous, and the retrograde American patriot is intimidated into silence. All our classic national touchstones are scrutinized through an unforgiving moral lens which grotesquely magnifies every flaw.

---

[21] Martinez, Bill, review of James Robbins' *Erasing America: Losing Our Future By Destroying Our Past*, October 1, 2018; <https://billmartinezlive.com/products-page/books/james-robbins-erasing-america-losing-our-future-by-destroying-our-past; or <https://www.bookpeople.com/book/9781684511679>.

[22] Robbins, James S., *Erasing America: Losing Our Future by Destroying Our Past* (Washington, DC: Regnery Publishing, 2018), pp.1-2.

> The attack extends to the national anthem, the American flag, and other symbols of nationhood.[23]

Reviewing Robbins' book, Linda Wiegenfeld, a retired teacher with 45 years of experience teaching children, laments the tearing down of traditional history and lack of civics education. She endorses Robbins' premise with her own assessment: "And with the growing intolerance for the exchange of ideas in our colleges and universities, basic knowledge of American identity has become confused. Students no longer know what America stands for. In fact, students are becoming more aware of what divides us than what unites us."[24] Robbins contends,

> Standards and frameworks based on the common understanding of history no longer exist. Ideas that were perfectly acceptable even a few years ago are now met with unhinged vitriol. Commonplace facts meet withering criticism and charges of political incorrectness. Traditional American reverence for the Founders and American symbols are recast as racist nationalism. The progressives want to eradicate the premises that formed the basis of American civic life for decades, even centuries. In so doing they have declared war on those who value American history and its unifying purpose. …Indeed, those who talk about rebuilding the traditional vision of the country are dismissed as hopelessly backward. "Church…family…police…military…the national anthem…Trump trying to call on all the tropes of 1950s-era nationalism," MSNBC's national correspondent Joy Reid tweeted out during the 2018 State of the Union speech. "The goal of this speech appears to be to force the normalization of Trump on the terms of the bygone era his supporters are nostalgic for."[25]

A couple of examples serve to illustrate the Robbins' thesis. After four years of war and tremendous damage to the South, Ulysses S. Grant drafted practical terms for peace because he wanted to unite the country again. "At Lee's request, Grant even allowed Confederates who owned their own horses to keep them so they could tend their farms and plant spring

---

[23] Ibid., p.3.

[24] Wiegenfeld, Linda, book review of *Erasing America* in *The Epoch Times*, October 15, 2018; <https://www.theepochtimes.com/book-review-erasing-america-losing-our-future-by-destroying-our-past_2684895.html>.

[25] Robbins, *Erasing America*, p.8; His quote ends with a tweet from Joy Reid, <https://twitter.com/JoyAnnReid/status/958528313563254784>.

crops... 'The war is over;' Grant told his staff, 'the rebels are our countrymen again.'"[26] The compromise that prevailed at Appomattox was the fervent desire of people in 1865—in the North and the South—and the priority of President Lincoln to unite and heal a house divided.

A surprising account of Robert E. Lee was told by a former state senator and Texas Land Commissioner, Jerry Patterson; that Lee declared, five years before the Civil War began, that he believed slavery was a moral and political evil. Acting on his convictions, he freed his inherited slaves long before there was a Confederacy.[27] Consistent with Lee's character, Jay Winik describes a beautiful event in his bestseller, *April 1865: The Month That Saved America*. A few weeks after his surrender at Appomattox, Lee attended worship at St. Paul's Episcopal Church in Richmond, Virginia, where he was a member. When worshipers gathered for Holy Communion, the tradition at the time was that black worshipers were required to wait in the balcony until whites had communed. When the priest invited people to come to The Lord's Table this time, however, a black man attired in a suit quickly arrived at the altar rail from the west gallery as an equal and knelt to receive the sacrament. No one knew what to do. The people were stunned. The pastor was stumped. Everyone froze. Within seconds, however, Robert E. Lee

> arose, his gait erect, head up and eyes proud, and walked quietly up the aisle to the chancel rail.... With quiet dignity, he knelt to receive communion with the black man.... Watching Robert E. Lee, the other communicants followed his faith, going forward to the altar, and with a mixture of reluctance and fear, hope and awkward expectation [walked] into the future.[28]

Reconciliation that month of April 1865 emerged in the form of Robert E. Lee. Just as his field commanders had been led by him into battle, the residents of the former capital of the Confederacy now followed him into the promise of the "Great Emancipator," Abraham Lincoln, whose famous words in his second inaugural address attempted to bring healing to the wounds of a divided nation, words which could serve as guidance for today:

> With malice toward none, with charity for all, with firmness in the right as God gives us to see the right, let us strive on to finish the work we are in, to bind up the nation's wounds, to care for him who shall have borne the battle and for his widow and his orphan, to do all which may achieve and cherish a just and lasting peace among ourselves and with all nations.[29]

---

26 <https://www.smithsonianmag.com/smithsonian-institution/gentlemans-agreement-ended-civil-war-180954810>.

27 <https://www.star-telegram.com/opinion/opn-columns-blogs/richard-greene/article27547456.html>.

28 Winik, Jay, *April 1865: The Month That Saved America* (New York: Harper Perennial, 2002), pp.362-363.

29 Lincoln, Abraham, "Second Inaugural Address;" <https://www.bartleby.com/124/pres32.html>.

Tearing Down Statutes

Heretic Effigy **Slave-Owning Presidents**

Martin Luther

President Andrew Jackson

President Thomas Jefferson

(Left) Martin Luther on top of a Column of Heresy: In 1520, Pope Leo X issued the bull *Exsurge Domine* that condemned Luther's Protestant views as heretical. A year later, at the Diet of Worms, on 17th April 1521 Luther was summoned to either renounce or reaffirm his views. He refused to retract, and on 25th May Luther was officially an outlaw. Pictured is Bernard of Luxemburg's popular *Catalogue of Heretics* that shows Luther on top of a 'Column of Heresy.' Catholic iconography is evident: while the heretic listens to the hot air bellowed into his ear by a winged demon, two other monsters below prepare to pull him with a chain into the flames of hell. Bernard described the Reformer Martin Luther as a fool, a piece of garbage, and a "toad of the Apocalypse," calling for the use of the secular sword in defense of the Church.

Image: Bernard of Luxemburg Catalog of Heretics Bernard of Luxemburg, Catalogus Hereticoru[m] (Cologne: Peter Quentel, 1526, Shoults Gb 1526 B.) <https://www.otago.ac.nz/library/exhibitions/luther>, and Catalogus Haereticorum (Cologne: Eucharius Cervicornus and Gottfried Hittorp, 1523, BRA0326) <https://www.smu.edu/Bridwell/SpecialCollectionsandArchives/Exhibitions/Luther/Controversies/BRA0326>

(Center) Statute of Andrew Jackson in D.C.'s Lafayette Square Pulled Down: During the summer 2020 protests, riots swept the nation, led by the Black Lives Matter movement in response to the death of Minneapolis resident George Floyd at the hands of the police. They demanded the removal of monuments and statues which they attacked, defaced with graffiti, and in many cases pulled down. Those of Confederate leaders were specifically targeted, along with those of U.S. Presidents who were slaveholders.

Image: REUTERS/Joshua Roberts Business Insider <https://www.businessinsider.com/andrew-jackson-statue-men-tried-tear-down-2020-6>

(Right) Statute of Thomas Jefferson in front of Portland's Jefferson High School: Thomas Jefferson, one of the Founding Fathers, has come under intense scrutiny over his seemingly contradictory history as the principal author of the Declaration of Independence while being a large slave owner. Jefferson was credited with writing 'all men are created equal' into the U.S. Constitution, but during his life he owned more than 600 slaves. Although he referred to slavery as 'moral depravity,' by 1782 Jefferson had become the largest slaveholder in Albemarle County, Virginia.

Image: Express Digest <https://expressdigest.com/thomas-jefferson-statue-brought-down-by-portland-protesters>

I find the current trend of defacing, destroying or removing monuments that were erected to honor our heroes, and changing the names on buildings and streets to deprecate these significant persons in our history, a dishonest approach to history's realities. Because a statue is removed, will there no longer be any remembrance of that person or event? History will always be there. Along with Robbins, I agree that "history is better served by adding than subtracting [heroes] from the American story."[30] Early in his book, Robbins explains why history matters:

> History is the source of all life's lessons, the good and the bad. We turn to history to see what to embrace and what to avoid.... It is also the storehouse of meaning and the wellspring of inspiration. The past is where we find our heroes and heroines, our stories of struggle and triumph. We look back to see forward, to trace our national destiny, to reinforce the idea that America has a purpose.[31]

George Santayana's original form of the quote we know as "Those who do not learn history are doomed to repeat it," actually reads, "Those who cannot remember the past are condemned to repeat it."[32] We look back to see forward with greater clarity. Often, we'll discover complex and long forgotten ideas and values that are germane to current events. Ignorance about our past, on the other hand, will lead to arrogance about the future. I find it helpful to be aware of the many people from the past who have built the place where I stand and have contributed to what I am privileged to enjoy, as I reach toward the future on a foundation formed by their witness, sacrifice and service. Those remembrances trace and give evidence to our national destiny, and reinforce my faith in the ideals upon which America was born.

The great German theologian and philosopher of the twentieth century, Ernst Troeltsch, wrote more than a century ago,

> The Present continually hovers before the backward looking glance, because it is by the aid of analogies drawn from the life of today—however little this may be consciously before the mind—that we reach the causal explanation of the events of the past. But what is still more important is that we always, either

---

[30] Robbins, *Erasing America*, p.79.

[31] Ibid., p.4.

[32] <https://bigthink.com/the-proverbial-skeptic/those-who-do-not-learn-history-doomed-to-repeat-it-really>.

> voluntarily or involuntarily, relate the course of past events to the complex of effects which lies before us in the present, and that we are constantly drawing either special or general conclusions from the past and making use of them in our task of shaping the present with a view to the future.[33]

Unfortunately, on many issues we are witnessing the stripping of meaning out of language and ideas. Love listens to the story behind the story. Our first service to others is to listen; but in our nation, we seem to have stopped listening to others. We have difficulty taking or seeing an individual life in context, and thus prohibit ourselves from empathizing. Instead, we are prone to devalue those who are also created in the likeness of God.

> Compromise has become a dirty word in these uncompromising times [according to Robbins]. But our political system, built on checks and balances, cannot function without it. The genius of the Founders was their insistence that many interests be balanced in the course of governing. They had little faith in universal theories of public good and even less in the power of flawed human beings to construct flawless societies. The more the utopian spirit dominates politics, the less will get done and the more problems will accumulate. James Madison famously observed that government is necessary because "men are no angels." ...This uncompromising posture widens the cleavages in American society, leaving a small group of radicals with outsized power and influence. These are the people Donald Trump referred to in his acceptance speech at the 2016 Republican National Convention when he said, "America is a nation of believers, dreamers, and strivers that is being led by a group of censors, critics, and cynics."[34]

Likewise, Luther's later alliance with the princes against the peasants, after he had supported their grievances, can appear to be not only callousness but adulteration of the Gospel, as were his anti-Semitic outbursts, especially without understanding the story behind the stories. As a result, Luther too has become as controversial in the twenty-first century as he was in the sixteenth.

---

[33] Troeltsch, Ernst, *Protestantism and Progress: A Historic al Study of the Relation of Protestantism to the Modern World*, trans. W. Montgomery (New York: G. P. Putnam's Sons, 1912), p.1-2.

[34] Robbins, *Erasing America*, p.9, quoting Donald Trump. <https://www.vox.com/2016/7/21/12253426/donald-trump-acceptance-speech-transcript-republican-nomination-transcript>.

4

God's Ways and Choices Are Not Always Our Ways and Preferences

In the Kingdom of God, we learn things are often upside down by our standards. The strong are called weak and the weak are strong. As St. Paul explains: *"But God chose what is foolish in the world to shame the wise; God chose what is weak in the world to shame the strong"* (1 Corinthians 1:27 NRSV). No one understood this more profoundly than Martin Luther, who could not, no matter how hard he tried—and try he did—please God in order to earn the Divine One's love and acceptance.

Recognizing his limitations, yet discovering God's gracious call, Luther became fully aware that God knows how to use the foolish and the weak to give Him glory and to extend His mission into the world He loves. It has always been like this: Abraham, the father of Israel, pimped his wife and was old; Moses, who led the people out of Egypt, was a murderer; Isaac lied; Jacob was a cheater; Elijah was depressed; Jonah was disobedient; David, the greatest king in all of Israel, lusted, committed brazen adultery, and sent his military leader into battle to be killed so he could have his widow (and yet David was acclaimed by God as *"a man after My own heart"* [1 Samuel 13:14, Acts 13:22 (NIV)]); Zacchaeus was a thief; the Samaritan woman was divorced five times and living with another man; Peter denied Jesus; Timothy was sick; Lazarus was dead; Saul, who became Paul, persecuted Christians. But none of these seeming flaws or negative characteristics were obstacles to God, who used these people in their weakness and struggles. God didn't write them off! How I rejoice that I'm not written off either by my sins, flaws or weaknesses! There is not even an attempt in the Bible to cover up the tragic flaws of these wayward sinners! Neither has there been an effort by Jews or the Church to revise and "clean up" the Biblical narrative by removing the "warts" of unsavory characters on display, as seems to be a prevailing cultural trend today.

Without going into the nuances and complexity of Apocrypha ("hidden") texts surrounding the Old and New Testament formation of the canon ("rule or measure") of Scripture, suffice it to say there were other "holy" books circulating amongst God's people. The Old Testament Apocrypha writings are more familiar due to the division between the Roman Catholic church and Protestant churches when, at the Council of Trent (1546), fourteen books including 1 & 2 Maccabees, 1 Esdras, Judith, Tobit, the Wisdom of Solomon, Sirach (Ecclesiasticus), and Baruch were officially regarded as Scripture by the Roman Catholic church. Luther had included these writings in a separate section in his German translation of *Die Bibel* between the Old and New Testaments. He prefaced the Apocrypha with his famous quotation, "These Books Are Not Held Equal to the Sacred Scripture but Are Useful and Good to Read."[35] He even saw them as worthy of being read as *anagignoskomena* (read aloud before those who gathered for worship), but they should not be used to define or create doctrine.

One of the primary reasons these books were viewed as secondary is the fact that neither Jesus nor the apostles referred to or quoted from them. In addition, neither Josephus nor Philo—key sources for our understanding of the scope of the Old Testament canon—used them as Scripture, and later rabbinic writers did not receive the Apocrypha, affirming only the Hebrew Scriptures already canonized which early Christians accepted from their Jewish forbearers.

New Testament Apocrypha refers to an array of books that look similar to and, indeed, imitate our New Testament writings in both style and genre, often falsely composed in the name of revered Apostles (*pseudepigrapha*). Within many of them lies a natural curiosity about the childhood of Jesus, tending to make Him a constant and effective miracle worker from the very beginning. *The Gospel of Thomas* "records" perhaps the most popular of these exaggerated miracles of young Jesus forming a bird ("sparrow") from the mud or clay by the water's edge and throwing it into the air where it flew away as a "real" bird to the jealousy and consternation of his playmates.[36] Other "apocryphal acts circulated in early Christianity, often with eccentric and embellished stories such as a dog talking, a man (Simon Magus) flying, a lion being baptized, [and even "gossipy" or excessive talk on trivial matters] including the *Acts of Paul*, the *Acts of John*, and the *Acts of Peter*."[37]

The amount of apocryphal material is overwhelming such as is our "fake news" and the "hyperbole" used to dramatize an account the "fact-checkers" can quickly dismiss or past video tapes discredit. Most of these dubious writings are dated to the second or third century or later and have no genuine claim to apostolic authorship. More importantly, many contain

---

[35] Brecht, Martin, Martin *Luther Vol. 3: The Preservation of the Church 1532-1546*, James Schaaf, trans. (Philadelphia and Minneapolis: Fortress Press, 1993) p.98.

[36] <https://www.gotquestions.org/infancy-Gospel-of-Thomas.html> and <https://thevcs.org/open-unexpected/jesus-raises-clay-birds>.

[37] Kruger, Michael J, "The Apocrypha," The Gospel Coalition. <https://www.thegospelcoalition.org/essay/the-apocrypha/>.

doctrines that are out of accord and contradict the rule of faith that has been passed down to the early Church. The Church's intent was to insure and present "inspired" Truth from God, and the Church's reception of a book as inspired became a sign that it is such.

I find it strikingly awesome that God saw fit in the process of delivering His Word and Truth, to preserve the memory of those He used to accomplish His purposes, including those parts we would probably rather forget or omit from the Sacred Scriptures "*delivered to the saints*" (Jude 1:3 NKJV) through the Church's discernment of His Spirit.

Nevertheless, there are many, including well-intentioned Christians, espousing self-righteous views that Trump's character should disqualify him from holding the most powerful position in the world. They highlight given "flaws" that under scrutiny may come to light in their own lives. It is always easy to point out the failures of others, especially past failures, while we conveniently ignore our own. I recall Jesus saying something very specific about this human behavior with regard to splinters and planks (Matthew 7:5). In the mind of John Witte, Jr.,* Professor at Emory University School of Law in Atlanta, Georgia, Luther accurately held the doctrine of the two-fold nature of the Christian person:

> Each person is at once a saint and a sinner, righteous and reprobate, saved lost—*simul iustus et peccator*[38] ...We are at once body and soul, flesh and spirit, sinner and saint, "outer man and inner man." These "two men in the same man contradict each other" and remain perennially at war.[39] ...On the one hand, as bodily creatures, we are born in sin and bound by sin. By our carnal natures, we are prone to lust and lasciviousness, evil and egoism, perversion, and pathos of untold dimensions.[40] ...Even the best of persons, even the titans of virtue in the Bible—Abraham, David, Peter, and Paul—sin all the time.[41] ...In and of ourselves, we are totally depraved and deserving of eternal death.

---

* John Witte, Jr. is an award-winning teacher, distinguished scholar, editor of the Cambridge Law and Christianity Series and *The Journal of Law and Religion*, long-serving director of the Center for the Study of Law and Religion (CSLR), and the series editor of the Emory University Studies in Law and Religion. The following footnote sources (38-44) are those Witte uses in the two paragraphs I quote from his article/lecture, "God is Hidden in the Earthly Kingdom," to cite Luther's writings. See footnote 44.

[38] LW 31:344-347, 358-361. *Career of the Reformer I*; "The Freedom of a Christian." See also LW 12:328; LW 27:230 ff., *Lectures on Galatians 5-6;* LW 32:173, *Career of the Reformer II;* WA 39/1:21, 492, 552.

[39] Ibid., LW 31:344. *Career of the Reformer I;* "The Freedom of a Christian."

[40] LW 31:344, 358-361, *Career of the Reformer I;* see also LW 25:120-130; and Luther's *Lectures on Romans,* trans Wilhelm Pauck (Philadelphia: Westminister Press, 1961), pp. 204-213.

[41] LW 19:47-48, *Commentaries on Minor Prophies II;* LW 23:146, *Sermons on Gospel of St. John 6-9.*

> On the other hand, as spiritual creatures, we are reborn in faith, and freed from sin. By our spiritual natures, we are prone to love and charity, goodness and sacrifice, virtue, and peacefulness. Even the worst of persons, even the reprobate thief nailed on the cross next to Christ's, can be saved from sin. In spite of ourselves, we are totally redeemed and assured of eternal life.[42]
>
> It is through faith in the Word of God, Luther argued, that a person moves from sinner to saint, from bondage to freedom. This was the essence of Luther's doctrine of justification by faith alone. No human work of any sort—even worship, contemplation, meditation, charity, and other supposed meritorious conduct—can make a person just and righteous before God. For sin holds the person fast, and perverts his or her every work. "One thing, and only one thing, is necessary for Christian life, righteousness, and freedom," Luther declared. "That one thing is the most holy Word of God, the Gospel of Christ."[43] To put one's faith in this Word, to accept its gracious promise of eternal salvation, is to claim one's freedom from sin and from its attendant threat of eternal damnation. And it is to join the communion of saints that begins imperfectly in this life and continues perfectly in the life to come. But a saint by faith remains a sinner by nature, Luther insisted, and the conflict of good and evil within the same person remains until death.[44]

Luther was a master of the dialectic, meaning he could hold two doctrinal opposites in tension while proceeding to explore ingeniously the intellectual power of this tension. We encounter this within our Christian tradition by such opposites as spirit and flesh, soul and body, faith and works, heaven and hell, Law and Gospel, sinner and saint, servant and lord.

As Christians Luther sees us at once both a lord who is subject to no one, and a priest who is servant to everyone. Being redeemed and gifted with faith by God's love and forgiveness expressed in Christ's action for us, we freely serve our neighbors, offering instruction, charity,

---

[42] LW 31:344-354, 368-377; *Career of the Reformer I.* "The Freedom of a Christian."

[43] Ibid., LW 31:345, *Career of the Reformer I.*

[44] *Luther: Lectures on Romans (1515-1516)*, trans. Wilhelm Pauck (Philadelphia: Westminister Press, 1961), p.120. See also LW 23:146; LW 12:328-330; LW 8:9-12. The above references to Martin Luther in footnotes 37-44 are cited by footnote designations in the quoted two paragraphs from John Witte's article "'God is Hidden in the Earthly Kingdom: The Lutheran Two-Kingdoms Theory as Foundation of Scandinavian Secularity." <https://ssrn.com/abstract=2517719> or <https://www.researchgate.net/publication/291196418>.

prayer, admonition, and sacrifice. We freely discipline and drive ourselves to do as much good as we are able, not that we may be saved, but that others may be served and experience God's love for them through us. We live for others which is our best witness to the One who has served us. St. Paul entreats us:

> *If you have any encouragement from being united with Christ, if any comfort from His love, if any fellowship with the Spirit, if any tenderness and compassion, then make my joy complete by being like-minded, having the same love, being one in spirit and purpose. Do nothing out of selfish ambition or vain conceit. Rather, in humility value others above yourselves, not looking to your own interests but each of you to the interests of the others.* (Philippians 2:1-4 NIV)

TIME Covers of Reform Warriors

Martin Luther
March 24, 1967
https://content.time.com/time/covers/0,16641,19670324,00.html

Donald Trump
December 19, 2016
<https://time.com/3742509/donald-trump-time-person-of-the-year-horns/>

In the cover story of Luther and the 450th anniversary of the Reformation, *TIME* magazine draws attention to this "human saint" whose complex paradoxes defy easy characterization:

> A limpid preacher of God's majesty and transcendence, he was capable of a four-letter grossness of language [that matched or exceeded Trump's, which we will explore later]. He was the archetype of individual Christian assertion; yet he could be brutally intolerant of dissent and acquiesced in

> the suppression of those he considered heretics. Prayerful and beer-loving, sensual and austere, he was the least saintly, but most human of saints.[45]

Many individuals have identified with some of those less flattering descriptions of Luther attributing them to President-elect Trump. Social Media was abuzz with comments about *TIME'S* annual "Person of the Year" on Dec 7, 2016 showing "devil horns" with the two black triangles under the red M of the *TIME* logo. Some wondered whether it was intentional, but research shows that 37 covers appear to give people horns. Even Luther suffered the indignity, albeit with smaller horns on *TIME*. As we will discover, both twins have been characterized as being the Devil.

It may surprise many readers that we have several Biblical accounts of how God even used nonbelieving pagan agents and leaders like Cyrus the Great, King of Persia, as His vessels. In this sixth century B.C. historic event to execute His divine plan, the exiled Jews were enabled to return to their homeland after 70 years of captivity as the Persians under Cyrus conquered Babylonia. The suggestion by some that Donald Trump is a modern-day Cyrus was significantly enhanced by the administration's decision to move the U.S. embassy from Tel Aviv to Jerusalem. It was further underscored with supporting reference from the Prime Minister of Israel, Benjamin Netanyahu, heavily implying Trump was Cyrus's spiritual heir.

Raised Up for Divine Purpose

King Cyrus the Great President Donald Trump
www.israel365news.com/103700/global-support-third-temple-coin/

The "Half Shekel" Temple coin contributed to the upkeep of the Temple in ancient times. The current coin was minted by the Israeli Educational Center to recognize the end of 70 years of Babylonian captivity after Nebuchadnezzar II had invaded the ancient Kingdom of Judah, taking prominent Jewish inhabitants into exile. The Persians under Cyrus, who is mentioned in several books of the Bible, conquered Babylonia and allowed the Jews to return to their ancestral homeland and rebuild the temple destroyed by Nebuchadnezzar. The connection between the two figures, recognized leaders of

---

[45] "Protestants: Obedient Rebel," *TIME*, March 24, 1967, 89:12, p.71.

the global superpowers of their respective times, is that they were both generous to the Jews, Cyrus permitting Jews to return to Israel and Trump formally recognizing Jerusalem as the capital of Israel, with the move of the U.S. Embassy from Tel Aviv. The '70' also reminds us of the seventieth commemoration of President Harry S. Truman being the first leader to recognize the Jewish State on May 14, 1948. While there are nearly 200 countries in the world today, Jewish tradition refers to global humanity as the '70 nations' to whom Israel was commissioned to be a light that the *"Lord's salvation may reach to the end of the earth"* (Isaiah 49:6 [NRSV]).

That historical comparison with an echo of an ancient emperor and the decision about recognizing Jerusalem as Israel's capital gave many evangelical Christians a compelling narrative in reconciling Trump's personal behavior (womanizing, multiple divorces, alleged sexual assaults and use of unflattering language) with what they could rationalize as his divinely ordained purpose to restore a Christian America. Instead of having to justify their views of Trump's controversial past or use of language, they can say his presidency was arranged by God and thus legitimize their support of someone who advocates policies that advance their point of view or agenda.

New York Archbishop Timothy Dolan captures the essence of the book currently in your hands through his op-ed in the *Wall Street Journal* of June 28, 2020, "Even the Bible Is Full of Flawed Characters." He begins by sharing an early experience in dedicating a new parish to St. Peter. He received a protest from a woman who wrote:

> 'Why would you name a Church after such a coward, a sinner who denied even knowing the Lord when Jesus needed him most, at the hour of His arrest and crucifixion?' Knowing her and what parish she was from, I wrote back. 'But you're a proud parishioner at St. Mary Magdalene Church. She was sure not a paragon of virtue for a chunk of her life. Yet, by God's grace, she became a radiant, inspirational saint. If we can't name churches after sinners, the only titles we'd have left would be [those that refer to Jesus, such as Savior, Redeemer, Lord, and King].'[46]

And then the archbishop asks, "Isn't the same true of America's historical personalities? All of them had flaws, yet all of them still contributed a lot of good to our nation's progress."[47]

---

[46] Dolan, Timothy, "Even the Bible is Full of Flawed Characters," *Wall Street Journal*, June 28, 2020. <https://www.wsj.com/articles/even-the-bible-is-full-of-flawed-characters-11593370160>.
[47] Ibid.

Or for an even more dramatic example, consider St. Matthew's genealogy of Jesus, the very Son of God, which extends roughly 840 years, and contains whores, pagans, pariahs and adulterers, and ends with the Virgin Mary! This is nothing less than the "intersection of incompatibles," the scandalous mystery of incarnation where "human imperfection meets divine perfection." Nowhere is there stronger evidence that God indeed chooses to use flawed human beings like Luther, Trump, even you and me, in His service through the cultures and times of then and now, to participate as partners in His plans and purposes.

God Uses Whom He Chooses

Do Not Be Afraid, I Am with You
I Will Strengthen and Uphold You

Jesus' Presence with Luther
By He Rice Tanned
angelfire.com/nyr/dhw/hrt.html
<https://www.angelfire.com/ny4/djw/hrt.html>

You Are Not Alone Mr. President
The Lord Thy God Is with You Always

Jesus' Presence with Trump
By Danny Hahlbohm
<https://pixels.com/featured/you-are-not-alone-danny-hahlbohm.html>

Two recent essays re-enforce this remarkable understanding of God's involvement in the lives of His ordinary and imperfect people. One is attributed to Karen Vaughn, mother of Aaron Vaughn, Navy SEAL, killed in action on August 6, 2011, entitled "The Salty Sailor and the Fireman."

Sometimes God uses the no-nonsense, salty sailor to get the job done. Appreciating what the man is doing doesn't mean we worship the salty sailor or even desire to be like the salty sailor. It doesn't even mean God admires the salty sailor. Maybe He just knows he's necessary for such a time as this.

I believe with all my heart that God placed that salty sailor in the White House to give this nation one more chance in November 2016. Donald Trump is what he is—and he is still the man he was before the election—and without guilt. I very much admire what that salty sailor is accomplishing.

He's not like me. That's okay with me. I don't want to be like him. I will never behave like him. I know we've NEVER had a man like him lead our nation before. It's crazy and a little mind-blowing at times. But I can't help admire the stamina and ability he has—acting with his heart rather than a calculated, PC, think tank-screened, carefully edited script. I still believe that is WHY he became our President and WHY he's been able to handle a landslide of adversity and STILL pass unprecedented amounts of good legislation for our country AND do great works for MANY other nations, including Israel.

I'm THRILLED with what he's doing for my nation, for the cause of Christ (whether intentional or unintentional, doesn't matter to me), and for the concept of rebuilding America and putting her FIRST. I will not be ashamed of my position because others don't see him through the same lens.

Should it matter to me if a fireman drops an f-bomb while he's pulling me from a burning building? Would I really care about what came out of his mouth in those moments? Heck no! I'd CARE about what he was DOING. He wasn't sent there to save my soul and I'm not looking to him for spiritual guidance. All I'm thinking in those moments is, "Thank you, Jesus, for sending the fireman."

This man is crass. Okay. He's not careful with what he says. Okay. You feel offended that he's not a typical statesman. Okay. But he is DOING THE JOB of rebuilding the nation my son died for...the nation I feared was on a

> fast track to becoming a hopeless cause. Forgive me if I'm smiling. KAREN VAUGHN.[48]

Then the *Houston Chronicle* and the *Dallas Morning News* reported that U.S. Energy Secretary and former Governor of Texas Rick Perry had claimed Donald Trump God's "chosen one" to lead the nation, comparing the President to several Old Testament kings who were flawed:

> I happen to believe that God used, you know, individuals who aren't perfect all through history...Donald Trump's not perfect. And I think the Christian teachings and the Christians that are around him in his cabinet and in his life are very important. And I hope I've been a bit of a minister, if you will, a person who's been able to share my faith with the President.... None of us got here by accident. I'm a big believer that the God of our universe is still very active in the details of the day-to-day lives of government.[49]

These testimonies from Perry and Vaughn reflect the sentiment of that familiar quote emanating from the Scriptures' teachings in 1 Corinthians 1:27-29, Exodus 4:10-13, Romans 9:11-12, and Hebrews 13:21: "God doesn't call the qualified. He qualifies the called." Luther, in his exposition of Psalm 118, references Daniel 4:17 and 5:21 (RSV): "*The Most High God rules over the kingdom of men and sets over it whom He will*," not whom *we* will. In Luther's words, "Daniel is simply saying that temporal government is purely and solely a gift and grace of God, which no man can establish or maintain by his own wisdom or strength."[50]

In all the accounts of national governance in Scripture, and all the stories of Israel's kings I have studied, I've never discovered God demanding moral perfection of those he thrusts into leadership roles. Even most of the Judges were deeply flawed vessels who God conscripted and empowered by his Spirit, and who through heroic acts of momentary reliance on God were able to accomplish His will (cf. Hebrews 11). Most, however, were

---

[48] Vaughn, Karen, "The Salty Sailor," *Bear Witness Central*, August 1, 2020 (written Feb. 8, 2018). <https://bwcentral.org/2018/02/the-salty-sailor>.

[49] Perry, Gov. Rick, quotes in *Dallas News* and the *Houston Chronicle*; <https://www.dallasnews.com/news/politics/2019/11/25/rick-perry-says-god-chose-both-trump-and-obama-to-be-president-says-great-leaders-have-flaws>; <https://www.houstonchronicle.com/news/politics/texas/article/Rick-Perry-says-Trump-is-God-s-chosen-one-14860699.php>.

[50] LW 14:54. *Selected Psalms III*, "Psalm 118."

not models of political leadership or virtue upon which to lavish praise, as much as they provide an honest look at deeply flawed individuals who God used in spite of themselves.

I share this perspective because in making the comparison between these twins, I am in no way presuming to know the heart and soul of the President's faith relationship to God by suggesting similarities with Martin Luther who has shared much about himself in this realm of faith. I am merely lifting up how our faith acknowledges an omniscient God whose ways are not our ways, and who can often work His purposes through those we'd never imagine as well as those who at times have difficulty practicing that which they proclaimed.

5

The Times They Are a-Changin'

Bob Dylan recorded his anthem-like hit song, "The Times They Are a-Changin'," in October 1963, less than two months after the March on Washington for Jobs and Freedom, which had occurred at the end of August. Written in the style of Biblical prophets, there are in the verses what one could infer as many Scriptural references from the prophets and John the Baptist, though without contradiction those phrases could function also as banner slogans, not only for peaceful anti-war protesters but also for revolutionaries. We associate the cultural context of the Sixties with the rise of the civil rights movement, the counter-culture movement, the anti-Vietnam War protests, emerging environmental awareness, the war on poverty, the start of the space race to the moon, the upcoming gay rights movement, and an outburst of feminism. However, the song is not a protest song. As Kees de Graaf puts it, we receive a prophecy, but without any preaching about what ought to be.

> We are simply told that the times will change and that we have to accommodate to and accept the new order or else we will drown and perish...change is inevitable and there is nothing one can do to stop it... At one time Dylan himself used these words as a banner for his theological stance. In a stage rap during a concert in the fall of 1979 Dylan said: 'I told you "The Times They Are a-Changin'" and they did. I said the answer was "Blowing in the Wind" and it was. I'm telling you now Jesus is coming back, and He is! And there is no other way of salvation.'[51]

Let's begin our exploration, then, by viewing the similarities of the times that were "a-changin'" when both Luther and Trump stepped out onto the world's stage. When one looks back on The Reformation, you cannot dismiss the apocalyptic climate the people of Luther's day were experiencing. They feared the end of times and thought that the Apocalypse was on the horizon. For Luther, the Last Day was at hand, and the Devil

[51] de Graaf, Kees, "Bob Dylan's 'The Times They Are A-Changin' – an analysis;" <https://www.keesdegraaf.com/index.php/241/bob-dylans-the-times-they-are-a-changin-an-analysis-by-kees-de-graaf>.

was insidiously at work, everywhere and potentially in everyone—through the Pope, the Emperor, and teachers. Luther's intent was not to start a new church, or for that matter to split the old one, but to protect the faithful from the jurisdiction of a corrupt papacy. For Luther, control of the papal office had been seized by the evil one, and thus became the agency through which a last furious attempt was being made to reverse the victory of the Cross and the Resurrection by attacking the faith from inside the Church.[52]

Albrecht Durer and Lucas Cranach both illustrated through their paintings and woodcuts the unfolding of St. John's prophecy in the Book of Revelation. The coming of the Antichrist was variously identified with the "Turks" and the threatening Ottoman expansion into Europe, the Anabaptist and "fanatic" Thomas Müntzer, and of course the Pope himself, who was the primary target of the reformers. It was an uneasy world, filled with scary spirits. "No other generation in Germany," according to Heinz Schilling, "has likely been so preoccupied with death and salvation as was that of the late fifteenth and early sixteenth centuries."[53]

In the visual arts and literature, concerns about the afterlife—reconciliation with God or the never-ending torments in the abyss of hell—found new introspective expressions. Devils, witchcraft, and the Dance of Death appeared as the fears of the age, in grotesque forms and surreal paintings that the modern mind dismisses as superstitions. Nevertheless, these anxieties about salvation, the end of time heightened by the apparently unstoppable advance of the Turks, deadly plagues, plus the fear of hellfire, were real and an ever-present possibility—all of which permeated the mind and spirit of both Luther and the populace in his time.

Much has been written and is still being written about our own times and the epidemic of anxiety disorders. Australian social researcher Hugh Mackay, who has been recording the way we live for the last 50 years, has dubbed our present time an "Age of Anxiety." He writes, "We have been plunged into a period of unprecedented social, cultural, political, economic, and technological change in which [our] way of life is being radically redefined."[54] All the old certainties have been turned upside down, and the only thing we are told we can rely on is an ever-increasing acceleration in change. "Since the early 1970s," Mackay continues, "there is hardly an institution or a convention of [our] way of life which has not been subject to serious challenge or radical change. The social, cultural, political, economic

[52] See Scott Hendrix's insightful analysis, "The Controversial Luther." <https://wordandworld.luthersem.edu/content/pdfs/3-4_Luther/3-4_Hendrix.pdf>.

[53] Schilling, *Upheaval*, p.34.

[54] MacKay, Hugh, *Reinventing Australia* (Pymble: Angus and Robertson, 1993), p.6.

landmarks which we have traditionally used as reference points for defining [our] way of life have vanished or been eroded or shifted."[55] People are awash in a sea of uncertainty. The anxiety epidemic manifests itself in high levels of stress, changes swirling faster and faster around us, living on a short fuse, drug abuse, domestic violence, distrust of institutions, and concentration on surviving, not dreaming about the future. People of The Reformation era were experiencing what we are presently witnessing: living through an age of redefinition—transitioning from the Medieval Age to the beginnings of the Modern Age. Indeed, "Times They Are a-Changin'!"

The European economy in the late fifteenth and early sixteenth centuries was improving for the first time in centuries, as a result of trade and new technologies, much like the upswing we are experiencing in the United States. Carl Raschke, Professor of Religious Studies at the University of Denver, makes the claim, so suggestive of those critical of the recent tax cut legislation, that

> the benefits were only accruing to the very wealthy entrepreneurial families and mercantile magnates of urban Europe, especially those of the Italian states. By the same token, this "one percent" also controlled the politics of the Church and exploited popular folk beliefs concerning heaven and hell to extract more than a regular pound of flesh from the masses of uneducated commoners. The violent and bloody peasant wars that erupted during the 1520s were a grim manifestation of this seething populist anger beneath the surface.[56]

We will discover later that Trump's tax cut has indeed benefited all segments of the population and not just the top one percent.

The legal historian Harold Berman describes the turn of the half-millennium in this way: "Everywhere in Europe, royal power over feudal nobility was increasing, secular authority was asserting itself against ecclesiastical authority, and territorial loyalties were intensifying. Everywhere in Europe strong voices were advocating reduction of ecclesiastical power and reformation of both Church and State. Everywhere the cities were seeking greater autonomy."[57]

---

[55] Ibid., p.17.

[56] Raschke, Carl, "Where is Martin Luther When You Need Him?" <https://politicaltheology.com/the-500th-anniversary-of-the-reformation-where-is-martin-luther-when-you-need-him-carl-raschke>.

[57] Berman, Harold J., "The Impact of the Protestant Reformations on the Western Legal Tradition," *Law and Revolution II* (Cambridge, MA: Belknap Press of Harvard University, 2003), p.38.

There were profound international tensions in the age of Luther, with the death of Emperor Maximilian in 1519 and the election of his grandson, Charles, who had recently inherited the Spanish crown. Through complicated negotiations, expensive bribes and institutional pressures, the ill-fated hope of a universal European Empire under the new Emperor was never realized. The Turks, who controlled large parts of southeastern Europe, continued their pressure on the eastern frontiers of the empire during Luther's ministry. Besides, the papacy in the sixteenth century was still a major political power that made alliances, fought wars, and acted like any other political kingdom. The Church had incurred enormous expenses warring with the Turks at the walls of Vienna and initiating an ambitious building campaign, including the reconstruction of St. Peter's Basilica in Rome, and had to borrow huge sums from Europe's biggest banks, including Germany's Fugger Bank.

Likewise, international tensions were part of the political landscape in the age of Donald Trump, with the European Union encountering potential fractures, trade deals and "payments" to secure treaties in order to appease opponents and threats posed on our electoral processes by foreign adversaries. He entered a political arena where folks were experiencing social fragmentation, feeling as if they had been forgotten with little sense of belonging or being heard, and of course they were anxious as well about kitchen table economics: work, food, housing, stagnant wages, healthcare, and the diminishing resources with which to keep up with rising expenses. Furthermore, the jittery population was divided and polarized by the role of government in their lives, and found themselves being surrounded by economic disparity, the sexual revolution, globalism, ideologies, bioethical changes, biomedical advances and multi-culturalism, and being branded with foul names through "identity politics" that focus on differences, which produce disunity and divisiveness over mutual understanding.

Such identity politics have introduced a host of strange and unfamiliar "tribal" words into our vocabulary that end with the suffix "ist," "ism," "ic," "phobe," or "phobic." Control the words and you control the debate. Characterizing this "Age of Outrage," Mathew Block, editor of *The Canadian Lutheran* magazine and Communications Manager for the Lutheran Church-Canada, observes how "mass demonstrations for purportedly noble purposes descend into violence and intimidation" in which participants revel. Those who disagree with the prevailing opinion of the mob are intimidated or drowned out. As a result, the average person is afraid of expressing any controversial opinion in a public forum, for fear of being exposed, cancelled, or ruined personally and/or professionally. "Rules and common decency be damned; we want to rage and rend and tear. And we will follow anyone who permits us to do so, anyone who feels and acts as we do." Into this diseased culture, Block argues, "argument has given way to anger, dialogue has given way to diatribe, and civility is considered a sign of weakness."[58] Tolerance for differing points of view has turned into being tolerant only toward those who share "our" views. Hysteria and threats of reprisals result with little enlightening discussion and much less historical understanding or context of the issues, as citizens thrash about for people to blame—the left, the right, blacks, whites, females, males, rich, poor, believers, unbelievers, Muslims, refugees, immigrants, terrorists, or police.

Another unsettling dynamic includes the resulting "Me-Centered Morality" as a symptom of America's rampant individualism on steroids. One can observe a large corporation such as Apple capturing this development in naming their products "iPhones" and "iPads," and *The Atlantic* in an article asking, "Have Smartphones Destroyed a Generation?"[59] The iGen life, with more time on Facebook, Snapchat, et al., and less time on in-person social interactions, is creating more isolation and loneliness, leading to depression. Yuval Levin in *The Fractured Republic* describes the effects of individualism we're experiencing today upon our institutions, including the Church:

> Individualism involves the corrosion of people's sense of themselves as defined by a variety of strong affiliations and unchosen bonds and its replacement by a sense that all connections are matters of individual choice and preference. It breaks up clusters of people into more isolated individuals held together by more casual affinities and more utilitarian relationships—each best understood in relation to the needs and wants of the individual. Politically such individualism tends to weaken mediating power centers that stand between the individual and the nation as a whole—from families to local communities (including local governments), religious institutions, fraternal bodies, civil-society organizations, labor groups, and the small and medium-sized businesses that make up much of the private economy."[60]

Erik Teller, an executive at Google, adds to the mix "the accelerating speed of scientific and technological innovations [that] can outpace the capacity of the average human being

[58] Block, Mathew, "The Age of Outrage," *First Things*, March 4, 2016; <https:///www.firstthings.com/blogs/firstthoughts/2016/03/the-age-of-outrage>.

[59] <https://www.theatlantic.com/magazine/archive/2017/09/has-the-smartphone-destroyed-a-generation/534198>.

[60] Levin, Yuval, *The Fractured Republic* (New York: Basic, 2016), pp.99-100.

and our societal structures to adapt and absorb them… Many of us cannot keep pace anymore and that is causing a lot of 'cultural angst.'"[61]

And of course, amplifying the cacophony has been the omnipresent scrutiny and the increasing and demanding expectations of being politically correct, which have become the order of the day. Undeniably, Trump has amplified the social tensions of our day, as Luther did in his day, but neither of them created them. As disruptors, they exposed divisions as real existential threats that must be met head-on.

We in our times feel anxious, partly because we have no idea whom to trust. We are drowning in media—more sources of information, including the 24-hour news cycle and social media "Fake News," than we know what to do with. In the process, we seem to have lost trust in the methods that we used to use to make sense of them. More to the point, we have cut ourselves off from the source of our convictions and traditions, convinced that the past has nothing to teach us. The result, as in the sixteenth century, are these enormous anxieties coupled with a propensity to see enemies, whether devils or racists, under every bush.

---

[61] Teller, Eric, quoted in "The Age of Acceleration," in *The Lisa Movement;* <https://www.thelisamovement.com/technology-acceleration>.

6

The Entitled Elite Establishment Scandalized

Was Martin Luther the 16th-century Donald Trump? Is Donald Trump the 21st-century Martin Luther? Or are they just twins who followed their beliefs, purely in an attempt to reform? In having the audacity to suggest such a comparison, I have been met with surprise if not outright disgust. Most often the reaction is laced with suspicion, if not rejection, or at least fraught with cynical disbelief by the Incredulous Class, the Smartest Guy in the Room Class, or those summarily identified as the Elite Establishment. The Sanctimonious Class, which includes many of my colleagues and religious folks within the Church, are literally shocked and scandalized by the prospect that similarities could exist between "playboy" Donald Trump and "holy man" Martin Luther.

As we will repeatedly discover, both Luther and Trump confounded the elite establishment who not only feel entitled but demonstrate a patronizing superiority toward those with dissenting views or who utilize unconventional ways of communicating and means of getting things done.

Consequently, it is not difficult to discern how these populist twins in their respective centuries effectively are identified and resonate with the Common Class who have felt put-upon. Both demonstrate the ability to tap into the deep vein of discontent and disillusionment many were experiencing in their respective time periods. They struck a chord with those who felt exploited and ignored while being fleeced to pay for the excesses and corruption in both Church and State. In each of these centuries, the forgotten and abused people felt they had a warrior who could speak for them, represent them, and lead them. Both Luther and Trump became viewed as heroes of the disenfranchised.

Of course, both were subsequently despised by all the "correct" people for having taken on the establishment: an improbable monk at an undistinguished university in the backwater, podunk town of Wittenberg "on the edge of civilization" (Luther's own description—"*in termino civilitatis*"[62]), light years away from the splendors of Renaissance Rome where Luther took on the powers of Church and State—the Pope and the Emperor—and in so

[62] Schilling, *Upheaval*, p.91 (for the term '*in termino civilitatis*' Schilling references Karlheinz Blaschke's *Wittenberg, die Lutherstadt* [Leipzig, 1977], p.13).

doing became synonymous with the concept of speaking truth to power; and a non-politician, outsider, real estate developer and TV celebrity, who broke the norms of American politics by not coming up through the ranks of elected office, taking on sixteen rivals within the Republican Party for the nomination, the Democratic Party with its dual "Obama-Clinton machines," as well as the bias of the national media, as he proceeded to defy respected pollsters.

Both populist reformers clearly, against incredible odds, disrupted the long-standing political establishment of their times, which had initially misjudged what they perceived to be, at most, a minor irritant unlikely to cause anything more than a hiccup. Trump, as we know, had been "chronically underestimated as a nonstarter for the Republican nomination until he clinched it; unelectable until he was elected; and likely to be impeached until the investigations fade and his accusers find themselves engulfed in suspicion"[63] by "trumped up" charges and bogus impeachments.

There are many who claim Pope Leo X initially dismissed Luther as "a son of iniquity," laughing off Luther's challenge to the Church as just another drunken German who when sober would change his mind.[64] If this was really the Pope's assessment, he obviously underestimated what he would be dealing with in this German monk who never really sobered up! This was just the beginning of the challenge between Luther and the Church, from the Ninety-five Theses until Luther's excommunication in April 1521. Variations of such a quote have even found their way into Luther's "Table Talks," a collection of dinner-table observations, but one wonders how Luther could even know of such a statement from the Pope. The quote is probably spurious, though it reflects the probability that the Pope and the Roman Curia were caught napping, as this Catholic dissident was whipping up a populist storm against the Church establishment. George, Duke of Albertine Saxony, enemy and rival to Luther's own patron prince, Frederick the Wise, expressed a similar succinct Nathanael's bewilderment about Jesus' origin (John 1:46: *"Can anything good come out of Nazareth?"*), saying, "That a single monk, out of such a hole [Wittenberg] could undertake a Reformation, is not to be tolerated,"[65] no more than a non-politician can be permitted to penetrate the Beltway in order to grab the reigns of control and power away from the entrenched.

---

[63] Black, Conrad, "Why Donald J. Trump is Truly a President Like No Other," *National Post*. <https://nationalpost.com/opinion/conrad-black-why-donald-j-trump-is-truly-a-president-like-no-other>.

[64] Schaff, Philip, *History of the Christian Church*, 8 vols. (New York, NY: Charles Scribner's Sons, 1910), 7:170–172.

[65] Schwiebert, Ernest G., "The Electoral Town of Wittenberg," *Medievalia et Humanistica*, (1945), pp.108-09, cited by Andrew Pettegree in *Brand Luther* (New York: Penguin, 2015), p.8.

Luther himself expressed negative views of Wittenberg, as he shared his disillusionment with his wife, Katie, writing to her in 1545 that he wanted to leave this worthless little sleepy, hickish, dirty backwater town in Saxony where only drunken, boorish and hypocritically pious people live. The President Emeritus of Concordia University in Texas, David J. Zersen, writes that Luther seemed to be echoing remarks of his contemporaries who "wondered why a university should have been established in such a remote place, and why God should choose it to be the starting point for the dissemination of His Word. 'It was,' wrote Dr. [Martin Pollich von] Mellerstadt, 'as if [we live] in a slaughter yard where people survive without culture, civilization or discipline.'"[66]

Flea Bites Trigger Revolutions

Frederick the Wise* had picked Wittenberg to become the home of a university he envisioned would rival the already well-established and prestigious schools in other areas of Germany. He chose Martin Pollich von Mellerstadt, a philosopher, astrologer, physician and theologian, to be the founding rector of the new university. Little did Pollich know that the young Augustinian monk he met in 1508 would bring more fame than he or Frederick could ever have imagined to Wittenberg. There on the eve of the feast celebrating that pantheon of holy intercessors, All Saints' Day, October 31, 1517, Luther's Ninety-Five Theses were reportedly posted on the doors of Wittenberg's Castle Church. John Naughton writes in *The Guardian*,

Frederick the Wise

> This rebellious stunt (posting the Ninety-Five Theses) by an obscure monk must have seemed at the time like a flea bite on an elephant. But it was the event that triggered a revolution in religious belief, undermined the authority

---

[66] Zersen, David J., "Did Luther Really Say? Contexts for Luther's Comments on the Wends," *Concordia Historical Institute Quarterly*, Fall 2017. <https://www.academia.edu/36898659/>. (Wends was the large territory between Hannover and Danzig which was once populated by various Slav ethnic groups typically described by the German word "Wends," but they referred to themselves by the Slav word "Serbs.")

* Frederick III known as "the Wise" was Elector of Saxony from 1486 to 1525, one of seven who selected the Emperor. He is mostly remembered for the worldly protection of his subject Martin Luther. Portrait by Lucas Cranach the Elder, c.1525. (Image: Public domain, retrieved from the website of the Barnes Foundation)

> of the Roman Church, unleashed ferocious wars in Europe and shaped the world in which most of us (at least in the West) grew up. Some flea bite![67]

In both Luther's and Trump's successful "bites" we witness how the long-standing political establishments fail to cope with disruptive outsiders, thus hastening their own fate. But with moral courage, and standing almost alone against clerical abuse and corruption, Luther courageously decided to risk all and challenge the authoritative teachings of the Church. His protest against the Church was theological and, at its heart, an attempt to recover the historic meaning of the Christian Gospel from what he saw as legalistic corruption.

Hostility of the Fake News Media

The audacity of a political neophyte's iconic descent on a golden escalator inside Trump Tower to launch a presidential bid was viewed by most as a spectacle, if not a joke:

> Nearly every member of his nascent political team urged Trump not to ride down a moving stairway to make his announcement. They fretted it would look amateurish and not remotely presidential.... Trump was insistent. "No, I'm going down the escalator," he said—an early example of him flouting the norms and conventions of politics at nearly every juncture and often prevailing.[68]

As we have come to experience, President Trump withstands daily onslaughts as he defies such "norms and conventionalities" expected by belligerent "Trump bashers," an outraged media, political opponents, and even some within his own party. Media Research Center reports 92% negative coverage and "spin" on Donald Trump from TV network evening news programs on ABC, CBS and NBC.[69] The center describes this as "the most hostile coverage of a President in history."[70] The Harvard Kennedy School on Media, Politics

---

[67] Naughton, John, "Why We Need a 21st-Century Martin Luther to Challenge the Church of Tech, *The Guardian*, Oct. 29, 2017; <https://www.the guardian.com/technology/2017/oct/29/why-we-need-a-21st-century-martin-luther-to-challenge-the-church-of-technology-95-Theses>.

[68] <https://www.washingtonpost.com/politics/im-going-down-the-escalator-the-spectacle-in-trump-tower-that-launched-a-presidency/2019/06/16/20fec336-8e1d-11e9-adf3-f70f78c156e8_story.html>.

[69] <https://www.investors.com/politics/editorials/media-trump-hatred->.

[70] <https://www.newsbusters.org/blogs/nb/rich-noyes/2018/10/09/study-econ-boom-ignored-tv-trump-coverage-hits-92-percent-negative>; <https://www.mrc.org/research>.

and Public Policy researchers likewise found Trump coverage on CNN and NBC was 93% negative and concludes that "the news media need to give Trump credit when his actions warrant it"[71] instead of ignoring or burying such positive reports on page 17.

According to Newt Gingrich, "this relentless hostility parallels what President Lincoln had to endure in the media of his day—newspapers and magazines." In his No. 1 *New York Times* bestseller, *Understanding Trump*, Gingrich wrote that

> many news organizations opposed Lincoln from the beginning—much as they have President Trump in our time. Upon Lincoln's election, the *Memphis Daily Appeal* wrote on November 13, 1860, "Within 90 days from the time Lincoln is inaugurated, the Republican Party will be utterly ruined and destroyed. His path is environed with so many difficulties, that even if he had the ability of Jefferson and the energy of Jackson, he would fail, but he is a weak and inexperienced man, and his administration will be doomed from the commencement..." The criticisms of Lincoln were not confined to the South.
>
> The northern newspaper editors also said of Lincoln: As President of the United States he must have enough sense to see and acknowledge he has been an egregious failure...(and he should) retire from the position to which, in an evil hour, he was exalted.... Even the general who Lincoln chose to lead the Union Army, George McClellan, dismissed President Lincoln as a frontier hack, an idiot, and the original gorilla.... Republican William M. Dickson of Ohio wrote in 1861 that Lincoln is universally an admitted failure, has no will, no courage, no executive capacity...his spirit necessarily infuses itself downwards through all departments.[72]
>
> Just as President Trump rails against 'Fake News,' President Lincoln felt that a significant front in his war to preserve the Union was against the news media. This made Lincoln highly critical and skeptical of the media...and he often said, "the worst feature about newspapers was that they were so sure

---

71 <https://www.washingtonexaminer.com/byron-york-harvard-study-cnn-nbc-trump-coverage-93-percent-negative>.

72 Gingrich, Newt, "The Surprising Thing Trump and Lincoln Have in Common," <https://www.foxnews.com/opinion/newt-gingrich-the-surprising-thing-trump-and-lincoln-have-in-common>; quote from Gingrich, Newt, *Understanding Trump*, NY and Nashville: Center Street, 2017.

to be ahead of the hounds, outrunning events, and exciting expectations which were sure to be disappointed."[73]

Media Word Clouds*

Images: Shutterstock

It is interesting to note that more than 300 newspapers were shut down by the federal government during the Lincoln administration, most of them Democratic papers that were sympathetic to the Confederacy.[74] Does any of this rankling with the media or hostility sound familiar? Supposed "bombshells" proved to be "Fake News," such as Buzzfeed reporting the President had ordered his former attorney and "fixer" Michael Cohen to lie, which none other than Special Counsel Robert Mueller had to discredit by raining down on the media parade during his two-and-a-half-year investigation that concluded there was no evidence of collusion with the Russians by the Trump team. However, the Democratic National Committee and Hillary Clinton's campaign did collude, paying for the Russian Dirty Dossier which was deceitfully used to obtain the FISA court warrants to investigate her opponent and his aides. Then too, during the efforts to impeach the President, much that was being gleefully reported from those closed-door testimonies as evidence that "the walls are closing in" was proven to be the opposite in the newly released documents, revealing the actual testimony given by those witnesses. Nevertheless, the media continued to provide their feeding frenzy of Fake News without apology, retraction or correction.

---

[73] Ibid.

* A "word cloud" is an image composed of words used in a particular text or subject, in which the size of each word indicates its frequency or importance.

[74] <http://ocean.otr.usm.edu/~w304644/ajha/americanjournalism/fall09.pdf>.

7

Reluctant Warriors, Compelled Reformers

I find it thought-provoking, the way the historic leaders we are comparing recount their entrances into and their role in their respective arenas as reluctant reform warriors. They were motivated not by a desire for power, fame or fortune, but rather were compelled or constrained by an inner conviction to correct the corrupt religious and political systems prevalent in their time.

Donald Trump, lamenting the failures of the Republican Party to achieve victory, said, "This time I'm going to do it myself, OK?"[75] which parallels Luther's constraining observation that "the distress and misery that oppress all the Christian states especially in Germany…have now forced me to cry out…"[76] The presidential candidate declares, "I had a great life. I don't need this. I am doing this for you: to Make America Great Again,"[77] and he confidently presents himself as the last hope of a political system in crisis.

"For Luther, there was no question," writes Heinz Schilling. "He wanted to make the Church more Bible-based and pristine again and he was convinced that he alone had been commissioned by God to speak as God's prophet."[78] He states that he was encouraged to initiate reform and to persevere through a prophetic word conveyed to him by his spiritual advisor and overseer, Johann Staupitz, the vicar-general of the Augustinian monks in Germany. When Luther was in Rome in 1511, he heard the prophecy publicly proclaimed, "An Eremite (the Augustinians were called Eremites) shall arise and spoil the papacy!" and through Staupitz, Luther learned that "a certain Franciscan at Rome had seen this in a vision."[79] Luther, confident and convinced that he was God's prophet and servant, stated, "I acknowledge my indebtedness to my Christian brethren, whom I am duty-bound to

[75] <https://grabien.com/story.php?id=49642>.

[76] Martin Luther, "An Open Letter to the Christian Nobility," *Three Treatises* (Philadelphia: Muhlenberg Press, 1960), p.11. See also LW 44:124.

[77] <https://www.reddit.com/r/The_Donald/comments/4a4k40/trump-after-being-attacked-i-had-a-great-life>.

[78] Schilling, *Upheaval*, p.243.

[79] <https://lexloiz.wordpress.com/2009/01/05/in-conversation-with-martin-luther-%E2%80%93-table-talk>.

warn so that fewer of them may be destroyed by the plagues of Rome, at least so that their destruction may be less cruel."[80]

In honest self-awareness, Luther describes himself as a rough woodsman and contrasts his behavior with Philip Melanchthon, his friend and colleague, saying,

> I was born to wage war against sects and devils, and that is why my books are so stormy and combative. I have to root out stumps and branches, cut out thorns and hedges, drain the swamps.... I am the great woodcutter who has to forge a path and therefore I have to destroy much. But Master Philip proceeds calmly and neatly, he builds and plants, sows, and waters, and does so with pleasure, totally employing the gifts that God has given him for this.[81] ...Master Philip cuts with the precision of a knife. I simply swing the ax.[82]

Trump's co-author of *The Art of the Deal*, Tony Schwartz, writes,

> To survive...Trump felt compelled to go to war with the world. It was a binary, zero-sum choice for him: You either dominated or you submitted. You either created and exploited fear, or you succumbed to it—as he thought his older brother had. This narrow, defensive outlook took hold at a very early age, and it never evolved. "When I look at myself in the first grade and I look at myself now," he told a recent biographer, "I'm basically the same...." In countless conversations, he made clear to me that he treated every encounter as a contest he had to win, because the only other option from his perspective was to lose, and that was the equivalent of obliteration.[83]

Many historians note and criticize the vehemence of Luther's polemical works against three groups named in the accusatory titles that have the ability to capture notice: "Against the Robbing and Murdering Hordes of Peasants" (1525, LW 46:45-55); "On the Jews and

---

[80] LW 31:336. *Career of the Reformer I*, "An Open Letter to Pope Leo X" in *The Freedom of a Christian*, or see *Three Treatises*, p.268.

[81] Seiderhuis, Herman, "The Many Faces of Martin Luther," *Christianity Today*, Nov. 2017, footnote 55.

[82] <https://www.ligonier.org/podcasts/5-minutes-in-church-history-with-stephen-nichols/philip-melanchthon> and <https://www.patheos.com/blogs/e2medianetwork/2017/05/5-minutes-church-history-philip-melanchthon>.

[83] Schwartz, Tony, "I Wrote '*The Art of the Deal*' with Trump," *Perspective*, May 16, 2017; *The Washington Post*; <https://www.washingtonpost.com/posteverything/wp/2017/05/16/i-wrote-the-art-of-the-deal-with-trump-his-self-sabotage-is-rooted-in-his-past>.

Their Lies" (1543, LW 47:121-306); and "Against the Roman Papacy, an Institution of the Devil" (1545, LW 41:257-376). Author Scott Hendrix, Emeritus Professor of Reformation History at Princeton Theological Seminary, states that

> Various attempts have been made by historians to explain and sometimes to tame the virulence of these attacks. Luther's health, worldview, and theology have all been suggested as explanations for his harshness, and all of them did play a role. In a new study, however, Mark Edwards* has attributed greater influence to factors outside Luther, namely to the political pressures exerted on Luther by his own prince and by the broader Protestant-Catholic conflict. These pressures exacerbated the anger which Luther recognized as his peculiar sin and, also strengthened his apocalyptic conviction that the Last Day was at hand. In this historical context, Luther's penchant for coarse and blunt expression was utilized and exploited by friends and foes. Most of Luther's polemical works produced during the later years were provoked or solicited by others, often by his aggressive prince, Elector John Frederick, in support of Protestant political decisions.[84]

Likewise, Attorney General William Barr, in releasing Special Counsel Robert Mueller's long-awaited report on the swirling investigation of Russian interference in the 2016 election, acknowledged factors and pressures outside Trump that undoubtedly affected the President's reaction by intensifying and heightening his outrage. "There is substantial evidence to show that the President was frustrated and angered by a sincere belief that the investigation was undermining his presidency, propelled by his political opponents and fueled by illegal leaks."[85] Facing daily belligerent "Trump-bashing," charges of being a traitor, a Russian agent beholden to Putin, colluding with Russia, "bombshells" and "walls closing in" that fizzled as wishful thinking, "fake" media accounts being discredited, the apparent coordinated attempts to take down this President and his family through spying, wiretapping, unmasking

---

* Mark U. Edwards, noted Reformation historian, professor at Harvard University Divinity School, and President of St. Olaf College, Northfield, Minnesota.

[84] Hendrix, Scott H., "The Controversial Luther," *Word & World*, 3:4, Fall 1983, p.392, citing Mark U. Edwards, Jr., *Luther's Last Battles: Politics and Polemics 1531-1546* (Ithaca and London: Cornell University, 1983), pp.205-207. <https://wordandworld.luthersem.edu/content/pdfs/3-4_Luther/3-4_Hendrix.pdf>.

[85] Wolf, Richard, "Mueller Report: Trump's Anger Over Russia Probe may have Saved Him from Obstruction Charge," *USA TODAY*, April 18, 2019; <https://www.usatoday.com/story/news/politics/2019/04/18/mueller-report-how-did-president-trump-dodge-obstruction-justice/3500784002>.

human sources, weaponizing the intel agencies to investigate private citizens…who wouldn't be frustrated and angered?

Disseminating Appealing Propaganda Visually

The Devil Playing the Bagpipes

Devil Calls the Tune
by Erhard Schön (c. 1530)
(Left): Public domain, retrieved from
thereformationroom.com/single-post/2017/03/13/

Vladimir Putin Playing Donald Trump

Virtuoso
by David Horsey, Los Angeles Times
(Right): Image: Los Angeles Times
July 10, 2017

The well-known satirical image on the left was created by Erhard Schön, a pupil of Albrecht Dürer, circa 1530. It was used as a broadside by the "reformers" against the Roman Catholic Church. The lower right-hand corner is where messages of dissent were placed before being posted around the town. The image depicts "the Devil perched on the shoulders of a monk, whose head forms the bagpipe and through whose ears and nose he 'plays his tune.'" It is a pungent image, reinforcing the idea that monks were instruments of the Devil. From the resemblance the head bears to Luther, and being that Luther was a monk, many are inclined to view this woodcut as an allegorical allusion of Satan instigating Luther while the Devil plays his tune on Luther's nose. However, no such print is known with the addition of a suitable anti-Lutheran text, though that is not to say that opponents did not copy the broadsheet and attach their own potent tool against Luther being in the service of Satan. Much like modern editorial cartoons, these woodcut compositions were intended to amuse, outrage, or enlighten the public, especially those who were unable to read.

During the campaign and transition, and from the beginning of his presidency, Donald Trump has been accused of collusion with the Russians, of being in Putin's pocket and under his control, and of being a Russian asset and thus a traitor to our country. His attributed "bromance" with Vladimir Putin fueled the "Russian investigations," leading the president to call the probes "witch hunts" or "Fake News." Nonetheless, the pundits and artists kept beating the drum and Trump found himself not winning the image duel as his twin had done, even though no evidence was ever discovered on which to convict him.

Writing in *USA Today* (April 18, 2019), Richard Wolf acknowledges that

> What might appear obstructive to others, [Attorney General] Barr implied, needs to be put in context. Trump faced an "unprecedented" situation coming into office in 2017, he said, in which his conduct was being scrutinized, and speculation about his personal culpability was rampant in the media [as were questions about his mental stability]. Further evidence that justice was not obstructed, Barr said came from the White House's willingness to cooperate with Mueller's team, both by turning over documents and allowing witnesses to be interviewed. "The President took no act [not even executive privilege] that in fact deprived the special counsel of the documents and witnesses necessary to complete his investigation," Barr said. "Apart from whether the acts were obstructive, this evidence of non-corrupt motives weighs heavily against any allegation that the President had a corrupt intent to obstruct the investigation."[86]

Scott Hendrix suggests in pointing specifically to Luther, but also applicable to Trump's controversies, that

> Instead of treating the ongoing controversy (Luther's apparent alliance with the princes against the peasants and the use of his anti-Jewish statements by National Socialists in the Twentieth Century) as an embarrassment, however, we can take advantage of the positive function that controversial figures from the past exercise. They remind us first not to distort the past by failing to include those parts of the story which now seem incomprehensible or unmentionable. Moreover, they alert us to the restrictions on our vision and invite us to inquire if insights might be present which still deserve

[86] Ibid., Wolf, "Mueller Report."

> consideration even though they might challenge our own comfortable assumptions. Not all disputes yield such insights, but the controversial Luther (and Trump) can on occasion cause healthy discomfort.[87]

In the eulogy Melanchthon delivered at Luther's funeral, he elevated his friend and colleague to one of the greatest figures in history, but did not shy from mentioning Luther's shortcomings:

> Some have complained that Luther displayed too much severity. I will not deny this. But I answer in the language of Erasmus (Luther's best-known intellectual adversary, the famous humanist, theologian, and Catholic priest): "Because of the magnitude of the disorders, God gave this age a violent physician." …I do not deny that the more ardent characters sometimes make mistakes, for amid the weakness of human nature no one is without fault. But we may say of such a one, "rough indeed, but worthy of all praise!" If he was severe, it was the severity of zeal for the truth, not the love of strife, or of harshness.… Brave, lofty ardent souls, such as Luther had must be divinely guided.… God was his anchor, and faith never failed him.[88]

God had indeed graciously filled the need for a "sharp physician" for the existing ailments within His Church.

Martin Luther believed many of the Church leaders had betrayed their faith by accumulating great wealth, thereby creating a culture of ecclesiastical luxury and abuse. In view of President Trump's efforts to "drain the swamp" of politicians and bureaucrats who profit from their service, and the attempts to get the President to disclose his tax records, I'm sure he would appreciate the quote of the day that has made its rounds on the internet: "America does not need to see the tax return of a billionaire who became a public servant. America needs to see the tax returns of those who became millionaires while being public servants."[89] Moreover, the President donates his salary back to the government.

---

[87] Hendrix, Scott H., "Controversial Luther." *Word & World*, 3:4, Fall 1983, p.393. <https://wordandworld.luthersem.edu/issues.aspx?article_id=453>.

[88] Melanchthon, Philipp, eulogy quote in Clyde Leonard Manschreck's *Melanchthon: The Quiet Reformer* (New York/Nashville: Abingdon Press, 1958), pp.275-76; Metaxas, Eric, *Martin Luther, The Man Who Rediscovered God and Changed the World* (New York, NY: Viking, 2017), p.431.

[89] <https://makeameme.org/meme/america-does-not-8d10a2e6da>.

8

A Visit Over Hell

The recognizable image of Luther with a hammer at the door of Wittenberg's Castle Church tells the legendary story of an incident which was the spark that set off a political and religious conflagration that would sweep across Europe known as the Protestant Reformation. This celebrated event portrays a rebel intent on overturning the tables of the Medieval Church to expose its "deep-rooted corruption and spiritual malaise in order to restore the heart and soul to the Christian faith." Bruce Gordon, in "Reading the Reformation in 2017," goes on to suggest that

> with the benefit of hindsight and more careful study into the period, we now understand that the medieval Church from which Luther broke was far from a cesspool of iniquity. For all its institutional flaws, popular and religious devotion flourished on the eve of the Reformation. The problem with indulgences, as Luther knew, was not that they were resented but that they were wildly popular.[90]

Luther was appalled not by the laity, but by the leaders of his Church abusing their powers, and thus sacrificing their spiritual responsibilities to their greed and lust. He saw within the hierarchical nature of the Church "grace" being mediated as a substance through sacramental pipelines overseen by priestly control. Indulgences were being marketed as "get-out-of-jail-free cards" with little likelihood for any direct encounter of the believer with the Lord through repentance. Instead, they provided a way for individuals to bypass a "faith experience" while being led to believe such purchases had reduced the impact sinning had on their salvation chances. For Luther, indulgences were a scam—the great salvation sell-off! The Church was selling bogus tickets, assuring sinners they would not only be exempt from purgatorial fire but would also benefit from being on an express route to heaven. Through its "tentacle-like system of clerical corruption throughout Europe…every church official from

[90] Gordon, Bruce. "Reading the Reformation in 2017," *Christianity Today*, Jan/Feb 2017. <https://www.christianitytoday.com/ct/2017/january-february/reading-reformation-in-2017.html>.

the local parish priest to the Pope himself was receiving a certain amount of undisclosed 'spoils' from indulgence peddling."[91]

Experiencing Life in the Capital

While Luther had been enthusiastic about visiting the Eternal City and the Capital of Christendom, his expectations were overthrown by disappointments. His trip in 1511 to the pinnacle of his spiritual aspirations would certainly shore up his failing spirituality, but his trip was to end in disillusionment and confusion. Corrupt clergy reduced religious ceremonies and practices to mere habits, performed mechanically without understanding and right feeling. He was disturbed at the frivolous and totally irreverent manner in which the priests celebrated the sacrament of the altar and disgusted by how they could rush through the mass so hastily as if they were performing an illusion. At one time when Luther had just reached the Gospel the patrico* next to him had already terminated the mass and shouted "'Pass, Passa,' make haste! Have done with it at once,"[92] Get away, wrap it up! Luther goes on to express the depth of his disenchantment, "If there is Hell, then Rome is built over it!" calling it a "cesspit of sin."[93]

We have been led to believe that in 1517, Europe was stuck in an era of spiritual lethargy, and the Roman Catholic Church was not only corrupt, but in a state of religious atrophy. Luther would understand that description applies to those in the highest offices of the Church, but not to those in the pews faithfully practicing their piety. In fact, Luther and the reformers struck a responsive chord in an intensely religious culture. Donald Trump describes those in the "Deep State" and those bureaucrats at the top levels of government agencies in Washington, D.C., acting as a cabal determined to undermine or overthrow his presidency in a coup attempt, but he doesn't implicate those in the rank and file of civil service any more than Luther did with the trusting laity. However, he must at times feel it's hell to be under such unproven and continued accusations and attacks.

---

[91] Raschke, "Where is Luther," <https://politicaltheology.com/the-500th-anniversary-of-the-reformation-where-is-martin-luther-when-you-need-him-carl-raschke>.

* an archaic term for a fraudulent priest

[92] Meredith, Roderick C., "The Break with Rome," *Tomorrow's World*, 2017 July-August, <https://www.tomorrowsworld.org/magazines/2017/july-august/the-break-with-rome> and quoting from D'Aubigne, Merle. *History of the Reformation*. (Delmarva Publications, Inc., 1846), p. 68.

[93] Keilo, Jacques, "Martin Luther in Rome: Piazza Martin Lutero in the Eternal Centre," *Centres and Centralities*, November 4, 2017, <https://centrici.hypotheses.org/1323> or see <https://lineagejourney.com/timeline-details/event/luthers-visit-to-rome>.

Indulgence-Gate: Get Out of Purgatory Passports

In addition to dishing out bishoprics to his favorite relatives, Pope Leo X* embraced the practice of simony—selling church positions to the highest bidder to support the papacy.

He also extended and encouraged the crude commercialization of indulgences—the purchase of "get out of purgatory" certificates guaranteeing forgiveness for inevitable sins without repentance. Luther might not have made a fuss if it weren't for the fact that these "purgatory" passports weren't actually free.

Pope Leo X

The granting of indulgences in exchange for good works and acts of piety dates to 1095, when Pope Urban II offered them to entice Christians to the Crusades. As History.com reminds us, "On November 27, 1095, Pope Urban II made perhaps the most influential speech of the Middle Ages, giving rise to the Crusades by calling Christians in Europe to war against Muslims in order to reclaim the Holy Land with the cry of 'Deus vult!' or 'God wills it!'"[94] Indulgences then became a stock item in the Medieval Catholic penitential system in dealing with moral transgressions. Today's media might call this Medieval supernatural version of the criminal justice system "Indulgence-gate." Penance was being dispensed through financial transactions, offering salvation in metric units of forgiveness. The records of those transactions would resemble an accountant's intricate ledger, where the quantification of one's sins and the quantification of good works or penance were recorded as demerits and merits, or debits and credits.

In the mix of this "monetized" system, there was also a "treasury of merit," analogous to a central bank. This "reserve bank" served as a repository of all good deeds and saintly virtues that had been accumulated over time, from which one could draw in a "pay-to-play" scheme to rebalance one's liabilities. Pope Sixtus IV widened the market opportunity in 1476 by offering the opportunity for this ingenious product called an "indulgence" to be purchased on behalf of another person. The "market share" thereby expanded exponentially beyond those who were alive and sinning, to millions who had already died, thus maximizing the revenue stream into the Vatican's coffers. Bereaved relatives could now get a deceased loved one, who was presumed to be suffering in the intermediate prison called "purgatory" and

* Pope Leo X, born Giovanni de' Medici, is quoted as having said, "God has given us the papacy, let us enjoy it." (Image: Public domain, retrieved at the Duke University website).

[94] <https://www.history.com/this-day-in-history/pope-urban-ii-orders-first-crusade>.

thus beyond the reach of confession and absolution, out early, thereby hastening their entry into heaven.

According to New York Times bestseller Eric Metaxas, "Indulgences became a surefire income stream that in time became an absolute necessity for the Church. It became so important that looking the other way when abuses occurred, as they must, was very easy to do."[95] What made Luther's Theses so egregiously offensive to the Church was how they undermined the very essence of papal authority and the business model upon which the entire Vatican was built. In essence, Luther was calling out the Pope as a liar for authorizing the sale of fake securities. The 6th Thesis questions the assertion that "the Pope can forgive sins only in the sense that he declares and confirms what may be forgiven by God."[96] *New Yorker* staff writer Joan Acocella suggests that

> In Luther's mind, the indulgence trade seems to have crystallized the spiritual crisis he was experiencing. It brought him up against the absurdity of bargaining with God, jockeying for His favor—indeed, paying for His favor. Why had God given His only begotten Son? And why had the Son died on the cross? Because that's how much God loved the world. And that alone, Luther now reasoned, was sufficient for a person to be found "justified," or worthy. From this thought, the Ninety-Five Theses were born.[97]

Badmouthing the Pope, however, has never been a vote-winner. In the Europe of 1517, Luther's attacks on the system were fighting words and certainly not a good career move for a young Augustinian monk. They would have been suicidal. People had been burned at the stake for less.

As the Theses were translated from Latin into German and found wide circulation, many who were already distrustful of the Church championed Luther's words and rallied around him with glee. They saw in him a standard-bearer against what they considered the shameful malfeasance of their religious authorities.

---

[95] Metaxas, Eric, *Martin Luther, The Man Who Rediscovered God and Changed the World* (New York, NY: Viking, 2017), p.45.

[96] LW 31:26. *Career of the Reformer I,* "Ninety-Five Theses."

[97] Acocella, Joan, "How Martin Luther Changed the World," *The New Yorker,* October 23, 2017. <https://www.newyoker.com/magazine/2017/10/30/how-martin-luther-changed-the-world>.

Peddling Purgatory Relief

Johann Tetzel, Dominican
Left: Public domain, retrieved at Wikimedia

Friar and preacher selling Indulgences
Right: The Book of Days Tales blog

Pope Leo X commissioned Dominican Johann Tetzel, an enthusiastic indulgence-hawker, to sell these indulgences in Germany, where there were many who were eager to "buy into" the hope perpetrated on them that by such "good works" a human soul could be led into the celestial joys of paradise! Randy Petersen, in *Christian History* magazine, characterizes Tetzel "a regular P.T. Barnum traveling through the towns and villages with his pitch for forgiveness of sins, cheap at any price," when the alternatives were considered. He used an alluring advertising slogan which captures this crudity nicely: "As soon as a coin in the coffer rings, the rescued soul from Purgatory to heaven springs."[98]

Indulgences were especially popular among the poor, just as lotteries and other gambling attract those today who have the least money to spare, but do so with the hope of "hitting it big." The writer of 1 Peter 1:18-19 (NRSV) proclaimed it clearly that believers have been ransomed "*not with perishable things like silver and gold, but with the precious blood of Christ...*" Likewise, the Apostle Paul confirms in Ephesians 2:8 (NRSV) that it is "*by grace you have been saved through faith, and this is not your own doing; it is the gift of God—not the result of works*" (or by indulgences). Grace is not for sale. Christ's shed blood was not only "sacred"—it was sufficient.

Things had gotten so out of hand, so ridiculous to our modern thinking, that there was even a pay-now-sin-later scheme for recidivists planning for their future sins: "I will take two robberies, two rapes, and a murder to go." And at the right price, believers could save up for the "cost" of their own future sins to insure their own way out of purgatory with a sort of

---

[98] <https://christianhistoryinstitute.org/magazine/article/selling-forgiveness-sparked-protestant-reformation>.

spiritual IRA. Such cynical manipulation of holy things for unholy gain was anathema to Luther. Later, he called the practice, which in his heart and mind clearly violated the Gospel, "the pious defrauding of the faithful"[99] by playing on their fears. "'Roman bloodsucking' was what many German princes called it."[100]

One cannot help but recognize the correlation between Luther and Trump in the way they respond to accusations, seemingly willing to "admit" but with a more biting indictment. Luther, in responding to being wrongly condemned in the Roman Bull, commented, "I was wrong, I admit it, when I said that indulgences were 'the pious defrauding of the faithful.' I recant and I say, 'Indulgences are the most impious frauds and imposters of the most rascally pontiffs, by which they deceive the souls and destroy the goods of the faithful."[101]

---

[99] Kittelson, James M., *Luther the Reformer* (Minneapolis: Augsburg Publishing House, 1986), p.104, citing LW 32:64 (WA:7, 126).

[100] Ibid.

[101] Bainton, Roland H., *Here I Stand: A Life of Martin Luther* (New York, Nashville: Abingdon Press, 1955), p.165; the paperback edition, A Mentor Book, p.127-28.

9

Draining the Swamp is Dirty Work

Luther captured the popular mood throughout Germany with his promise to clean up a corrupt and bloated Rome. The consequences for Luther tackling such monumental corruption resulted in his being charged as "an enemy of the State," a capital offense, and excommunication as a condemned heretic for challenging and calling the all-powerful Church to be accountable. In the face of all he encountered, Luther had the audacity to dub the citadel of faith—the Vatican in Rome—a "Lernaean* swamp full of hydras and other monsters,"[102] that needed to be drained. This was only one of the several unflattering descriptions he bestowed upon the Holy City.

Remembering later in life his visit to the Eternal City, Luther reflected on the disappointment he experienced with "*Sancta Roma*" (the "Holy City of Rome"). Lyndal Roper,† in her three-dimensional portrait of *Martin Luther: Renegade and Prophet*, shares his damning verdict of what he had witnessed first-hand: "I saw the head of all wickedness and the seat of the Devil" or the "*Sedes Diaboli.*"[103] She is further descriptive in her footnote by quoting what Luther immediately added recalling this experience later in life: "'And the Devil shat his thanks on the Pope,' as if the city's reputation for holiness still needed a bit of prophylactic mud-slinging"[104]

---

* A reference to the swamp at Lerna, Greece, near Argos, in which Hercules and Iolaus were said to have killed the hydra, a multiheaded serpentine monster, which was a terror to the people of Lerna. According to Greco-Roman mythology, every effort to destroy the creature was futile, for with every head that was chopped off, the hydra regenerated two more, until Hercules slew it using fire to seal the wounds.

[102] Metaxas, *Rediscovered*, p.134.

† Lyndal Roper is a distinguished and respected historian of early modern Europe and is the first woman to hold the prestigious Regius Chair at Oxford University. Her newest book, *Luther's World, Body and Soul* (Princeton 2018) focuses on the social and cultural themes connected with Luther.

[103] Roper, Lyndal, *Martin Luther: Renegade and Prophet*, New York: Random House (2017); p.48, quoting from WT 5, 5344, 75:2 summer 1540.

[104] Ibid., p.431 in her Chapter 3 Notes, "The Monastery," footnote 38 quoting from WT 5, 6059.

He was horrified as he witnessed the moral decrepitude of the clergy. The young monk had found Rome to be a hotbed of corruption; and worse, the Catholic Church did not stop such sinfulness, greed and otherworldly desires, but was a key player in it. As Bainton puts it, "Luther commented that he had gone to Rome with onions and had returned with garlic."[105]

The Twin Warriors Caricatured as Fighting Swamp Creatures

Luther as "The German Hercules"

Luther Dealing Crushing Blows to His Opponents

Left: Public domain, retrieved at the Red Brick Parsonage blog

Trump as "The American Superhero"

Trump Dropping the Hammer on America's Enemies

Right: *TIME* magazine, retrieved at the Patriot Minear blog

In a 1519 woodcut by Hans Holbein the Younger (left), Luther is portrayed as Germany's Hercules after the famed Greek hero. Luther with his tonsure (hair shaved off top of head) and Augustinian habit, from which a lion's skin hangs down protracted, holds down the neck of the Flemish Dominican theologian and inquisitor Jacob van Hoogstraaten. In his right hand, he holds a knotty club with long, sharp spikes, in order to deal crushing blows to his opponents, past and present. A string is drawn from Luther's nose, which has the strangled Pope, identified by his triple crown, hanging from the end of it. His already slain victims, lying on the ground powerless, include the philosopher Aristotle; Thomas Aquinas; William of Ockham; an unnamed monk; Nicholas of Lyra directly beneath Luther's feet with his commentary on the Bible in hand; Peter Lombard, wearing a beret, virtually crushed by those around him, holding his book (which reads "L. IV SENTENCIAR"—short for *Libri IV Sententiarum* [Four Books of Sentences]—in reflected letters); Robert Holcot, an English Dominican scholastic philosopher, theologian, and influential Bible scholar; and Duns Scotus, who was known for his commentary on Lombard's *Sentences*, but who is not visible. In the background are some houses in a small village below a mountain. Between the village and the foreground, another hooded and tasseled figure makes good his escape. Beneath the woodcut are six Latin distichs (a two-line verse or couplet), the first of which reads:

> Do you not shudder, wicked Rome, at your enemy Luther,
> the German Hercules, as he does away with monsters?

---

105 Bainton, *Here I Stand*, Abingdon, p.51; Mentor pb, p.38.

In the image on the right, *TIME* magazine accidentally turns Trump into a superhero in what was intended as a hit piece. Their goal was to show him oblivious to the chaos around him. Instead, they inadvertently showed him as unflappable. The President is dropping the hammer on America's enemies; some within his party, others from the swamp, including his opposition, the "Deep State," and the "Fake News media."

As if taking a page from Luther's playbook, Donald Trump described groups of miscreants in Washington, D.C., as the quixotic "swamp" needing to be drained. He identified this "swamp" of rogue scoundrels operating within the Washington Beltway as being comprised of cronies and large donors, legislators in both parties, lobbyists, assorted special interests of all types, and the embedded "Deep State"—the steady creep and entrenchment of government bureaucrats that drain the vitality and wealth of the people—who grow unimaginably wealthy at the expense of the American citizens. Such a depiction of Washington corresponds to Luther's view of Pope Leo X's Rome:

> The Church of Rome, once the holiest of all, has become the most licentious den of thieves, the most shameless of all brothels, the kingdom of sin, death, and hell. It is so bad that even the Antichrist himself, if he should come, could think of nothing to add to its wickedness. ...Is it not true that under the vast expanse of heaven there is nothing more corrupt, more pestilential, more offensive than the Roman Curia? It surpasses beyond all comparison the godlessness of the Turks so that, indeed, although it was once a gate of heaven, it is now an open mouth of hell..."[106]

The notion that corrupt politicians would rather promote policies beneficial to themselves, their donors and lobbyists than their constituents was also a similar concern to Luther:

> Often the Councils [especially Constance and Basel] have made some pretense at reformation, but their attempts have been cleverly frustrated by the guile of certain men and things have gone from bad to worse. With God's help I intend to expose the wiles and wickedness of these men, so that they are shown up for what they are and may never again be so obstructive and destructive."[107]

---

[106] LW 31:336-337. *Career of the Reformer I*, "Letter to Pope Leo X" prefacing *The Freedom of a Christian*; or *Three Treatises*, p.268-69, 270.

[107] LW 44:124-25. *The Christian in Society, I*, "An Open Letter to the Christian Nobility;" and also, *Three Treatises*, p.11.

We discover Martin Laidlaw's 2016 post graduate thesis, "These Walls of Straw and Paper" exploring key complaints raised against religious institutions in the Reformation era and pointing to the similarity he views between our two populist leaders: "Trump's complaints against the Washington political establishment ultimately mirror Luther's criticisms of the papacy: that the Court of Rome serves only the popes and cardinals whom it allows to live in splendor; that the sale of indulgences grants absolution only to those with financial means to obtain them."[108]

Regardless of personal opinions or political persuasion, it is unmistakable that both disruptors

> believe they are fighting a vast and uncompromising enemy, one which has the backing of larger political and media entities. Whereas Luther promotes adherence to Scripture (*Sola Scriptura*), it is the upholding of the U.S. Constitution and Federal Law that Trump seeks to enforce (*Sola Lex*).... What is also fundamental to both is their desire to enact real change on procedure and practice of sacred institutions. Like Trump, Luther...was met with intense opposition from the establishment he wished to permanently alter.[109]

It doesn't take long walking around a swamp to become aware that while the water is murky and smelly in its stagnant state, when it is stirred and disrupted the stench gets even worse. Perhaps Luther was closer in downgrading his descriptive word for Rome from "swamp" to "cesspit" or cesspool; and since Trump has entered the White House, he too has suggested the same degradation as Luther. Addressing the Boy Scout Jamboree on July 24, 2017, he said, "I go to Washington, and I see all these politicians, and I see the swamp, and it's not a good place. In fact, today, I said we ought to change it from the word 'swamp' to the word 'cesspool' or perhaps to the word 'sewer.'"[110]

---

[108] Laidlaw, Martin, "These Walls of Straw and Paper: Trump, Luther and Political Populism," *Histories of Emotion*, October 7, 2016. <https://historiesofemotion.com/2016/10/07/these-walls-of-straw-of-straw-and-paper-trump-luther-and-political-populism>.

[109] Ibid.

[110] Nilsen, Ella, "5 Bizarre Moments from President Trump's Speech to the Boy Scouts," *Vox* magazine, July 25, 2017. <https://www.vox.com/2017/7/25/16024928/trump-boy-scout-jamboree-speech>.

Die Luterisch Strebkatz

Luther's Tug of War with the Church

Draining the Swamp

Trump Confronts the Deep State and Corruption

Warriors Taking a Stand with Enormous Odds Against Them

(Left) Martin Luther and the Pope are engaged in the popular game of *"Strebkatznziehen,"* a tug-of-war between two opponents, gripping between their teeth a wooden rod at each end of a connecting rope. The Pope is helped by Luther's main theological opponents with the heads of animals symbolically associated with the Devil: John Eck as the pig, Jerome Emser as the goat, Murner as an Alsace cat, and Jacob Lemp as a dog wearing a scholar's cap. In the background are peasants who proved difficult to convert in southern Germany, and were mocked for being ignorant and superstitious beasts. Despite the appearance of an uneven match, the Pope has fallen to his knees with his triple-tiered crown toppling off his head. His purse full of coins has burst open on the ground in a sign of papal greed. Keeping Luther steady is a large cross signifying that Christ is on his side and therefore stands for the true Word of God. His opponents were not only on the wrong side, but on the side of traitors with the greedy Pope of Rome. The rat-infested king has likewise been corrupted as the aristocracy had a share in the wealth received from indulgences.

<https://danarehn.com/2017/10/16/exhibition-luthers-reformation/>.

(Right) "Drain the Swamp" originally meant to get rid of the malaria-carrying mosquitoes by draining the swamp. Figuratively, it became a familiar theme of President Trump's mission to "exterminate something that is harmful" or anything that people hate such as corruption, government waste, or criminality in weaponizing and targeting agencies such as the FBI, DOJ against political opponents. Trump also claimed the media as the enemy of the people supporting the swamp creatures along with the deep state unaccountable bureaucrats and self-perceived elitists who desire to dictate to *"We the People"* what they believe we are unable to decide or determine as best for ourselves.

(retrieved from <https://www.pinterest.com/pin/339740365626042503/>).

Candidate Trump presented his opponent, Hillary Clinton, as a representative of this den of corruption and establishment cronyism residing in the swamp. Postgraduate research student at the University of Dundee, Martin Laidlaw, points to what he saw as a major hindrance to her campaign, and still unresolved "is the charge of deleting (and subsequently destroying) 33,000 subpoenaed emails that were held on an illegally created private server" which risked national security, a crime for which others have been incarcerated. With a "Lutherish" understanding, Trump "has cast Hillary as 'the buyer of indulgences' who escapes unpunished despite evidence of guilt."[111] Luther had asserted that the temporal Christian power must exercise its office like the symbolic blindfolded Lady Justice without considering whom it may strike, whether pope or bishop or priest; whoever is guilty, let him suffer for it.[112]

Trump thus echoes Luther's conclusion: "Where sin is, there is no escape from punishment."[113] The candidate focused on his opponent to illustrate how the justice agencies of our country are being "weaponized" and abused for political gain and to call attention to how our system of government is rife with unethical practice by making charges of financial improprieties, nepotism, pay-to-play, embezzlement, and unfavorable deals and treaties. He observed many embedded in the swamp who sought financial gain and promoted policies beneficial to donors over the reward of serving their countrymen. Both Church and State had abandoned their very purpose and thus neglected the needs and desires of the people they were to serve.

The "anti-Trumpers" seem incensed, embarrassed, and perhaps threatened that an outsider successfully shattered the crystal ceiling of the governmental palace and penetrated the inner sanctums of the political process and power without having met any of the select elite "club" prerequisites, including prior military or elected experience. Or maybe the rub or the insult was his boasting and strutting about just such inoculation from Washington. Even worse perhaps was the realization that he would have access to much which covered up existing corruption and the ability to expose the ways those in power nefariously pursued their own political agenda and exalted privileges. Here was a warrior who viewed the administrative State's reach going beyond government. It embraces and enhances the media, political consultants, related professions (especially the legal establishment), academia, and identity groups. They all mutually give legitimacy to each other while strengthening the administrative State's grip over the citizens. Here comes a reformer challenging and shaming the media's dishonest participants, who belie their claim of professionalism by reporting "Fake News" or purposefully withholding stories or facts that are inconvenient to their biased agenda. In addition, he was willing to take on bureaucrats who are not accountable to the electorate but serve special interest clients/ lobbyists with favorable regulations.

---

[111] Laidlaw, "Straw."

[112] LW 44:131. *The Christian in Society I*, "Letter to the Christian Nobility;" also *Three Treatises*, p.18.

[113] Ibid., LW 44:133; and in *Three Treatises*, p. 20.

The double standard and two-tiered justice administered politically has also come under the scrutiny of the Trump administration. Those, including Congress, who have been exposed for their duplicity and hypocrisy hate him for shining the light upon them, and in a coordinated fashion, their response is, "Impeach!" because they are being uncovered and discovered. Above all, imagine how an amateur politician bringing his new brand of politics with its distinctive style of Twitter-based ad hominem to the White House must infuriate them as he penetrates the shroud his opposition and detractors have operated behind.

The implausible candidate and President has repeatedly defied expert predictions and has proven himself to be a far more astute student of politics and culture than his critics understand. His cavalier attitude, by not conforming to "orthodox" protocol or acting "presidential," enrages his foes. As a result of his election, their singular focus has centered on delegitimatizing his presidency by continually resisting and obstructing the President's efforts to drain the "Washington swamp" and by peeling back the onion's layers of deceit and intrigue covering corruption. Through the dismantling of the establishment's power and control of the "Deep State" or "the centralized administrative State," Trump is seeking to return the government to the people.

From the beginning of his presidency, Trump has been charged with "colluding with the Russians," obstructing justice and treason, and has faced the hostile threats of impeachment which began minutes after he was sworn in. The *Washington Post*'s headline, published seventeen minutes after the inauguration, read, "The Campaign to Impeach President Trump Has Begun."[114] He has been the target of rude and derogatory insults and character assassinations, not only for being inept but being psychologically unfit to hold the office, along with personal attacks on his family and members of his administration.

---

[114] <https://www.washingtonpost.com/news/post-politics/wp/2017/01/20/the-campaign-to-impeach-president-trump-has-begun>.

10

The Oppressed and the Vulnerable Find a Voice

Rising to prominence on the wave of anti-establishment discontent among those who felt themselves shut out and left behind by the powers that be, both of our twin warriors were suggesting that the people could liberate themselves from the tarnished and abusive powers of the Church and State. Luther clearly saw a Church hierarchy that was no longer in love with the Truth and the pursuit of the same. Trump saw a nation squandering its distinctive role of being a democracy of representative self-government that is "of the people, by the people and for the people." Our twin disruptors both observed good and honest questions being answered with an imperious, "Be silent and do as we say, or else."[115]

At the foundation of these populist reformers was a rejection of "experts" or "elites" who mistakenly presume to instruct those they characterize as "the masses," the "retrograde lot," "barbarians," "deplorables," "dregs of society" and "smelly Walmart shoppers" because they are thought to be too ignorant to know what's good for them. Our twin contentious warriors each derived much of their power as avatars from the wide swath of the population that felt put down, silenced, and then stigmatized by their self-styled betters. The aristocrats in both centuries speak from the privileged ranks of presumed superiority and the heights of idealism rather than going "down" and "out" among those they abhor, where they might experience, empathize and learn. Instead, "we know what's best for you" was the condescending message heard from the loftiness of academia's ivory towers and the Church's high pulpits, through government officials and bureaucratic regulations mandated by those not held accountable to the electorate. People were told what to do and how to do it, what to think and value, and how to live and achieve (buy) salvation.

Conscience: The Dog that Can't Bite, but Never Stops Barking

Luther championed conscience, which some have described as "living with yourself for the rest of your life." It is like a compass; and for Luther, one's conscience is guided by faith

[115] Metaxas, *Rediscovered*, p.94.

bestowed through divine grace and informed by reading the Scriptures, over the deceitful dictates of Church rules and regulations. We have witnessed the effect on the economy after President Trump freed businesses from unnecessary bureaucratic regulations and controls:

> Luther and Trump would also quickly have discovered a shared impatience with law and lawyers: A single wise prince was worth a battalion of pen-pushers, Luther thought, and he was often alarmingly ready to give carte blanche to a ruler whose favor he needed—even to the point of winking at some very unorthodox marital arrangements.[116]

The Wittenberg professor liked rulers (could he be thinking about his own prince, Frederick the Wise, his protectorate?) who cut through convention to get stuff done, and who left him alone to do his own thing without being unnecessarily bridled. Lest one be led to believe Luther was advocating an "anything goes" license by upholding individual conscience, one needs to take to heart the full impact of those words he had declared at his trial in Worms: "Unless I am convinced by Scripture and plain reason…my conscience is captive to the Word of God. I cannot and I will not recant anything, for to go against conscience is neither right nor safe. God help me. Amen."[117]

Roland Bainton adds that "The earliest printed version added the words: 'Here I stand, I cannot do otherwise.' The words, though not recorded on the spot, may nevertheless be genuine, because the listeners at the moment may have been too moved to write."[118]

In pointing to the enduring relevance of Martin Luther in a masterful commemoration of the Reformer's 500th birthday in the *New York Times*, Jaroslav Pelikan joins those who have called Luther the "rediscoverer of conscience:" "Part of his universal appeal, across the boundaries of history and of belief, comes from his spirited defense of the sanctity of the individual, who cannot, and therefore must not, be forced to say 'I believe' if it is not true."[119]

Each of our disruptors, separated by 500 years, sought to make those in positions of authority more responsive and accountable to the people they were to serve. They thus

---

[116] Ryrie, Alec, "Martin Luther Was the Donald Trump of 1517," *Foreign Policy*, May 23, 2017; <https://foreignpolicy.com/2017/05/23/martin-luther-was-the-donald-trump-of-1517>.

[117] LW 32:112 *Career of the Reformer II*, "Luther at the Diet of Worms," LW 32:112.

[118] Bainton, *Here I Stand*, Abingdon, p.185; Mentor paperback, p.144.

[119] Pelikan, Jaroslav, "The Enduring Relevance of Martin Luther 500 Years After His Birth," *The New York Times Magazine*, Sept 18, 1983. <https://www.nytimes.com/1983/09/18/magazine/the-enduring-relevance-of-martin-luther-500-years-after-his-birth.html>.

addressed the abuse and attempted to eradicate criminality in their effort to affect real change on procedures and practices within the institutions they loved and viewed to be sacred.

Both Trump and Luther inaugurated creative and effective means of appealing to the masses of those alienated and deemed uneducated in the "scholarly" and "ecclesiastical" language of the "cosmopolitan" cultural elites by fluently speaking the language of the street. As ironic as it sounds, they were not just bypassing the traditional gatekeepers by circumventing the media but were now waging a populist insurgency by engaging and speaking directly with the people on the streets over the heads of the "experts." The significance of Luther writing in German "for the laity" also had the positive effect of de-mystifying religious, political, legal and economic systems which communicated formally in Latin. Both recognized the power of an existing medium and transformed it into an influential political tool used to bypass established media conventions and communicate directly with the people.

Core Convictions—Back to Basics

One could call "Marty" and "The Donald" voices crying in the wilderness in a straight-shooting manner that broke the norms. (Remember, Scripture even calls our attention to the strange "dress" and "diet" of John the Baptist!) Trump is the product of a corrupt, oppressive political environment, and Luther is the product of a Church that had clearly lost its bearings. They both gave voice to what the "common rabble" was thinking and the frustrations the forgotten were experiencing.

Our brash president, like the 16th-century monk, has a singular talent for calling us back to the basics of our beliefs. For Trump, it is returning to the foundational values of our country by upholding the Declaration of Independence for "We the People," and the Constitution limiting the role of government over the people in a top-down manner. Trump entered the political arena identifying with those who felt a willful disregard for the "rule of law" by the powerful elite, and feared the decline of traditional "American exceptionalism" through slow national deference to other nations, which he felt was to our own detriment. It was the erosion of the distinctiveness of "The American Experiment" caused by ignoring the constitutional boundaries laid out by the Founding Fathers that Trump feared. He spoke to and for the people in a simple but stirring affirmation, like Ronald Reagan did in his successful 1980 presidential campaign slogan "Let's Make America Great Again." The emphasis on "again" presupposes a departure Trump perceives as radical and destructive to our constitutional republic. It was an affirmation as stirring and as simple as that of Martin Luther calling the nobles to "take back their country" from the Roman bureaucracy that had been feeding on their money. Luther denounced the vast money-hungry bureaucracy of papal officials as "a crawling mass of reptiles."[120]

Though excommunicated by Pope Leo X in 1521, Luther challenged the Pope's authority and continued his proud stance against the perceived corrosion of the Catholic faith and intolerable corruption of the established Catholic Church. For Luther it was a return to the sources of Scripture, and "Scripture Alone" (*Sola Scriptura*), that provided authority above the Pope and Councils of the Church. Simply put, for Luther it was Scripture that created the Church, while for his adversaries, it was the power of the Church which had created the Scriptures.

Luther struck a chord with the people who felt exploited as they were being bilked through the sleazy spiritual extortion racket of indulgences to pay for lavish basilicas and other architectural glories, such as the rebuilding of St. Peter's in the Eternal City, and wages paid to Michelangelo and Raphael for their Renaissance art. German gold and money were leaving the country to enrich the grandeur of the Vatican in Italy, and in return Pope Leo X was sending worthless pieces of parchment known as "indulgence vouchers" that gave people a reduction in their purgatorial stay by "guaranteeing" an earlier berth in heaven for departed loved ones (or for themselves).

Furthermore, Luther clearly understood the economic concern the princes were experiencing, which parallels Trump's alarm regarding the unfavorable balance of trade for our country. In attacking this fundraising scheme, Luther threatened the Church's mainstay with the loss of financial revenue as well as political power. He saw the monetizing of forgiveness as a devious stratagem for the benefit of the institution, instead of the institution serving the people by assuring the faithful that they are the recipients of God's mercy and grace as a "free gift." For Luther, this was the Church's purpose: the proclamation of the "*Gospel*" which is *Good News!* This was to become the foundation of his whole system of thought—his theology—for which he was plainly ready to lay down his life.

Both men were driven by certain core convictions that never seem to waver. Rather than engaging with Luther's ideas, the Church simply labeled him a heretic, ordering him to "shut up" or face the legal consequences and be happily consigned to a fiery death. Just as the Church hierarchy lashed back at Luther, so have those formerly in power and their allies in both political parties, the "Deep State," the media and academia lashed out at Trump. We have been subject to massive displays of projection, accusing him of corruption, collusion, treason, even being mentally unbalanced, as "the resistance" obstructs every nomination he makes or position he takes. In both cases, the more these warrior reformers are attacked and

---

[120] Kittelson, *Reformer*, p.112.

criticized by those who feel their power threatened and their influence waning, the more the legions of supporters seem to rally, grow, and stand firmer against the elite establishment. In Luther's experience, "The world cannot truly charge me with public crimes; that angers it all the more…"[121]

And so it also seems to be with the opposition's unproven allegations of collusion with Russia toward Trump, or in defending their articles of impeachment of the President. The more militant enemies have a way of always emphasizing and exaggerating flaws, creating fake claims, and distorting what is true. A quote attributed to various "notables" (Mark Twain, Jonathan Swift, Thomas Jefferson, John Randolph, Charles Spurgeon, Winston Churchill, etc.) expresses the reality we, unfortunately, know all too well: "A lie can travel halfway around the world while the truth is still putting on its shoes." While the phrasing and figurative language of the quote has been evolving, the Quote Investigator website shares comments made by Swift in 1710:

> Besides, as the vilest Writer has his Readers, so the greatest Liar has his Believers; and it often happens, that if a Lie be believ'd only for an Hour, it has done its Work, and there is no farther occasion for it. Falsehood flies, and Truth comes limping after it; so that when Men come to be undeceiv'd, it is too late; the Jest is over, and the Tale has had its Effect…[122]

Actually, an extensive MIT study of Twitter posts published in *Science* finds that fake, misleading, or false news online travels "farther, faster, deeper, and more broadly than truth. And the effect is more pronounced for false political news than for false news about terrorism, natural disasters, science, urban legends or financial information. Falsehoods are 70 percent more likely to be retweeted on Twitter than the truth, researchers found."[123]

Similarly, and unfortunately, like any oft-repeated lie, the long-term, systematic defamation of Luther and Trump's characters attain the status of truth in the minds of many—especially those who can't be bothered to investigate history or verify claims for

---

[121] Oberman, Heiko A., *Luther—Man between God and the Devil*, translated by Eileen Walliser-Schwarzbart (New York, NY: Image Books Doubleday, 1982), p.321.

[122] <https://quoteinvestigator.com/2014/07/13/truth>, citing an article written by Jonathan Swift, November 2, 1710, in *The London Examiner*, No. 15, p.2.

[123] Church, Zach. "Study: False News Spreads Faster Than the Truth," MIT Sloan School of Management, March 8, 2018; <https://mitsloan.mit.edu/ideas-made-to-matter/study-false-news-spreads-faster-truth>; or Carr, Nicholas, "Unfortunately, Lies Can Trump Truth," *Political Magazine*, Nov. 19, 2020. <https://www.politico.com/news/magazine/2020/11/19/roundup-what-trump-showed-us-about-america-435762>.

themselves and give evidence of having no real clue as to what these warriors are genuinely like. They will believe and report only that narrative that agrees with their pre-existent views and predetermined agenda.

In our twisted world we have experienced several high-profile cases where "rushes to judgment" were wrongly made by high officials and advanced by false media accounts, with nary an apology when proven false. The critically important constitutional guarantees of presumption of innocence, due process and rule of law are ignored in favor of rumor, prejudices and false narratives to further biased positions that support their schemes, not truth. We can point to how fake media got it wrong on Baltimore, Charlottesville, Freddie Gray, Rodney King, the George Zimmerman shooting of Trayvon Martin, the Ferguson uprising with the fatal shooting of Michael Brown, the Cambridge Police, the Duke Lacrosse rape case, Richard Jewell, and of course the Covington High School student Nick Sandmann, the Steele document, Russian collusion, and Russian disinformation. The same predictable cast of characters don't seem to care about truth or justice, equal justice, or equal application of our laws. They only care about their narrative, which had already spread like a contagion before the facts were fully known. And when their feelings are derailed by facts and logic, their response is not a retraction, nor admission of getting it wrong, let alone acknowledging their violating the ethics and standards of journalism. Instead, their *modus operandi* is to resort to derogatory screams of racism or other accusations which intimidate, demean and polarize. Trump has called these purveyors of "'Fake News' the enemy of the people.... They're very dishonest people." He then cites that deception in the way "they dropped off the word 'fake' and all of a sudden the story became 'the media is the enemy'...I called the 'Fake News' the enemy of the people—the 'Fake News.'"[124]

Sadly, this is not just too frequently occurring within the media and from our lofty governmental officials, but even more lamentably, we experience it within the Church. Our Evangelical Lutheran Church in America (ELCA) is not alone in this practice, but certainly is in lock step as it journeys with Protestant liberalism in reflecting our society and culture. St. Paul instructs the Church in Romans 12:2, *"Do not be conformed to this world"* (NRSV, RSV). John Bertram Philllips' Modern English Version (PME) translates the passage as *"Don't let the world around you squeeze you into its own mould,"* while Eugene Petersen's *The Message, The Bible in Contemporary Language*, renders it *"Don't become so well-adjusted to your culture that you fit into it without even thinking."*

In "A Pastoral Message on the Rittenhouse Acquittal," ELCA Bishop Elizabeth Eaton quotes verse 19:15 (NRSV) from the book of Leviticus, *"You shall not render an unjust*

---

[124] <https://www.nytimes.com/2018/07/19/business/media/trump-media-enemy-of-the-people.html>.

judgment; you shall not be partial to the poor or defer to the great: with justice you shall judge your neighbor." She proceeds to cite our ELCA social message on "Community Violence"* which "urges us to become more involved in countering the reality and fear of violence in our communities and our neighbors' communities, pursuing justice and seeking peace no matter how long the journey or complex the challenge." She then, in my view, rushes to judgment in her comments:

> When a child is allowed to become a vigilante without recourse, we are forced to confront the idols of our society: guns, violence and white supremacy. To be sure, this is not about one person, but indeed about all of us, together.
>
> Today's acquittal is an injustice. It points to the disorder in which we all live. As we seek to restore justice; so also will we restore God to God's rightful place at the center of our life together.[125]

She wrote this, as she admits, on the day the acquittal was rendered by a jury. Is it fair to ask whether she had viewed all the evidence the jury had seen, some of which, from my understanding, was only released after the verdict was rendered? Or whether she would defend herself with everything and anything she had while being pursued and about to be beaten with a skateboard? When is defending oneself a vigilante action? It is easy for religious zeal to be compromised by pre-determined assumptions of intellectual and moral infallibility. As the Church we must not neglect our responsibilities and, as we will later discover, to exercise our right to call for justice in government and society, though as we learn also from St. Paul, we cannot forfeit our commitment to observing the rule of law, due process, presumption of innocence until proven guilty, and trial by jury. While our bishop commands that we do not render an unjust judgment, she makes premature judgments by calling Kyle Rittenhouse a vigilante, implying he was a white supremist and his acquittal by a jury an injustice in the same epistle. A criminal trial's sole purpose is to determine the guilt of the one charged, not to be a reflection on a social justice statement. Yet as the Presiding Bishop she frequently writes such pastoral messages which appear to espouse her political view or bias as the judgment or pronouncements of the Church.

---

* "A Social Message on…Community Violence" is available to read or download from the Evangelical Lutheran Church In America; <https://www.elca.org/faith/faith-and-society/social-messages/community-violence>.

[125] Eaton, Bishop Elizabeth, "Pastoral Message," November 19, 2021; <https://www.elca.org/News-and-Events/8125?>.

In today's arena of identity politics, within society, and especially within the Church as we will further explore with immigration, sanctuary denomination, double standards of "justice," racism, environmentalists, et al., condemnation and judgement toward the "other" is not in short supply. Within these contexts, ill-considered advocacy and rush to judgements can compound confusion, conflict and division within churches and in culture. A more adequate "teaching office" (magisterium) in the Church and congregations providing open discussion of papers or presentations on these controversial topics could provide the people of God with a firmer foundation in understanding and voicing God's Law and Gospel, while honoring different voices or viewpoints by upholding Luther's view of the freedom of individual conscience. After all, God saw fit to provide us with four renderings of the Gospel in Matthew, Mark, Luke and John.

As we will further discover, our junior warrior shares his senior's counsel in his "Sincere Admonition to All Christians:"

> But when you see these same liars pour their lies and poison into other people, then you should boldly take the offensive and fight against them, just as Paul in Acts 13 [:10-11] attacked Elymas with hard and sharp words, and as Christ called the Pharisees a "brood of vipers [Matthew 23:33]. You should do this, not for their sake, for they will not listen, but for the sake of those whom they are poisoning. Just so does St. Paul command Titus to rebuke sharply such empty talkers and deceivers of souls [1:10-13].[126]

---

[126] LW 45:71. *The Christian in Society II*, "A Sincere Admonition to All Christians to Guard Against Insurrection and Rebellion," 1522.

11

Character, Style and Speech

Many leaders do not possess what it takes to set themselves against a ruling class or the establishment the way Luther and Trump have done. With traits of authoritarianism, they challenged the establishment with a courage that was as stubborn as it was fearless. Both warriors display an absolute bullheadedness in their convictions and leadership style, which is often misinterpreted and thus runs the risk of garnering many unneeded enemies. Nevertheless, they do not back down if they feel they're right, and neither of them find it easy to admit the possibility that they might be wrong. As a matter of fact, one could say that even setbacks are rarely admitted or accepted, and if they are acknowledged they are perceived as moral victories or preludes to victory. Both identify with those who are sick and tired of the status quo and politics as usual, and those who are willing to rock the boat. Both leave no doubt about their designations as disruptors and anti-establishment figures.

Trump will take on the world, the media, Congress, Russia, China, Iran and North Korea. You oppose him and he will counterpunch harder, fighting the opponent to the finish no matter how much criticism results. In Conrad Black's assessment, Trump is "a battle-hardened veteran of very difficult businesses full of unethical people (and he is no Eagle Scout). He is a very tough and an almost demiurgically energetic man.... His exterior is uneven, but his history is one of astounding accomplishment.... He admires strength and respects earned success in every field."[127] His personality can be garish and flamboyant. He is one you may not want to take literally, but you'd be mistaken not to take him seriously. He repeatedly outwits his opponents and seems to relish those opportunities to create chaos to throw them off their game. In addition, he possesses that singular, unique talent in drawing out and exposing people for who they really are. One could say he knows how to "play people to a 't'."

Luther relished the support of friends, but when wounded by disagreement, he was naturally inclined to flatten perceived opponents who didn't follow his preferred path. Characteristically he was unapologetically ungracious toward his opponents and was always

---

[127] Black, Conrad, "Why Donald J. Trump is Truly a President Like No Other," *National Post*. <https://nationalpost.com/opinion/conrad-black-why-donald-j-trump-is-truly-a-president-like-no-other>.

ready to apply the label "fanatic" to those who crossed him. The scathing rebukes he could dish out to even some of his closest friends caused many to bite their tongues lest they become his enemies. One can find such parallels as Tony Schwartz recalling his experiences with Luther's twin when he was collaborating on the book *The Art of the Deal.* He recalls

> ...how Trump got angry about some perceived slight. Everyone around him knew that you were best off keeping your distance at those times, or, if that wasn't possible, that you should resist disagreeing with him in any way. In the hundreds of Trump's phone calls, I listened in on with his consent, and the dozens of meetings I attended with him, I can never remember anyone disagreeing with him about anything. [And he fears that] the same climate of fear and paranoia appears to have taken root in his White House.[128]

Could not the assessment of Martin Luther in James R. Payton, Jr.'s review of Craig Harline's *A World Ablaze: The Rise of Martin Luther and the Birth of the Reformation* also apply to Luther's twin, Donald Trump? "Luther could be irascible and stubborn. He could exhibit both dramatic bravery and fearful hesitation. He manifested extraordinary humor and could display undeniable pettiness. That is to say, he was a genuine human being."[129]

Luther recognized the trait he shares with Trump by admitting that while others "prick with pins and needles...I stab with a heavy pike used to hunt boars."[130] CBS News reported that an "unnamed confidant" of the President referenced this medieval weapon in warning GOP senators, "You vote against the President and your head will be on a pike."[131] Luther's closest ally, with whom he shared a scholarly symbiosis and lifelong personal and

---

[128] Schwartz, Tony, "I wrote '*The Art of the Deal*' with Trump. His Self-Sabotage is Rooted in his Past," May 16, 2017 op-ed in the *Washington Post*; <https://www.washingtonpost.com/posteverything/wp/2017/05/16/i-wrote-the-art-of-the-deal-with-trump-his-self-sabotage-is-rooted-in-his-past>.

[129] Payton, Jr., James R. review of Craig Hartline's *A World Ablaze*; <https://www.christianitytoday.com/ct/2017/november-web-only/reliving-reformation-as-it-happened.html>.

[130] LW 54:50. *Table Talk*, "Difference Between Luther and Melanchthon, No. 348."

[131] <https://www.marketwatch.com/story/gop-senators-told-their-heads-will-be-on-a-pike-if-they-vote-against-trump-report-2020-01-24>.

spiritual bond, Philipp Melanchthon,* described his admired colleague as having a "'militant temperament' and a 'cocky self-righteousness.'"[132]

Philipp Melanchthon

In spite of that honest appraisal, Melanchthon recorded that "[he] would rather die than be parted from this man."[133] In writing about having to "bear the burden…Melanchthon complained to a trusted friend: 'I bore an almost dishonorable servitude, for Luther more often allowed his temperament to rule, which contained a not insignificant pugnacity and bossiness, than he would have done if he had paid attention to his reputation and to the common good.'"[134] Those words could equally apply to Donald Trump, and we might say if Trump were solely concerned with his reputation or his showing in the polls, he would surely at times hold his temperament (and some of his tweets!) in check.

For both, because of their disposition and zest for action, everything moved too slowly. Luther would generally respond immediately to his opponents, adopting the uncompromising, combative style of debate that was in keeping with his unconditional responsibility to the truth. Trump likewise is action-oriented, championing "Promises Made, Promises Kept" and almost rejoicing in defying predictions of what can't be done, while at the same time resenting the opposition bent on obstructing and resisting through legislative roadblocks and parliamentary maneuvers, and the media who are willing to interpret anything he says or does in the worst possible light.

Sharp Tongues and Foul Mouths

As one would imagine, both populists were bristly and untamable, plain-spoken and direct, no doubt due to the pent-up aggravation they were confronting and felt compelled to bear.

---

* Philipp Melanchthon, original name Philipp Schwartzerdt, colleague and collaborator at Wittenberg and Luther's friend, who was a professor of Greek and a theologian, composed the first systematic treatment of the new Wittenberg theology, and authored the Augsburg Confession. (Image: Public domain, retrieved at the Reformation 500 website)

[132] James III, Frank A. "The Many Faces of Martin Luther," *Christianity Today*, November 20, 2017; <https://www.christianitytoday.com/ct/2017/november-web-only/many-faces-of-martin-luther.html>; in reviewing Herman Selderhuis' book, *Martin Luther: A Spiritual Biography*, Wheaton Illinois, Crossway, 2017.

[133] Schilling, *Upheaval*, p.111.

[134] Ibid., Schilling is citing Melanchthon, *Corpus Reformatorum* 6, no. 880, April 1548, to Christoph von Carlowitz, p.549.

But we should also note that coarse polemics were standard fare in the sixteenth century as they are now, unfortunately, in the twenty-first. Each one could speak tenderly and compassionately and yet lash out in anger using incendiary and foul language. It is not only what they say, but how they said it. Like Trump, Luther was a virtuoso of insult who could cut his more established opponents down to size. Both proved to be unrelenting disruptors. Keeping quiet was certainly not a strength, and neither minced words in their unreserved criticisms. They offered their opinions, sought or unsought, on most matters that crossed their desks.

There are times, as we shall see, when both exhibit few filters between their sharp minds and their unbridled mouths, which appeals to some but is repulsive to others. Yet, as is so common, a person's strengths can also be their weaknesses. Their words, "misspeaks," gaffes and rhetoric would often get them in trouble. Case after case can be made about those "times they divided when they might have united; alienated when they could have reconciled, and where they used a sledgehammer when a scalpel was needed."[135] As we also know, one's right view can lose the hearing of others by going about sharing it in the wrong way. But as we have also noted, both needed to be who they were even when such honesty and integrity may have detracted from their cause or lessened the adulation received. Do we wish they may have spoken forthrightly but in more sophisticated ways? Yes. But as Dennis Prager reminds us, "I also wish that cheesecakes were not fattening. But just as cheesecake comes with sugar [our twin populist warriors] come with unsophisticated rhetoric. People are packages, not a la carte menus."[136]

While Bernhard Lohse* finds Luther's crudeness shameful, he notes that Luther's "vulgarity increased according to whether or not he was under attack, and according to the ferocity of the attack."[137] Eric Metaxis comes to the same conclusion: "As Luther's sense of his own danger increased, so did his boldness. He thought, what do I have to lose? I am speaking the truth and therefore my life is in danger, so I might as well say what I can while I have breath in me. His willingness to go further and further, wherever he felt the truth led

---

[135] <https://askdrbrown.org/library/what-martin-luther-and-donald-trump-have-common>.

[136] Prager, Dennis, "10 Thoughts on the President and the 'S--- hole Countries;" *RealClear Politics*, January 16,2018. <https://www.realclearpolitics.com/articles/2018/01/16/10_thoughts_on_the_president_and_the_s---hole_countries_136014.html>.

* Bernhard Lohse was a preeminent church historian and Professor of Historical Theology at the University of Hamburg, Germany and author of *A Short History of Christian Doctrine, Martin Luther: An Introduction to His Life and Work,* and *Martin Luther's Theology.*

[137] Lohse, Bernhard, *Martin Luther: An Introduction to His Life and Work,* trans. Robert C. Schultz (Philadelphia: Fortress Press, 1986), pp.85-86.

him, became breathtaking."[138] "The truth," Luther wrote in May 1522, "is mightier than eloquence, the Spirit greater than genius, faith more than education."[139] These were the ingrained "*credo*" principles directing his thoughts, words and actions.

Waging war on the Devil for the sake of God left Luther little room for subtlety. We certainly know his behavior was decisively molded by his conviction that "*If God is for us, who can be against us!*" (Romans 8:31 [KJV]). Heiko Oberman finds

> Many of Luther's diatribes resemble public exorcisms [which] are futile as attempts to persuade persons of different opinions of the rightness of his position. Thus, it is probably no coincidence, and only seemingly a consequence of rhetoric, that Luther rarely used the commonly employed scholarly qualification "if I am not mistaken"—*ni fallor*—but made generous use of his favorite expression, "certainly"—*immo*. Luther's certainty left its mark on German academic linguistic usage. Where Anglo-American scholars qualify their statements with an "I am inclined to believe," the Germans say, "it is patently obvious." This, too, is part of the Luther heritage—its negative aspect, and a watered-down version at that.[140]

Trump, likewise not beholden to anyone, could be just as wild and aggressive in attacking individuals, the media, and policies, having no patience for considering how it might come across. One can hear Trump affirming what Luther had written in "To The Christian Nobility of the German Nation:" "The time for silence is past, and the time to speak has come..."[141] There are times we must speak out, as Luther reminds us, saying, "timidity is no help in emergency; I must proceed. I must try to instruct poor bewildered consciences, and take up the matter boldly."[142] Characterizing what could be considered "fake news" in Luther's time, Oberman reports that "Lies are passed off as truth and...even codified into law..."[143] Luther says, with a hint that he is speaking from his own bitter experience that with which Trump was also familiar: "the whole world hates the Truth if it hits someone...

---

[138] Metaxas, *Rediscovered*, p.180.

[139] Oberman, *Devil*, p.300, quoting Luther writing to Erasmus in 1522; *WABr* 2/544. 12f.; 28 May 1522.

[140] Ibid., p.299.

[141] LW 44:123. *The Christian in Society I*, "To the Christian Nobility," and in *Three Treatises*, p.9.

[142] LW 45:17. *The Christian in Society II*, "The Estate of Marriage (1522)."

[143] Oberman, *Devil*, p.43.

For the Truth is the most unbearable thing on earth."[144] We witness both straight-shooting warriors communicating with a vivid directness whose impact cannot be denied, leaving half the country scandalized, half of it delighted, and all of it paying attention!

Neither Luther nor Trump used the language the establishment expected, and neither observed the etiquette the elite demanded. In fact, both were "vulgar, foul-mouthed, vindictive, brash, cantankerous, full of bravado, and often spoke with a very tasteless, earthly sense of humor."[145] They are not puritans. Both openly acknowledge they are not paragons of the Christian life and both admit to having worldly impulses and view the world and its pleasures as created for enjoyment. Luther, knowing himself, acknowledged, "I do not set myself up as a saint..."[146] and could easily join Trump in affirming, "I never said I'm a perfect person, nor pretended to be someone that I'm not."[147]

Neither of our warrior leaders was ashamed of revealing that they were anything but genuine human beings—real people. They both possessed potty mouths, had a flair for bluntness and drama, a famously oversized appetite, an enjoyment of sex, and a grouchiness toward anyone who crossed them.

We learn much from notes taken and logged by students who hung on Luther's every word, and from friends and dinner guests of Luther who recorded his pronouncements in social conversations at the table and private offhanded comments. These jewels were collected and assembled into a large anthology from multiple sources, edited and published in six German volumes of the Weimar edition of *Luther's Works* under the title *Tischreden*, which translates as "Table Talk."

For John MacArthur,* "Table Talk" yields

> A fascinating window into the mind and personality of Martin Luther. His wit, his keen insight, his boldness, and the strength of his convictions

---

[144] Springer, Carl P.E., "Luther's Aesop," *LOGIA, A Journal of Lutheran Theology*, Reformation 2008, Vol. XVII, No.4, pp. 17-24, here pages 19 and 20 (quoting Luther WA 50:453 and WA 50:454). Springer is Professor of Classics at Southern Illinois University, Edwardsville and is known for his studies of Martin Luther's knowledge and use of the classics.

[145] Ryrie, Alec, "Martin Luther Was the Donald Trump of 1517." <https://www.foreignpolicy.com/2017/05/23/martin-luther-was-the-donald-trump-of-1517>.

[146] LW 32:111. *Career of the Reformer II*, "Luther at the Diet of Worms."

[147] <https://www.cbsnews.com/news/donald-trump-defends-lewd-2005-conversation-about-women-as-locker-room-banter>.

* John MacArthur is pastor of Grace Community Church in Sunday Valley, California and is known for his internationally syndicated Christian teaching radio program, "Grace to You."

> are clearly discernible. He is, as we would expect, passionate, opinionated, articulate, provocative, and zealous for the truth. Somewhat surprisingly, he is also jovial, engaging, well-versed in many subjects, and full of good-natured mischief. Unlike the younger Luther of the monastery, the Luther of Table Talk comes across as confident, mature, and secure in his faith. He was clearly a fascinating dinner host[148]

who was blessed with a hostess possessing the "mostest," as we will discover!

There at the long refectory table in the cavernous Luther home, we get a front-row opportunity to observe with up to 50 other friends and students his humor, his serious side, his likes, dislikes, sarcasm and passions. "This was Luther's especial domain," writes Andrew Pettegree* in his biography, *Brand Luther.* "The day's labors past, he would sit with his friends and talk. Fueled by his wife's excellent beer, conversation would become general, discursive, and sometimes unbuttoned."[149] Some would claim "unbuttoned" is an understatement. Energetic, loquacious and knowledgeable, he could zig-zag between the sublime and the scatological. MacArthur further observes that "It's *not* necessarily clear in the 'Table Talk' entries when Luther is joking, purposely overstating his case, speaking satirically, playing the devil's advocate, or just trying to get a rise out of his dinner guests."[150] Many of these accounts truly humanize the rebellious monk and we discover some of Luther's "Table Talk" banter coming close to Trump's "locker-room" bravado. While the *Access Hollywood* tapes purport to expose Trump's bragging about his sexual prowess and his delight in grabbing women, Luther makes plain his distaste for "large and flabby breasts."[151] One can wince as he seems to revel in providing too much information about his sexual habits or his own defecation.

---

148 MacArthur, John, "Foreword" in R.C. Sproul and Stephen Nichol's book, *The Legacy of Luther,* (Reformation Trust, Sanford, FL, 2016), p,3; also "John MacArthur on The Legacy of Martin Luther." <https://www.gty.org/library/Print/Blog/B170111>.

* Andrew Pettegree is a professor of modern history at the University of St. Andrews in Scotland where he was the founding director of the St. Andrews Reformation Studies Institute.

149 Pettegree, Andrew, *Brand Luther: 1517, Printing, and the Making of the Reformation* (New York, NY: Penguin Press, 2015), p.3.

150 MacArthur, "Foreword," *Legacy of Luther,* p.4.

151 LW 54:321. *Table Talk,* "Discussion at Table About Mothers' Milk, No. 4105."

While Luther was troubled with chronic constipation, "He was not too modest to admit that he took particular pleasure in the successful evacuation of his bowels!"[152] There in the lavatory he spent much of his time in contemplation and reading with his head in the heavens and his ass on the toilet, while also taking the opportunity to denigrate the Devil by "throwing" fecal language, such as "I shit on the Devil." Today, many people keep books and magazines near the toilet to help the user relax or to redeem the time that must be spent there each day. Author Dr. Lee Gatiss, Director of Church Society in the Reformed and Evangelical Tradition of the Church of England, suggests it can be "revealing to see which volumes people choose to shelve next to their porcelain chamber pots." He affirms that he knows some people who have even installed bookshelves in their bathrooms. He attests:

> Luther also kept books next to the loo [toilet]. Especially the books written against him by his fiercest opponents. This was not a tactic to help him unwind by reading—it would hardly have been soothing for an intense and feisty man like him to read inflammatory material at such a crucial moment. But it did have one advantage. They were soft, strong, and thoroughly absorbent: he used these books as toilet paper.[153]

There are many historians who suggest that Luther even wrote his Ninety-Five Theses "in cloaca" on "*das Klo*" (as the Germans call it), which had become a makeshift study or library in the warm comfort of a heated privy in the annex of the Tower. Whether Luther had that "Tower Experience" (*Turmerlebnis*) sometime after the Theses were posted, or whether his inspired understanding of "*faith alone*" served as a backdrop for his complaints against indulgences, is disputed by scholars, but can affect how one interprets his earlier writings. Whichever way, Anton Szandor LaVey jests, "Martin Luther dreamed up Protestantism while sitting on the toilet at the Wittenberg monastery, and we know what a big movement

---

[152] Gordon, Bruce, "Reading the Reformation in 2017," *Christianity Today*, January/February 2017, 61:1, p.46. <https://www.christianitytoday.com/ct/2017/january-february/reading-reformation-in-2017.html>.

[153] Gatiss, Lee, "When Scatology Informs Theology: The Bowels of the Reformation," *The Good Book* Blog. <https://www.thegoodbook.co.uk/blog/interestingthoughts/2017/01/31/when-scatology-informs-theology-the-bowels-of-the-/>.

that became."[154] The poet W.H. Auden references the "seat of the Reformation" in a poem: "Revelation came to / Luther in a privy."[155] Or perhaps Luther accidentally drank holy water with his laxative before he started a religious movement!

Such "eureka" moments are never planned but can and do occur in the oddest of places. As Oberman writes, "No spot is unholy for the Holy Ghost; this [cloaca] is the very place to express contempt for the adversary through trust in the crucified."[156] The cloaca is not just a privy. It was where the Devil hung out, and yet in that very place Luther

> found salvation where he was most debased. "*Mouse dirt that I am:*" he habitually thought of himself sans Christ in excremental metaphors. So Luther's latrine *is* the primal scene of Lutheranism… [and the] Devil is especially king of the cloaca where man cannot but viscerally recognize that his life is already involved with death, each turd a calling card from his own corpse. It is here we are lost, and it is here, if at all, that we must be saved. Which is precisely what the incarnation manages. For Luther, the child '*wrapped in swaddling clothes, lying in a manger*' is a sign that God has divested Himself of omnipotence to redeem our mortality from the Devil. He has hallowed it, potentially restoring to us life in all its fullness.[157]

As for Luther, we could say he finds his voice while sitting on the toilet. In like manner, many pundits picture President Trump tweeting his thoughts on the affairs of State while sitting on the "golden throne" and not just pronounced from the Oval Office. We discover Luther didn't just do his theology in an ivory tower. He also did it in the bathroom. It may well be a profound realization if we're intimidated or awestruck by imagining some great celebrity or prominent individual "on the john." As unpalatable and unseemly as this levelling comedy may be, it is nevertheless an imaginative way of reminding ourselves that they are just as human as you and I are.

---

[154] LaVey, Anton Szandor; <https://quotefancy.com/quote/1493405/Anton-Szandor-LaVey-Martin-Luther-dreamed-up-Protestantism-while-sitting-on-the-toilet>.

[155] Auden, W.H., "The Geography of the House (for Christopher Isherwood)." <https://hellopoetry.com/poem/793/the-geography-of-the-house>.

[156] Oberman, *Devil*, p.155.

[157] Fernie, Ewan, *The Demonic: Literature and Experience* (New York and London: Routledge, 2013), p.39.

Slinging and Tweeting Messages

The Reformer "slinging" his fecal message at the Devil from the "Seat of the Reformation"

(Image: PartisanHotel.co.uk)

The Commander-in Chief tweeting on his "Golden Throne" in the White House

(Image: UselessThingsToBuy.com)

Scatology: God's Word in Filthy Language

"Scatology" is the word used to define interest in or preoccupation with excrement, and often refers to obscene literature such as woodcuts at the time of The Reformation or, in the use of gross words, as "weapons of ridicule" to belittle and degrade one's enemies. Luther's frequent use of scatological language, repugnant to any modern sense of decorum or modesty, provided him a sharper sword than the weapons of clean erudite discourse in his battle against his enemies, both human and demonic. This method of degradation with foul language was especially common in Germany as an acceptable and powerful way to speak even in academic circles, and thus not limited solely to "street talk" or to those at the bottom rungs of German society.

Luther spoke emphatically, as we have noted. He talked tough; and in 16th-century Germany, that meant having a "potty mouth." Luther could obviously turn a filthy phrase with the best of them. In her work *German Hercules: The Impact of Scatology on the Image of Martin Luther*, Danielle Mead Skjelver* notes that "in Luther's time, vulgarity and scatology (a strong focus on excretory functions and their products, or more simply, poop) were part of (sometimes) even polite society."[158]

---

* Danielle Mead Skjelver, Collegiate Professor of History with the University of Maryland Global Campus, which was founded to serve the U.S. military around the world and is the Coordinator of the History Capstone Series.

158 <http://www.todayifoundout.com/index.php/2014/11/talking-tough-martin-luthers-potty-mouth>.

Spreading feces on the doorknob of a foe's home was not unheard of in Luther's era. In that vein, Luther and his allies would use copies of his detractors' scathing pamphlets as their toilet paper—"and then sent the used pages back to its authors—initiating the world's first 'smear' campaign. …This was in keeping with the practice of the German nobility who sometimes dipped their enemies' coats of arms in excrement and then carried that insult into battle."[159]

Pastor and author John MacArthur underscores Skjelver's portrayal: "The vernacular of that time was frequently earthy to the point of obscenity—even in supposedly genteel settings such as courtrooms, palaces, and ecclesiastical settings. Death was always imminent. Minds were rife with irrational fears."[160]

The mastery of language and the use of words had both pragmatic and theological implications for Luther. "While often able to defeat enemies in his field with lofty and truly towering intellect," Danielle Mead Skjelver acknowledges that "only the educated in German society could fully comprehend these battles. When [Luther] used 'scatology,' however, he set forth in common language unanswerable insolences and dominated his enemies in a way that every German could understand,"[161] and in so doing, increased his stature both as a victor and a national and spiritual champion for the people.

"[Luther] knew himself to be fighting not against ethnic minorities and cultural sub-classes, but against *principalities and powers*—against Satan and all his minions (Ephesians 6:12 [KJV]). For such warfare," former President of Concordia University Texas David J. Zersen asserts, "[Luther] needed the big guns, not only Scripture itself and the power of logical argument…. Two-fistedly, he occasionally snatched-to-hand street-talk and ethnic slurs to make his points. It was a matter of urgency. Luther was not going to give the Devil his due. The Kingdom was at stake."[162] Heiko Oberman summarizes, "In the total historical context…Luther's scatology-permeated language has to be taken seriously as an expression of the painful battle fought body and soul against the Adversary, who threatens both flesh and spirit."[163] Oberman believes that modern analysts rob Luther's abusive language of

---

159 <https://partisanhotel.co.uk/Vallance-II>.

160 MacArthur, "Foreword" in *The Legacy of Luther*, p.2; and <https://www.gty.org/library/Print/Blog/B170111>.

161 Skjelver, Danielle Mead, "German Hercules: The Impact of Scatology on the Image of Martin Luther as a Man, 1483-1546;" pp. 42-43; <https://www.academia.edu/1016951>.

162 Zersen, David J., "Did Luther Really Say?" *Concordia Historical Institute Quarterly*, Fall 2017. <https://www.academia.edu/36898659>.

163 Oberman, *Devil*, pp.108-9.

its significance if it seeks to close in on young Martin via his father Hans and his mother Margaret:

> We find here far more than upbringing and environment. Inclination and conviction unite to form a mighty alliance fashioning a new language of filth which is more than filthy language. [When] Luther's lifelong barrage of crude words hurled at the opponents of the Gospel [is] taken seriously, it reveals the task Luther saw before him: to do battle against the greatest slanderer of all times![164]

Another overly simplistic analysis is

> suggesting that Luther's negative comments about the Wends [or about the Jews as we will later discover] imply racism [when such criticism really] inserts a modern context into a sixteenth-century one. As an intellectual who championed education and an interpretation of the Gospel that required linguistic and historical insight, he can be forgiven for challenging rural people without a written language who had not yet discovered Grace's redeeming potential[165]

by using their slang and colorful speech.

Luther's *Bierstube* ("bar room") banter or uncouth language has troubled many, because as Zersen also claims,

> they mistakenly imply that his invectives against individuals or groups were intended quite personally rather than participating in speech patterns known in his context. Additionally, Luther's condescending views of diverse ethnic and cultural groups are often regarded from a modern perspective as racist prejudices rather than as off-the-cuff comments known among the people in his area.[166]

---

164 Ibid. p.109.

165 Zersen, "Did Luther Really Say?"

166 Ibid.

As mentioned, his vulgarity and castigating remarks were not reserved for the "unlettered," or just "for the sake of simple folk,"[167] but spoken equally to his fellow clerics and his elite academic colleagues; and even in his sermons, the scatological language was spoken and received without blushing. In a 1515 sermon, speaking of "stench from the abyss of all filth," Luther told Satan to "Stuff it.... Get lost Satan! Eat your own shit!"[168] As Oberman notes, "Immediately following that sermon, Luther was elected to be the right hand of Vicar General of the Augustinians, Johann Staupitz, and placed in charge of eleven monastic houses and the only two *studia* (schools or universities) in Erfurt and Wittenberg—the very 'foundation of the Order.'"[169]

Danielle Mead Skjelver points out how Martin Luther's employment of vulgarity, especially scatological vulgarity, in his writings and speech has drawn criticism, embarrassment and accusations—even entire books—suggesting Luther was troubled, not only spiritually but psychologically as well, suffering from some kind of mental illness. Some critics, psychologists and historians claim Luther exhibited an aberrant personality...a pathological head-case obsessed with shitting. Pundits and politicians in our time have likewise made accusations about President Donald Trump being unfit psychologically to lead and have called for family or staff to stage an intervention to implement the 25th Amendment—designed for one disabled, not disliked, to remove him from the Oval Office. Militant enemies of both Luther and Trump have emphasized and exaggerated the warriors' flaws; and with oft-repeated claims, systematic defamation of their character attains the status of truth in the minds of many, especially those who want to believe such accusations which they cannot substantiate.

As we have noted, there was real power in this crude and filthy language, especially as "Martin Luther's combative use of scatology defined him as a virile male in sixteenth-century Germany. Brash and full of bravado, the scatology of Martin Luther lent him the appearance of fearlessness,"[170] much as Trump's tough, blustery New York style reflects language more typical on the streets than from polished statesmen in the halls of government. Trump's tougher-than-tough-guy posturing, often described as machismo, obviously plays well to those males who have lost or are fearful of losing the "manliness" from which they benefited, and the culture had previously embraced. Many would suggest Trump's use of

---

[167] Oberman, *Devil*, pp.107-109.

[168] Oberman, Heiko A., *The Impact of the Reformation: Essays* (Grand Rapids, MI: William B. Eerdmans Publishing House, 1994), p.61, citing WA 1.51.24-25.

[169] Ibid., pp.59-60.

[170] Skjelver, "German Hercules;" p.2.

vulgarity is not so much obscene language itself as it is the ways in which he has chosen to deploy it.

There are those who say that our surnames guide our fates. In that vein, it is interesting to note that "The name 'trump' has a long history in UK slang. It means 'breaking wind.'"[171] Since the early 15th century, "trump" has served as a synonym for "fart," or rather to denote an especially noisy fart.[172] Rather comical, considering Luther's superior, Staupitz, having told his mentee that he did not need to confess every fart! Even more curious are those who speculate that the U.S. President is "the last trump" mentioned in the Bible, and that his geopolitical moves such as recognizing Jerusalem as the capital of Israel are heralding the End Times. Specific "proof texts" singled out by current "prophetic" preachers include:

> First Thessalonians 4:6 (KJV) reads: *"For the Lord Himself shall descend from heaven with a shout, with the voice of the archangel, and with the trump of God: and the dead in Christ shall rise first."*
>
> First Corinthians 15:52 (KJV) states: *"Behold, I show you a mystery; We shall not all sleep, but we shall all be changed in a moment, in the twinkling of an eye, at the last trump: for the trumpet shall sound, and the dead shall be raised incorruptible, and we shall be changed."*

The wording, however, only works in the English translation from Greek in the King James Version and some older translations. Other translations have "trumpet" instead of "trump." People have long been making predictions about U.S. presidents playing a role in End Times prophecy, all the way back to Abraham Lincoln, using faulty exegesis in not carefully understanding the texts they cite, and all obviously have proven to be wrong. Jesuit Church historian Hartmann Grisar, writing in the early twentieth century, viewed Luther as a precursor of all those proclaiming the end of the world and Judgment Day. In his six volume "opus" on Luther, he writes:

> Luther was convinced that he was the "last trump," which was to herald in the destruction, not only of Satan and the Papacy, but also of the world itself.

---

[171] Green, Jonathan, "A Lexicographer Explains the Sneaky Agenda Behind Trump's Dirty Mouth," *QUARTZ*, April 6, 2016; <https://qz.com/655502/>.

[172] Crapper, John [?], "What Does 'Trump' Mean in British Slang? *Holy Shitters*, October 19, 2017; <https://holyshitters.com/2017/10/what-does-trump-mean-in-british-slang>.

> "We are weak and but indifferent trumpeters, but, to the assembly of the heavenly spirits, ours is a mighty call." "They will obey us and our trump, and the end of the world will follow. Amen!"[173]

Weaponizing Language to Fight Flesh, World and Devil

The excitement with which Luther looked forward to the approaching end of the world gradually became an absolute certainty. That the end was nigh created a sense of urgency within him that "colored" much of his understanding, his sense of mission, his attitude, and his language usage, as we will experience in his relationship with peasants and Jews, especially in his later years. While we hear about "Covid-19 super-spreaders," Joseph Schmidt and Mary Simon refer to Luther as a "theological shit-spreader," and say further that Luther "provided the scatological with a fervor never read or heard before."[174] And historian Danielle Meade Skjelver concurs that "clearly Luther's scatology went beyond the rules of decorum even for his own era," while drily noting that "it seemed to work for him."[175]

Journalists, politicians and academicians alike have accused Trump of cheapening and demeaning public discourse by producing some of the most foul-mouthed speeches ever offered from a political podium. Many, including church people, while they may welcome his policies and what he has accomplished, have difficulty embracing the linguistic taboos he seems to be breaking as they confront his use of foul and bawdy language. While not excusing Trump or Luther, it must be remembered that politicians have never been polite:

> Yet while politicians have long vituperatively damned their rivals, they typically stay within the realm of socially acceptable speech. Trump does not—hence the outcry.... For his part, Trump claims such squeamishness is yet another example of the mealy-mouthed elitism that plagues the U.S. 'It's stuff like this that people in this country are tired of today,' he told a reporter who inquired about his vulgar language...[176]

---

[173] Grisar, Hartmann, *Luther*, Vol. 5, tran. E.M. Lamod (2014), p.239, quoting Luther's letter to Ratzeberger, the Elector's medical advisor, August 6, 1545, "Briefe," 5, p.754: "*Credo nos esse tubam illam novissimam*," etc.

[174] Schmidt, Josef, and Simon, Mary, "Holy and Unholy Shit: The Pragmatic Context of Scatological Curses in Early German Reformation Satire," *Fecal Matters in Modern Literature and Art*, eds. Jeff Persels and Russell Ganim (Surrey: Ashgate, 2004), pp.112.

[175] Simon, Ed, "Fecal Fridays," p.4. <https://queenmobs.com/201712/fecal-fridays--martin-luther-toilet>.

[176] Green, Jonathan, "Trump's Dirty Mouth."

During the campaign, Mr. Trump contended that the Republican establishment was being run by a bunch of "mealy-mouths" who lacked conviction. The term "mealy-mouthed" has likewise been used about Trump's mutterings and explanations that didn't go far enough, especially in denouncing white supremacist movements in the United States. His comments were judged to be inadequate and lacking straightforwardness by the media. But as the *Wall Street Journal* notes, "The alliterative expression, meaning 'unwilling to speak forthrightly, as from timidity or hypocrisy,' goes back to the 16th Century," where Luther in "Table Talk" "used the idiom, 'Mehl im Maule behalten,' literally 'to carry meal in one's mouth,' to describe those who were less than forthcoming in their views…,"[177] being vague, equivocal or one who "beats around the bush."

Lexicographer Jonathon Green explains what he describes as the sneaky agenda behind Trump's dirty mouth:

> Paradoxical though it may appear, his use of vulgar language is about winning friends and influencing people—while strategically alienating others…. On the surface, it's easy to see how supporters might view his use of foul language as a refreshing contrast to the jargon, double-talk, and downright untruths we've come to expect from politicians…. His supporters say they're sick of political correctness. They don't want to be lectured about micro-aggressions and xenophobia; they're eager to be liberated from what they see as linguistic censorship.[178]

One cannot ignore the shift taking place in societal taboos surrounding so-called "dirty" or curse words. As Matthew J.X. Malady writes in *Slate,*

> The word "bastard," yet another of Trump's insults, was once a hot-button slur questioning the legitimacy of one's parentage. Now that we've become more adjusted to the idea of having children out of wedlock, "bastard" is seen as a relatively mild insult. And frequent swearing in action movies and cable-television has further inured many people to vulgarity.[179]

---

[177] Zimmer, Ben, "How 'Mealy-Mouthed' Moved on From Luther to White House Critics," *The Wall Street Journal,* Aug. 18, 2017; <https://www.wsj.com/articles/how-mealy-mouthed-moved-on-from-luther-to-white-house-critics-1503067157?ns-prod/accounts-wsj>.

[178] Green, "Trump's Dirty Mouth."

[179] Ibid., Green quotes Matthew J.X. Malady writing in *Slate.*

The culture of Luther's Germany witnessed artists, writers and theologians employ urine, feces, and flatulence as a means of diminishing the stature of their enemies by reducing them to objects of mockery and derision. Such vulgar talk, often aided by filthy woodcuts, was specially directed at the Pope, and resulted in giving Luther the perception of power by his vulgar degradations; not only because his followers and allies would understand, because they used the same language, but because Luther also used these scathing and degrading insults as a rhetorical device in the service of defending pure doctrine against tyranny and godlessness. We often find mercenaries depicted in woodcuts depositing their feces into the papal tiara to demean and diminish the Pope with a weapon stronger than the sword. To be honest, however, many of his followers, especially those less interested in theology than in German independence from Rome, would have found such talk of "putting the Pope in his place" as music to their ears.

More than just a stronger weapon to the popular mind, Luther's scatology served to link the Pope and his followers with the Devil through fecal matter. The latrine or privy was viewed as the playground or haunt of demons and evil spirits, and yes, where the Devil hung out.[180] The Devil, whom Luther took seriously, was an enormous threat, far greater than the Pope, and thus it was easy for Luther to make the fecal connection. "Associating the Devil with the latrine and with all things fecal, Luther quipped back to the Devil that God deserved Luther's praise anywhere and everywhere, while the Devil deserved only Luther's ordure (dung)."[181] If the Satanic fiend could not be driven away with mere flatus from his own heavenly posterior—"It is often with a fart that I chase him away"[182]—Luther would use stronger words with the Devil: "I have shat in my pants and breeches, hang them on your neck and wipe your mouth with them.[183] ...But if that is not enough for you, you Devil, I have also shit and pissed; wipe your mouth on that and take a hearty bite."[184]

Luther saved his most bitter polemic writing for "The Most Hellish Father, St. Paul III" in 1545, in a tract entitled "Against the Papacy, An Institution of the Devil." In this treatise, Luther pulled out all the stops, as if he had been saving his best attacks for last. Disgusted with papal power over secular leaders throughout history, Luther wrote, "They are temporal

---

180 Scribner, R.W., *For the Sake of Simple Folk: Popular Propaganda for the German Reformation* (Oxford: Clarendon Press, 1994), p.84.

181 Skjelver, "German Hercules," p.28. <https://www.academia.edu/1016951>.

182 LW 54:16. *Table Talk*, "Treatment of Melancholy, Despair, Etc.," No. 122."

183 WATr 2:132. Luther quoted by Skjelver, "German Hercules," p.29; see also <http://www.todayifoundout.com/index.php/2014/11/talking-tough-martin-luthers-potty-mouth/>.

184 Oberman, *Devil*, p.107 (quoting from WAT 6:6827; 216, 9-11; see also Skjelver, "German Hercules," p.29).

lords, ordained by God. Why do they tolerate such things from such a rotten paunch, crude ass-pope, and fart-ass in Rome?"[185] He described the practices of indulgences as "an utter shitting, [swindle] with which the Hellish Father fooled all the world and cheated them of their money."[186] He had further claimed that "the dearest little ass-pope"[187] would "not only worship [Satan], but "also lick [his] behind"[188] (the equivalent to our modern expression "kiss ass" or literally, "being a 'brown' nose"). He also said the Pope farted so thunderously and powerfully that "it is a wonder that it did not tear his hole and belly apart."[189] Could it be, Oberman asks, that these drastic literal scatological expressions reflect the proverbial call "Devil, get thee behind me" (Matthew 16:23)?[190]

Sensing the Divine While on the Pot

As Eric Metaxes explains in his volume, *Martin Luther—The Man Who Rediscovered God and Changed the World,* Luther could not resist making a joke even while making a terribly serious point. A year before his death, the Reformer again recalled the "breakthrough" which he says took place in early 1517—that the righteous live by a gift of God, namely by faith. Jesting in 1532, Luther claimed his earthshaking "Tower Experience," or his "intestinal epiphany," occurred in that most humbling and humiliating of places "while on the john" in the Cloaca Tower at the Black Cloister in Wittenberg. "Cloaca" was the ancient Latin term for "sewer" and at the time of Luther had come to mean "outhouse:" "The heated room that was Luther's study for decades—and where he, therefore, did his Biblical exegesis—was in that part of the monastery [now the Luther residence] located in the tower. It so happened, however, that in the base of this tower there was an outhouse."[191]

> This realization occurred to [Luther] while he was contemplating Romans 1:17 "in the sewer," that is while he was pooping. He writes that the foundational cornerstone of the Reformation, of *sola Fide,* was "given to me by the Holy Spirit on this *Cloaca* in the tower," with "cloaca" a Latineuphemism for the

---

185 "LW 41:335. *Church and Ministry III;* "Against the Roman Papacy, An Institution of the Devil,"

186 Skjelver, "German Hercules," p.32.

187 LW 41:280. *Church and Ministry III,* "Against the Roman Papacy," See also Skjelver, "German Hercules," p. 32.

188 Ibid., LW 41:334.

189 Ibid., LW 41:344-5.

190 Oberman, *Devil,* p.107.

191 Metaxas, *Rediscovered,* p.96.

> toilet. [Luther] writes that following that successful evacuation of his bowels... he "felt totally newborn, and through open gates I entered paradise."[192]

Obviously, Luther felt that straining, tense, uncomfortable—even painful—holding onto matter better dispelled which is experienced by a traveler in search of a bathroom. Then, when the blissful evacuation finally occurs, relief is experienced with an abundance of exuberance, in this case for Luther not just physically but also spiritually, with an awareness of cleansing renewal of having been purified, having been made new. Princeton gastroenterologist Dr. Anish Sheth dubs the sense of ecstasy and exhilaration from the passing of a large mass of stool which distends the rectum and stimulates the vagus nerve, "Poo-phoria."* He along with co-author Josh Richman explain in *What's Your Poo Telling You?* that "To some [poo-phoria] may feel like a religious experience, to others like an orgasm, and to a lucky handful it may feel like both. This is the type of poo that makes us all look forward to spending time on the toilet."[193]

One could say that at that moment, experiencing such inspiration and a euphoric sense of freedom, Luther found his voice while sitting on the "pot." Adding significance to Luther's "experience" is the rendering of most historians who liken Medieval Christianity to a cluttered and constipated Church coated in filth—until Luther's mighty evacuation frees and purifies it, realizing that flesh-and-blood Luther argued for a more "earthy Christianity," which regarded the entire human body—and not just the soul—as God's creation. One can surmise Luther was extremely grateful that Jesus took away his sins and the Church was being cleansed, but he must have been somewhat disappointed that he was still left with his hemorrhoids!

Eric W. Gritsch† argues that Luther's earthiness was part of his theology as well as his humor, especially his scatological humor for which he was notorious. For Terry Lindvall and Morgan Stroyeck "Luther was no mere man of the mind, he was also a man of the

---

[192] Simon, Ed, "Fecal Fridays," p. 5, <https://queenmobs.com/2017/12/fecal-fridays-martin-luther-toilet>.

* Dr.Anish Sheth and co-author Josh Richman of *What's Your Poo Telling You?* reveal that the feeling of a "poo-phoria" high can accompany a large movement experienced by some people when going to the toilet. They further define the term with the synonyms Holy Crap, Mood Enhancer, The Tingler.

[193] Sheth, Anish and Josh Richman, *What's Your Poo Telling You?* (San Francisco, CA: Chronicle Books, 2007), p.22; see also <https://partisanhotel.co.uk/Vallance-II>; <https://www.mirror.co.uk/news/weird-news/going-toilet-can-like-having-3152190>.

† Eric W. Gritsch was an American Lutheran ecumenical theologian who served as Professor of Church History at Lutheran Theological Seminary, Gettysburg, Pennsylvania. He was a Luther scholar and author of several books and articles on the Reformer.

bowels."[194] While his humor may be unseemly and vulgar, it is nevertheless orthodox to remind ourselves that "The One Who shared in all things with humanity, also shared the blessed dual humiliations of digestion and defecation."[195]

> The scandal of Christianity has always been that Christ was incarnated as a man and died the indignant death of man. In between His nativity and crucifixion, He inevitably must have shit as well. To be offended by that reality is to be offended by Christianity, but to acknowledge that the living God is One who has to have shat, is to embrace the living God.[196]

In Luther, we find a sensual life that walked with God in self-awareness of the reality of his own body and its weakness, especially as he experienced severe bouts of constipation among other ailments. Using Luther's descriptive and profound language, shitting is a rather central aspect of the human condition which is often obscured with our awkward laughter. Not being prudish at all with the realities of life, Luther provides "a profane reminder that humans are born naturally between piss and shit;"[197] and later in life, contemplating his own death, he compared himself to a "turd" about to be expunged, as referenced and cited below.

We need to be reminded that these bodily functions were more properly acknowledged and, one might even say, celebrated in the late Medieval and early Reformation periods. Maybe in our esteemed propriety, we don't often connect with St. Paul's admonition to honor the unseemly or "uncouth" members of the lower body, those "*less honorable*" (1 Corinthians 12:22-23 [NRSV]) with the transcendent. Instead, the crass and derogatory thoughts, associations and usages come to mind and easily slide off our tongues in "crass" and "vulgar" speech.

Throughout his life, Luther was eternally grateful for that intestinal theophany that freed him from always striving to get from earth to heaven, in the realization that "Christ came to us from heaven to earth; we did not ascend from earth into heaven to Him."[198] It is compelling in Scripture that we discover the "downs" are followed by "ups" to clearly inform our theology. For example, in Exodus 3:8 (NRSV), the Lord says, "*I have come*

---

[194] Lindvall, Terry and Morgan Stroyeck, "Holy Dung: Comic Signs of Consubstantiality in Martin Luther Films." <https://www.mdpi.com/2077-1444/7/3/20/html>.

[195] Ibid.

[196] Simon, "Fecal Fridays," p.17.

[197] Ibid., p.11.

[198] LW 42:41. *Devotional Writing I*, "An Exposition of The Lord's Prayer."

down** to deliver them from the Egyptians, and to bring them **up** out of that land to a good and broad land, a land flowing with milk and honey."* Or Jesus going **down** into the water for His baptism and came "up** out of the water*" (Mark 1:10). In the Apostles' Creed, we confess He [Christ] "**descended** into hell [to the dead]" and then "**ascended** into heaven" [all emphases added].

Luther emphasized his own humble earthy humanity when he told his wife just before he died, "I'm fed up with the world, and it is fed up with me. I'm quite content with that.... I'm like a ripe stool and the world is like a gigantic anus, and so we're about to let go of each other."[199] Luther's excremental humor is filled with meaning, and Gritsch asserts, "deserves to be integrated into his legacy.... [It] is testimony of his conviction that 'between birth and death and between the first and second advent of Christ, one must trust the promise of the Holy Scripture that all will be well after the final hour of earthly time'"[200] as grace invades and shines a light on all that is decaying to bring forth new life!

Metaxas suggests perhaps Luther was jesting about that momentous bathroom revelation coming to him while sitting "on the john" grunting. Yet, he too notes that Luther made it a perfect illustration of his theological foundation which was in keeping with everything he knew about the incarnate God of the Bible:

> the infinite and omniscient and omnipotent Creator God of heaven did not descend to earth on a golden cloud. He came to us through screaming pain, through the bloody agony of a maiden's vagina, in a cattle stall filthy with and stinking of dung.... It was the only way to reach us *where we are* and *as we are*...and because of His love for us...God reached down not halfway to meet us in our vileness but all the way down, to the foul dregs of our broken humanity. And this holy and loving God dared to touch our lifeless and rotting essence and in doing so underscored that this is the truth about us...we are fatally befouled with death and fatally toxic filth and require total redemption. If we do not recognize that we need eternal life from the hand of God, we remain in our sins and are eternally dead. So, because God respects us, He can reach us only if we are honest about our condition. So, it fit well with Luther's thinking that if God were to bestow upon him—the

---

[199] LW 54:448. *Table Talk*; "Luther Suffers Pain and Expects His End, No. 5537."

[200] "The Scatological Luther," *The Wilson Quarterly*; <https://www.wilsonquarterly.com/quarterly/summer-2012-american-vistas-the-scatological-luther>, referencing Eric W. Gritsch, "Martin Luther's Humor," *Word & World* 32 (2012); <https://wordandworld.luthersem.edu/issues.aspx?article_id=1601>.

unworthy sinner Luther—such a divine blessing, it must needs be done as he sat grunting in the "cloaca." This was the ultimate antithesis to the gold and bejeweled splendor of papal Rome. There all was gilt, but here in Wittenberg it was all *Scheisse.* But the shit in its honesty *as shit* was very golden when compared to the pretense and artifice of Roman gold, which itself was indeed as shit when compared to the infinite worth of God's grace. That was cheap grace, which was to say it was a truly satanic counterfeit. True grace was concealed in the honesty—in the unadorned shit—of this broken world, and the devil's own shit was concealed in the pope's glittering gold.[201]

Birthplace of the Reformation in the "Cloaca"

Excavation in 2004 around the Black Monastery, which became the "Lutherhaus" and now houses the Luther Museum, shows that there was indeed a "stone room" annex equipped with a heated lavatory or "cloaca" on the first floor of the tower. Well advanced for its time, the toilet had a cesspit underneath attached to a drain. "Director of the Luther Memorial Foundation, Stefan Rhein, matter-of-factly said of the 30cm stone seat with a hole in the center that 'This is where the birth of the Reformation took place.'"[202] This archaeological discovery, however, does not necessarily validate that Luther's evangelical breakthrough "hit him in the latrine" while sitting on the toilet, but should serve to remind us that "God would go anywhere to reach His children."[203]

Lewis Spitz, a Reformation historian, notes that

> phrase "*in cloaca*" was used not only with reference to location or place but also to describe a state of melancholy in a way similar to our colloquial expression "down in the dumps." Thus Luther, troubled in conscience, fearful and anxious, suddenly understands that St. Paul is speaking of the righteousness God bestows on man through forgiveness, and he is lifted out of the depths into the joy of paradise.[204]

---

201 Metaxas, *Rediscovered*, pp.97-98.

202 Simon, "Fecal Fridays," p.5.

203 Skjelver, "German Hercules," p.29.

204 Spitz, Lewis, *Psychohistory and Religion* (Philadelphia: Fortress Press, 1977), p.80.

The expression "in cloaca" has profound medieval roots. "In 1012, Thietmar of Merseburg tells us that demons arise from the cloaca to tempt monks…and later in the Middle Ages, falling into *the 'cloaca'* meant *'to fall into sin.'*"[205] "On the meaning of 'cloaca,'" opines Steven Ozment, professor of Ancient and Modern History at Harvard University,

> …historians have done their homework better than the psychologists. In the late Middle Ages, the descriptions of oneself as being "*in cloaca*," "*in stercore*," or "*in latrina*" were common religious rhetoric, actually derived from the Bible and connoting a state of utter humility and dependence on God. When Luther described his Reformation insight as occurring "*in cloaca*," he was saying no more than that he received his understanding of the righteousness of God after a long period of humble meditation in the tower room—actually the library—of the monastery. Once again an understanding of the religious culture of the period proves more illuminating than conjectures based on modern clinical psychology.[206]

By Luther's time, "cloaca" was used in conventional speech and was a bit of monastic slang, meaning being "in the dumps" or "in the pits." Thus, perhaps the realization occurred to Luther when he was despondent or depressed. Or perhaps it is possible the Reformer meant it both metaphorically and literally when he claimed to have been inspired while "sitting on the throne," as we know he did frequently since he suffered from obstipation and chronic disorders in his bowels. Thus "he would spend time in the outhouse, thinking and reflecting on what and how to say what he wanted. His world was packed down with words like 'Scheisse' (shit), 'Mist' (manure), 'Dreck' (dirt/shit) and 'Arsch' (ass)."[207]

As we have learned from Danielle Mead Skjelver's vast research on scatology, Luther's language was hardly unique in early modern Europe. Describing the time somewhat more crassly, Ed Simon, Associate Editor at *The Marginalia Review of Books*, affirms Luther "was part of an ongoing tradition, for this was an era *awash* in shit." While "Luther produced thousands of pages of vibrant, visceral, vernacular German prose which explored faith, grace, and ritual…he also developed a profound rhetoric of shit." He cites the numerous times Luther references flatulence, shit and anuses in his "Table Talk" and "the analysis of his close to four hundred letters, almost 40% of which had some sort of reference to either

---

205 <http://beggarsallreformation.blogspot.com/2016/10/luther-tower-bathroom-and-faith-alone.html>.

206 Ozment, Steven, *The Age of Reform, 1250-1550* (New Haven: Yale University Press, 1980), p.230.

207 Lindvall, Terry, *God Mocks: A History of Religious Satire* (New York: NYU Press, 2015), p.88.

butts, shitting, shit, and anuses, in that order of descending popularity."[208] In one "Table Talk," Volker Leppin translates Luther as saying, "If our Lord God in this life—in this shithouse, this abominably shitty life—has given us such noble gifts [as music], what will happen in that eternal life, where everything will be perfect and delightful?"[209]

Scheisshaus or Shit House

Here, like Trump, Luther phrases his thoughts bluntly and very earthly: this life is a "Scheisshaus" (toilet or "shit house") compared to the glories of heaven. So, Luther was speaking with tongue in cheek, or figuratively and seriously at the same time, as he so often did.

> The "*cloaca*" was not only literally that place in the tower where he went to the bathroom, but also the essence of this world, a world not merely begrimed with, but filled with and consisting of sin, shit, misery, and death. For God to come into this foulest world, is for Him already to come most of the way into hell…and unless we allow the God of Life to come here, we do not allow Him to redeem us. He cannot redeem and resurrect what is not foul and dead, but we are both.[210]

Simon also points to the theological significance of Luther's preoccupation with feces, reminding us "from that rich manure would come good trees," and Luther understood that "good trees bear good fruit." In *Rabelais and His World*, Mikhail Bakhtin writes that while using the scatological rhetoric of excrement to degrade, it is referring to the "lower stratum of the body, the life of the belly and the reproductive organs and therefore relates to acts of defecation and copulation, conception, pregnancy, and birth…it [thus] has not only a destructive, negative aspect, but also a regenerating one…it is the fruitful earth and the womb. It is always conceiving."[211]

---

[208] Simon, "Fecal Fridays," (here pp. 9, 4, and 5).

[209] Leppin, Volker, "Becoming a Reformer," *Martin Luther and the Reformation: Essays* (Dresden: Sandstein Verlag, 2016), p.87, quoting WATr 4:191. (Referenced in Metaxas, *Rediscovered*, p.98.)

[210] Metaxas, *Rediscovered*, p.98.

[211] Bakhtin, Mikhail, *Rabelais and His World*, trans. Helene Iswolsky, (Bloomington: Indiana University Press, 1984), p.21.

To pass over Luther's fecal utterances with disgust, or awkward and embarrassed laughter, is to abandon part of the "rich" inheritance we receive from one who perceived meaning in even the most mundane and rudimentary aspects of living, such as defecating and urinating, which tend still to be disregarded as uncomfortable realities of life. Shit is very much real, and as the adage undeniably declares, "Shit Happens!"

Without being snarky, Ed Simon shares his appreciation for

> the freshness of Luther's "shit theology." "Please" [he cautions us,] "do not read the second to last word in the previous sentence as an adjective, but as a noun. In that I mean to say that Luther took waste seriously, used it to great rhetorical effect and took part in intellectual disputations...with adversaries from Ulrich Zwingli and Thomas More that could best be described as 'shit-fests.'" [He concludes his article by stating:] "Shitting, it should go without saying, is a rather central aspect of the human condition. If theology is that which simultaneously deals with the most profound of questions as they intersect with the human condition, to ignore shitting is gross negligence. A squeamishness Luther did not have, for salvation which doesn't grapple with shit is no salvation at all. The rest of us it seems have found that where we are too embarrassed to speak, we have rather decided to pass over with a silent fart."[212]

Luther's insight—this "Bathroom Revelation" or "Tower Experience"—in the "scheisshaus" is profound and obviously more Biblical and theologically meaningful than the President's careless use of the phrase in a news conference on January 10, 2018, referring to countries from which third-world immigrants are seeking entry into the United States. Yet, in many ways, the use of the term "shit house" or "shithole" acknowledges the same reality or inferences as the words we use but deem "more acceptable." Our "sanitized" terms—"the other side of the tracks," "the ghetto," or "slums"—while less offensive are just as derogatory in describing undesirable locales in our own country or communities where God's children, whom He loves, also exist. Why are not the repeated descriptions of America being "systemically racist" with its white majority not the moral equivalent of the word "shithole" and just as offensive?

In a letter of February 1520 to George Spalatin, Luther accounts for the strong language he often uses: "I cannot deny that I am more vehement than I should be.... But they [his

---

[212] Simon, "Fecal Fridays," (here pp. 4 and 18).

enemies] assail me and God's Word so atrociously and criminally that...these monsters are carrying me beyond the bounds of moderation."[213] He was keenly aware that he was a fallen man with sinful proclivities, and also not above offering "justifiable" rationalization!

In writing a dedicatory letter to Pope Leo X which prefaced his "Treatise on Christian Liberty" or "The Freedom of a Christian," Luther wrote:

> I have, to be sure, sharply attacked ungodly doctrines in general, and I have snapped at my opponents, not because of their bad morals, but because of their ungodliness. Rather than repent this in the least, I have determined to persist in that fervent zeal and to despise the judgment of men, following the example of Christ who in His zeal called His opponents *"a brood of vipers," "blind fools," "hypocrites," "children of the devil"* [Matt. 23:13, 17, 33; John 8:44]. Paul branded Magus [Elymas, the magician] as the *"son of the devil...full of all deceit and villainy"* [Acts 13:10] and he calls others *"dogs," "deceivers,"* and *"adulterers"* [Phil. 3:2; 2 Cor. 11:13; 2:17].... No person is more stinging and unrestrained in his denunciations than Paul. Who is more stinging than the prophets? Nowadays, it is true, we are made so sensitive by the raving crowd of flatterers that we cry out that we are stung as soon as we meet with disapproval.... What is the good of salt if it does not bite? Of what use is the edge of a sword if it does not cut?[214]

Luther never denied having an overly sharp tongue. His tendency to use such heavy ammunition genuinely damaged his reputation in cultured circles in the same way as Trump's often flagrant, flippant insults and intemperate words offend the elite establishment today, including political pundits, and which are latched onto by media commentators. They both use invectives and exhibit the ability to know when and how to throw the verbal bombs or threats that are called for without the need for conscious reasoning. Hyperbole, truthful and otherwise, is Trump's common parlance, and he is attacked with snobbery, envy and spitefulness. Conrad Black observes that Trump's opponents have "committed all their energy to proving their assumed self-evident proposition that Trump could not win,

---

[213] "Luther on His Vehement Polemics," *What Luther Says—An Anthology*, Vol. II, compiled by Ewald M. Plass (St. Louis, MO: Concordia Publishing House, 1959), p.1058 (WABr 2:44f).

[214] LW 31:335. *Career of the Reformer I*, "The Freedom of a Christian." Also, the *"Open Letter to Pope Leo X"* can be found in Martin Luther's *Three Treatises*, (Philadelphia, Muhlenberg Press, 1960) p.267.

then that his victory could be undone, and then that it could be vitiated by scorched-earth obstruction, or, destroyed completely by investigations and indictments."[215]

Trump is unpredictable, unorthodox, and somewhat erratic, and his stridency and ill-tempered outbursts are not what most Americans expect of their presidents. In his fierce ideas, vehement language, and combative intellectual style, Luther prefigured Trump, who often does not show charity in "turning the other cheek," but rather punches back harder. Both seem to have recognized that it is not always "nice" to be "nice," especially when confronting the hypocrisy and double standard of the entrenched, entitled and privileged elite.

Language: Words and How They Are Used Have Meaning

Speaking, writing and reading are integral to everyday life, where language is the primary tool for expression and communication. Yet we are also aware that from our experience we bring different meanings to the same words others use, and that the way words are spoken may convey an entirely different message. We're familiar with the quote from Robert McCloskey: "I know that you believe that you understood what you think I said but I'm not sure you realize that what you heard is not what I meant."[216] In addition, we possess expectations about how others are to speak to us.

Many conclude that President Trump not only sounds different but uses speech and means unlike that from what they have come to expect from our public leaders. Politicians, especially Presidents, are to be impressive orators, delivering a crafted speech eloquently and always prepared with stock answers in which to reply to anticipated questions.

With Trump, the mold of oratory and focus-group, poll-tested, carefully selected words has been broken. Rhetoric and linguistics scholars who have studied Trump's speaking style conclude it is persuasive precisely because his sentences are grammatically awkward, repetitive, and composed of highly simplistic words. His word choice is simple, frequently using the words "stupid," "very," "terrific," "great," "terrible," "incredible," "best" or "worst" instead of stronger adjectives. He punctuates his speech with repetition to hammer the point home, and relies heavily on superlatives. Edward Schiappa, Professor of Rhetoric and Media at MIT, notes that Trump's simplicity of language is appealing: ""Trump's prepared

---

[215] Black, Conrad, "Why Donald J. Trump is Truly a President Like No Other," *National Post*, May 11, 2018. Excerpted from his book *Donald J. Trump: A President Like No Other* (Regnery Publishing, 2001). <https://nationalpost.com/opinion/conrad-black-why-donald-j-trump-is-truly-a-president-like-no-other>.

[216] <http://quodid.com/quotes/10994/robert-mccloskey/i-know-that-you-believe-that-you-understood>.

speeches are pedestrian' and his language is 'plain style,' which gives the impression that politics is straightforward."[217]

George Lakoff, a linguist at UC Berkeley, adds that many of "Trump's most famous catchphrases are actually versions of time-tested speech mechanisms that salesmen use… and Trump has 50 years' experience as a salesperson." Trump chooses to show his credibility through an outspoken, honest-sounding style. Take, for example, Trump's recurring "use of 'Many people are saying…' or 'Believe me…' [which] tends to make him sound more trustworthy since Trump implies that he has direct experience with what he's talking about. At a base level," Lakoff argues, "people are more inclined to believe something that seems to have been shared."[218]

All this leads Jennifer Sclafani, a professor in Georgetown University's Department of Linguistics who for two years has studied Trump's language, to conclude that Trump is a "unique politician because he doesn't speak like one…he speaks like everybody else." As for the criticism that he sounds erratic when he changes subjects in the middle of a speech or sentence, or makes rambling remarks full of digressions, Sclafani reminds us that "this is something that we all do in everyday speech." She claims he engenders a "spectacle" in the way he speaks and this "creates a feeling of strength for the nation, or it creates a sense of determination, a sense that he can get the job done through his use of hyperbole and directness."[219] He comes across as a straight shooter rather than one who is "dodgingly" trying to avoid a question.

According to Richard Wilson, a professor of anthropology and law at UConn School of Law, his "clunky style" of speaking like regular folks forces people to listen more closely to make sense of his words:

> [Using] unusual speech patterns and ungrammatical phrases and long pauses…of pulls you in…. This style of speech is effective: [He] wants to speak like regular folks…and it forces us to listen more closely…audiences have to pay closer attention to make sense of his words. And this focus means audiences are more likely to be persuaded, just as one is more likely to be convinced by a lecturer if you pay close attention, listening intensely, rather than allowing those words drift over you.[220]

---

217 <https://qz.com/965004/rhetoric-scholars-pinpoint-why-trumps-inarticulate-speaking-style-is-so-persuasive>.
218 <www.vox.com/2016/8/18/12423688/donald-trump-speech-style-explained-by-linguists>.
219 <https://www.washingtonpost.com/news/the-fix/wp/2017/07/07/this-linguist-studied-the-way-trump-speaks-for-two-years-heres-what-she-found/?utm_term=.0566c951eaf0>.
220 <https://qz.com/965004/rhetoric-scholars-pinpoint-why-trumps-inarticulate-speaking-style-is-so-persuasive>.

Trump uses language to enhance his "brand" as a "non-politician" who is not scripted, but rather speaks "from his gut" or "off the cuff." He wears on his sleeve who he is. His speeches are not meant to be read, and thus for many, their incoherence stems from the big difference between written and spoken language. The patterns of rhythm and sound, along with gestures, posture and gazes, are subtle clues that make Trump's digressions and rambles easier to follow. As Lakoff observes, this allows Trump's sentences to trail off with no ending because "He knows his audience can finish his sentences for him."[221] He makes vague implications with a raised eyebrow or a shrug, turning his back to look at those seated behind him, allowing his audience to reach their own conclusions. And that conversational style can be effective, coming across as being more intimate than one orchestrated to give a rehearsed, ghostwritten, scripted speech.

Twentieth-century American literary theorist, poet and novelist Kenneth Burke asserted that "one can persuade others only insofar as you can talk his language in speech, gesture, tonality, order, image, attitude, idea, identifying your way with his."[222] People walk away from Trump feeling as though he was casually talking to them by using sensory language, allowing them to finish his thoughts, often with sentiments that resonate on an emotional level.

Luther was likewise people-centric possessing a commanding charismatic personality. In a Patheos Blog, Lutheran Librarian Nathan Rinne* quotes the appraisal of Andrew Pettegree, author of *Brand Luther*, to which Nathan adds his own assessment:

> '[Luther] had a sort of personal magnetism which somehow carried people over their natural borders and boundaries,' Pettegree says. He often talked very convincingly and practically about the importance of being simple and humble in his writings. None of this however precluded having a deep understanding of his times and environment, nor the need to be quite strategic as well. Luther [like Trump] was politically savvy, a master of media manipulation, and a creative marketer[223]

which we will soon explore.

---

[221] <www.vox.com/2016/8/18/12423688/donald-trump-speech-style-explained-by-linguists>.

[222] Burke, Kenneth, A *Rhetoric of Motives* (Berkeley: University of California Press, 1969), p.55.

* Nathan Rinne has master's degrees in both theology and library science and works full-time in the library at Concordia University, St. Paul, providing technical services with the library's electronic resources. He teaches the online class "Biblical Christianity for Thoughtful Persons," and frequently blogs on sites beyond his own, "Theology Like a Child," and publishes in both library and theology journals.

[223] <http://www.patheos.com/blogs/justandsinner/semper-vendenda-was-the-reformation-about-creative-marketing-with-disruptive-technology>.

Luther, like Trump, was not offering a "new product" but sought a course correction for a train that had gone off the rails. In "The Unrefined Reformer," Eric Gritsch writes,

> Luther also admitted he could be rude. He considered foul language an appropriate weapon to combat evil.... By anyone's standard, Luther was bull-headed, coarse-tongued, and intemperate at times. In many ways he behaved like other people of his time. But his speech and actions were always more intense. No matter how high or low the cause, he seemed to rise or sink to any occasion.[224]

Derisive Nicknames and Insulting Monikers

One wonders if Trump did not take another page out of Luther's playbook in the Reformer's battle with the Pope. Luther used a vast lexicon of unflattering yet colorful monikers, labels and pejorative nicknames with which he identified his opponents and detractors. Convinced that the Pope was the Antichrist, Luther would use forceful diatribes, well-tuned and defiant phrases describing the Pope as we have already evidenced. Other denigrating descriptions used by Luther to belittle "His Holiness" include the "devil's mouthpiece," a "vulgar boor, blockhead, and lout," the "Whore of Babylon," "hellish scum," and "snot-nose." In his treatise "Against the Roman Papacy," Luther calls the Pope "a vicar of the devil, an enemy of God, and adversary of Christ, a destroyer of Christ's churches; a teacher of lies, blasphemies, and idolatries, an arch church-thief...a brothel-keeper over all brothel-keepers and all vermin...an Antichrist, a man of sin and child of perdition [II Thess. 2:3]; a true werewolf ."[225] Addressing "The Most Hellish Father, St. Paul III," Luther asserts that the Pope and his Curia are "mad asses who do not know they are asses."[226] That's a sentiment one could expect President Trump to assert about his adversaries, or perhaps he would not give them that much credit because they really do know the intentional deceit within which they operate.

---

[224] Gritsch, Eric W., "The Unrefined Reformer," *Christian History*, Issue 39 (Vol. XII, No. 3), p. 35; Christianity Today, Issue 39: <https://www.christianitytoday.com/history/issues/issue-39/unrefined-reformer.html>.

[225] LW 41:357. *Church and Ministry III*, "Against the Roman Papacy, An Institution of the Devil."

[226] Ibid., LW 41:361. (For more interesting "descriptions" see <https://churchpop.com/2014/08/10/29-of-martin-luthers-most-hiliariously-over-the-top-insults>.)

Bad-mouthing the Pope or anyone has never been a productive means of seeking endearment or respect. Yet, we cannot suppress Luther's ravings, especially his scatology-permeated discourse, out of embarrassment, nor treat him gingerly, for that would mean not taking him at his word. And, as we have previously witnessed, Luther's raunchy scatological expressions were used especially in his contempt for the satanic fiend and his operatives, as he fought body and soul against the Adversary who threatens the Church as the Body of Christ.

"Luther's propaganda wars with the Catholic Church," according to Chandra Johnson, "gave rise to the forerunner of today's internet memes where each side mocked the other for the public to see. No one came close to matching his prolific output, and his penchant for insult could give any modern-day Twitter trolls or meme generators a run for their money."[227] "Luther's language is so physical and earthy that in his wrathful scorn he can give the Devil 'a fart for a staff' and advocated the only appropriate retort to the Devil's dung: 'You go eat it!'"[228] In writing "Against the Roman Papacy, an Institution of the Devil," Luther offered one of his most picturesque insults hurled at the Pope:

> May God punish you, I say, you shameless, barefaced liar, devil's mouthpiece, who dares to spit out, before God, before all the angels, before the dear sun, before all the world, that you alone are the shepherd of all Christ's sheep, regardless of the Gospels and the Epistles of the apostles Peter and Paul, against whom you so knowingly spit and throw your devil's filth.[229]

The filthy, harsh, abrasive vocabulary of Reformation propaganda was aimed at inciting the common man, and Luther admittedly used a great deal of invective. In Constance Furey's* assessment, some of Luther's writing aimed at Luther's opponents and the Catholic Church are laced with no small amount of entertainingly scathing insults that can shock even a jaded reader:

---

[227] Johnson, Chandra, "5 Things I Learned at the Martin Luther: Art and the Reformation Exhibit," *Deseret News.* <https://www.deseretnews.com/article/865671316/5-things-I-learned-at-the-Martin-Luther-Art-and-the-Reformation-exhibit.html>.

[228] Oberman, *Devil,* pp.108-109.

[229] LW 41:349. *Church and Ministry III,* "Against the Roman Papacy."

* Constance M. Furey is professor of religious studies at Indiana University, Bloomington, an author and scholar of Renaissance and Reformation Christianity.

> In the prefatory letter to *The Babylonian Captivity of the Church* (1520) Luther begins by wishing for "grace and peace in Christ" before launching his attack on the "brainless and illiterate beast in papist form" and its "whole filthy pack of…asses," and concludes by exhorting his reader to rise up against the Catholic hierarchy: "Continue courageously, noble sir; in this way, the disgrace of the Bohemian name will be abolished, and the sludge of the harlot's lies and whoring shall again be taken up in her breast."[230]

Luther used many crass words in good humor, and often in complete sarcasm. His insults could be serious and biting. As we have pointed out, he was a product of his times, and as Pastor Tyler Rasmussen of Trinity Lutheran Church in Coopersburg, PA, reminds us about Luther we must realize his derogatory words and insults are extremely contextual and used as a common rhetorical device in the polemical literature of the sixteenth century in defense of pure doctrine and against tyranny and godlessness:

> They were spoken in hopes of defending the pure faith against impure doctrine and guiding the church of his day back into the faith of the Church. …their original context, including the work in which they are found and the socio-political context of sixteenth-century Germany where insulting was a norm, is vital for understanding both their meaning and Luther's vehemence.[231]

As we have already pointed out, Luther had a flair for indelicate and blunt expressions in his harsh and abrasive attacks, and condemnations on the papacy, peasants and Jews. In his notorious "On the Jews and Their Lies," he bitterly denounces Jews as "boastful, arrogant rascals," "real liars and bloodhounds," and "the vilest whores and rogues under the sun." When Jews would not convert, Luther concluded that "a Jewish heart is as hard as a stick, a stone, as iron, as a devil." Others were labeled "fanatics," "false brethren," "a snail," and "poop in the street." During Luther's preparation in writing this anti-Jewish tract, tragedy

---

[230] Furey, Constance M., "Invective and Discernment in Martin Luther, D. Erasmus, and Thomas More," *Harvard Theological Review*, 98:4, October 2005, p.469. <https://www.cambridge.org/core/journals/harvard-theological-review/article/invective-and-discernment-in-martin-luther-d-erasmus-and-thomas-more/DA7DB0B30D8BEF11F35330A4D4B17C51>.

[231] Rasmussen, Tyler, "Luther's Insults Explained." <http://ergofabulous.org/luther/insults-explained.php>.

struck the Luther household when his beloved daughter Magdalene died in his arms on September 20, 1542. The wounds were still raw dealing with such devastation, yet his hope remained resolute. He completed the book near the end of that year. Obviously, the tragedy does not excuse his violent tone, yet it would be unrealistic for one to dismiss this important part of the context for this book.

There were many others on both sides who exhibited their own graphic language and disparaging descriptions to attack their enemies. Tom Standage* of *The Economist* writes that the papal court theologian Sylvester Mazzolini in his defense of the Pope, called Luther "a leper with a brain of brass and a nose of iron."[232] Pope Leo X himself proclaimed that Luther was "the wild boar" that has invaded the Lord's vineyard, and "we can no longer suffer the serpent to creep through the field of the Lord.... We cannot suffer the scabby sheep longer to infect the flock."[233] Other dismissive and defamatory words or phrases to address Luther included a "pestilential buffoon," "the Leipzig Goat," "the Wittenberg Bull," a dolt, "a pig," an "ape," "Dr. Liar," "wily Fox," "Child of Satan," the "Seven-Headed monster," "a piece of scurf," "a demon in disguise as a man," and the "Beast of the Apocalypse." "Much as they wanted to be rid of 'this petty monk,' as Pope Adrian VI, [who succeeded Leo X,] labeled him," Peter Stanford† reminds us "the establishment could not hand him over to his fate for fear of igniting an uprising. So, Luther, unlike those earlier would-be-reformers, lived to put his theories into practice."[234]

---

* Tom Standage is a journalist and author from England, and the Deputy Editor of *The Economist.*

[232] Standage, Tom, *Writing on the Wall: Social Media—the First 2000 Years* (New York: Bloomsbury, 2013), p.55, and in "How Luther Went Viral," <https://www.economist.com/christmas-specials/2011/12/17/how-luther-went-viral>.

[233] <http://mluther.ccws.org/stand/1.html>; see also <https://www.pastormelissascott.com/martin-luther/letters-leo.html>; "The Vatican, July 8, 1520;" and <https://sermons.faithlife.com/sermons/207555-sola-scriptura:-swazi-lecture>.

† Peter Stanford is an award-winning English writer, journalist and broadcaster known for his biographies including *Martin Luther: Catholic Dissident*, (Hodder Stoughton, 2017) and writings on religion and ethics.

[234] Stanford, Peter, "Five Centuries On, Martin Luther Should be Feted as Hero of Liberty and Free Speech," *The Guardian*. <www.theguardian.com/world/2017/mar/19/martin-luther-relevance-anniversary>.

The Seven-Headed Beast Mentioned in the Book of Revelation

SEVEN HEADED MARTIN LUTHER

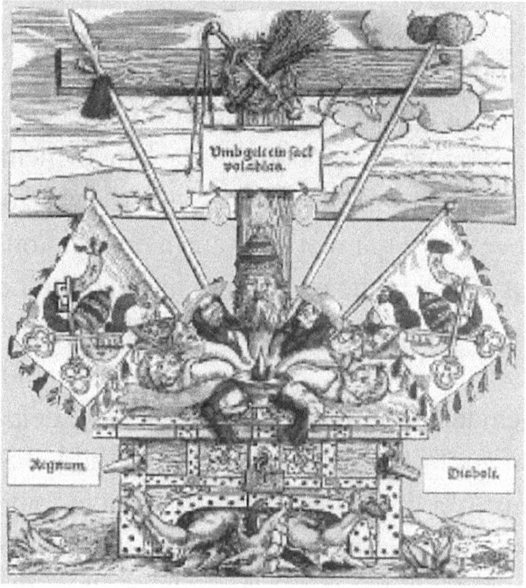

SEVEN HEADED PAPAL BEAST

(Images: Public domain, retrieved at the Salem [New Jersey] Community College website)

In mocking Luther, the Catholics portray the Reformer as having seven heads or guises under which Luther corrupted Christendom. Each head bears a different title intended to belittle him: Doctor (of theology); Martinus (as a monk); Heretic Luther (as a Turk wearing a turban); a priest (Ecclesiastes) who preaches what the mob wishes to hear; "Suermer" as the fanatic/enthusiast with his hair on end surrounded by hornets; a Church supervisor/visitor who revises the laws, thus accusing Luther of being a new Pope; and Barabbas (alluding to the thief who should have been executed instead of Jesus) as a wild man with a club. It is both a caricature of Luther and a defamation of him as the Antichrist (the seven-headed beast of the Apocalypse). Luther is portrayed as reading a book. One of Luther's most vigorous Roman Catholic opponents, polemicist Johannes Cochlaeus, engaged artist Hans Brosamer to construct this broadsheet circa 1529.

Lutherans countered with an image representing instruments of the papacy as a diabolical institution. The woodcut shows a cross bearing the instruments of Christ's passion and crucifixion, and the flags show the papal arms with symbols of the keys and the tiara. Between them is the seven-headed papacy, a diabolical monster made up of the pope, cardinals, bishops and monks. The beast sits on top of an altar which has been degraded into a treasure chest of indulgence money in what is identified as the kingdom of the Devil, who lies beneath it. The sign on the cross, replacing the INRI designation, reads in German, "For Money, a Sack Full of Indulgences." The Latin words on the sides say "Reign of the Devil." In explaining the woodcut, the writers note under the image, "The beast had received a mortal wound, signifying that Doctor Martin has struck the papacy a deadly blow. May God grant that it will soon be overthrown. Amen."

As we read the Gospels, we discover Jesus himself using sharp derogatory words and names for the Pharisees, scribes and Sadducees. One could reasonably assume His word about how we are to treat others, even our enemies, with kindness and gentleness is being contradicted. "*You blind fools*" (our "moron") in Matthew 23:17; "*hypocrites*" and "*snakes and brood of vipers*" (Matthew 23:33); "*tell that fox*," or in Jesus' day, "a weasel," referring to Herod as that cunning and crafty leader. Or take His instructing the woman in Matthew 7:6 not to give dogs what is sacred or throw pearls to pigs. He doesn't seem to be playing nice with the Pharisees, saying they are like "*whitewashed tombs*" (Matthew23:27-8), appearing nice on the outside but filled inside with hypocrisy. Contrary to our perceived expectations, Jesus doesn't always treat people with kid gloves, but rather confronts them head-on. There are times when He calls a spade a spade, acknowledging the benefit of using nicknames and words that hold truthful meaning and significance.

Or we read in Acts 13:9-10, "*But Saul, who was also called Paul, filled with the Holy Spirit, looked intently at him* [a magician named Elymas, a prophet and most likely a soothsayer] *and said, 'You son of the devil, you enemy of all righteousness, full of all deceit and villainy, will you not stop making crooked the straight paths of the Lord?'*" That doesn't sound considerate or caring, but rather biting with sharp words. We discover Spirit-prompted boldness, which doesn't mince words about the wickedness of this magician. With Luther, the Apostle Paul uses speech motivated and animated by God's Spirit in ways that insult, with pointed and direct words that are harsh and seem cruel and out of character.

As a maverick presidential candidate, Trump routinely denigrated his opposition by using schoolyard taunts and acerbic rhetoric in ways that parallel Martin Luther's. By referring to his rivals and opponents by a belittling nickname, Trump evokes negative feelings about them right off the bat. Trump's racially charged nickname for Senator Elizabeth Warren is "Pocahontas." That moniker was given to Warren when he revived a dispute about the senator's heritage, arguing she falsely claimed Native American ancestry to advance her academic career. University of Wisconsin communications professor Dietram Scheufele explains that "In one word, he basically mentions that story that most of his voters won't remember, but they kind of know what he's referencing, so they find themselves all of a sudden like 'Yeah, yeah, I remember that' without really any rational thought or way of thinking through the story."[235] Not only providing emphasis but repetition also strengthens the association. From there, Trump can say something completely unrelated about Warren, like his tweet, "Pocahontas wanted V.P. slot but wasn't chosen…" For his supporters, the damage is already done.

Similarly, calling Hillary Clinton "Crooked Hillary" ensures that, no matter the content of the sentence that follows, the reference about her email controversy easily slips into the mind of the hearer as a presupposed truth. These little nuggets are packed with enormous linguistic power, especially as the media creates a circus surrounding Trump's insults, ensuring they make it in the soundbite, headline or meme on social media. Name-calling and the hurling of insults have always been a raw, primal assertion of power, according to Professor Emeritus Jack Zipes at the University of Minnesota. He credits Trump having "a unique intuition. He's able to use these pejorative adjectives in a way which really does overpower the opposition." Jon Allsop,* a freelance journalist who interviewed Dr. Zipes, adds that "Trump is a highly skilled wielder of the fairy tale insult. Devastating when well-applied, it can stick to recipients with indelible persistence and ruin presidential bids, reputations, and careers altogether."[236]

North Korea's leader is known as "Rocket Man" when few can recall his name as Kim Jong Un. Another political rival was Senator Bernie Sanders, who was dubbed "Crazy Bernie," and fellow 2016 candidate Marco Rubio received the punching epithet "Little Marco." "Lyin' Ted" was applied to Senator Ted Cruz, "Low Energy Jeb" to Jeb Bush, "Cryin' Chuck" to Senate Minority Leader Chuck Schumer, and "Sleepy Joe" to then Vice President Joe Biden. Assaulted by an amateur politician who brought his distinctive brand of Twitter-based ad hominin to the campaign and then to the White House, what does the opposition do? They do as did Luther's opponents. They make use of their own degrading nicknames for the President: "womanizer," "Benedict Donald," "Boss Tweet," "The Antichrist," "Agent Orange," "Adolf Twitler," "Trumpty Dumpty," "Hair Fuhrer," "Orange Julius," "Alpha Molester," "Assaulter-in-Chief," "The Donald," "Cheddar Boy," and "Lady Fingers Trump."

---

[235] Abadi, Mark, "There's an Interesting Reason Why Donald Trump's Nicknames for His Enemies are so Effective," *Business Insider*, No. 2, 2016; <https://www.businessinsider.com/why-donald-trump-gives-nicknames-to-his-political-enemies-2016-11>.

* Jon Allsop writes the *Columbia Journalism Review's* daily newsletter, "The Media Today," and freelances on the side with bylines in *The Atlantic*, *The Nation*, *Hartford Courant*, *New York Daily News*, and *Limpopo Mirror* in South Africa.

[236] Allsop, Jon "Inside the Fairy Tale Mind of Trump," *Columbia Journalism Review*, September 27, 2017. <https://www.cjr.org/special_report/trump-fairy-tale.php>.

Both Trump and Luther recognized the value of branding their adversaries and dissenters with descriptive monikers that project, while hammering home, in a word or two, negative feelings about a person that can be easily shared in conversations. They could cast aspersions in slamming their opponents while cheering defenders in simplistic terms.

Trump understood also that the average news soundbite had shrunk from 43 seconds in 1968 to about 8–9 seconds now. This coincides, interestingly, with how long it takes someone to speak a text or tweet, which Trump has mastered.[237]

A large part of Trump's success with his new brand of politics is his ability to resonate almost intuitively with an audience with just a few words. Bestowing a nickname to his opponents and detractors is a signature trademark of Donald Trump's political strategy, and the shorthand messaging works as it jibes with Trump's confident persona. Labels stick and leave little room for debate or contradiction and require little additional information beyond knowing what the names are meant to apply. "When Luther dubbed the Pope the 'Antichrist' and Catholics 'anti-Christians,' …the Pope responded by not only anathematizing Luther as a 'heretic,' but he 'denominated' Martin's followers 'Lutheran' so that they might share in his punishment and shame."[238] These labels have stuck for centuries.

---

[237] Kottke, Jason, "The Shrinking Political Soundbite," Jan 3,2011; <https://kottke.org/11/01/the-shrinking-political-soundbite>.

[238] Bejan, Teresa, "You don't have to be nice to Political Opponents. But You do have to Talk to Them," *The Washington Post*, March 8, 2017. <https://www.washingtonpost.com/posteverything/wp/2017/03/08/you-dont-have-to-be-nice-to-political-opponents-but-you-do-have-to-talk-to-them/?utm_term=.5f3fe228f1ac7>.

12

Bawdy and Ballsy Humor

One may think I have resorted to the use of off-color language, but the word "ballsy" is an apt description of how our twin rebels use language even in their humor. While there is a "manly" or "macho" association, its meaning and synonyms focus on being tough and courageous, gutsy, intrepid, valorous, daring and bold.

Many find Trump to be no laughing matter, or have trouble finding lighthearted spots in an ongoing stream of hyperbole and bile. They often take his words literally or superficially, without recognizing the penetrating truth he is espousing sarcastically. But his standup "shtick" is powerful when it makes his supporters feel they're in on his jokes in a way the establishment and media are not, or pretend not to be. In *Politico* magazine, Joanna Weise writes that

> this effect is an extension of the 2016 campaign formulation, likely coined by GOP strategist Brad Todd and popularized by Peter Thiel, that Trump supporters "take him seriously, but not literally." Because Trump's fans take him seriously, they recognize when he isn't being serious, and laugh when his opponents miss the joke.... Trump's jokes give his supporters a way to feel superior to the elites, to mock what they see as a humorless and predictable political establishment.[239]

Examples of his sarcastic and insulting humor are his jokes kidding about wanting to purchase the Danish territory of Greenland, promising not to build a "gold-plated Trump Hotel" on its craggy shore; seeking a third term or leaving office in six years, or maybe 10 or 14 years; that Russia might help find the 30,000+ subpoenaed Hillary

[239] Weiss, Joanna, "Trump Pokes Fun at Himself. Why Do Only Some People See It?" *Politico*, November 9, 2019. <https://www.politico.com/magazine/story/2019/11/09/trump-pokes-fun-at-himself-why-do-only-some-people-see-it-229908>.

emails; that China should investigate Hunter Biden; and posting a photo of a frowning Nancy Pelosi, Chuck Schumer and Steny Hoyer, accompanied by the question, "Do you think they like me?" Such jokes or satirical comments about his political rivals' hatred of him conveys more than a sense of humor. It also underlines the fact that Trump has become President while facing down deep hostility and is now in a strong position to joke about it, as accomplishments mount in defiance of repeated investigations based on false claims.

Now investigations into the "investigators" are peeling back the corruption, layer by layer, of the so-called "scandal-free" administration of his predecessor, which threaten to expose their schemes to indict and overthrow a duly elected president. While the reports have not yet been fully announced, enough have already shown how the intel community was weaponized against Trump, like the IRS was against conservative organizations applying for tax-exempt status. This is proving to be no laughing matter but rather the biggest hoax ever perpetrated on "We the People," and has the potential of becoming the darkest moment in the political history of our country.

To be sure, "Trump's brand of humor," described by Andrew Restuccia and Ben Schreckinger as "cutting, insulting and sometimes even downright mean—has long offended and shocked the president's critics"[240] while being elusive to many. But for his supporters and allies, Trump's irreverent jokes are used much as Luther's rhetorical device in using demeaning, insulting words, and graphic, comedic depictions. In fact, they have become a central feature of Trump's "performance" at rallies held across the country. Many "Trumpers" come to these rallies, where he is at his absolute best, to be entertained. "His speaking style is what endears him to his supporters," said Brian O. Walsh, president of the pro-Trump group America First Action. "It's a big part of what fueled him through the primaries and the general election. The unpolished 'everyman' who says what he thinks."[241]

The subtle humor of Trump was spotlighted in his 2020 acceptance speech from the White House and accented by his facial expressions of a smirking smile with the rolling and twinkling of his eyes and that comedic styling stance as he turns to a portion of the audience, then to another, to say without uttering a sound, "You know what I'm *really* saying!" Trump was exposing his rival's 47 years of being a "swamp creature" in Washington,

---

[240] Restuccia, Andrew and Ben Schreckinger, "In MAGA World, Trump's Jokes Always Land;" <https://politico.com/story/2018/10/19 trump-rallies-comedy-916795>.
[241] Ibid.

"taking donations of blue-collar workers, gave them hugs, and even kisses, [then Trump intentionally pauses to slap that confused expression on his face to help the audience focus on the obvious reference to the former Vice President's creepy proclivity of sniffing women's hair or neck] as he [Biden] told them he felt their pain, and then he flew back to Washington and voted to ship our jobs to China and many other distant lands."[242]

Another classic example was his ridiculing Senator Elizabeth Warren for claiming Native American heritage at his rally in Mosinee, Wisconsin, September 17, 2020:

> Pocahontas, you know Pocahontas? Did anybody ever hear of her? She's another great one. Pocahontas. I said to her a long time ago, I've got more Indian blood in me than you do, and I have none, I have none. Sadly. I'd love a little bit of it, but I have none, I said...I turned out to be right. She choked and she went for a blood test. Remember? Was it 1024th? Meaning maybe nine hundred years ago, there was a little action going on. Crazy Pocahontas, she's a nasty one though, isn't she?[243]

The Trump presidential humor brand can be as indecorous as Luther's excremental humor, in that both are deeply scathing and can easily be weaponized to effectively assassinate an opponent's character. Perhaps in addition to the more acceptable usage of scatological language in Luther's culture, his developing glee in being liberated from God's judgment seems to have given him license to indulge in language that would surprise the pious, even to those in our day. This "Church Father," according to Luther scholar Eric Gritsch, is the only one

> who incorporated humor into his life and work. He did so by posing as a court jester (an advertised self-image*), a quick wit, a facetious wag, and a sit-down comedian with humorous comments in more than five thousand "table talks." His humor has to be taken seriously as an integral part of his literary legacy in the still-incomplete Weimar Edition of more than a

---

242 <https://www,nytimes.com/2020/08/28/us/politics/trump-rnc-speech-transcript.html>.

243 <https://www.rev.com/blog/transcripts/donald-trump-mosinee-wi-rally-speech-transcript-september-17>.

* "I shall for the time being become a court jester," wrote Luther in his letter "To the Christian Nobility of the German Nation" in LW 44:123.

> hundred oversized volumes, published since 1883. Though known for many proverbial witticisms ("No one can become an expert among ignoramuses"*), Luther made humor an integral part of his theological reflections...using it to enhance his Biblical witness, to ridicule those in power, and to mock death and the devil.[244]

Gifted with a keen sense of the ridiculous, it was almost second nature for Luther to delight in drollery and particularly to clothe his ideas in playful imagery. His mind was indeed an inexhaustible source of rich and homely humor even amidst the trials he faced. His conversation with friends, colleagues and pupils was rendered more stimulating and attractive with his witticisms and under the cover of a jest he was often able to convey good instruction more easily. Nature had indeed endowed Luther from his cradle with that rare talent of humor which also proved valuable to him amidst the trials and hardships of life. Admittedly, his use of that gift was anything but refined although it certainly proved to be a powerful resource for reforming Christ's Church.

In the Guise of a Fool

Court jesters conjure images of medieval feasts where the fool, brightly dressed and belled, would entertain his lord's guests with mockery, mimicry and jests. The role of the fool, however, predates the medieval period, going back to the Egyptian pharaohs, and is found in all cultures and nations, addressed in Scriptures and embodied by our twin reformers. The Bible contains words and usages about the fool that are familiar in our experiences and applied by many to describe actions and thoughts of these warriors, as well as some of our acquaintances, and of course ourselves: acting unwisely or imprudently, lacking sense or judgment, laughing at or turning eyes away from truth.

---

* Gritsch references three German proverbs in Luther's treatise *On the Councils and the Church* (1539), in *LW* 41:76.

[244] Gritsch, Eric W., "Martin Luther's Humor," *Word & World* 32:2, 2012 p.132. <https://wordandworld.luthersem.edu/issues.aspx?article_id=1601>.

"The Bible also uses the word 'fool' in another way," says Napp Nazworth, the Executive Director of American Values Coalition in Washington, D.C., informing his readers that "the second type of 'fool' can be one who upends the wisdom of the world, who turns weakness into strength, who makes the lowly powerful, who flips the script on all we thought we knew. In this sense of the word, God is the greatest Fool of all."[245] St. Paul affirms this truth in his first letter to the Church in Corinth, as he announces that he was sent by Christ to proclaim the Gospel: "For the message about the cross is foolishness to those who are perishing, but to us who are being saved it is the power of God (1:18 [NRSV]). …For God's foolishness is wiser than human wisdom… (1:25 [NRSV])." Later in the letter, Paul refers to himself and the other Apostles as "fools for the sake of Christ" (4:10). As Nazworth notes, "He's not saying that he's an actual fool, in the first sense of the word, but that he's willing to appear to be a fool to the world for the sake of Christ."[246]

Court jesters function in the same way as powerful critics of the existing order. Luther and Trump use humor and mockery to ridicule and violate the norms their onlookers live by. It is much like that which happens at Washington's storied White House Correspondents' Dinner, an annual event where the most powerful leader in the world "officially" acts the "jester," delivering a joke-laden monologue and enduring caustic jibes thrown back. Gritsch notes the similarity of St. Paul's willingness to be a "fool for Christ" with Luther, who believed "he had been destined to appear in the guise of a monk. Ringing his bells and tapping his shoes. The melody originated in the mind of God and was heard through Holy Scripture and the best of Christian tradition. Not everyone, he said, would be able to understand what the jester said or did, for it had to be ambiguous, often offensive."[247]

---

245 Nazworth, Napp, "Race-Baiter, Misogynist, and Fool," *The Spiritual Danger of Donald Trump*, edited by Ronald J. Sider (Eugene, OR: Cascade Books, 2020), p.40.

246 Ibid.

247 Gritsch, Eric W., "The Unrefined Reformer," *Christian History*, No. 39, 1993. <https://christianhistoryinstitute.org/magazine/article/luther-unrefined-reformer>.

Court Jesters of Epic Proportions

Der Schalksnarr

The Fool by Heinrich Vogtherr
Left: Public domain, retrieved at the Public Domain Clip Art blog

Entertainer in Chief

Modern Trump meme
Right: Foolocracy.com

The role and images of jesters and fools were a common staple in medieval culture. Here is Heinrich Vogtherr the Younger's most striking—and colorful—depiction of a fool, "cocking a snoot" at the authorities (c.1540). The most identifiable part of a medieval jester's outrageous costume was the "fool's hat" which had three points with bells at the end that jingled. Jesters used a special scepter called a "bauble" or "marotte" with various heads embedded. Woodcuts of the jester were used to caricaturize Luther, often being humorous in his deft lampooning of his enemies, while his opponents like Thomas Murner, a German Franciscan monk, return the "favor" by making fun of the "Great Lutheran Fool." Some pundits and commentators have bequeathed to President Trump those caricatures of being the jester or clown in their depiction of the "Entertainer in Chief."

Luther gave himself the image of being God's court jester and described his mission in these words:

> Perhaps I owe my God and the world another work of folly *[besides the* Theses*]*. I intend to pay my debt honestly. And if I succeed I shall for the time being become a court jester. And if I fail, I still have one advantage—no one need buy me a cap or put scissors to my *head [his monk's cowl would serve as a jester's cap]*. It is a question of who will put the bells on whom *[that is, who is the bigger fool]*. ...Paul says, *"He who wishes to be wise must become a fool."* [I Cor. 3:18]. Moreover, since I am not only a fool, but also a sworn doctor of Holy Scripture, I am glad for the opportunity to fulfill my doctor's oath, even in the guise of a fool."[248]

---

[248] LW 44:123-4, *The Christian in Society I*, "To the Christian Nobility of the German Nation," quoted by Eric W. Gritsch in *The Wit of Martin Luther* (Minneapolis: Augsburg Fortress, 2006), p.21.

Even in the midst of physical pain and suffering through extraordinary hardships, Luther's humor served him well, keeping his wits especially since he had experienced that liberating serenity. Because of his confidence in Christ's promise and belief in His imminent return, he could even face death with satirical wit: "For one person I've done enough. All that's left is to sink into my grave. I'm done for, except for tweaking the pope's nose a little now and then."[249] In Eric Gritsch's words,

> Serenity in the face of earthly "*Anfechtung*"* and the imminent end of the world generated Luther's gallows humor. It was anchored in an unconditional loyalty to Jesus Christ who had promised to overcome sin, evil, and death. That is why Luther could joke about his illnesses, especially headaches and kidney stones. They were agents of the devil, attempting to destroy Christian discipleship and its discipline. The devil created headaches by riding through the brain looking for a spa.[250]

Kidney stones are deadly torture and Luther makes a play on words with the stones that struck and killed St. Stephen (Acts 7:54-60) and the kidney stones that were causing him excruciating pain. Luther concedes "I am obliged to be stoned to death like Stephen and to give the pope an occasion for pleasure, but I hope he won't laugh very long. My epitaph shall remain true: While alive I was your plague, when dead I'll be your death, O pope."[251]

Luther could mock even death as that last enemy with the assurance of eternal life carrying him through life's troubled times. He could joyfully face life's anxieties by anticipating eternal joys. The Wittenberg theologian never lost his sense of humor and its intimate connection with faith. Keeping faith in times of distress often requires a sense of humor, with laughter, smiling, and even mocking, as Luther exhibited and as many today have discovered in the humor generated by Covid-19. He understood clearly that divinely comedic element of the One who sits in the heavens and laughs (Psalm 2:4 [NRSV]) in the face of Satan's defeat.

---

[249] LW 54:343. *Table Talk,* "Luther Says that that He is Tired, Worn Out, No. 4465 (1539)."

* "*Anfechtung*" is the German word for anguish, tribulation, inner spiritual struggle, the feeling of being forsaken by God, or a deeply seated soul struggle.

[250] Gritsch, Eric W., "Martin Luther's Humor," *Word & World* 32:2, 2012, p.139. <https://wordandworld.luthersem.edu/issues.aspx?article_id=1601> with the "spa" comment referencing Luther's Letter to John Frederick (March 28, 1532) in WA-Br 6:277.

[251] LW 54:227. *Table* Talk, "Gravely Ill, No. 3543A (1537);" His epitaph is mentioned also in LW 34:49.

Can one conceive of Luther envisaging himself as a prescription for the devil? "If he devours me, he shall devour a laxative (God willing) which will make his bowels and anus too tight for him. Do you want to bet?"[252] In the play and subsequent film *Luther,* John Osborne captures this humor as he jauntily focuses on Luther's constipation, with Johann von Staupitz urging Luther to do something about those "damned" bowels that were a constant source of discomfort. In response, Luther famously quips, "Who knows—if I break wind in Wittenberg, they may smell it in Rome."[253]

Alan Wolfe, who wrote *The Politics of Petulance: America in an Age of Immaturity,* uses the humorous quote in a little different translation while making the observation, "Even among believers themselves, not everything religious was treated as sanctified: Martin Luther, the Don Rickles of the Protestant Reformation, was a master of one-line putdowns, as in…'When I fart in Wittenberg, the Pope in Rome wrinkles his nose.'"[254] At another time, our comedian with a highly developed sense of smell, used flatulence to express a laughable witticism: "Out of a desperate ass never comes a cheerful fart."[255] Or as it is also translated, "A happy fart never comes from a miserable ass."[256]

Flatulence and pooping were obviously among Luther's favorite subjects for silliness and satire. Being the Greek scholar translating the Bible from the Greek manuscripts, he not only recalled the contrast St. Paul made in writing to the Philippians but could personally resonate with it from his welcomed evangelical discovery regarding righteousness. In Philippians 3:8 (NRSV), Paul writes,

> *I regard everything as loss because of the surpassing value of knowing Christ Jesus my Lord. For His sake I have suffered the loss of all things, and I regard them as* "**rubbish,**" *in order that I may gain Christ and be found in Him, not having a righteousness of my own that comes from the law, but one that comes through faith in Christ.*

---

[252] LW 49:329. *Letters II*, "215 To Philip Melanchthon [Coburg], June 29, 1930."

[253] Osborne, John, *Luther, A Play* (Woodstock, IL: Dramatic Publishing Company, 1961), p.54.

[254] Wolfe, Alan, *The Politics of Petulance: America in an Age of Immaturity* (Chicago and London: University of Chicago Press, 2018), p.128.

[255] Gritsch, Eric W., *Wit of Martin Luther,* (Minneapolis: Fortress, 2006), p.114.

[256] <https://www.quotetab.com/quote/by-martin-luther/a-happy-fart-never-comes-from-a-miserable-ass?source=fart>.

The contrast of "all things" with knowing Christ is called "*skubala*." Unfortunately, the word gets sanitized in translation as "rubbish," "garbage" or "refuse." It is the King James Version, remarkably, that more accurately uses the word's stronger meaning: "dung." St. Paul is saying that everything I think that brings me meaning, security and identity is like a pile of human excrement when compared to the surpassing greatness of knowing Christ. Can you imagine the shock our genteel congregations would experience upon hearing the word "shit" or "crap" being read in the lesson for the day from St. Paul?

Luther often wrote with uninhibited flamboyancy in offering fecal tirades against the Pope, such as saying he is the "cuckoo who devours the Church's eggs and then craps out cardinals."[257] Then there is that unforgettable anecdote we encountered earlier. Knowing he would soon die, he shared with his wife, "I'm like a ripe stool and the world's like a gigantic anus, and we're about to let go of each other."[258]

Luther had a Biblical conviction of the papacy being the Antichrist. Of course, as we have seen, the Catholics returned the "compliment" in their caricature of Luther as the seven-headed beast portrayed in Revelation 13:1 with blasphemous names on the heads. In February and March 1545, Luther gave full unrestrained venting to his pent-up frustration with the Pope who had already convoked the Council of Trent. The result was his treatise *Against the Papacy in Rome, Instituted by the Devil*, printed at the end of April.

The late Francis Betten, Prussian-American priest and professor at John Carroll University, reminds us that

> When Luther rose in rebellion against the ecclesiastical authority, the art of printing was about seventy years old. A large number of books that had been produced by that time were illustrated. The art had given an impetus to the sister art of wood engraving; that is the production of pictures by means of figures cut inversely into wooden blocks. (Copper engraving, too, saw a rapid development, but was not so extensively utilized by Luther.) In Luther's time the renown masters of drawing and painting, Albrecht

[257] Schmidt, Josef, and Simon, Mary, "Holy and Unholy Shit: The Pragmatic Context of Scatological Curses in Early German Reformation Satire," *Fecal Matters in Modern Literature and Art*, edited by Jeff Persels and Russell Ganim (Surrey: Ashgate, 2004), pp.109–17.

[258] LW 54:448. *Table Talk*, "Luther Suffers Pain and Expects His End, No. 5537."

> Dürer and Lucas Cranach, also engaged extensively in wood engraving. But before Luther the illustrations of books rarely served the purpose of ridiculing, vilifying, and slandering an adversary or any particular class of people. It was Martin Luther that introduced the cartoon, the caricature, into the productions of the press. He made it one of his favorite and most effective weapons, and he used it to an extent such as probably no one since has equaled.[259]

In his book *The Art of Controversy: Political Cartoons and Their Enduring Power,* Victor S. Navasky* embraces "anthropologist David Thorn's idea that the man responsible for the birth of political cartoons and caricatures is, of all people, Martin Luther."[260]

While working on that treatise against the papacy, Luther also designed a series of ten depictions or cartoons defaming the papacy—not in the sense of drawing them himself, but in the sense of describing what he wanted artist Lucas Cranach to produce for him. He also composed a short poem, consisting of two distichs—a two-line verse or couplet—to accompany each illustration. Cranach then created the woodcuts according to his impression of Luther's proposal and had them published with a Latin title at the top and Luther's poem as the caption at the bottom of each. Today this collection of woodcuts is called "*Abbildung des Papsttums*" or "Portrayal of the Papacy."

The quintessential artist, Cranach had partnered with Luther and together they had become a dynamic duo. Luther wrote and Cranach fused the Reformer's words with images drawn and carved as woodcuts, as well as painting exquisite works of art, many of which graced altars. As a creative thinker, the illustrator's job is to visualize someone else's ideas. This the talented artist and friend of Luther succeeded in doing, especially for the benefit of the illiterate. For example, he

---

[259] Betten, Francis S., "The Cartoon in Luther's Warfare against the Church," *The Catholic Historical Review,* 11:2, 1925, pp.252. <https://www.jstor.org/stable/25012186>.

* Victor S. Navasky is an American journalist, editor and professor emeritus at Columbia University. He was the editor of *The Nation* from 1978 until 1995 and its publisher and editorial director until 2005.

[260] Navasky, Victor S., *The Art of Controversy: Political Cartoons and Their Enduring Power* (New York: Alfred A. Knopf, 2013), p.29. See also David Thorn's "Political Satire: The Influence of Humor." <https://www.littlewolf.us/politicalsatire.html>.

> illustrates the Pope holding a literally flaming anti-Protestant encyclical whose fires are being tamed by the winds of the farting German peasants, whose asses are directed at the throne of St. Peter and its current occupant.... In that same pamphlet, Cranach plays even bluer, when he presents an image of Landsknecht mercenaries electing to challenge the Pope with a "weapon other than the sword"...one determined fellow is poised crouching over a positively massive papal tiara, taking a dump into its cavernous beehive like interior [as if it were a privy].[261]

The powerful image maker devoted to Luther's cause skillfully combined medieval devotional imagery with polemical images of the Pope to create a visual theology that complemented Luther's verbal theology. Citing Matthew 12:34 or Luke 6:45 (NRSV), "*Out of the abundance of heart the mouth speaks*," logical questions have been raised about how the torrent of conscious slander and indecency could come from the mind and heart by one claiming to be guided by the Spirit of Truth. These cartoons or caricatures rank among the most hideous, vulgar and obscene, and were, as we have stated, of Luther's own conception. They make a satirical, witty point humorously as an effective means of criticizing the establishment. Most political cartoons are directed at the common person, the masses of people who can make or break a political idea, and it has proven to be as effective today at stirring and directing public opinion as it was during the Reformation.

---

[261] Simon, "Fecal Fridays," p.10.

Reformation Humor Expressed in Woodcuts

A prototype of modern comic strips, woodcuts were the first items produced to serve as a means of visual mass communications, in one of history's best examples of a successful public relations campaign in the Protestant Reformation. Woodcuts were cheap, easy to produce, and could communicate effectively to the large percentage of people who were illiterate.

ORTUS ET ORIGO PAPAE

"Here the Antichrist is Born"

HIC OSCULA PEDIBUS PAPAE FINGUNTUR

"The Kissing of the Pope's Feet is Taunted"

(Left) A she-devil gives rectal birth to the pope and cardinals. In the background on the right Megaera, one of the Furies* in Greek mythology, serves as the baby pope's wet-nurse. Alecto, another of the Furies, serves as his nursemaid, rocking him and feeding him honey. Tisiphone, the last of the Furies, teaches the toddler pope to walk. Luther criticized Cranach for depicting the Pope's birth so crudely, saying that he should have been more considerate of the female sex. The birthed pope and cardinals are identified by their traditional dress. (**Furies* were creatures from Greek mythology who exacted divine retribution from those guilty of wrongdoing.)

(Right) German peasants bare their buttocks and release flatulence in answer to the Pope's decree of excommunication which is emanating rays. The two peasants had been summoned to kiss the Pope's feet in repentance. Instead, they curse his ban, turn around and moon him, and pass gas at him before they go. Luther often referred to the Pope as the "fart-ass." Luther wrote, "They are temporal lords, ordained by God. Why do they tolerate such things from such a rotten paunch, crude-ass in Rome" (LW 41:335). The caption reads, "Don't frighten us Pope with your ban...or else we will show you our rears."

<https://redbrickparsonage.wordpress.com/tag/lutheran-reformation-500th-anniversary/>

Reformation Humor Expressed in Woodcuts

Woodcuts like these accompanied "letters of insult," a common custom among the German nobility, which aimed at gaining revenge for unredressed grievances. Such letters of insult heaped abuse upon the enemy, intended to insult by showing the person under assault suffering death by dishonorable means through hanging, for example, or dismemberment, or disembowelment.

ADORATVR PAPA DEVS TURRENVS

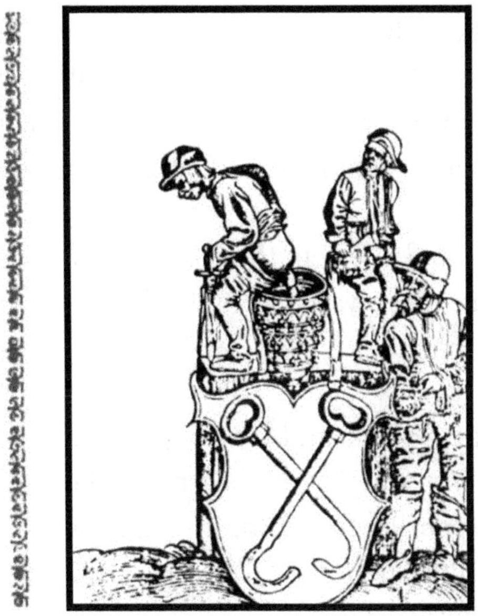

"Defecating into the Papal Tiara"

DIGNA MERCES PAPAE SATANISSIM

"Just Rewards of the Satanic Pope"

(Left) Luther had a Biblical conviction of the papacy being the Antichrist. In this woodcut a peasant is defecating in an inverted papal tiara or crown, while another one gets ready to do so. Luther's poem reads, "'Pay her back double,' says the Spirit. 'Go ahead and fill it up,' it is God who says so." To paraphrase Luther, "After all the crap the Pope, as fallen Babylon, has given you true Christians, put twice as much 'crap' in his crown for him to wear," making a play on his translation of Revelation 18:6-7.

(Right) *The Just Rewards of the Most Satanic Pope and His Cardinals*: In his poem, Luther said that if the pope and cardinals were to receive what they deserved in the form of earthly punishment (and not just the eternal punishment they can anticipate), this is what it would look like. The pope (on the far right) and three cardinals hang from a gallows. Because of their blasphemies against God and His Word, their cut off tongues are nailed to the gallows next to their heads (the hangman is in the process of nailing the pope's tongue to the crosspiece at the right). Demons receive their souls and carry them away. Luther often penned a text verse or couplet to accompany the woodcut; here "If the Pope and Cardinals were / To be justly punished here on earth / Their slanders would merit / What you see depicted here."

<https://pages.uoregon.edu/dluebke/Reformations441/ReformationSatires.html>

In addition to Luther's intellectual successes in winning battles with his clean scholarly academic language, he continued to win many verbal and visual battles with foul language and "indelicate" cartoon illustrations provided by Cranach, as we have just sampled. This side of Luther's activity is very little-known. Yet to fully understand the Reformer's character it needs to be taken into consideration and in the context of his day where vulgar degradation gave the perception of power to the degrader. And, as we have previously learned, the use of such coarse excremental words in the late Medieval and early Reformation periods enhanced one's stature as a victor; and for Luther, it gave him re-enforcement, especially in his fight against the Devil. Adding "toilet humor" gave weight or gravity to the transcendent, bringing the holy down into the everyday life of ordinary people. (Could the colloquialism "holy shit" have its origin with Luther and the Reformation?!) "Although Luther did make derogatory comments and use his pen to ridicule his opponents," Gritsch reports that "Luther avoids that so-called '*schadenfreude*' [joy at other's hardships]."[262]

In the later polemic pictures against the papacy and Church, the coarseness increases beyond bounds. The sole purpose of these cartoons in his warfare against the Church, in Francis Betten's appraisal, was

> to give the papacy and its Church over to the ridicule and lowest contempt of the beholder.... Luther assures us in his last year that he had not by far done enough in this regard, and that he despairs of ever doing enough. He confides to a friend that he considers his filthy pictures of the pope as a special heirloom which he bequeaths to posterity.[263]

It is helpful to keep in mind that Luther and his followers were focused initially and primarily on the positive goal of reforming the German Church to conform to the true religion of Christ through faith alone. I believe Luther saw the depth of corruption in the papacy, which lent urgency to the task he believed he was called to address, much as Trump discovered the magnitude and complexity of the Deep State and the scandalous swamp he attempted to drain. The President may have indeed come to a similar realization

---

[262] Maschke, Timothy, "Review of *The Wit of Martin Luther* by Eric Gritsch," *Concordia Theology*. <https://concordiatheology.org/2010/03/the-wit-of-martin-luther-by-eric-gritsch->.

[263] Betten, "The Cartoon," p.264. Fr. Hartman Grisar's *Luther* translates the Reformer declaring "that he would bequeath his hatred of the Papacy as an heirloom to his disciples." (Cp. Our vol. iii, p. 435). Grisar, *Luther*, Vol. 5, p.101. <https://www.gutenberg.org/files/49171/49171-h/49171.htm#c84>.

the Reformer had deduced: the Devil was at work in the office of the Bishop of Rome, to the extent that that office had become the prophesied figure of the Antichrist and the End Times were at hand.[264] Dr. Robert L. Rosin* of Concordia Seminary detects in Luther's innovative antipapal rhetoric a distinction that it is the office, and not the person of the pope, who is in effect the Antichrist.[265] Yet, as Dr. Bobbi Dykema of Strayer University in Herndon, Virginia, acknowledges, those in the hierarchy of the Church

> do not, in Luther's reckoning, escape condemnation. By promulgating the notion that the papacy was and is Antichrist, Luther and his colleagues by implication indicted all of its officeholders, past, present, and future as being in league with evil—possibly the most damning assassination of character possible, particularly for those who ostensibly were tasked with the care of the souls of all of Christendom.[266]

Our preconceptions would lead us to think that our historical religious heroic twin would indeed speak and protest boldly, but with stern propriety and reverence, not with irreverent lambastes, fecal invectives or bawdy prose. Yet as Dr. David Bagchi† of Hall University reminds us, "Luther is not trying to offend indiscriminately, but quite specifically to offend the Devil… with scorn…. The Devil wants to be taken seriously, but in fact, he has no real power over us: that is why Luther says, 'we can destroy his pride with a simple word.'"[267]

---

[264] Oberman, Heiko A., *The Reformation: Roots and Ramifications*, translated by A. C. Gow (Grand Rapids, MI, Eerdmans, 1994), p.30.

* Rev. Dr. Robert Rosin was Professor of Historical Theology for 35 years at Concordia Seminary and served as editor of Concordia Seminary publications and Director of the Center for Reformation Research. He has been a guest instructor or lecturer in many countries and is the author of numerous books and articles.

[265] Rosin, Robert L., "The Papacy in Perspective: Luther's Reform and Rome." *Concordia Journal*, 29:407-26, October 4, p.424.

[266] Dykema, Bobbi, "The Ass in the Seat of St. Peter: Defamation of the Pope in Early Lutheran *Flugschriften*," *Character Assassination Throughout the Ages*, ed. Martijn Icks and Eric Shiraev (Palgrave, 2014). Also <https://www.academia.edu/9540882> p 10.

† David Bagchi, professor at the University of Hull, England. He has a special interest in the theology of Martin Luther, early modern religious polemic, and the use of the printing press for dissemination of theological ideas. He is Co-Director of the Andrew Marvell Centre for Medieval and Early Modern Studies, coeditor of *The Cambridge Companion to Reformation Theology*, and author of *Luther's Earliest Opponents*.

[267] Bagchi, David, "The German Rabelais? Foul words and the Word in Luther," *Reformation and Renaissance Review* 7:143-62, 2005. (Francois Rabelais was a French Renaissance writer, physician, humanist, monk and Greek scholar known for his satire, grotesque and bawdy jokes and songs.) <https://www.academia.edu/6423382/>.

This reminds us of the words Luther includes in his most famous hymn, "A Mighty Fortress Is Our God":

> *Let this world's tyrant rage; In battle we'll engage!*
> *His might is doomed to fail; God's judgment must prevail!*
> *One little Word subdues him.*[268]

This "little Word" gives power to Luther's foul words and renders the Devil powerless against us to the extent that we, through faith, confess Christ's victory over him. According to Bagchi, Luther used scatological outbursts as an efficacious remedy against diabolically inspired assaults.

> Luther's language is not gratuitously offensive but serves a specific function…. The Devil tries to undermine our confidence in Christ by reminding us of our excrement, that is our sins. The only solution is to say to the Devil: "Yes I know I am a sinner and here are my sins—I make no secret of them." Or, to say that same thing and at the same time offend him, "Here is my shit, why don't you eat it as well?"[269]

Luther admitted that he was, on occasion, bull-headed, coarse-tongued and intemperate like his later twin brother Donald exhibited. Their speech and actions were frequently intense. Gritsch characterizes Luther as "The Unrefined Reformer." "No matter how high or low the cause he seemed to rise or sink to any occasion…he spoke freely and unguardedly about himself and others…Once when Luther was being publicly criticized, he declared, 'I am a tough Saxon, a peasant. I've grown a thick skin for this kind of_____.' But for Luther, 'to curse for the sake of God's Word is just.'"[270]

There were other arenas in which Luther mastered the use of humor as he connected with the people. As Luther's protectorate, Frederick the Wise, had a collection of 19,013

---

[268] Martin Luther, "A Mighty Fortress Is Our God," LBW Hymn 229; ELW Hymn 503; LW Hymn 297; and LSB Hymn 656.

[269] Bagchi, "The German Rabelais;" quoting Luther, WA 1:50.25; 4:681.20-30; <https://www.academia.edu/6423382/> or <https://doi.org/10.1558/rarr.v7i2-3.3.143>, or <https://www.tandfonline.com/doi/abs/10.1558/rarr.v7i2-3.3.143>.

[270] Gritsch, Eric W., "The Unrefined Reformer," *Christian History* 39, 1993. <https://christianhistoryinstitute.org/magazine/article/luther-unrefined-reformer>, also <http://reformationsa.org/index.php/reformation/396-libel-against-luther>.

relics (purported to be bits of petrified remains) of dead saints, so did his long-time nemesis, Archbishop Albrecht of Mainz. It was to Albrecht that Luther had sent a copy of his 95 Theses, inviting a debate on what he saw as the Church's ultimate perversion, selling indulgences. Twenty-five years later, in 1542, an anonymous pamphlet alerted the public to a showing of Albrecht's collection, including a piece of bread allegedly from the Last Supper and sacred remains, that if viewed solemnly, the faithful (who paid an admission fee) would be granted an indulgence. And if that were not enough to entice pilgrims, a "Black Friday Special" of sorts was also being offered: Newly discovered relics, so momentous, would be exhibited, so that viewers would receive a special indulgence offered by Pope Paul III. The new relics included in this fantastic new collection included (and I quote):

- A nice section from Moses' left horn (Exodus 34:29, Vulgate: 'his face was horned from the conversation with the Lord');
- Three flames from the burning bush on Mount Sinai (Exodus 3:3);
- Two feathers and an egg from the Holy Spirit;
- A remnant from the flag with which Christ opened hell;
- A large lock of Beelzebub's beard, stuck on the same flag;
- One-half of the archangel Gabriel's wing;
- Two ells (about ninety inches) of sound from the trumpets on Mount Sinai (Exodus 19:16);
- A whole pound of the wind which roared by Elijah in the cave on Mount Horeb (1 Kings 19:11);
- Thirty blasts from the trumpets on Mount Sinai;
- A large, heavy piece of the shout with which the children of Israel tumbled the walls of Jericho (Joshua 6:20);
- Five nice, shiny strings from David's harp;
- Three beautiful locks of Absalom's hair, which got caught in the oak and left him hanging (2 Samuel 18:9).

Whoever paid one guilder at the exhibition would receive (an additional) papal indulgence remitting all sins committed up to the time of payment and for ten more years thus giving the people of the Rhineland a unique opportunity to attain a special state of grace.[271]

[271] Gritsch, Eric W., "Two Feathers from The Holy Spirit," *Christian History*, 39:12, Vol. XII No. 3; <https://www.christianitytoday.com/history/issues/issue-39/two-feathers-from-holy-spirit.html>. See also Gritsch, *Wit*, pp.29-30.

What a deal! Sometime after this anonymous "New Pamphlet from the Rhine" had been widely circulated that provided boisterous laughter throughout the populace, Luther admitted he was the rascally author. He could not resist speaking out on indulgences once more in a humorous and belittling way to annoy Archbishop Albrecht, who was the most notorious advocate of indulgence traffic.

"Luther used humor to express his theological ideas in all sorts of ways," in Jane Voigts'* observance:

> Perhaps it's because he struggled with melancholy as well as profoundest opposition to his passionately held ideas; his humor served as a life-raft keeping his spirits and Spirit buoyed. In addition, humor often proves a great tool for winning the sway of the crowd, be it a crowd of peasants or scholars; perhaps that's why Luther regularly went for the funny.[272]

Championing the Virtues of Marriage and Sex

While Luther had much to say about sex, some of it too was crude, earthy and as explicit as Donald Trump's. He ventured unhesitatingly into areas where even a layperson, much less a priest, feared to tread, into questions of adultery, impotence, fornication, and masturbation. But as we have revealed, even in reference to feces, Luther found no area of life as unspiritual or unholy.

> Whoever is ashamed of marriage is also ashamed of being and being called human, tries to improve on what God has made. Adam's children are and will remain human; that is why they should and must beget more men. Dear God, we see daily the effort it costs to live in a marriage, and to keep the marital vows. And we try to promise chastity as if we were not human, had neither flesh nor blood.[273]

Luther did not hesitate to speak plainly about the healthy elemental force of sexual desire present within human beings.

---

*Jane Voigts is a comedian, writer and an ordained United Methodist pastor in Palm Springs, California.

[272] Voigts, Jane, "You Say Scatological, I Say Eschatological – The Humor of Martin Luther," personal blog, October 25, 2014. <janevoigts.com/blog/2014/10/24/luther-laughter>

[273] Oberman, *Devil*, pp.272-73, quoting WA 18:277, 26–36. Also quoted by Metaxas, *Rediscovered*, p.342.

> A young woman, if the high and rare grace of virginity has not been bestowed upon her, can do without a man as little as without food, drink, sleep, and other natural needs. And on the other hand: a man too, cannot be without a woman. The reason is the following: begetting children is as deeply rooted in nature as eating and drinking. That is why God provided the body with limbs, arteries, ejaculation, and everything that goes along with them. Now if someone wants to stop this and not permit what nature wants and must do, what is he doing but preventing nature from being nature, fire from burning, water from being wet, and man from either drinking, eating, or sleeping?[274]

His marriage to Katie gave him more than the strongest hint towards the bodily, earthily sensual side of humanity to which we all can relate. Luther was a man of God, but nevertheless a man! He discovered even more fulfillment in the sexual desire and physical act of sexual union within the bonds of marriage that is healthy, beautiful and holy, because it is God-given and intended.

One particular passage of a letter to his friend George Spalatin was removed from later editions of Luther's letters because it was, quite frankly, too embarrassing:

> When you sleep with your wife Catherine and embrace her, you should think: "This child of man, this wonderful creature of God has been given to me by my Christ. May He be praised and glorified." On the evening of the day on which, according to my calculations, you will receive this, I shall make love to my Catherine [von Bora] while you make love to yours, and thus we will be united in love.[275]

In Herbert David Rix's *Martin Luther: The Man and the Image*, the author quotes Luther sharing his counsel thru correspondence to the young tutor, Jerome Weller, hired for the Luther children. Weller was apparently noted for depression and Luther was advising him how he often responded to "evil thoughts" that assailed him:

> "How often have I grasped my wife and rubbed against her naked body that by arousing sexual desire in this way, I might drive away those thoughts that

[274] Ibid., pp.275-76. Oberman is quoting WA 10 II. 156, 13–22. Also see Metaxas, *Rediscovered*, p.343.
[275] Johnston, Andy, "Enjoy Sex and Defeat the Devil," Think Blog. <https://thinktheology.co.uk/blog/article/enjoy_sex_and_defeat_the_devil>.

> come from Satan." Other suggestions Luther offers Weller are "arousing in himself other thoughts such as of beautiful girls, or by hearty eating and drinking.... I recommend these things, although the best of all remedies is to believe in Jesus Christ."[276]

Few individuals ever examine their "sins" as exactingly as Martin Luther did, and too few come to that repentance of which he spoke in the Ninety-Five Theses. Fewer yet would speak so openly about their sins, lavatorial and bedroom activities as he did. "I have a lot of spiritual failings," he might remark, as Harry Haille writes, "'but I am about beyond my sins of the flesh. Avarice does not trouble me, because I have enough money. Lust doesn't trouble me either.' He looked impishly over at Kate—'I get plenty of what it takes to remedy that.'"[277]

One of Luther's major contributions emerging from The Reformation was his belief that celibacy was unnatural, and his championing the virtues of marriage. Healthy marital sex was ordained by God as the natural expression of one's physicality being made in the image of God. The gift of marital sex was not just for procreation, but for Luther the sex drive was a divine force for the deep fulfillment found in the giving and experiencing of pleasure. He was not hesitant, nor was he embarrassed, to speak plainly about this immanent healthy natural force of desire. In typical style, as he launched a crusade to permit monks to marry, he argued that the Curia could "just as easily have banned shitting."[278] His prolific comments on sexual matters, according to Heinz Schilling, was "not from obsession or frivolity,"[279] but because he was asked for his opinion and as he sat around the table with his friends, the subject would come up, often in humorous discourse.

Throughout his career as a reformer, he elevated not only marriage, sex and family, but also the status and role of women in society and, surprisingly for his time, the intimacies of the marital relationship. He counseled men of their responsibility in seeking the sexual fulfillment of their spouse as well as their own:

---

[276] Rix, Herbert David, *Martin Luther: The Man and the Image* (New York: Irvington Publishers, Inc., 1983), p.188 (T.R. #32986).

[277] Haile, Harry Gerald, "Knocking the Grand Heads," *Luther: An Experiment in Biography* (Princeton, NJ: Princeton University Press, 1980, Press Edition 1983), p.149.

[278] Schulz, Matthias, "Archaeologists Unveil Secrets of Luther's Life." <https://www.spiegel.de/international/germany/the-reformer-s-rubbish-archaeologists-unveil-secrets-of-luther-s-life-a-586847.html>; and <https://belover.medium.com/martin-luther-comedian-f4e5f0f8b6bd>.

[279] Schilling, *Upheaval*, p.278.

> It is one of the worst of sins, he informed the audience of a lecture on Genesis, to be like the Old Testament Onan, "to produce semen and excite the woman and to frustrate her at that very moment." His words were an admonition against coitus interruptus, the standard form of contraception of his time, but they also told of a sexual interaction that took the female partner seriously."[280]

"On May 19, (1521), during his early days at the Wartburg," James Reston, Jr. writes that Luther

> touched on the subject of physical love in a letter to Nicolas Gerbel, a jurist, doctor of canon law, and humanist from Strasbourg who would become an important supporter in subsequent battles and was deeply interested in Luther's literary life. It is not clear just how the two had first established their friendship or when Luther had met Gerbel and his wife. But from this letter, it's evident that in Gerbel's marriage the Reformer perceived a romantic model.
>
> "Kiss and re-kiss your wife," Luther wrote. "Let her love and be loved. You are fortunate in having overcome, by an honorable marriage, that celibacy in which one is a prey to devouring fires and to unclean ideas. That unhappy state of a single person, male or female, reveals to me each hour of the day so many horrors, that nothing sounds in my ear as bad as the name of monk or nun or priest. A married life is a paradise, even where all else is wanting."[281]

As physical beings, God has given us physical things for our enjoyment. For Luther, body and the mortal world were given by God to enjoy with love and laughter. And of course, being the Biblical scholar, Luther inevitably

> found Biblical validation for the sporting that goes on between husband and wife. "We are permitted to laugh and have fun with and embrace our wives, whether they are naked or clothed," just as Isaac fondled his wife in Genesis 26:8. (Later he would refer to sex between spouses as precious

---

[280] Ibid., p.279. Schilling is quoting Luther, *Lectures on Genesis, Chapters* 38-44, LW 7:21.

[281] Reston, Jr., James, *Luther's Fortress: Martin Luther and His Reformation Under Siege* (New York: Basic Books, 2015), pp. 87-88.

> and beneficial.) And female companionship was an excellent antidote to a man's melancholy. "When you are assailed by gloom, despair, or a troubled conscience, you should eat, drink, and talk with others. If you can find help for yourself by thinking of a girl, do so."[282]

Despite his joking and his obvious satisfaction with sexual pleasures, the sex drive for Luther, being a divinely created force, was an intrinsic part of God's creation. No area of life should be thought of as unspiritual or unholy—not even dung or sex. Sexual desire and fulfillment are healthy and God-given. He dignified the estate of marriage and sex, taking them from the "unholy" and the "dark hours of the night" and elevating them to a whole new level, just as he had done with the role and dignity of women.

In a letter to George Spalatin, inviting him to the wedding, Luther writes, "I have made the angels laugh and the devils weep."[283] Luther obviously loved his wife, professing it openly throughout his life, modeling what he believed when he said, "There is no bond on earth so sweet nor any separation so bitter as that which occurs in a good marriage."[284] He sums up this proactive view of love within marriage with the wise counsel of experience: "Let the wife make the husband glad to come home, and let him make her sorry to see him leave."[285]

He ardently "boasted to his table colleagues in 1531: 'I would not trade my Katie for France or Venice'...and continued his rapturous admiration for his beloved wife: 'The greatest gift of grace a man can have is a pious, God-fearing, home-loving wife, whom he can trust with all his goods, body, and life itself, as well as having her as the mother of his children.'"[286]

Luther considered "marital sex as a positive good in itself and not simply because it leads to procreation; sex increases affection between spouses and promotes harmony in domestic life."[287]

---

[282] Ibid., p.88. Reston quotes Luther, *Lectures on Genesis Chapters 26-30*; LW 5:37.

[283] Bainton, *Here I Stand*, Abingdon, p.289; Mentor pb, p.226.

[284] Ozment, Steven, "Re-inventing Family Life," *Christian History*, 39:25, Vol. XII No. 3 ("Martin Luther: The Later Years"), 1993, p.25.

[285] <https://jimdaly.focusonthefamily.com/three-things-martin-luther-teaches-us-marriage> or <https://www.hargraveshomeandhearth.com/martin-luther-and-katharina-von-bora-their-love-story-and-its-impact-on-the-church-a-guest-post-by-emilie-cubino>.

[286] O'Reggio, Trevor, "Luther on Marriage and Family," Faculty Publications, Andrews University, March 2012, quoting WABr 3:900, WATr 1:49.

[287] Karant-Nunn, Susan and Wiesner-Hanks, Merry, *Luther on Women: A Sourcebook* (Cambridge: Cambridge University Press, 2003), p.137.

> For Luther, the perpetuation of the species and the channeling of sexual drive were primary reasons for marriage.... Marriage serves the dual purpose of forestalling immorality and assuring the reproduction of the species. To abstain from sex or to engage in sex outside of marriage leads to fornication or secret sin.... If sexual desire is inevitable, it needs to be safely channeled into marriage...since it kept a lid on evil.[288]

While Luther wrote many positive things about marriage, Trevor O'Reggio* likens Luther's understanding of "marriage similar to the way in which he described the role of the political order 'to restrain greed and wickedness.' He saw marriage as a kind of remedy against sin. Marriage acted as a kind of restraint against the flood of human sensuality and immorality. Marriage was necessary because of the weakness of the flesh after the fall."[289] Luther writes

> For is it not a great thing that even in the state of innocence God ordained and instituted marriage. But now this institution and command are all the more necessary, since sin has weakened and corrupted the flesh. Therefore, this comfort stands invincible against all the doctrines of demons (1 Timothy 4:1), namely that marriage is a divine kind of life because it was established by God Himself.[290]

While rejecting celibacy because he thought it was impossible, he preached a sermon in 1522 on marriage entitled "Increase and Multiply," which is shocking even to this day. "As little as we can do without eating and drinking," he preached, "just as impossible is it to abstain from women.... He who resolves to remain single, let him give up the name of human being.... Let him prove that he is an angel or a spirit.... If the wife refuses, let the servant maid come."[291]

---

288 Deifelt, Wanda, "For God is also the God of Bodies: Embodiment and Sexuality in Martin Luther's Theology," *Journal of Lutheran Ethics*, February 1, 2007. <https://www.elca.org/JLE/Articles/529>.

* Trevor O'Reggio is professor of Church History and director of the M.A. in Religion program, Seventh Day Adventist Theological Seminary, Andrews University, Berrien Springs, MI.

289 O'Reggio, Trevor, "Martin Luther on Marriage and Family," Faculty Publications. Paper 20, 2012. <http://digitalcommons.andrews.edu/church-history-pubs/20>.

290 LW 1:134. *Lectures on Genesis, Chapters 1-5* (here expounding on 2:22).

291 Reston, *Fortress*, pp.222-223.

As if to be fair and balanced, Luther made further surprising concessions. He argued that a woman married to an impotent man ought to be allowed intercourse with another, perhaps the man's brother: "the woman is free through divine law and cannot be compelled to suppress her carnal desires. Therefore, the man ought to concede her right and give up to somebody else the wife who is his only in outward appearance."[292]

Such passages seem shocking, but Jonathan Poletti reminds us

> It is his bizarre genius to pelt you with sexual images. As [Luther] talks, you're imagining *yourself* as a monk having wet dreams, cleaning up, and going to listen to women telling you all about their sins. Such passages would barely register in Christian treatments, and often not be mentioned. But it is shocking and lurid. Luther holds out the image of himself, a Catholic priest covered in semen, as the female confessions are then perceived sexually, to be imagined by male listeners. *What did they say?*[293]

Yet throughout this seemingly unexpected use of scat and sexual language from a religious person, Luther reveals himself to be very realistic, human and earthy. While Poletti, a religious education instructor at Immaculate Heart of Mary Parish in Lansing, Michigan, is "shocked" to find Luther a comedian with a very dirty mouth rising to power with dark, sexual humor, he acknowledges the Biblical truth the Reformer espouses: "Some marriages were motivated by mere lust, but mere lust is felt even by fleas and lice," he remarks. "Love begins when we wish to serve others."[294]

Jonathon Green, the slang lexicographer we encountered earlier, reminds us that if our other twin is indeed lowering the standards of our public discourse, "his audiences don't seem worried…. Every breach of taboo brings a roar of approval. This is also a way for Trump to flex his muscles and emphasize his alpha-male status [much like Luther's usage of scatological language identified himself with "plain folks".]…. Trump, self-appointed man of the people, is trying through his unrestrained manner of speech to position himself of 'us' not 'them.'"[295]

---

[292] Ibid., pp.90-91.

[293] Poletti, Jonathan, "Martin Luther, Sick Comic?" <https://belover.medium.com/martin-luther-comedian-f4e5f0f8b6bd>.

[294] Ibid.

[295] Green, "A Lexicographer Explains the Sneaky Agenda Behind Trump's Dirty Mouth," *Quartz*, April 6, 2020. <https://qz.com/655502/a-lexicographer-explains-the-sneaky-agenda-behind-trumps-dirty-mouth>.

Both our reform warriors are noted for the forthright expression of their ideas. They are famous for being straightforward in speaking the unvarnished truth, and not afraid to say what they believe, no matter how much criticism they receive. Often humor confounds the hearer, especially if they are the adversary; yet both Luther and Trump used their gift of humor effectively, even though many of their opponents were guilty of misunderstanding because of their inability to appreciate the humor in statements which were never meant in earnest.

Creating change is messy. One can hate it or love it, but we can all agree it's not neutral. Neutrality doesn't change much. It's an open question as to whether Luther or Trump could create change without their arrogance, potty mouths, and flung insults in a captivating style. But as has been my premise, God can use flawed yet passionate individuals—or in the words of Ryan MacDiarmid, "jackasses"—to accomplish His work, and it isn't always pretty or neat. As we are aware,

> Jesus hurled a few insults too, and so did John the Baptist (insert brood of viper motif) as they brought about the biggest change of all time—THE GOSPEL. It got messy, like crucifixion messy. So, change isn't always pretty, but when change is needed it's worth fighting for, maybe sometimes it requires some frank speech and a little name calling. Maybe other times change happens despite the frank speech and name calling...
>
> There are things in the current Christian culture that I believe are compromising the spread of the Gospel and the joy of the Gospel. I'm not talking about megachurch culture, loose doctrine, or politicians. It comes from our infighting, which directs our energies at one another, and shifts our eyes away from our Heavenly Father, who desperately wants all of his kids to come home to a family meal.
>
> They [Jesus, Luther, and I believe Trump], are directing their negative energy and insults at hypocrisy in the Church [and State] as a means to bring everything back to THE MAIN POINT. I truly believe this is the heart of Jesus, Luther, [Trump]...and so many other leaders who are trying to bring about change. Of course, Jesus's harsh words were on point; Luther and [Trump] are humans and thus guaranteed to veer into '*jackassery*' at some point...no matter the decade or context, change can be messy. I'm not sure

> that is a bad thing. Nor do I need to agree with everything a human does and says to derive value from their battle against the status quo.[296]

Here's another insult from Martin Luther directed toward Dr. Karlstadt, who would latch onto a single word or verse in Scripture to

> smear his spittle as he pleases, but meanwhile, he does not take into account other texts which overthrow him…so that he is upended with all four limbs in the air…. He is like the ostrich, the foolish bird which thinks it is wholly concealed when it gets its neck under a branch [head in the sand emu like the Liberty Insurance commercial]. Or like small children, who hold their hands in front of their eyes and seeing nobody, imagine that no one sees them either.[297]

We cannot ignore the immense power humor has in exposing misguided values and destructive practices. Satire is not only funny but also enormously forceful and effective in the unmasking of vice, folly and, as we have experienced, the flip-flopping mandates during the Covid-19 virus.

Luther used humor to meet his rhetorical goals to enhance his Biblical witness, to ridicule those in power, and to mock death and the devil. Gritsch says in the preface to his book, *The Wit of Martin Luther,*

> I chose "wit" as the single word to describe Luther's humor. It describes a quick mind that can tell a "joke" (*Witz* in German), knows how to have fun through "jesting" (*scherzen* in German), and is a "wag" (*Schalk* in German). Luther presented himself as a "court jester" (*Hofnarr* in German, "a fool at court") to German politicians, and he was an amusing wit (*Spassvogel* in German, "a funny bird") at the dinner table. His wit relaxed anxious minds and annoyed angry foes. May it continue to do so today.[298]

---

[296] MacDiarmid, Ryan, "Martin Luther's Potty Mouth," *Jackass Theology*, March 25, 2019. <https://jackasstheology.com/2019/03/25/martin-luthers-potty-mouth>.

[297] LW 40:186. *Church and Ministry II*, "Against the Heavenly Prophets."

[298] Gritsch, *The Wit of Martin Luther* (Minneapolis: Augsburg Fortress, 2006) p.x.

Trump loves to joke around too. His wit, however, is so subtle, so nuanced, that sometimes it takes time for many to decipher without a spokesperson to clarify it. The President uses the style of an "insult comedian" like Don Rickles at his rallies. Andrew Restuccia and Ben Schreckinger quote David Litt, a former Obama speechwriter who helped craft jokes for the 44th president, saying Trump "weaponizes what he would call jokes to an unprecedented extent," adding that the laughter at Trump's rallies "is about solidifying a tribal identity…. It's laughter in agreement rather than laughter because something is funny."[299]

The authors of "In MAGA World, Trump's Jokes Always Land," furthermore write that

> Trump's advisers say the president's crass sense of humor is at the core of his appeal to a conservative base that has rejected political correctness – and they're betting that his jokes, paired with his broader say-anything attitude will help deliver a repeat of the success he saw in 2016…helping him get reelected in 2020…and have urged him to incorporate more wisecracks into his speeches…. Aides argued that Trump makes plenty of jokes that aren't acerbic or biting, adding that his aggressive attacks are often in response to what he views as a slight. "He's very much a counter-puncher," counselor to the president Kellyanne Conway said [much like Luther stabbing with a pike, not pins and needles]…. "He rarely draws first blood and he always gets the last word."… "He has a great sense of humor that he doesn't get credit for," said another senior White House official…boosting the belief that the media don't understand the president's sense of humor.[300]

Joanna Weiss views the President's self-aware sense of humor as a powerful weapon, but with the caveat "if you can spot the joke." If one is only seeking pre-determined or slanted frames of reference, one will miss "some striking moments (and tweets) when Trump isn't just raging outward, but making fun of himself…. At a rally in Louisiana, he poked fun at the rambling rhetoric that sometimes gets him into trouble: 'I do my best work off-script…I also do my worst work off-script.'" Along with other examples, she is convinced that "These were

---

299 Restuccia, Andrew, and Ben Schreckinger, "In MAGA World, Trump's Jokes Always Land," *Politico*, 10/19/2018. <https://www.politico.com/story/2018/10/19/trump-rallies-comedy-916795>.

300 Ibid.

genuine, self-aware, sometimes even self-depreciating jokes—if you were in the mindset to receive them. Of course, many Trump opponents aren't."[301]

While both of our "stand-up comedians" had similar yet distinctive manners in the use of speech, humor and caricatures, they shared that common yet essential talent for knowing their audience and speaking to it with truthful concern, often sprinkled with barbed humor to accent their point.

[301] Weiss, "Trump Pokes Fun at Himself."

13

Peasants as Victims and Assailants

In defending the cause of Christ, Luther was as uncompromising and bellicose as Trump is in his attempt to "Make America Great Again." Populist ideas were not always well-received in Europe during Luther's time. Kings, princes, bishops and abbots would snuff them out and crack down on all who sought to apply them. Having long idealized peasants as those who embraced the directives they found in Scripture even as they were losing out, Luther sympathized with their plight. He admired the peasants for their ceaseless work in a harsh economy and offered strict criticism to nobles for the unjust way they treated their workers. Much like many in our time, peasants were under great taxation—even the imposition of a death tax (*Todfall*)—and they experienced oppression from both secular and ecclesiastical authorities. Minor gentry and impoverished agricultural workers saw Luther's movement as a way of redressing those social grievances which were mounting. Groups of peasants in 1525 met in Memmingen, where their demands were formulated into "Twelve Articles."

Inspired by Luther's new evangelical theology espoused in three of his most famous treatises published in 1520—"To the Christian Nobility of the German Nation," "The Babylonian Captivity of the Church," and "On Christian Freedom"—the peasants had called upon Luther to formulate their grievances and to adjudicate their demands. Their rallying cry championed Luther's assertion that "A Christian is a perfectly free lord of all, subject to none."[302] Offering Christian exhortation to all parties, Luther hoped the conflict could be stilled without violence. In response, he published his verdict in a pamphlet entitled "Admonition to Peace," where he appealed to the conscience of each side.

To the princes and lords, he says,

> we have no one on earth to thank for this disastrous rebellion, except you princes and lords, and especially you blind bishops and mad priests and monks, whose hearts are hardened, even to the present day. You do not

[302] LW 31:344, and Martin Luther, *Three Treatises*, "Freedom of a Christian," (Philadelphia, PA, Muhlenberg Press, 1960), p.277.

> cease to rant and rave against the Holy Gospel, even though you know that it is true and that you cannot refute it. In addition, as temporal rulers you do nothing but cheat and rob the people so that you may lead a life of luxury and extravagance. The poor common people cannot bear it any longer.[303]

To the peasants he says,

> you say that the rulers are wicked and intolerable, for they will not allow us to have the Gospel; they oppress us too hard with the burdens they lay on our property, and they are ruining us in body and soul. I answer: The fact that the rulers are wicked and unjust does not excuse disorder and rebellion, for the punishing of wickedness is not the responsibility of everyone, but of the worldly rulers who bear the sword...[and] are instituted by God for the punishment of the wicked.[304]

Injustices committed by governing authorities do not justify peasant injustice, which Luther deemed would bring about inevitable revolt and bloodshed. In addition, and being pragmatically concerned, Luther expressed anxiety over the implications for his reform movement if it was associated with law-breaking and the collapse of public order. In like manner, immigrants entering the United States illegally have been a major concern, not only of President Trump but also his predecessors and legislators who were just as adamant in their denunciation of those breaking the law.

While acknowledging and rendering praise to the peasants, Luther reminds them that they themselves confess in the preface to the Articles that "all who believe in Christ become loving, peaceful, patient and agreeable." Then he instructs them, saying:

> Your actions, however, reveal nothing but impatience, aggression, anger, and violence. Thus, you contradict your own words.... You may do anything that God does not prevent. However, leave the name Christian out of it. Leave the name Christian out, I say, and do not use it to cover up your impatient, disorderly, un-Christian undertaking (1 Peter 2:16). I shall not let you have

---

303 LW 46:19. *The Christian in Society III*, "Admonition to Peace."

304 Ibid., 25.

> that name, but as long as there is a heartbeat in my body, I shall do all I can, through speaking and writing, to take that name away from you.[305]

He then makes them aware that it is not his intention "to justify or defend the rulers in the intolerable injustices which you suffer from them. They are unjust and commit heinous wrongs against you" but that does not entitle the use of force, destruction, and violence:

> Christians do not fight for themselves with sword and musket, but with the cross and with suffering, just as Christ, our leader, does not bear a sword, but hangs on the cross. Your victory, therefore, does not consist in conquering and reigning, or in the use of force, but in defeat and in weakness, as St. Paul says in 2 Corinthians 10:4, "*The weapons of our warfare are not material, but are the strength which comes from God...*" and "*Power is made perfect in weakness*" (2 Cor. 12:9).[306]

In Eric Metaxas' assessment,

> Luther was most bothered by the "*Schwarmer*"* who had incited this rebellion with their careless words. All of them ought to have known better. Like his namesake Martin Luther King Jr., Luther was not advocating doing nothing, but he was strongly advocating against violence as a Christian means of solving social injustices. Luther's advice was to trust God and to trust him radically. His message was scriptural.... To make his point, Luther quoted Romans 12:19: "*Beloved, never avenge yourselves, but leave it to the wrath of God.*" Then he wrote, "Indeed, our Leader, Jesus Christ says in Matthew 7 [5:44] that we should bless those who insult us, pray for our persecutors, love our enemies, and do good to those who do evil to us. These, dear friends, are our Christian laws."[307]

---

[305] Ibid., 31–32.

[306] Ibid., 32.

* Luther coined the derogatory word "*Schwarmer*" to designate zealots, swarming like bees, whom he considered to be false prophets, enthusiasts, extremists or irrational spiritualists led astray by the thoughts and feelings of their own heart, in wanting to force Reformation principles and practices ahead of where the people were.

[307] Metaxas, *Rediscovered*, p.329.

> Already in 1522 from the Wartburg [Luther] had written his pamphlet *Sincere Admonition to All Christians to Guard Against Insurrection and Rebellion.* He wrote it in response to the rabble-rousing and worse that had been going on in Wittenberg at that time [it was after all a university community and enthusiasts were forcibly pushing extremist views!] and in it he put forth his conviction that the Gospel must never proceed through force or violence. The Word of God would accomplish its own ends peacefully, if only people would preach it patiently and humbly.[308]

Luther was confident that Christ's victory over the powers of darkness surrounding the chaos would prevail, but according to Heinz Schilling,

> that victory required that the princes do their duty as Christian authorities [who should] not hesitate to re-establish order and peace, cost what it will at this decisive moment in the history of the world and salvation when Satan threatened to crush the rediscovered Gospel. As the prophet of God, Luther believed himself duty-bound constantly to remind the authorities of their responsibilities.[309]

He took as his watchword Romans 13:1 (RSV): "*Let everyone be subject to the governing authorities.*" "The donkey needs to feel the whip, and the people need to be ruled with force. God knew that full well, and so He gave the rulers not a feather duster ['*Fuchsschwantz*,' literally a foxtail], but a sword,"[310] in order that they might take action against evil in the kingdom of earth with all severity.

As we often experience in the reporting of events today, accounts are frequently shaped to fit a narrative and thus disregard factors that could lead to divergent conclusions. Robert Kolb,* professor emeritus of Systematic Theology at Concordia Seminary, St. Louis, reminds us that

---

308 Ibid., p.328.

309 Schilling, *Upheaval*, pp.258-9.

310 LW 46:76. *The Christian in Society III*, "An Open Letter on the Harsh Book."

* Dr. Robert A. Kolb is a professor emeritus of Systematic Theology at Concordia Seminary, St. Louis. He has served as the director of the Seminary's Institute for Mission Studies and had been director of the Center for Reformation Research held various teaching roles in the religion and history departments at Concordia, St Paul, MN. He is the author of several books including *The Christian Faith: A Luther Exposition*; *The Genius of Luther's Theology: A Wittenberg Way of Thinking for the Contemporary Church* and more than 100 articles and essays.

> the writing of history has always included a mixture of facts and interpretation, a mixture of what really happened with what the historians and their patrons wish had happened, a mixture of the past that is beyond our reach with the inventions and fabrications that serve our propaganda purposes.[311]

Typical textbooks' retelling of Luther's embroilment with the Peasants' Rebellion portray the Reformer as advocating oppression of the "lower class." Those who had viewed Luther as their champion now saw him favoring their oppressors, the lords and princes who ruled over them. The larger context reveals a different picture, as we have already noted. Luther's primary "concern focused neither on peasants as peasants nor princes as princes but on public order and justice as well as the need for princes and peasants alike to repent of their sins and trust in Jesus Christ."[312] For Luther, Christians must exercise proper personal responsibility according to God's commands within their respective callings. This includes secular officials as God's agents, entrusted with maintaining the peace by restoring public order within society. He furthermore objected to the way in which both sides used the name of Christ for the propagation of their ideas, and how they tried to use the Gospel for implementing their political power by claiming to act on Christ's authority. Are we not experiencing the same claims being made to support conflicting views regarding illegal immigrants and open borders, as well as the violence created by the rioters in the summer of 2020?

Bands of peasants were plundering towns, monasteries and castles in Thuringia under Thomas Muntzer's leadership, against the feudal landlords in their efforts to realize the Christian freedom Luther had promised to those who were oppressed. Luther accused them of using the Gospel to justify violence, and asked representatives of the princes and city councilmen to mediate the conflict to avoid bloodshed. He concluded his detailed commentary on the peasants' "Twelve Articles:"

> If you don't follow this advice—God forbid!—I must let you come to blows. But I am innocent of your souls, your blood, or your property. The guilt is yours alone. I have told you that you are both [princes and peasants] wrong and that what you are fighting for is wrong.... I, however, will pray to my

---

[311] Kolb, Robert, "Luther on Peasants and Princes," *Lutheran Quarterly*, Vol. XXIII, 2009, p.125. <wp.cune.edu/twokingdoms2/files/2017/05/Luther-on-Peasants-and-Princes-by-Robert-Kolb.pdf>.
[312] Ibid.

> God that he will either reconcile you both and bring about an agreement between you, or else graciously prevent things from turning out as you intend.[313]

As tensions and violence began to escalate, Luther attempted to forestall further violence by preaching, but discovered that was not the solution as he met hecklers, much the way our politicians, including Trump, are confronted. Fearful that the rebellious peasants would stop at nothing short of complete revolution and overthrow of the existing social order, Luther made a sharp, harsh call for action to restore peace and stability to the general populace. He was infuriated that the peasants had

> (1) violated their oaths of loyalty to their rulers [or divinely instituted government] and were therefore subject to temporal punishment; (2) they had robbed, plundered, and murdered, and were subject to death in body and soul; and (3) they had committed their crimes under the cover of Christ's name, thereby shamefully blaspheming God.[314]

Intended as an appendix to a new printing of "Admonition to Peace," Luther composed "Against the Robbing, Murdering Hordes of Peasants" to call upon secular rulers to oppose the destruction Satan was spreading across the land like a raging fire, as we have seen in Australia and California:

> Anyone who can be proved to be a seditious person is an outlaw before God and the emperor; and whoever is the first to put him to death does right and well. For if a man is in open rebellion, everyone is both his judge and his executioner; just as when a fire starts, the first man who can put it out is the best man to do the job. For rebellion is not just simple murder; it is like a great fire, which attacks and devastates a whole land...with murder and bloodshed; it makes widows and orphans, and turns everything upside down, like the worst disaster.[315]

---

[313] LW 46:43. *The Christian in Society III*, "Against the Robbing and Murdering Hordes."

[314] Schultz, Robert C., revised Introduction and translator of Luther's "Against the Robbing and Murdering Hordes of Peasants" in *The Christian in Society III*, LW 46:48.

[315] LW 46:50. *The Christian in Society III*, "Against the Robbing and Murdering Hordes."

The secular rulers could restore order through armed force, which Luther believed God had called them to do, as agents of His desire for civil peacekeeping in society. They were to put down the rebellion by force and, if necessary, "smite, slay, and stab secretly or openly" those who were visiting destruction upon people and property, if the peasants did not lay down their arms and end their rebellion. His harsh and violent words continued by reminding the government officials "that there is nothing more poisonous, hurtful, or devilish than a rebel. It is just as when one must kill a mad dog; if you do not strike him, he will strike you and a whole land with you."[316]

Luther reminded the peasants that secular authorities are divinely instituted for human good and must assume their responsibility to crush the uprising. In this realm, the law has its rightful place in its function of structuring and protecting human life and human relations. He went on to state that

> anyone who is killed fighting on the side of the rulers may be a true martyr in the eyes of God, if he fights with the kind of conscience I have just described for he acts in obedience to God's Word. On the other hand, anyone who perishes on the peasants' side is an eternal firebrand of hell, for he bears the sword against God's Word and is disobedient to Him and is a member of the devil.[317]

German rulers had already launched their retaliation against the peasants by the time this brief tract appeared in print. Estimates in the range of 100,000 were put down during the Peasants' War, including the savage bloodletting in the Battle of Frankenhausen where 5,000 peasant soldiers fell, and the captured renegade prophet and leader Thomas Muntzer was beheaded. It is interesting to note that Luther had earlier written to his friend George Spalatin in 1520 that no one should think that the Gospel "can be advanced without tumult, offense and sedition.... The Word of God is a sword, it is war and ruin, an offense, perdition, and poison,"[318] with Luther obviously referencing Jesus' words in Matthew 10:34 (NRSV): *"Do not think that I have come to bring peace to the earth; I have not come to bring peace, but a sword...to set one against another."*

---

[316] Ibid.

[317] Ibid., LW 46:53-54.

[318] Martin Luther, *Luther's Correspondence and Other Contemporary Letters, Vol. 1: 1507-1521*, "Letter 228 Luther to Spalatin, Wittenberg, between Feb 12 and 18, 1520," translated and edited by Preserved Smith, Ph.D. (Philadelphia, PA: Lutheran Publication Society), p.287.

Rather than disavow his harsh position in "Against the Robbing and Murdering Hordes of Peasants," he restated it in even starker terms with a brief defense entitled "An Open Letter on the Harsh Book Against the Peasants." To those who charged that he was being unmerciful, he wrote, "This is not a question of mercy; we are talking of God's Word. It is God's will that the king be honored, and the rebels destroyed; and He is as merciful as we are."[319] Luther maintained that

> the necessity of restoring public order had superseded any other consideration because all would be harmed by the chaos and arbitrary carnage of the insurgency. He also rejected the criticism that he was currying the ruler's favor and support and repeated his call to them to repent of their injustice and of their excessive use of force in suppressing the Revolt, sharply reprimanding those who were undertaking oppressive measures after the peasant defeat as "furious, raving, senseless tyrants," bloodthirsty dogs who belonged to the devil and were bound for hell.[320]

I cannot help but think Luther would empathize with the corresponding dilemma his twin has been encountering with the "caravans" and other "invading" immigrants entering the country illegally, or the rioters in the streets of our cities, as we will address in the following chapter. We hear many of our politicians and others, including Christians, urge mercy and compassion over the rule of law and over the protection of citizens from those intent on doing harm. To demonstrate how contemporary Luther is, I am quoting several paragraphs from his "Open Letter on the Harsh Book Against the Peasants" which sets forth his rationale that could also be applied to dealing with illegal immigrants and rioters. Luther says,

> Here I do not want to hear or know about mercy, but to be concerned only about what God's Word requires. On this basis, my little book was and remains right, even though the whole world take offense at it. If it pleases God, I do not really care whether you like it or not. If He will have wrath, and not mercy, what business do you have being merciful? Did not Saul sin by showing mercy to Amalek [Agag] when he failed to execute God's wrath as he had been commanded [I Sam. 15:4-24]? Did not Ahab sin by having

---

[319] LW 46:66. *The Christian in Society III*, "An Open Letter on the Harsh Book."

[320] Kolb, "Luther on Peasants," pp. 133-134.

mercy on the king of Syria and letting him live, contrary to God's Word [I Kings 20:42]? If you want to have mercy, then do not consort with rebels, but respect authority and do good; "*but if you do wrong, be afraid,*" Paul says, "*for He does not bear the sword in vain*" [Romans 13:4].[321]

This ought to be answer enough to all who are offended by my book and make it useless. Should not a man keep quiet when he hears that God says this, and that this is God's will? Or does God have to give reasons to such empty babblers, and tell them why this is His will? I would think that the mere wink of His eye would be enough to silence every creature, to say nothing of what should happen when He speaks. God's Word says, "*My son, fear the Lord and the king; if you do not, disaster will suddenly come upon you*" [Proverbs 24:21-22]. And in Romans 12 [13-2], "*Whoever resists God's authority will incur judgment.*" Why is not St. Paul merciful? If we are to preach God's Word, we must preach the Word that declares His wrath, as well as that which declares mercy. We must preach of hell as well as heaven and help extend God's Word and judgment and work over both the righteous and the wicked so that the wicked may be punished and the good protected.[322]

I have taught and written more about mercy than any other man in a thousand years. It is the very devil himself who wants to do all the evil that he can, and so he stirs up good and pious hearts and tempts them with things like this while he tries to deck himself out in a reputation for mercy…. You praise mercy so highly because the peasants are beaten; why did you not praise it when the peasants were raging, smiting, robbing, burning, and plundering, in ways that are terrible? …Why were they not merciful to the princes and lords, whom they wanted to exterminate completely? No one spoke of mercy then. Everything was "rights"; nothing was said of mercy, it was nothing. "Rights, rights, rights!" They were everything. Now that the peasants are beaten, and the stone that they threw at heaven is falling back on their own heads,* no one is to say anything of rights, but to speak only of mercy.[323]

---

[321] LW 46:66. *The Christian in Society III*, "An Open Letter on the Harsh Book."

[322] Ibid.

* Luther referencing Ecclesiasticus 27:25 (*"Who so casteth a stone on high, casteth it on his own head, and a deceitful stroke shall make wounds." KJV*) Cf. Ernst Thiel, Luthers Sprichwortersammlung (Weimar, 1900), No. 135. Ecclesiasticus is more properly known as the Wisdom of Sirach in the Apocrypha.

[323] Ibid., p.67.

And yet they are stupid enough to think that no one notices the rascal behind it! Ah, no! We see you, you black, ugly devil! You praise mercy not because you are seriously concerned about mercy, or you would have praised it to the peasants; on the contrary, you are afraid for your own skin, and are trying to use the appearance and reputation of mercy to escape God's rod and punishment.... You, however are trying to do wrong and yet escape wrath by praising mercy.... Suppose I were to break into a man's house, rape his wife and daughters, break open his strong box, take his money, put a sword to his chest, and say, 'If you will not put up with this, I shall run you through, for you are a godless wretch'; then if a crowd gathered and were about to kill me, or if the judge ordered my head off, suppose I were to cry out, "Hey, Christ teaches you to be merciful and not to kill me," what would people say?[324]

That is exactly what these peasants and their sympathizers are now doing. Now that they have, like robbers, murderers, thieves, and scoundrels, done what they pleased to their masters, they want to put on a song and dance about mercy, and say, "Be merciful, as Christ teaches, and let us rage, as the devil teaches: do good to us and let us do our worst to you; be satisfied with what we have done and call it right, and call what you are doing wrong." Who would not like to get away with that? If that is mercy, then we shall institute a pretty state of affairs; we shall have no sword, ruler, punishment, hangman, or prison, and let every scoundrel do as he pleases; then when he is to be punished, we shall sing, "Hey, be merciful, as Christ teaches." That would be a fine way of doing things![325]

Where have I ever taught that no mercy should be shown? Do I not in my book beg the rulers to show grace to those who surrender?[326] Why do you not open your eyes and read it? ...But you are so full of poison that you seize upon the one part of it in which I say that those who will not surrender or listen ought to be killed without mercy; and you skip over the rest of it, in which I say that those who surrender are to be shown grace.... It is not true that you condemn the peasants or love mercy—what you would really like

---

[324] Ibid., pp 67-68.

[325] Ibid., p. 68.

[326] Referring to his "book" *Against the Robbing and Murdering Hordes of Peasants* (see LW 46:54–55).

> to see is wickedness go free and unpunished, and the temporal sword made ineffective.... So much for the un-Christian and merciless bloodhounds who praise the sayings [of Christ] about mercy so that sheer wickedness and mercilessness may rule in the world as they please! ...There are two kingdoms, one the Kingdom of God, the other the kingdom of the world.[327]

Dr. John Witte, Jr., Professor and Director of the Center for the Study of Law and Religion at Emory University, makes an interesting contrast: "The Peasant's War of 1524-26 was fought in the name of Christian freedom but was harshly repressed in the name of Christian order."[328] Luther is often criticized for not supporting the peasants, as if he owed complete loyalty to the populist wave. Lyman Stone* reminds us, these

> rebels were not democratic reformers, but apocalyptic radicals seeking the institution of heaven-on-earth. When a group of radicals took the city of Munster in 1534, they formed a polygamous death-cult centered around charismatic leaders (Thomas Muntzer, fanatical leader of the Anabaptists) who duped their followers into a disastrous siege in the hope of initiating the End Times. Their campaign was more Jonestown than Yorktown. Thus, when Luther condemned the rebellion, he did not condemn a political platform. Indeed, he supported many of the practical reforms the peasants demanded and pushed the German nobles to adopt them! Rather, he condemned the mobs for trying to institute cultic theocracies based on their idiosyncratic and often violently repressive readings of Scripture. He argued that the conflict was basically civil in nature—neither side could claim to be representing God.[329]

---

327 LW 46:69. *The Christian in Society III*, "An Open Letter on the Harsh Book."

328 Witte, Jr., John, "The Legacy of the Protestant Reformation in Modern Law." <https://politicaltheology.com/the-legacy-of-the-protestant-reformation-in-modern-law>.

* Lyman Stone is an author and economist who researches demography and migration and is an advisor for the consulting firm Demographic Intelligence. He writes about economics, population and related family issues for the Federalist, the Institute for Family Studies, and Vox. He and his wife are serving currently as missionaries for the Lutheran Church-Hong Kong Synod.

329 Stone, Lyman, "Two Kingdom Theology in the Trump Era," *First Things*, 4/26/18. <https://www.firstthings.com/web-exclusives/2018/04/two-kingdom-theology-in-the-trump-era>.

A few years later, in his commentary on Psalm 118, Luther points back to the Peasants' War, saying,

> Here lords and princes, as well as subjects, should learn that the government of a land and the obedience of the people are a gift of God—a gift bestowed out of nothing but His pure goodness.... Some mad princes and lords presumptuously claim that they rule land and people with their power and govern them by their reason. Especially the haughty bigwigs among the nobility and the smart alecks in the cities imagine that they run everything, as though God could not get along without them...
>
> Certainly, in the recent insurrection God demonstrated clearly that neither human power nor skill, but He alone governs the world. For these very same bigwigs who would rob God of His honor by bragging and boasting of their role in suppressing the insurrection were at that time the most fear-stricken wretches I have ever seen. Now they forget the God who rescued them when in sheer fright they filled their pants. We still smell the stench whenever one of these bigwigs is near.... [Their] impudence and pride lead me to believe that they defy and tempt God to send a new insurrection, that He could show them once more whether the bigwig or God's goodness and power holds the mob in leash.[330]

Gritsch makes the assessment that

> The peasants' uprising in 1525 led Luther to the conclusion that any attempt to transform the communication of the Gospel into a political crusade was doomed to produce only misery for anyone involved. Moreover, he thought Germany was plagued by a general lack of law and order precipitated not only by peasants but also by rulers.[331]

He cites Luther's exposition of Psalm 118, where the Reformer complained

> that in the present time there is not a single soul in Germany who would preserve law and order in the face of these lawless and robbing nobles or

---

[330] LW14:52-53. *Selected Psalms III*, "Psalm 118 (vs.2)."

[331] Gritsch, Eric W., *Martin—God's Court Jester: Luther in Retrospect* (Ramsey, NJ: Sigler Press, 1990), p.60.

> protect government from such faithless and thievish subjects. Robbery and stealing abound; assassins follow their singular practices; men plot and rage. Yet no one's conscience is pricked by these sins against God. I am of the opinion that our present peace hangs by a silk thread; in fact, it is solely in God's hands, above and beyond our will and despite the fuming and the raving of all the devils. If human wisdom and the power of man were governing Germany today, she would be lying in ruins tomorrow.[332]

Not to be overlooked is Luther's concern regarding the "bigwigs" among the "nobility" and "smart alecks" in the cities (aka the elite establishment of today, located predominantly in American cities on the east and west coasts) presuming to know what's best for the rest of the population, and foreseeing the divide between heavily populated metropolitan centers and the rural heartland. It was also the genius of the framers of the Constitution to consider such implications to the extent that the Electoral College was included in our Constitutional system. The same considerations influenced the establishment of a House of Representatives that would reflect the population—disadvantaging the small states—but a Senate that would give the small states equal representation with the large ones. Interestingly, however, we are engaged in a debate over the Electoral College versus direct popular vote, resulting from the recent elections where George W. Bush and Trump won elections without the majority of the popular vote. However, few are aware that Bill Clinton did not receive the majority of the popular vote in either of his elections, yet he had the legitimacy to speak for the American people because he won the Electoral College.

---

332 LW 14:54. *Selected Psalms III*, "Psalm 118."

14

Peaceful Protesters and Lawless Rioters

The Reformation Luther triggered in the 16th century not only affected the Church and theology, but also brought fundamental reforms to law and the State. As we will discover with his doctrine of Two Kingdoms *("Zweireichelehre")*—the heavenly and earthly—God is Lord in and over both the spiritual and temporal realms. It is through the spiritual rule, Luther writes, that God, through

> the Holy Spirit, produces Christians and righteous people under Christ; and the temporal, which restrains the un-Christian and wicked so that—no thanks to them—they are obliged to keep still and to maintain an outward peace. Thus does St. Paul interpret the temporal sword in Romans 13[:3], when he says it is *"not a terror to good conduct but to bad."* And Peter says it is for the *"punishment of the wicked"* [1 Peter 2:14].[333]

For Luther, temporal authority has the responsibility to punish the lawless to maintain an outward peace and prevent a sinful world from falling into chaos.

Undisputedly, Trump must share the disappointment, frustration and dishonesty Luther experienced with the peasants as they

> forgot their promise and violently took matters into their own hands and are robbing and raging like mad dogs. All this now makes it clear that they were trying to deceive us and that the assertions they made in their *Twelve Articles* (grievances Luther assisted the peasants in writing against the lords) were nothing but lies presented under the name of the Gospel. To put it briefly, [Luther writes,] they are doing the devil's work.[334]

---

333 LW 45:91. *The Christian in Society II*, "Temporal Authority: To What Extent It Should Be Obeyed.".

334 LW 46:49. *The Christian in Society IIIL*, "Against the Robbing and Murdering Hordes of Peasants."

In his treatise "Against the Robbing and Murdering Hordes of Peasants," we have heard Luther speak graphically and forcibly as he arraigned the peasants on charges of violating their oath of obedience to their masters; robbing, plundering and murdering; and covering their crimes under the cover of Christ's name. In the words of Robert C. Schultz, writing the introduction to this assessment, Luther was "convinced that the rebellious peasants would stop at nothing short of complete revolution and overthrow of the existing social order, Luther decided to publish his opinion…"[335] He had returned to Wittenberg after learning of the full-scale attacks peasants were making on their landlords and rulers as they plundered and destroyed castles, monasteries and churches, and hearing from relatives reports of peasant violence.

Guarding Against Insurrection

In his book *Luther and His Times*, Ernest G. Schwiebert, Professor of History at Wittenberg University in Springfield, Ohio, writes,

> As is often the case, the new movement suffered from the over-enthusiasm of its followers who substituted vigorous action for their lack of understanding and levelheaded thinking. The men who now felt duty bound to carry on the struggle in Luther's absence were not very clear on either Luther's objectives or the methods which as Christians they might employ. The result was a radicalism and mob rule, which often result from impulsive action not based on clear thinking.[336]

The peasants' leader was Thomas Muntzer, who believed himself to be a "prophet" executing the will of God he received by direct revelation. Remarkably, Schwiebert in 1950 uses the familiar terminology we hear today in the Black Lives Matter rioting for the religious fanatics in the Peasants' Rebellion of Luther's time. Muntzer did not find it difficult to gain the support of overzealous peasants who believed it was their special assignment to be part of the "priesthood of believers" through their participation in affecting a reformation of the Church.

---

[335] LW 46:48. Schultz, Robert, C. "Introduction," and Translator of Luther's "Against the Robbing and Murdering Hordes of Peasants."

[336] Schwiebert, E.G., *Luther and His Times* (St. Louis, MO: Concordia Publishing House, 1950), p.536.

> Muntzer was the leader of the extreme left wing of those religious fanatics who thought it their duty to inaugurate the Kingdom of God by force and social revolution rather than waiting for the tedious process of conversion. This revolution, if need be, was to be "blood red," and he believed himself to be the divinely commissioned emissary of the Holy Spirit to inaugurate such a social transformation.[337]

Do those words not sound all too familiar, and the destructive actions taken by the angry and "righteous" peasants not reflect what we are witnessing from the radical far-left rioters who are violently pushing by force social revolution and the transformation of our society?

Muntzer preached violence, destruction of statues and stained-glass windows of churches for their idolatry, as well as defiance of all accepted authority, except for God, as the only means of establishing the new order to transform society. Luther's position was too conservative in his concern for moving too far out in front of the people. Luther chose to follow the practice of St. Paul in Athens (Acts 17:16ff), who pleaded with the people to forsake their heathen altars, temples and idols, but did not advocate their destruction by force. Their destruction accomplishes nothing; it is the Spirit that matters. Instead, he sought to teach the fundamentals of the faith and the basic doctrines of the Church, and let the Word alone affect the needed reforms within the hearts of the people. The Christian faith, in short, was not to be advanced by violence. However,

> The doctrine of "The Freedom of the Christian" was changed from Luther's meaning of an inner freedom of the reborn man to mean freedom from the economic bondage of feudalism. Although Luther's doctrine of the "priesthood of believers" originated with the New Testament and was not meant to favor any particular class, it became potential dynamite in the hands of the unrestrained masses. It was this gross misinterpretation of his doctrines which caused Luther to modify his views on lay control when the Church in Germany was reorganized after the Peasants' War.[338]

Through his famous Invocavit sermons in March of 1522, Luther was able to restore order in Wittenberg. He summarized his views on political violence and disturbance in the treatise "A Sincere Admonition by Martin Luther to All Christians to Guard Against

---

[337] Ibid., p.546.

[338] Ibid., p.560.

Insurrection and Rebellion." Luther believed that God alone "reserved punishment to Himself," but realistically recognized

> how the princes and nobles disagree among themselves and evince no willingness whatsoever to improve matters...[they] are not thereby excused; they ought to do their part and use the power of their sword in the effort to ward off and moderate to the best of their ability at least some of God's wrath as Moses did in Exodus 32 [:27-28].[339]

We have heard President Trump express a similar concern and frustration with mayors and governors not exercising their rightful role in providing protection and security for their citizens from lawless rioters. Trump has basically expressed the view Luther espoused:

> [Insurrection] never brings about the desired improvement. For insurrection lacks discernment; it generally harms the innocent more than the guilty. Hence, no insurrection is ever right, no matter how right the cause it seeks to promote. It always results in more damage than improvement, and verifies the saying, "Things go from bad to worse".... I am and always will be on the side of those against whom insurrection is directed, no matter how unjust their cause; I am opposed to those who rise in insurrection...because there can be no insurrection without hurting the innocent and shedding their blood.
>
> [Furthermore, Luther states] God has forbidden insurrection: "*Revenge is mine; I will repay*" (Deuteronomy 32:35).... Insurrection is nothing else than being one's own judge and avenger, and that is something God cannot tolerate...God is not on the side of insurrection.[340]

Firmly grounded in the Scriptures, Luther was compelled to insist that God is in charge of the world He created and loves. Speaking like Trump as he exalts all that he has accomplished despite the resistance and investigations, Luther exclaims, "See what I have done. Have I not, with the mouth alone, without a single stroke of the sword, done more

---

[339] LW 45:62. *The Christian in Society II*, "A Sincere Admonition to All Christians to Guard Against Insurrection and Rebellion."

[340] Ibid., p 63.

harm to the pope, bishops, priests, and monks than all the emperors, kings, and princes with all their power ever did before? St. Paul says, *"He (the evil one) will be destroyed by the mouth of Christ"* [2 Thessalonians 2:8]."[341] We are to let our mouths become the mouth of the Spirit of Christ and continue the work that has begun, by speaking and writing so that the knowledge of Christ and His love may be known and experienced throughout the world. To his followers, he further reminds them:

> Every man whether it be I or another—who speaks the Word of Christ may boldly assert that his mouth is the mouth of Christ. I for my part am certain that my word is not mine, but the Word of Christ; my mouth therefore must also be the mouth of Him whose Word it speaks. Therefore, there is no need for you to demand an armed insurrection. Christ Himself has already begun an insurrection with His mouth, one which will be more than the pope [or any man can bear]. Let us follow that One and carry on. What is now transpiring in the world is not our work. No mere man could possibly begin and carry on such an affair by himself. It has come thus far without my consideration and counsel; it will also be completed without my advice, and the gates of hell shall not stop it [Matthew 16:18]. A far different Man is the driving power [the devil making the wheel go round] who would like to see an armed insurrection develop which would hinder and bring into disrepute this spiritual insurrection. But God willing, there should be and will be no such help for him. He must be destroyed "by no human hand" but "by the mouth" alone; nothing will prevent that. Get busy now; spread the Holy Gospel, and help others spread it; teach, speak, write, and preach… [it.][342]

Schwiebert continues his narrative of the Peasants' Revolt:

> By the spring of 1525, the movement had fanned out in all directions and the clashes were becoming increasingly violent in some sections. Virtually the whole Empire was inflamed…. The worst region was Thuringia, where Muenzer [Muntzer] and his followers had preached violence and defiance of all accepted authority as the only means to the new order…. When Luther

[341] Ibid., p. 67.

[342] Ibid., pp. 67–68.

> learned, however, that he was being quoted in support of their violence and lawlessness, he decided that he could not remain silent any longer.[343]

Luther's advice to rulers was to first take the matter to God, humbly praying for help against the devil, and offering the "mad peasants" opportunity to come to terms; if they are unwilling, then swiftly take up the sword. Note how he reminds the princes and lords of their responsibility as well as their culpability if they do not respond to violence and lawlessness:

> According to Romans 13 [:4 "*authority does not bear the sword in vain! It is the servant of God to execute wrath on the wrongdoer.*"] he is God's minister and the servant of His wrath and that the sword has been given him to use against such people. If he does not fulfill the duties of his office by punishing some and protecting others, he commits as great a sin before God as when someone who has not been given the sword commits murder. If he is able to punish and does not do it—even though he would have had to kill someone or shed blood—he becomes guilty of all the murder and evil that these people commit. For by deliberately disregarding God's command, he permits such rascals to go about their wicked business, even though he was able to prevent it and it was his duty to do so. This is not a time to sleep. And there is no place for patience or mercy. This is the time of the sword, not the day of grace.[344]

With a clear conscience, rulers must press on, confident that God has appointed them to fulfill the duties of their office as His wrathful arm against evildoers. If magistrates have done what Luther called for, and it does not quell the rioting, "then swiftly take to the sword.... [P]ress on and take action in this matter with a good conscience..."[345] Luther is aware that there were many good peasants who had been forced and compelled to join the wicked rebels and he asks the lords to "release, rescue, help, and to have mercy on these poor people."[346] Nevertheless, believing that rebellion is intolerable, Luther emphatically announces:

---

343 Schwiebert, *Luther and His Times*, p.562.

344 LW 46:52-53. "Against the Robbing and Murdering Hordes of Peasants."

345 Ibid., pp. 52-53.

346 Ibid., p. 54.

> These are strange times, when a prince can win heaven with bloodshed better than other men with prayer! …Let whoever can stab, smite, slay. If you die in doing it, good for you! A more blessed death can never be yours, for you die while obeying the divine Word and command in Romans 13 [1, 2], and in loving service of your neighbor whom you are rescuing from the bonds of hell and of the devil. And so, I beg everyone who can to flee from the peasants as from the devil himself…[347]

No doubt about Luther's position: Swift action was being called for, not idle words sounding religiously pious that fall flat, failing to motivate obedient behavior; there is no time to cower in the face of intimidation; no stand-down orders that permit violence to override law and order in keeping the peace for law-abiding citizens.

> For the man who thus sympathizes with the rebels makes it perfectly clear that he has decided in his heart that he will also cause disaster if he has the opportunity. The rulers, therefore, ought to shake these people up until they keep their mouths shut and realize that the rulers are serious. If they think this answer is too harsh, and that this is talking violence and only shutting men's mouths, (i.e., that Luther is advocating the use of force rather than persuasion) I reply, "That is right." A rebel is not worth rational arguments, for he does not accept them. You have to answer people like that with a fist, until the sweat (Luther probably means blood) drips off their noses. The peasants would not listen; they would not let anyone tell them anything, so their ears must now be unbuttoned with musket balls till their heads jump off their shoulders. Such people need such a rod. He who will not hear God's Word when it is spoken with kindness (a reference to Luther's *'Admonition to Peace'*) must listen to the headsman, when he comes with his axe.[348]

Let Reverence for Law Become the Political Religion of the Nation

Abraham Lincoln sought to address a similar circumstance to what Luther encountered and as we have experienced in the summer of 2020, which we will soon examine. Lincoln

---

[347] Ibid., pp. 54-55.

[348] LW 46:65-66. *The Christian in Society III*, "An Open Letter on the Harsh Book."

spoke before the Young Men's Lyceum of Springfield on January 27, 1838, concerning a major challenge he foresaw: "The Perpetuation of Our Political Institutions." He saluted our peaceful possession of the "fairest portion of the earth" and being the legal inheritors of the fundamental blessings of liberty and equal rights. As beneficiaries, he saw the task of his generation to express their gratitude to "our fathers" by faithfully observing the laws of the country and by transmitting to our posterity the legacy of freedom and liberty bequeathed to us. To violate the law, in Lincoln's mind, was to trample on the blood of our fathers while simultaneously divesting our children of their liberty.

> Let reverence for the laws be breathed by every American mother…—let it be taught in schools, in seminaries, and in colleges—let it be written in Primers, spelling books, and in Almanacs;—let it be preached from the pulpit, proclaimed in legislative halls, and enforced in courts of justice. And in short, let it become the *political religion* of the nation; and let the old and the young, the rich and the poor, the grave and the gay, of all sexes and tongues, and colors and conditions, sacrifice unceasingly upon its altars.[349]

Yet he was wary, as are many today, in sensing "something of ill-omen amongst us. I mean the increasing disregard for law which pervades the country; the growing disposition to substitute the wild and furious passions, in lieu of the sober judgment of Courts; and the worse than savage mobs, for the executive ministers of justice."[350] He was referring to accounts of outrages committed by mobs in reacting to the hanging of gamblers in Mississippi, to

> negroes, from negroes to white citizens, and from these to strangers; till, dead men were seen literally dangling from the boughs of trees upon every roadside.… Such are the effects of mob law; and such are the scenes, becoming more and more frequent in this land so lately famed for love of law and order; and the stories of which, have even now grown too familiar, to attract anything more, than an idle remark.… And so; the innocent…fall victims to the ravages of mob law; and thus, it goes on, step by step, till all

[349] Lincoln, Abraham, "The Perpetuation of Our Political Institutions," (Lyceum Address); <https://quod.lib.umich.edu/j/jala/2629860.0006.103/--perpetuation-of-our-political-institutions-address>, p.4, or <http://www.abrahamlincolnonline.org/lincoln/speeches/lyceum.htm>.
[350] Ibid., p.2.

> the walls erected for the defense of the persons and property of individuals, are trodden down, and disregarded.[351]
>
> But all this even, is not the full extent of the evil. By such examples, by instances of the perpetrators of such acts going unpunished, the lawless in spirit, are encouraged to become lawless in practice; and having been used to no restraint...they thus become, absolutely unrestrained.... While, on the other hand, good men, men who love tranquility, who desire to abide by the laws, and enjoy their benefits, who would gladly spill their blood in the defense of their country; seeing their property destroyed; their families insulted, and their lives endangered; their persons injured; and seeing nothing in prospect that forebodes a change for the better; become tired of, and disgusted with, a Government that offers them no protection.... Thus, then, by the operation of this mobocratic spirit, which all must admit, is now abroad in the land, the strongest bulwark of any Government, and particularly of those constituted like ours, may effectually be broken down and destroyed...
>
> Whenever this effect shall be produced among us; whenever the vicious portion of population shall be permitted to gather in bands of hundreds and thousands, and burn churches, ravage and rob provision stores, throw printing presses into rivers, shoot editors and hang and burn obnoxious persons at pleasure, and with impunity; depend on it, this Government cannot last... which for the last half century, has been the fondest hope, of the lovers of freedom, throughout the world.... Yet, notwithstanding all this, if the laws be continually despised and disregarded, if their rights to be secure in their persons and property, are held by no better tenure than the caprice of a mob, the alienation of their affections from the Government is the natural consequence; and to that, sooner or later, it must come.[352]

As if taking his cue from Luther, Abraham Lincoln, who also openly confronted the news media, expresses the reality of living in a society governed by law and order, and foreshadowed President Trump's position on the primary role of government in protecting its people and their property, as we will soon discover. "When I so pressingly urge a strict observance of all the laws," Lincoln clarifies emphatically,

---

[351] Ibid., p.3.

[352] Ibid.

> "let me not be understood as saying there are no bad laws, nor that grievances may not arise, for the redress of which, no legal provisions have been made. I mean to say no such thing. But I do mean to say, that, although bad laws, if they exist, should be repealed as soon as possible, still while they continue in force, for the sake of example, they should be religiously observed. So, also in unprovided cases. If such arise, let proper legal provisions be made for them with the least possible delay; but, till then, let them if not too intolerable, be borne with. There is no grievance that is a fit object of redress by mob law.[353]

The Power of the Sword to Establish Law and Order

While the entire nation was united in anger, horror, and grief watching the video of George Floyd's death on the streets of Minneapolis, Minnesota, on May 25, 2020, our country has been anything but united in the resultant civil unrest, destruction, violence, and harm to life and property that has ensued following that appalling tragedy. Peaceful protests broke out over the brutality exercised by a white police officer who knelt on a black man's neck for over eight minutes while three fellow policemen stood by, not intervening. The protests turned to rioting and lawlessness, leading the President to address the nation from the Rose Garden on June 1st. Reminding the country that his first and highest duty as President is to defend our great country and the American people, he said,

> I swore to uphold the laws of our nation and that is exactly what I will do. All Americans were rightly sickened and revolted by the brutal death of George Floyd. My administration is fully committed that for George and his family, justice will be served. He will not have died in vain, but we cannot allow the righteous cries and peaceful protestors to be drowned out by an angry mob. The biggest victims of the rioting are peace-loving citizens in our poorest communities and as their President, I will fight to keep them safe. I will fight to protect you. I am your President of law and order and an ally of all peaceful protestors. But in recent days, our nation has been gripped by professional anarchists, violent mobs, arsonists, looters, criminals, rioters, Antifa, and others.

[353] Ibid., p.4.

> A number of state and local governments have failed to take necessary action to safeguard their residents. Innocent people have been savagely beaten… small business owners have seen their dreams utterly destroyed. New York's finest have been hit in the face with bricks…. A police precinct has been overrun here in the nation's Capital; the Lincoln Memorial and the World War II Memorial have been vandalized. One of our most historic churches was set ablaze…. A Federal officer in California, an African American enforcement hero was shot and killed. These are not acts of peaceful protest, these are acts of domestic terror. The destruction of innocent life and the spilling of innocent blood is an offense to humanity and a crime against God. America needs creation, not destruction; cooperation not contempt; security not anarchy; healing not hatred; justice not chaos. This is our mission, and we will succeed 100%…we will succeed. Our country always wins. That is why I am taking immediate presidential action to stop the violence and restore security and safety in America…

He then announced that he would be

> mobilizing all available federal resources, civilian and military, to stop the rioting and looting to end the destruction and arson and to protect the rights of law-abiding Americans…immediately! …Today I have strongly recommended to every governor to deploy the National Guard in sufficient numbers that we dominate the streets. Mayors and governors must establish an overwhelming law enforcement presence until the violence has been quelled.[354]

We read Luther's corresponding words:

> The Scriptures, therefore, have good, clear eyes [Matthew 6:22-23] and see the temporal sword aright…it must exercise wrath and severity. As Peter and Paul say, it is God's servant for vengeance, wrath, and punishment upon the wicked, but [also] for the protection, praise, and honor of the righteous [1 Peter 2:14; Romans 13:4]…. The merciless punishment of the wicked is

---

354 Trump, Donald, "June 1, 2020 Speech." <https://www.rev.com/blog/transcripts/donald-trump-speech-transcript-june-1-trump-may-deploy-us-military-to-cities>.

> not being carried out just to punish the wicked and make them atone for the evil desires that are in their blood, but to protect the righteous and to maintain peace and safety. And beyond all doubt, these are precious works of mercy, love, and kindness, since there is nothing on earth that is worse than disturbance, insecurity, oppression, violence, and injustice. Who could or would stay alive if such things were the rule? Therefore, the wrath and severity of the sword is just as necessary to a people as eating and drinking, even as life itself.[355]

After announcing the steps he would be taking, the President concluded:

> America is founded on the rule of law. It is the foundation of our prosperity, our freedom, and our very way of life; but where there is no law, there is no opportunity. Where there is no justice, there is no liberty; where there is no safety, there is no future. We must never give in to anger or hatred. If malice or violence rains [reigns], then none of us is free. I take these actions today with firm resolve and with a true passionate love for our country.[356]

Luther would obviously concur and affirm the position the President was taking, and that which President Lincoln had earlier enunciated. "Peace," Luther wrote, "is certainly worth more than all law, and peace is not made for the sake of the law; rather the law is made for the sake of peace."[357]

Our Constitution's First Amendment guarantees "the right of the people peaceably to assemble, and to petition the Government for a redress of grievances."[358] The right to protest is enshrined within the Constitution, and the means and ways of affecting change are provided in many ways, including the ballot box. But terrorizing the people by rioting, destroying property, physically harming or taking the life of another are not forms of protest, but rather violent acts of "mobocracy."

Surprisingly I discovered that "We have laws, in every state, against obstruction of streets, sidewalks and freeways, even if you are engaged in a free speech rally or protest. Enforcing

---

355 LW 46:73. *The Christian in Society III*, "An Open Letter on the Harsh Book."

356 Trump, "June 1, 2020 Speech."

357 LW 46:288. *The Christian in Society III*, "On Marriage Matters."

358 <https://www.law.cornell.edu/constitution/first_amendment>.

them should have been our first line of defense against BLM rioters," according to Linda Jordan in *The Post & Mail*. She writes,

> Roads are the weapon of choice for BLM and Antifa mobs. They are the conduit through which all their disruption and violence flow, including arson, assaulting police officers, refusing to disperse, beating innocent citizens, murdering people, attacking drivers in cars, destroying buildings and statues, looting businesses, threatening people in their homes, in stores and at restaurants, and holding drivers and passengers hostage on every road they block.[359]

As President Trump carefully makes clear, he is not speaking of peaceful protesters, but rather of those who have maliciously co-opted the demonstration against police brutality and turned it into mob rule, where neither rational understanding nor an explanation for the action taken can be given for why innocent people, including merchants serving that community, are targeted with domestic terror, looting, destruction of their property, and harm to their bodies.

No thoughtful person can support or justify the brutality we saw in the killing of George Floyd. Such brutality is inexcusable in every sense of the word, even in police matters. I know there has been much said about the slogan "Black Lives Matter," and to be sure, black lives do matter. Some would substitute the word "All" for the adjective, saying "All Lives Matter;" or perhaps as some suggest, just "Lives Matter." On the mere face of the slogan, I would assert the slogan is racist, as I am sure others would eagerly assert that "White Lives Matter" is racist and evidence of "white supremacy." I recoiled the first time I heard "BLM" expressed. It is for the very same reason I dislike "identity politics" which only polarizes and divides people, rather than uniting. I prefer St. Paul's understanding in this vein: *"For in Christ Jesus you are **all** children of God, through faith. As many of you as were baptized into Christ have clothed yourselves with Christ. There is no longer Jew or Greek, there is no longer slave or free, there is no longer male and female; for **all** of you are one in Christ Jesus"* (Galatians 3: 26-28 [NRSV]) [emphasis added].

Strange, isn't it, in an election year, with the nominations for President and Vice President, we heard the media speaking of the choice of his running mate made by then Vice President Joe Biden as having checked the most boxes—being black, from immigrant parents, being female—all lifted higher in terms of priorities than the qualities Luther

[359] <https://www.thepostemail.com/2020/09/23/taking-it-to-the-streets>.

sought in leaders: being wise, competent and prudent, as well as serving the people and not one's self or ambition. We could, and perhaps we should, ask, "What really matters?" Checking the most boxes? What race? Gender? LGBTQIA? I once followed a car with a bumper sticker which read, "What Matters Is Who You Are!" St. Paul says it for this Paul: "A *child of the living God!*" (Romans 9:26).

I often cite the "bookends" of my ministry…that first parish, Trinity in Sebring, Ohio, that risked calling a seminarian just out of school and green behind his ears. They taught me the value and excitement of being "*ephphatha*," which in Greek means "be open." They were not only "open" to me, but open to the possibilities God had in store for the congregation. Willing to risk it all, selling the inadequate church building and parsonage, they chose to embark on a journey of trusting God's providence for their future, including the "promised land" of a site for relocation. While the congregation's staff was housed in offices and meeting rooms above the bank on the town square, we worshiped in an elementary school's multi-purpose space. In this period of transition, Trinity came to grips with their deepening response to being part of God's mission by initiating a creative ministry called "The Concern Food and Goods Center" to which other congregations in the area soon joined. The cooperative ministry gained national recognition for serving the people of Western Mahoning County and was bequeathed a large empty store from which to better serve the people in the area. Soon, a highly desirable site we had been previously told by the realtors and city fathers could not be purchased became "mysteriously" available, and building plans quickly ensued.

At the other end of my "life bookshelf" was…First Trinity in my Re-Firement! (You've heard it said that the "*first shall be last and the last first?!*") There, unlike any other congregation I've served (and there have been 130 parishes to which I have provided pastoral care and support to their pastors and families, while resourcing their congregations' ministries as an assistant to the Bishop), I learned the richness of community in being the family of God. Rarely is that crucial component of our faith so genuinely experienced: the accepting and embracing Church, reflecting God's embracing love that makes you

"THUMBODY." They were a small multicultural congregation in Indianapolis' Eastside, who enjoyed sharing fellowship meals following Sunday worship, and were just as eager to learn, grow and serve their community as they were to engage in fellowship as a family while eating. It didn't matter who you were as to the color of your skin, your gender, your marital or financial status, or any other "boxes" one could check. What mattered was that you knew you were "THUMBODY"* special because you are loved and belong to God as His child and thus to each other. Yes, there were Caucasians, Blacks, Asians, Hispanics, married, divorced, singles, a gay couple, a transgendered couple, widows, widowers, single mothers, youngsters, and a Jewish pianist who enlivened our worship.

Unfortunately, in a world that seems at times to be upside-down, we have witnessed peaceful demonstrations and protests against police brutality, and many of those protests were soon overshadowed by violence, destruction and looting, with businesses destroyed, buildings burned, police precincts burned to the ground or overtaken in many of our largest cities. A sense of "community" was forsaken for division and heightened polarization. People, including police and National Guard soldiers, were injured and some killed in the riots, which included vandalizing, destruction and the tearing down of monuments and statues, with demands that funding for the police be cut. Crime and shootings have increased substantially, with killings that included the lives of small children, much of which was done under the banner and umbrellas of Black Lives Matter and Antifa. With the black-on-black crimes and shootings, especially in Chicago, there is 5-year-old Cannon Hinnant tragically shot and killed in North Carolina, a 4-year-old boy, LeGend M. Taliferro, in bed sleeping when he was killed by gunfire from outside, and Bernell Trammel, a black political activist and businessman who ran the *eXpressions Journal*, a political and spiritual publication in Milwaukee, shot and killed presumably because he carried a sign supporting Donald Trump even though he supported the BLM movement. With black children becoming victims and with the number of black infants aborted—1,000 a day, as we will soon examine—I must ask, which black lives *really* matter? Only the few noted and picked up by the press that seemingly involve white fingers on the trigger of a gun aimed at a black person, especially if it is a white policeman's finger? Where have the civil rights leaders—like the Reverend Al Sharpton, those leaders in the Democratic Party, and the BLM movement—been in speaking out and condemning the destruction, violence, injuries and deaths of those whose lives matter too?

* Thumbprints were used in a children's message at the height of the Black Lives Matter protests. Badges with "I'M THUMBODY" printed over the top of a thumbprint were used with the children. Fingerprints are unique, just as everyone is distinctively unique. What is most important is that we are "THUMBODY" because we are a child of God, and loved not because of the color of our skin, our gender or our nationality, but because we are His. Through one of the public school teachers in our congregation, this became the theme for Black History month in the school, for which it was awarded a $15,000 library technology grant.

Luther reassures his readers and, perhaps offering counsel to his younger twin, makes it perfectly plain that he is

> speaking of those who were first approached in a friendly way, and [they] would not respond. All my words were directed against the obdurate, hardened, blinded peasants, who would neither see nor hear, as anyone may see who reads them; and yet you say that I advocate the merciless slaughter of the poor captured peasants. If you are going to read books this way and interpret them as you please, what book will have any chance with you? Therefore, as I wrote then so I write now: Let no one have mercy on the obstinate, hardened, blinded peasants who refuse to listen to reason; but let everyone, as he is able, strike, hew, stab, and slay, as though among mad dogs, so that by so doing he may show mercy to those who are ruined, put to flight, and led astray by these peasants, so that peace and safety may be maintained. It is better to cut off one member without mercy than to have the whole body perish by fire, or by disease [Matthew 5:29-30]. How do you like that? Am I still a preacher of the Gospel who advocates grace and mercy? If you think I am not, it makes little difference, for you are a bloodhound, and a rebellious murderer and destroyer of the country, you, and your rebellious peasants, whom you are flattering in their rebellion.[360]

Fascinating how Luther implies that he, too, is bedeviled with the misreading and lack of understanding of his views by his opponents who run with false narratives to support their pre-determined and biased opinions. Luther would clearly understand that without forceful pushback and restraint; with revolving-door justice as New York institutes "no-bail release" for those arrested, and disbanding the "Anti-Crime Unit" (undercover police); with commanding enforcement officers to pull back; with the takeover of police precincts, even a section of downtown Seattle that bars police and emergency personnel from entering their "autonomous zone" called the "summer of love" in the mayor's words; with proposals to reduce assaulting a policeman to a misdemeanor crime; with monuments and statues defaced and ripped down, buildings destroyed by fire, business storefronts shattered, and stores looted; with demands to abolish or defund police departments; with vandals, agitators and terrorists being emboldened in their reign of terror, intimidation and raw power to do as they please. No civil society can survive without safety and protection, without law and

---

360 LW 46:73-74. *The Christian in Society III*, "An Open Letter on the Harsh Book."

order. “Rebellion is no joke,” says Luther, “and there is no evil deed on earth that compares with it. Other wicked deeds are single acts; rebellion is a flood of all wickedness.”[361]

Not on My Watch!

Standing before Mount Rushmore in a July 4th event, President Trump sadly recognized the

> growing danger that threatens every blessing our ancestors fought so hard for, struggled, they bled to secure. Our nation is witnessing a merciless campaign to wipe out our history, defame our heroes, erase our values, and indoctrinate our children. Angry mobs are trying to tear down statues of our founders, deface our most sacred memorials, and unleash a wave of violent crime in our cities. Many of these people have no idea why they're doing this, but some know what they are doing. They think the American people are weak and soft and submissive, but no, the American people are strong and proud, and they will not allow our country and all of its values, history, and culture to be taken from them.
>
> One of their political weapons is “cancel culture,” driving people from their jobs, shaming dissenters, and demanding total submission from anyone who disagrees. This is the very definition of totalitarianism, and it is completely alien to our culture and to our values and it has absolutely no place in the United States of America. This attack on our liberty, our magnificent liberty must be stopped, and it will be stopped very quickly. We will expose this dangerous movement, protect our nation's children from this radical assault, and preserve our beloved American way of life.
>
> In our schools, our newsrooms, even our corporate boardrooms, there is a new far-left fascism that demands absolute allegiance. If you do not speak its language, perform its rituals, recite its mantras, and follow its commandments, then you will be censored, banished, blacklisted, persecuted, and punished. It's not going to happen to us. Make no mistake. This left-wing cultural revolution is designed to overthrow the American Revolution. In so doing they would destroy the very civilization that rescued billions from poverty, disease, violence, and hunger, and that lifted humanity to new heights

---

[361] Ibid., LW 46:81.

> of achievement, discovery, and progress. To make this possible, they are determined to tear down every statue, symbol, and memory of our national heritage.... Not on my watch![362]

In response to those being critical of him for not showing mercy to the rebellious peasants, Luther defended his position by example: "...a savage beast is bound with chains and ropes so that it cannot bite and tear as it would normally do, even though it would like to; whereas a tame and gentle animal needs no restraint, but is harmless despite the lack of chains and ropes."[363] In another writing, Luther states, as if he were supporting his brother in dealing with rioters and rebels, "you may deal harshly with the liars and hardened tyrants, and act boldly in opposition to their teachings and their works, for they will not listen.... With wolves you cannot be too severe; with weak sheep, you cannot be too gentle."[364]

The Rev. Dr. Thorsten Prill* comments on the criticism directed toward Luther's lack of empathy in not extending mercy to the peasants:

> A sinful fallen world cannot be ruled by the Gospel, but only by law and coercion. To abolish the law [*aka defund and/or abolish the police*] and to apply, for example, the ethical principles of the Sermon on the Mount in politics would endanger peace in society and lead to destruction. It would be, writes Luther, like "loosing the ropes and chains of the savage wild beasts and letting them bite and mangle everyone, meanwhile insisting that they were harmless, tame and gentle creatures" [*aka peaceful protesters*].[365]

President Trump began his remarks at the Kennedy Space Center, on the launch of two astronauts to the International Space Station on May 30, 2020, by acknowledging his call to

---

362 Trump, Donald, "Speech at Mount Rushmore July 4th Event, July 3, 2020." <https://www.rev.com/blog/transcripts/donald-trump-speech-transcript-at-mount-rushmore-4th-of-july-event>.

363 LW 45:90. *The Christian in Society II*, "Temporal Authority: To What Extent It Should Be Obeyed."

364 LW 45:73. *The Christian in Society II*, "A Sincere Admonition to All Christians to Guard Against Insurrection and Rebellion."

* Thorsten Prill is a Lutheran theologian teaching Systematic Theology and Missiology at Namibia Evangelical Theological Seminary in Windhoek.

365 Prill, Thorsten, "God's Two Kingdoms and the Christian's Two Citizenships," quoting Luther, "Temporal Authority," LW 45:91. <https://www.researchgate.net/publication/283118904>.

the Floyd family to express the nation's sorrow on the disturbing death of George who was killed in Minneapolis:

> It should never have happened, [the President said.] It has filled Americans all over the country with horror, anger, and grief. I stand before you as a friend and ally to every American seeking justice and peace. And I stand before you in firm opposition to anyone exploiting this tragedy to loot, rob, attack, and menace. Healing, not hatred; justice, not chaos are the mission at hand.... I understand the pain that people are feeling. We support the right of peaceful protesters, and we hear their pleas. But what we are now seeing on the streets of our cities has nothing to do with justice or with peace. The memory of George Floyd is being dishonored by rioters, looters, and anarchists. The violence and vandalism is being led by Antifa and other radical left-wing groups who are terrorizing the innocent, destroying jobs, hurting businesses, and burning down buildings.
>
> The main victims of this horrible, horrible situation are the citizens who live in these once lovely communities. The mobs are devastating the life's work of good people and destroying their dreams. Right now, America needs creation, not destruction; cooperation, not contempt; security, not anarchy. And there will be no anarchy. Civilization must be cherished, defended, and protected. The voices of law-abiding citizens must be heard, and heard loudly. We cannot and must not allow a small group of criminals and vandals to wreck our cities and lay waste to our communities. We must defend the rights of every citizen to live without violence, prejudice, or fear...
>
> In America, justice is never achieved at the hands of an angry mob. I will not allow angry mobs to dominate. It won't happen. It is essential that we protect the crown jewel of American democracy: the rule of law and our independent system of justice. Every citizen in every community has the right to be safe in their workplace, safe in their homes, and safe in our city streets. This is the sacred right of all Americans that I am totally determined to defend and will defend. My administration will always stand against violence, mayhem, and disorder. We will stand with the family of George Floyd with the peaceful protesters and with every law-abiding citizen who wants decency, civility, safety, and security. We are working toward a more

> just society, but that means building up, not tearing down; joining hands, not hurling fists, standing in solidarity, not surrendering to hostility.[366]

In Luther's understanding, a twofold divine government exists, and while not all the people are Christians, and Christians are not ethically or morally perfect, they too must submit to and honor the temporal authority over them. Thus, because Christians stand before God, but also live in the world, they have dual citizenship—earthly citizenship, which comes with birth, and heavenly citizenship, which comes through faith:

> Because the sword is most beneficial and necessary for the whole world in order to preserve peace, punish sin, and restrain the wicked, the Christian submits most willingly to the rule of the sword, pays his taxes, honors those in authority, serves, helps, and does all he can to assist the governing authority, that it may continue to function and be held in honor and fear.... [Believers are called to be model citizens and] so he serves the governing authority primarily for the sake of others, that they may be protected and that the wicked may not become worse. He loses nothing by this; such service in no way harms him, yet it is of great benefit to the world. If he did not so serve, he would be acting not as a Christian but even contrary to love; he would also be setting a bad example to others who in like manner would not submit to authority, even though they were not Christians. In this way, the Gospel would be brought into disrepute, as though it taught insurrection and produced self-willed people unwilling to benefit or serve others, when in fact it makes a Christian the servant of all.*[367]

The purpose statement of the United States Justice System is

> to enforce the law and defend the interests of the United States according to the law; to ensure public safety against threats foreign and domestic, to

---

[366] Trump, "Kennedy Space Center Speech." <https://www.whitehouse.gov/briefings-Statements/remarks-president-trump-kennedy-space-center>.

* See Luther's 1520 "The Freedom of a Christian" where Romans 13 and Matthew 17 are also cited in illustrations of the Christian's willing service to others. LW 31:343-377, especially p.369 and in *Three Treatises*, pp. 265-316, expressly pp. 306-307.

[367] LW 45:94. *The Christian in Society II*, "Temporal Authority."

> provide federal leadership in preventing and controlling crime; to seek just punishment for those guilty of unlawful behavior; and to ensure fair and impartial administration of justice for all Americans.[368]

Our elder twin was quite explicit in his understanding of the role of civil government in maintaining and cultivating a peaceful earthly life by restraining sinful conduct under the threat of punishment. John Witte, Jr. interprets this civil use of the law that

> God wants even the worst of sinners to observe—the basic law of God and the State—to honor their parents, to avoid killing and stealing, to respect marriages and households, to testify truthfully, and the like, so that "some measure of earthly order, concourse and concord may be preserved." Sinners, not naturally inclined to observe the law, may be compelled to do so by fear of punishment—divine punishment as well as human punishment. "Stern, hard civil rule is necessary in the world," Luther wrote, "lest the world be destroyed, peace vanish, and commerce and common interests be destroyed.... No one need think that the world can be ruled without blood. The civil sword shall and must be red and bloody."[369]

Witte adds Luther's additional sentiment from the same passage: Indeed, if the magistrate "does not punish murder and bloodshed, although he could, he is himself guilty of the same murders and wrongs that those villains commit." The magistrate must apply the law equitably and to do so, Witte understands Luther cautioning them not to rashly relax laws and discipline[370] as Trump witnessed civil officials doing in the summer riots of 2020.

In his "Admonition to Peace," Luther had addressed the princes and magistrates sharply, claiming they along with "blind bishops and mad priests and monks" are to blame for the disastrous rebellion of the peasants.

---

368 "Front Page." *The United States Department of Justice*, 26 Oct. 2017, <www.justice.gov>. Or see <https://www.reidlawalabama.com/guest-blog/2017/10/31/the-protestant-reformations-effect-on-modern-law>.

369 Witte, Jr., John, "Martin Luther's Influence on Legal Reforms and Civil Law," *Oxford Research Encyclopedia of Religion* (March, 2017), quoting Luther WA 10:454; WA 11:251; and WA 15:302. <https://doi.org/10.1093/acrefore/9780199340378.013.503>; <https://hcommons.org/deposits/item/hc:25395/>; or <https://www.researchgate.net/publication/334707670>.

370 Ibid. Witte quoting Martin Luther "Against the Robbing and Murdering Hordes" in WA 18:360 or *The Christian in Society III*, LW 46:53.

> To make your sin still greater, and guarantee your merciless destruction, some of you are beginning to blame this affair on the [Reformation] Gospel and say that it is the fruit of my teaching. Well, well, slander away dear lords! You did not want to know what I taught or what the Gospel is; now the one who will soon teach you is at the door unless you change your ways. You, and everyone else, must bear witness that I have taught with all quietness, [without inciting rebellion]...this rebellion cannot be coming from me. Rather the murder-prophets,* who hate me as they hate you, have come among these people and have gone about them for more than three years, and no one has resisted and fought against them except me.[371]

The three year period dates from the Wittenberg riots at the beginning of 1522 and the activity of the Zwickau prophets preceding them. Luther took firm and decisive action against them, as he did against Muntzer and Karlstadt, while the civil authorities were still uncertain about what to do. In his Mount Rushmore address, Trump called attention to the executive order he signed that would ensure a minimum of ten years in prison for those who damage or deface federal statues or monuments:

> Our people have a great memory. They will never forget the destruction of statues and monuments to George Washington, Abraham Lincoln, Ulysses S. Grant, abolitionists, and many others. The violent mayhem we have seen in the streets and cities that are run by liberal Democrats in every case, is the predictable result of years of extreme indoctrination and bias in education, journalism, and other cultural institutions. Against every law of society and nature, our children are taught in school to hate their own country and to believe that the men and women who built it were not heroes but that they were villains. The radical view of American history is a web of lies, all perspective is removed, every virtue is obscured, every motive is twisted, every fact is distorted, and every flaw is magnified until the history is purged and the record is disfigured beyond all recognition. This movement is openly attacking the legacies of every person on Mount Rushmore. They defiled the memory of Washington, Jefferson, Lincoln, and Roosevelt.

---

* By "murder-prophets," Luther means the religious revolutionaries who were inciting the people to revolt and were using the Gospel to support their position. (Cf. LW 46:19, ftn 5). LW 46:20.

[371] LW 46:20-21. *The Christian in Society III*, "Admonition to Peace."

> Our founders launched not only a revolution in government, but a revolution in the pursuit of justice, equality, liberty, and prosperity. No nation has done more to advance the human condition than the United States of America and no people have done more to promote human progress than the citizens of our great nation. It was all made possible by the courage of 56 patriots who gathered in Philadelphia 244 years ago and signed the Declaration of Independence. They enshrined a divine truth that changed the world forever when they said, "All men are created equal." These immortal words set in motion the unstoppable march of freedom. Our founders boldly declared that we are all endowed with the same divine rights, given us by our Creator in Heaven, and that which God has given us, we will allow no one ever to take away...ever![372]

He continued his Mount Rushmore address with the acknowledgment and praise of those who came before us to establish a foundation upon which we can build, but also with the caution and warning of the threats that imperil our nation's future. He could well have reminded the country of President Theodore Roosevelt's first message to Congress after succeeding President William B. McKinley, who was assassinated by an anarchist on September 6, 1901, while attending the Pan-American Exposition in Buffalo, New York. Harshly denouncing anarchism, President Teddy Roosevelt said, "The man who advocates anarchy directly or indirectly, in any shape or fashion, or the man who apologizes for anarchists and their deeds, makes himself morally accessory to murder before the fact." He went on to describe the anarchist as a criminal whose perverted instincts lead him to prefer confusion and chaos to the most beneficent form of social order. "The anarchist is everywhere not merely the enemy of system and of progress, but the deadly foe of liberty."[373] Below the towering Mount Rushmore where President Teddy Roosevelt is enshrined, Trump spoke similar words:

> No movement that seeks to dismantle these treasured American legacies can possibly have a love of America at its heart. Can't happen! No person who remains quiet at the destruction of this resplendent heritage can possibly lead

---

[372] Trump, "Mount Rushmore Speech," July 4, 2020; <https:///www.rev.com/blog/transcrripts/donald-trump-speech-at-mount-rushmore-4th-of-july-event>.

[373] Roosevelt, Theodore, "First Address to Congress," <https://millercenter.org/the-presidency/presidential-speeches/december-3-1901-first-annual-message>, or see <https://historynewsnetwork.org/article/274>.

> us to a better future. The radical ideology attacking our country advances under the banner of social justice, but in truth, it would demolish both justice and society. It would transform justice into an instrument of division and vengeance, and it would turn our free and inclusive society into a place of repression, domination, and exclusion. They want to silence us, but we will not be silenced.
>
> We will state the truth in full without apology. We declare that the United States of America is the most just and exceptional nation ever to exist on earth. We are proud of the fact that our country was founded on Judeo-Christian principles, and we understand that these values have dramatically advanced the cause of peace and justice throughout the world. We know that the American family is the bedrock of American life. We recognize the solemn right and moral duty of every nation to secure its borders and we are building the wall. We remember that governments exist to protect the safety and happiness of their own people. A nation must care for its own citizens first. We must take care of America first. It's time.
>
> We believe in equal opportunity, equal justice, and equal treatment for citizens of every race, background, religion, and creed. Every child of every color, born and unborn, is made in the holy image of God.... We believe our children should be taught to love their country, honor their history, and respect our great American flag. We stand tall, we stand proud, and we only kneel to Almighty God. This is who we are. This is what we believe, and these are the values that will guide us as we strive to build an even better and greater future.... My fellow Americans, it is time to speak up loudly and strongly and powerfully and defend the integrity of our country.... For the sake of our honor, for the sake of our children, we must protect and preserve our history, our heritage, and our great heroes. Here tonight before the eyes of our forefathers, Americans declare again, as we did 244 years ago, that we will not be tyrannized, we will not be demeaned, and we will not be intimidated by bad, evil people. It will not happen.[374]

In that excellent op-ed in the *Wall Street Journal*, June 28, 2020, New York Archbishop Timothy Dolan is critical of the destruction and defacing of our monuments and the tearing

---

[374] Trump, "Mt. Rushmore Speech."

down of statues and hiding portraits. He views such action as today's version of Puritan book burning, which unfortunately would not be in the memory of most rioters. Much as we discovered early in this book, citing James Robbins' *Erasing America: Losing Our Future by Destroying Our Past* and Jay Winik's *April 1865: The Month That Saved America* (see chapter 3), the renowned Archbishop expresses concern that the effect of such criminal action only impoverishes our sense of history:

> Our children need to know their country's past, its normative figures and their virtues and vices.... Yes, there are scandalous parts of our history, and countless episodes when popes, bishops, priests, and others—including some who are now saints—didn't act as they should have.
>
> God forbid we'd go through a cultural revolution as China did five decades ago. Beware of those who want to purify memories and present a tidy—and inaccurate—history. And who's to say which statues, portraits, books, and dedications are spared? Remember when some objected to raising the status of Martin Luther King Jr.'s birthday to a national holiday, citing his self-admitted flaws?
>
> If literature that depicts prejudice, or words or scenes that are today rightly abhorred, is to be banned, I don't know if even the Bible can survive.... I want to remember the good and the bad and recall with gratitude how even people who have an undeniable dark side can let light prevail and leave the world better. I want to keep bringing classes of schoolchildren to view such monuments, and to explain to them how even such giants in our history had crimes, unjust acts, and plain poor judgment mixed in with the good we honor.[375]

Thomas Paine could have been honestly describing Luther's "time" as well as our own in this epidemic year of the coronavirus, economic collapse and disastrous rebellions, as well as his own times that literally "pained" him.

> THESE are the times that try men's souls. The summer soldier and the sunshine patriot will, in this crisis, shrink from the service of their country;

[375] Dolan, Timothy, "Even the Bible Is Full of Flawed Characters," *The Wall Street Journal*. <https://www.wsj.com/articles/even-the-bible-is-full-of-flawed-characters-11593370160>.

> but he that stands by it now, deserves the love and thanks of man and woman. Tyranny, like hell, is not easily conquered; yet we have this consolation with us, that the harder the conflict, the more glorious the triumph. What we obtain too cheap, we esteem too lightly: it is dearness only that gives everything its value. Heaven knows how to put a proper price upon its goods; and it would be strange indeed if so celestial an article as FREEDOM should not be highly rated.[376]

What Would Jesus Say?

Bill Tenny-Brittian* provides, I believe, wise counsel and a crucial understanding in his "The Effective Church" post. He reminds us how the Romans used crucifixions along the roadside to deter those who might be tempted to break the law; how racist Jews were in Jesus' day, especially against those who weren't Jewish living on the "other side of the tracks in Samaria;" and how John the Baptist, Jesus' cousin, was imprisoned and executed without the due process of a trial, judge and jury, for having spoken out against the immorality of a public figure. The list can go on and on and folks can ask, as they often do: "What would Jesus do? What did Jesus say or do about these injustices or travesties?" Surprisingly, He was completely silent. Not a word!

"So…what 'sin' and 'injustice' *did* Jesus choose to directly address over and over again?" Pastor Bill asks. "Hypocrisy of the religious leaders—not about the way they did or didn't address social issues, but because of their holier-than-thou attitudes toward those in the community."[377] Does that not seem to resonate with the self-anointed elite establishment we have encountered in both Luther and Trump's times? Not just those in the Church, but also in the government and media? There are those in positions who presume to instruct others about proper behavior, what to do, what not to do, how to do it, what viewpoints are to be held and espoused, and how to speak with political correctness, but do not follow their own advice or the mandates they impose on others.

---

376 Paine, Thomas; Quote retrieved from <https://www.goodreads.com/quotes/175410-these-are-the-times-that-try-men-s-souls-the-summer>.

* Bill Tenny-Brittian is a pastor and presently Managing Partner at The Effective Church Group. He joined Bill Easum's consultation group to resource congregations and is the editor of *Net Results*, as well as the author of nine books.

377 Tenny-Brittian, Bill, "When Protesting Doesn't Work," June 12, 2020. <https://effectivechurch.com/when-protesting-doesnt-work>.

New York Times opinion editor Bari Weiss, in her letter of resignation, gives a devastating "beat down" in making the salient point that journalism is dead at the *New York Times* while exposing, in blistering terms, internal operations:

> I was hired with the goal of bringing in voices that would not otherwise appear in your pages: first-time writers, centrists, conservatives, and others who would not naturally think of *The Times* as their home. The reason for this effort was clear: The paper's failure to anticipate the outcome of the 2016 election meant that it didn't have a firm grasp of the country it covers.... But the lessons that ought to have followed the election—lessons about the importance of understanding other Americans, the necessity of resisting tribalism, and the centrality of the free exchange of ideas to a democratic society—have not been learned. Instead, a new consensus has emerged in the press, but perhaps especially at this paper: that truth isn't a process of collective discovery, but an orthodoxy already known to an enlightened few whose job is to inform everyone else. Twitter is not on the masthead of *The New York Times*. But Twitter has become its ultimate editor...
>
> My own forays into Wrongthink have made me the subject of constant bullying by those who disagree with my views. They have called me a Nazi and a racist.... Still *New York Times* employees publicly smear me as a liar and a bigot on Twitter with no fear that harassing me will be met with appropriate action. They never are...
>
> Showing up for work as a centrist at an American newspaper should not require bravery. Part of me wishes I could say that my experience was unique. But the truth is that intellectual curiosity—let alone risk-taking—is now a liability at *The Times*. Why edit something challenging to our readers, or write something bold only to go through the numbing process of making it ideologically kosher, when we can assure ourselves of job security (and clicks) by publishing our 4000th op-ed arguing that Donald Trump is a unique danger to the country and the world? And so self-censorship has become the norm.
>
> What rules that remain at *The Times* are applied with extreme selectivity. If a person's ideology is in keeping with the new orthodoxy, they and their work remain unscrutinized. Everyone else lives in fear of the digital thunder

> dome. Online venom is excused so long as it is directed at the proper target... standing up for principle at the paper does not win plaudits. It puts a target on your back.
>
> All this bodes ill, especially for independent-minded young writers and editors paying close attention to what they'll have to do to advance in their careers. Rule One: Speak your mind at your own peril. Rule Two: Never risk commissioning a story that goes against the narrative. Rule Three: Never believe an editor or publisher who urges you to go against the grain. Eventually, the publisher will cave to the mob, the editor will get fired or reassigned, and you'll be hung out to dry.
>
> I can no longer do the work that you brought me here to do—the work that Adolph Ochs described in that famous 1896 statement: "to make of the columns of *The New York Times* a forum for the consideration of all questions of public importance, and to that end to invite intelligent discussion from all shades of opinion."
>
> Ochs's idea is one of the best I've encountered. And I've always comforted myself with the notion that the best ideas win out. But ideas cannot win on their own. They need a voice. They need a hearing. Above all, they must be backed by people willing to live by them.[378]

Interesting how those who verbally support diversity and encourage tolerance are so frequently intolerant of views other than their own. Do we not notice, also, how selective they are with their pontifications that "nobody is above the law?" While that truth was espoused by many to bolster their claims during the impeachment, we don't hear those same voices chanting that confident assertion during the chaos, vandalism and destruction rendered by rioters who are clearly breaking the law. Instead, we experience and tolerate those who intimidate and even bully, by their use of unflattering innuendoes and accusations that label and belittle those who disagree into submission, even into bowing!

That's not to imply the Church should not make its presence known in the public square nor speak out against injustice. Indeed, that is one of the roles assigned to the Church, and expected as responsible actions of Christian citizens. But isn't it equally unjust to operate on a double standard or a two-tier system of justice? The Old Testament prophets regularly

[378] Weiss, Bari, "Letter of Resignation," personal website. <https://www.bariweiss.com/resignation-letter>.

called attention to our responsibility, and to the responsibilities of their leaders. But, as Tenny-Brittian points out,

> the Church has a deplorable record on addressing social ills when using society's tools (lobbying, protesting, politicking, etc.). In the 20s we got our noses bloodied in the war against alcohol (I guess we forgot Jesus made 120 gallons of wine in a single sitting). In the 1940s, we looked pretty bad when the U.S. Church vehemently supported Isolationism and suggested the Jews fend for themselves. In the 1960s, we didn't do so well trying to defeat abortion. In the 1980s, we lost face in the face of homosexuality. And in the 2000s, the battle against same-gender marriage was seriously lost.[379]

In addition to these social issues that seem to dominate the Church's ministry, there is the Biblical concern for those in poverty and the resulting condition of our inner cities. As Michael Tanner points out, "This year the federal, state, and local governments will spend close to a combined $1 trillion to fund more than 100 separate anti-poverty programs. In fact, since Lyndon Johnson declared a 'War on Poverty' in 1965, government efforts to fight poverty have cost more than $23 trillion."[380]

According to the Heritage Foundation analysis, Senior Research Fellow Robert Rector reports there has been no improvement at all in improving self-sufficiency:

> Many groups are less capable of self-support today than when Johnson's war started. The culprit is, in part, the welfare system itself, which discourages work and penalizes marriage. When the War on Poverty began, 7% of American children were born outside of marriage. Today (2014) the number is 41%. The collapse of marriage is the main cause of child poverty today. The welfare state is self-perpetuating.... Johnson sought to help the poor help themselves. He aimed to free the poor from the need of government aid, rather than to increase their dependence. That's a vision worth recapturing.[381]

---

[379] Tenny-Brittian, "When Protesting Doesn't Work."

[380] Tanner, Michael D., "Spotlight on Poverty and Opportunity," Cato Institute, January 23, 2019. <https://www.cato.org/publications/commentary/whats-missing-war-poverty>.

[381] Rector, Robert, "The War on Poverty: 50 Years of Failure," Heritage Foundation. <https://www.heritage.org/marriage-and-family/commentary/the-war-poverty-50-years-failure>.

The stated goal of the War on Poverty, as enunciated by Lyndon Johnson on January 8, 1964, was "…not only to relieve the symptom of poverty, but to cure it and, above all, to prevent it."[382] This is what President Trump was succeeding in achieving before the pandemic hit the country—unemployment numbers the lowest for all the minority sectors, highest number of employed, lowest number on food stamps, and the establishment of Opportunity Zones in the inner cities.

Church and other non-profit organizations have contributed mightily to hunger's and poverty's "elimination," but we still have poverty, as Christ recognized, "*you always have the poor with you*" (Matthew 26:11 [NRSV]). To be sure, the persistence of poverty is not a reason to ignore the plight of the poor, but instead to be even more generous, because the poor will always be with us (Deuteronomy 15:11). But that also necessitates the far more difficult challenge in addressing the very heart of concern that underlies the symptoms our political leaders say they are seeking to address on the surface.

As reported on Father.com, "More than 20 million children live in a home without the physical presence of a father. Millions more have dads who are physically present, but emotionally absent. If it were classified as a disease, fatherlessness would be an epidemic worthy of attention as a national emergency,"[383] just as the coronavirus has been. From data gathered by the Census Bureau, the U.S. Department of Health and Human Services, the Centers for Disease Control and numerous other studies,

> children from fatherless homes are more likely to be poor, become involved in drug and alcohol abuse, drop out of school, and suffer from health and emotional problems. Boys are more likely to become involved in crime, and girls are more likely to become pregnant as teens…children of single-parent homes are more than twice as likely to commit suicide.[384]

Back on July 29, 2013, CNN's Don Lemon said, "Just because you can have a baby, it doesn't mean you should, especially without planning for one or getting married first.

---

[382] Woodhill, Louis, "The War on Poverty Wasn't a Failure—It Was a Catastrophe," *Forbes*, May 19, 2014. <https://www.forbes.com/sites/louiswoodhill/2014/03/19/the-war-on-poverty-wasnt-a-failure-it-was-a-catastrophe/#6cf0eb976f49>.

[383] <http://fathers.com/statistics-and-research/the-extent-of-fatherlessness>.

[384] <http://fathers.com/statistics-and-research/the-consequences-of-fatherlessness>. See also <https://datacenter.kidscount.org/data/tables/107-children-in-single-parent-families-by-race#detailed>.

More than 72 percent of children in the African American community are born out of wedlock.... That means absent fathers. And the studies show that lack of a male role model is an express train ride to prison and the cycle continues."[385] One wonders if he could get away with reporting that fact today. But he was correct! Two population experts—Tom W. Smith, a senior fellow at the National Opinion Research Center at the University of Chicago, and Douglas Massey, Professor at Princeton University's Office of Population Research—agreed that the statistic is the best available.[386]

In his Fatherhood Speech at the Apostolic Church of God in Chicago on Father's Day, June 15, 2008, then-Senator Barack Obama affirmed the role of fathers in their children's lives, signaling out African American communities:

> Of all the rocks upon which we build our lives, we are reminded today that family is the most important. And we are called to recognize and honor how critical every father is to that foundation. They are teachers and coaches. They are mentors and role models. They are examples of success and the men who constantly push us toward it.
>
> But if we are honest with ourselves, we'll admit that what too many fathers also are missing—missing from too many lives and too many homes. They have abandoned their responsibilities, acting like boys instead of men. And the foundations of our families are weaker because of it.
>
> You and I know how true this is in the African-American community. We know that more than half of all black children live in single-parent households, a number that has doubled—doubled—since we were children. We know the statistics—that children who grow up without a father are five times more likely to live in poverty and commit crime; nine times more likely to drop out of schools and 20 times more likely to end up in prison. They are more likely to have behavioral problems, or run away from home or become teenage parents themselves. And the foundations of our community are weaker because of it...

---

385 <https://www.politifact.com/factchecks/2013/jul/29/don-lemon/cnns-don-lemon-says-more-72-percent-africa>.

386 Ibid.

> Yes, we need more cops on the street. Yes, we need fewer guns in the hands of people who shouldn't have them. Yes, we need more money for our schools, and more outstanding teachers in the classroom, and more after-school programs for our children. Yes, we need more jobs and more job training and more opportunity in our communities.
>
> But we also need families to raise our children. We need fathers to realize that responsibility does not end at conception. We need them to realize that what makes you a man is not the ability to have a child—it's the courage to raise one.[387]

Fatherless homes, for the most part, are by any measure disastrous for the future generation and, needless to say it, so is abortion. The impact on our black communities is hard to fathom. According to the Guttmacher Institute, which generally supports abortion, in 2011 360,000 black babies were aborted. CDC statistics for 2011 show that 287,072 black deaths occurred from all other causes, excluding abortion. By these numbers, abortion is the leading cause of death among blacks.[388] In New York City, thousands more black babies are aborted each year than born alive.[389]

Abortion is not just a woman's issue. "It's a human rights issue that impacts African Americans at a higher rate than any other population group. Today, with more than 28% of all black pregnancies ending in induced abortion, it is a human crisis. Abortion is the number one killer of black lives in the United States. So why don't these Black Lives Matter? According to the Centers for Disease Control and Prevention, abortion kills more black people than HIV, homicide, diabetes, accident, cancer, and heart disease… combined…. Abortion kills 1,000 Black babies every day in America…. In 2014, African American women comprised 13.3% of the U.S. population, but black women had 36% of all abortions.[390] The Guttmacher Institute records 37% of abortions are obtained by black women compared with 34% for white women.[391] Viewed from the perspective of ratios, the

---

[387] Obama, Barack, "Fatherhood Speech," June 15, 2008. Retrieved at *Politico*. <https://www.politico.com/story/2008/06/text-of-obamas-fatherhood-speech-011094>.

[388] <https://azcapitoltimes.com/news/2020/02/25/abortion-the-overlooked-tragedy-for-black-americans>.

[389] <https://www.wsj.com/articles/lets-talk-about-the-black-abortion-rate-1531263697>.

[390] <https://www.grrtl.org/genocide>.

[391] <https://www.guttmacher.org/gpr/2008/08/abortion-and-women-color-bigger>.

Guttmacher finds that black women are almost five times more likely than white women to undergo an abortion."[392]

Guttmacher said it was impossible to identify exactly what factors are driving the declines in abortions the past twenty-five years, but pointed to fewer pregnancies, contraceptive access and use, a decline in sexual activity, and infertility as possible causes. Researchers noted, however, that it is possible that the drop is not as large as it appears, due to a potential increase in self-managed abortion, which is not reflected in the data. Self-managed abortions are those that occur outside of healthcare settings and might include the use of medication, chemical abortifacients like mifepristone (which rose from 16.4% in 2008 to 39.4% in 2017), and herbs or other methods without the direct supervision of a medical professional.[393] Looked at from another perspective, of the 62 million abortions since *Roe v. Wade* in 1973, based on numbers reported by the Guttmacher Institute, nearly 19 million would be black babies.[394] With such statistics, I have to ask whether those babies whose lives were taken really matter, and how does that reflect on the value we place on life other than our own?

Who Really Matters?

An article from the *New York Post* points to another issue that both of our warriors have encountered: the attempted radical transformation and/or overthrow of their countries by fanatic rioters. We've seen that in former Luther supporter Thomas Muntzer, leading misguided peasants into war. Mike Gonzalez and Andrew Olivastro reveal that "The Agenda of Black Lives Matter Is Far Different from the Slogan:"

> Many see the slogan "Black Lives Matter" as a plea to secure the right to "life, liberty, and the pursuit of happiness" for all Americans, especially historically wronged African Americans.... Tragically when [people or corporations] donate, they are likely to bankroll a number of radical organizations, founded by committed Marxists whose goals aren't to make the American Dream a reality for everyone—but to transform America completely.... Just ask BLM

392 <https://www.motherjones.com/politics/2016/10/true-stories-hard-choices-documentary-abortion-black-women>. See also <https://azcapitoltimes.com/news/2020/02/25/abortion-the-overlooked-tragedy-for-black-americans>, <https://www.guttmacher.org/gpr/2008/08/abortion-and-women-color-bigger>.

393 <https://www.washingtonpost.com/health/2019/09/18/us-abortion-rate-falls-lowest-level-since-roe-v-wade/> and <https://nrlc.org/uploads/factsheets/FS01AbortionintheUS.pdf>.

394 <http://www.numberofabortions.com>.

> leaders Alicia Garza, Patrisse Cullors, and Opal Tometi. In a revealing 2015 interview, Cullors said, "Myself and Alicia, in particular, are trained organizers. We are trained Marxists..."
>
> Visit the Black Lives Matter website, and the first frame you get is a large crowd with fists raised and the slogan "Now We Transform." Read the list of demands, and you get a sense of how deep a transformation they seek. One proclaims: "We disrupt the Western-prescribed nuclear-family-structure requirement by supporting each other as extended families and "villages" that collectively care for one another…"
>
> The goals of the Black Lives Matter organization go far beyond what most people think. But they are hiding in plain sight, there for the world to see, if only we read beyond the slogans and the innocuous-sounding media accounts of the movement…. The group's radical Marxist agenda would supplant the basic building block of society—the family—with the State and destroy the economic system that has lifted more people from poverty than any other. Black lives, and all lives, would be harmed.[395]

Robert Stilson, a former student of mine, and a member with his family at King of Glory Lutheran Church in Carmel, Indiana, where I served, runs several specialized projects for Capital Research Center, a Washington-based nonprofit that examines how foundations and charities spend money. One of those projects has been taking a deeper look at Black Lives Matter, its organizational structure, its impact, and its financial relationships. He discovered

> a number of distinct entities operate to one degree or another within the broader Black Lives Matter framework, and they make use of the term or a closely related variant. Two groups in particular—the Black Lives Matter Global Network Foundation and the Movement for Black Lives—appear to be networks of particular coalescence.[396]

"BLM Global Network Foundation stands out as the closest thing to an organizational standard-bearer for the very decentralized Black Lives Matter movement that exists," Stilson

---

395 <https://nypost.com/2020/07/01/the-agenda-of-black-lives-matter-is-far-different-from-the-slogan>.

396 Stilson, Robert, "The Organizational Structure of Black Lives Matter." <https://capitalresearch.org/article/the-organizational-structure-of-black-lives-matter>.

told *The Daily Signal* in an email. "It operates the BlackLivesMatter.com website, claims the movement's co-founders as its own co-founders, and functions as the center of its officially affiliated Black Lives Matter chapters…of which there are 12 state chapters in the U.S., one in the nation's capital, and three in Canada."[397]

He also determined that Black Lives Matter Global Network Foundation's fiscal sponsor is Thousand Currents, a left-of-center grantmaking nonprofit based in Berkeley, California. "Fiscal sponsorship is an arrangement through which an organization that does not have its own IRS tax-exempt status can operate as a 'project' of an organization that does. In the case of 501(c)(3) fiscally sponsored projects, this allows for tax-deductible donations."[398]

Investigative reporter for *The Daily Signal*, Kevin Mooney, reports that

> The W.K. Kellogg Foundation, based in Battle Creek, Michigan, used Thousand Currents as a conduit to provide Black Lives Matters chapters with a three-year grant totaling $900,000 according to Influence Watch, a project of Capital Research Center. NoVo Foundation donated more than $1.5 million from 2015 to 2019 and Borealis Philanthropy donated $343,000 from 2016-2018…the Ford Foundation in 2015 gave a grant of 1.3 million to BLM Foundation. Other donations from big corporations include Amazon giving $10 million to a slew of left-leaning groups, including BLM; Intel making a $1 million to "address social justice and racism" that includes BLM; and Microsoft pledged to give $250,000 to the BLM Global Network Foundation and to other groups the tech giant views as advancing "social justice"…For such a young movement, its impact appears to be everywhere. Corporations and foundations are shoveling money its way, perhaps without understanding the movement's broader stated goals.[399]

One who certainly knows what his Open Society Foundations supports is business magnate George Soros. His philanthropic group, according to the *New York Times*,

> announced on July 13, 2020, that it was investing $220 million in efforts to achieve racial equality in America, a huge financial undertaking that

[397] Mooney, Kevin, "A Deeper Look at Black Lives Matter and Its Impact." <https://www.dailysignal.com/2020/07/02/a-deeper-look-at-black-lives-matter-and-its-impact>.

[398] Stilson, "Black Lives Matter."

[399] Mooney, "Black Lives Matter."

> will support several Black-led racial justice groups.... The initiative... will immediately reshape the landscape of Black political and civil rights organizations...$150 million will fund five-year grants for selected groups, including progressive and emerging organizations like the Black Voters Matter Fund and Repairers of the Breach...and more established Black civil rights organizations like the Equal Justice Initiative.... The Open Society Foundations will invest an additional $70 million in local grants supporting changes to policing and criminal justice. This money will also be used to pay for opportunities for civic engagement and to organize internships and political training for young people.
>
> Patrick Gaspard, the president of the Open Society Foundations, said in an interview that the group believed the investment was about harnessing the momentum toward racial justice, but also giving organizations room to think long-term.... So it's time to double down. And we understood we can place a bet on these activists—Black and white—who see this as a moment of not just incrementalism, but whole-scale reform...we need these moments to be sustained. If we're going to say Black Lives Matter, we need to say Black organizations and structures matter.[400]

While the stated goals or "demands" of Black Lives Matter vary from region to region, they certainly extend the coalition's agenda beyond the slogan. The movement advances the LGBT (lesbian, gay, bisexual and transgender) political agenda, including abolishing the nuclear family, ending violent attacks against protesters, the immediate abolishment of ICE, the closing of all prisons and privately owned detention facilities, defunding or abolishing the police, ending qualified immunity for police, vandalizing statues and monuments, retroactive decriminalization and expungement of all drug-related offenses, and decriminalization of prostitution. The Toronto chapter even claims "it favors decriminalization of 'poverty, drugs, HIV and sex work.'" BLM also calls for reparations, a progressive restructuring of tax codes at the local, state and federal levels to ensure a radical and sustainable redistribution of wealth. Guiding principles include collective value, loving engagement, empathy, restorative practices, black families and villages, kinship families, queer and transgender affirming,

---

400 Herndon, Astead W., "George Soros's Foundation Pours $220 Million into Racial Equality Push," *New York Times*. <https://www.nytimes.com/2020/07/13/us/politics/george-soros-racial-justice-organizations.html>.

and globalism. They remain "committed to dismantling White Supremacy, Patriarchy, Capitalism, Imperialism, and the role of the State in supporting them."[401]

> In terms of finances, Stilson finds that Thousand Currents played a key role in getting Black Lives Matter off the ground as a viable organization. "BLM Global Network Foundation's sponsorship by Thousand Currents lets us see some of the numbers behind their operations, including some of the nonprofits and foundations that have contributed to it," Stilson said… "With fiscally sponsored projects you rarely get the complete financial picture, but you can piece together parts of it."[402]

Kevin Mooney concludes his article by writing, "Although it remains difficult to assemble a complete picture of Black Lives Matter finances and structure, the organization's ideological underpinnings and historical antecedents are becoming more clear." Scott Walter, president of Capital Research Center, just published a report highlighting the radical history of Susan Rosenberg, vice chairwoman of Thousand Currents' board of directors. Walter writes:

> If there were any question whether Black Lives Matter has ideological ties to the Communist terrorists of the 1960s, the story of Susan Rosenberg should put that issue to bed. Rosenberg, who started out as a member of the 1960s revolutionary group Weather Underground, graduated into even more violent, and arguably successful, forms of terrorism in the 1970s and 1980s—including bombings at an FBI field office in Staten Island, the Navy Yard Officers' Club in Washington, D.C., and even the U.S. Capitol building, where she damaged a representation of the greatest of the Democrat defenders of slavery, John C. Calhoun.[403]

Not surprisingly, Mooney reports that Thousand Currents scrubbed its website shortly after Capital Research Center published its expose on Rosenberg, but assures his readers that the details are archived at the Center. Likewise, the Black Lives Matter websites have also scrubbed references to their Marxist views and their intent on abolishing the nuclear family.

---

[401] Mooney, "Black Lives Matter."

[402] Ibid.

[403] Walter, Scott, "A Terrorist's Ties to a Leading Black Lives Matter Group." <https://capitalresearch.org/article/a-terrorists-ties-to-a-leading-black-lives-matter-group> or <https://www.dailysignal.com/2020/07/02/a-deeper-look-at-black-lives-matter-and-its-impact>.

15

God's Mission Has the Church!

Having briefly looked at several significant but very complex issues confronting and impacting the Church, State, and society in general, I return to Bill Tenny Brittian's article where he identifies and has focused on the core concern and fundamental challenge that should more than rattle and haunt the Church in its present existence:

> Jesus charged the church with making disciples of Jesus Christ, and I think I can safely argue that a *faithful follower* of Jesus Christ (not just a "Christian" or a "church member") has a pretty good handle on the Golden Rule and on Paul's admonition that in Christ there is no gender, no race, no ethnicity, no social distinctions, etc. The only "cure" for our nation's ills, or the world's ills, for that matter, is Jesus Christ, and the only effective tool the Church has for making that a reality is evangelism and discipleship.
>
> Which is to say, if the church had been faithful for the last 2000 years with the Great Commission, and if the U.S. Church spent as much time, energy, and resources engaging in effective evangelism as it has trying to right all of society's ills using society's tools (something even Einstein suggested was futile), then MLK, Rodney King, Ferguson, and now Minneapolis might not have happened in the first place.
>
> We must all be good citizens. We must vote. Write letters. Even protest. But the CHURCH, the organized Body of Christ has a single mandate… to make disciples. When we get sidetracked with *anything* else, we cease being the Church and become just another non-profit organization. We've been protesting racial injustice since well before Martin Luther King, Jr. Things have changed…but only incrementally. Perhaps it's time for the Church to put Jesus' plan for global redemption onto the front burner…

> And that is why I teach evangelism, church growth, preaching, and pastoral leadership…because if we were faithful and effective at those four, the U.S. might not be rioting in the streets tonight.[404]

It is only to the Church to whom Christ has given this mission: "*You are a chosen race, a royal priesthood, a holy nation, God's own people, in order that you may proclaim the mighty acts of Him who called you out of darkness into His marvelous light*" (1 Peter 2:9 [NRSV]). Some translations use the terminology that we are a "*peculiar people*," because of our distinct purpose. But that is who we are, and when Christ bestowed that mission to "*Go therefore and make disciples of all nations*" (Matthew 28:19 [NRSV]), He did not leave us on our own nor powerless to accomplish what He has entrusted to us: "*Remember, I am with you always, to the end of the age.*"

Christianizing Christendom

We don't often connect "mission" and "reformation" together, and conceivably that has been an unacknowledged failure for the Church, especially for those believers who identify themselves with Luther's name. Luther could not entertain those concepts as being unconnected. He viewed every person as a helpless sinner in the eyes of God, and thus in need of hearing God's Word as Law and Gospel. The Law commands and requires us to do certain things. The Gospel shares the Good News of what God has done for us in His Son which inspires us to live fully in His justifying grace and forgiveness with renewed hearts, gratitude and purpose by loving the neighbor as we have been loved.

Even if we do not find our typical mission terminology in Luther's writings and sermons, we can find what Ingemar Oberg* came to call "mission universalism" in Luther's theology.[405] God's mission is to save the lost, and for that purpose He instituted the Church, enlisting it to believe, practice and preach the Gospel. That "Good News" of sinners being "found" by

---

[404] Tenny-Brittian, "When Protesting Doesn't Work."

* Ingemar Oberg, one of Scandinavia's foremost Luther scholars served as professor at the School of Mission and Theology, Stavanger, Norway and has written major works on Luther's theology of the keys and his hermeneutics. His groundbreaking book on Luther and World Mission provides an interpretation of a mission-minded servant of the Gospel who laid the foundation for an evangelical Lutheran theology of mission.

[405] Oberg, Ingemar, *Luther and World Mission: A Historical and Systematic Study with Special Reference to Luther's Bible Exposition*, translated by Dean Apel (St. Louis: Concordia, 2007). Oberg specifically points to Luther's interpretations of Matthew 6:10, 13, 22:1–4, and Luke 14:16–24.

God's mercy, forgiveness, love, and acceptance is proclaimed not only from the Church's pulpits but is lent credibility through Christians' witness, as they put into real-life practice what they've "heard" and believe by fulfilling their human callings or vocations.

In his announcement from the lavish Trump Tower on Fifth Avenue in New York, on June 16, 2015, Donald J. Trump declared "I am officially running for President of the United States, and we are going to make our country great again! …Sadly the American dream is dead, but if I get elected president I will bring it back bigger and better and stronger than ever before."[406] He laid out a vision to match his incoming campaign slogan, "Make America Great Again." In his final debate with then Vice President Joe Biden, ahead of the November 3rd election, Trump said, "You know Joe, I ran because of you. I ran because of Barack Obama, because you [as a team] did a poor job. If I thought you did a good job, I would have never run."[407]

The future President sensed a decline and foresaw further threats on the horizon to the constitutional values that had made our democratic republic great, and perceived his mission as one that could work to correct the country's downward trajectory by restoring that "beacon of hope," especially for its forgotten citizens and for the world. He was obviously echoing Ronald Reagan's farewell address to the nation, in which the former President defined his vision of the country as being "the shining city upon a hill." The origin of that phrase is from Matthew 5:14-16 (NRSV): *"You are the light of the world. A city built on a hill cannot be hid…"* Earlier in his address, Reagan acknowledged his nickname of "The Great Communicator":

> I wasn't a great communicator, but I communicated great things, and they didn't spring full bloom from my brow, they came from the heart of a great nation—from our experience, our wisdom, and our belief in the principles that have guided us for two centuries. …[F]or me it always seemed more like the great rediscovery…of our values and our common sense.[408]

Both our reform leaders possessed the gift of penetrating vision into the temper of their day, and the urgent need for course correction, beginning with the most pressing

---

406 Trump, Donald, "2016 Announcement," <https://www.cnn.com/2015/06/16/politics/donald-trump-2016-announcement-elections/index.html>.

407 <https://www.boston.com/news/politics/2020/10/23/trump-tells-biden-he-sought-presidency-because-you-did-a-poor-job>.

408 <https://ourlostfounding.com/ronald-reagan-and-the-shining-city-upon-a-hill>.

deficiencies they identified and then guided by the perceptive insights and wisdom they drew from going back to the original sources, which have formed our faith for Martin Luther and our democracy for Donald Trump.

For Luther, as we know, reform revolved around schemes of human merit, promoted by the Church and reinforced by superstition in its various forms, which ignored God's free gift of grace within Medieval Christendom. For Trump it meant returning government to the people, from the bottom-up, not from the top-down, and restoring greatness to the country.

Following his visitations to the parishes in 1528, Luther was appalled by the dire state of Christianity he encountered in Germany. In his assessment, Christians had constructed their faith "on their own way of life, devotion, and good intentions and did not know anything about Christ. That sort of room was just equipped for the devil, and he could gleefully upset it and throw it all into a heap."[409] Luther knew well that human focus on merits and rewards induces a sense of self-righteousness which dethrones God in the human heart and replaces Him with a human imposter. Earlier he surmised that "at present we are almost completely pagan and only Christian in name"[410] with the emphasis being on works of righteousness, which he attacked. This seemingly omnipresent focus on human merits led him to exclaim:

> in our day this life [i.e., true Christian life] is unknown throughout the world; it is neither preached about nor sought after; we are altogether ignorant of our own name and do not know why we are Christians or bear the name of Christians. Surely, we are named after Christ, not because He is absent from us, but because He dwells in us, that is, because we believe in Him and are *Christs* one to another and do to our neighbors as Christ does to us. But *in our day, we are taught by the doctrine of men to seek nothing but merits, rewards, and the things that are ours; of Christ we have made only a taskmaster far harsher than Moses.*[411]

Both Luther's "missionary" zeal and agenda were heightened by his Saxon visitation experience. The subsequent *Catechisms* were a direct response to reset and clarify the evangelical message of the Gospel. He desperately desired to effect spiritual renewal by "reChristianizing" a population that supposedly presumed to be Christian but had grown

[409] LW 21:283.*The Sermon on the Mount*, "The Seventh Chapter."

[410] LW 36:264. *Word and Sacrament II*, "Receiving Both Kinds in the Sacrament" (1522).

[411] LW 31:368. *Career of the Reformer I*, "The Freedom of a Christian," (emphasis added). Also, *Three Treatises*, p. 305.

ungodly and idolatrous. Adding to his sense of urgency, Luther believed he was living in the final days before the imminent apocalyptic closure of history. Therefore, it was crucial that "real Christians" be provided resources to live in repentance, ever renewed as they grow in faith, hope and a new life of love, whereby they could become "Christs" one to another and in their service and witness to their neighbor. Reformation pamphlets, Christian art and woodcut engravings, Luther's evangelical catechesis and postils (devotional homilies), commentaries on the Scriptures and prayers all became useful and effective missionary tools to nurture and strengthen believers to refocus from their efforts to obtain God's grace to gratefully receiving the free gift of faith in their loving response of joyful service and witness to others.

Christianizing Earthdom, Including Heathendom

As we will discover, Luther's central focus was on the Word, and the Bible was foundational in his theological reflections. He realized that the Bible was an instruction manual for life (**BIBLE** capable of being an acronym for **B**asic **I**nformation **B**efore **L**eaving **E**arth), as well as a missionary book beginning in Genesis, especially with that champion of faith, Abraham, who Luther identifies as being a "missionary bishop." Abraham erected an altar "in order to perform his duty as bishop; that is, he instructs his church concerning the will of God, admonishes them to lead a holy life, strengthens them in their faith, fortifies their hope of future blessing, and prays with them."[412] In a sermon on Genesis 12:14-16, Luther even interprets the wandering of the people of God from one place to another not just as a means to prove their faith, but also in light of the missionary purpose of God "so that they may benefit other people." He argues that "Abraham certainly could not remain silent…*it would be insufferable for someone to associate with people and not reveal what is useful for the salvation of their souls.*"[413]

Michal Valco, Professor of Theology and Religious Studies and Lutheran Theological faculty member at Comenius University in Bratislava, Slovakia, declares that

> The strong emphasis in that sentence is impossible to overlook. Luther cannot imagine that those who know the treasure of salvation would not

[412] LW 2:286. *Lectures on Genesis, Chapters 6-14*, "Chapter 12."

[413] WA 24:261, 26:262,1. *Sermons on the First Book of Moses (1523-1524)*. English translation cited from *The Church Comes from All Nations: Luther Texts on Mission*, edited by Volker Stolle, translated by Klaus Detlev Schulz and Daniel Thies (St. Louis: Concordia, 2003), p.16 (emphasis added).

> reveal it to others—it would be "insufferable" to them. Luther goes even further when he claims that one cannot be a genuine Christian without having this burning desire to share the saving Word of God with others and enacting this inner urge in real life.[414]

Valco reminds us of writings and sermons where Luther asserts that there is no doubt that Mary and Joseph could have remained silent about their miracle Child as they preached and brought others to faith and salvation in Egypt, just as the Wise Men did in returning to their land as they taught their people about the Child, and the Ethiopian eunuch likewise who had an encounter with Philip.

It would be accurate to assert that Luther wished other people to experience what he had experienced when the liberating Gospel of undeserved grace was imparted to him through the power of God's Word. He understood clearly that he was being commanded by God to *"proclaim the mighty acts of Him who called [me] out of darkness into His marvelous light"* (1 Peter 2:9 NRSV). In a private letter to Philip Melanchthon while Luther was at the Wartburg Castle, Luther's desire to spread the Gospel is evidenced early on in his reforming efforts:

> For goodness' sake, *do you want the King of God to be proclaimed only in your town? Don't others also need the Gospel?* Will your Antioch not release a Silas or a Paul or a Barnabas for some other work of the Spirit? I tell you: although I would be very happy to be with you all, yet I would not be disturbed if the Lord deigned to open to me a door for the Word either at Erfurt or Cologne or anywhere else, since you already have a surplus [of preachers and teachers]. Look how big a harvest there is everywhere—and how few are the harvesters! You all are harvesters. Certainly, we have to consider not ourselves but our brethren who are spread out all over the country, lest we live for ourselves, that is, for the devil and not for Christ.[415]

In Luther's understanding, every "real Christian" lives on mission for the sake of proclamation and has the duty of giving a missionary witness by willingly participating in

---

[414] Valco, Michal, "Martin Luther's Views on Mission and Christianization," *Oxford Research Encyclopedia of Religion* (Oxford, UK: Oxford University Press, 2016), p.3. See also Stolle, *The Church Comes from All Nations*, pp.18 and 19 with specific reference to the African treasurer's conversion Luther mentions in "On the Institution of the Ministry of the Church (1523)," WA 12:192, 15:23.

[415] LW 48:262. *Letters I*, "To Philip Melanchthon, Wartburg, July 13, 1521," (Italics added).

that movement of the Spirit that began with the Apostles and continues until Judgment Day. Pointing to Christ's promise that the Gospel would be preached in all the earth before the end comes, and believing that he was living shortly before the final Apocalypse, Luther's missionary zeal extended to Jews, whom he was convinced could be converted, and to Turks, though he found it unlikely that they might come to faith in Christ, though he wanted to leave the door open. Then in his commentary on that short Psalm 117, Luther addresses the need to witness to the heathen.

> the Psalmist prophesies and proclaims the great work and wonder of God, namely, the Gospel and the Kingdom of Christ, which was foretold but not yet revealed at that time, and says: "Praise the Lord, all heathen!" This is the same as saying that God is not only the God of the Jews but the God of the heathen also, and not only of a small part of heathendom but of all heathen throughout the world. For to speak of "all heathen" is to exclude none. Thus *we* heathen are assured that *we*, too, belong to God and in heaven, and that *we* shall not be damned, even though *we* are not of Abraham's flesh and blood as the Jews boast...but the distinction of being God's children and heirs of His kingdom of heaven is not theirs alone. This Psalm sings and proclaims that *we* heathen also have the same distinction.
>
> Now if all heathen are to praise God, this assumes that He has become their God. If He is to be their God, then they must know Him, believe in Him, and give up all idolatry...if they are to believe, they must first hear His Word and thereby receive the Holy Spirit.... One cannot come to faith or lay hold on the Holy Spirit without hearing the Word first, as St. Paul has said (Romans 10:14).... If they are to hear His Word, then preachers must be sent to proclaim God's Word to them...[416]

Throughout all places on earth and among all nations, Luther affirms people have a hunger for God, so that those who have lived in darkness hear the message of light, their hearts become stirred, and they are then attracted to the emerging "Church of God" already in the Old Testament. We see this in the witness of Abraham, Jacob, Joseph, Daniel and Jonah, which prompts Luther to claim

---

[416] LW 14:8-9. *Selected Psalms III*, "Psalm 117."

> I have often stated that it is quite credible that when the patriarchs were teaching, many of its heathen flocked to them, for they saw that the patriarchs were godly and holy men and that God was with them, and therefore they heard and embraced their doctrine…outsiders…who all undoubtedly heard the Word….Therefore God gathered a church in the world not only from one family of the patriarchs but from all nations to which the Word made its way.[417]

This is the very reason for the existence of the Church. God's mission has the Church—the children of God—to proclaim the Good News, and to be the physical presence of Christ's Body in the world until the End Times. The power of God's proclaimed Word produces not only a new life-view or true faith to those newly become believers, but also new life outcomes in all areas of life:

> Christianity, to Luther, has been the true religion of the world ever since the beginning of God's interaction with humans in the Garden of Eden. Based on Luther's understanding of Biblical promises, all other religions or philosophies are to a greater or lesser degree deviations from this one, original, true religion…. In his exposition of the prophet Zechariah (1527), Luther expressed his conviction that before the end came, the Spirit of God would bring all scattered Christians into one true faith through the ministry of evangelical preachers.[418]

Luther acknowledges that the "living voice of God," the preached Word, is the Spirit's main tool of evoking faith and a good conscience in the inner being of the hearer. Isaiah (55:11) promised that God's Word *"shall not return empty but it shall accomplishes that which He purposes,"* and St. Paul asserts that *"faith comes from hearing"* (Romans 10:17). Luther writes:

---

[417] Stolle, Volker, ed., *The Church Comes from All Nations: Luther Texts on Mission,* translated by Klaus Detlev Schulz and Daniel Thies (St. Louis: Concordia, 2003), p.17, citing Martin Luther "Lectures on Genesis" (1523), LW 6:227 or WA 44:168.14-19.

[418] Valco, "Views on Mission," p.4, citing LW 20:296, *Minor Prophets III Zechariah, Luther's Lectures on Zechariah 1527,* "Chapter Nine" (vs. 16).

> the world has always been full of idolatry, factions, and error, so that even the Romans, the cleverest and mightiest of all, had more than a hundred gods.* The world is divided into countless errors, and yet this Psalm (117) dares include these thoughts and boldly declare that all such factions and idolatries must cease, and that all the heathen must turn to one faith and praise and honor one God. Through the Word of God there is to come out of such a variety of worship one harmonious flock under one Shepherd (John 10:16). It is truly wonderful that a human heart can dare conceive of this, believe in it, and firmly prophesy that it will happen, especially when one considers how hard the devil will oppose, resist, and block it with all the power and wisdom of this world, so that it would seem to be a sheer impossibility. Nevertheless, the Psalmist has the courage to say it, and in spite of all of it has come to pass. Both are great miracles: that a man should believe this, and that it should actually happen.[419]

In "A Simple Way to Pray," Luther writes about the first petition of the Lord's Prayer, "*Hallowed be Thy Name,*" (Matt. 6:9 [RSV]), saying that the Lord God's name should be "hallowed" throughout the world. The mission is clear: Go to all people and share the Good News of Jesus Christ and bring them into fellowship with other Christians and teach them about the love and forgiveness Jesus has for them. Then he prays:

> Dear Lord God, convert those who are still to be converted that they with us and we with them may hallow and praise Thy Name, both with true and pure doctrine and with a good and holy life. Restrain those who are unwilling to be converted so that they be forced to cease from misusing, defiling, and dishonoring Thy holy Name and from misleading the poor people. Amen.[420]

---

* The editors of LW suggest that the source of this information may be Augustine, *The City of God,* III ch. 12, and reference Luther's exposition of Psalm 118 (LW 14:70) where Luther says, "The Romans could bear their several hundred gods; only Christ they could not tolerate."

[419] LW 14:10. Selected Psalms III, "Preface to Psalm 117."

[420] Martin Luther, *Devotional Writings II,* "A Simple Way to Pray, 1535;" LW 43:195.

For Luther and the Augsburg Confession, it's all about the Gospel—"*evangelisch*"—says Edward H. Schroeder,* as opposed to "other" gospels that were threatening to supplant the genuine one, even in the very first generation of Christ-confessors.

> Martin Luther's thesis about missions—if he had one—would be this: "A mission field is anywhere that other gospels are being proclaimed and trusted. Therefore, Luther's mission field was the Church and the world.... [He asks] Is our day any different? Where are "other gospels" to be found in our day? As much inside our churches as out there in the "secular" world. Not much different from what was confessed in Augsburg on June 25, 1530.[421]

This Scriptural witness and Luther's understanding of the Church's Christianizing purpose didn't seem to inform our Evangelical Lutheran Church in America when it issued its Declaration of Inter-Religious Commitment (DIRC), cautioning the Church to be careful about claiming to know God's judgments regarding another religion, as we will soon further consider. Perhaps this reflects our lack of connecting The Reformation with the concept of mission, and our reluctance or timidity in sharing the "treasure of our salvation" with others, even though we speak of being "evangelical" much as Luther discovered his German brothers and sisters considered themselves "Christian." That possibility would surely explain why we would not likely consider Luther as the first theologian of the Reformation to compose a "missionary" hymn. Entitled "May God Bestow on Us His Grace" ("*Es woll' uns Gott genadig sein*"), the hymn is based on Psalm 67:

> *May God bestow on us His grace, With blessings rich provide us;*
> *And may the brightness of His face To life eternal guide us,*
> *That we His gracious work may know, and what is His good pleasure,*
> *And to the unbelieving show Christ's riches without measure,*
> *And unto God convert them.*

---

* Edward H. Schroeder was educated at Valparaiso University and the University of Hamburg. He taught theology at Valparaiso University, Concordia Seminary, Seminex, and seminaries in Australia, Ethiopia and Lithuania, in numerous seminars and through a ten-year email ministry, The Crossings Community.

421 Schroeder, Edward H., "Lutheranism's Crying Need: A Mission Theology for the 21st Century." <https://crossings.org/lutheranisms-crying-need>.

To You shall be the highest praise And thanks of ev'ry nation,
And all the world with joy shall raise The song of exultation.
For You will judge the earth, O Lord, Nor suffer sin to flourish;
Your people's pasture is Your Word, Their souls to feed and nourish,
In righteous paths to keep them.

Oh, let the people praise Your worth, In all good works increasing;
The land shall plenteous fruit bring forth; Your Word is rich in blessing.
May God, the Father, and the Son And Holy Spirit, bless us;
Let all the world praise Him alone, Let solemn awe possess us.
Now let our hearts say, "Amen."[422]

Michal Valco submits,

> An acute sense of apocalyptic urgency stimulated in Luther not only a highly focused, disciplined, courageous stance and action, and a strong prophetic self-perception, but also impatience with his opponents, which resulted in some inexcusable statements against Peasants, Jews, "papists," Anabaptist, and other dissenting groups of his time.... Any dissenting view on a subject that Luther held important was perceived by him as being inspired by a "different spirit" (i.e., an evil spirit).[423]

With the use of polemic language and hyperbole, Luther would frame those dissenters as opponents of the Gospel, and therefore in the service of the Antichrist. Indeed, his black-and-white rendering of the world could be partially "colored" by his eschatological impatience, but also must be viewed through the lens of his missionary zeal "to keeping the Gospel afloat in the world's last ravaged hour."[424]

---

422 Martin Luther, "May God Bestow on Us His Grace," (LBW Hymn 335; LSB Hymn 823; LW Hymn 288).
423 Valco, "Views on Mission," p.2.
424 Oberman, Heiko, *The Roots of Anti-Semitism in the Age of Renaissance and Reformation*, translated by J.I. Porter (Philadelphia: Fortress, 1984), p.122.

Luther's Felt Urgency Comically Portrayed

<http://janevoigts.com/blog/2014/10/24/luther-laughter>

Luther liked to refer to his bathroom as the "tower room" which served as his alternative "office" or "study" where he found solace from distress, both physically and spiritually. Although they didn't have "tp" in his day, he found "suitable" substitutes as we will discover. This photo however, fits with the urgency he "felt" living in the end of time and thus the limited season he and the Church had to share the "Good News." Jane Voigts concludes her article on the "Humor of Luther" exclaiming, "I can hear Luther and his wife singing it now...'You say scatological, I say escatological....'"

Luther clearly saw himself as the Christ-appointed head of a new missionary movement within Christendom and, as he came to believe, the last one in his lifetime just shortly before the apocalyptic end of times that would center on his beloved Germany. Like God's spokespersons of old, Luther did not hesitate to prophetically call his countrymen to "make use of God's grace and Word while it is there," for as he saw it,

> If we let it slip by without thanks and honor, I fear we shall suffer a still more dreadful darkness and plague. O my beloved Germans, buy while the market is at your door; gather in the harvest while there is sunshine and fair weather; make use of God's grace and Word while it is there! For you should know that God's Word and grace is like a passing shower of rain which does not return where it has once been. It has been with the Jews, but when it's gone it's gone, and now they have nothing. Paul brought it to the Greeks; but again,

> when it's gone its gone, and now they have the Turk.* Rome and the Latins also had it; but when it's gone it's gone, and now they have the pope. And you Germans need not think that you will have it forever, for ingratitude and contempt will not make it stay. Therefore, seize it and hold it fast, whoever can; for lazy hands are bound to have a lean year.[425]

Urging his people to "seize *it* and hold *it* fast, whoever can" certainly expresses a sense of urgency, but also draws attention to the sobering realization that not everyone *can* or *will.* He therefore reminded his parishioners in a 1523 sermon on John 10:12 that the Gospel must continue to be preached, even unto the end of the world, giving opportunity to all—those who are nominal Christians in name only, as well as to the heathen—to grasp the treasure of salvation before it is too late and the opportunity passes. Thus, both aspects of the mission—the effort to deepen the faith of Christians, and the challenge to reach out to people of other faiths or no faith—were part of Luther's understanding of his role in spreading the one true Gospel found in Jesus Christ. Luther's sincere conviction that he was living in the End Times, the final stage before the imminent apocalyptic closure of history helps to explain the urgency he felt in fulfilling his God-given mission. Likewise the newly reChristianized evangelical Church needed to use all its resources for the sake of the faithful proclamation of Gospel. The gravity of the limited time with his commitment and compassion for saving souls obviously affected why he could be so vulgar and dismissive of differing views. We see this played out time and time again in his excessive polemic against the peasants, the Jews, and the papacy.

"American exceptionalism" has long been a staple of American foreign policy and presidential speeches but considering the more recent history of long-term foreign entanglements with the cost of American blood and treasury, doubt and disillusionment has set in about the nation's role in being the guarantor of global peace and security. When Donald Trump spoke of a "glorious destiny" for the country in his Inaugural Address on January 20, 2017, he was not suggesting America as a "chosen nation" whose destiny is to preach democracy to others by embarking on another worldwide crusade. His desire was to revitalize the domestic economy and to deliver for the "forgotten men and women" with

---

* From the conquest of Syria beginning in 635 until the fall of Constantinople in 1453, the Byzantines were constantly pressed by Islam, and the Greek Church gradually lost its best territories to the Turks.

[425] LW 45:352-353 (WA 47:565-566). *The Christian in Society II*, "To the Councilmen of All Cities in Germany that They Establish and Maintain Christian Schools." LW 45:352-353 (WA 47:565-566).

whom he identified, and who in turn swept him into office. In like manner, his idea of an America "winning again" was a clarion call to bring back jobs and economic growth, not the spoils of war, nor was it a summons for the exporting of American liberty and democracy. With this focus, President Trump exclaimed, America would "shine as an example…for everyone to follow."[426]

For Trump, America's uniqueness lies in its origins, not in the prevailing winds of globalization with the goal of ushering in a "New World Order." The need for our country, according to Trump, is a return to our founding principles. In his mind, an appreciation for the titans who wrote the Declaration of Independence and the Constitution is essential to a fresh era of national greatness, which can provide a shining example of people taking ownership of their future. Consistent with that view, he called for a "great reawakening of nations, for the revival of their spirit, their pride…and their patriotism"[427] in his address to the General Assembly of the United Nations on September 19, 2017. He spoke of nations that are rooted in their histories and has repeatedly made the connection between culture, sovereignty, nationhood, sacrifice, and respect for the past.

Former Washington bureau chief for *The Economist* David Rennie observes, "Countries are made unhappy by idiotic liberal internationalists…countries are like families, and they are happiest when they look after their own."[428] James Curran, a Fellow at the Lowy Institute and Professor of History at the University of Sydney, Australia, points to how Trump

> elevates the founding documents, especially the U.S. Constitution with its invocation of "*We the People*", as "America's source of strength." Such sentiments are repeated in the 2017 National Security Strategy, which likewise invokes the intellectual heroes of the revolution: Thomas Jefferson's writing of the Declaration of Independence and Alexander Hamilton's observation from New York in April 1784 that the "influence of our example has penetrated the gloomy regions of despotism."[429]

---

[426] Trump, Donald, "Inaugural Address January 20, 2017." <https://www.politico.com/story/2017/01/full-text-donald-trump-inauguration-speech-transcript-233907>.

[427] Trump, Donald, "Remarks by President Trump to the 72nd Session of the United Nations Assembly," September 19, 2017. <https://www.whitehouse.gov/briefings-Statements/remarks-president-trump-72nd-session-united-nations-general-assembly>.

[428] Interview with David Rennie, Washington DC, September 27, 2017, quoted in James Curran's "'Americanism, not Globalism,' President Trump and the American Mission," The Lowy Institute, July 2018.

[429] Curran, James, "'Americanism, not Globalism,'" quoting from *The National Security Strategy of the United States of America*, 1:37.

For Trump, these founding documents and statements show that America leads by example, as the introduction to the National Security Strategy affirms:

> Our founding principles have made the United States of America among the greatest forces for good in history. But we are also aware that we must protect and build upon our accomplishments, always conscious of the fact that the interests of the American people constitute our true North Star.[430]

We should note that the classical ideal of a republic held by the founders is one in which the origin and authority of government should come from the people. The Strategy's conclusion reiterates the conviction that "America's renewed strategic confidence is anchored in [its] recommitment to the principles inscribed in [its] founding documents."[431] Returning to these founding ideals and traditional values undergirds the impetus for Trump's mission to "Make America Great Again."

Addressing his first joint session of Congress, President Trump acknowledged that he had inherited many problems domestically and overseas, and then began to outline what he believed needed to be addressed: job creation by restarting the engines of the American economy; slashing corporate taxes and regulations; reevaluation of America's policies related to international trade; overhauling the immigration system; increasing defense spending to strengthen our national security; and "draining the swamp." These were major components of his "America First" vision. He concluded his address by

> asking all citizens to embrace this renewal of the American spirit. I am asking all members of Congress to join me in dreaming big, and bold, and daring things for our country. And I am asking everyone watching tonight to seize this moment and—believe in yourselves. Believe in your future. And believe, once more, in America.[432]

Trump's concluding words at the rallies he has held throughout the nation summarizes his intent and has provided guidance, direction and coherency to his presidency: "Because we are Americans and our hearts bleed red, white, and blue. We are one people. We are one family. And we are one glorious nation under God. And together we will make America

---

[430] Ibid.

[431] Ibid., p.2.

[432] Trump, <https://www.businessinsider.com/trump-State-of-the-union-2017-2>.

wealthy again. We will make America strong again. We will make America safe again. And we will 'Make America Great Again!'"[433]

Both reform warriors have held the same basic ordering in their mission priorities, preceding from local to global goals. Our Wittenberg Biblical scholar followed Scripture's directive of beginning locally then globally, which we will again encounter, especially with living in the midst of a pandemic. The first priority centered on the home and the nuclear family; followed by the family of God, the local congregation; the local community in which one lived, specifically the "neighbor;" then wider into the regions of Germany; and then beyond, globally "to the ends of the earth" (Acts 1:8). For the 45th President, it was "We the People" and "America First" before international concerns, unless those concerns were a threat to the homeland and its citizens. Both, as we have witnessed previously, tapped into real and visceral feelings of people who felt neglected by the entrenched elite, who assumed they were smarter and more virtuous than the people, and neither was hesitant in reaching back to draw their values from the sources upon which the Church and Nation were founded.

Guiding Political Decisions and Influence

Today we observe Christians who make no separation between religious convictions and secular politics, and others who simply see no relation between their faith and their political life. For the latter, Sunday does not connect with Monday. These sectarian Christians believe religion should remain a private hobby, and thus confuse the separation of Church and State with the separation of Church and politics. Yet historically we discover many religious individuals and groups expressing their political will, from the American Revolution to anti-slavery, Prohibition, civil rights and the pro-life movement. The First Amendment in our Constitution guarantees not only freedom of speech, the freedom to assemble, and the freedom to worship, but also its "free exercise," which most assuredly includes the political expression of religiously based moral values. As we will discover in Luther's doctrine of the Two Kingdoms, Christians are called to be good citizens by their conscientious participation in the political process, by holding their government accountable to God's law, and by their obedience to civic officials. Separation of religion and politics is not possible.

I have never favored nor advocated a straight-line vote for candidates based on a specific party, policy, or issue, any more than on a single characteristic such as appearance (i.e. gender or race) or personality trait. Any candidate is far more complex and, might I say, even

---

433 Trump, <https://www.tampabay.com/florida-politics/buzz/2018/08/01/heres-a-full-transcript-of-president-trumps-speech-from-his-tampa-rally>.

contradictory in their views at any particular time, and perhaps even hopefully so, because they have the integrity to act on being enlightened or persuaded by new information or circumstances. Robert Benne,* Professor Emeritus of Religion at Roanoke College in Salem, Virginia, offers sound advice to the Church, especially in light of the political challenges we face as a people today:

> A case for serious Christian resistance to a candidate or program can be called for, I believe, only when there is a direct and systematic denial of the principles and processes of our constitutional democracy, which would of course include the Amendments to the Constitution. Further, its ideology would have to be thoroughly anti-Christian: racist, xenophobic, warlike, brutal messianic…in short, idolatrous. Such characteristics are not always obvious; dangerous movements often clothe their appeal in rhetoric familiar and attractive to the ordinary populace. Let us hope and pray that we as American Christians can recognize such dangers when they do arise, but yet have enough wisdom not to "cry wolf" when we merely disagree strongly with a legitimate candidate or program.[434]

Benne believes if the Church is really the Church, those formed by its Gospel message will possess core convictions that will guide their political decisions and find indirect ways to influence political life:

> Serious lay persons will be committed to the dignity and value of each person created in the image of God, and they will prize just behavior and policies based on that fundamental Christian commitment. A vibrant Church will produce laity who will take those values into the public sphere; it may even produce politicians with such convictions. The Church can also enable its laity to "critically participate" in the political process by teaching the Lutheran doctrine of vocation: that we are called to be good citizens thinking through

---

* Robert Benne was Professor of Church and Society at the Lutheran School of Theology at Chicago before going to Roanoke, and is the author of twelve books. Upon his retirement in 2012, Roanoke College renamed the center which he directed for thirty years in his honor as The Robert D. Benne Center for Religion and Society.

[434] Benne, Robert, "Lutherans and the Political Challenges of 2016," *Journal of Lutheran Ethics*, 10/01/16, p.6. <https://www.elca.org/JLE/Articles/1181>.

> and acting out our core Christian convictions in the public realm. It can even help Christians make Sunday-Monday connections by discussing political issues in the light of Christian teaching in its adult forums, though it must be open to differing Christian trajectories from core to policy. Pastors can preach sermons emphasizing how the Gospel leads to core moral convictions and how those relate first to private Christian behavior and then to political issues of the day...[435]

Like Bill Tenny-Brittian, Benne cautions the Church against attempting to employ direct ways to influence political life through social statements, pronouncements, Papal Encyclicals and Bishops' letters, as if to be the "social conscience" of society. One major reason he cites for their modest effect, as Tenny-Brittian has also pointed out, is their frequency from too many sources that contradict each other:

> Another reason is they seem to be fused with the political predilections of the agencies and leaders who make them, which robs them of any religious authority [as we have pointed to with the ELCA's "Sanctuary Denomination" pronouncement]. A wise Church makes such public statements rarely and on the most serious of issues. And then it is better to call attention to those issues than to opt for specific policies to address them. The most noble examples of this "social conscience" approach have historically occurred when the Church simply says, "No" to a wicked public policy or program, especially when no one else in society is raising an alarm.[436]

Fusing the Christian faith with a particular political figure or program has proven to be disastrous in the history of Christianity. From the Holy Roman Empire to the horrid attempt of "German Christians" to fuse Christianity to the Nazi movement, we have witnessed attempts to religionize politics and politicize religion. This "blurring process" Luther understood as dangerous to both realms, since it turns the Gospel into the Law and the Law into the Gospel. We are, in my view, experiencing the Church today attempting to turn the Gospel into a partisan political instrument by many well-intentioned Christians. However, politics never saves. Only Christ can save. Politicizing the Church's message destroys the transcendent character of the Gospel, by merging it with mundane and partisan human

[435] Ibid.

[436] Ibid., p.7.

actions that become our "works." Benne concludes by making an astute observation and a prophetic view we need to hear:

> It may be a melancholy truth that the combination of high affluence and unfettered human freedom leads to the deterioration of the cultural values of a society. I believe we are in that process now. We are perhaps getting the politics we deserve. Orthodox Christianity is now counter-cultural; it is being whittled down to a disciplined community of faith that can again be salt and leaven. What an opportunity for the Church to renew a society at its roots, not by political agitation but by the proclamation of the Gospel. Then moral regeneration and political health will follow.[437]

Certainly, our self-interest is a legitimate concern in political life; but for the Christian, and especially for Luther, it can never be so narrow as to forget our care and concern for "neighbor love." Self-interest must be tempered and even expanded by Christian values. Christian norms of love and justice must transcend any candidate, political figure, party, or program. By our human nature alone, however, the self becomes primary in all occasions and decisions.

The "Old Adam" is Alive and Well in the Subjective Self

Captain Russell Graef,* writing in the *Lutheran Forum* journal, points to the prevailing "hermeneutic of subjectivity" he sees in the Church, as it willingly gives priority to the subjective self over affirming beliefs like creeds, confessions and even Scripture. In his critique of the ELCA's adoption of "A Declaration of Inter-Religious Commitment (DIRC)" to guide our denomination's relationships to people of other faiths, he writes: "By giving priority to these individuals' subjective experience, the ELCA has established a canon within the canon. The Bible, creeds, and confessions retain authority insofar as they align with the subjective experience of individuals. They surrender authority when they fail that test."[438] While the institution may thus avoid appearing authoritarian, such comfort comes

---

[437] Ibid., p.8.

* Captain Russell Graef retired in 2019 after twelve years of service in parish ministry and twenty-four years of service in the United States Navy Chaplain Corps.

[438] Graef, Russell, "The Subjective Self and the ELCA's Decline," *Lutheran Forum*, 54:2, Summer 2020, pp.55-56.

at a cost: "Eventually the subjective self will find the Church unnecessary in its quest for personal fulfillment."[439] In effect, the "subjective self" places oneself "in a protected zone where creeds, confessions, and Scripture are not allowed to intrude, thus they have immunity from critique or correction. Within such a protected zone, discussion about faith is not allowed to explore doctrinal Truth as it relates to life and faith."[440]

"The subjective self" is what St. Paul and Lutherans would call "the old Adam and Eve." Could this "woke" or "cancel culture" we are experiencing represent a real ideological crisis, a genuinely revolutionary moment? Or is it just a kind of digital-age playacting, in which young people dissatisfied with a past they don't really know, nor attempt to understand, pretend to be fascists and Marxists on the internet, reenacting the 1930s and '60s? "This phenomenon is also referred to as 'creative destruction'—destruction of the old ways to make way for the supposedly better ways. Ross Douthat referred to this movement as the decadent society."[441]

In Douthat's newest book, *The Decadent Society: How We Became the Victims of Our Own Success*, the *New York Times* opinion columnist senses a cultural and intellectual exhaustion, along with a world weariness brought about by various forces—economic stagnation, loss of trust in our government and institutions, technology, malaise within our cultural enterprises, and even biological through our low birth rate. That's our present predicament in a nutshell. We live in the midst of material plenty, but we're not really getting "richer." Art and literature were once innovative, creative and beautiful, but now seem to be just repetitive. Government appears to be broken and doesn't seem to work anymore for "we the people," but only for those with power who can maintain their control. The author's analysis of these forces leading to our "decadence" weighs various hypotheses that might explain us to ourselves.

Douthat is obviously searching for clarity that can bring an end to both optimistic pretense and hysteria. He worries that our predicament seems to be sustainable as he observes,

> 'What fascinates and terrifies us about the Roman Empire is not that it finally went smash,' wrote W.H. Auden of the last world empire in its endless autumn, but rather that 'it managed to last for four centuries without creativity, warmth, or hope.'

---

[439] Ibid., p.57.

[440] Ibid., pp.54-55.

[441] Clark, James A. (Rev. Dr.) of St. Martin Lutheran Church, Atlanta. <https://www.facebook.com/saintmartinlutheranchurcht/posts/403567127716339#_=_>.

> 'There was nothing left that could conquer Rome,' G. K. Chesterton wrote on the same theme, 'but there was also nothing left that could improve it.... It was the end of the world, and the worst of it was that it need never end.'
>
> Whether we are waiting for Christians or barbarians, a renaissance or the Singularity,* the dilemma that Auden and Chesterton described is now not Rome's but ours.[442]

I believe that we, the Church, are more inclined to allow the culture to set the agenda for the Church than focus on being the salt and light that is to "season" and "illuminate" the world by living on mission, as directed by our Lord. It is He who is the Light of the world, who compliments us by affirming we, the Church, His people, are called to be *"the light of world"* and let *"our light shine before others so that they [too] may see our good works and [respond by] giving glory to our Father in heaven"* (Matthew 5:14-16 [NRSV]). Unfortunately, as in our secular or political life, we in the Church are just as likely to "cave in"—to acquiesce—being merely a reflection of our society, and "go along for the ride" instead of confidently trusting the promise and be "re-Christianized"...or in Luther's terminology, become "real Christians," "true Christians," and thus the "true Christian Church."[443]

Amplifying Douthat's grim prophetic observation of our decadent society [with my emphasis], we sit or recline as

> we are aging, [materially] comfortable and stuck, cut off from the past, and no longer optimistic about the future, spurning both memory and ambition [while attempting to spur both with "supplements"] while we await some saving innovation or revelation, [revival, or re-awakening of the woke,] burrowing into cocoons [now intensified by Covid-19 lockdowns] from which no chrysalis is likely to emerge, growing old unhappily together in the glowing light of tiny screens."[444]

---

* The Technological Singularity—also, simply, the Singularity—is a hypothetical point in time at which technological growth becomes uncontrollable and irreversible, resulting in unforeseeable changes to human civilization.

[442] Douthat, Ross, *The Decadent Society: How We Became the Victims of Our Own Success* (New York: Avid Reader Press, 2020), p.13.

[443] See Martin Luther's usage of "evangelized" in LW 29:160; "real" in LW 21:15; and "true" in LW 22:197.

[444] Douthat, *Decadent*, p.13.

In an edifying sermon from 1531 based on 2 Corinthians 13:8 *("For we can do nothing against the Truth, but only for the Truth" [NRSV]),* Luther argues that there are those who oppose Christ outside as well as within the Church, notably the Pope and his princes. He also identified his evangelical opponents as fanatics and false prophets who were tools of the devil, trying to defeat the Gospel by attacks from the inside. In Luther's day, as well as our own, there were Christians who thought peace and unity are all that matter. Luther's reply in this sermon was that in matters of faith, we must be inflexible, unyielding and adamant. We should not give in to avoid creating waves, nor cower, nor be so intimidated that we overlook differences by going along to get along, thinking that is the way to

> preserve brotherly and Christian unity and fellowship. No, my dear man, do not recommend to me peace and unity when thereby God's Word is lost, for then eternal life and everything else would be lost. In this matter there can be no yielding nor giving way not for love of you or any other person, but everything must yield to the Word whether it be friend or foe. The Word was given to us for eternal life and not to further outward peace and unity. The Word and doctrine will create Christian unity or fellowship. Where they reign, all else will follow. Where they are not, no concord will ever abide. Therefore, do not talk to me about love and friendship, if that means breaking with the Word, or the faith, for the Gospel does not say that love brings eternal life, God's grace, and all heavenly treasures, but that these come from the Word.[445]

Patrick Henry in his famous "Give Me Liberty or Give Me Death" address to the House of Burgesses meeting in Richmond, Virginia, at St. John's Church on March 23, 1775, stated clearly and emphatically wisdom we, and especially our leaders in both Congress and the Church, need to hear, assimilate and heed:

> No man thinks more highly than I do of the patriotism, as well as abilities, of the very worthy gentlemen who have just addressed the House. But different men often see the same subject in different lights; and, therefore, I hope it will not be thought disrespectful to those gentlemen if, entertaining as I do opinions of a character very opposite to theirs, I shall speak forth my

[445] Martin Luther, *Day by Day We Magnify You: Daily Readings* (Minneapolis: Augsburg Books, 2008), p.379; also WA 34:II.387.

> sentiments freely and without reserve. This is no time for ceremony. The questing before the House is one of awful moment to this country. For my own part, I consider it as nothing less than a question of freedom or slavery; and in proportion to the magnitude of the subject ought to be the freedom of the debate. It is only in this way that we can hope to arrive at truth, and fulfill the great responsibility which we hold to God and our country. Should I keep back my opinions at such a time, through fear of giving offense, I should consider myself as guilty of treason towards my country, and of an act of disloyalty toward the Majesty of Heaven, which I revere above all earthly kings.
>
> Mr. President, it is natural to man to indulge in the illusions of hope. We are apt to shut our eyes against a painful truth, and listen to the song of that siren till she transforms us into beasts. Is this the part of wise men, engaged in a great and arduous struggle for liberty? Are we disposed to be of the number of those who, having eyes, see not, and, having ears, hear not, the things which so nearly concern their temporal salvation? For my part, whatever anguish of spirit it may cost, I am willing to know the whole truth; to know the worst, and to provide for it.[446]

Notice the discerning perspective Ed Stetzer* brings to the Church as he succinctly focuses on the active imperative our Lord has entrusted to us:

> Mission is rooted in the identity of God Himself. God is on a mission, and Jesus is the embodiment of that mission. He identifies Himself as being sent more than forty times in the Gospel of John. Then, near the end of the Gospel of John, He says, "*As the Father has sent me, I am sending you*" (John 20:21). The Church is sent on mission by Jesus. It's not that the Church has a mission, but rather that the mission has a Church. We join Jesus on His mission. A missional Church is one that seeks to engage all of the Church

---

[446] Henry, Patrick, "Give Me Liberty or Give Me Death." <http://hrlibrary.umn.edu/education/libertyordeath.html>.

* Ed Stetzer is a speaker, author of numerous books, and pastor of Grace Church in Hendersonville, Tennessee. He is also President of LifeWay Research, a contributing editor for *Christianity Today*, and a columnist for *Outreach* magazine. In addition, he teaches as a visiting professor of Research and Missiology at Trinity Evangelical Divinity School and at Southeastern Baptist Theological Seminary.

> in the activity God has for them—His mission. Our goal should be to move them from just sitting in rows to living in such a way that they are engaged in the work God has for them. That mission might be in, through, or beyond the Church, but it is ultimately rooted in obedience to Christ and obedience to His call.[447]

Church leaders don't have the freedom or the luxury other organizational leaders have—the freedom to whiteboard, discuss, and create a mission for their organizations. We already have our mission, as we are drawn into Christ. To be sure, we can state the mission in contextual language for our congregations and time, but the mission has already been given and it is clear and constant—every Christian is called to live on mission. If evangelism—the "Go" portion of the Great Commission (Matthew 28:19)—does not result in discipleship, it is not the evangelism that Jesus envisioned. We are to care for and teach those we reach, so they can grow and deepen their faith. And if discipleship—the helping believers "grow" portion of the Great Commission—does not result in more evangelism, then it is not really "teaching people to obey." Those we reach must also be sent out to impact their world. The end result of discipleship is not "teaching them everything" but "teaching them to obey everything." The mission has the Church to make disciples and teach them to obey all Jesus has commanded. Churches are to focus on both sides of the Great Commission, convinced that the two sides are inseparable.

Unchanging Mission

In *Unchanging Mission*, Douglas Webster's* monograph written in 1965, I discovered a memorable framework that has informed and "structured" my understanding of the Church's exclusive purpose. While historical situations alter ways and means of responding to questions and human needs, the essential mission of the Church never changes. Mission and the Gospel are the constants. Perhaps Ed Stetzer also read Douglas Webster, who begins his little treatise with the statement, "We begin, then, where mission begins, with God."[448]

---

[447] Stetzer, Ed, "God's Mission Has a Church: An Interview with Ed Stetzer." <https://www.ligonier.org/learn/articles/gods-mission-has-church>.

* Rev. Canon Douglas Webster served as Education Secretary for the Church Missionary Society from 1953-1961, and was Professor of Mission at Selly Oak Colleges, Birmingham, England.

[448] Webster, Douglas, *Unchanging Mission: Biblical and Contemporary* (Philadelphia: Fortress Press, 1965), p.1.

He treats the directional terms—down, up, out and in—in spiritual rather than in spatial dimensions. Action and response take place in pairs.

Mission is a movement of God's initiative and response between God and man. "The Downward Reach" embodied in the words of the Nicene Creed—"He came down from heaven"—creates "The Upward Lift" as the love of Christ transforms us and gives structure to mission by compelling the horizontal dimension of engagement between the Church and the world. "The Outward Thrust" from Christ propels us to invite and share that love we experience with others, so they too are drawn by "The Inward Pull" of Christ to Himself (John 12:32) to be His body and His instrument or agent in mission. It is thus through our words and actions as "little Christs" to our neighbors that they experience "The Downward Reach" of God's love personally as we have, and the movement of mission continues onward. St. Paul (in 2 Corinthians 5:20 [NRSV]) characterizes this privileged dynamic as being "*ambassadors for Christ since God is making His appeal through us*"—the Church! God's mission has the Church!

It is instructive to note that when these two pairs of prepositions are used theologically by Webster, their normal order is reversed. In worldly speech we usually say "up and down" and "in and out." But with God, things are often turned "upside down" and "inside out" to keep the focus away from ourselves and our "doing." Thus, the theological order becomes down and up, out and in. To illustrate, Webster explains:

> Mission is the operation in time and space through which the Savior of the world is drawing men—all men—to Himself. We should notice, perhaps with some surprise and discomfort, that the Church features in none of these sayings. Yet the Church is both His body and His chief instrument or agent in mission. But the drawing is *by* Himself and *to* himself, not by the Church or to the Church. The calling of the Church is to mediate Christ, not to obscure Him. There are occasions in the Gospel narratives when the disciples are depicted as coming between the Lord and the crowd in the wrong kind of way, as obstacles instead of mediators, keeping people away from Jesus instead of bringing them to Him..."[449]

In many respects, is not this happening within contemporary Christianity? How many people cannot see the greater light of Christ because of the lesser light of the Church in between, like a partial eclipse when the moon is between Earth and the sun, even

[449] Ibid., pp.55-56.

though the Church itself takes its light from the same source, as does the moon from the sun? However, mission, like ministry, is the reverse of status seeking; it always involves the surrender of status, as St. Paul taught in Philippians 2:5-7 NRSV: *"Let the same mind be in you that was in Christ Jesus, who though He was in the form of God, did not regard equality with God as something to be exploited, but emptied Himself, taking the form of a slave, being born in human likeness."*

Does this not also reflect the pattern witnessed within our own political realm, where identity politics, narcissism, political correctness, Fake News, hypocrisy, corruption, double standards, the ends justify the means, and lack of honesty and integrity hold sway over truth, qualifications, experience, objectivity, tolerance, honor, patriotism, constitutional law, authority and justice? Desire for power and control eclipse (or shall I say with pun intended—"trump") serving "We the People" for whom Luther and Trump championed. They had realized what a placard being waved at a rally I saw on the news said: "'We the People' have More Power than the People in Power."

More than a Namesake, We Are to Bear Fruit

Often in my mentioning of Martin Luther and the book I've been writing, individuals immediately fix their mind on Dr. Martin Luther King, Jr., unfamiliar with the earlier Martin Luther; and if they are by chance aware of the two "Martin Luthers," most are not cognizant of the connection between these two reformers. What they share is far greater than a name. The Senior Pastor of Ebenezer Baptist Church in Atlanta was born Michael King, and had a son born January 15, 1929, named after his father, Michael King, Jr. The congregation gifted their pastor with a trip to the Holy Lands and to Europe:

> In 1934, King's father traveled to Berlin to attend the Fifth Baptist World Alliance Congress. There, he and 29 other black ministers helped racially to integrate the Congress in the face of a "color ban." They also condemned the rising anti-Semitism they saw in Nazi Germany. (The Baptist Alliance responded to the hatred with a resolution deploring "all racial animosity, and every form of oppression or unfair discrimination toward Jews, toward coloured people, or toward subject races in any part of the world.')
>
> While in Berlin, Michael King Sr. (as he was then known) learned about Luther's denunciations against the injustices of the medieval penitential

system. Luther's struggle resonated with King, who wondered what such boldness might mean for racial injustice in the United States."[450]

He was also inspired by Luther's advocacy for non-violence unless "magistrates" were left no choice to maintain peace and order than by force, or the power of the sword granted to government by God. In short, Luther's legacy left such an impression on King that he changed his name to Martin Luther King, Sr. and the name of his then 5-year-old son to Martin Luther King, Jr. Name changes have long been a part of Biblical and religious history (most familiarly, Abram to Abraham, Simon to Peter, and Saul to Paul), often used to announce the existence of a "new person." Although King Sr. would go on to make his own courageous stand for social justice, his son's life and legacy was destined to more closely mirror that of the monk from Germany.

MARTIN LUTHER—AND MARTIN LUTHER KING, JR.

(Image: Cision News)

(Image: Public domain, retrieved at the "He Rice Tanned!" blog)

King Jr. centralized the cross of Christ as the particular revelation of God's love that empowers and guides social action. When He was arrested and unjustly tried, Christ did not respond with retaliation or passivity. Rather, He responded with self-giving nonviolent action. This redemptive pattern guided and empowered the entire nonviolence movement. Like Luther, who believed that the Gospel was not advanced through violence, King Jr. saw the cross which demonstrates love having the final say over injustice.

In my favorite Baptism/Easter hymn, "*We Know That Christ Is Raised*," we have what I believe is a great summary of Tenny-Brittian, King and the Wittenberg Reformer's understanding and concern about being who we are: a "new creation" privileged to share in

---

[450] Edmondson, Mika, "How the Protestant Reformation Led to Martin Luther King, Jr.," *The Washington Post*, Jan. 14, 2017.

the mission our Lord has entrusted to us, the Church, which is being "Christ's new Body" physically in our world today by *our* presence!

> *We know that Christ is raised and dies no more.*
> *Embraced by death He broke its fearful hold.,*
> *and our despair He turned to blazing joy. Hallelujah!*
>
> *We share by water in His saving death.*
> *Reborn, we share with Him an Easter life,*
> *As living members of our Savior Christ. Hallelujah!*
>
> *The Father's splendor clothes the Son with life.*
> *The Spirit's fission shakes the Church of God.*
> *Baptized, we live with God the Three in One. Hallelujah!*
>
> *A new creation comes to life and grows*
> *As Christ's new body takes on flesh and blood.*
> *The universe restored and whole will sing: Hallelujah!*[451]

In a sermon on the fifteenth chapter of St. John, Luther recalls the teaching of Christ to His disciples, which underscores and affirms the need to "be" who we are without shame or intimidation. Yet, do we not find ourselves bowing to the pressures of not speaking about politics or religion in public? We don't want to be characterized as either a "holy roller" or religious fanatic, or to be put down for expressing support for Trump and his "Make America Great Again" policies. The tendency, as we have noted, is to go along to get along. Here is Luther's conviction:

> Christ has said, "*I appointed you that you should go and bear fruit*" *[Jn 15:16]*. This is a repetition of what He had said earlier: "*You are My friends*" *[Jn 15:14]*,' that is, people who are chosen by Me and who receive everything good from Me. But this does not mean that you are to be idle, or that you may live as you like. It is true, you need to do nothing to receive forgiveness and eternal life. You have all this through Me. But just because it is yours, still you must demonstrate this outwardly through your love for your neighbor; your life must be a token of your faith in Me.... This is the meaning of the words "*that*

[451] Geyer, John B., "We Know That Christ Is Raised," (LBW Hymn 189; ELW Hymn 449; LSB Hymn 603).

> *you should go and bear fruit.*" *You* need not go to Rome or to Jerusalem, but you are to go to your neighbor. You are not to sit still without fruit and works, but you are to come into the open and let other people benefit from you and gain from your message, confession, service, and help. Thus, they can surely see that your fruit is genuine. For in the absence of faith you will certainly not risk, do, or suffer anything for the sake of the Gospel. But when a person is willing to risk life, goods, and honor for Christ's sake, is eager to bring all to the faith, serves his neighbor faithfully, treats him justly and brotherly—then you have a sure sign that such a person is a sincere and believing Christian.[452]

Professor Eric Gritsch writes,

> There is little debate about the fact that Luther's reformation was propelled by the power of the Word. He was, as Gerhard Ebeling put it, a "language event (Sprachereignis)."[453] Church and empire soon regarded this event as incendiary, rebellious, and treasonable. Luther's outburst against the ecclesiastical establishment before the Diet of Worms, his violent words against peasants and Jews, and the anti-papal obscenities of his final years made him *the* revolutionary of his age. His crudeness (*Grobianismus*) was...a means by which he exposed the roots of ecclesiastical and political satanism,[454]

much as Trump exercises his distinctively unique ability or intuition in drawing out his opponents. In so doing, he reveals their real motivations, and so often, unwittingly they let slip their hypocrisy and rage toward how the 45th President envisions the government's role in serving its citizens coupled with its mission in the world:

> Luther soon became identified with all those who plotted the overthrow of government to further their own interests! The German knights regarded him as the protector of "States' rights" against the imperial central government;

---

[452] Martin Luther, *Sermons on the Gospel of St. John Chapters 14-16*, "John 15:16," LW 24:262-3.

[453] Ebeling, Gerhard, *Luther: An Introduction to His Thought*, tr. R.A. Wilson (Philadelphia: Fortress Press, 1970), title of ch. 1, unfortunately rendered into English as "linguistic innovation."

[454] Gritsch, Eric W., "Martin Luther and Violence: A Reappraisal of a Neuralgic Theme," *The Sixteenth Century Journal*, Vol. 3, No. 1, Apr. 1972, pp. 40-41. <https://www.jstor.org/stable/pdf/2539903.pdf?seq=1>.

> many humanists saw in him the forerunner of a new age filled with peace and harmony after the status quo had first been overthrown by force; and peasants considered him the emancipator who would free them from the yoke of feudal slavery. Thus, the pope's and emperor's fears of imminent revolution in Europe seemed justified, in view of Luther's violent oratory. Luther's writings were banned; church officials accused him of heresy; he was finally excommunicated in a papal bull, and, condemned in an imperial edict. Bull and edict leave no doubt that Luther was considered the most dangerous man in Europe.[455]

Curiously, in the portrait of her uncle, clinical psychologist Mary L. Trump explores the family dynamics and life events she claims formed Trump, and draws the same conclusion about her uncle as others had about Luther. The title of her newly released book incorporates that descriptive term: *Too Much and Never Enough: How My Family Created the World's Most Dangerous Man.*[456]

There is no doubt that both Donald Trump and Martin Luther have been viewed as dangerous and revolutionary men in the eyes of the elite establishment and the Deep State, who are threatened by being exposed as those who view power and control as pre-eminent priorities over truth and service to others. For both our twins, I believe we witness a reminder that faith without action is dead, as the Apostle James (2:17 [NRSV]) affirms: "So *faith by itself, if it has no works, is dead,*" and action without love is idolatrous, as the Apostle Paul teaches in 1 Corinthians 13:1-3 (NRSV): *"If I...do not have love, I am nothing."* 1 John 3:18 (NRSV) combines both tenets *("...let us love, not in word or speech, but in truth and action")* when that "love" is sourced in God and personified in Christ. If our actions are not motivated by love, even if our outward conduct is immaculate, we are and have nothing. Our relationship with others flows out of our relationship with our Maker, and thus prepares us to love others rightly, in relation and submission to God who has enlisted us to be His missioners.

---

455 Ibid.

456 Trump, Mary L., *Too Much and Never Enough: How My Family Created the World's Most Dangerous Man,* (New York: Simon & Schuster, 2020).

16

From Revolting Peasants and Lawless Rioters To Illegal Immigrants

We have already observed the striking parallels between Luther's "Open Letter on the Harsh Book," which explains and defends his position on the Peasants' Rebellion, with Donald Trump's position on immigrants illegally entering our southern border, as he follows the prescribed laws enacted by Congress. It is ironic that Trump has been under attack by lawmakers who participated in drafting and supporting the laws the Trump administration was enforcing, and were proponents of strict border control reinforced with walls that they now oppose with hostility. The President has simultaneously attempted to work with Congress to close loopholes and make meaningful and relevant changes to our immigration laws. These contemporaneous concerns dealing with the revolting peasants and the illegal immigrants focus attention on one's understanding of the juxtaposition of Law and Gospel, the rightful roles of civil as well spiritual governance, and discerning the need for administering justice while concurrently demonstrating compassion.

Throughout history, the State has always possessed power over who it allows into its borders, and how immigrants and refugees become citizens. One does not discover an "inalienable right" to access a land or territory without following the procedures of the "host" country. Even as a tourist, I must possess a passport to enter a foreign country. In his inaugural address of January 20, 2017, Donald Trump reminded his fellow citizens that "We've defended other nations' borders while refusing to defend our own.... From this moment on, it's going to be 'America First.'"[457]

This is not the policy of an isolationist America, or the lifting up of narrow self-interest, but rather follows John Quincy Adams's view of presenting ourselves as an exemplary nation, in the manner of that sixth President of the United States in his address celebrating the Declaration of Independence on July 4, 1821.

> The interest which in this paper (The Declaration of Independence which he had just read) has survived the occasion upon which it was issued; the

[457] Trump, "Inaugural Address," <https://www.whitehouse.gov/briefings-Statements/the-inaugural-address>.

> interest which is of every age and every clime; the interest which quickens with the lapse of years, spreads as it grows old, and brightens as it recedes, is in the principles which it proclaims. It was the first solemn declaration by a nation of the only legitimate foundation of civil government. It was the cornerstone of a new fabric, destined to cover the surface of the globe.... It stands, and must forever stand alone, a beacon on the summit of the mountain, to which all the inhabitants of the earth may turn their eyes for a genial and saving light, till time shall be lost in eternity, and this globe itself dissolve..."[458]

President Trump, in his July 4th Salute to America in 2019, traced the truly extraordinary heritage of our

> great nation whose people have risked everything for what they know is right and what they know is true. It is the chronicle of brave citizens who never give up on the dream of a better and brighter future. [He went on to reference examples of that American spirit and rugged American character emboldened by ideals that] forever changed the course of humanity...and built this country into the most exceptional nation in the history of the world.... We will always be the people who defeated a tyrant, crossed a continent, harnessed science, took to the skies, and soared into the heavens.... We are one people, chasing one dream, and one magnificent destiny. We all share the same heroes, the same home, the same heart, and we are all made by the same Almighty God.[459]

In spite of the "oneness" patriotically saluted by citizens and by President Trump, who reminds us, "No matter the color of our skin, we all bleed the same red blood"[460] and the "oneness" in Christ professed by devout Christians and stated succinctly by St. Paul in Galatians 3:28 (NRSV) *("There is no longer Jew or Greek, there is no longer slave or*

---

[458] Adams, John Quincy, "Independence Day Speech," <https://teachingamericanhistory.org/library/document/speech-on-independence-day>.

[459] Trump, "July 4 Salute to America," <https://www.whitehouse.gov/briefings-Statements/remarks-president-trump-salute-america>.

[460] Trump closed his 100th day rally in Pennsylvania with this message of unity: <https://www.youtube.com/watch?v=xlyn7s99Vdw>.

free, there is no longer male and female; for all of you are one in Christ Jesus"), we discover profound differences on the issues confronting our society and culture. One of the most complex and hotly debated issues of our time, immigration, serves to illustrate the discord and fragmenting of our people in both civic and religious life.

The Biblical Perspective: God's Design for Borders and Boundaries

Scripture informs us that God "scattered" the people who chose to honor how great they were, instead of honoring "*How Great Thou Art.*" They built a tower celebrating their one-nation mentality, as recorded in Genesis 11:6-8. Here we have recorded God's reaction to the "empire builders" and their Tower of Babel, which signified the amassing of personal power. God "scatters" the people over the face of the whole earth in order that there be a diversity of nations with different languages, cultures and boundaries. This portrayal was to demonstrate God's way of counteracting man's fallen nature, which is inclined to accumulate and then misuse power. We're familiar with the axiom "Power corrupts, and absolute power corrupts absolutely." It was understanding that basic principle which informed the Founding Fathers in their establishing a government with checks and balances, and separation of powers. Luther likewise understood that human tendency to allow power and position to inflate one's self-perception and role by describing them as "haughty bigwigs" and "smart alecks…as though God [Himself] could not get along without them."[461]

If this is God's design for independent nations to exist, then of necessity there will be borders and boundaries, which over the course of history we have seen being violated by many would-be conquerors. With borders, however, it follows that enforcement becomes a primary responsibility of the State whose authority God has ordained, as St. Paul reinforces in Romans 13:1 (NRSV): *"Let every person be subject to the governing authorities; for there is no authority except from God, and those authorities that exist have been instituted by God."* God is not only the author of independent nations, but chooses to manifest His sovereignty through the governments of those nations, as we will further discover in Luther's understanding of the Two Kingdoms.

For me this Biblical insight clearly dispels the view that God would favor a "borderless" world or a "one nation" form of world governance, where we worship our own greatness

---

[461] LW 14:52-53. *Selected Psalms III*, "Psalm 118,".

like the people at the time of Babel, or within the Humanism being perpetuated today. As President Trump asserted in his United Nations address,

> Looking around and all over this large, magnificent planet, the truth is plain to see: If you want freedom, take pride in your country. If you want democracy, hold on to your sovereignty. And if you want peace, love your nation. Wise leaders always put the good of their own people and their country first. The future does not belong to "Globalists." The future belongs to patriots. The future belongs to sovereign and independent nations who protect their citizens, respect their neighbors, and honor the differences that make each country special and unique.[462]

The President has publicly professed that he was elected to be President of the United States, not the president of the world, in his defense and rationale for a focused priority in making and keeping "America First."

Biblical Distinctions of Aliens or Foreigners in the Land

It may surprise many that migration is a prevalent theme throughout the Bible. The pages of Scripture are rich with theological reflection, portraying our journey through life as "aliens" in this world, which is not our permanent home (cf. Hebrews 13:14 NLT). The Old Testament portrays "the chosen people" (Deuteronomy 14:2, 1 Peter 2:9) as a people on the move. And as is true today, there were various reasons for migration in Biblical times. Today, many are classified as refugees, having been driven from their homes due to desperate situations caused by racial, political or religious persecution, war, and local economic or natural disasters. Others seeking food and shelter, along with the lure of opportunities for a new and a more comfortable life, likewise claim asylum.

As is the case with our language, descriptive words are used to reflect and distinguish the circumstances groups of migrants or individuals faced in Old Testament times, as they became outsiders in a new land. The challenge becomes discerning the different nuances these words convey, as well as the various translations made, especially when there is no consistency in the way various versions of the Bible translate the terms. As M. Daniel

---

462 Trump, "United Nations Speech," September 24, 2019. <https://www.whitehouse.gov/briefings-Statements/remarks-president-trump-74th-session-united-nations-general-assembly>.

Carroll R.* writes in "Immigration and the Bible," "The same English word can be used for several Hebrew and Greek terms, and a Hebrew or Greek term may be translated by different English words! The most common translations of these words are 'alien,' 'resident alien,' 'foreigner,' 'stranger' and 'sojourner.'"[463]

What are these Hebrew terms that get translated into English as if they were synonymous, when there are subtle but significant distinctions? In a compelling Bible study, Ralph Drollinger,† President and Founder of Capitol Ministries, provides helpful Hebrew background, showing the importance of distinguishing three types of people in the land of Israel that are essential in understanding a Biblical perspective to the current immigration debate within our country. "An Israelite citizen is referred to as a ***countryman*** (*'ach'*) in Scripture, whereas a legal immigrant is referred to as a ***sojourner*** (*'ger'* or *'toshab'*) and a foreigner is called an ***illegal*** (*'nokri,' 'nekhar'* or *'zar'*)."[464]

Drollinger illustrates the significance of these distinctions in the Old Testament by explaining that an illegal did not possess the same benefits or privileges as a sojourner or countryman. He points to Ruth the Moabite and her response to Boaz the Israelite in Ruth 2:10 (NRSV): "Why have I found favor in your sight, that you should take notice of me, when I am a foreigner?"

> Not only was Ruth a ***foreigner*** (*nokri*), an ***illegal*** immigrant, she was a Moabite ***illegal***, who according to Deuteronomy 23:3 was forbidden to migrate into

---

* M. Daniel Carroll R. (Rodas) is the Scripture Press Ministries Chair of Biblical Studies and Pedagogy at Wheaton College where he was previously Blanchard Professor of Old Testament, and prior to Wheaton he was Professor of Old Testament at Denver Seminary. Half Guatemalan and raised in a bilingual and bicultural household and the realities and challenges of politics, poverty and war in Central America fostered his passion for the Old Testament Texts and social ethics. He is the author of *Christians at the Border* (Baker, 2008) and *The Bible and Borders: Hearing God's Word on Immigration* (Brazos Press/Baker, 2020) in addition to this paper among other articles.

[463] Carroll R. (Rodas), M. Daniel, "Immigration and the Bible," *MissioDei*, No.19; <https://www.mennonitemission.net/Downloads/MissioDei19.E.pdf>.

† Ralph Drollinger, a clergyman and retired professional basketball player who along with his wife founded Capitol Ministries in 1996, starting dozens of ministries in capitols throughout the world to make disciples of Jesus Christ in the political arena through out the world. He birthed a study to U.S. Senators in 2015, and under President Trump's Administration, he led a Bible study to Members of the White House Cabinet which he continues to teach remotely every week to former members.

[464] Drollinger, Ralph, "What *the* Bible Says About Our Illegal Immigration Problem," Capitol Ministries. <https://capmin.org/what-the-bible-says-about-illegal-immigration>.

> Israel altogether! For **citizen** Boaz to entertain Ruth at all was remarkably generous and gracious, and possibly even against the law of the land. (Perhaps Boaz already had in mind legitimizing her status by marriage.) The point is that Ruth's self-declaration serves to underscore the classification of people in and by ancient Israel.
>
> Furthermore, a ***citizen/countryman*** was expressly forbidden to take advantage of or mistreat a ***legal immigrant***, known as a ***sojourner***, per Exodus 22:21 and Deuteronomy 10:19 respectively: "*You shall not wrong or oppress a resident alien/sojourner, for you were aliens in the land of Egypt.*" "*You shall also love the stranger, for you were strangers in the land of Egypt.*"[465]

Biblically, a "*ger*" was a migrant who came to live in Israel as a legal resident or refugee with the permission of a host or proper authority, while a *foreigner* could be likened to an illegal immigrant or undocumented alien today.

Another Biblical expert on this subject, Dr. James Hoffmeier,* explains the differentiation in this way: "A **sojourner** (sometimes translated as 'stranger') was a person who entered Israel and followed legal procedures to obtain recognized standing as a **resident alien** ('*ger*')." He underscores how Israel treated "illegal immigrants" differently making the parallel analysis: "**Illegal immigrants** should not expect these same privileges from the State whose laws they disregard by virtue of their undocumented status."[466]

Teaching Elder K.J. Tromp† of the Christian Reformed Church in Australia concurs that in the Old Testament,

> the "**resident alien**" *(ger)* is often differentiated from the "foreigner" *(nokri)*. Often carrying negative connotation (e.g. Genesis 31:15; Psalm 144:7; Isaiah 2:6; 62:8), the *nokri* is defined as an individual who comes from another country and has no links with the tribal system of the covenant community

---

465 Ibid.

* James K. Hoffmeier is Professor of Old Testament and Near Eastern Archaeology at Trinity International University, Divinity School (Deerfield, IL). He has consulted for many TV programs on Egypt and the Bible for the Discovery, the Learning, and History channels and National Geographic and is the author of numerous articles and books, including *The Immigration Crisis* quoted here.

466 Hoffmeier, *The Immigration Crisis: Immigrants, Aliens, and the Bible* (Wheaton, IL: Crossway Books, 2009), p.52.

† K.J. Tromp is the Teaching and Discipleship Pastor of Open House Church in Queensland, Australia.

> and seemingly follows his own religion. This is concluded from the fact that the *nokri* is never listed among those who take part in Israel's religious ceremonies, and is specifically excluded from eating the Passover (Exodus 12:43).[467]

Dr. M. Daniel Carroll R. (Rodas), Professor at Wheaton and author of *Christians at the Border: Immigration, the Church, and the Bible*, likewise asserts

> that Israel made distinctions among those who came from elsewhere, "*Nekar*"/ "*nokri*" and "*zar*," refer to something or someone who is foreign to Israel. They often have a negative connotation of being a corrupting influence or threat ("*nekar/nokri*"—Joshua 24:20; 1 Kings 11:1-8; Ezr 9-10; Nehemiah 13:23-27; and "*zar*"—Deuteronomy 32:16; Proverbs 22:14; Isaiah 1:7)…. The nekhar/ nokri are excluded from participating in certain festivals (Exodus 12:43). Perhaps, these individuals had no plan to stay for a lengthy period and were not interested in integrating themselves into Israelite life. [He postulates that] they might have been, for example, merchants, mercenaries or traders.[468]

Alternatively, Pastor K.J. Tromp assigns that possibility to a further distinction he makes within legal foreigners living in another country by citing "temporary residents" (*tosab/ toshab*), which is in proximity but not synonymous with "*ger*," even though they are often used together:

> The "*tosab*" is not entitled to partake in the Passover (Exodus 12:45; cf, v. 48); meanwhile, the "*ger*" is listed as a participant in public worship (Leviticus 16:29; 17:8-9; 22:18) implying that the "stranger" (*tosab*) is less integrated into Israelite society than the "resident alien" (*ger*). The term "*tosab*" carries with it the sense of a transitory existence within the host community; it designates someone who has another destination in mind.[469]

---

467 Tromp, K.J., "Aliens and Strangers in the Old Testament," *Vox Reformata*, 2011, p.5. <http://www.rtc.edu.au/RTC/media/Documents/Vox%20articles/Aliens-and-Strangers-in-the-Old-Testament-KJT-76-2011.pdf>.

468 Carroll Rodas, <https://www.mennonitemission.net/Downloads/MissioDei19.E.pdf>.

469 Tromp, "Aliens and Strangers."

For these reasons, some scholars suggest the designation *"tosab/toshab"* could be comparable to those non-citizens who are legally in our country by possessing a temporary worker visa, a student visa, or even a tourist visa. Thus, the term *"gers"* would refer to assimilating aliens while *"toshab"* would signal non-assimilating aliens. In either category, they would have received permission to enter the country legally, and be granted not only civil justice and thus enjoy legal protection, but also the privileges and social benefits of native citizens on certain conditions. Both *"gers"* and *"toshabs,"* however, would be required to adhere to the laws and regulations that applied to native citizens.

From the early narratives in Genesis, we learn the Patriarchs had to negotiate treaties and agreements to "sojourn" in the territory of other lands and obtain water rights from local authorities. Such an example among several would include the Children of Israel asking Pharaoh for permission in Genesis 47:4: "And they said to Pharaoh, 'We have come to reside as aliens in the land; for there is no pasture for your servants' flocks because the famine is severe in the land of Canaan. Now, we ask you, let your servants settle in the land of Goshen.'" With permission from no less than Pharaoh, the King of Egypt, they were permitted to settle. The Hebrews, though foreigners, were residing in Egypt as legal residents, *"gers."*

Hoffmeier cites another example of Moses becoming a "sojourner," "stranger" or "alien" after striking and killing an Egyptian taskmaster. He fled Egypt, crossed the Sinai, and ended up in Midian. Meeting the daughters of Jethro, the local priest, at a well where they were being harassed by shepherds, Moses came to their aid and helped them water the flock. Exodus 2:18-22 reports that the daughters were asked by their father how they accomplished their task so quickly, and when told what had happened, the father responded by telling his daughters to invite this rescuer and helper in for dinner. Moses was content to dwell with Jethro and called himself a sojourner (*"ger"*), not a foreigner (*"nekhar"*), even though he was living in a foreign land. The eldest daughter, Zipporah, was given to Moses and she later gave birth to a son who Moses named Gershom, containing the term *"ger,"* reflecting his change of status.[470]

Showing Hospitality and Welcoming the Stranger

There are many Christians who cite the Scripture's emphasis on practicing hospitality, such as Genesis 18 with Abraham welcoming visitors, Mary and Joseph being immigrants (Matthew 2:16-21), the admonition given in Hebrews 13:2 (NRSV) *("Do not neglect to show*

[470] Hoffmeier, "The Use and Abuse of the Bible in the Immigration Debate," Center for Immigration Studies; <https://cis.org/Report/Use-and-Abuse-Bible-Immigration-debate>.

hospitality to strangers, for by doing that some have entertained angels without knowing it"), and 1 Peter 4:9 (NRSV) (*"Be hospitable to one another without complaining"*), and endeavor to apply those teachings as a basis for our national immigration policy. But as Scott Aniol, Founder and Executive Director of Religious Affections Ministries and Chair of the Worship Ministry Department at Southwestern Baptist Theological Seminary, says,

> this blurs important Biblical distinctions between the common kingdom, which includes sovereign nations ruled by civil governments, and the redemptive kingdom, which includes Christians gathered together in local churches. These commands were given to churches, not governments. The responsibility churches have toward others is different from the responsibilities governments have toward citizens and non-citizens.[471]

Christ's own teachings are also used to underscore the hospitality imperative: *"I was hungry and you gave me food, I was thirsty and you gave me something to drink, I was a stranger and you welcomed Me, I was naked and you gave me clothing, I was sick and you took care of me, I was in prison and you visited Me.... Truly I tell you, just as you did it to one of the least of these who are members of my family, you did it to Me"* (Matthew 25:35-36, 40 [NRSV]).

Defenders of illegal aliens are quick to cite many positive statements from the Bible about the hospitality and compassionate treatment people of faith are to extend to "strangers" in their midst. As an Old Testament scholar, James K. Hoffmeier was intrigued by the way the Bible was being used in the current immigration debate, knowing that the Bible was not being read seriously. As a result, he wrote a small book, *The Immigration Crisis: Immigrants, Aliens, and the Bible* (Crossway, 2009):

> The very positive statements about the treatment of strangers in the Bible [is to] show compassion for the alien in ancient Israel. The defenders of illegal aliens point to these passages as the rationale for rewriting current laws. The problem [Hoffmeier saw] was that people make a simplistic correlation between the ancient Israelite social law and the modern situation as if the Bible was addressing the same problem.[472]

---

[471] Aniol, Scott, "The Two Kingdoms and Immigration policy." <https://religiousaffections.org/articles/articles-on-culture/the-two-kingdoms-and-immigration-policy>.

[472] Hoffmeier, "The Use and Abuse of the Bible in the Immigration Debate," Center for Immigration Studies, December 1, 2011. <https://cis.org/Report/Use-and-Abuse-Bible-Immigration-Debate>.

In another article, Hoffmeier asserts that many religious leaders

> agree God's central message to the Israelites is to protect and defend the stranger. Leviticus 19:33 is one passage quoted in this regard: "*When a stranger resides with you in your land, you shall not oppress the stranger. The stranger who resides with you shall be to you as the citizen among you.*" This wonderful passage has nothing to do with illegal immigrants in America…. Old Testament laws were primarily intended to promote an orderly society for a nation—ancient Israel. Simplistic application of 3,000-year-old laws to American society is ill-advised until one thoroughly understands what was meant by "stranger" in this verse. The Bible is not "a living breathing document" that can mean whatever you want it to say.[473]

As we will discover, this issue must be viewed contextually and based on what the key words meant when they were written, before applying them as if they mean the same in our time. For Hoffmeier,

> The most significant Hebrew word for our discussion is "*ger*" translated variously in English versions, which creates some confusion, as "*stranger*" (KJV, NASB, JB), "sojourner" (RSV, ESV), "*alien*" (NEB, NIV, NJB, NRSV), and "*foreigner*" (TNIV, NLT). It occurs more than 80 times as a noun and an equal number as a verb (*gwr*), which typically means "to sojourn" or "live as an alien." The problem with more recent English translations (e.g. TNIV and NLT) is that they use "*foreigner*" for "*ger*," which is imprecise and misleading because, as we have learned, there are other Hebrew terms for "foreigner," namely "*nekhar*" and "*zar*." The distinction between these two terms and "*ger*" is that while all three are foreigners who might enter another country, the "*ger*" had obtained legal status.[474]

To reiterate, "*nekhar*" and "*zar*" foreigners did not have the same standing in Biblical law as the "alien" "*gers*" who enjoyed legal protection, social benefits and religious inclusion like their native-born citizen/neighbors ("*Achs*").

---

473 Hoffmeier, "Jeff Sessions Got it Right on Immigrants and the Bible."
<https://religionnews.com/2017/01/10/jeff-sessions-got-it-right-on-immigrants-and-the-bible>.
474 Hoffmeier, "Use and Abuse."

Scripture carefully notes for our instruction that the Israelites were fully aware of the need to respect territorial sovereignty. After the exodus from Egypt, the Hebrew people lived a nomadic existence for 40 years in the Sinai Peninsula, over which no country claimed hegemony. When they left, they had to pass through Edom, and Moses sought permission from the king: "*Thus says your brother Israel…here we are in Kadesh, a city on the edge of your territory. Now let us pass through your land. We will not pass-through field or vineyard, or drink water from any well; we will go along the King's Highway, not turning aside to the right hand or to the left until we have passed through your territory…*" (Numbers 20:14-21 [NRSV]). Similarly, Moses petitioned the Amorite King to pass through his territory (Numbers 21:21-31 [NRSV]).

People often mistake examples of Bible characters fleeing persecution as a broad mandate of open borders, as if none exists. The most notable reference is to Mary and Joseph's flight to Egypt, forgetting why they ever went to Bethlehem. "They were obeying an inconvenient law they could have easily ignored. And they fled to Egypt for reasons already permitted under current immigration law: to escape the murder of their child. Joseph and Mary are models of the law-abiding immigrant, not illegal immigrants"[475] argues Tom Hobson* as their compliance with the Roman census demonstrates. As far as we know, they did not demand any special privileges from Egypt. "This act did not constitute illegal immigration," is also the analysis of James R. Edwards,† a Fellow at the Center for Immigration Studies (CIS). "Nothing indicates that the Holy Family broke any Egyptian laws. Their intent was finding temporary humanitarian relief. They stayed only until they could return to Israel."[476] Their "sojourn" into Egypt was always intended to be a brief one, not driven by a desire to seek higher economic gains by relocating. This flight is motivated by life and death concerns which most nations honored, and not for the material comforts of economic gain.

---

475 Hobson, Tom, "'Ger' – The Immigrant in the Hebrew Bible," *The Aquila Report*, May 20, 2010; <https://www.theaquilareport.com/ger-the-immigrant-in-the-hebrew-bible>.

* Tom Hobson is Assistant Pastor at Bonhomme Presbyterian Church (ECO a Covenant Order of Evangelical Presbyterians) in Chesterfield, MO and author of *What's on God's Sin List for Today?*

† James R. Edwards, Jr. joined the Center for Immigration Studies in 2009. He was Legislative Director for a member of the House Immigration Subcommittee and had been an Adjunct Fellow with the Hudson Institute and was selected as a 1996 Lincoln Fellow by the Claremont Institute. He has written several papers and authored with James G. Gimpel, *The Congressional Politics of Immigration Reform* (Longman, 1998).

476 Edwards, James R. "A Biblical Perspective on Immigration Policy," p.7. <https://cis.org/sites/cis.org/files/articles/2009/immigration-Biblical-perspective.pdf>.

Egypt is merely providing the Holy family with the same practice most nations exhibited then as they do today, in accepting foreigners as temporary residents because of warfare, natural disasters, and political or religious persecution in their homelands that make it impossible for these people to continue residing there without exceptional danger. "It is wrong," Dr. Hoffmeier reiterates, "to confuse these two Biblical categories of foreigners, [sojourners or '*gers*' with illegals, '*nekhar*' or '*zar*'] and then use passages regarding the '*ger*' as if they were relevant to illegal immigrants of today."[477] Dr. Hoffmeier concludes that this is a faulty application of these Biblical laws. On the other hand, he finds merit in these Biblical laws which urge us today to help and incorporate foreigners who are legally among us, especially because they can be easily exploited (Deuteronomy 24:14-15). Israelite identity was shaped by their history of being a transient people in strange settings, and thus should be able to empathize with aliens in their midst who could likely experience oppression and marginalization as they had.

As Israel was continually reminded to "remember" their history, they developed and shared a deep and meaningful bond with the strangers and aliens of their world. As the Church comes to grips with its responsibility to immigrants, refugees and asylum-seekers, we too are reminded that we, like all humanity, are "foreigners and strangers in this world" (1 Peter 2:11 [NIV]) which is not our true home. Most fair-minded Americans acknowledge that we are an "immigrant" nation and an immigrant Church. There are plenty of legal aliens among us who feel disenfranchised due to their cultural, religious or ethnic backgrounds, who need help fitting in with their host culture but often are ignored, even by those who advocate helping those who are illegal.

In the ancient world, there were no governmental assistance programs as we experience today, so the extended family was the primary resource in times of need. The sojourners ("*gers*") in the Old Testament were often displaced and at-risk persons being separated from their kinship networks, and thus at the mercy of others for provision, work and protection. As outsiders, even though having received permission to enter another country, "*gers*" were easily taken advantage of, so Old Testament law classified "*gers*" with widows, orphans and the poor, which qualified them with gleaning privileges at harvest time and to participate in the triennial tithe for charity. Furthermore, they were not to be oppressed but treated equally under the law, paid wages on par with the native-born citizens, and be allowed to participate in the rituals of Israel's religious life and culture.

---

477 Hoffmeier, "Use and Abuse."

Providing Sanctuary for Who and Why?

The Biblical practice of "sanctuary" is also misunderstood, but nevertheless used and abused to justify cities and states who refuse to cooperate with federal authorities in matters related to illegal immigrants by defying the 1996 Illegal Immigration Reform and Immigrant Responsibility Act. The word "sanctuary" had its origin in the Sinai wilderness period after the exodus from Egypt. There, the entire community lived with the Tabernacle and Israel's "sanctuary," in the middle of the camp.

Murder was a capital offense and was specifically highlighted in the Ten Commandments God delivered to His people on Mt. Sinai, which forbade killing a person (Exodus 20:13). Yet, as is so apparent with the law, there are often exceptions and distinctions made as we witness in Exodus 21:12-14, which Dr. Hoffmeier emphasizes

> *'Anyone who strikes a person with a fatal blow is to be put to death. However, if it is not done intentionally...they are to flee to a place I will designate. But if anyone schemes and kills someone deliberately, that person is to be taken from my altar (in the tabernacle) and put to death.'* Cases of involuntary manslaughter or negligent homicide (Exodus 21:12-15) were not capital offenses. So to keep the *lex talionis* (law of retribution) 'eye for eye, tooth for tooth...life for life' (Exodus 21:23-25) from being carried out by family members [most often by the oldest male relative of the deceased or an "*avenger of blood*" (Joshua 20:5) enlisted by the family to seek justice], the offender was to run to the sanctuary where he would be safe until his case could be heard.[478]

Once the populace spread throughout their new homeland, it was impractical to have just one place of sanctuary. Consequently, six cities of refuge were designated, three on either side of the Jordan River (Numbers 35:11-30; Joshua 20:1-6). Sanctuary, then, is explicitly a "safe zone" for one to flee in order to get a fair hearing in the case of accidental death, or in the words of Joshua 20:3 (NRSV) for "*anyone who kills a person without intent or by mistake*" but for no other crime. Hoffmeier reminds us that "the cities of refuge were not a place to avoid trial or punishment. American cities that use their communities to circumvent the

[478] Ibid.

law to help the illegal alien in the name of justice are doing a gross injustice to the letter and spirit of Biblical law."[479]

Cities of refuge were rooted in laws of the Torah, in contrast to sanctuary cities which are illegal and outside the justice system. The whole point for cities of refuge—authorized under the Mosaic Code as part of Israel's justice system (Numbers 35 and Joshua 22)—

> was to provide safe zones to which the person who had accidently killed someone could flee, be protected from excessive retribution, and have the case heard by an impartial judge.... The person may be guilty of killing, but not murder according to Biblical law. A defendant was to flee ahead of the avenger to one of the sanctuary locations where he could "*state his case before the elders of that city*" (Joshua 20:4-6). The Biblical practice of sanctuary, then, was to protect the offender from vigilante justice and to guarantee one received a fair trial [according to Hoffmeier]. A person who was found guilty of intentionally murdering someone should be removed from the protection of the sanctuary and receive his punishment. This practice is clearly stated in Exodus 21:14: "*take him away from my altar and put him to death.*"[480]

Sanctuary protection was thus limited exclusively to offenders who had accidentally or unintentionally killed someone, and was never intended as a place to "avoid the law" and the consequences of criminal behavior, but rather to allow the law to take its proper course:

> In other words, the purpose of a city of refuge was to make sure the rights of the accused to due process were observed. But sanctuary cities,* in contrast, do not exist to protect due process. They exist to enable the guilty to escape punishment altogether. The mere presence of an illegal alien on American soil is an illegal, a criminal act which is the proper subject of law enforcement. Those, no matter how well-meaning they are, who help others avoid facing the legal consequences of such criminal conduct are subverting the system of justice, not cooperating with it. A city of refuge worked with

---

[479] Ibid.

[480] Hoffmeier, "Does the Bible Really Advocate Sanctuary Cities?" <https://religionnews.com/2017/02/15/does-the-bible-really-advocate-sanctuary-cities>.

* Nearly 500 jurisdictions (cities, counties and states) now shield illegal immigrants from deportations according to *The Washington Times*, March 14, 2017.

> law enforcement; a sanctuary city works against it. A city of refuge served to guarantee a man his day in court, a sanctuary city works to prevent the accused from ever facing a day in court. A city of refuge existed to ensure that every man received a fair trial; a sanctuary city exists to enable a man to avoid a fair trial altogether. So, no, sanctuary cities are not a modern embodiment of Biblical cities of refuge, and only Christians with a shallow understanding of Scripture could believe they are. As James Hoffmeier of Trinity Evangelical Divinity School puts it, such Christians "are twisting Biblical statues to political ends and subverting federal law."[481]

This article concludes with its author, Bryan Fischer, host of "The Focal Point" on American Family Radio, asking the question, "Should not the role of the Church of Jesus Christ be to help its members become law-abiding disciples rather than law-breaking ones?"[482] Uncontrolled border crossing by people whose motivations are not life and death, but rather economic or sinister, become an injustice not only toward those who have lined up waiting their turn to enter the country legally, some up to ten years, but also toward the citizens who bear the costs on many fronts.

Financial and Social Costs of Illegal Immigrants

Consider the financial and social impact illegal immigrants are presently adding to the millions of undocumented residents (estimates vary from 12–20+ million) already within America's borders. The State would go bankrupt allowing unlimited immigration through an open borders policy that would swell the ranks of entitlement recipients, especially with such attractive magnets being offered as free college tuition, medical care, and other benefits to those who are not its citizens... benefits many citizens do not even receive. Is bestowing citizenship rights to undocumented immigrants fair to those who have been waiting in line to enter the country legally, or to millions of other potential immigrants from more distant but far more impoverished lands, not to mention those who are being actively persecuted for their political or religious faith?

Could it not be argued in America that we are disregarding "equality" by favoring or bestowing preferential treatment on those who have the ability to "walk up" from Central America on "terra firma" through Mexico to enter our country illegally over those who

---

[481] Bryan Fischer, "Sanctuary Cities Like Biblical Are Cities of Refuge," American Family Radio. <https://www.afa.net/the-stand/culture/2017/03/are-sanctuary-cities-like-Biblical-cities-of-refuge>.

[482] Ibid.

would also like to enter the country, say from Africa, to claim asylum, but cannot walk on water to enter our shores? Could one not assert in the all-too-common allegations so easily thrown about that it is "racist" to favor "browns" from Central America over "blacks" from Africa? Is this not a justice issue? Likewise, is giving automatic citizenship to illegal immigrants coming over the border to enhance their economic status, or to undocumented immigrants already in the country, fair to millions of other potential immigrants or refugees who would desire to live in the United States? And as we know, there are those in other parts of the planet who are being persecuted for their political or religious faith.

Biblical Understandings and Insights

Several factors need to be restated and highlighted: Countries in ancient Biblical times had borders that were protected and respected, and foreigners had to seek permission to enter for residency or to merely pass through. City-states had walls and gates and thereby controlled entry and exit. National sovereignty included the right to determine the grounds for admitting foreigners into the jurisdiction, and on what conditions. At all times, the local governments or rulers held not just the ultimate control over admission, but also over expulsion, and they set the terms of stay (Nehemiah 13:15-22). Native-born Jews and naturalized citizens ("*Achs*") were to treat these legal alien residents or "*gers*" like a native-born Hebrew, respectfully and fairly according to Leviticus 19:33-34 (NRSV): "When an alien resides with you in your land, you shall not oppress the alien. The alien who resides with you shall be to you as the citizen among you; you shall love the alien as yourself, for you were aliens in the land of Egypt..." As wonderful as this passage is, it has nothing to do with illegal immigrants in America and "to infer some open borders or mass-amnesty mandate from what actually appears in Scripture is wrong,"[483] asserts Dr. James R. Edwards.

Leviticus 19 is one of Judaism's greatest ethical statements in the view of Stephen Steinlight,* Policy Analyst at the Center for Immigration Studies.

---

483 Edwards, James R. "A Biblical Perspective on Immigration Policy," p.3. <https://cis.org/sites/cis.org/files/articles/2009/immigration-Biblical-perspective.pdf>.

* Stephen Steinlight is one of the nation's most insightful voices on immigration. He is a Fellow at the Center for Immigration Studies (CIS) in Washington, DC and has testified before the Judiciary Committees of the House and Senate and has provided expert testimony before state legislatures. Prior to joining CIS he was Executive Director of the American Anti-Slavery Group, and for eight years he was National Affairs Director at the American Jewish Committee (AJC) where he oversaw its public policy agenda on First Amendment issues, civil rights, immigration and social policy. He also served as Vice President of the National Conference of Christians and Jews (NCCJ).

> It makes empathy, and even love, for non-Jews a binding duty, asserting ethical universalism and reminding us that the God who commands it is the God of all humankind, not only of Jews. Moreover, this universalism is exceptional; strictures surrounding it are addressed to the Children of Israel as a people set apart, a "chosen people".... However [it] is not Judaism's only word on the treatment of strangers, and it is in reading other Biblical passages that it becomes clear that key terms have been mistranslated for what can only be political purposes.[484]

In testimony on May 22, 2007, before the House Judiciary's Subcommittee on Immigration, Citizenship, Refugees, Border Security and International Law, Dr. Stephen Steinlight supported the distinctions we have already encountered in Hebrew Scripture regarding immigrants.

> It doesn't require much hermeneutical acumen to see the meaning of a key term—***sojourn***—has been misconstrued for political purposes. The word in the Hebrew Bible for stranger is "*Ger v'toshav.*" The precise English equivalent is **sojourner**. It first appears in Genesis 4:23 describing Abraham when he dwells briefly with the Hittites in what is now Hebron. It last appears in Chronicles 29:15 where King David employs it to contrast the transitory nature of human existence with the eternality of God, creator and steward of the earth on which we briefly dwell as wanderers. Richard Elliot Friedman, a leading authority on Biblical Hebrew, translates it as "*alien*" and "*visitor.*" Every English dictionary defines sojourn as a temporary stay. Thus, this passage [Leviticus 19] offers no Scriptural sanction to argue some 12 million [some estimates go as high as into the 20+ millions] illegal aliens should be permitted to remain permanently in the United States.[485]

While "*gers,*" legal immigrants or alien residents, were not full citizens, they did have rights and were entitled to receive all the social benefits and protection afforded a citizen, as we pointed out in defining the Hebrew distinctions in Scripture. Should "*gers*" desire to

---

484 Steinlight, Stephen, "Cease Citing Bible to Defend Bush's Immigration Bill." <https://cis.org/Cease-Citing-Bible-defend-bushs-immigration-Bill>.

485 Steinlight, Stephen, "Faith-Based Approaches to Immigration Policy." <https://cis.org/FaithBased-Approaches-Immigration-Policy>.

become citizens, they could go through what would constitute a process of naturalization: circumcision, abandoning idolatry, and pledging allegiance to their new country.

In our current immigration debate, a significant factor is often ignored. "*Gers*" living within ancient Israel were, in turn, expected to strictly conform to Israelite law, diligently observing the one law (Numbers 15:15-16; 15:29; Leviticus 24:22) for both natural-born citizens and for "*gers*" residing among them. While a lot of focus is directed toward Israelites showing compassion toward the "stranger" and refraining from oppressing or taking advantage of the "*gers*"—for example, in the area of employment, where they would be paid less than their fellow Israelites—little attention seems to be given to the behavior expected of the "*gers*" living in their midst. "*Gers*" were explicitly instructed not to undermine the legal fabric of Israelite society but to obey the laws of the nation, including observing the Sabbath. As James Edwards emphatically points out, the Old Testament passage commands aliens to assimilate into the Hebrew culture. They were "not to impose their own customs, language, etc. and remake the receiving society in their own image."[486] Scripture passages such as Deuteronomy 16:9-15 illustrate the Biblical assimilation ethic which even includes observing dietary and holiness laws governing holidays. In fact, the Israelites are "warned numerous times against letting the aliens' pagan practices corrupt God-given moral standards."[487] Through the advocacy of those supporting illegal immigration, one can witness in our society a trend leaning certainly in the direction of accommodating the "stranger" in our midst rather than facilitating means by which they are assimilated.

Edwards further opines,

> Aliens granted permission to reside in a nation owe a moral duty to the accepting nation to abide by its laws and assimilate to its customs. Such is morally responsible individual conduct in the context of immigration... forcing oneself on an existing nation is both unjust and unjustifiable. In other words, illegal immigration is morally wrong. Lawbreaking aliens bear moral responsibility for their unlawful actions.[488]

Punishment as well as the expulsion of those aliens who do not abide by the civil laws, including immigration laws, is also the host country's prerogative. We find the following warning given in Scripture: "But whoever acts high-handedly, whether a native or an alien,

---

486 Edwards, "A Biblical Perspective," p.8.

487 Ibid., p.3.

488 Ibid., p.8.

affronts the Lord, and shall be cut off from among the people. Because of having despised the Word of the Lord and broken His commandment, such a person shall be utterly cut off and bear the guilt" (Numbers 15:30-31 [NRSV]).

In referring to his dissertation "Cut Off from (One's) People," Tom Hobson repeats his understanding of the term "cut off" to mean expelled or deported.

> To cross our modern border without legal permission can hardly be an accident, and is almost always an act of deliberate defiance. Much of the substance of the immigration debate hangs on the meaning of the verb "oppress" in the command not to "oppress" the "***ger.***" The pro-illegal-immigration crowd wants to define oppression as broadly as possible. But the language, in context, does not permit us to equate oppression with enforcement of legitimate laws.

He goes on to acknowledge that

> While it is true that many immigrants in ancient Israel may have been fugitives from punishment elsewhere, the only non-extradition clause found in the Torah is for runaway slaves (Deuteronomy 23:15-16), not for murderers or even for political refugees. There is no obligation in the Torah to protect any immigrant other than runaway slaves from being deported to their country of origin for crimes they have committed…. To claim that illegal immigrants have an inalienable right to be here in America, based on Scripture, is a stretch far beyond what the meaning of "***ger***" will allow…. The truth is that our immigration laws are already far more generous than those of other countries who criticize us.[489]

The illegal immigrant has been compared to the person who breaks into your home, then claims that they have the right to bunk down and raid your refrigerator, and then further claims that the residents or the community must provide the means for their living. Readers may judge for themselves whether the comparison fits. Ironically, from a Biblical perspective, even desperate circumstances do not justify illegal immigration. Proverbs 6:30-31 (NRSV) clearly acknowledges that "*Thieves are not despised who steal only to satisfy their appetite when they are hungry. Yet if they are caught, they will pay sevenfold; they will forfeit all the goods of their house.*" While one can empathize with his circumstances, the

---

[489] Hobson, Tom, "'Ger'—The Immigrant in the Hebrew Bible."

fact remains that he stole and restitution must be made, even to the point of bankruptcy. Yes, the private owner can make an exception, but the civil government cannot. As James R. Edwards puts it, "Civil government exists to preserve the peace. Were the government not to hold lawbreakers accountable, that laxity would send the wrong message to others who might not be in quite as dire circumstances. The forgiven lawbreaker might take the government's mercy as lack of will to enforce its laws."[490]

This we observe not only with illegal immigrants, but also the lawless criminals in our cities' streets wreaking havoc, destruction, and harm to property and life. We are currently witnessing a rise in shoplifting and theft in states where the decision to downgrade the theft of property valued below an arbitrary figure from a felony to a misdemeanor, together with selective enforcement that focuses on more "serious" crimes, has resulted in thieves knowing they can brazenly shoplift and merchants knowing the police will not respond to their complaints. Likewise, alleged looters and rioters arrested by the New York Police Department were being immediately released due to the state's new bail-reform law, which has now been somewhat amended in response to the outcry from those who asserted that the new law was turning the criminal justice process into a mockery. Edwards concludes, "In other words, the action here of both the government and the lawbreaker have consequences for the rest of society."[491] Merchants will take those losses as a cost of doing business and pass those costs along to the consumer, in the form of higher prices for their goods and services.

---

[490] Edwards, "A Biblical Perspective," p.8.

[491] Ibid.

17

Just Societies Require Just Laws

God, in His economy, created nations and governments and intends for the leaders of nations to protect its citizens and to exercise justice. While Micah 6:8 (NRSV) *("to do justice; and to love kindness, and to walk humbly with your God")* is also frequently referenced, especially in regard to showing mercy, the role of justice is often neglected. We're witnessing those today who believe immigration is a "right," not a "privilege," and out of compassion and mercy they seek to fit the immigration policy to the demands of those who desire to immigrate to the United States. Justice and mercy are complementary principles, along with a godly life, which we will explore as we examine Martin Luther's insights into what is termed his doctrine of the "Two Kingdoms" and how those kingdoms interact Biblically.

David C. Steinmetz* summarizes the heart of Luther's social and political ethics in his volume *Luther in Context*, writing:

> For Luther, the vertical relationship to God and the horizontal relationship to the neighbor are so inseparably joined in the act of faith that one is unthinkable without the other. In principle…there is no place in Luther's conception of the Gospel for that variety of evangelical Christianity…which cultivates individual piety but is utterly unable to identify with the weak, the poor, and the oppressed, with whom Christ is identified.

Yet he continues to say that, at the same time,

> Luther has no patience with a social gospel which lacks religious depth and which substitutes ethical analysis and moral obligation for inner liberation and joy.[492]

---

* David C. Steinmetz, was a scholar of Medieval and Reformation history and theology, Professor Emeritus of the History of Christianity at Duke Divinity School and a former president of the American Society of Church History, author of several books including *Luther and Staupitz, Luther in Context, Reformers in the Wings*, and *The Cambridge Companion to Reformation Theology.*

[492] Steinmetz, David C., *Luther in Context* (Grand Rapids: Baker Academic, 2002), p.124.

Obviously, immigration is one of the most complicated issues of our time. Voices on all sides argue strongly for action and change. Christians find themselves torn between the desire to uphold laws and the call to minister to the vulnerable. Unfortunately, instead of engaging in a study to discover how the Bible speaks to contemporary issues such as immigration, Dr. John Scott Redd, Jr., an Associate Professor of Old Testament at the Washington, D.C. campus of Reformed Theological Seminary, as well as its president, laments the "all-too-common practice in which a person starts with a political opinion and then mines Scripture for verses that corroborate the foregone conclusions. Not only is this approach unhelpful…it is sinful, because it places the reader in a position of authority over the divinely inspired text."[493]

There is no denying that throughout redemptive history in both the Old and New Testaments, we discover God's heart imploring His people to care for and demonstrate concern for those who are poor, orphaned, widowed, afflicted and oppressed: "the least of these…the hungry, the naked, the stranger, the prisoner" (Matthew 25:31-46). In lifting up such Biblical passages, including the classic teaching of mercy in Luke 6:27-31 which contains what we know as the "Golden Rule," and the neighborliness illustrated by the Good Samaritan, we are reminded by Dr. James Edwards that these instructions are directed toward individuals instead of governments. Such acts of kindness coming from individuals investing themselves in someone in need, instead of governments, best reflects the "mercy" the Bible teaches.

> At the policy level, it would be too easy for the State to demand conduct best exercised voluntarily by individuals, not under compulsion. Such is not mercy, nor is it motivated by love. The same goes for the State erroneously regarding foreigners as "neighbors" and treating them better in certain ways than its own citizens [which underscores a justice issue] …For each national government, "*the least of these*" will be native-born sufferers, the less fortunate of its own nation, those who stand to lose if forced to compete for jobs or education, for example, with people who would immigrate from some other nation (whose own civil authorities are responsible for their welfare) … Government can only exercise mercy through its agency. Compassion and mercy, when individuals exercise them, amount to their decision willingly to bear an injustice. It is merciful when a private person turns the other cheek,

---

[493] Redd, Scott, "Immigration and the Kingdom of God." <https://rts.edu/resources/immigration-and-the-kingdom-of-god>.

> gives up his tunic, and gives to a beggar. However, the government cannot do any of those things; it only can obligate the members of its society to do so.[494]

In the Sermon on the Mount, Luther makes a distinction between God's inward kingdom and the outward kingdom of the world. As mentioned above, we as Christians may turn the other cheek when we are treated unfairly. Yet as collective members of society with responsibilities towards people other than ourselves, Christians must make room for the law in the earthly kingdom, advocating for justice by restraining those who have wronged neighbors in our community. In Luther's own words, as these concerns are brought into harmony with one another, we read:

> At one and the same time you satisfy God's kingdom inwardly and the kingdom of the world outwardly. You suffer evil and injustice, and yet at the same time you punish evil and injustice; you do not resist evil, and yet at the same time, you do resist it. In the one case, you consider yourself and what is yours; in the other you consider your neighbor and what is his. In what concerns you and yours, you govern yourself by the Gospel and suffer injustice toward yourself as a true Christian; in what concerns the person or property of others, you govern yourself according to love and tolerate no injustice toward your neighbor.[495]

Today, we, as with those of former times, should have a special, irrepressible desire to care for the poor and outcast, the orphan and widow, the sick, naked, hungry and homeless. Citizens of this kingdom ought to love the poor and oppressed in a manner fitting for followers of the King. These general principles or values that Christ teaches to His disciples may certainly inform certain public actions, but it would be wrong to conclude that they mandate funding of government programs, foreign or domestic, that can result in dependency while at the same time failing to consider the obligations and responsibilities entailed, which will be borne by its citizens. "When considering mercy as public policy, however, an important distinction must be drawn. Not every moral or ethical teaching in

---

[494] Edwards, "A Biblical Perspective," pp.4-5.

[495] LW 45:96. Martin Luther, *The Christian in Society III*," "Temporal Authority: To What Extent It Should Be Obeyed."

the Bible fits cleanly or applies equally to both individuals and societies. This is certainly true with justice and mercy,"[496] exclaims Dr. Edwards.

Those in need are all around us, and while Christians should be concerned with those outside our borders who seek entry, we cannot ignore the needs of those within the country who are near us, for whom we are responsible. Dr. Scott Redd reminds us that "The Good Samaritan is not faulted for all the needy people whom he never encountered, but he shows that he is a loving neighbor by the way he treats the one he encounters on the road (Luke 10:25-37)."[497] As we consider the immigration crisis, Dr. Redd argues that

> we need to consider how our decisions at the border will affect other realities for the poor in our own society, many of whom are themselves immigrants. The issues are related. For instance, decreased border security would have a significant effect on our nation's social safety net and would make other programs like health care, labor policy and, yes, national security much more difficult to maintain.[498]

Dr. Edwards makes the case that it is far more challenging for the government to exercise mercy than to fulfill its role to ensure justice. He cites some "rifle-shot" examples such as granting a pardon or early parole, but these examples are of limited scope and infrequent application. The implication of policymakers establishing a program of "mercy" results in public cost. He sees "the adverse effect of immigration on the economic well-being of our most vulnerable fellow Americans, particularly blacks and those with a high school education or less [which] results in economic injustices that advantage the foreign worker over the American in the American's own nation." [499] In other words, in the view of Dr. Edwards, we evidence the practical consequences of civil government's "mercy" toward some affecting an injustice being borne by the citizen.

He illustrates the conundrum in our immigration system by citing amnesty proposals.

> Forgiving foreigners for entering the country illegally or staying when their visas expire might be seen as "merciful" or "compassionate," at least in its effect on the people gaining legal status without having to suffer the

[496] Edwards, "A Biblical Perspective," pp.3-4.

[497] Redd, "Immigration and the Kingdom of God."

[498] Ibid.

[499] Edwards, "A Biblical Perspective," p.10.

> consequences of the law that otherwise would be required of them. However, the government, as agent, has acted in such a way that coerces innocent citizens and law-abiding immigrants to suffer the consequences.
>
> In recent amnesty proposals, 12 million or more illegal aliens would be legalized. These amnestied lawbreakers would tie up the immigration bureaucracy; introduce through chain migration millions of relatives into an already clogged system; qualify for scarce public resources such as Medicaid, welfare, and other public assistance; and the cost of all these things would be borne by American taxpayers. Furthermore, the scale of such "mercy" would do harm to many Americans and communities, and lead to more illegal immigration by the signal such policies would send (and indeed have sent with previous amnesties).[500]

Dr. Edwards concludes, "As for mass amnesty, by legalizing millions of illegal immigrants, government does not show mercy. Rather, it obligates its citizens to bear the injustices aliens have committed against the body politic…"[501] while providing them at the same time with a leg up over those who wait to enter the country legally because they have succeeded in taking the law into their own hands, crossing the border illegally.

Francis Scott Key, a lawyer and the author of "The Star-Spangled Banner," provides an instructive understanding of the temporal allegiances one has. Being a Christian himself, Key explains how believers appropriately fulfill their Biblical calling as citizens of both the "City of God and the City of Man:"

> Finding himself associated with numberless fellow-creatures, "framed with like miracle, the work of God," he has been solicitous to learn his relation to them. He is told that they are his brethren, that he is to love them, and that it is to be his business to fill up the short measure of his life by doing good to them. Engaged in this work, he has perceived himself peculiarly connected with some, who are brought nearer to him, and therefore more within the reach of his beneficence. He has observed that he is a member of a particular social community, governed by the same laws, exercising the same privileges, and bound to the same duties. His obligations therefore to this community,

---

[500] Ibid., p.5.

[501] Ibid., p.10.

> are more obvious and distinct. His own country, to which he is immediately responsible, by whose institutions he has been cherished and protected, has therefore a peculiar claim upon him.[502]

Maybe this is the time for Americans, particularly those who are Christians, to not only acknowledge the great "divide" immigration is causing in our political life, but to become better informed as such divisiveness and polarization are rendering cracks to the very foundation of our country. To better appreciate and act on the sacred privileges we have as citizens, we need to return to the sources of our faith and republic, as Luther and Trump respectively have urged, so that with enlightenment (from years past) we may become "wise as serpents and innocent as doves" (Matthew 10:16) in all matters that contribute to our well-being and that of our neighbor. Tom Hobson reminds us,

> One of the curses on a nation that abandons YHWH [the Lord] is that "*the aliens residing among you shall rise higher and higher, while you shall sink lower and lower*" (Deuteronomy 28:43). When illegal aliens ("*nokri*", "*nekhar,*" or "*zar*") have grown so powerful that they have created a double standard that allows them immunity from laws which the rest of us have to obey, we might want to think deeply about what is happening to us and why.[503]

As we have witnessed from St. Paul, the passage of all laws should stem from a desire to protect the nation and its citizenry (Romans 13:1-4). The protection afforded by the laws embedded in the Constitution was motivated by and is meant to "ensure domestic tranquility" and to "provide for the common defense." That protection, along with immigration laws passed by Congress, should serve the public good and

> deter a myriad of intrusions by illegals: weapons of destruction, disease, property and job theft, the importation of illegal drugs, [trafficking in sex and child abuse,] and the like, which could result from illegals who have never pledged their allegiance to the nation and its laws, but rather have broken the laws of the land by entering the country illegally.[504]

---

[502] Delaplaine, Edward S., *Francis Scott Key: Life and Times* (Stuarts Draft, VA: American Foundation Publications, 1998), pp.114-115.

[503] Hobson, "'*Ger*'—The Immigrant in the Hebrew Bible."

[504] Drollinger, "What the Bible Says About Our Illegal Immigration Problem."

In his Bible Study with the legislators on Capitol Hill, Dr. Drollinger shared that

> there are those who believe that because God calls us to be impartial and because God created all mankind in His image of God (Lat: *Imago Dei*) that believers should be the leading proponents of a borderless world—one without classifications or categorizations of people within a given country! [Dr. Drollinger believes] Such a perspective misunderstands what Biblical impartiality and *Imago Dei* mean and do not mean. For instance, Leviticus 19:15 defines and properly contextualizes the concept of Biblical impartiality: *"You shall not render an unjust judgment; you shall not be partial to the poor or defer to the great: with justice you shall judge your neighbor."*
>
> In discussing impartiality, God does not scrub the aforementioned distinctions of various people in Israel; impartiality nowhere in Scripture negates the aforementioned precepts of one's legal status in a given nation. This passage points to the fact that to treat one illegal immigrant who possessed wealth differently from one without money is what is partial. To say that God created everyone in His image does not negate the Biblical concepts of, in this case, legal status in the land: To clarify the point, a bank robber, a murder, and an illegal immigrant are all created in God's image, but that fact does not place them above the law of land! Often, attempts are made to foist impartiality or *"Imago Dei"* onto the discussion about immigration policy. Such attempts however serve to reveal the proponents' ignorance or else deliberate twisting of Scripture.[505]

The delineation between the legal "alien" or "stranger" ("*ger*") and the foreigner or illegal ("*nekhar*" or "*zar*") in Biblical law is stark indeed. The "*ger*" could receive social benefits (Leviticus 19:9-10; Deuteronomy 24:19-22; Deuteronomy 26:12-13) and all the benefits and protections of a citizen as has been previously noted, whereas the foreigner ("*nekhar*") could not.

"To remain Biblical, these distinctions between citizens, immigrants and (illegal) foreigners should never be obliterated. To eradicate these distinctions postures oneself as more knowledgeable and insightful than God"[506] who obviously had these distinctions in His mind when He scattered the people into different nations in Genesis 11.

---

[505] Ibid.

[506] Ibid.

Furthermore, is it not helpful to be reminded by Mark D. Tooley,* President of the Institute of Religion and Democracy, that much of the Hebrew Scriptures portray

> the Jews attempting to get back home from their various exiles, not about their trying to immigrate elsewhere, legally, or otherwise? This point seems to be lost on many modern religious advocates of unrestricted immigration, many of whom shun all national borders and nation states, the U.S. in particular. For some of these theologians and religious activists, the U.S. is not a nation worthy of protection but merely a smorgasbord of special benefits that good manners require must be offered to all.[507]

Hospitality to the Stranger in our Midst

Martin Luther in his "Lectures on Genesis," Chapter 18, portrays Abraham as not only the "father of faith" but also a "father of good works"[508] as he praises the patriarch for being "a beautiful moral example of hospitality"[509] at Mamre. Abraham's service to three strangers is viewed as an embodiment of the Church's hospitality toward the Lord Himself. Our sixteenth-century Biblical scholar and theologian optimistically asserts that "There is hospitality wherever the Church is"[510] and thus depicts hospitality as a mark of the Church's holiness. "To be true members of the Church, remember to practice hospitality"[511] and like Abraham, offer "not only a kindly heart but also a bounteous and beneficent hand toward strangers…" Notice, however, the caveat that follows: "But, as I have said, this virtue exists solely ***in*** the Church"[512] [emphasis mine].

---

* Mark D. Tooley is layman and lifelong member of the United Methodist Church who became president of the Institute of Religion and Democracy (IRD)in 2009, an ecumenical religious think tank that makes Christian arguments for democracy, human rights and religious freedom. His articles have appeared in the *Wall Street Journal, World, National Review*; has contributed chapters to numerous books, and authored *Taking Back the United Methodist Church, The Peace That Almost Was,* and *Methodism & Politics in the 20th Century.*

507 Tooley, Mark D., "Jesus Christ: Illegal Immigrant?" *FrontPage Magazine*, September 15, 2006. <https://archive.ph/t40VD> or <http://www.politicsforum.org/forum/viewtopic.php?p=968716>.

508 LW 3:190. *Lectures on Genesis Chapters 15-20*, "Chapter 18," LW 3:190.

509 Ibid., LW 3:177.

510 Ibid., LW 3:178.

511 Ibid.

512 Ibid., LW 3:181.

Luther was making a distinction that many well-intentioned Christians overlook even to this day. He maintains that

> when the Word lets its light shine, persecutions and exiles were most common. In our own age, too, there is the great light of the Word, kindled as the result of God's goodness. For this reason, Satan rages and through the pope, the bishops, and tyrannical princes fills the entire world with poor people and exiles who roam about in misery, thirst, hunger, and are oppressed in various ways. Hence there should be…an Abraham, and there should be some little domain of a godly prince in which there can be room for such people; for where there is no house, there can be no hospitality.[513]

He continues offering cautious and practical insight:

> Here Abraham believes that he is seeing true strangers of this kind; for I am calling true strangers those who live in exile because of the Word, not those vagrants of whom there has been a very great supply under the papacy, who either out of wantonness and flippancy or because of hope in their own righteousness went into exile of their own accord without being compelled to do so by persecution.[514]

Luther is identifying these three strangers as those who live in exile because of the Word, in contrast to the monks who chose forms of self-imposed exile to show off and trust their own self-righteousness. "This is a very beautiful picture of a man who is generous and bounteous toward brethren afflicted because of their profession of the Word, for Abraham believed that they were men of this kind."[515]

Obviously an astute student of human nature, Luther is aware of people who trick the Church into giving them things, even though they are not truly in need:

> There is no lack of idle hypocrites who are accustomed to begging; and if you give them a handout, they at once spend it on gambling and carousing; and where they know of churches ready to assist the needy, they flock together as for prey and for a time simulate godliness solely in the hope of richer gain. Thus Paul

---

[513] Ibid., LW 3:179.

[514] Ibid., LW 3:179-180.

[515] Ibid., LW 3:181.

> (1 Timothy 5:16) complains about the wanton widows who were being supported at public expense and were a burden to the churches. If this happened at that time, it is not remarkable if today many come to us too under the pretense of being exiles in distress, as though they had been deprived of their means because of their confession of the Word. So far as they are concerned, it is not hospitality but rapine and an unfair burden which is imposed on the churches. Therefore, caution is needed here, so that we may beware of such vagrants.[516]

"Undoubtedly," Luther acknowledged, "idle men frequently took advantage of Abraham by abusing his generosity and flocking to him for they knew that a table was prepared for them where he lived and that everything was placed at their disposal"[517] and thus "very many abuse the generosity of the godly."[518] Luther had a concern about wasting kindness on imposters that could best be used toward those truly in need. Such kind acts which are lost on evil, however, are not lost on Christ. Nevertheless, there is indeed a balance between caution and kindness that should be exercised.

Luther proceeds to call attention to important differentiations in regard to providing "prudent generosity" and hospitality. While he is focusing on exiles who flee for their lives due to religious persecution, he reminds his listeners and readers that a Christian's first responsibility is obviously to those within their own families, then to those within "the household of faith" or to the "brethren," followed by fellow citizens who experience misfortune, and to those exiled because of their confession or who have fled from persecution. He then enthusiastically encourages the faithful to extend their generosity toward those "who are strangers in the State, provided that they are not manifestly evil, as for example, if a Turk (in today's language, a Muslim) were to come to us, not because of our doctrine, but as a beggar" and as a stranger in distress. "Even though he is not suffering because of the Word but is in distress in other respects, he should not be disregarded by us."[519]

"The basic lesson we can draw from Luther's teachings for the Church today," according to Leopoldo A. Sanchez M.* of Concordia Seminary (director of the Center for Hispanic Studies),

---

[516] Ibid., LW 3:182.

[517] Ibid., LW 3:183.

[518] Ibid., LW 3:189.

[519] Ibid., LW 3:183-184.

* Leopoldo A. Sanchez M., is Professor of Hispanic Ministries, Professor of Systematic Theology and Director of the Center for Hispanic Studies at Concordia Theological Seminary, St. Louis. He was the main drafter for The Lutheran Church—Missouri Synod's report *Immigrants Among Us: A Lutheran Framework for Addressing Immigration Issues (2012)*, and has served Lutheran Women's Missionary League, Lutheran Hour Ministries, and the Lutheran Immigration and Refugee Service (LIRS) as a theological consultant for various projects.

> is that we become the House of Abraham in the world extending the hand of mercy to exiles, both Christian and others regardless of factors such as their religious commitments or their legal status in the State. Such hospitality will be exercised within the bounds of the law and it can include assisting people with food, clothing, shelter, medical assistance, psychological counseling, childcare, schooling, immigration legal service and visiting immigrants in detention centers.[520]

Sanchez concludes that we, like Luther, should not lump all strangers into the same category, but take into consideration the circumstances. He also is aware of how Luther

> balances his concern for hospitality toward exiles with an equally valid concern for the needs of the residents of the State which is an important consideration about public policy on refugees and immigrants today.... [He cautions, however, that we should not] retreat into a default position of fear, suspicion, or shaming of the stranger, but rather lead with hospitality even if at times we might be taken advantage of in doing so.... A hospitable disposition toward exiles must remain a constant in the lives of Christians and give guidance to their thinking on refugees and immigrants. Even though Luther himself allows Christians to exercise a certain priority of love toward those of the family of faith in the realm of the Church and toward their fellow citizens and residents in the realm of the State, the basic virtue of hospitality toward all exiles remains one of her unique identity marks in the world.[521]

Luther conceded that some "strangers" may have evil intent, and some beggars are lazy opportunists and not really in need. He was also a realist in weighing the options, advocating the practice of wise discernment while upholding Christ-like values even within the Peasants' Revolt that brought terror, destruction, and death. Like Donald Trump, who never claimed all refugees and travelers from the Middle East are radical Muslims intent on killing Americans, or that all illegal immigrants

---

[520] Sanchez M., Leopoldo, A., "The Church Is the House of Abraham: Reflections on Martin Luther's Teaching on Hospitality Toward Exiles," *Concordia Journal*, 44:1, p.23. <https://issuu.com/concordiasem/docs/thechurchisthehouseofabraham?e=2445893/92039284>.

[521] Ibid., p.36.

at the southern border are criminals, rapists or "bad hombres," he acknowledged the probability of deception in order to pursue self-interests that would be harmful to others. Both Luther and Trump thus affirmed the role and importance of the law, and the responsibility of Christians, citizens, non-citizens, and immigrants to obey civil authorities.

Neither one would close their eyes to those who would intentionally break the law of the land to advance their status by cutting ahead of those who were legally entering the country, and then knowingly game the system by claiming asylum and refugee status. Just as Luther called out the indulgence peddlers who were taking undue advantage of his fellow countrymen at great expense, economically as well as spiritually, so does Trump (as did his Democratic predecessor, along with other Democratic leaders) call out those entering the country illegally without proper vetting to gain legal documentation as an immigrant. Without proper vetting, there could be—and indeed, there have been—illegals coming across our border who desire to do us harm, commit rape and murder, endanger the populace through drug smuggling, and engage in human trafficking and child sexual exploitation. In addition, one cannot dismiss those "undocumented immigrants" who have previously committed felonious crimes and have been deported, only to re-enter the country again illegally as repeat offenders.

Being a Sanctuary Denomination

To proclaim the Gospel, follow the teachings of the Sermon on the Mount, and do the works of mercy and compassion, one can foster an unwillingness to deal with immigration laws that Christians are also commanded to obey. If such laws, or any law, are judged to be unjust, then our responsibility as citizens of both the Church and the State should be to promote serious consideration of a more just state of affairs. Eugene Brueggemann* acknowledges that "while no one of significance is calling for the establishment of a Christian theocracy in America today, there are many Christians who believe that the government should legislate and govern in a way that conforms to Christian values."[522]

---

* Eugene Brueggemann, a Lutheran pastor on the Editorial Board of *The Daystar Journal: Gospel Voices in and for the Lutheran Church—Missouri Synod.*

[522] Brueggemann, Eugene, "Luther's Doctrine of the Two Kingdoms in Today's World," *The Daystar Journal*, Fall 2006. <thedaystarjournal.com/luthers doctrine-of-the-two-kingdoms-in-todays-world

The Capstone Report comments:

> Making [mercy] the only consideration is nothing short of setting up a progressive-Christian theonomy in a dangerous attempt to realize the eschaton [trying to make that which belongs to the afterlife happen here and now] and usher in a "Gospel Utopia" [which, in Luther's theology is solely God's domain.] At the heart of such claims is a childish political theology that mercy and love are good things and with justice are important. However, they cannot be the only consideration when viewing a policy. Any evangelical political theology must contain at its core a respect for God's created intention for government…[otherwise it will] confuse the purpose of the State with the purpose of the individual and the Church…"[523]

I am convinced we are witnessing within my denomination, the Evangelical Lutheran Church in America, such confusion with the passage of a resolution making the ELCA the *first* "Sanctuary Denomination." Often political ideology clouds clear Biblical interpretation, as well as good theology. Several concerns suggest such deficiencies in Biblical and theological insights that should guide crucial discussion and action, instead of rushing to advance political bias. It is my opinion that such blatant action sprung surprisingly upon the ELCA will lead inevitably to further confusion about the role and mission of the Church in the world today. This can be attested by the passage of "A Declaration of Inter-Religious Commitment (DIRC)" which we have previously referenced.[†]

This Declaration states, "We must be careful about claiming to know God's judgments regarding another religion." An amendment, recalling the words of Jesus in John 14:6 (NRSV)—*"I am the way, and the truth, and the life. No one comes to the Father except through Me"*—reads, "We have a clear statement from Jesus, who is fully God and fully man. We do therefore have a basis to know God's views on religions that do not require faith in Jesus Christ as God's Son." That amendment was overwhelmingly defeated by voting members to our national Assembly.

On that very issue, Dennis D. Nelson, Executive Director of Lutheran CORE, asks how that document (DIRC) could be recommended by the ELCA Conference of Bishops and approved by the ELCA Church Council when it "rejects clear teaching of Scriptures." He asks,

---

523 <http://capstonereport.com/2018/01/21/repairing-evangelical-political-theology-getting-the-State-right/31843>.

† See Chapter 15.

> How can there be any doubt that God means what He says in the First Commandment? *"You shall have no other gods before Me."* (Exodus 20:3) In Acts 4:12 Peter said, *"There is salvation in no one else, for there is no other name under heaven given among mortals by which we must be saved."* First Timothy 2:5 says, *"There is one God and also one mediator between God and humankind, Christ Jesus."* It was bad enough that the document rejects the clear teaching of Scripture. It was even worse that in so solidly rejecting the amendment the Assembly was rejecting the words of Jesus.[524]

Consider another example. Why adopt the phraseology of "Sanctuary Denomination" in a declaration to "publicly state that walking alongside refugees and immigrants is a matter of faith?"[525] We have been assured that the Assembly just wanted to reaffirm the commitment of the ELCA as "we continue and deepen what we have been doing as a church for some time in support of refugees and immigrants."[526] Could the difference perhaps be hidden, but signaled, in the word "deepen?" Indeed, we Lutherans have had a proud and distinguished ministry of supporting immigrants and refugees by partnering with agencies like the Lutheran Immigration and Refugee Services (LIRS) in years past, but such immigrants and refugees were legal and documented by the government, and further channeled through the Church in their placement with hosts and sponsors.

The refugees my parents assisted and supported, those my home congregation of Emmanuel Lutheran in New Philadelphia, Ohio, sponsored, as well as the two young Vietnamese men my wife and I housed and supported along with our newly formed congregation in Brecksville, Ohio, had no need of being "sheltered" or "protected" from authorities in "sanctuary cities" nor "sanctuary states." Neither would their status have been enhanced being associated with a "sanctuary denomination." If the goal of the Assembly was true as stated, would not "Renewing and Celebrating Our Church's Commitment to Refugees and Immigrants" and "Welcoming the Stranger in Our Midst" better describe our "evangelical" mission stance than using language associated with jurisdictions refusing to cooperate with federal officials on immigration enforcement?

---

524 Nelson, Dennis D., "Letter to Friends," September 2019.

525 Eaton, Bishop Elizabeth, "Pastoral Email to Siblings," August 14, 2019.

526 Gafkjen, Bishop William, "Pastoral Letter to Members and Friends," August 12, 2019.

And notice how the explanations, so conspicuous by their absence, avoid making the distinction between immigrants who enter the country legally and those who enter illegally. Obviously, the use of such descriptive adjectives or distinguishing categories as we find in the Old Testament is deemed as not being politically correct. Illegal immigrants who break the law entering the United States to "claim asylum" or justify "refugee" status are often treated the same as those who abide by the rule of law and often receive priorities and benefits as we have previously mentioned, ahead of those who have been standing in line, which should be viewed as a justice issue. America, it seems to me, should be a sanctuary for law-abiding Americans, legal immigrants and refugees, not a sanctuary for illegal immigrants.

Here, for example, is how the misinterpretation or distortion of Biblical distinctions is used intentionally to bolster appropriate Christian empathy toward illegal immigrants. Quoting my bishop, The Rev. Dr. William O. Gafkjen of the Indiana-Kentucky Synod, from his pastoral letter explaining the action of the Assembly declaring the ELCA as a "sanctuary church body:"

> Please note: The Churchwide Assembly did not call for any illegal actions, all actions mentioned by the Churchwide Assembly are legal. Whether any person or organization chooses to engage in civil disobedience (and therefore accept the consequences) is up to them. Nevertheless, one panelist in one of the news reports that I saw misguidedly proclaimed that the ELCA is violating both federal law and the Word of God in declaring itself a sanctuary church body. To make his point he quoted Romans 12:1ff: "*Let every person be subject to the governing authorities.*" Of course, the Word of God also says, in many places, that we are called to welcome, accompany, advocate for, and protect those who come from other places to live among us:
>
> > "*Do not oppress a foreigner; you yourselves know how it feels to be foreigners, because you were foreigners in Egypt.*" [Exodus 23:9]
> >
> > "*For I was hungry and you gave me something to eat, I was thirsty and you gave me something to drink. I was a stranger and you invited me in.*" [Matthew 25:35]
> >
> > "*The stranger who resides with you shall be to you as the native among you, and you shall love him as yourself, for you were aliens in the land of Egypt; I am the Lord your God.*" [Leviticus 19:34]
> >
> > "*Do no wrong to the **resident alien**.*" [Jeremiah 22:3] (Emphasis added)

> Ministries of welcome, advocacy, accompaniment, and protection for refugees and other immigrants are rooted in God's Word and enlivened by the Spirit of Jesus. Freed in Christ crucified and risen, we are sent to love our neighbor as Jesus has loved us. We disagree with one another about how that love is expressed in the context of a dysfunctional immigration system and in light of the vulnerability of many refugees and immigrants among us. We also disagree with one another about whether, how, and when to resolve the tension between the call to "*be subject to governing authorities*" *and* the call to invite the stranger in and to "*do no wrong to the* ***resident alien***."[527] (Emphasis added)

As already shown, many English translations of the Hebrew terms use the word "foreigner" for all those individuals coming from other countries, not making crucial distinctions the Israelites understood and set forth in their laws which are embodied in the Old Testament. "Aliens" would come closest to our understanding when using the term "foreigner," as opposed to native-born citizens. Strangers or sojourners and "resident aliens," as we have discovered, would be those from other countries who had permission to live as permanent residents, and who basically enjoyed the same rights and responsibilities as native-born citizens or to those who had permission to reside temporarily in the host country. We have witnessed the same distinctions in our country with those possessing permission to be within our borders by having a passport and visa, or having made an application for citizenship. In Hebrew, "foreigner" carries negative overtones and would come closest to what we describe as an "illegal immigrant" or an "undocumented" immigrant without standing.

One could further point to the distinction we have made in who our neighbor is by Jesus' parable of the Good Samaritan and His obvious understanding of Christians residing among us as citizens, brothers and sisters in Christ, but who are "strangers"—those "unknown" who might even be next-door neighbors. Those neighbors may also be people of other faiths, or unaffiliated religiously (often referred to as "Nones"), or of a different race, ethnicity or culture, but they are living in our country as legal citizens or temporary residents. The concern then, still very real today, is not to oppress or take advantage of those who are different from us. The relevant application is practicing hospitality and demonstrating mercy to all who are of differing nationalities, races and faiths legally living in our midst. This would reflect the hospitality Luther portrays as a mark of the Church's holiness. It is also the fullest meaning of "resident alien" in the Hebrew sense, not those

---

[527] Ibid.

who are illegally living here or those who have been deported, but have again entered the country illegally.

"Undocumented" is used sparingly in the parlance of the ELCA, perhaps because so many immigrants have previously entered the country illegally that they cannot be ignored. We don't really know exactly how many "undocumented" there are in our midst, residing in our country, some of whom were children when first arriving, brought with parents or through traffickers, and thus did not enter under their own volition.

Yes, we have a dysfunctional immigration system, but it does not help having a dysfunctional hermeneutic in understanding Scriptures to support a political bias without the necessity of engaging in "discernment [through] deep and honest discussion, debate, prayer and study" as Bishop Gafkjen now suggests after the fact. Yet he and Presiding Bishop Eaton did not obviously encourage such "discernment" to stand in their way, nor the Assembly's, Synods' and congregations', as they could have by suggesting a motion to refer for study and reflection before acting on the motion, which I believe was entirely premature and now requires damage control.

And yes, for the most part, the ELCA is an immigrant church, made up of descendants of immigrants who chose to follow the laws properly, controlling immigration into the host nation of which they desired to become proud citizens. And for the most part, those immigrants and refugees worked hard in fulfilling the Old Testament expectation of lawful immigrants assimilating into their new homeland of America. Isn't that exactly what we have prided ourselves as being when we say "America is a melting pot" where many people—people of different races, cultures and nationalities—blend together as one? As a matter of fact, that is the motto of the United States: "*E pluribus unum*," or "Out of many, one!" From his Inaugural Address on, President Trump has been fond of stating his deeply felt belief: "We all bleed the same red blood."[528]

Talking Points

Our Presiding Bishop, Elizabeth Eaton, felt compelled to send out her "Talking Points" about what she felt the Assembly meant when the voting members had already, after the vote, *specifically* requested the church through its appropriate units and offices provide guidance for the three expressions of the church (national, synodical and congregational) on what it means to be a sanctuary church body, with a report to the 2022 Churchwide Assembly. Was this an after-thought for having placed the cart before the horse?

528 Trump, <https://www.whitehouse.gov/briefings-Statements/the-inaugural-address>.

A better practice, in my view, was that followed by our fellow Lutherans in the Missouri Synod prior to the approval of their Commission on Theology of Church Relations' (CTCR) report, "Immigrants Among Us: A Lutheran Framework for Addressing Immigration Issues" in November 2012:

> During the process of reflection and writing of the draft, the CTCR benefitted from feedback given by a variety of individuals with a wide range of experience and expertise dealing with immigration issues, who came together at a Consultation on Immigration Issues in El Paso, Texas, September 17-19, 2011. Speakers represented fields such as law, law enforcement, national and local government, social services, ethics, history, as well as church workers serving among immigrants including pastors, district staff, and theological educators.[529]

Utilizing the terminology of "Talking Points" also carries the weight of negative connotations associated with one-sided propaganda funneled through the echo chambers, which continually repeat the same opinions using the same phrases and words in a filibustering drumbeat way, which seems designed to prevent anyone from distracting the messenger with any other point of view. A Washington-based nonprofit advocacy firm, which we will later encounter, The Democracy Integrity Project or TDIP, pumps out daily "research" (stilted propaganda) to prominent Washington journalists and Democratic congressional staffers,[530] which in turn is quickly utilized by passing on the created words and phrases that are repeated over many media outlets, as if the reporters were incapable of formulating their own words, thoughts or opinions.

Would not the "teaching" function of the Church be better served with considerations captioned by "Biblical Insights on Hospitality: A Guide to Understanding Law and Gospel as We Live Simultaneously in Two Kingdoms?" And can one ignore the possibility of how much "hubris" was being attached to boastfully proclaim: "The ***First*** Sanctuary Denomination?"

Interpreting the action of the Assembly, several synodical bishops reiterated Bishop Eaton's talking points, including the following by my bishop, William Gafkjen, who at the time was head of the ELCA Conference of Bishops:

> There is no requirement that any particular synod, congregation, or person provide sanctuary or engage in advocacy or other ministry with or on behalf

---

[529] <https://concordiatheology.org/2013/03/immigrant-neighbor-on-my-mind>.

[530] <https://thefederalist.com/2019/03/21/soros-funded-pr-shop-constructing-media-echo-chamber-push-impeachment>.

> of refugees or other immigrants. In other words, the Churchwide Assembly's declaration that the ELCA is a sanctuary denomination binds only the ELCA Churchwide Organization; it does not bind congregations, synods, or other organizations.[531]

Are our Church leaders unaware that the first thing Article VII of the "Augsburg Confession" states about the Church is that it "is the assembly of saints (or the assembly of 'all believers') in which the Gospel is taught purely and the sacraments are administered rightly?"[532] The Church is not the hierarchy of officials or the bureaucracy of the Pope, Curia and Bishops, but rather the people—the community of believers—those who the elite ecclesiastical establishment had neglected, then in Luther's time and now in the present. The Church is an organism rather than an organization that reflects the ways of the world. The Church is a living body of which each believer is a member possessing the gift of grace. Faith for Luther thus no longer consisted in merely assenting to the Church's teachings, but of trusting the promises of God and the merits of Christ.

One can detect a direct parallel between Martin Luther and President Trump's continual reference to "returning power to the people" for whom the institutions of the Church and government exist to serve. I found it, therefore, not only ironic but disturbing that Bishop Gaflkjen's explanation contradicted the ELCA Assembly's theme and logo under which he published it: "***WE*** ARE CHURCH" (emphasis added), not just the bureaucracy of the Churchwide organization. While historically we have asserted sound theological values as Lutheran Christians (contained in *The Book of Concord*, which includes the "Augsburg Confession"), we actually now turn those foundational Biblical and theological principles on their head as many of our political leaders are doing with our Bill of Rights and the U.S. and state constitutions. We follow the hypocrisy we witness politically by asserting "We the People" on the one hand, but discover we are expected to function as if we are marionettes at the ends of strings controlled by those above who believe we don't have the capacity or sufficient "gray matter" to think clearly for ourselves. Politically these "controllers" can be elected individuals who forsake their role as "representatives" for the benefit and privilege of their elite status, which provides a sense of power and control, or they can be entitled

---

[531] Gafkjen, "Pastoral Letter."

[532] *The Book of Concord: The Confessions of the Evangelical Lutheran Church*, "The Augsburg Confession, Article VII, [The Church] ," translated and edited by Theodore G. Tappert (Philadelphia: Fortress Press, 1959), p.32.

bureaucrats who are not accountable to the electorate or to the "believers" who make up the Church.

Bishop Eaton goes on to clearly explain that "being a sanctuary denomination…may mean providing space for people to live; providing financial and legal support to those who are working through the immigration system; of supporting other congregations and service providers."[533] Who are "***WE***" if not those who are members of the ELCA that provide financial support through ***OUR*** benevolent offerings to fund the operational functions, ministries and staffs of our Churchwide organization—or to use the corresponding governmental and political terminology, "bureaucracy?"

Our presiding bishop seems to be following one of the all too frequent patterns of "Fake News" in presenting material that supports a predetermined position or narrative while simultaneously neglecting to reveal additional "exculpatory material"* that substantially illuminates the "rest of the story,"† which may, if revealed, actually contradict her prejudice. We have now discovered through the Inspector General's report and through the rare ruling of the head of the FISA Court that such abusive practices were committed by the FBI and the Department of Justice to fraudulently obtain warrants that would deprive citizens of their rights in order to substantiate a desire to uncover evidence to impeach President Trump.

As an individual, Bishop Eaton may indeed disagree with positions Martin Luther took, or those of the President, but as the Presiding Bishop of the ELCA speaking for the denomination and its members, she does not have the privilege of distorting or even casting the Reformer's or the President's position in a way that perverts reality or conflates ideas to add support to her own political predisposition, which she desires to propagate.

Acknowledging the Truth revealed in Scripture, and affirming our theological interpretation of that Truth, the Church has a responsibility to speak out and work for more just laws even as we subject ourselves to our authorities (Romans 13:1). Interesting, then, that the Presiding Bishop joined or led 600-700 voting members or participants at the Assembly in protest as they marched to the door of the Immigration and Customs Enforcement (ICE)

---

[533] Eaton, Bishop Elizabeth, "Pastoral Email."

* In the judicial system, "The Brady Rule" requires prosecutors to disclose materially "exculpatory" evidence in the government's possession to the defense.

† "The Rest of the Story" was a weekday radio program originally hosted by Paul Harvey, begun in 1976 and continued until his death in 2009. It consisted of stories presented as little-known forgotten facts on a variety of subjects, with some element of the story held back until the end, when the host would conclude with the tag line "And now you know the rest of the story."

building in Milwaukee—to an office of the Government which is charged with "enforcing the law"—and not to a legislator's office, who has responsibility for writing just laws or re-writing laws that seem unjust.

ICE is a federal law enforcement agency, and the primary investigative arm, of the U.S. Department of Homeland Security, tasked with securing the borders of the United States and safeguarding the integrity of the U.S. immigration system. There the protestors themselves broke the law, taping 9.5 Theses to the front door—supposedly re-enacting a celebrated portrayal of Luther nailing his Ninety-Five Theses to the doors of Wittenberg's Castle Church—which a security guard immediately removed because it was an illegal action! Most historians and scholars dismiss Luther's posting action as historical fact, but assert it was merely legend, perpetuated at a historic celebration of The Reformation, as we will further explore. Nevertheless, whether Luther had actually posted his Theses as is so frequently portrayed, or posted by someone else, it would have been legal, as those church doors served as a community bulletin board for such announcements, not an illegal occurrence like we witnessed being exhibited in Milwaukee.

ABC News reports "ICE issuing fines to [undocumented] immigrants who have taken sanctuary in churches" as they seek to avoid deportation orders as well as to those who "facilitate their presence." They note that "ICE has had the authority to issue civil fines for decades."[534] I may not agree with all the laws enacted or even how they are adjudicated, but I am bound to work to right those perceived injustices through the legal means provided.

Luther and Trump are far more complex individuals than a simple snapshot view can ever present, or a simple highlighting of a mere facet of one's speech or action. Without acknowledging the wider context or crucial details, one can obviously distort the true picture to achieve the specified end in making one's point. Consider this particular example: Bishop Eaton is quoted in the press as saying:

> Luther wanted to make it clear there is no barrier, no boundary between the believer and between God, and nothing should stand in the way. And in the same way, there should be no boundary between those who are seeking freedom and opportunity and safety.... Luther tried to break down walls. We're trying to do the same thing.[535]

---

[534] <https://abcnews.go.com/Politics/ice-issuing-fines-immigrants-sanctuary-churches/story?id=64094018>.

[535] <https://www.wuwm.com/post/lutheran-activists-borrow-martin-luther-protest-immigration-policies-milwaukee#stream/0>.

The press, of course, immediately linked that statement to President Trump's "call for an expanded wall between the U.S. and Mexico to deter illegal immigration."[536] Certainly, Bishop Eaton knows such conflation serves her partisan purpose, when Luther in fact had called for the repair and strengthening of the wall around Wittenberg to protect its residents and his students, as we shall soon examine in greater detail. It is, however, disappointing that the leaders of our church, including the Presiding Bishop, do not know our own history surrounding Luther, nor obviously even bothered to check the facts before uttering a false claim to substantiate their political posturing. One could understand if the news media did not fact-check Bishop Eaton's remarks covered nation-wide and beyond but assumed given her position she would know what she was asserting. Likewise, one would presume she understands the difference and significance between walls that exist to protect people from walls that "jail" and "enslave" them as President Reagan so effectively called attention to with the Berlin Wall. Credit must be given to those in the press who covered the event and accurately used the word "illegal," which the Bishop with her "talking points" and our synodical Bishop conveniently failed to acknowledge, in favor of utilizing the nondescript or their "politically correct" terms: "immigrants" and "refugees."

There is a world of difference between immigrants who legally enter the country and those who illegally cross the border by breaking the law. As we have already observed, Luther, in his extensive commentary on Abraham, cautioned about extending hospitality to those with evil intent, or who abuse the claim of persecution to seek asylum, by going into exile on their own under false pretense to game the system for their economic benefit.

It is disappointing to see the leaders of our Church use eisegesis (interpreting a text in a way that introduces one's own presuppositions, agenda, or bias), rather than proper exegesis (the systematic process and analysis of a text to arrive at a coherent sense of meaning, viewed in its historical context and surrounding setting), which is the hermeneutic method I was taught in seminary. To understand how the Holy Spirit speaks to us in our time, Scripture must be interpreted, contextualized and understood by its original audience in its own time. There is a consequential difference between exegesis and eisegesis. Exegesis means that one allows the text to speak for itself within its context, whereas eisegesis indicates that one makes the text say what he or she wants it to say. In specific reference to Scripture, eisegesis is cherry-picking a verse or text to provide confirmation for a pre-held view or agenda, without acknowledging its context (including surrounding verses)

---

[536] Ibid.

or the implications of other texts which may reveal diverse applications or contradictory interpretations.

Even more harmful is the dishonesty of intentionally misleading the people of God who are not as well-versed in Scripture as those schooled to lead, having been entrusted to do so faithfully. Luther, addressing "The Councilmen of Germany," had some appropriate words regarding such malfeasance in the interpretation given to texts by those within our religious realm, just as applicable to our political realm today:

> When men attempt to defend the faith [or a political view] with such uncertain arguments and mistaken proof texts, are not Christians [citizens and reporters] put to shame and made a laughingstock in the eyes of adversaries who know the language? The adversaries only become more stiff-necked in their error and have an excellent pretext for regarding our faith as a mere human delusion. When our faith is thus held up to ridicule, where does the fault lie?" [Luther suggests it is with the language,] "missing the sense of the text and twisting it to suit their fancy."[537]

I'm convinced Luther could probably hear a loud "Amen!" from President Trump and a resounding, thunderous, standing ovation from supporters.

It is true, both left and right use this methodology, especially on such issues like immigration, to strengthen their arguments. It is revealing that the contributing editor of *The Christian Century*, Jason Byassee, who teaches Homiletics and Biblical Hermeneutics at the Vancouver School of Theology, honestly admits in a column for the religious left leader Jim Wallis' *Sojourners* website that "occasionally it's the liberals who are the literalists about the Bible."[538]

Mark D. Tooley, a Methodist layperson and President of the Institute of Religion and Democracy, whose article on "Jesus Christ: Illegal Immigrant?" includes the above quote by Byassee, believes

> many religious leftists practice a politically and expediently expansionist interpretation of the Scriptures. Biblical admonitions to treat strangers kindly become political demands for abolishing immigration law.

[537] LW 45:362. *The Christian in Society II*, "To the Councilmen of Germany."

[538] Tooley, "Jesus Christ: Illegal Immigrant?" <https://archive.ph/t40VD>.

> Biblical commands to feed the hungry become political demands for an unrestricted welfare state. Biblical aspirations for peace become political demands for unilateral disarmament. In fact, the Scriptures almost never offer the specific public policy guidance that the Religious Left, even more than the Religious Right, effusively likes to claim. Serious Christian moral reasoning calls for more than the Religious Left's kind of bumper sticker sloganeering.[539]

In the same manner, we discover in the impeachment of President Trump that the framers of the Constitution or our founders are being continually cited or credited literally when it seems helpful and sounds appropriate to do so. We hear of Alexander Hamilton from those who probably do not even recognize his image on a ten-dollar bill. At the same time, these very individuals ignore or shred the same documents by violating principles and values espoused therein, such as upholding due process and being presumed innocent until proven guilty. They also tend to practice a double standard that does not meet the "shoe on the other foot" test, as they practice "rules for thee, but not for me." All the "reverent references" to the framers become fraudulent with hypocrisy when such rights are denied, or new laws suggested to eliminate, for example, the right to bear arms, the abolishment of the Electoral College, or the packing of the Supreme Court. Then the Constitution and the Bill of Rights are conveniently ignored, just as other portions of Scripture are disregarded by many who find them inconvenient to their narrative.

Sadly, the caution and fear Dr. William Lazareth* and other theologians of note had expressed prior to the formation of the ELCA in 1988 centered on whether the "Christian fellowship would regenerate in 'fruits of the Spirit' or degenerate into 'works of the law.' Passion for the law-free Gospel will alone determine whether the Lutheran Church will remain a confessional movement within the Church Catholic or slowly succumb to the lures of American mainline, Protestant denominationalism."[540]

---

[539] Ibid.

* Dr. William Lazareth, former Bishop of the Metropolitan New York Synod of the Evangelical Lutheran Church in America (ELCA) had a distinguished career as a college and seminary professor, author and leader with the ELCA, the former Lutheran Church in America (LCA), and the World Council of Churches (WCC), Geneva.

[540] Lazareth, William, "Love and Law in Christian Life," *Journal of Lutheran Ethics*, November 1, 2001. <https://www.elca.org/JLE/Articles/1005>.

Law and Justice

To be sure, there are "justice issues" to be considered in the multifaceted immigration debate within our country, and we should not preclude mercy and compassion from being part of the discussion and consideration to enlighten new legislation or reform. But, as Luther quickly discerned, altruism and mercy cannot be the only consideration, as if the State is the compassionate arm of society. "All utopian political hopes were alien to Luther," according to George Forell.* "Luther advocated a sober realism in regard to human beings and their possibilities. He had no illusions about their innate goodness. He had no utopian hopes that humans could through their efforts establish God's kingdom on earth."[541]

Forell points to the confusion some Christians have when they attempt to use the State as an instrument of the Gospel. Likewise, Herbert Butterfield† has enunciated the view that "It is essential not to have faith in human nature. Such faith is a recent heresy and a very disastrous one."[542] He is articulating an insight which was part and parcel of Luther's counsel which, when ignored by the Church, leads to "*Schwarmerei*," the enthusiastic confusion of Law and Gospel. I believe this great secular historian speaks clearly to our current discourse, as well as to the awkward and embarrassing situation in which the ELCA finds itself after having thrust itself forward with the pronouncement on being a "Sanctuary Denomination." In making a very "Lutheran" observation, Butterfield says,

> Somewhere or other there exists a point at which our ambitions, however well-meaning, do become a defiance of the providential order. At that point there would be better hope for the world if we would try to see rather how to make the best of it and accept some of our limitations and discomforts as the decree of Providence, lest by too feverish an activity we only make matters worse.[543]

The gift of "Good News" comes to those who hear and receive Christ's promises with saving faith, enabling one to repent and believe in the assurance of forgiveness. This forgiveness overcomes sin through Christ's saving death and resurrection, described as

---

541 Forrell, George, "Luther's Theology and Foreign Policy." <https://www.elca.org/JLE/Articles/993>.

* George W. Forell was a pastor, author, and professor at Gustavus Adolphus College, Chicago Lutheran Theological Seminary, and the School of Religion of the State University of Iowa. He also served as President of The American Society for Reformation Research.

† Herbert Butterfield was a British historian, philosopher, and Vice Chancellor of the University of Cambridge.

542 Butterfield, Herbert, *Christianity and History* (London: Fontana, 1957), p.66.

543 Ibid., p.135.

justification, the bedrock of Luther's theology. It comes outwardly and establishes a vertical relationship that restores our broken relationship with God and equips us to lead new and transformed lives. For Dr. Paul J. Seastrand,*

> This vertical relationship, however, is misconstrued when the Gospel is equated with human accountability under the law, such as moral imperatives to love the neighbor and projects of social transformation addressing racism, sexism, poverty, earth care, etc. In its "spiritual" use, the law accuses, denounces, punishes, and drives to the Gospel; in its "political" use, the law in the public arena orders society, punishes crime, and directs justice; yet in neither its spiritual nor its political use does the law justify or save humanity from the deep schism and self-centeredness within human nature that is the root condition of sin.
>
> The Gospel is what God does, the law is what the justified do with renewed hearts, gratitude, and purpose. Justification does lead "horizontally" to the love and justice that Christians are to demonstrate to all persons (the "new obedience" ["faith should produce good fruits and good works"] spoken of in Article 6 of *The Augsburg Confession*[544]). However, identifying the Gospel with ethical idealism and social activism reduces it to an anemic moralism and a civil works righteousness that obscure the divine source and power that authors "faith active in love." This danger tempts all Christian churches.[545]

While asserting that no individual Christian and no Christian denomination can be free of cultural conditioning, nor should we want to be, Seastrand maintains

> The relationship between faith and culture is not an "either-or," but is a "both-and."...The larger question is whether any church can avoid reflecting back to society the values of society. Since its inception, the ELCA has run the risk of ceding its distinctive evangelical language and interpretation to the language and interpretation of postmodern liberal culture.[546]

---

[544] "The Augsburg Confession," *The Book of Concord*, p.31.

* Paul J. Seastrand, now a retired pastor living in Billings, MT, has served the ELCA in numerous congregational, synodical, and churchwide capacities.

[545] Seastrand, Paul J., "The Risky Engagement of Gospel and Culture in the ELCA," *Lutheran Forum*, Vol. 55, No. 3, Fall 2021, pp.55-56.

[546] Ibid.

When that occurs, the Gospel is not serving, but is sacrificed to, social action. As I have understood Scripture and our Lutheran theology, the inclusion of all people being "in Christ" is based on grace, not race or any other label. I am reminded of my pastor while growing up in New Philadelphia, Ohio, James N. Fisher, who continually reminded worshippers that "the road to hell is paved with good intentions." The central problem challenging the Church has its roots not in our intentions or goals, but in the processes that direct and flow from our values and beliefs as we witness in our reform warriors. The problem is not the love, fairness, justice and goodness the ELCA or any denomination wants to express in its social ethics, but whether our church has maintained sufficient clarity and resolve about our evangelical theology to direct those policies and actions.

It often appears that the Church "rushes to judgments" as in the ELCA's pronouncements of being a "Sanctuary Denomination" or in justice and advocacy issues as well as "Pastoral Letters" from the Bishop often written seemingly with naivete, in order to "sound" or "appear" good and, as we have noted in A Declaration of Inter-Religious Commitment (DIRC), to guide the ELCA's relationship to people of other faiths being "careful about claiming to know God's judgments." In the process, we surrender the sources and norms of Law and Gospel, of justification and sanctification, for those cultural sources and norms that are associated with race, color, and gender identities; wealth disparities and equity; climate change; theories of social transformation; etc. When public leaders, especially those within the Church, fail to interrogate their own views and remain captive to prejudicial ideologies, the danger we witness is an increasing division and polarization which, within the Church, suppresses the spiritual and social realities of unity and equality empowered by Christ. The Church alone has been commissioned to proclaim first and foremost the authentic voice and Truth of the Gospel in and above the many other voices of culture.

Professor Lamin Sanneh* of Yale Divinity School has been quick to remind us that "Governments cannot love."[547] It is not that America lacks hospitality or generosity, as our country admits large numbers of legal immigrants each year and grants asylum to thousands of refugees. The United States, as the number-one destination country for immigration around the world, has been a world leader in refugee resettlement.

---

* Lamin Sanneh, born in Gambia and eventually a naturalized U.S. citizen, was Professor of Missions and World Christianity at Yale Divinity School, and Professor of History at Yale University.

547 Elowsky, Joel, "Luther, Religious Freedom and the Two Kingdoms," <https://www.academia.edu/7033810>.

> America's big heart in welcoming tens of thousands of refugees and asylum seekers from war-torn and disaster-ravaged nations comes with a huge cost.... The Federation of American Immigration Reform put the five-year price tag at...nearly $80,000 per refugee. There are some 18 federal and state programs refugees can tap for financial help, including food stamps, child-care, public housing and school loans.[548]

In addition, many of these same governmental programs provide support to those who have illegally entered our country. The Federation for American Immigration Reform (FAIR) uses the figure of $116 billion a year as the cost of undocumented, illegal immigrants to the taxpayers.[549] Congregations, charitable organizations, and individuals also provide support and assistance, and we cannot dismiss our country's largesse in bestowing billions annually in foreign assistance for peace, security, health, humanitarian efforts, education, social services, and economic development throughout the world. Never in the history of the world has any country amassed so much wealth and power and used it for the benefit of others outside their country as the United States of America.

Compassion and Mercy

We need to be reminded that the Biblical teachings and commands about compassion, mercy, and welcoming the stranger were given to religious people—to the Jews and Christians, not to governments. Critically, one could view the results we are witnessing as an indictment on the Church, and at the very least underscore the responsibilities churches have toward others who are strangers in our own communities, and even more locally within our congregations, where visitors should be treated as guests we have invited and welcomed into our midst. As we will discover in Luther's understanding of Scripture from his doctrine of "Two Kingdoms," God has established specific responsibilities for governments and civil authorities: preserving order, protecting citizens and their property, and punishing wrongdoers.

---

548 <https://www.washingtonexaminer.com/refugee-costs-88-billion-80-000-per-immigrant-free-welfare-medicaid>.

549 <https://markets.businessinsider.com/news/stocks/new-fair-study-illegal-immigration-costs-116-billion-annually-1002644791>, also <https://www.fairus.org/press-releases/new-fair-study-illegal-immigration-costs-116-billion-annually>.

> The authority God delegates to civil government focuses on justice, not mercy (though, as we have pointed out, this is not to say that laws should not be tempered by mercy). Biblical teachings of mercy generally apply to individual conduct, not to civil authorities. Further, standards of justice are not fully moral if they are not accompanied by judgment and punishment. These two elements (judgment and punishment) are integral, or else justice is not just, [according to Dr. Edwards. He further explains,] On some matters of public policy, the Bible speaks clearly. On other issues, there is less clarity and more room for prudential judgment. The rub comes where there is a lack of scriptural clarity on a particular issue, significant differences between the particular society of Old Testament Israel and the United States, or some other factor. Christianity teaches that God, His Word, and His precepts are unchanging, but believers may struggle to find the most appropriate guidance from Scripture for handling a very specific public policy issue for their day and age in their nation. This conundrum of finding and applying the right, timeless principles to a modern policy issue in a specific nation challenges both the laity and clerics.[550]

The rulers in the Church and in the secular government of Luther's day were seeking to extend their sphere of influence into each other's realm, where they did not belong. As we will discover, both the temporal and religious kingdoms depend upon each other, as they share common concerns such as hospitality, but rulers and their subjects need to know that there are limits to each and what those limits are. Compelling "people to get rid of certain books [such as those Luther had written] and to believe and conform to what the rulers prescribe" [551] is cited by Dr. Joel C. Elowsky, Professor of Historical Theology at Concordia Seminary, as an example which Luther referred to as rulers putting themselves in a place where only God belonged, ruling over men's "conscience and faith."

> This is not the domain of the State, however, but of God.... There is a higher authority than the State when it comes to matters of virtue, self-worth, freedom, and what in essence it means to be a human being. The Kingdom

---

[550] Edwards, "A Biblical Perspective."

[551] LW 45:83-84. *The Christian in Society II*, "Temporal Authority."

> of God has something much more enduring, much more all-encompassing to say in this regard than the kingdom of this world.[552]

Writing *The Coming World Civilization* back in 1956, William Ernest Hocking* exposed the weakness of the idea that the government is the answer to all of humanity's problems and aspirations. "We rely...on the political community to do its part in the making of men, but first of all to furnish the conditions under which men can make themselves." We have a misplaced faith in the political community, believing it can deliver more than it is actually capable of doing. "The State, purely as secular, comes to be regarded as capable of civilizing the human being, and in doing so of remaking him, training his will, moralizing him."[553] But governments cannot love, nor can they inculcate virtues such as love, although they may provide a mechanism in which love, freedom and responsibility can be expressed. Yet, even then, as Sanneh realizes,

> the political community is inherently deficient in enabling human beings to mature fully as moral agents. Loving God and our neighbor, giving ourselves for the care of the weak and vulnerable, inspiring, and inculcating virtue and fostering acts of altruism—for these and more, we need another and higher realm of reality.[554]

Hocking reminds us that

> human nature has indeed another mirror, and there with another source of self-training. It is often the religious community—let us call it in all its forms "the Church"—which has promised to give the human individual the most complete view of his destiny and of himself. It projects that destiny beyond the range of human history...It provides standards of self-judgment not alone in terms of behavior, as does the law, but also in terms of motive and principle—of the inner man which the State cannot reach.[555]

---

552 Elowsky, "The Two Kingdoms."

* William Ernest Hocking was an American idealist philosopher at Harvard University.

553 Hocking, William Ernest, *The Coming World Civilization* (New York: Harper, 1956), pp.1-2.

554 Sanneh, Lamin, "Christianity, Politics, and Citizenship," Lausanne Conference at Cape Town, South Africa, p.44.

555 Hocking, p.2.

"The inner man" is the purview of the Kingdom of God, not the kingdom of the world. And yet the State, the kingdom of the world, often becomes the *de facto* lens, the mirror through which we view truth, virtue, and freedom, rather than viewing these things in the kingdom better suited to them, the Kingdom of God.

Blurring the Realms

To blur these distinctions usually means ignoring other clear Biblical principles. For example, attempting to apply Church mandates for hospitality to the national government tends to ignore the authority granted to civic governments to punish wrongdoing and protect and defend its citizens and resources. To believe Luther was not concerned for the peasants and the underprivileged in the society of his day is to misunderstand his pastoral heart. He is credited with developing the concept of the Common Chest, or as we know it, the Community Chest or United Way within our communities for organized charitable giving today. In German it is known as "*gemeinen kasten*," which expanded to become the centralized poor relief system.[556] For Luther, the Common Chest was never to be an alternative to acts of charity and compassion which were to be part of one's Christian lifestyle in the practice of neighbor-love.

Like Donald Trump, who quietly bestows his generosity on people in need, and has demonstrated his concern about restoring dignity to individuals by lifting them off welfare and out of unemployment, so Luther's heart so freely responded to individual needs that his wife had to hide items in their household lest he give them away and upset the family budget. Luther was not very concerned because he was confident God would provide. And God did, primarily through the hard work, wisdom, and good business sense of his wife who, with respect and appreciation, he referred to as "lord" of the house.

Luther was convinced that charity belonged to the compassionate lifestyle of the Christian. Since local churches were unable to supply adequate support for the poor, he expected all sectors of society to contribute toward relief of the poor, as well as support for exiles and refugees, but was still disappointed by the overall lack of generosity: "Today nobody gives anything."[557]

---

[556] Hall M.S.W., Susannah, "The Common Chest Concept: Luther's Contribution to 16th Century Poor Relief Reform," *Journal Social Thought*, 5:1, 1979. <https://www.tandfonline.com/doi/abs/10.1080/15426432.1979.10383279>.

[557] LW 3:182. *Lectures on Genesis, Chapters 13-20*, "Genesis 18."

For Luther, the quandary was this.

> If the heart expects and puts its trust in divine favor, how can a man be greedy and anxious? Such a man is absolutely certain that he is acceptable to God: therefore, he does not cling to money; he uses his money cheerfully and freely for the benefit of his neighbor. He knows full well that he will have enough no matter how much he gives away. His God, whom he trusts, will neither lie to him nor forsake him...[558]

I had a pastor-mentor friend in my home congregation, Dr. Ralph Wheadon, who loved to share the conviction that "God loves a cheerful giver, but He'll also accept from a grudge." The implication, of course, was that the money given with the wrong motivation can be used just as effectively to benefit others, but it will not bring satisfaction to that donor like that experienced by the one who gives joyfully out of the abundance of what he or she has received.

What makes such issues as immigration and refugees so challenging is the reality of the human faces we encounter, especially children. Here Luther suggests that Christians by their actions must exceed expectations when it comes to treating not only Christian exiles, but also those outside the Church.

I believe Luther's basic goal in his teaching on Abraham's hospitality goes beyond the reality that Christians are often inconsistent and thus not always practicing what they preach or teach. Perhaps Luther is speaking prophetically to the Church of our day, calling the Church back to that spiritual disposition or virtue in the heart that must precede and prepare the way for imagining more specific "Church practices" and/or "State policies" regarding the social issues of our day. For example, in the immigration crisis we are currently experiencing, how can we provide a more sensible and realistic framework that balances the needs of our country and its citizens with those legitimately seeking to immigrate from countries throughout the world, as well as those who are fleeing disasters, tyranny or persecution? How do we as citizens of the State and members of the Church more adequately and justly provide hospitality for the strangers—not just immigrants and refugees from other countries, but also new residents among us—in our neighborhoods, congregations and communities? How can we, for example, more effectively teach and instill respect for human life, especially when it comes to gun and knife violence or abortion of the most vulnerable? If the heart is not dealt with first, little holiness can be expected from God's people.

---

[558] LW 44:108. *The Christian in Society I*, "Treatise on Good Works."

In the *Daystar Journal*, Eugene Brueggemann reminds us that,

> no one should question that the Church's preaching and teaching should influence attitudes and actions in the political life of the nation, the Left Hand of God. But for the Church *as Church*, whether it be a denomination, a congregation, or a loose confederation of congregations to get actively involved in party politics is to abdicate or compromise the unique and imperative responsibilities as the Kingdom on the Right. The mission of the Church is **not** to create a kingdom of this world.[559]

Problems surface when issues are addressed as action agendas, as opposed to the teaching agenda of the Church to which individual Christians can respond freely, acting as their conscience dictates. Ordination or holding an office within the Church certainly does not disqualify an individual from government service, with the caveat that they do not present themselves as speaking for the Church.

Pastor Brueggemann summarizes his caution by saying,

> Whether American Lutherans are Republicans or Democrats, ELCA, LCMS, or whatever, it falls on them particularly to distinguish between the work of the right and left hands of God. It is, after all, a confessional position that distinguishes us from many Protestant groups. Witnessing to the Word of God in addressing the great moral issues of the day in pulpits, classrooms, and national assemblies is essential as well as legitimate. Individual members may certainly enter the political arena with the blessings of the church. But for the Church or its officeholders to enter that same arena as *Church* violates the Biblical distinction between the two kingdoms, and it compromises and undermines the mission and ministry assigned to us by our gracious Lord.[560]

In another article, Brueggemann cautions that "we must not assume that the phrase *Evangelical Lutheran* in our Church's name has the same meaning as the word *evangelical* in our national political life." The latter descriptive usage describes conservative Protestant churches and leaders in today's American culture, not our

---

[559] Brueggemann, Eugene, "Luther's Doctrine of the Two Kingdoms in Today's World," *The Daystar Journal*, Fall 2006. <http://thedaystarjournal.com/luthers-doctrine-of-the-two-kingdoms-in-todays-world>.

[560] Ibid.

European religious heritage. While he acknowledges that we are all Protestants, that there is some overlap in our love of the Gospel, and that we hold many traditional doctrines and moral values in common,

> we differ in the confessional principle of the two kingdoms doctrine, which is anchored in Christ's words to Pontius Pilate, *"My Kingdom is not of this world [John 18:36],"* and in Saint Paul's counsel in Romans 13. As a [Church] we are designed to engage society not as a political player, but as a witness to the Truth embodied in Christ and His mission. Our political influence is our faith at work in promoting justice and peace at home and abroad in personal life and in charitable organizations...
>
> It is most certainly true that Lutherans are free to identify with any political party or movement whose values and objectives they share, with the essential caveat that they do not replace the Christian faith and Church as their primary identity. ...[T]he use of the word *evangelical* in American politics today is a cultural indicator with little or no association with the same word in our religious heritage. ...We are Evangelical Lutherans (a traditional religious category), who may or may not be Lutheran evangelicals (a contemporary political category). It is one more way to differentiate between the law and the Gospel as we wend our pilgrim way through the thickets of political clamor into the future where God is leading us.[561]

Dr. Thorsten Prill, our Namibian theologian, finds Luther's doctrine of the Two Kingdoms still relevant today, both for individual Christians and for the Church.

> The doctrine teaches the Church what her main duties are: to preach the Gospel of Christ to her members and to a lost world. Where secular issues dominate the Church's preaching, teaching and worship, it is not the Kingdom of God that radiates into the world, but a fallen world that forces its way into God's Kingdom. The result is a Church that commits a kind of self-secularization, as it can be currently observed, for example in the American Episcopal Church, the Evangelical Lutheran Church in

---

561 Brueggemann, Eugene, "Evangelical—What's in a Name?" *The Daystar Journal*, Fall 2021. <http://thedaystarjournal.com/evangelical-whats-in-a-name>.

> America, the Lutheran Church of Sweden, and unfortunately also in some mainstream Protestant denominations in southern Africa.[562]

For most fair-minded citizens, there is a recognition that our immigration system is broken as well as arcane. It has not kept pace with the legitimate needs of our country, nor has it been able in our highly politicized climate to effectively deal with "immigration outside the law." It is a highly complicated arena where each of us in our own little ways—whether as employers, consumers or homeowners—have counted on and benefited from this force of extralegal immigrants. For example, guest workers are exploited as cheap labor in harvesting our food, maintaining our lawns and landscape, painting our homes, and rendering repairs, often with their compensation being rendered "under the table" and thus not taxable, which presents another justice issue. As we have already witnessed, Hebrews were commanded not to oppress the "stranger" or "sojourner" ("*gers*" or legal immigrants) in their midst, but to treat them equally as fellow citizens and with wages that were commensurate with what native-born citizens would earn.

We once again encounter CIS Fellow James R. Edwards, co-author of *The Congressional Politics of Immigration Reform*, drawing the inference from his research that

> We may fairly conclude that it displays questionable judgment to rigidly construct an immigration policy for 21st Century America based on a handful of Scripture passages taken out of context or from particular instances of migration spanning centuries, vastly different nations and kingdoms, wholly different circumstances, etc. than found in Scripture. Rather, carefully discerning applicable principles better fits the situation.[563]

What seems clear, however, from Biblical witness and from that which Luther argues in presenting his "Two Kingdom" theory, is that except in the rarest of instances, disobedience of duly adopted laws not only dishonors God but displays hatred toward one's neighbor. We read in 1 John 4:20 (NRSV) "*...for those who do not love a brother or sister whom they have seen, cannot love God whom they have not seen.*" Viewing that passage in the context of members of nations, Edwards interprets one's neighbors as

---

562 Prill, "God's Two Kingdoms and the Christian's Two Citizenships."

563 Edwards, "A Biblical Perspective," p.9.

> those people who share one's citizenship, patriotic allegiance, and sacred duty to the body politic...obeying civil law is the normative, Biblical imperative for Christians as discussed above. National sovereignty is part of the authority God has delegated to civil authorities. Whatever the immigration laws of a particular nation, determining the policies of how many immigrants to admit and the terms and conditions applying to immigrants are the prerogative of the national body. Each society may set or change its nation's immigration laws. Those decisions rest within the society, and outsiders have no legitimate voice in that exercise of national sovereignty.[564]

The duty of the sovereign State in dictating the course of justice and the exercise of the sword was also espoused by John Calvin, reformer and statesman, who wrote in his *Institutes of the Christian Religion*:

> If they [civil authorities] ought to be the guardians and defenders of the laws, they should also overthrow the efforts of all whose offenses corrupt the disciplines of the laws.... For it makes no difference whether it be a king or the lowest of the common folk who invades a foreign country in which he has no right, and harries it as an enemy. All such must equally be considered as robbers and punished accordingly.[565]

We have long prided ourselves as being a nation of immigrants and a nation of laws. The ensuing tension between those two distinct national features centers on an immigration system that is not well-tailored to the country's traditional values and current needs. Thus, we see our immigration system predictably and strategically being used politically to incentivize people to come to our country, or remain here, in violation of the law. It is entry into the country illegally that is not sustainable without considerable expense to communities and society at large. We cannot wait any longer to reform America's immigration laws in the midst of the magnitude of the challenges arising from decades of legislative inaction. Only through reform can faith in the system be rebuilt and respect for the rule of law be restored in a way that is in concert with our country's values.

---

564 Ibid.

565 Calvin, John, *Institutes of the Christian Religion*, trans. Ford Lewis Battles (Grand Rapids, MI: William B. Eerdmans Publishing Co., 1975), p.214.

Breaking the law, including immigration laws, flouts God's provision for each person's well-being, because civil authorities have been delegated by Heaven to craft, enact and enforce those laws deemed suitable to their unique circumstances of time and place. We cannot dispute, even though we may not agree with all the laws and policies on the book, that they were adopted through lawful, legitimate, democratic processes. But as Edwards irrefutably articulates:

> [T]his nation is blessed with a republican process for making laws. There is a just and fair way, through the political process, to modify statutes. Thus, the will of the Congress, as manifested in U.S. laws, represents the collective wisdom of the people's representatives, and the will of the American people as a whole as it informed lawmakers' decisions throughout the political process. This is how "the consent of the governed," a solemn principle in American life, operates—as messy and unsatisfying as that at times may be.[566]

566 Edwards, "A Biblical Perspective," p.10.

18

Dual Status of All Christians: Citizens of Two Kingdoms

The mission of the Church is to bring God's saving grace, love, and forgiveness to all (Matthew 28:19). The responsibilities churches have toward members and neighbors differs from the responsibilities governments have toward citizens and non-citizens. Blurring these two distinctions, as we have already noted, usually means ignoring other clear Biblical principles. Those who seek to apply, for example, the Biblical mandate for the Church to demonstrate hospitality as a requirement for the national government tend to ignore the mandate for governments to punish wrongdoers and protect its citizens. Often Scripture is quoted out of context, as we have also shown, and Christians who hold opposing views are often demeaned as if they are somehow less Christian. Scripture itself makes a distinction between the specific responsibilities assigned to the Church and those for which the civic governments are accountable, which we will soon examine.

But first, to better understand that distinction, it will be helpful to recognize a couple of underlying misconceptions that can easily distort Biblical teachings. During the Reformation, there were those who rejoiced at being "freed" by the Gospel. These individuals concluded that the Law, therefore, had no place in the Christian life and that pastors did damage to the Gospel by preaching the Law's demands. It was the Gospel which worked repentance, not the Law which they feared would take the Church back into the legalisms that would mandate "works" as leading one to righteousness. They did, however, recognize the need for the Law in the civil realm, especially for non-believers. Luther identified this gross misinterpretation of his doctrine of "the freedom of a Christian" as "antinomian" ("*Nomos*" is Greek for "law" and "*anti*" means "to be opposed").

In preparing guidance for those who were to inspect the condition of the churches in Electoral Saxony in 1527, Philipp Melanchthon wrote some "Instructions For the Visitors of Parish Pastors," where he stressed the necessity of preaching the Law as well as the Gospel. "Many now talk only about the forgiveness of sins and say little or nothing about repentance.[567] "But," as Martin Bertram* writes in the introduction to his translation of Luther's "Against the Antinomians,"

> true repentance and contrition for sin—which are to be instilled by rigorous preaching of the Law—are the necessary preconditions of genuine faith. Furthermore, the preaching of the Law, e.g., the Ten Commandments, is useful and necessary, he (Luther) insisted, as a guide to the good works which are to follow true faith.[568]

For Antinomians, the Holy Spirit works only through the Gospel; and while not denying the presence of sin in the life of the Christian, the preaching of the crucified Christ alone would lead to true repentance. During the Antinomian Disputations which took place between 1537 and 1540, Luther opposed Johannes Agricola, a former colleague and supporter of The Reformation, who became known as "the Father of the Antinomians."

It is fascinating to discover that Luther experienced many early supporters and colleagues at Wittenberg who later disagreed with him for not going far enough or for having gone too far, much as Trump has experienced. Some of the President's early advisors, and even members within his cabinet, were dismissed or quit because of disagreements with the administration. Among those who fell into disfavor were Anthony Scaramucci, Steve Bannon, Michael Cohen, James Comey, John Bolton and Rex Tillerson, some of whom set out eagerly to write exposés in "tell-all" books and newspaper op-eds, or welcomed the opportunity to give interviews to embarrass the President. For Luther, it was not only Agricola but also Andreas Bodenstein von Karlstadt, Thomas Muntzer, Johann Eck, Huldrych Zwingli, Desiderius Erasmus and others who turned on the Reformer and became his antagonists, with Eck even organizing the Catholic opposition to The Reformation. From what we have discovered about our twin warriors, one can only imagine the difficult challenge of working alongside either one!

In the Antinomian Controversy, Luther asserted that while the Christian remains in the flesh, one is at the same time justified while yet a sinner. As such, the Law still speaks to believers, since lust, greed, ambition, pride, etc. continue to cling to one's flesh. More emphatically, as Rev. Jesse Burns quotes Luther, "[Since] the saints in this life do not entirely

---

[567] LW 40:274. *Church and Ministry II*, "Instruction for the Visitors of Parish Pastors."

* Martin H. Bertram is an independent researcher, based in Hamburg, Germany, specializing in manuscripts of medieval law and a renowned translator of Luther's writings including several volumes of Luther's Works: Sermons on the Gospel of John; Lectures on Galatians; Luther's treatise On The Jews and Their Lies; and the fourth volume of The Christian in Society.

[568] Bertram, Martin, "Introduction to Luther's 'Against the Antinomians,'" *The Christian in Society IV*, LW 47:101.

leave the old man and feel the Law in their members rebelling against the Law of their mind and bringing it into captivity (cf. Romans 7:23), the Law must not be removed from the Church, but must be retained and faithfully driven home."[569]

Again, Luther writes,

> To be sure, man is to be led to repentance through the cross and suffering of Christ. But it does not follow from there that the Law is totally useless, inefficacious, nothing, and to be removed completely. Quite the contrary, we rather come to repentance through the knowledge of the Law as well as through the knowledge of Christ's cross or of salvation.[570]

Pastor Burns at the Lutheran Church in Ventura, Iowa, summarizes Luther by saying "…if one would lose the proclamation of the Law, one would also lose the sweet Gospel which sets sinners free from condemnation."[571]

Here we view Luther 500 years ago, encountering the threat of a radical divide, much like we are witnessing in our political and religious lives today. How contemporary Luther sounds:

> Yet it is safest to turn to a middle road, to turn too much neither to the right or to the left. For both are dangerous, and, as I said already, for this reason also, the office of the Word was instituted, that we might teach both, that is, the Law and the Gospel. The one cannot properly be taught or dealt with safely without the other.… So here too one must divide well, lest only one part be taught in the churches—either fear and sorrow or consolation and joy—but both at the same time.[572]

In his letter to Dr. Casper Guttel, a former Augustinian monk, convert to the cause of the Reformation, and friend of Luther who became the pastor in Eisleben, our Reformer addressed his concerns about this false spirituality in "Against the Antinomians." He asks his friend,

---

569 Burns, Jesse, "The Antinomian Disputations," citing Martin Luther, *Solus Decalogus Est Aeternus: Martin Luther's Complete Antinomian Theses and Disputations*, ed. Holger Sonntag (Minneapolis, MN: Lutheran Press, 2008), p.63. <https://lutheranreformation.org/history/the-antinomian-disputations>.

570 Ibid., Burns citing Martin Luther, *Solus Decalogues*, p.117.

571 Burns, "Antinomian Disputations."

572 Burns, "The Antinomian Disputations," citing Luther's *Solus Decalogus*, p.157.

> Should it be unbearable that the holy Church confesses itself a sinner, believes in the forgiveness of sins, and asks for remission of sin in the Lord's Prayer? How can one know what sin is without the law and conscience? And how will we learn what Christ is, what He did for us, if we do not know what the law is that He fulfilled for us and what sin is, for which He made satisfaction? …For who could know what and why Christ suffered for us without knowing what sin or law is? Therefore, the law must be preached wherever Christ is to be preached, even if the word 'law' is not mentioned…[573]

Both Law and Gospel are therefore necessary for repentance: The Law reveals the guilt of sin, and the Gospel works faith in the gracious promise and assurance of forgiveness.

William Lazareth sums up his article "Antinomians: Then and Now" with these words:

> An antinomian is opposed to all law in the Christian life. Luther, following Paul, taught rather that the Christian is (1) wholly free from the Law as a way of salvation, but also (2) still bound to the Law both religiously insofar as one acts sinfully, and ethically insofar as one acts civilly. Existing at once both righteous (in Christ) and sinful (in self), a Christian is divided into two times: "To the extent that he is flesh, he is under the Law; to the extent that he is spirit, he is under the Gospel."[574]

The reactions that President Trump continually encounters exhibit the same traits of resistance and opposition Luther faced in dealing with so many opponents such as these Antinomians, who argued that the Law has no relevance within the spiritual realm. Can one imagine the heights to which such anger would rage were Trump to identify his opponents with being expressions of the Devil himself, as Luther did? Listen to the Wittenberger:

> God's Word flourished somewhere and His little flock was gathered, the devil became aware of the light, and he breathed and blew and stormed against it with strong, mighty winds from every nook and corner in attempt to extinguish this divine light. And even if one or two winds were brought under control and were successfully resisted, he constantly stormed and blew

---

573 LW 47:113. *The Christian in Society IV*, "Against the Antinomians."

574 Lazareth, William, "Antinomians: Then and Now," (quoting Luther LW 26:342), *Journal of Lutheran Ethics*, 08/01/2005; <https://www.elca.org/JLE/Articles/651>.

> forth from a different hole against the light. There was no let up or end to it, nor will there be until the Last day.
>
> I believe that I alone—not to mention the ancients—have suffered more than twenty blasts and rabbles which the devil has blown up against me. First there was the papacy. Indeed, I believe that the whole world must know with how many storms, bulls, and books the devil raged against me through these men, how wretchedly they tore me to pieces, devoured and destroyed me. At times I, too, breathed on them a little, but accomplished no more with it than to enrage and incite them all the more to blow and blast me without ceasing to the present day.[575]

Can we not hear Donald Trump expressing the same sentiment as Luther, wondering who else could withstand the daily onslaught of "storms," attacks and accusations he has endured since he came down the escalator to announce his candidacy for the highest office of the land? Luther goes on to cite the examples of Muntzer, Karlstadt and the Anabaptists, who "flung the door and windows open as they tried to extinguish the light… but did not achieve their aim."[576] Both our twins were masters at creating rage, as if "on cue," to expose the opposition for who they are and to shed light on the hypocrisy they espouse.

Beyond the sound of Luther's assessment, Trump would certainly identify with the advice as well as the terms Luther used that are still currently employed to summarily describe opposing party positions or political leanings, both "Left" and "Right." We witness the rise of today's Antinomians urging open borders, when ironically it is many of the same voices on the Left favoring more gun control laws. Such apparent and seemingly contradictory positions abide on both sides of the political spectrum today, be it within the secular or the spiritual realms. Another example, however, cannot be ignored. I find it disturbingly pathetic to consider the frequency with which the position "Nobody is above the law" is so pompously pontificated, especially within the impeachment investigation, except as we have noted for those who cross the border "illegally," or for those not being charged with a felony for looting, aggravated assault, torching buildings, or having stolen something under

---

[575] LW 47:115-116. *The Christian in Society IV*, "Against the Antinomians."

[576] Ibid., LW 47:116.

the value of $950 in California, $1,500 in New York, and $2,500 in Texas and Wisconsin,[577] resulting in a dramatic escalation of shoplifting and organized "smash and grab" thefts.

Dr. Lazareth "prays that our official reaffirmation of such updated ecclesiastical applications of Luther's historic theological ethic might greatly contribute to authentic signs of piety…(or) the antinomian adherents of Agricola could soon carry the day politically in reflecting our morally autonomous and secularized society."[578]

In responding to the status of the Decalogue* in Christian ethical life, William Lazareth quotes Luther's significant opinion, shared by John Bugenhagen and Philip Melanchthon:

> This is what should be preached: First, the law should be preached in order to expose and punish sin. As Christ says, "*Repentance and forgiveness of sins should be preached in Christ's name*" (Luke 24:27); and Paul's words, "*The law is our custodian*" (Galatians 3:24)…. Further, God also desires that the law should be preached for the sake of social peace and order against those godless and crude men who live immoral lives.[579]

Both Law and Gospel must be taught and are necessary for repentance. The law reveals sin and works contrition while the Gospel reveals the "Good News" and works faith in the promise of forgiveness. In the words of Paul Speratus's hymn:

> *The Law reveals the guilt of sin*
> *and makes us conscience-stricken;*
> *But then the Gospel enters in*
> *The sinful soul to quicken.*[580]

Pastor Burns concludes his article, "As we remain in the fallen flesh we will have need for God's holy Law, not as a means to make ourselves righteous, but in order that we

---

577 <https://www.themarshallproject.org/2017/08/09/what-s-the-punishment-for-theft-depends-on-what-State-you-re-in>.

578 Lazareth, William, "Antinomians: Then and Now." <https://www.elca.org/JLE/Articles/651>.

* Decalogue is the Greek term for the Ten Commandments or "the Ten Words" in Exodus 20:3-17.

579 Lazareth, William, "Love and Law in Christian Life," (citing WA 15:299). *Journal of Lutheran Ethics*, November 1, 2001, <https://www.elca.org/JLE/Articles/1005>.

580 Speratus, Paul, "Salvation unto Us Has Come (No. 555, vs. 8)," *The Lutheran Service Book* (St. Louis, MO: Concordia Publishing House, 2006).

acknowledge our sinful state so that we take hold of the depth of Christ's saving work for us, delivered in the Gospel message of Christ's forgiveness"[581] and our redemption.

In his treatment of "Secular Authority: To What Extent It Should Be Obeyed"—a treatis within *The Christian in Society II (1523)*, Luther sharply distinguishes the aims of Church and State, limiting the reach of authority for each kingdom. The primary role of the kingdom of the world is to restrain evil and keep the chaos under control. Otherwise, if the law of human nature were allowed to prevail without any temporal authority to keep it in check, human beings would prey on each other and take advantage of one another without any fear of retribution. For that very reason, the temporal government is limited, according to Luther, having

> laws which extend no further than to life and property and external affairs on earth, for God cannot and will not permit anyone but Himself to rule over the soul. For over the soul God can and will let no one rule but Himself. Therefore, where the temporal authority presumes to prescribe laws for the soul, it encroaches upon God's government and only misleads souls and destroys them.[582]

Rejecting the notion of a Christian commonwealth, Luther insisted that the State possesses neither the competence nor a mandate from heaven to intrude into spiritual matters. "The soul is not under Caesar's power;" he wrote, "he can neither teach nor guide it, neither kill it nor give it life, neither bind it nor loose it*, neither judge it nor condemn it…"[583]

The State cannot compel faith or bind the conscience.

> [I]t is futile and impossible to command or compel anyone by force to believe this or that…. Furthermore, every man runs his own risk in believing as he does, and he must see to it himself that he believes rightly…. How he believes or disbelieves is a matter for the conscience of each individual, and since this takes nothing away from the temporal authority the latter should be content to attend to its own affairs and let men believe this or that as they are able and willing, and constrain no one by force. For faith is a free act, to which no one can be forced.

---

[581] Burns, "The Antinomian Disputation."

[582] LW 45:105. *The Christian in Society II*, "Temporal Authority,"

[583] Ibid., LW 45:111.

* Reference to the "Power of the Keys" known also as the "Office of the Keys" derived from Matthew 16:19. It references the power Christ has given to His Church on earth to forgive the sins of repentant sinners, and also to withhold forgiveness from the unrepentant as long as they do not repent.

> Indeed, it is a work of God in the spirit, not something which outward authority should compel or create.... For no matter how harshly they lay down the law, or how violently they rage, they can do no more than force an outward compliance of the mouth and the hand; the heart they cannot compel, though they work themselves to a frazzle. For the proverb is true: "Thoughts are tax-free".[584]

Human rules and regulations "cannot possibly extend [their] authority into heaven or over souls; it is limited to the earth, to external dealings men have with one another, where they can see, know, judge, evaluate, punish, and acquit."[585] To underscore this point, Luther emphatically makes the claim that "Christ Himself made this distinction, and summed it all up very nicely when he said in Matthew 22[:21], *'Render to Caesar the things that are Caesar's and to God the things that are God's.'*"[586]

The kingdom solely under Christ is governed by the Gospel. This redemptive realm includes Christians gathered together in local congregations or parishes. Its laws extend to the spiritual condition of humanity, the soul, and the conscience; but this is as far as its rule is to extend. Nevertheless, rulers in the Church and in the secular government of Luther's day were seeking, as they are doing today, to extend their realm into areas where they do not belong. There is one King but two kingdoms which are both ultimately under God's rule and they actually need each other. Luther distinguishes between them, but he does not divorce them. "Other reformers sought a radical separation of Church and State, a concept that Luther ultimately rejected."[587]

In his 1534 "Commentary on Psalm 101," Luther succinctly summarized his compelling theology of Church and State:

> The spiritual government or authority should direct the people vertically toward God that they may do right and be saved; just so the secular government should direct the people horizontally toward one another, seeing to it that body, property, honor, wife, child, house, home, and all manner of goods remain in peace and security and are blessed on earth. God wants the

---

584 Ibid., LW 45:107-108.
585 Ibid., LW 45:111.
586 Ibid., LW 45:111.
587 <https://www.nationalgeographic.com/news/2017/10/martin-luther-freedom-protestant-reformation-500>.

government of the world to be a symbol of true salvation and of His Kingdom of heaven, like a pantomime or a mask.[588]

Anders Nygren,* Swedish Lutheran theologian, Professor of Systematic Theology at Lund University, and then Bishop of Lund, wrote:

> We may seek in vain for any fully-evolved doctrine of the State in Luther's thought. But he has given us what is more valuable still: he has shown us the Christian way of looking on the State and its responsibilities. In these days, so full of brutal lust for power and of the deification of the State, often according to a feignedly Christian concept, there is a very special need that we should see the true purpose of God concerning temporal power. And for that there is no better guide than the New Testament, and Martin Luther, its greatest interpreter.[589]

The Role of the Church: Mercy and Compassion

The State can never fully represent God's Kingdom on earth, but encouraging the State to do its job-creating order by balancing security and justice is a legitimate role for the Church. "The ruler helps the Christian toward the good…if he is a just ruler, by providing him with encouragement to do good and discouragement from doing evil…and by curbing the worst excesses of other men's sinfulness and providing them with selfish reasons for acting justly."[590]

Likewise, Luther realized that the Church betrays an essential part of its mission if it does not continually, by exhortation and warning, remind those in earthly authority of the Law of God to which they are subject. While Thorsten Prill emphasizes that the primacy

---

588 Martin Luther, *Selected Psalms II*, "Psalm 101," LW 13:197.

* Bishop Anders Nygren, Swedish Lutheran theologian who was Professor of Systematic Theology at Lund University and elected as Bishop of Lund in 1948. He was an important figure in the ecumenical movement and served as President of the Lutheran World Federation. He is best known for his two-volume work *Agape and Eros*.

589 Nygren, Anders, "Luther's Doctrine of the Two Kingdoms," *Journal of Lutheran Ethics*, August 1, 2002. <https://www.elca.org/JLE/Articles/931>.

590 Cranfield, C.E.B., A *Critical and Exegetical Commentary on the Epistle to the Romans, International Critical Commentary* (London; New York: T&T Clark International, 2004), p.666.

of the Church's task is to preach the Gospel, he does not minimize its office of being a "political guardian," but within certain boundaries.

> The Church exists in this world and cannot withdraw from it and occupy a neutral position. God rules in both realms, and it is the Church's task to remind the secular authorities of this. As a political guardian, the Church has to speak up and interfere in politics where she is hindered by the government to fulfil her calling to preach the Gospel or where the fundamental values of God's commandments are clearly violated.[591]

Bishop Anders Nygren explains that

> The Church is not merely to protest when temporal authorities interfere with its own freedom to preach and to live as a Church; it is commissioned to interpret the will of God in regard to the various ordinances He has instituted in the world to regulate man's relation with his neighbors, and to stand forth uncompromisingly against injustice and tyranny. "To rebuke the authorities," writes Luther, "is certainly not a revolutionary act when it is done at the Divine command and in accordance with the Law of God, openly, fearlessly and honestly. It would, in fact, be much more dangerous to the public weal if a preacher were not to rebuke authority for its injustices."[592]

Joel Elowsky of Concordia Seminary asserts, "The kingdom of the world needs the kingdom of the Church, even if at times it may be ignorant of this fact. As Luther demonstrated in the third part of his treatise on '*Temporal Authority*,' rulers would do well to listen to the voice of the kingdom of God on how to use the authority that has been given to them by God."[593]

It is certainly therefore within the Church's purview to prophetically critique the State and to provide comments and recommendations, while also being subject to its authority. This mandate to speak to the world is illustrated in Jesus' analogy of the Church being salt and light (Matthew 5:13-16). The function of salt is to "season and preserve" while the function of light is to "illuminate." This is a particularly difficult challenge when the

---

591 Prill, "God's Two Kingdoms and the Christian's Two Citizenships."

592 Nygren, Anders, "Luther's Doctrine of the Two Kingdoms."

593 Elowsky, Joel, "Luther, Religious Freedom and the Two Kingdoms." <https://www.academia.edu/703>.

Church seems all too eager to reflect the "ways" and "practices" of the world rather than to "enlighten" the world with the Word which makes us *"a peculiar people"* (Deuteronomy 14:2 [KJV]; 1 Peter 2:9 [KJV]). Luther was deeply troubled that the practices and teachings of his Church acquiesced to the ways of the world.

In 1959, Hermann Sasse, German pastor, theologian and author, considered one of the foremost confessional Lutheran theologians, called attention to a profound spiritual disease, like an epidemic, sweeping through churches which have grown out of The Reformation.

> Everywhere in the Protestant world, the ability seems to have been lost to reject error and to condemn heresy.... If one sees these modern churches of various denominations, among them Lutheran bodies, which one or two generations ago were very conscious of their confession, one is reminded of ships drifting with a broken rudder.... [The] present generation of Christendom is losing, or has lost, the great charisma of "discerning the spirits" without which the Church cannot exist.[594]

Yet it is instructive, according to Dr. Prill, to recognize

> those issues where a straightforward ethical decision cannot be made on the basis of God's law, where one cannot clearly distinguish between good and evil or true and false. There are situations where one can only choose between two "evil" options. In such cases, the Church as an institution has to keep silent.... The Church has no mandate to comment on political or economic issues, where Christians on the basis of their conscience can and always will have different views. To deal with such matters of discretion, all that is needed is human reason.... The problem with a Church that claims to have the right to be heard on every political issue [i.e., a country joining a particular international organization, moving the Israeli embassy, implementing new ID cards, or increasing the price for gasoline or VAT taxes] is that it will soon be a church that is not listened to at all. But that does not mean that individual Christians should stay away from such issues.[595]

---

[594] Sasse, Hermann, "The Crisis of Lutheranism 1959," *The Lonely Way: Selected Essays and Letters, Volume II*, (St. Louis: Concordia, 2002), p.295.

[595] Prill, "God's Two Kingdoms and the Christian's Two Citizenships."

Also instructive for the Church's understanding of its role or mission are these following passages from Scripture: "*For I am not ashamed of the Gospel; it is the power of God for salvation to everyone who has faith, to the Jew first and also to the Greek. For in it the righteousness of God is revealed through faith for faith; as it is written, 'The one who is righteous will live by faith.*'" Romans 1:16-17 (NRSV) is not only the thematic verses for the exposition of the Gospel that St. Paul sets forth, but also the passage that awakened Luther's understanding of "Justification by Faith." Perhaps not as well recognized is how it served a missional directive for the young Church to reach out first to the Jews.

It seems clear to me that Scripture suggests a pattern which may perhaps appear parochial, not only in terms of benevolent care and compassion, but also in the order and mission priorities Christ gives to the Church. We read in Acts 1:8 (NRSV), "*But you will receive power when the Holy Spirit has come upon you; and you will be my witnesses in Jerusalem* (right where you are in the community in which you live and sleep), *in all Judea* (in the surrounding region), *and Samaria* (places where you'd least likely want to go), *and* (then) *to the ends of the earth.*"

St. Paul instructs the Galatians (6:10 [NRSV]), "*So then, whenever we have an opportunity, let us work for the good of all, and* ***especially*** *for those of the family of faith*" [emphasis added].

The Gospel of John 13:34-35 (NRSV) says, "*I give you a new commandment, that you love one another. Just as I have loved you, you also should love one another. By this everyone will know that you are my disciples.*"

Ever the lawyer and Church Father from Northern Africa, Tertullian (ca. 160-220) subscribed to the view that the best defense is a good offense. In the assessment of one whose focus is on the early Church Fathers, Dr. Warren Smith* attests Tertullian arguing the Christian life as taught in Scripture and *practiced* by the Church was the most effective witness the Church could make to the Gentiles. Smith writes "He imagined pagans looking at Christians and saying, 'Look…how they love one another (for they themselves [pagans] hate one another); and how they are ready to die for each other.'"[596]

---

* J. Warren Smith, Professor of Historical Theology and Director of the Th.D. Program at Duke Divinity School, is a John Wesley Fellow and ordained elder in the North Carolina Conference of the United Methodist Church. His interest is on early Christianity with a focus on the theology of the Church Fathers (patristic theology).

596 Smith, J. Warren, "See How These Christians Love One Another," *Christian History Magazine*, Issue 105, 2013. <https://christianhistoryinstitute.org/magazine/article/see-how-these-christians-love>.

The pattern seems to suggest that one's subjects, be they citizens, parishioners, or family members, receive first priority in terms of exercising responsibility, care, and compassion. That is not to exclude others from concern, but it does give substance to the witness given when such priorities are so valued and practiced. I sense this fundamental truth underlying President Trump's policies and endeavors focused on "America First."

Luther taught us that we are beloved by God, which is not something we can obtain or change by what we have done or fail to do. As God gifts us with forgiveness regardless of how broken we may be, He sends us forth to be His heart, hands and voice—the very body or enfleshment of God's love on earth today—while remaining faulty and imperfect in doing so. Cynthia D. Moe-Lobeda* writes in the *Journal of Lutheran Ethics*: "According to Luther, our shortcomings in fulfilling this calling are vast. Vaster yet is God's unfailing forgiveness of them and love for us despite them."[597] To hear Luther, we ought to think,

> Although I am an unworthy and condemned man, my God has given me in Christ all the riches of righteousness and salvation without any merit on my part, out of pure, free mercy, so that from now on I need nothing except faith which believes this is true. Why should I not therefore freely, joyfully with all my heart, and with an eager will do all things which I know are pleasing and acceptable to such a Father who has overwhelmed me with His inestimable riches? I will therefore give myself as a Christ to my neighbor, just as Christ offered Himself to me; I will do nothing in this life except what I see is necessary, profitable, and salutary to my neighbor, since through faith I have an abundance of all good things in Christ.[598]

Justified sinners gradually are transformed through the indwelling presence of Christ and become the body of God's love in the world, who like their Lord are now more attuned to seeking the well-being of others. Human works do not and cannot cause salvation, but good works naturally flow from salvation. Salvation for Luther was no longer the destination

---

* Cynthia D. Moe-Lobeda is the writer of the article "Luther's Economic Ethic of Neighbor-love and Its Implications for Economic Life Today—A Gift to the World," and the author of *Healing a Broken World: Globalization and God.* She holds a joint appointment in ethics at Pacific Lutheran Theological Seminary and Church Divinity School of the Pacific.

[597] Moe-Lobeda, Cynthia D., "Luther's Economic Ethic of Neighbor-love," *Journal of Lutheran Ethics*, 06/01/2019; <https://elca.org/JLE/Articles/1266>.

[598] LW 31:367. *Career of the Reformer I*, "The Freedom of a Christian," or in *Three Treatises*, p.304.

for people but the starting point of their new journey together with a loving God. "Faith is a divine work in us which changes us..." says Luther. "O it is a living, busy, active, mighty thing, this faith. It is impossible for it not to be doing good works incessantly. It does not ask whether good works are to be done, but before the question is asked, it has already done them, and is constantly doing them." Then, as if to underscore the startling converse, he states: "Whoever does not do such works, however, is an unbeliever."[599] Using picturesque metaphors, Luther explains, "Faith is followed by works as a body is followed by its shadow"[600] and it becomes "impossible to separate works from faith, quite as impossible as to separate heat and light from fire."[601] Genuine faith arouses and motivates good works through love which will not sleep but seeks concretization and validation in loving works toward one's neighbor. The fruits bear testimony to the tree that produces them. Thus, for Luther, works are a vital part of life for people justified by Christ, for as he preaches, "God makes love to our neighbor an obligation equal to love to Himself."[602] The Church's blest role is to teach and equip individuals in "being the Church"—the very "physical" body of God's love—so that we seek the well-being of the neighbor in every aspect of life since the very presence of Christ dwells within us. By Christ's directive, the poor were to receive justice which Christians are to demonstrate through neighbor-love in their practice of exercising charity and through their encouragement of the government to enact legislation that provides a safety net for those in poverty.

The Program Director of Hunger Education for ELCA World Hunger, Ryan Cumming, calls attention to "the crucial difference between ministry that *responds* to problems and ministry that *solves* problems. Responding to problems is carrying out charity; solving problems is achieving justice."[603] But solving the problem of poverty involves more than just meeting immediate needs. It means addressing the root causes, of which there are a myriad of interconnected and tangled systems that underlie hunger and poverty—mental illness, unemployment, low wages and high rent, single-parent households, just to name a few of the causes contributing to the "root ball."*

---

599 LW 35:370. *Word and Sacrament I*, "Prefaces to the New Testament."

600 WA 44:135. *Genesis 31-37.*

601 LW 35:371. See also Luther's explanation of the crucial inherent connectedness of faith with its consequent incarnate works in his lectures on Galatians, especially chapter 5 in LW 27:30.

602 Martin Luther, *Sermons of Martin Luther (Reprinted Edition), Volume 7*, ed. John Nicholas Lenker (Grand Rapids, MI: Baker Book House, 1983), p.69.

603 Cumming, Ryan, "BREAD and JUSTICE" newsletter of the Metropolitan New York Synod Hunger Committee, Spring 2017. <https://www.mnys.org/assets/1/6/bread_and_justice_2017.pdf>.

* A root ball is the main mass of different types of roots at the base of a plant, such as a shrub or tree.

Luther, therefore, admonishes pastors to unmask hidden injustice, saying

> Christ has instructed us preachers not to withhold the truth from the lords but to exhort and chide them in their injustice.... [W]e must rebuke the Pilates in their crime and self-confidence. Then they say to us, "You are reviling the majesty of God," to which we answer, "We will suffer what you do to us, but to keep still and let it appear that you do right when you do wrong, that we cannot and will not do"...for one should not remain silent about injustice nor let sin go unrebuked.[604]

For Luther, one of the preaching functions of the church is to unmask hidden injustice, by opening the eyes of secular authorities to fulfill their mandate to establish a civil society. Specifically, he maintains that the function and honor of preaching is "to make sinners saints, dead men live, damned men saved, and the devil's children God's children..."[605] What a haunting yet glorious privilege!

Addressing economic life in our contemporary world from the perspective of the neighbor-love ethic of Luther, Cynthia Moe-Lobeda asserts that "the Church today is called to disclose, denounce, and counter economic policies, practices, and assumptions that harm economically vulnerable neighbors whom we are called to love.... Christians as objects of Christ's love become subjects of that love because it abides within them."[606]

A crucial role for the Church is to inspire and train individuals for public service. Politics should be no more a dirty business than coaching a team, operating a business, or tilling the land. We have the responsibility to encourage members to fulfill their calling as Christian citizens in a republic "of the people, by the people and for the people," where we elect the men and women who govern us. Exercising our right to vote and supporting Christian politicians in their vocation as servants of Christ's Kingdom of the left hand, is also a religious duty.

The Role of the Government: Justice and Security

For Luther,

> worldly government is a glorious ordinance and splendid gift of God, who instituted and established it and will have it maintained as something

---

604 WA 28:360-1, LW 69:236-37, see LW 44:51 cited by Carter Lindberg in his chapter "Luther and the Common Chest" in the book *Forgotten Luther: Reclaiming the Social Economic Dimension of the Reformation* he co-edited with Paul Wee, (Minneapolis: Lutheran University Press, 2016), p.22.

605 LW 46:237. *The Christian in Society III*, "A Sermon on Keeping Children in School."

606 Moe-Lobeda, "Neighbor-love."

> men cannot do without. If there were no worldly government, one man could not stand before another; each would necessarily devour the other, as irrational beasts devour one another.... It is the function and honor of worldly government to make men out of wild beasts and to prevent men from becoming beasts. It protects a man's body so that no one may slay it; it protects a man's wife so that no one may seize and defile her; it protects a man's child, his daughter or son, so that no one may carry them away and steal them; it protects a man's house so that that no one may break in and wreck things, it protects a man's fields and cattle and all his goods so that no one may attack, steal, plunder or damage them. Protection of this sort does not exist among the beasts, and if it were not for worldly government there would be none of it among men either; they would surely cease to be men and become mere beasts...[607]

Without a capable and wise government, we would see our society devolve to the survival of the fittest, or perhaps in our times, the wealthiest. Luther continues, "It is certain, then that temporal authority is a creation and ordinance of God and that for us men in this life it is a necessary office and estate which we can no more dispense with than we can dispense with life itself..."[608]

Christians and Jews have basically held that God-ordained civil government pre-dates the Mosaic Law through natural revelation. As St. Paul affirms in Romans 2:14-15, God has not left Himself without a witness, in that He has revealed a moral law in the hearts and consciences of all people. Civil law is based on the cultural mandate given in Genesis 1:28 to subdue all things in creation. This was reinforced by God ordaining the sword for capital punishment in Genesis 9:6. The nature of human government is also clearly spelled out in Romans 13:1-7 and 1 Peter 2:13-14. Appropriately, to preserve "law and order," fight off invaders, and execute punishment on those who break the law, earthly governors "bear the sword" on behalf of those who live under their jurisdiction:

> Christians understand this delegation of authority to protectors in the civil realm to be a tangible safeguard against the consequences of the sin

---

[607] LW 46:237, *The Christian in Society*, "Children in School."

[608] Ibid., LW 46:238.

> nature that inherently resides in every person. Hence, national defense and police powers manifest the central role given to the government. A given government's responsibility under God is to safeguard its citizens.[609]

Isaac Watts argued that the "design of civil government has been deemed a necessary thing, according to the 'light of reason,' to protect and preserve the life and properties of individuals as well as the just liberty and peace of humankind from the invasions and injuries of their neighbors."[610] He was emphatic in stating that "The Gospel of Christ does not pretend to erect a kingdom of this world, and therefore it alters nothing in the nature of civil government but leaves to Caesar the things that are Caesar's" (Matthew 22:21).[611]

Jesus certainly was not questioning the legitimacy of civil government, nor was He being critical of the role of civil government, in this passage of rendering to Caesar. And while Jesus indeed told the ruler in Luke 18:22 to sell all that he owns and distribute the money to the poor, He never advocated a public policy enforced by the power of the sword bestowed on civil government to extort or impoverish those in the "upper class" or "the one-percenters." From such Biblical teachings, we may conclude such actions are being appropriately directed toward individuals as acts of kindness they may consider taking, not for governments to mandate.

Can one imagine the absurdities of trying to force Gospel principles on the State? Consider our Lord's teaching in Luke 6:27-31. Such attempts are out of place and would confuse the purpose of the State with the purpose of the individual and the Church, and thereby weaken both, as it undermines God's created order. Biblical principles for individuals such as "*turning the cheek*," "*forgiving 70 times 7*," and "*giving away your shirt if your coat is taken*" provide ethical guidance in our personal relationships with our family and neighbors. The principles governing the State, however, are to foster order by protecting us, so that we may be empowered to carry out those acts of love and mercy and to assume our responsibility to strive for goodness, peace and justice.

---

609 Edwards, "A Biblical Perspective," p.2.

610 Watts, Isaac, *The Works of the Rev. Isaac Watts, D.D., Volume* 3 (Leeds: Edward Baines, n.d.), p.328.

611 Ibid., p.361.

Dragon Slayers in the Spiritual and Temporal Realms

Martin Luther as Knight Jorge
By Heinrich Goding
(Left: Public domain, retrieved at Wikimedia)

Donald Trump as Knight in Shining Armor
By Hira Lie
(Right: Know Your Meme)

Heinrich Goding, a student under Lucas Cranach, took his master's portrait of Martin Luther as Junker Jorge when the Reformer emerged from hiding to make a short expedition to Wittenberg, and portrayed the full stature of a noble knight who carried a sword at his side. While in protective custody at the Wartburg Castle, Luther had become incognito as the bearded Junker Jorge, or "Knight George" in English, in honor of the patron saint of Eisenach, St. George. It was also the name of the parish school he had attended when he was young. He was persuaded to sneak back into Wittenberg to quell the enthusiasts, fanatics, and dragons who had taken violent means to advance the Reformation in Luther's absence. Cranach had entitled his woodcut "Portrait of Martin Luther showing how he appeared when he returned from Patmos to Wittenberg, AD 1522." The artist was drawing a parallel between Luther's accomplishment at Wartburg in translating the New Testament into the language of the German people and the Apostle John's writing of Revelation while exiled on the island of Patmos. In the commemorative portrait, Goding places the dragon slayer in front of the cityscape of Worms, where Luther made his stand before the Emperor. His translation of the New Testament lays open and features verses from Matthew, Mark and John.[612]

As the Knight in Shining Armor, President Trump is portrayed with a devastating sword by which magistrates could exercise their God-appointed responsibilities to keep the peace and order within the community by fighting off the "dragons" that threatened the lives and property of its citizens.

---

[612] Hofer, Michelle, "Part 3—Martin Luther Dragon Slayer." <https://michellehofer.com/2017/11/14/martin-luther-dragon-slayer-part-3>.

Rescuing People from the Jaws of Roman and Washington Dragons

St. George and the Dragon
By Albrecht Dürer (ca. 1504)
(Left: Public domain, retrieved at the Museum of Metropolitan Art website)

Vanquishing the Evil Satan
(Right: Retrieved at a public online forum)

There is an historical figure known as St. George who lived at the end of the second century, boldly proclaiming the faith and being a wonder worker, who was then martyred following his stand before the Roman Senate. The legend, however, purports that he rose from the dead to deliver the people of his native city from a dragon who had been terrorizing them. Rushing in while riding a white steed, he gave the dragon a crushing blow, piercing it with his spear and trampling it with his horse. Martin Luther had his own St. George moment denouncing the injustices, schemes and abuses inflicted on the innocent by the Church and the Holy Roman Empire. Albrecht Durer's woodcut was used as propaganda to promote Luther's movement. Luther had adopted the pseudo-name of "Junker Jorge," or "Knight George" in English, during his hideaway stay in the Wartburg Castle with other knights. He was persuaded to sneak back into Wittenberg to quell the "enthusiasts" under Andreas von Karlstadt, who had taken over the reins of the movement in Luther's absence and was leading it in a literal destructive way, destroying images in the Church. He then returned to the solitude of Wartburg to work on a German translation of the New Testament, which he completed in 11 weeks. This noble knight had rescued the people from the jaws of the Roman Dragon by slaying many dragons.

Donald Trump in this caricature is preparing to slay Hillary Clinton as the symbolic dragon of the Deep State's swamp in Washington, D.C. which he intends to drain. The artist has given wings to the President and portrays a beam of heavenly light behind him as if, like St. George, he has come to rescue the people from the ever-threatening dragon of the government. The President holds the sword and scales of Justice in his hands, to signal no one is above the law. Like Luther, who returned to Wittenberg from his "Patmos" at the Wartburg to resume command of his movement, so too history may see Donald Trump re-elected to return to Washington in 2025 to continue his efforts to Make America Great Again, by draining the swamp and restoring those fundamental principles that have distinguished the United States from other nations. Should that possibility become reality, I am sure the 45th President would have similarly appropriate words as the 47th President as Luther expressed in the caption below Cranach's portrait of "Junker Jorge," which was printed and circulated in 1522 when Luther emerged from his hiding as evidence that he was indeed alive: "As much as I have been sought and pursued by you, Rome, see that I, Luther, still live through Christ. Jesus is my hope and has not deceived me. As long as I have this, fare thee well, false Rome."[613] It would be as if St. George, raised from the dead, has galloped into town on his valiant steed; and like Luther, returned to rescue the people from the jaws of the Washington Dragon!

Unlike today, "secular authority" for Luther was not that which is without or opposed to God, but rather rulers "of the world" who were regarded as guardians and embodiments of divinely instituted government for the sake of peace and order in God's creation. Magistrates were a "god" on earth, as we read in Psalm 82:6, and not only represented God's authority and majesty but were to be obeyed as if God Himself were exercising His judgment and wrath against human sin. "Princes and magistrates are the bows and arrows of God,"[614] Luther wrote, equipped to hunt down God's enemies in the earthly kingdom. He vigorously argues that God honors the power of the sword He has instituted, and further maintains that the hand of the Christian magistrate, judge or soldier "that wields the sword and kills with it is not man's hand, but God's; and it is not man, but God who hangs, tortures, beheads, slays, and fights. All these are God's works and judgments."[615]

In his volume *The Ethics of Martin Luther*, noted Luther scholar and theologian Paul Althaus* observes that a primary task of Christian preaching is to remind people that secular government and other stations in society are God's will.[616] Luther clearly views government as a gift of God's goodness and understands that those who govern are sitting in God's place and thus are to be respected and honored.[617] When magistrates apprehend violators of the law and criminals are punished, Luther maintains that government officials are acting as

---

613 Hofer, "Dragon Slayer."

614 LW 17:117. *Lectures on Isaiah Chapters 40-66*, "Isaiah 40."

615 LW 46:96. *The Christian in Society III*, "Whether Soldiers too Can Be Saved."

* Paul Althaus was a German Lutheran theologian, Professor of Practical and Systematic Theology at the University of Göttingen and when a professor at the University of Erlangen and leading Luther authority of his day, he welcomed the emergence to power of Adolf Hitler. He held the position of university preacher from 1932 to 1964. His major works, *The Theology of Martin Luther* and *The Ethics of Martin Luther,* remain standard works.

616 Althaus, Paul, *The Ethics of Martin Luther* (Minneapolis: Fortress Press, 1972), p.60.

617 Ibid., pp.113-114, 116.

"God's jailers and hangmen, and his divine wrath makes use of them to punish the wicked and maintain outward peace."[618]

Roland Bainton views the demarcation of the spheres of Church and State corresponding in a rough way "to dualism running through the nature of God and man. God is wrath and mercy. The State is the instrument of His wrath, the Church of His mercy. Man is divided into outward and inward. Crime is outward and belongs to the State. Sin is inward and belongs to the Church. Goods are outward and fall to the State. Faith is inward and falls to the Church."[619]

> As St. Paul says (Romans 13:4) *"It [government] is God's minister to you for good."* For where there is no government, or where government is not held in honor, there can be no peace. Where there is no peace, no one can keep his life or anything else, in the face of another's outrage, thievery, robbery, violence, and wickedness. Much less will there be room to teach God's Word and to rear children in the fear of God and His discipline (Ephesians 6:4). God will not have the world desolate and empty but has made it for men to live in, to till the land and fill it, as written in Genesis 1:29-30. Because this cannot happen where there is no peace, He is compelled, as a Creator, preserving His own creatures, works, and ordinances, to institute and preserve government and to commit to it the sword and the laws.[620]

For Luther, the Biblical witness is clear: the State exists to restrain evil, create order, protect its citizens (including Christians), and ensure tranquility. St. Paul instructs the Church in Rome:

> For rulers are not a terror to good conduct, but to bad. Do you wish to have no fear of the authority? Then do what is good, and you will receive its approval; for it is God's servant for your good. But if you do what is wrong, you should be afraid, for the authority does not bear the

---

618 Hopfl, Harro, *Luther and Calvin on Secular Authority* (London: Cambridge University Press, 1991), p.30.

619 Bainton, *Here I Stand*, p.242 Abingdon, or p.187 Mentor pb.

620 LW 13:44-45. *Selected Psalms II*, "Psalm 82."

> sword in vain! It is the servant of God to execute wrath on the wrongdoer (Romans 13:3-4 [NRSV]).

Here Paul tells us that government is God's servant (*diakonos*) that punishes lawbreakers. We are continually called to keep in mind that the service the State renders to God is twofold in helping its subjects toward good and preventing evil. By restraining human beings from their chaotic tendencies, such as breaking the law, entering the country illegally, rioting that is destructive to property and harmful to fellow citizens, looting, and arson, magistrates keep the peace and protect their subjects from threats or violations to their persons, properties, and reputations. As Paul Althaus argues, secular government is a gift of God's goodness, even as political rulers fulfill their God-given responsibilities of making those who violate the law and break the peace feel the wrath of God in order to protect the innocent and righteous. Thus, wrath also stands in the service of mercy by maintaining outward peace.[621] "God administers justice but is at the same time nothing else than love itself. God must use force against those who rebel against Him, and yet His heart burns with love for them. God's love appears in our evil world also in the broken form of His wrath—as His 'strange work.'"[622]

Several passages in Scripture (e.g. Romans 13:1-7; 1 Peter 2:13-17) acknowledge the early Church's awareness of civil government as an institution ordained by God. A leading Roman Catholic theologian and professor at The Catholic University of America, Joseph A. Fitzmyer, wrote: "Hence even Christians, 'freed' by Christ Jesus from the powers of this world, cannot resist the political authority that comes ultimately from God, even if that authority is at the time in the hands of heathens."[623]

Noted lawyer, professor and Lutheran theologian John Warwick Montgomery highlights the truth that even bad law is preferable to disorder. He emphatically declares: "Scripture clearly holds that even bad law is nonetheless law and that there is something worse than even bad law—namely, anarchy."[624]

---

[621] Althaus, *The Ethics of Martin Luther*, pp.55-56.

[622] Ibid., p.77.

[623] Fitzmyer S.J., Joseph A., *Romans: A New Translation with Introduction and Commentary, Volume 33*, (New Haven; London: Yale University Press, 2008), p.667.

[624] Montgomery, John Warwick, *Christians in the Public Square: Law, Gospel & Public Policy* (Edmonton: Canadian Institute for Law, Theology and Public Policy, 1996), p.137.

> It would seem problematic within this view of government, if people, (Dreamers though they might be) are rewarded for violation of the law.... Yet this is what so many evangelicals want when it comes to immigration. They want to reward the perceived weak by ignoring the law and rewriting the rules to favor their preferred class. This is fraught with danger because it confuses the purpose of law. Law is not meant to realize the eschaton.[625]

Montgomery helpfully explains that while Christians should work for a more just society, that must be tempered: "Politically, the law is regarded as a restraint for the wicked, not as a means of building the 'perfect society.'"[626] Besides, if one willfully breaks immigration laws, is it not reasonable to surmise that he or she may be more likely to break traffic laws, driving without a license or while drunk? And why pay taxes or observe other laws?

While open border activists cite passages in Scripture that they claim mandates that a society welcome any and all foreigners, Dr. Edwards asserts "No such passages [in Scripture] state or imply overlooking illegality committed on the part of the alien in his entry." To underscore how highly God regards borders as meaningful and important, he references Proverbs 22:28 and Proverbs 23:10-11 (warnings against removing the landmarks designating borders and encroaching):

> Consider, also, Deuteronomy 32:8: "*When the Most High gave to the nations their inheritance, when he divided mankind, he fixed the borders of the peoples according to the number of the sons of God.*" Ezekiel 47:13-23 details the Promised Land's boundaries. Numbers 34:1-15 describes the borders the Lord established for each tribe of Israel. Deuteronomy 19:14 commands against moving a neighboring tribe's boundary stone marking a given tribe of Israel's inheritance in the Promised Land.[627]

---

625 <https://capstonereport.com/2018/01/21/repairing-evangelical-political-theology-getting-the-State-right/31843>.

626 Montgomery, *Christians in the Public Square*, p.142.

627 Edwards, "A Biblical Perspective."

As we have witnessed, "migration chronicled in Scripture provides no sanction for open borders." Professor Edwards further explains that

> These movements of people across territories generally deferred to the national sovereignty of the local authorities regarding whether or not to grant entrance. The theme given the Hebrews of fairly treating aliens and sojourners resembles "equal justice under the law" more than an admonition to take all comers without conditions. Even humanitarian migration (fleeing persecution, etc.) did not trump national sovereignty, as preserving law and order even as it relates to immigration is a duty of governing authorities and a manifestation of general blessing (under common grace) of all lawful residents of a jurisdiction.[628]

Realistically, can our country or any nation receive unrestricted numbers of immigrants and still remain a viable nation? How will the numbers of illegals entering, added to the undocumented already residing in our country, affect the living standard of legal immigrants, and those citizens who are impoverished, homeless, and living on the streets of our cities, and those without benefits and social programs mandated or being proposed for illegals? What about illegal immigration's impact on crime in the U.S., or the long-term implications of "anchor babies" born on American soil to non-citizen mothers being given automatic citizenship, thus providing an advantage to family members seeking to secure citizenship or legal residency? "Maternity hotels" now accommodate the growth of a cottage industry which recruits women, particularly from China, to come to the United States on tourist visas to have their babies born on American soil as birthright citizens, ensuring life-long public benefits and privileges to their new offspring, including having a legal foothold in securing eventual citizenship for the entire family's future immigration to America.

In fairness, even though immigration in the past has been viewed as benefiting the needs and economies of welcoming countries, who addresses the moral implications entailed by favoring a "merit-based" immigration policy for refugees, where we seek to admit the "best and the brightest"—the very ones, perhaps, most needed to rebuild their war-torn, corrupt or devastated homelands? Is giving automatic citizenship to illegal immigrants fair? Tooley concludes his article by opining that these concerns and "questions are not likely to get

---

[628] Ibid.

serious answers from Religious Left activists, who, while twisting the Bible grossly out of context, prefer to portray the immigration debate as a battle between pious Good Samaritans and frothing xenophobes."[629]

Luther learned from St. Paul to take a realistic view of the Christian's earthly status living within both the spiritual and temporal realms, both of which are under the rule of God who never drops the reins. That realization for Bishop Nygren of Lund is all-important. "We are sometimes in danger of looking on the temporal as something profane, as if God were active only in the spiritual. The temporal is not foreign to God, and Luther does not regard it as such. To him there is nothing which is profane, and no sphere in which God is not at work."

The good Bishop goes on to state,

> God is in command in every sphere of life. It is with Him that we have to do in both the heavenly and the earthly kingdoms, in both spiritual and temporal rule. He meets us in both, though in different ways—in the spiritual with the Gospel, in the temporal with the Law. But His will is made manifest to us in both Law and Gospel. The two kingdoms exist side by side, both instituted directly by God for two different reasons. His purpose in the spiritual realm is to make men Christian and to hallow them in Christ, and the instrument He uses to this end is only and always the Word and the preaching thereof, and the sacraments. In the temporal realm His purpose is to sustain justice and peace in the world, and His characteristic instrument here is power, the use of the sword. In both realms He uses men as His agents. "Servants of the Lord" is a name applying not only to those who fill religious offices: rulers are also "servants of the Lord"...
>
> In the midst of our present existence God lays His mandate upon us, and His mandate is unvarying. In the final analysis, it is always a ministering love which He requires of us, whatever our station is in this life. In love and service, the preacher of the Word must work for the salvation of men through the Gospel. In love and service, the ruler must administer law and justice, defend the country against attack, punish the offender. The strict enforcement of this latter might seem to be the antithesis of love but for all

[629] Tooley, "Jesus Christ: Illegal Immigrant?"

> that it is the work of God's love which the ruler performs for the good of society. If, for the sake of giving to his conduct the appearance of love, the ruler were to permit law and justice to be trampled under-foot, or to let his country be overrun by an invader, he would be false to the task entrusted to him by God: he would be false to love.[630]

From the writings of Scripture cited above, the State not only acts as the avenger in punishing evil but in so doing provides an environment of safety. A Capstone report on "Getting the State Right" addresses the need to acknowledge some basic concepts about the role of the State as an institution ordained by God, as well as the need to live and minister in a way that honors Biblical teachings.

> This requires us to understand the State must be powerful enough to protect itself from inside rebellion and outside invasion. Security then should be part of the political evaluation Christians use when evaluating public policy. Key here is that Christians must recognize God created government for a specific purpose: To punish evil by the power of the sword so that Christians and all people can live quiet lives and this arrangement furthers the spread of the Gospel. It isn't wrong to keep the salvation of men in our thoughts. However, the best way to fulfill the Great Commission is not to ignore security and economic considerations for the State, but to make sure the State picks the policies that balance justice and security.[631]

Personal Opinions Are Not Necessarily God's Opinions

Before pursuing Luther's understanding of "Two Kingdoms," it is critical that one understand and underscore that as Christians, we have neither been given clarity nor divine prescription in the Biblical record for many of the issues we confront as human beings within society. Scripture, for example, makes no pronouncements concerning governing policy on something like borders and immigration. A sovereign nation's protection of her borders, and decisions regarding who is allowed or who is not allowed to enter the country, falls

---

[630] Nygren, Anders, "Luther's Doctrine of the Two Kingdoms."

[631] <http://capstonereport.com/2018/01/21/repairing-evangelical-political-theology-getting-the-State-right/31843>.

squarely within the realm of governmental authority. That these are debatable issues is to affirm that one may make a persuasive claim, giving reasoned arguments for a specific view or policy one thinks is best, but Christians must not give the impression that there is only one Biblically correct view which alone is correct for Christians to hold. As Montgomery cleverly and wisely counsels, "Christians can fight for non-revelational viewpoints, but they must make plain these are their own personal opinions, not necessarily God's opinions."[632]

Likewise, Scripture does not mandate the kind nor specific form or structure civil government should take. On his "Commentary on Psalm 101," Luther stated

> nothing is taught in the Gospel about how it (secular government) is to be maintained and regulated except that the Gospel bids people honor it and not oppose it. Therefore, the heathen can speak and teach about this very well, as they have done. And, to tell the truth, they are far more skillful in such matters than the Christians; Christ Himself says (Luke 16:8) that "*the children of this world are wiser than the children of Light.*"[633]

In the *Journal of Lutheran Ethics*, John R. Stephenson even makes the assertion that

> Secular government can function quite independently of the Christian faith, so that Luther could point from the pulpit that the emperor need not be a saint or even Christian: "*Satis est ad Caesarem, ut habeat rationem.*"[634]
>
> It would be quite mistaken, [Stephenson continues,] "to infer from Luther's admission that secular authority can be exercised independently of the ethos of Christendom that he deemed this an ideal state of affairs. On the contrary, [the Reformer was] firmly convinced that the business of government 'as a special way of serving God pertains to Christians above others on earth.'"[635]

Being an ordinance of God and therefore God's servant, the State extends its "ministry" into "our most basic human relationships and enduring social life and institutions (family, work, citizenship and other institutional arrangements for creating and preserving

---

[632] Montgomery, *Christians in the Public Square*, p.66.

[633] LW 13:198. *Selected Psalms II*, "Psalm 101."

[634] Stephenson, John R., "The Two Governments and the Two Kingdoms in Luther's Thought," citing WA 27.418, 4. <https://www.elca.org/JLE/Articles/947>.

[635] Ibid.

human and environmental well-being)," according to Professor Gary Simpson at Luther Seminary in St. Paul, Minnesota. As such, Professor Simpson maintains, it is through these networks that

> …we also discover what God would have us do and not do in order for earthly life to flourish rather than flounder. Finally, we discover how God uses dissuading and rewarding consequences to prevent sin and evil from proliferating and to preserve and promote both human flourishing and the well-being of creation. Luther also called God's left-hand governing God's "political" or "civil use of law…"[636]

"Of course, God rules even the international affairs of nations," Dr. George Forell reminds us, but for Luther, he asserts "this does not excuse the role of political leaders and individual citizens from taking their proper responsibility in these matters. Luther insists that God has chosen to exercise authority through human beings. All the preparations and activities of humankind are ways in which God accomplishes His purpose."[637] "Indeed," as Luther himself states using a favorite metaphor, "one could very well say that the course of the world, and especially the doing of His saints, are God's mask, under which He conceals Himself and so marvelously exercises dominion…'"[638]

One King and Two Kingdoms

Prior to and following his refusal to comply with the order of the highest temporal authority, the Emperor, to recant the numerous books he had written and published, Luther engaged in discussion with his followers about a Christian's obligation to submit to *"the governing authorities"* (Romans 13:1). Having been excommunicated, he was secretly taken to the Wartburg Castle for his protection. From this "fortress" he sent Melanchthon his thinking on this subject they had frequently discussed, regarding the authority of the State. In a letter from July 13, 1521, Luther expounded on his view that "the Gospel, as such, had nothing to

---

636 Simpson, Gary, "How Luther Helps Today's Citizens," *Living Lutheran*, October, 2016. <https://www.livinglutheran.org/2016/10/luther-helps-todays-citizens>.

637 Forell, George, "Luther's Theology and Foreign Policy," *The Journal of Lutheran Ethics*, 1/1/2002. <https://www.elca.org/JLE/Articles/993>.

638 LW 45:331. *The Christian in Society II*, "Exposition of Psalm 127, Sermon at Riga."

do with the temporal sword, and that a truly Christian society had no need of it."[639] "But in the Gospel, the law of the sword also is not forbidden. It is rather affirmed and commended to us. We certainly do not read this about things that are only permitted…"[640] Luther was making the point that if all people obeyed the Gospel, the sword would not be needed. But if it were abolished, he asks Melanchthon how long he thought the Church of God would exist amid the licentiousness of the wicked who are in the majority?[641]

In communication with George Spalatin on May 5, 1522, Luther stated "it was the elector's duty to provide for the 'salvation' of his subjects and to keep the 'wolves' from destroying them" and "in response to a number of questions, some of which concerned the relationship between the Gospel and the worldly sword, Luther wrote Baron Schwarzenberg* that he intended soon to publish a special treatise on the subject."[642]

When Luther returned to Wittenberg to quell the fanatics' disturbances there, he preached a series of eight sermons during the first week of Lent, known as the Invocavit Sermons, that provided the outline and served as the forerunner of his 1523 treatise "Temporal Authority: To What Extent It Should Be Obeyed." Here he set forth his political ideas which would, in turn, inform the position he was to take on the Peasants' Rebellion. He believed that the Church and State must have some kind of separation, while simultaneously acknowledging that they are related, since both are the means by which God sustains and redeems the world in the face of sin, death and evil. This position became known as Luther's Doctrine of the Two Kingdoms, as distinguished from the principle of "separation of Church and State" which had its roots in the Enlightenment.

"Although this theory may sound complicated," says Janet Leigh Gesme in her Portland State University thesis, she contends that

---

639 LW 45:77. *The Christian in Society II*, "Temporal Authority."

640 LW 48:259. *Letters I*, "To Philip Melanchthon, July 13, 1521." (fn 15: "Permitted things" for Luther are things neither commanded nor prohibited by God's Word; they are neutral in themselves and have no direct relationship to man's salvation. See also pp.156f., 278).

641 Ibid.

* Johann Freiherr (Baron) von Schwarzenberg, friend and supporter of Luther, greatest living authority on jurisprudence in the Empire, chancellor/judge in the court of Bamberg, author of the reforms in the criminal code. He was "troubled by apparent disharmony of Scripture which could affirm the coercive power of the sword in the apostolic writings while at the same time, supremely in the Sermon on the Mount, seeming to rule out recourse to or participation in its operation." See John R. Stephenson's "The Two Governments and the Two Kingdoms in Luther's Thought" <https://www.elca.org/JLE/Articles/947>.

642 LW 45:78. *The Christian in Society II*, "Introduction to Temporal Authority."

> at its core it represents one of the simplest concepts known to mankind: the concept of heaven and earth. The basic idea is familiar to most people—there are two kingdoms, one of them is heaven and the other is earth. In heaven everything is perfect. There one finds perfect peace and love, and no one suffers from sickness or poverty. On earth, however, there are many problems. On earth mankind searches for perfect peace and love, but it is hard to find. People suffer under many maladies: sickness, crime, unfulfilled longings, fear, and death. Although defining and delineating between these two kingdoms seems quite simple on the surface, the complexities become evident when one tries to explain the effect of the two realms on the human experience. Martin Luther's treatise about this subject is still hotly debated, almost 500 years after he wrote it. What seems to be a simple concept, God's Kingdom, and the Kingdom of the World, turns out to be a type of Pandora's box, which continues to instigate arguments about religion, politics, and the interaction of God with mankind.[643]

Luther found Biblical origins for the "Two Kingdoms" in the parting words of Jesus to His disciples in Matthew 28 (*"All authority in heaven and on earth has been given to Me"*), the testimony of Jesus before Pilate in John 18 (*"My kingdom is not of this world"*), and in the teaching of St. Paul in Romans 13 (*"Every person [should] be subject to the governing authorities, for there is no authority except from God"*).

Central to this resulting theological view of the "Two Kingdoms" is the tenet which holds that while God is over both realms, God *alone* rules in the "right-hand kingdom" and empowers humans to rule in the "left-hand kingdom." It is through His right hand that He rules over the Church through His Word and Spirit, and bestows salvation as a gift to those who place their faith in Christ. On the other hand (literally His left hand), God rules over the world through the agencies of government. In this worldly or temporal realm, God enlists men and women, both Christians and non-Christians, to partner with Him to effect order and peace in society by exercising their stewardship within the structures of political, social and economic life, and in interpersonal relations.

Luther also found a basis for his "Two Kingdoms" theory in the Decalogue or Ten Commandments, in which he saw a moral spreadsheet with two dimensions: The first three Commandments focus on our relationship with God—the vertical dimension—while the

---

[643] Gesme, Janet Leigh, "Martin Luther's 'Two Kingdoms Theory,'" *PDX Scholar, 2013*. <https://pdxscholar.library.pdx.edu/cgi/viewcontent.cgi?article=2512&context=open_access_etds>.

remaining seven give shape to our relationship with our neighbors—the horizontal. Thus, Luther explains how God exercises his sovereignty over all people through two governments, represented by authorities in both the spiritual and secular realms.

I appreciate the way in which Dr. Edward H. Schroeder* of Concordia Theological Seminary distinguishes Luther's own favorite Biblical terms for the different works done by God with differing hands:

> God's right-hand mission is centered in the One who now "sits at the right hand of God the Father," Christ the world's Redeemer. That's God's salvation work from way back at the beginning of the Old Testament culminating in Christ and continuing right on up to the *Parousia* [second coming of Christ]. God's left-hand mission is all the other works of God that preserve and continue creation, protect it from total destruction, hold us humans accountable as caretakers of that creation, but do not (yet) turn sinners into Christ-trusters.
>
> If my suggestions are "too Lutheran," [Dr. Schroeder states,] then [go] back to St. John's "Moses and Christ" in his prologue, or St. Paul and his use of the umbrella terms "*law*" for God's left-hand agenda and "*promise*" for God's salvific work of His right hand.[644]

In the words of a 1927 spiritual which became an international pop hit in 1957-58, we can affirm that God has the whole world in His hands, but always adding, "Yes, both of them!"

Edmund Schlink† in *The Theology of the Lutheran Confessions* summarizes the Lutheran position on temporal and spiritual authority, especially in Article XXVIII of the Augsburg Confession and its Apology: (1) The function but not the concrete form of both authorities is revealed in God's Word (pp. 247-254). (2) God demands of every person obedience to both

---

* Edward H. Schroeder was educated at Valparaiso University and the University of Hamburg and taught theology at Valparaiso, Concordia Seminary, Seminex, and seminaries in Australia, Ethiopia, and Lithuania, in numerous seminars and via a ten-year email ministry through the Crossings Community.

644 Schroeder, Edward H., "Lutheranism's Crying Need: A Mission Theology for the 21st Century." <https://crossings.org/lutheranisms-crying-need/>.

† Edmund Schlink was a leading German Lutheran theologian in the modern ecumenical movement, especially in the World Council of Churches. He was a professor of Systematic Theology at Heidelberg University, Germany.

authorities when that can be done without sin (pp. 254-259). (3) The ecclesiastical and civil offices must not be intermingled but differentiated (pp. 259-263). (4) The limit of obedience to each of the two offices is God's commandment (pp 263-268). (5) In the mingling of civil authority and ecclesiastical authority, the tyranny of Satan's kingdom invades both of them (pp 268-269).[645]

In addition, Professor Gary Simpson, reminds us that "Luther's teaching of the Two Kingdoms is a corollary of [the Reformer's] understanding of the Scripture's teaching of Law and Gospel, both of which contend with sin and evil, though in different ways, and both of which seek to bless the world, though also in different ways."[646]

Living in God's Two Realms

Two postage stamps portray Luther's Two Kingdom doctrine of living in both the spiritual and earthly realms over which God rules. Luther's portrait on the Lithuania 2017 stamp is placed before the University Castle All Saints Church in Wittenberg where is he buried. The heavenly rule or right hand of God's governance is the realm of redemption, of spiritual and eternal life where a person operates primarily by faith and love. The Togolaise stamp commemorating Trump's 75th birthday in 2021 points to the temporal rule through the governance of civic leaders who serve as God's left hand commissioned with the power of the sword to enforce the law to protect and defend the people so citizens may live in peace. President Trump is portrayed before a podium flanked by a bank of American flags. Our warriors don't represent the separation of Church and State, but rather God's two modes of rule which He has established. These two kingdoms interact and depend upon each in a variety of ways, but they ultimately remain distinct.

---

645 Schlink, Edmund, *Theology of the Lutheran Confessions*, translated by Paul F. Koehneke and Herbert J.A. Bouman (Philadelphia: Fortress Press, 1961), pp.247-269.

646 Simpson, Gary, "How Luther Helps Today's Citizens."

Luther's Rose Seal

The Presidential Seal

Luther's Rose Seal is surround by the "Five Solas" (which summarize Luther's theology: Christians are saved by grace alone, through faith alone, in Christ alone, as revealed by Scripture alone, to the glory of God alone) and of course the presidential seal.

Luther recognized that the individual Christian had to live in both the spiritual and the temporal realms as a believing member of the Church and an obedient citizen of the State. While the Two Kingdoms ultimately remain distinct, they interact and depend on each other, especially as citizens exercise their vocation in the earthly life. Luther explains the distinction between the roles of the Two Kingdoms in his open letter explaining his harsh language against the peasants' revolt.

> There are two kingdoms, one the kingdom of God, the other the kingdom of the world. I have written this so often that I am surprised that there is anyone who does not know it or remember it. Anyone who knows how to distinguish rightly between these two kingdoms will certainly not be offended by my little book, and he will also properly understand the passages about mercy. God's kingdom is a kingdom of grace and mercy, not of wrath and punishment. In it there is only forgiveness, consideration for one another, love, service, the doing of good, peace, joy, etc. But the kingdom of the world is a kingdom of wrath and severity. In it there is only punishment, repression, judgment, and condemnation to restrain the wicked and protect the good. For this reason, it has the sword, and Scripture calls a prince or lord *"God's wrath,"* or *"God's rod"* (Isaiah 14:5–6).
>
> The Scripture passages which speak of mercy apply to the kingdom of God and to Christians, not to the kingdom of the world, for it is a Christian's duty

not only to be merciful, but also to endure every kind of suffering—robbery, arson, murder, devil, and hell. It goes without saying that he is not to strike, kill, or take revenge on anyone. But the kingdom of the world, which is nothing else than the servant of God's wrath upon the wicked and is a real precursor of hell and everlasting death, should not be merciful, but strict, severe, and wrathful in fulfilling its work and duty. Its tool is not a wreath of roses or a flower of love, but a naked sword; and a sword is a symbol of wrath, severity, and punishment. It is turned only against the wicked, to hold them in check and keep them at peace, and to protect and save the righteous [Rom. 13:3–4]. Therefore, God decrees, in the law of Moses and in Exodus 22 [21:14] where He institutes the sword, *"You shall take the murderer from My altar, and not have mercy on him."* And the Epistle to the Hebrews [10:28] acknowledges that he who violates the law must die without mercy. This shows that in the exercise of their office, worldly rulers cannot and ought not be merciful—though out of grace, they may take a day off from their office.

Now he who would confuse these two kingdoms—as our false fanatics do—would put wrath into God's kingdom and mercy into the world's kingdom; and that is the same as putting the devil in heaven and God in hell. These sympathizers with the peasants would like to do both of these things. First, they wanted to go to work with the sword, fight for the Gospel as "Christian brethren" and kill other people, who were supposed to be merciful and patient. Now that the kingdom of the world has overcome them, they want to have mercy in it; that is to say, they are unwilling to endure the worldly kingdom, but will not grant God's kingdom to anyone. Can you imagine anything more perverse? Not so, dear friends! If one has deserved wrath in the kingdom of the world, let him submit, and either take his punishment, or humbly sue for pardon. Those who are in God's kingdom ought to have mercy on everyone and pray for everyone, and yet not hinder the kingdom of the world in the maintenance of its laws and the performance of its duty; rather they should assist it.

Although the severity and wrath of the world's kingdom seems unmerciful, nevertheless, when we see it rightly, it is not the least of God's mercies. Let everyone consider and decide the following case. Suppose I had a wife and children, a house, servants, and property, and a thief or murder fell upon me, killed me in my own house, ravished my wife and children, took all

> that I had, and went unpunished so that he could do the same thing again, when he wished. Tell me, who would be more in need of mercy in such a case, I or the thief and murderer? Without a doubt it would be I who would need the most that people should have mercy on me. But how can this mercy be shown to me and my poor, miserable wife, and children, except by restraining such a scoundrel, and by protecting me and maintaining my right, or, if he will not be restrained and keeps it up, by giving him what he deserves and punishing him, so that he must stop it? What a fine mercy to me it would be, to have mercy on the thief and murder, and let him kill, abuse, and rob me![647]

Two Kingdoms Distinguished But Not Autonomous

Citing Luther's immense respect for constitutional authority, author and Professor of Lutheran Historical Theology John Stephenson points to the Reformer counseling "the Christian prince in 'On Secular Authority' to trust God and to be diligent in prayer; to use his office for the service to his subjects; to sift his minister's advice with due discrimination and to deal firmly with evildoers, yet erring on the side of lenience rather than severity."[648] These pages are imbued with Luther's characteristic appeal to common sense, urging "the prince to have the law as firmly in hand as the sword, and determine in his own mind when and where the law is to be applied strictly or with moderation, so that law may prevail at all times and in all cases, and reason may be the highest law and the master of all administration of law."[649] It would thus appear, according to Stephenson, "that Luther can hold that theoretically secular government and Christendom have nothing to do with each other while averring at the same time that practically they have everything to do with each other. His view of the ideal relationship of God's two modes of rule is that while they ought to be distinct from one another, they are yet inextricably linked."[650] In Luther's understanding,

> Both must be permitted to remain; the one to produce righteousness, the other to bring about external peace and prevent evil deeds. Neither is

---

[647] LW 46:69-71. *The Christian in Society III,* "An Open Letter on the Harsh Book Against the Peasants, 1525."
[648] Stephenson, "The Two Governments and the Two Kingdoms."
[649] LW 45:119. *The Christian in Society II,* "Temporal Authority."
[650] Stephenson, "The Two Governments and the Two Kingdoms."

> sufficient in the world without the other. No one can become righteous in the sight of God by means of the temporal government, without Christ's spiritual government…. For without the Holy Spirit in the heart no one becomes truly righteous, no matter how fine the works he does.[651]

Within the coalition of these two strains of governance, one can witness the Reformer's pastoral motive as he explains the entirety of divine activity in both preserving the fallen Creation and leading it to salvation in Christ.

As Thorsten Prill describes Luther's understanding of the two kingdoms, they

> are clearly distinctive but at the same time they are inextricably linked with each other. They are not rivals, but they are related to one another and belong to one another…the two kingdoms are supposed to serve one another…. By maintaining order in society, the temporal authority and the kingdom of the world support the work of the Gospel. On the other hand, it is the task of the spiritual kingdom to radiate into the kingdom of the world…preaching the Gospel…admonishing secular authorities, [and encouraging people to] respect their secular rulers.[652]

The exercise of governmental power to preserve the fallen creation and prevent sinful human beings from tearing God's world apart is not founded on the consent of the governed, as has been assumed since the Enlightenment, but rather on the ordinance of God to which Luther points by citing Romans 13 and 1 Peter 2:13. Here civil authority acts with the power of the sword, as we have repeatedly underscored, to curb evil and keep outward peace with the coercive threat of punishment as a tool of God's wrath and, paradoxically as it seems, as a true manifestation of divine love.

Stephenson cautions that our

> Perception of divine benevolence which undergirds the exercise of order-creating authority in all spheres of life ought not, however, lead to an unbalanced, "enthusiastic" and ultimately idolatrous estimates of the function and competence of secular rule. The business of government at all levels is to patch up and preserve a non-ideal reality, and were its task to be

---

651 LW 45:92. *The Christian in Society II*, "Temporal Authority."

652 Prill, "God's Two Kingdoms and the Christian's Two Citizenships."

> compared with that of the modern hospital, then it might more properly be likened to the casualty department than to that of plastic surgery.[653]

He then points to the parable Luther uses in "On Secular Authority," which speaks directly to the wariness Luther directs toward the enthusiasm of those who espouse a "social gospel." Stephenson clearly articulates that as it is customarily employed, the term "social gospel" is theological nonsense as Luther illustrates:

> To rule the world with the Gospel would, [Luther contends,] be like a shepherd putting wolves, lions, eagles and sheep all together in the same fold. In blissful naivete the shepherd bids these creatures of disparate temperament, enjoy their fodder in peace unhindered by the coercion of dogs or clubs. The sheep, [surmises the Reformer,] will indeed follow the ways of peace, but not for long."[654]

To abolish the law and to apply, for example, the ethical principles of the Sermon on the Mount in politics would endanger peace and lead to destruction, as the sheep would quickly discover!

Three Estates within the Earthly Kingdom

Recognizing that we live under God's two modes of rule, Luther explains how God has further established three estates in which all people exist. He identifies these three spheres and explains how sovereigns in each exercise their roles to accomplish their assigned task and responsibilities: the *politia* (government and State), the *ecclesia* (Church), and the *oeconomia* (household or family). According to this schema, he saw all human life organized through hierarchically structured relationships, all of which are under God's care. Those who are set over others must acknowledge that the source of all authority is God, who stands at the top. No one in authority is to see their position as a self-serving privilege nor as a basis for tyranny and abuse, but rather as means of bearing responsibility for the well-being of those entrusted to their care and governance.

Civil leaders' or magistrates' first thoughts are to be for the well-being of their citizens by guarding, protecting, and defending the citizens, and enforcing the law and public policies,

---

[653] Stephenson, "The Two Governments and the Two Kingdoms."

[654] LW 45:92. The Christian in Society III; "Temporal Authority."

as President Trump has enunciated in his "America First" maxim. Pastors are to shepherd, tend, feed, preach, and oversee those entrusted to their care. Parents, of course, are to care for, provide for, and rear their children, teaching them and their dependents the law of God by word and deed. Reciprocally, citizens, parishioners and children have an obligation of paying respect, obedience, and honor to their rulers, clergy and parents. These three hierarchies are ordained by God and represent different dimensions through which His authority and law are exercised in the earthly kingdom. The State, Church, and household stand equal before God and each other in discharging their essential tasks in preserving law and order, and thus the preservation of life itself.

Although the three spheres are continuously distorted by sin, the earthly kingdom was much more clearly recognized as a realm of divinely ordained authority, as each had responsibility for exercising the justice and wrath of God against sin in its own orb. As Luther articulates in his "Commentary on Psalm 111:"

> These divine stations and orders have been established by God that in the world there may be a stable, orderly, and peaceful life, and that justice may be preserved.... For if God had not Himself instituted these stations and did not daily preserve them as His work, no particle of right would last even a moment.... But these divine stations continue and remain throughout all kingdoms, as wide as the world and to the end of the world.[655]

Our senior twin believed that God wanted the "government of the earthy kingdom [in its three stations] to be a symbol...of the heavenly kingdom, like a mime or a mask."[656]

We are reminded by Dr. Jonathan Mumme, Professor of Theology at Concordia University-Wisconsin in Mequon, that

> Though Luther writes no treatise on the matter [of Three Estates and finds people less familiar with it than the category of the Two Kingdoms], it percolates almost ubiquitously through his writings. A familiar example is his exposition of the Fourth Commandment in the Large Catechism. In the Small Catechism Luther identifies the Fourth Commandment as not only

---

655 LW 13:369. *Selected Psalms II*, "Psalm 111."

656 WA 51:241, quoted by John Witte, Jr. in *Law and Protestantism—The Legal Teaching of the Lutheran Reformation* (Cambridge and New York: Cambridge University Press, 2004), p.93. <https://www.scribd.com/document/136320559/52992141-Law-and-Protestantism>.

> speaking of the family (the *oeconomia*), but also of "other authorities," whom we are to honor, serve and obey, love, and cherish. In his exposition of the Fourth Commandment in the Large Catechism Luther notes that not only biological fathers and heads of households are here indicated, but "fathers of the land" and "spiritual fathers," thereby indicating the *politia* and the *ecclesia* along with the *oeconomia*.[657]

To summarize, Luther teaches in his Doctrine of the Two Kingdoms that Christians are to have a positive attitude toward State and society and are encouraged to play an active role in both. As Christians, given our dual citizenship in the temporal and spiritual realms, we do not have the option of opting out of society. Perhaps these "categories" are ignored in our day because they evoke visceral reactions to all forms of "paternalism," "authoritarianism," and other "isms" of hierarchical disregard, and so we seek to avoid or at least minimize the social and institutional offense. Despite the unpopularity of such usage by the "woke crowd," or the "PC police," I hope we Christians, committed to the Scripture's witness, will not relinquish the conviction that at the foundation lies the Truth: the source of all authority is God! To organize life and authority on premises ignorant of that reality will be nothing more than a passing trend on the grand stage of history.

---

[657] Mumme, Rev. Dr. Jonathan, "The Three Estates." <https://lutheranreformation.org/theology/the-three-estates>.

19

Role of Rulers (Or, Caesar Doesn't Need to Be a Saint)

Luther not only believed that civil government is ordained by God, but that just as religious authorities are neither different nor superior to other Christians, the same applies to governmental authorities. They each have special roles to exercise as leaders and we owe them obedience and respect.

> Therefore, just as those who are now called "spiritual," that is, priests, bishops, or popes, are neither different from other Christians nor superior to them except that they are charged with the administration of the Word of God and the Sacraments, which is their work and office, so it is with the temporal authorities. They bear the sword and rod in their hand to punish the wicked and protect the good. A cobbler, a smith, a peasant—each has the work and office of his trade, and yet they are all alike consecrated priests and bishops. Further, everyone must benefit and serve every other by means of his own work or office so that in this way many kinds of work may be done for the bodily and spiritual welfare of the community, just as all the members of the body serve one another [1 Cor. 12:14-26].[658]

"Good governing is a service to God," in Lewis Spitz's* assessment, "and poor or evil governance is an affront to God. Luther frequently referred to rulers as a 'father and helper,' a 'gardener and caretaker,' or 'God's official.' He emphasized that individual rulers were

[658] LW 44:130. *The Christian in Society I*, "To the Christian Nobility of the German Nation," or in *Three Treatises* pp. 16-17.

* Dr. Lewis W. Spitz, world-renowned expert on Luther and scholar of Renaissance and Reformation history, author of *The Protestant Reformation, 1517-1559*, (Harper & Row, 1985), was a professor at Stanford University.

divinely instituted to restrain evil and prevent anarchy and chaos."[659] Magistrates were to care for their subjects as though they were one's children, like a loving father to his own, or as a gardener nurtures and sustains one's crops. We have witnessed that concern from our President not only in protecting the border, but in relief from forces of nature, and from the current coronavirus, as well as offering support to cities being torn and ravaged by rioters bent on destruction and mayhem. For Luther, such political authority was divine in origin but earthly in operation.

Referencing Luther's "Commentary on Psalm 82" verse 1, Eric Gritsch underscores Luther's conviction

> that good and just government is anchored in the Biblical view that both those who rule and those who are ruled belong together, forming God's "community" (*Gemeinde*) on earth.... When a ruler is aware of his dependence upon God, he is a jewel and a treasure, enriching the ministry of the Gospel which is God's most essential work on earth. In this sense, the Bible calls just rulers "gods" because they are "partakers of His divine majesty and help Him to do divine and superhuman works."[660] God has endowed some of these rulers with special gifts so that they become clearly visible embodiments of His wisdom and grace. Such people can be found throughout the history of the world and include Christians, Jews, pagans, and even politicians, who are generally not very trustworthy.[661]

Luther recognized that

> Since the beginning of the world a wise prince is a mighty rare bird, and an upright prince even rarer. They are generally the biggest fools or the worst scoundrels on earth; therefore, one must constantly expect the worst from them and look for little good, especially in divine matters which concern the salvation of souls. They are God's executioners* and hangmen; His divine

---

[659] Spitz, Lewis W., "The Political Luther," *Christian History*, Issue 34, Vol. XI, No.2 ("Martin Luther: The Reformer's Early Years"). <https://www.christianhistoryinstitute.org/magazine/issue/martin-luther-the-reformers-early-years>.

[660] Gritsch, quoting Luther, LW 13: 54, 55, *Selected Psalms II*, "Psalm 82."

[661] Gritsch, *Jester*, p.121.

* The term *stockmeyster* translated "jailer" has meaning beyond that of being a guard or warden. It refers literally to one who flogs, inflicts or otherwise enforces legal punishment in execution of a sentence.

> wrath uses them to punish the wicked and to maintain outward peace. Our God is a great lord and ruler; this is why He must also have such noble, highborn, and rich hangmen and constables. He desires that everyone shall copiously accord them riches, honor, and fear in abundance. It pleases His divine will that we call His hangmen gracious lords, fall at their feet and be subject to them in all humility, so long as they do not ply their trade too far and try to become shepherds instead of hangmen. If a prince should happen to be wise, upright, or a Christian, that is one of the great miracles, the most precious token of divine grace upon the land.[662]

In his final sermon, Luther lamented the lack of wisdom in government.

> In worldly affairs and government…a few people are often endowed with great wisdom and understanding, unlike ordinary people. Often God gives us a fine, noble, intelligent man, who could serve principalities and people with wisdom and counsel. But such persons flee from the business of government, and it is hard to bring them to govern. On the other hand, however, there are others who want to be and do it, but they have no ability.[663]

Could it be that Luther's perceptive insight into human nature, and his discerning understanding of the political realm, provided him with the prophetic ability to foresee what his twin would encounter in becoming the leader of the free world from the perspective of the business world, rather than from the self-perceived, all-knowing elite political sector? Every success is disparaged or even overlooked, and actions are taken by the opposition to thwart the possibility of a "win" for the President, even though those critical political opponents had previously advocated exactly what he is doing or attempting to accomplish. After all, how can such a one who has never been elected to any political government office be "schooled" sufficiently to hold the highest office in the land? He must therefore be everybody's pupil, first and foremost of those so-called "political pros" he defied, his opponents whom he defeated, as well as their surrogates within the media, who imagined they alone were wise, and thus react with resentful anger that he succeeded in penetrating their sanctimonious ranks. He not only ascended to the highest pinnacle over them and succeeded in getting things done previous administrations only talked about doing, but was

---

[662] LW 45:113. *The Christian in Society II*, "Temporal Authority."

[663] LW 51:385. *Sermons I*. "The Last Sermon, Eisleben, 1546."

in a position to reveal the very shenanigans he alleged during the campaign and continued during the transition. Manufacturing charges and conducting faulty investigations served their purpose of deflecting attention from their own malfeasance, which led to the saddest ordeal the country has endured politically.

Perhaps that's the largest component driving the anger and behavior of Trump's opponents. They are fully aware that the President would have access to documentation that could expose, prove, and potentially indict those in the former "scandal-free" administration for their fraudulent conduct, and unravel the complex coup attempt designed to bring down a sitting President—spying on one's opponent and the American citizens associated with the campaign, or those selected to be part of the administrative team; purchasing a salacious dossier used to deceive the FISA Court four times; and accusing Trump of colluding with the Russians and being a traitor. In addition to conducting faulty "witch-hunt" investigations and calling for a special prosecutor, legislators gleefully lied to the public by announcing "bombshell" revelations heard in closed-door testimonies, signifying that the "walls were closing in," only to discover the actual transcripts of those witnesses revealed a complete contradiction of the promised "coming attraction" of the President's removal from office. Just as the public had been falsely and intentionally misled about Trump's collusion with the Russians, so it continued with the impeachment, aided of course and supported by the omnipresent "Fake News" media.

Holding those closed-door hearings in the bowels of the Capitol Building, ignoring Constitutional provisions such as due process, rights and rules of the House, and ignoring established precedents for initiating impeachment procedures with a vote of all members, should have invalidated the proceedings as well as the subpoenas issued.[664] Biased political partisans involved in fraudulent conduct seem to have served the purpose of creating heightened negativity by casting aspersions on the President, thereby directing attention away from their own criminality and attempts to cover up in order to protect themselves and their cohorts. Why, after the fact, would a resolution be passed in the House telling investigating committees to keep doing what they are already doing in conducting hearings, if not to provide some cover for not having had the entire body initially vote on an impeachment inquiry? Instead, one single person, Speaker Nancy Pelosi, solely directed six different House committees to launch the impeachment probe. A matter as serious and as important as removing a duly elected president should demand the fundamental principles of fairness

---

[664] <https://www.whitehouse.gov/wp-content/uploads/2020/01/Trial-Memorandum-of-President-Donald-J.-Trump.pdf>, p 41. More than 200 years of precedent confirms that the House votes to begin an impeachment inquiry, thus making subpoenas issued before House Resolution 660 invalid. See pp.41-42.

and the integrity of the democratic process, with an inquiry conducted in as transparent a manner as possible.

Ignoring the need for the whole House to vote on the impeachment inquiry; denying the minority party their right to be able to call witnesses and cross-examine the majority's witnesses; and the unbelievable fact that members of other committees, who had jurisdiction over the impeachment inquiry, were barred from participating in the questioning, are not just some minor technicalities, as some leaders of the majority in the House have claimed.

As discoveries continued to be made, it is not difficult to conclude that Trump's adversaries were projecting onto the President their own scandalous machinations they know so well. Ex-FBI lawyer Kevin Clinesmith was willing to plead guilty to falsifying a document to obtain a FISA warrant on former Trump campaign adviser Carter Page during the Russian investigation. Documents also disclosed Hillary Clinton's involvement in the scheme. Could the accusations against the President have been designed and intended to deflect attention away from those in the high ranks of the intel community who were involved in the spying and attempted coup? Some pundits concluded that whatever allegations the Democrats directed toward Trump reveal exactly their own transgressions. Did Trump not campaign on "draining the swamp?" From the very beginning, prior to the election, we continually discovered evidence of plotting to derail and "spy" on Trump and the campaign, even to crafting an "insurance policy" of malicious back-up actions if he were to be "mistakenly" elected.

Within minutes after President Trump's inauguration, we read headlines in *The Washington Post* saying "The Campaign to Impeach President Trump Has Begun," and heard incessant cries of "Impeach '45.'" The rationale "for cause" became a moving target and included lengthy and costly investigations into collusion with Russia, and charges that Trump was a Russian asset and a traitor to the country. In discovery, however, it was revealed that his opponents were accusing the "intruder" of the very acts which they themselves were guilty of having committed: collusion with the Russians by Representative Adam Schiff, anxious to receive the salacious material offered by Russian imposters; funding for opposition research and the "Dirty Dossier" provided by the Hillary Clinton campaign and the Democratic National Committee;[665] and the Hillary campaign seeking anti-Trump information from the Ukrainian government. Throughout all the investigations, those indicting legislators and media critics ignored the need to investigate the accusers when evidence revealed the destruction of subpoenaed emails, computers and phone messages by the Clinton campaign; the purchase of a "dirty dossier," used to fraudulently obtain FISA

[665] <https://apnews.com/article/7b7d698b9a660997f5e755d92b775d98>.

warrants to spy on a campaign; the wiping of the Mueller team phone records; collusion with a foreign government to aid their candidate; and when an obvious "quid pro quo" was publicly bragged about by Joe Biden, all seemingly to establish a pattern of double standards supported by a two-tier system of justice, as revelations now suggest that our nation's intel agencies were weaponized against Donald Trump, his campaign, and his resulting administration. Simply put, there seems to be a set of rules and laws for "me" that differs from those imposed on "thee."

Likewise, during the impeachment inquiry, the focus moved from "quid pro quo" in a phone conversation with the newly elected Ukrainian head of State to "bribery," "extortion," "abuse of power," and "obstruction of Congress," without evidence of any "high crimes" having been committed, nor the naming of who the victim was. Ironically, in the view of some eminent Constitutional scholars, not only were the subpoenas issued for witnesses invalid because the Speaker alone ordered the impeachment, when that power is granted solely to the entire House, but they suggest the very Articles of Impeachment could therefore be levied against the Speaker herself. In their opinion, she began the proceedings with "abuse of power" by not holding a formal vote to begin the inquiry, and was further guilty of "obstruction of Congress" by withholding the Articles from the Senate, thus thwarting the will of the House action as she attempted to forge her own "quid pro quo" with the Senate:

> "This is a major point," says Hans von Spakovsky, "that Democrats [have glossed] over as an insignificant technicality. Crucially, the Constitution gives the 'sole Power of Impeachment to the House of Representatives—not the Speaker of the House. Page 614 of the 2017 manual on the 'Rules, Precedents, and Procedures of the House'—written by the three individuals who have been the parliamentarians of the House of Representatives since 1994—states that under 'the modern practice, an impeachment is normally instituted by the House by the adoption of a resolution calling for a committee investigation of charges against the [federal] officer in question.' This means that Pelosi has violated the modern practice of the House by not having the entire body vote on such a resolution.[666]

[666] von Spakovsky, Hans, "In Trump Impeachment Probe, Democrats Refuse to Follow Nixon and Clinton Precedents," *The Daily Signal*, October 30, 2019. <https://www.dailysignal.com/2019/10/30/in-trump-impeachment-probe-democrats-refuse-to-follow-nixon-and-clinton-precedents>.

Luther exhibits little patience with those who camouflage their attitude and actions by saying:

> In this way the schismatic spirits can brag and swear that the reason they teach differently is not any pride or envy, but only their desire for the glory of God and the salvation of their neighbor [country?] They make it all so beautiful and bright, and they make their humility and God's glory so great that they cannot see anything else. In matters of life, it is the same. As soon as people begin judging and criticizing one another, we see the same camouflage and the same boast: "I am not doing this out of hostility to the person but out of love for righteousness [love of country]. I am a friend to the person but an enemy to the cause." This tickles a person so gently beneath his lovely exterior that he never becomes aware of any log...[667]

in his own eye, but sees only the speck in the brother's eye, referencing Jesus' teaching in Matthew 7:3 and Luke 6:41.

He goes on to say that passing judgment by "invoking the glory and the righteousness of God...is a demonic addition, decorating and beautifying itself with this camouflage."[668] One wonders how Luther would describe the current situation where views, positions and attitudes are not merely camouflaged but actually expose blatant hatred and hostility, as opponents of the President demonstrate their hypocrisy from their adamant positions taken before Donald Trump became President. To cite just a few views: the timing of Supreme Court nominations in the last year of a President's term, or the so-called "Biden rule;" protecting the southern border from illegal entry; and the impeachment process, which certainly did not follow honored precedents, Constitutional guarantees, or House rules, and could not pass "the shoe on the other foot" test, as Constitutional lawyer Alan Dershowitz describes the partisan charges. Most recently we witnessed Speaker Pelosi saying she has no "hatred" in her heart against President Trump, but yet observed her angrily tearing up the President's State of the Union address, as well as hearing Senator Romney justify his impeachment "half-vote."

---

[667] LW 21:222-223. *The Sermon on the Mount and the Magnificat*, "The Sermon on the Mount (Matthew 7:6)."

[668] Ibid., p.223.

Observe how contemporaneous Luther is as we compare the remarks of the President at the 68th Annual National Prayer Breakfast, February 6, 2020, with his twin's commentary on Jesus' Sermon on the Mount:

The President:

> As everybody knows, my family, our great country, and your President, have been put through a terrible ordeal by some very dishonest and corrupt people. They have done everything possible to destroy us, and by so doing, very badly hurt our nation. They know what they are doing is wrong, but they put themselves far ahead of our great country. Weeks ago, and again yesterday, courageous Republican politicians and leaders had the wisdom, the fortitude, and strength to do what everyone knows was right. I don't like people who use their faith as justification for doing what they know is wrong. Nor do I like people who say, "I pray for you," when they know that that's not so. So many people have been hurt, and we can't let that go on.[669]

The Theologian:

> Oh, this is a thing that ought to be known to all princes and rulers who, not content with confessing the right, immediately want to obtain it and win the victory, without the fear of God; they fill the world with bloodshed and misery and think what they do is right and well done because they have, or think they have, a just cause. What else is that but proud and haughty Moab, which calls itself worthy to possess the right, that fine and noble good and gift of God; while if it regards itself right in the sight of God, it is not worthy to live on earth or eat a crust of bread, because of its sins. Oh, blindness, blindness![670]

So, intently focused on impeachment from before the inauguration with allegations proven to be false; the repeated investigations coupled with resistance and obstruction; and the denial of the Constitutional rights of due process, presumption of innocence until proven guilty, to confront one's accuser, to call witnesses, and opportunity to cross-examine,

---

[669] President Trump, "National Prayer Breakfast Remarks," <https://www.whitehouse.gov/briefings-ments/remarks-president-trump-68th-annual-national-prayer-breakfast>.

[670] LW 21:336-37. *The Sermon on the Mount and the Magnificat*, "The Magnificat (Luke 1:50)."

have prevented legislation that otherwise could be deemed sensible and helpful to the country. This, Luther claims, is the "shameful wisdom of the world."[671] In his analysis, he maintains that whatever God "institutes and ordains must always be not only perverted but also reviled and discredited by the devil and his followers. And then the world even thinks that God should be pleased and look with approval upon the fact that every fool wants to master and rule Him."[672]

Luther continues:

> The devil has slobbered us with fools. And Aristotle, who observed in governments that few people are properly qualified to govern, makes a distinction between the truly wise and understanding and others whom he calls "*doxa, id est opinione sua sapientes*," the wise who only think they are wise and understanding; just as we say in German: "Conceit keeps the dance going." They imagine that because they are in government and are higher-ups, they must surely be wise. And one such fool in counsel hinders the others from getting on with anything at all; for he wants to be wise by force in the devil's name and still he is a fool.
>
> Now, if in worldly affairs one is quite rightly opposed to these people who want to be wise and are not, how much more irksome are those people, whom both God and men rightly dislike, who want to be wise in the holy Christian Church and are not. For these people hinder the ministry, so that the people cannot come to God. Such in our time were Munzer, [Thomas Muntzer, enthusiast, fanatic, and leader in the Peasant's War.] and the anti-Sacramentarians, who prevent and obstruct the course of the Gospel and mislead the people, imagining that they alone are wise and understanding because they are in the office and government of the Church.[673]

To make it perfectly clear, Luther reiterates that

> the Lord Christ will not tolerate in His Christian Church [those] whether they be pope, emperors, kings, princes, or learned men...[who] want to make

---

[671] LW 51:384. *Sermons I*, "The Last Sermon, Eisleben, 1546")

[672] Ibid., LW 51:385.

[673] Ibid., LW 51:385-386.

> themselves masters of His divine Word and with their own wisdom rule in the high, great matters of faith and our salvation.... He has no intention of being a pupil, they are to be the pupils. He is the eternal wisdom, and He knows very well what He wishes to do or not to do. They think that, because they sit at the top of government, they are the wisest, that they see more deeply into the Scriptures than other people...and because they are in the government, God cannot get along without their counsel and rule.[674]

As we noted in introducing this comparative exploration of our twin populist reformers, God can use whomever He deigns—even those for whom we may have contempt—to partner in effecting His will. Luther brought a new respect for what has been called "the sacredness of the secular." This is most clearly witnessed with his emphasis on equality in the "Priesthood of all Believers" as well as in his understanding of governance being divine in origin, even though it may be administered by those who may be godless and abuse the trust placed in them.

In his "Commentary on Psalm 101," Luther claims that

> God has two kinds of people on earth in all walks of life. Some have a special star before God; these He teaches Himself and raises them up as He would have them. They are also the ones who have smooth sailing on earth and so-called good luck and success. Whatever they undertake prospers; and even if all the world were to work against it, it would still be accomplished without hindrance. For God, who put it into their heart and stimulates their intelligence and courage, also puts it into their hands that it must come to pass and must be carried out; that was the case with Samson, David, Jehoiada, and others. He occasionally provides such men not only among His own people but also among the godless and the heathen, and not only in the ranks of nobility but also among the middle classes, farmers, and laborers. For instance, in Persia He raised up King Cyrus; in Greece, the nobleman Themistocles and Alexander the Great; among the Romans, Augustus, Vespasian, and others. In Syria, too, He brought all success and prosperity through one-man Naaman (2 Kings 5:1). I do not

674 Ibid., LW 51:387. See also LW 51:384 where Luther views "the wise and understanding" feel the need to improve on what God has done; "God must be everybody's pupil as they want to be His teacher."

> call such people trained or made but rather created; they are princes and lords directed by God.[675]

Perhaps the Reformer, reflecting honestly from his own introspection, was being prophetic in anticipating his twin's role in the governance of the United States! We are reminded by Luther scholar and ethicist George Forell that

> in this practical area Luther's thought is characterized by an unexpected combination of realism, conservatism, and pragmatism. His analysis of the political situation is singularly free from the common sentimental illusions of amateur politicians. His advice is a lively combination of caution, courage, and prudence. Of course, politics in general and foreign policy in particular belong for Luther in the realm of the law. It is, therefore, proper that reason should rule and guide people in these decisions. It is not even necessary that a ruler, in order to rule competently, should be a Christian. Luther says, "Caesar does not need to be a saint."* For the ruler, it suffices that he uses reason; in this way God maintains all government, even that of the Tartars and Turks.[676]

For Luther, the kingdoms of this world and their rulers are tools in the hands of a sovereign God, and regardless of whether these temporal rulers acknowledge His role, God can affect and accomplish His sovereign purpose through them. Forell contends that in the practical results of statecraft, Luther was led

> to suggest that it might actually be better, politically speaking, to have a competent and intelligent ruler who is personally evil than to have a ruler who, though personally a model of virtue, is politically incompetent and stupid. Indeed, Luther insists that a good and wise ruler is the ideal head of government, but if this ideal is not available it may turn out to be in the long-range interest of the commonwealth if a personally evil person rules the

---

[675] LW 13:154-55. *Selected Psalms II*, "Psalm 101."

* George Forell quoting from *Luther's Sermons* (1528), WA 27:418.

[676] Forell, "Foreign Policy," *Journal of Lutheran Ethics*, January 1, 2002, p.4; <https://www.elca.org/JLE/Articles/993>.

> State intelligently and with skill than if someone who is personally virtuous rules without intelligence and competence.[677]

Here's how Luther puts it:

> The question has been properly raised whether a prince is better if he is good and imprudent or prudent and yet also evil. Here Moses certainly demands both. Nevertheless, if one cannot have both, it is better for him to be prudent and not good than good and not prudent; for the good man would actually rule nothing but would be ruled only by others, and at that only by the worst people.[678]

Could this observation not have been prophetic for the 2020 reality where Joe Biden, as the Democratic Party's presidential nominee, is viewed as being a "nice man" and "fun" to be around, but has little in accomplishments to show for his more than four decades in government service that would commend him for the highest office in the land? Then too, there are concerns about his "cognitive skills" and his acumen to handle the demands of the Presidency. In fact, many cite the concerns they have already perceived in his inability to clearly explain his views, his past positions (especially those related to segregation), his gaffs, and his propensity to invade the personal space of females. Indeed, some have concluded he is merely a vessel into which handlers and others, whose support he needs, can pour in their positions which are not necessarily his, and thus cannot adequately articulate or defend them.

Luther had too much respect for the technical demands of a competent government to believe good intentions are all a ruler needs. Political action taken by leaders, in Luther's view, needs to reflect a common-sense approach that guides, judges and endeavors, not according to theories, presumptions or hearsay, but according to its effect on the welfare of the citizens. Such advice seems to be ignored by those who would vilify Trump in favor of political gain. Luther's counsel, therefore, always expressed his concern for the practical political results of an action, not to maintain power and control. In his "Treatise On Good Works" published in 1520, he wrote:

---

677 Ibid., p.9.

678 LW 9:19 (WA 14:553). *Lectures on Deuteronomy.* "Deuteronomy 1: 13 Choose Wise Men." Also quoted in Ewald Plass, *What Luther Says*, 2:582, "No. 1774 Prefer a Wise but Wicked to a Saintly but Stupid Ruler."

> A prince must also be very wise and not always try to impose his own will, even if he has the right and best of all reasons to do so. For it is a far nobler virtue to put up with a slight to one's own rights than [it is to risk damage] to life and property, where this is to the advantage of the subjects. As we know, worldly rights are valid only with respect to the things of this world.[679]

Luther then proceeds to praise Caesar Augustus, who "did not wish to wage war, however right he was unless there were sure indications of greater benefit than harm, or at least of a bearable harm." Luther liked quoting Emperor Augustus: "War can be likened to fishing with a golden net—you never catch as much as you risk losing."[680] He referenced this Roman saying* in his "Commentary on Psalm 82" and added, "One must not begin a war or work for it; it comes unbidden, all too soon. One must keep peace as long as one can, even though one must buy it with all the money that would be spent on the war or won by the war. Victory never makes up for what is lost by war."[681]

In our comparison, one can view President Trump adhering to the wisdom offered to leaders in the temporal realm by his twin. While we hear bluster, which can be annoying, we also experience action and witness accomplishments from the President that in many sectors have broken all-time records. His restraint in retaliating to the alleged provocations from Iran (piracy on the high seas, seizing oil tankers, shooting down an American drone, missile and drone attacks on Saudi Arabia's oil infrastructure) with military strikes, follows Luther's counsel to take time to calibrate the risks, benefits and costs. The Commander in Chief's repeated declarations that "he doesn't want war with Iran," accompanied with the assertion that "the United States is more prepared for conflict than any other country in history,"[682] seem to reflect that practical advice offered by the Reformer to those who hold responsible positions in government. This advice would also be directed to the papacy,

---

[679] LW 44:94. *The Christian in Society I*; "Treatise on Good Works."

[680] Ibid.

* In his Lecture on Deuteronomy 20, Luther pointed to Augustus, who always preferred peace to war, which the emperor said was "like a golden fishhook, where the cost is greater than the yield; and when it is lost, one catch cannot make up for it." Augustus Caesar had become proverbial for promoting peace through the Pax Romana (LW 9:203 fn.3; *Lectures on Deuteronomy*).

[681] LW 13:57. *Selected Psalms II*, "Psalm 82," (vs.2).

[682] <https://www.usatoday.com/story/news/politics/2019/09/16/donald-trump-u-s-doesnt-need-mideast-oil-discusses-iran-response/2339329001>.

whose international intrigues had been more than just dabbling in foreign affairs. Luther continues with an illustration to underscore his point:

> He who drives a cart must act differently than if he were walking alone. When he is on his own, he can walk, jump, and do what he likes, but when he is driving, he must control and guide so that the horse and cart can follow. He has to pay greater regard to the horse and cart than to himself. A prince is in the same position. He stands at the head and leads the multitude and must not go or do as he wants but as the multitude are able. He has to pay more regard to their needs and necessities than to his own will and pleasure.[683]

In essence, Luther is arguing that any other behavior by those who govern is destined to lead to disaster, both to those who rule and those who are under their care: "When a prince rules according to his own mad will and follows his own opinion, he is like a mad driver who rushes straight ahead with his horse and cart through bushes, hedges, ditches, streams, uphill and downdale, regardless of roads and bridges. He will not drive for very long. He is bound to smash up."[684]

Luther understood the need for those who govern in the temporal sphere to face the complexities of political life realistically. During Turkish attacks, he viewed the Emperor as the protector of Germany and its freedom, which entailed defending the borders and protecting the life and property of its citizens. Likewise, we witnessed President Trump building the wall on the southern border, and his willingness to provide troops to aid our cities during the violent riots to protect innocent lives and citizens' property from destruction.

In the exposition on that same Psalm (101), Luther describes the rightful role of an ecclesiastical leader:

> Now if a preacher in his official capacity says to kings and princes and to all the world, "Thank and fear God, and keep His commandments," he is not meddling in the affairs of secular government. On the contrary, he is thereby serving and being obedient to the highest government. Thus, the entire spiritual government really does nothing else than serve the divine authority, which is why they are called servants of God and ministers of Christ in the Scriptures. Indeed, St. Paul even calls it a service to the Church and to all

683 LW 44:94. *The Christian in Society I*, "Treatise on Good Works."

684 Ibid., LW 44:94-95.

> heathen (Rom.15:16). Thus, if David or a prince teaches or gives orders to fear God and to listen to His Word, he is not acting as a lord of that Word but as an obedient servant. He is not meddling in spiritual or divine government but remains a humble subordinate and a faithful servant. For with respect to God and in the service of His authority, everything should be identical and mixed together, whether it be called spiritual or secular—the pope as well as the emperor, the lord as well as the servant. No distinctions and no respect of persons apply here: one is as good before God as the other. For He is one God, the same Lord of all, of the one as well as of the other. Therefore, they should all be identical in their obedience and should even be mixed into one another like one cake, every one of them helping the other to be obedient. Therefore, in service or submission to God there can be no rebellion among the spiritual or the secular authorities. Even in the world, rebellion never stems from obedient service but from an ambitious desire to rule.
>
> But it is a confusion and a mingling of the secular and the spiritual realms when those sublime and meddlesome spirits want to change and correct the civil law in a dictatorial and dominating fashion, even though they have no directive or authority to do so, either from God or from men. The same is true when spiritual or secular princes and lords want to change and correct the Word of God in a dictatorial and dominating fashion, when they themselves dictate what should be preached and taught, even though they have no more right to do this than the lowest beggar. Such people want to be God themselves, and not to serve Him or to remain subordinate to Him. Like Lucifer, (Isaiah 14:12) they seek equality with God, even superiority to Him. Thus, they cease to be subject to Him, they meddle in His government, and finally they set themselves above Him. Therefore, all the wrangling and complaining about the confusion of the spiritual and the secular realms are in the interest of domination and not of service. Everyone wants to produce and make something new; no one wants to serve and obey, either in divine or in secular matters.[685]

No candidate or public official is immune to or above Biblical principles and moral standards, nor above the law; and while we'd like to expect our leaders to exemplify the best

[685] LW 13:195-96. *Selected Psalms II.* "Psalm 101," (vs.5).

character qualities of decency, morality, respect, and kindness toward others, we cannot expect, much less demand, perfection or even devout behavior in our leaders.

Again, here Scripture is helpful to us and clear in its instruction that goes beyond the "strictness" of the letter of the law by stating, for example, that "lusting" is tantamount to having committed adultery in your heart, and "hating" is the equivalent of having committed murder. In addition, we are cautioned about judging others lest we be judged, as is visibly apparent in pointing a finger at others only to discover three fingers pointing back at us.

It is clear in my understanding that Jesus is warning us against taking pride in a "works-based" view of salvation that allows us to think that because we have not literally committed such outward offensive acts, we have not sinned. Instead, Jesus is undeniably urging us to be genuinely honest and sensitive about the motives we can harbor but eagerly attempt to conceal for appearance's sake. We may not actually do the deed, but with pretense, we still falsely camouflage or withhold expressing our true feelings. In other words, one can obey the law perfectly in a literal sense, but one's heart and motivations, known to God, are still sinful. At the same time, it is instructive to be mindful of a very human tendency I am all too aware of in myself: being critical of actions I see in others that I am prone to exhibit.

In governance both within the Church and State, Luther and Trump recognized and faced the complexities of political life realistically. That is not at all easy as both quickly discovered. Luther observed what Trump certainly experienced, stating perceptively that

> Nobody thinks he is too clumsy or inept. If he were the government [or Church], he would really do splendidly; and he is dissatisfied with anything done by others....Those are the Master Smart Alecks who are so clever that they can bridle a steed in its hind end. All they can do is to condemn other people. When they get control of things, they ruin everything. It is as the saying goes: "Whoever watches the game knows best how to do it."[686]

Luther is convinced that critics are often spectators who assume no responsibility and often fail to be informed or aware of the intricacies of governance in the midst of divergent views, some of which neglect consideration of unintended consequences and others that defy common sense for the sake of expedience, political power or to masquerade an ulterior motive.

---

686 *Luther's Sermons* (1528), WA 27:149.

Ultimately, Eric Gritsch writes that Luther "favored rulers whose reasonable government was enlightened by faith. While reason is able to provide a just administration of wise laws, faith adds a healthy distrust of merely human power." Citing the Reformer's "Commentary on Psalm 127" (verse 1 [NRSV]: *"Unless the Lord builds the house, those who build it labor in vain"*),

> Faith in God shields a statesman against the arrogance of power as well as against despair when human policies fail. That is why, Luther argued, rulers ought to be Christians, although he was quite skeptical about a purely Christian government exemplified in the territorial rule of bishops. He nevertheless favored Christians in government since they ought to know the limitations of secular power rather than being preoccupied with themselves and their own authority. Christians should be able to discern better than anyone else the differences between legalism and justice as well as between law and love.[687]

---

[687] Gritsch, *Jester*, p.122.

20

Role of Subjects: Obedient to God First for Christians

Luther took seriously St. Paul's words in Romans 13:1 (RSNV): "*Let every person be subject to the governing authorities; for there is no authority except from God, and those authorities that exist have been instituted by God.*" In a similar vein, the author of 1 Peter (in 2:13-17 [NRSV]) sets forth the same focus on the subject's role as a servant:

> *For the Lord's sake accept the authority of every human institution whether of the emperor as supreme or of governors, as sent by Him to punish those who do wrong and to praise those who do right. For it is God's will that by doing right you should silence the ignorance of the foolish. As servants of God, live as free people, yet do not use your freedom as a pretext for evil. Honor everyone. Love the family of believers. Fear God. Honor the emperor.*

To Luther, we all have duties primarily as subjects of an earthly, a divine, and a household sovereign. As we have observed, the three states and the roles of ruler, pastor and parent were all ordained by God to carry out their responsibilities in equipping and enabling all to exercise their vocation as subjects, parishioners and family members. In the other direction, subjects or citizens, laity or parishioners, and children owe their rulers, clergy and parents obedience as embodied sources of God-given authority.

As citizens, Christians are expected and encouraged by St. Paul (1 Timothy 2:1-3 [NRSV]) foremost to pray for their leaders: "*First of all, then, I urge that supplications, prayers, intercessions, and thanksgivings be made for everyone, for kings and all who are in high positions, so that we may lead a quiet and peaceable life in all godliness and dignity. This is right and is acceptable in the sight of God our Savior...*" This passage acknowledges the Church's awareness of civil government as an institution ordained by God, as well as to our need to live and minister in ways that observe our responsibility.

Our democratic and participatory government and many other modern nations place duty and responsibility upon citizens. They do not have a ruler in the sense that Christians did, to whom St. Paul wrote his letters. However, the Scriptural teachings about governments still apply, even though in a democracy Christians cannot be viewed as mere subjects of the State. By having a voice, it is incumbent that we keep ourselves informed to be responsible participants in the election of leadership for our governance, and serve in such a government as a way to express our love and concern for our neighbor.

As such, we interact and depend upon each other in a variety of ways, especially through the faithful discharge of our vocations in earthly life. Professor Simpson confidently writes:

> Luther taught that God fervently desires that all humans share in His own left-hand governing. We are called and sent in our various vocations to be God's "masks" in the world, as he liked to say, through which God's left-hand governing happens. As God's co-creative creatures, we serve our neighbors in solidarity and love, seeking justice, peace, and well-being. God thereby endows human beings with remarkable capacities of "reason," making it possible for humans to participate in God's left-hand governing. Reason was Luther's shorthand to identify the broad scope of worldly wisdom, including the sciences, the arts and humanities, and especially the traditions of moral wisdom.[688]

In other words, as Christians we are privileged to be the heart, hands, and voice of Christ, as together we become the "Body of Christ"—His physical presence—in the world today.

In exercising our citizenship, we thus have the joyous experience of sharing in God's left-hand governance, which is to be accomplished with other Christians, with those of other faiths, and with those of no faith at all. However, Luther encouraged Christians to "put on" our neighbors as Christ has "put on" us in His service. He urged citizens and political authorities to promote social justice by giving special attention to the most vulnerable among us, especially the weak, the widows and the orphans. The synthesis of our various duties, roles, interests and talents are thus to be utilized in the service of others as we become "partakers of Divine majesty" working together for the preservation, protection and development of human life and the resources of nature.

"So that we may accomplish this task," Lyman Stone cites and affirms Luther's teaching that "God has established three estates in which all people exist and find their roles: state, church, and family." Our place and role in life, fulfilling our responsibilities and exercising our talents and skills is called our "vocation." Stone contends "Luther practically invented the

---

[688] Simpson, Gary, "How Luther Helps Today's Citizens."

modern usage of the word 'vocation.' Before Luther, the word had meant almost exclusively the spiritual calling to priesthood or monasticism. But for Luther, God works in the Kingdom of Man through vocation, through observable means or 'masks'" and makes the observation that "...this extension of spiritual and moral significance to mundane, secular work in the earthly realm is what is meant by the 'Protestant work ethic.'"[689]

"This is about the way Luther conceives of man as a 'fellow worker' with God," writes Gustaf Wingren.* Through one's vocation cooperation takes place as one does work which effects the well-being of others and the neighbor is profited.

> In his "Kirchenpostille" (sermons or homilies and Biblical commentaries) we find the concept of a Christian as a conduit or channel, which receives from above, from God through faith, "and then gives forth below" to others, through love. Luther makes it clear that God's own love reaches out to others through Christians as channels [or masks]. God is present on earth with His goodness when a Christian directs his service downward to others. God dwells in heaven, but now He is near and working on earth with man as his co-operator. In The Large Catechism it is said that all creatures ("parents and all in authority" are specially mentioned) are God's hands, channels and means through which He gives us all things....If I thus receive God's gifts through the faithfulness of others in their vocations, the same is true about my vocation in relation to others.[690]

The State has a crucial role to play in the ordering of society through its civil "servants," but that doesn't mean that the Church has nothing to say to the State except to submit, acquiesce and support it in its earthly duties. The Church in Luther's view, as we have said, has the sacred responsibility of reminding magistrates—the loving "fathers" of the community, as he liked to refer to the sovereigns—of the burden placed on them to care for their subjects as though they were his children, by providing for their needs as he guides the State morally and ethically. In addition, citizens have the responsibility of not only holding our leaders accountable when they fail to discharge their duties, but to exhort all public servants, from schoolteachers to the President, to live up to the demands of their vocations.

---

689 Stone, Lyman, "Two Kingdom Theology."

* Gustaf Wingren was Professor of Systematic Theology at Lund University and one of the most influential, best known and creative theologians in twentieth century Sweden and author of several theological books.

690 Wingren, Gustaf, *Luther on Vocation*, Tr. By Carl C. Rasmussen, (Philadelphia, Muhlenberg Press, 1957), p.126. Wingren is quoting Luther, WA 30, 136 (1529).

Citizens in a democracy are more than subjects of the state. They are to be participants in the governance of their state by having "voice." How we discharge those privileges and duties of citizenship—whether by passively accepting the creeping authoritarianism of the State usurping our "God-endowed rights" or by raising our voices and taking action in support of constitutional law and democratic norms that have sustained our country—is obviously a question of moral conscience with which we as responsible citizens are honorably obliged to wrestle and certainly suitable for confession, and demanding repentance if we err.

Since all authority comes from God (Romans 13:1), St. Paul assumes and makes clear elsewhere that human authority cannot in any way usurp God's authority over the individual. Believers are always to obey and submit to their government, which is in power whether just or unjust—even oppressive and heathen governments. No conditional clauses are lifted up such as "obey governments only if they are just" or "pay taxes only if the government is using one's money for moral causes." Biblically we are to obey all that are in actual authority over us and work diligently to bring about constructive change when we discover encroachment of the State or, as Christ-followers, the subordination of the Church and the Gospel of God to the State as we discharge our sacred responsibilities and privileges as self-governing citizens with conscientious care.

Civil Disobedience

Disobedience is permitted only when government usurps God's authority, as Professor Norman L Geisler of Dallas Theological Seminary articulates adroitly:

> Whereas believers are always to obey government when it takes its place '*under*' God, they should never obey it when it takes the place '*of*' God. In short, governments and laws can *permit* evil, but they cannot *command* it. For example, they can *allow* citizens to worship idols, but they cannot *insist* that all do so. The authority of government ends where conscience of the believer begins.[691]

We have navigated some choppy seas during the pandemic balancing our freedoms to assemble and worship, guaranteed in the First Amendment of the Constitution, with the dictates of government closing down "gatherings" and limiting the number who

---

[691] Geisler, Norman L., "A Premillennial View of Law and Government," *Journal of Bibliotheca Sacra,"* 142:567, July 1985. <https://www.galaxie.com/article/bsac142-567-05>.

can assemble, out of concern for one's neighbor. Where is the voice of the people? Does not the public get to decide in a democracy? Who determines what businesses are essential to remain open? Casinos and tattoo parlors or churches? Or mandating social distancing and wearing masks for rallies or sporting events, but not for mass rioters in the street?

We will be examining later the role "conscience" played in Luther's career, and the lasting legacy he established by courageously upholding this cherished value. While it may be necessary to take a rebellious stand, it is crucial to note those Biblical limits on how and when believers can disobey the government. While every subject should strive to be a good citizen and obey valid laws, if a regime establishes laws that are contrary to the natural law of love, the law written on human hearts (Romans 1:19-20), the subject is then bound to obey God rather than man (Acts 5:29). Under such conditions, it is the duty of one to resist tyrannous rulers and to withhold obedience to the government. When "the government mandates teachings or practices that are contrary to Scripture" Geisler says

> the Christian should refuse to comply. That is, the government must eliminate religious freedom not simply regulate it before the believer should disobey the government.... Second, Christian noncompliance to oppressive laws should be *refusal*, but not a *revolt*. That is, their disobedience should be *passive*, not *active*. They can be insubmissive, but they must not be insubordinate. Even when a believer cannot submit to the law, he must be willing to submit to the consequences of that law.[692]

When such occasions prevail, such as government ordering its citizens to violate Scripture and their Biblically informed consciences, and civil disobedience is rightfully taken, the Christian must be prepared to accept the consequences. Peter refused to stop preaching Jesus when ordered to do so, but he did not refuse to go to prison (Acts 5). The Israelites refused to obey Pharaoh's command, but they didn't revolt, attack, or use the sword against him, and Daniel refused to pray to the king but did not refuse to go into the lion's den (Daniel 6). In such incidents, Luther advised his people to say to their prince or temporal ruler, "I owe you obedience in body and property; command me within the limits of your authority on earth, and I will obey. But if you command me to believe or get rid of certain books, I will not obey; for then you are a tyrant and overreach yourself, commanding where you have neither the right nor the authority."[693]

---

692 Ibid.

693 LW 45:112. *The Christian in Society II*, "Temporal Authority."

Summing up the Biblical teachings on civic authority, The Augsburg Confession of 1530 states this key confessional text of the Lutheran Reformation: "Christians are obliged to be subject to civil authority and obey its commands and laws in all that can be done without sin. But when commands of the civil authority cannot be obeyed without sin, we must obey God rather than men (Acts 5:29)."[694]

Luther firmly believed there was evil in government, just as there is in any other segment of society, and he experienced it firsthand. Not one to naively accept or endorse whatever the government promoted or magistrates did, he urged the clergy to preach against evils in government, and that did not preclude exposing personal as well as political sins. Once he thundered: "There are lazy and useless preachers who do not denounce the evils of princes and lords, some because they do not even notice them.... Some even fear for their skins and worry that they will lose body and goods for it. They do not stand up and be true to Christ!"[695]

This was not idle talk for Luther. He himself refused to keep silent when his city governor persisted in fornication. Yet he believed that one of the best ways to encourage godly government was to praise the good and experienced in government and to encourage Christians to pursue politics, even though he was a realist regarding most politicians just doing and commanding only what they want. Professor Spitz also notes that Luther's "correspondence especially during the last fifteen years of his life, shows him constantly involved in political situations, advising and urging city councils concerned with 'urban reformation,' and chastising episcopal and secular princes."[696]

As Christians, we are called to care about the state of the law, even to debate and disagree on various aspects of it, but then to work to make laws better as we are able. "Far from being an affront to the rule of law, such critical and non-violent Christian political engagement can indeed reflect a true respect for the rule of law and God's gift of temporal government."[697] Leopoldo A. Sanchez M (Merino) of Concordia Seminary continues his commentary, affirming what should be openly acknowledged:

> Each Christian can work to make laws better and collaborate with other like-minded individuals to do so. Still, we are faced with the reality that not all Christians will agree on the moral failure of immigration laws. Christians

---

[694] *Book of Concord*, "The Augsburg Confession," p.38.

[695] As quoted in Lewis W. Spitz's "The Political Luther," *Christian History* <https://christianhistoryinstitute.org/magazine/article/political-luther>.

[696] Ibid.

[697] *Immigrants Among Us: A Lutheran Framework for Addressing Immigration Issues*, LCMS's Commission on Theology and Church Relations, pp.25-26.

> are called to obey the authorities, and the laws they enact, unless such laws are against God's law. But when exactly is this or that immigration law or policy explicitly against God's command? In dealing with such questions, genuine diversity of opinion is inevitable even among Christians who share a common confession. We are thus reminded that politics cannot dictate the Church's evangelical identity and mission in the world.[698]

Quoting himself, Sanchez says,

> Affirming God's action in both realms (citizens of the State and citizens of Heaven) allows us to disagree with other Christians on immigration law without destroying our unity in Christ. The unity of the Church is anchored in the Gospel and not in this or that law.... Affirming God's governing in both realms helps us to acknowledge the duty of every citizen (or resident) to obey the law without letting such duty affect negatively his commitment to promote the proclamation of the Gospel and the works of mercy that ultimately define the Church's mission to all without distinction.[699]

In what is one of the most complex and hotly debated issues of our time, I believe Lutheran theology has much to contribute to its understanding of Scriptural and Confessional guidelines. However, I discover much of the debate obscured by the avoidance of referring specifically to what I believe is the stumbling block for those within our Church and many outside the Church. The battle over immigration is exacerbated by the reluctance of many to use the term "illegal" in making the distinction between those entering the country. We have examined how the Hebrews made helpful distinctions that guided actions and the application of laws. So often, those entering the country "illegally" are subsumed within the broad category of "immigrants" or within the sub-identifiers of being "undocumented," "refugees," or "asylum seekers." From my experience, objection is not directed toward a bias people have against immigrants so much as it is toward those who enter illegally by placing themselves above the law. An unintended consequence then easily develops into bias or prejudice against particular neighbors or sets of neighbors, even toward those who have legally gained entry. They can easily discover themselves experiencing scorn, instead of the best construction we are expected to place on our neighbor—including legal immigrants among us.

---

[698] "Lutheran: Who is My Neighbor? Immigration Through Lutheran Eyes," *Immigrant Neighbors Among Us: Immigration Across Theological Traditions*, edited by M. Daniel Carroll R. and Leopoldo A. Sanchez M. (Eugene, OR: Pickwick Publications, 2015), pp.32-33.

[699] Ibid. p.33, quoting himself in "Mission e immigracion," p.74.

I am not advocating an uncritical, passive, or even idolatrous attitude toward government and civil law, but rather a critical examination of current immigration law to reform the potential problems and injustices discovered. Likewise, as we have discovered in the Gospel, works of mercy and acts of compassion cannot blind us to the use of reason, which can unfortunately lead us to unintended consequences by not taking seriously the desire and need to promote the rule of law and God's command to obey the authorities.

The Lutheran Church–Missouri Synod's *Immigrants Among Us* study concludes with an exhortation:

> All of this reminds us of the struggle of Christian life in a fallen world. "*Our sin is ever before us*" (Psalm 51:3), and our whole life remains one of repentance [as Luther reminds us in the first of his 95 Theses*] The Gospel's absolution is constantly needed, both for our obvious sins and for the many times when we see no recourse other than to choose what appears to be "the lesser of two evils." None of this shakes our confidence in God's Word of forgiveness, even as we seek again and again to do better. We must all acknowledge that we do fail to help some neighbor and do not fulfill all that the law demands of us. We all sin in various ways as we seek to fulfill our vocations in the left-and right-hand realms and kingdoms.[700]

In Paul Althaus's study of *The Ethics of Martin Luther*, he writes,

> [W]e cannot fulfill any vocation without being involved in sin. Here again it is very important that all Christian ethos is ethos under justification. This is particularly true of our vocation, whatever that may be. Thus, the work that we do in our vocation cannot be acceptable apart from the certainty that our sins are forgiven. No matter how impossible it is to avoid sins in our station and vocation because of our sinful nature, however, our station as such remains pure and holy because it is established through God's Word.[701]

---

[700] *Immigrants Among Us: A Lutheran Framework for Addressing Immigration Issues, a Report of the Commission on Theology and Church Relations, The Lutheran Church—Missouri Synod, November 2012* (Concordia Publishing House, 2013), p.46.

* LW 31:25. *Career of the Reformer I*, "*NINETY-FIVE THESES*," '1. When our Lord and Master Jesus Christ said 'Repent' [Matt. 4:17] He willed the entire life of believers to be one or repentance.'

[701] Althaus, *Ethics*, p.41.

21

Jews and Anti-Semitism That Is Not Racist

In many instances, like Trump, Luther was incapable of apologizing or backing off. Compromise was difficult and not an easy natural back-up position for either one. Yet, "Here I Stand!" is the position of principled individuals guided by Scripture, which we cherish and admire.

While Luther's enduring passion was the Gospel and his central message was love, he was often prone to displays of anger and expressions of hatred, as we have witnessed in his sharp words for the peasants' actions in using his teachings as an inducement to start wars to end feudalism, his anger with the princes for continuing their persecution of peasants after the uprising, and which we will now witness in his infamous "anti-Semitic" writings.

But before we venture into this arena, I believe Courtney Cherest* offers a discerning caution: "…it is absolutely critical to understand Martin Luther's utter hatred for anything that would hinder the Truth of the doctrine of 'Justification by Grace alone through Faith alone' and how he rightly recognized that any type of works righteousness was (and still is) Satan's calling card."[702] I share her counsel, because a certain character quality can be viewed as both the best and worst thing about us, and indeed, about our twins. The biggest criticism I've discovered directed toward Luther and attributed to Trump centers on the use of their seemingly ungodly, untamed tongues, which obstructs any possibility for favorable consideration of positions taken regardless of their merit. Cherest concedes

> Most often, people have a certain quality, characteristic, or gifting that serves as their greatest asset, yet simultaneously can be their greatest vice. Martin Luther was no exception. The Lord gifted him with a unique boldness, a

---

* Courtney Cherest resides outside of Washington D.C., leads One19 Ministries, and serves as the Communications Director for Grace Church in Waldorf, MD. She has worked in communications and leadership with incredible ministries and organizations across the country.

702 Cherest, Courtney, "Luther's Untamed Tongue: The Man, the Mistakes, & the Mission." <https://wearepatrol.com/blog/part03>.

> fiery zeal, a passionate anger, a skillful tongue, and a sharp mind. He used all of those things to further the Kingdom of God on this planet during his life. His giftings were undeniably used to demolish strongholds of works righteousness in the culture around him and to spread the Gospel through the entire world for the next five hundred years. His passion for the doctrine of Grace is arguably unmatched among men. And Jesus' name was glorified in and through Martin Luther.[703]

Whether it be Luther, Trump, or other historical figures, we are obligated to do our best in evaluating the whole person and interpreting them in the complete context of their life and culture, and of course, not ignoring their human sinfulness. Luther not only acknowledged but saw his angry fervor as a most valued commodity that promoted his prayer, preaching, and pen activity in the most significant and beneficial ways. While both warriors are fascinating individuals, they can also be frustrating characters.

As claimed by Jaroslav Pelikan, the Sterling Professor of History at Yale University, Luther's theology could be most accurately labeled "Christocentric." Luther was "a Christ-intoxicated man," who often repeated the words of the Apostle Paul: "*Not to know anything… save Jesus Christ, and Him crucified*" (1 Corinthians 2:2 [KJV]). Understanding "the depth of Luther's conviction about the centrality of Christ must also, I believe, be the starting point for any effort to understand his attitude toward Jews and Judaism."[704]

Luther had stressed that the Old Testament faithful, like Abraham and David, who believed the promises of God, were models of Christian faith. After all, the Old Testament pointed to Jesus as the Messiah[705] and Luther's

> commentaries on the Hebrew Bible were filled with extravagant praise for the Jewish people before Christ. They were the "chosen people" of God, the only true Church… [and so he] reminded his fellow Christians in a treatise bearing the title "*That Jesus Christ Was Born a Jew*," that the historical setting for the redemption of the world was Judaism."[706]

---

[703] Ibid.

[704] Pelikan, "The Enduring Relevance of Martin Luther."

[705] Hendrix, Scott H., "The Controversial Luther," *Word & World* 3/4, 1983. <https://wordandworld.luthersem.edu/content/pdfs/3-4_Luther/3-4_Hendrix.pdf>.

[706] Pelikan, "The Enduring Relevance of Martin Luther."

That work, published in 1523, could be considered an eloquent denunciation of anti-Judaism which predates Luther, and in a real sense discloses a favorable view of the Jewish people that was counter-cultural for his time. Luther was convinced, according to Jaroslav Pelikan,

> that the principal reason for the separation between the Jewish Church and the Christian Church was the concealment of the authentic Gospel under the papacy. Therefore, he was hopeful that the "*rediscovery*" of this Gospel, as brought about through the Reformation, would have as one of its consequences a large-scale return of Jews to the true faith, which was the faith of Abraham, "the father of all believers," Christian and Jews alike.[707]

It is, however, imperative to keep in mind Luther's counter to the Jewish boast and pride of their lineage in being descendants of the patriarch Abraham. Their special status by virtue of physical descent was not of concern to Luther. Their future was dependent, like everyone's, on whether they will turn to Christ or not. What sets Abraham and his descendants apart, according to Luther, is not a common race, but rather a common faith.[708] Neither does circumcision put Jews in a special relationship with God, but rather only a circumcised heart produces a people of God, and that can take place independent of physical circumcision.[709]

Indeed, there were hopeful signs as the younger Luther, with pastoral optimism, reached out to Jews, and in Heinz Schilling's observance, thought that "rapprochement might be in the offing, with Luther telling Jews of an end to medieval oppression, and with some Jews speaking in celebratory terms of the Reformer as liberator and anticipating that he would bring about lasting improvement in the relationship between Jews and Christians."[710] Luther lambasted the Catholic Jew-haters and chided the Church for being a bad example to the Jews, in their subhuman treatment of those who had not received the pure Word of God. Instead, Jews had been persecuted and marginalized by "the crude asses' heads" (referring to "our fools, the popes, bishops, sophists, and monks") which drove them away from the

---

707 Ibid.

708 LW 47:140-50. *The Christian in Society IV*, "On the Jews and Their Lies."

709 Ibid. LW 47:153.

710 Schilling, *Upheaval*, p.474.

Gospel. Luther had pleaded for toleration of Jews, which he sincerely believed could be the first step towards their conversion, for he was not unmindful that they were, after all, the first people to receive God's promise of salvation. Luther wrote that "If I had been a Jew and had seen such dolts and blockheads govern and teach the Christian faith, I would sooner have become a hog than a Christian. They have dealt with the Jews as if they were dogs rather than human beings...show[ing] them nothing of Christian doctrine and life, but only subject them to popishness and mockery." He goes on to draw the unhappy conclusion, "... if the apostles, who also were Jews, had dealt with us Gentiles as we Gentiles deal with the Jews, there would never have been a Christian among the Gentiles."[711]

At this point Luther's stance was against the prevailing cultural trends of treating Jews inhumanely. Instead, Luther unashamedly exhorted his fellow Christians to embrace their Jewish neighbors in friendship and community. He believed Gentiles owed a spiritual debt to the Jews, which could be repaid with compassion and clear proclamation of the Gospel. "Since they [the Apostles] dealt with us Gentiles in such brotherly fashion, we in our turn ought to treat the Jews in a brotherly manner in order that we might convert some of them. For even we ourselves are not yet all very far along, not to speak of having arrived."[712] He further expresses the desire that we "do a service to the Jews on the chance that we might bring some of them back to their own true faith, the one which their fathers held."[713] Early on, Luther elevated Jews at a time when their race was regarded as second class. Luther had worked hard using his influence to encourage equality and acceptance of Jews in Germany.

Luther's high expectations for the advent of evangelical theology, however, after having recovered the blessed Biblical precept of "Justification by Faith" that had long lain buried under an avalanche of well-meant ecclesiastical clutter including Catholic dogma and papal traditions permitting preposterous misuse of hierarchical privilege, were soon to dissipate. Jews didn't *en masse* convert. Every effort to reach the Jews with the truly Good News was being rebuffed; and even worse, Luther came to understand that many Christians were "Judaizing" their faith by embracing Old Testament Law and practices. It became apparent that both parties had misplaced their projections on misunderstanding, and his disillusionment gave way to anger over the Jews' stubborn rejection of their Messiah. His

---

[711] LW 45:200. *The Christian in Society II*, "That Jesus Was Born a Jew."

[712] Ibid., LW 45:200-201.

[713] Ibid. LW 45:213.

tone clearly changed. "Jews were no longer errant brothers who could be won over for evangelical Christianity by instruction; they were now Satan's agents who must be forced onto their knees without mercy in order that their evil-intentioned perversion of Scripture would not lead faithful Christians into error."[714] Therefore, Luther wrote, "I do not wish to have anything more to do with any Jew. As St. Paul says, they are consigned to wrath; the more one tries to help them the baser and more stubborn they become. Leave them to their own devices."[715] It was then that Luther demonstrated the vehemence of his personality coupled with his flair for language, in unleashing his vituperative rhetoric in the treatise "On the Jews and Their Lies:"

> The fabricated tales that two decades earlier [Luther] had condemned as inventions of the medieval Church were now set out as actual events; there was every reason to believe the accusations of "contaminating wells, of kidnaping and piercing children".[716] Even the presence of the sow sculpture (Judensau*) on the parish church facade in Wittenberg was used as an opportunity to spread in all their degrading detail the established stereotypes of the everyday life of Jews.[717]

Medieval Europe's anti-Semitism Literally Carved in Stone

A *Judensau* is a folk art image of Jews in obscene contact with a large sow, which in Judaism is an unclean animal, according to the Torah, resulting in the prohibition of Jews eating pork (Leviticus 11:2-8). The arrangement of Jews surrounding a sow, suckling or having intercourse with the animal, signaled a mockery of Judaism and also served as a stark message that Jews were not welcome in their communities, places of worship or other gathering places.

---

[714] Schilling, *Upheaval*, p.484.

[715] LW 47:192. *The Christian in Society IV*, "On the Jews and Their Lies."

[716] Ibid. LW 47:217; see also LW 47:276, 284 and 170.

* Judensau is a folk-art image of Jews in obscene contact with a large sow (female pig), implying that Judaism is an unclean animal.

[717] Schilling, *Upheaval*, p.485.

The Judensau on the façade of Wittenberg's Town Church, St. Mary's

The *bas relief* sculpture on the facade of Wittenberg's Town Church, St. Mary's, where Luther frequently preached, married his wife Katharina von Bora, and baptized their six children, dates to 1305. The graphic stone image shows Jews drinking from the teats of a sow as a rabbi looks under its tail. "Written above the relief is an inscription with the words: '*Rabini Schem Hamphoras*'. This nonsensical reference to the Jewish appellation of God's name, added after Luther's time, quotes a derogatory comment in one of Luther's writings."[718]

In *Vom Schem Hamphoras* (*On the Holy Name*, 1543), Luther comments on the Judensau sculpture at Wittenberg, echoing the anti-Semitism of the image and locating the Talmud in the sow's bowels:

> Here on our church in Wittenberg a sow is sculpted in stone. Young pigs and Jews lie suckling under her. Behind the sow a rabbi is bent over the sow, lifting up her right leg, holding her tail high and looking intensely under her tail and into her Talmud, as though he were reading something acute or

---

[718] Pardo-Kaplan, Deborah, "Anti-Semitic Sculpture Outside Luther's Church Creates Controversy," *Christianity Today*, October 12, 2016; <https://www.christianitytoday.com/ct/2016/october-web-only/anti-semitic-sculpture-on-luthers-church-creates-controvers.html>. See Gritsch's *Jester*, pp.141-42.

> extraordinary, which is certainly where they get their *Shemhamphoras* [the explicit name of God].[719]

Deborah Pardo-Kaplan, a Messianic Jew, acknowledges as she writes in *Christianity Today* how the use of the pig deliberately escalates the offense of the image:

> The interpretation of the imagery of the "Judensau" has contributed to the darker part of Luther's legacy. In 1543 in his work, *On the Schem Hamphoras,* Luther insults the Talmud (rabbinic writings) and the Jewish name for God by linking them to the actions of the Jews on the sow sculpture.... What began as a symbol of a particular vice such as gluttony, reluctance to repent, uncleaniness, sinfulness, later becomes a clearly defamatory representation of the Jewish people.[720]

Efforts more constructive than those imposed by rioters tearing down statues of historical individuals, or by intimidation affecting their removal, along with streets and buildings being re-named within our country during the summer of 2020, were attained in Germany. Discussions about the defamatory *Judensau* sculptures were underway prior to the reunification of Germany as the Town Church leaders spoke with the Jewish community who supported the decision to keep the sculpture in place. In response, the youth group at the church created a memorial plaque laid on November 11, 1988, to commemorate the 50th anniversary of *Kristallnacht* (when Nazis burned Jewish stores and synagogues):

> The German text of the monument is translated into English on an additional wall plaque as, "The true name of God, the maligned '*Chem Hamphoras,*' which Jews long before Christianity regarded as almost unutterably holy, this name died with six million Jews under the sign of the cross." On the margins of the plaque in Hebrew are the words from Psalm 130, "*Out of the depths, I cry to you.*"[721]

---

719 Wolffsohn, Michael, *Eternal Guilt?: Forty Years of German-Jewish-Israeli Relations* (Columbia University Press, 1993), p.194.

720 Pardo-Kaplan, "Anti-Semitic Sculpture."

721 Ibid.

In anticipation of the 500th anniversary of The Reformation in 2017, a loose coalition of activists seized the opportunity to argue that the sculpture in its current location where Luther preached in German remains a dangerous symbol of intolerance. While even the evangelical community may have had mixed opinions on the issue of removing the *Judensau*, they agreed on rejecting anti-Semitism.

The congregation's council and the town council adopted resolutions that the sculpture should remain. This action was supported by German Chancellor Angela Merkel, herself the daughter of a Lutheran pastor, who said it was essential that Luther's anti-Semitism never be scrubbed from his theological legacy. The church's pastor, Johannes Block, told reporters, "We are convinced that history means not forgetting the dark side of the past but confronting it." Micha Brumlike, professor of education, who was leading the local movement to maintain the image, agrees: "It would be historically incorrect to remove the sculpture."[722] He expressed the view of expanding the adjacent memorial against anti-Semitism, which was installed under communism, to give a more complete explanation and more fully place the "Judensau" in context. Despite the calls for its removal, the panel of judges in the Naumburg court ruled on February 4, 2020, that the 1305 AD sandstone carving in question didn't harm Jewish people because it is "presented in a memorial context.... There is an informational sign, placed on the ground in 1988 next to the church's wall, and the church itself is a protected United Nations cultural site."[723]

Luther did indeed utter appalling incitements and was shamefully intolerant of his Jewish contemporaries. His later sermons and writings were marked by highly offensive, despicable sentiments, and wince-inducing rhetoric that the Nazis would later use to justify their brutal persecution efforts toward the extinction of the Jews. The writer of the screenplay *Luther*, Aaron Armstrong, says:

> It's tempting to ignore the more unsavory aspects of Luther, the man. To focus only on the great Reformer and all the powerful ways God used him and offer (at most) a quick but ultimately dismissive acknowledgement of unpleasant things he said and did. To gloss over the inconvenient truths. At the same time, there's the opposite temptation: to vilify the man and only focus on the horrible or embarrassing moments. We want to see him either as a hero or

---

722 <https://www.thelocal.de/20171031/anti-jewish-sculpture-splits-opinion-on-500-anniversary-reformation-wittenber-luther>.

723 Lateshia Beachum, *The Washington Post*, February 5, 2020. <https://www.washingtonpost.com/world/2020/02/05/germany-anti-semitic-sculpture-church>.

heretic. As brilliant or a buffoon. But to present either is to present a fictional Luther; a caricature that bears a passing resemblance but is, ultimately, empty. **"The Truth is far more complex, and far more beautiful."**

That's what I realized as I waded through a sea of biographies, articles, and essays, trying to make sense of this man. For me to honor Luther, to tell his story honestly, I needed to embrace this tension. To strip away all the mystique we've built up around him, and get to the heart of Luther as he really was: a normal, frail, fallen, sinful human being who was used extraordinarily by a gracious God.

That sounds strange, doesn't it? To say that Luther, this giant in the history of the world, was a normal man in as much need of grace, and forgiveness, as you and I are. A man who, undoubtedly, entered into his Master's rest, and was shocked by what he got wrong, just as you and I will be. It seems absurd, if not bordering on blasphemous.

And yet, this is the Truth. The man God used to change the world was just that—a man. And we need to embrace that. If we want to honor Martin Luther, we need to not recast him as a modern North American evangelical. We need to go past the legendary (but contested) words, "Here I stand," and meet a 16th century German Augustinian Monk with a tender conscience. One so deeply assailed by guilt and shame that he confessed even the tiniest of infractions until his confessors demanded he leave until he'd done something worth confessing! One who would wrestle with the Word of God until it beat him into submission at every turn. Who would pen awe-inspiring hymns and sermons, and abhorrent insults. Who would fight back against the condemnation of the devil, admitting that he deserved death and hell, but, "I know One who suffered and made satisfaction on my behalf. His name is Jesus Christ, Son of God, and where He is, there I shall be also!"

This is Martin Luther. And this is the Luther we want you to meet because it is the Martin Luther we discovered as we made this film. And, by God's grace, this is the Martin Luther you and I will be spending eternity alongside as we worship before the throne—a man who was loved and redeemed by Christ.[724]

---

[724] Armstrong, Aaron, "What to Do With Martin Luther: Holding the German Reformer in Tension." <https://wearepatrol.com/blog/2017/3/29/part04>.

It is only honest, however, to acknowledge upfront that Luther was anti-Jewish in his stance of being rebuffed, though he was not an anti-Semite. Luther's criticism, as we shall soon discover, was rooted in theological disagreement over the reading of shared Scriptures, not in racial animus. Judaism was and is based solely on keeping the tenets of God's Law, thus depending on one's own righteousness and not Christ's. His passionate anger and the ferocity of his language was against works of righteousness that opposed the Gospel of Grace—against law-based teaching, not of their person, being or ethnicity. Dr. Phillip Cary, Professor of Philosophy at Eastern University in St. Davids, PA, points out that "Luther's attacks were not about personalities, but what he saw as threats to the Gospel by the devil. Those Luther suspected of seeking to undermine the absolute certain truth of justification would be met with an intolerant, harsh, unforgiving, vulgar, abusive, malicious and at times violent responses."[725] Justification by faith, for Luther, was true with "no ifs, ands or buts." In the opinion of Dr. Harry Loewen, teacher, minister, and founding Chair of Mennonite Studies at the University of Winnipeg, "the doctrine of justification was of such importance [to Luther] that not to accept it was to blaspheme God and to repudiate the Christian religion."[726]

On a variety of other issues like a person's outward morality or views, Luther could be less rigid and even kind, but on the veracity of justification and private conscience of a person there was no compromise. In spite of Luther's abhorrent, repugnant, and even diabolical outbursts toward the Jews that scandalized his colleagues and continue to appall his theological descendants, it is difficult to appropriate or connect our 20th-century anti-Semitism with the Medieval anti-Semitism experienced in Luther's time. That is not to whitewash or exonerate "*Martin Luther's Anti-Semitism: Against His Better Judgment*"[727]—using the title of Eric W. Gritsch's 2012 volume—but being honest in understanding how historical heroes are not flawless in practicing what they preach. There is no question that Luther was contradicting the Gospel as he sought to be a faithful witness of Christ and to that Gospel.

Luther's position was nevertheless absolute and irreversible. His concern was to safeguard his position on rediscovering the Gospel. After all, God had called him to take up the fight

---

725 Cary, Phillip (n.d.), "Luther and His Enemies – Luther: Gospel, Law and Reformation," academic lecture. <https://www.thegreatcourses.com/courses/religion/luther-gospel-law-and-reformation.html>.

726 Loewen, Harry, *Ink Against the Devil: Luther and His Opponents* (Waterloo: Wilfrid Laurier University Press, 2015), p.284.

727 Gritsch, Eric W., *Martin Luther's Anti-Semitism: Against His Better Judgment* (Grand Rapids: W.B. Eerdmans Publishing, 2012).

and cleanse the Church, returning it to being a more faithfully authentic Church just as Trump believed he was to return government to the people and drain the swamp. As the prophet, Luther was to return the people to the path of salvation, including Jews, who were "God's chosen people." Thus, any measure against the Jews was now justified in his mind. He was certainly aware of the human suffering that would result in their banishment and the destruction of their communities, just as he knew and was willing to accept the implications of the peasants whom he had supported but who were led astray by Muntzer and the fanatics and, with his urging, defeated at the hands of the civil authorities in the Peasants' War.

In his egregious and infamous 1543 pamphlet, "On the Jews and Their Lies," Luther asks, "What shall we Christians do with this rejected and condemned people, the Jews?" Since all hope of their conversion appeared to be lost and time was running out, he urged Christians to take radical measures in the sliver of hope that some would convert in the face of threaten destruction. Before Luther begins with his recommendations he writes:

> Since they live among us, we dare not tolerate their conduct, now that we are aware of their lying and reviling and blaspheming. If we do, we become sharers in their lies, cursing and blasphemy. Thus, we cannot extinguish the unquenchable fire of divine wrath, of which the prophets speak, nor can we convert the Jews. With prayer and the fear of God we must practice a sharp mercy to see whether we might save at least a few from the glowing flames.... I give you my sincere advice:[728]

In harsh and ferocious words, his proposals call upon those in authority "to set fire to their synagogues or schools...raze and destroy their houses...confiscate their prayer books and Talmudic writings...forbid rabbis to teach...abolish safe conduct on the highways... prohibit usury practices when lending money...and, make them work with their hands."[729] As a last resort, Jews should be driven out of Germany, which was hardly a novelty in the sixteenth century, as there had been a long history of Jewish expulsion in Europe. For our twenty-first-century ears, his language and the aggression he advocates is undoubtedly offensive. It cannot be explained away or excused, nor should it be. For Mark D. Thompson, Head of Theology and Academic Dean of Moore Theological College in Sydney, Australia, "...it bears all the marks of a man pushed too far, of disillusionment and betrayal and even

---

[728] LW 47:268. *The Christian in Society IV*, "On the Jews and Their Lies."

[729] Ibid., LW 47:268-69.

of grief. He may have explained it as '*sharp mercy*' but even some of his closest friends found it difficult to swallow."[730]

Luther had reverted to an endemic anti-Semitism which permeated Medieval Europe, fueled in part by Jewish usury practices—the exploitation of people by charging excess interest rates—and thereby saying Jews "are nothing but thieves and robbers who daily eat no morsel and wear no thread of clothing which they have not stolen and pilfered from us by means of their accursed usury. Thus, they live from day to day, together with wife and child, by theft and robbery, as arch-thieves and robbers, in the most impenitent security."[731] There had also been latent suspicions that Jews favored the Turks and were assisting the Muslims against the Christians.

Luther's Larger Agenda and Paramount Concern

What the professor of the Bible was really interested in was following the lead of the Apostle Paul, who recognized as a Jew, that the Old Testament pointed to Jesus' coming as the promised Messiah. For Luther in his later years, he was especially sensitive to the threat rabbinic exegesis (critical interpretation of Scripture) was posing in undermining that distinctive claim. He saw it as a betrayal of Christ and the Gospel. For him, it was a challenge to the Truth of Christianity, which had inflamed Christian opposition to Judaism since the earliest days. Thus, Luther sought to prove that Jewish exegesis and teachings were a lie that made God Himself a liar in His Word. This was not an ethnic motivation on Luther's part, but rather a theological one.

Believing he was living on the eve of the Last Judgment further exacerbated his harsh attacks against the Jews, according to Mark Edwards in his book *Luther's Last Battles*:

"[W]ith the establishment of The Reformation and exposure of the papal antichrist within the Church, the devil had unleashed his last, most violent attack on the true Church. The devil's servants in this final assault were the papists, the fanatics, the Turks, and the Jews. Luther saw it as his duty in this apocalyptic struggle to attack the devil with all the vehemence at his command and to defend the Church against all the devil's thrusts."[732]

---

[730] Thompson, Mark D., "Luther and the Jews," Edersheim Lecture. <https://www.academia.edu/7250539/Luther_and_the_Jews>.

[731] LW 47:242. *The Christian in Society IV*, "On the Jews and Their Lies."

[732] Edwards, Jr., Mark U., *Luther's Last Battles: Politics and Polemics 1531-46*, (Ithaca and London: Cornell University Press, 1983), p. 142.

Heiko Oberman also observes that Luther's identification of the Church's perversions in the sale of indulgences were a sign of the Last Days, which intensified the imperativeness in preaching the Gospel. Love directs missionary zeal for Luther. For him, time was running out. "This urgency breeds impatience, and impatience an uncompromising stance against all opposition."[733] The rise of the papacy as Antichrist was to him a signal that the end is near, demanding emergency measures so that as many men and women as possible could be rescued. Luther understood "God's Reformation" to be that final act of bringing all things to their proper order through the Final Judgment. For Luther, God's ultimate victory was never in doubt for a moment. Yet that conviction did not squelch his awareness that Satan would employ any strategy, distort any Truth, and enlist any ally in his frantic attempts to silence the Gospel and arrest its progress. To quote Oberman again,

> According to Luther's prediction, the Devil would not "tolerate" the rediscovery of the Gospel; he would rebel with all his might and muster all his forces against it. God's Reformation would be preceded by a counterreformation, and the Devils progress would mark the Last Day. For where God is at work – in man and in human history – the Devil, the spirit of negation, is never far away.[734]

Gripped by the Gospel

It is significant to keep in mind the guiding light Luther's pathfinder, Johann von Staupitz, provided the conscience-stricken monk who kept coming to confess before him. Given the task of memorizing the Scriptures in the Erfurt cloister, the assignment of teaching the Bible at the new University of Wittenberg, Luther spent his entire life studying and expounding the Scriptures. He was known and praised for his deep knowledge of the Scriptures, and was even referenced as "the living concordance."[735] In his Edersheim Lecture on "Luther and the Jews," Dr. Mark Thompson of Australia notes Luther's passionate attachment to the Scriptures, and his paramount concern for the careful and appropriate reading of Scripture.

---

[733] Oberman, *Devil*, p.71.

[734] Oberman, *Devil*, p.12.

[735] Cherest, Courtney, "Luther's Story: Threatened by a Thunderstorm, Gripped by the Gospel." <https://wearepatrol.com/blog/Luther-part2>.

> After all, it was through his study of the Bible that he came to understand the true dimensions of what had been *done* for him in the cross of Christ...and liberated him from the cycle of religious effort and despair...that plagued him all his life, his *Anfechtungen*....
>
> These are all important observations for understanding what was happening when Luther wrote against the Jews. For him, the Scriptures are honoured when their intention of 'driving home' Christ is taken seriously. To make use of the Scriptures with some other intention was to abuse them. And Luther made clear his attitude to anyone who dishonoured Christ by manipulating or evading the clear teaching of Scripture...[736]

Martin Brecht,* a leading Luther scholar, accurately confirms that "Luther's theological controversies were always a struggle over the interpretation of the Bible"[737] whether in his early debates with Catholic theologians, his dispute with Erasmus, Zwingli, or his writings about the Jews over key Messianic texts.

> Explaining Scripture clearly and showing where others had erred in their reading of Scripture was his responsibility as a "doctor of the Church"... Luther's absolute devotion to Jesus Christ [was the result of recognizing] he owed everything to Christ, who was the only hope of men and women in the Last Days. Once again it was Staupitz who had pointed him in this direction. Through Staupitz, Luther learnt to look to Christ when confronted with the reality of God's wrath rather than be drawn into despair by his own wretched state or his inadequate performance of penitential acts. Christ has done all that is necessary, and the Christian belonged body and soul to his Saviour. In the midst of his struggle with spiritual despair Luther would often repeat the pray of Psalm 119:94: *"I am yours; save me."*[738]

---

[736] Thompson, "Luther and the Jews," pp.5-6. Some suggest Luther adopted this practice on the advice of Staupitz; see Oberman, p.182.

* Martin Brecht, Church historian and Professor of Reformation and Modern Church History at the University of Munster, Westphalia, Germany, and author of a three-volume work on Martin Luther.

[737] Brecht, Martin, *Martin Luther: The Preservation of the Church 1532-1546*, trans. James Schaaf (Philadelphia: Fortress, 1993), p.336.

[738] Thompson, "Luther and the Jews," pp.6-7.

His inflammatory rhetoric, as we have witnessed, was not just reserved for Jews. In this, he was really an equal opportunity offender. After Luther gave up the hope for the conversion of the Jews, he included them in the notorious company of the "Papists," Turks, fanatics, nominal Christians, and peasants that formed an ever-existing unholy coalition of God's enemies who were in the service of the Devil. Against each of his opponents, Luther, using hyperbole and exaggeration like Trump, "...passed on what could be construed as libelous tales and gave credence to improbable charges. In all of these respects Luther treated the Jews no differently than he treated his other opponents."[739]

Like Luther even to this day being denigrated as "Hitler's spiritual ancestor" with his anti-Semitic remarks and compared to Robespierre in the context of his Two Kingdoms doctrine emerging from the Peasants' War,[740] President Trump all too frequently elicits vicious accusations of being a traitor, a racist, a bigot, one with blood on his hands, and a white nationalist. It is perhaps too easy to conclude that their caustic and inflammatory rhetoric solicits immediate media response that exceeds inuendoes. Luther, as we have seen, was characterized as a seven-headed monster and Trump portrayed as being decapitated. The media seems all too eager to break out the "r-word" (racist) which is recklessly flung around these days simply to try to silence, punish, and suppress people with differing views or supporters of the President. The actual meaning of "racist" is being lost, and many Americans are getting tired of being beaten up, put down with condescension, and treated as if they cannot think for themselves or exercise their right to freedom of speech. Those who seem to pride themselves on their pious advocacy of being tolerant of others are often the very ones who demonstrate so arrogantly their own intolerance.

John Fund of the *National Review* expresses his view and request:

> So, if we wonder why our conversation has become so stilted and so unable to incorporate language that helps us solve problems, let's acknowledge that crying racism in today's political theater is sure to create both more smoke and more fire. Before it gets any worse, let's have as many people of good will as possible declare that, for at least a bit, we should stick to the dictionary definition of racism. After all, dictionaries exist for a reason. Let's use them to clear the air.[741]

---

[739] Edwards, *Luther's Last Battles*, p.141.

[740] Stephenson, "Two Kingdoms," citing Richard Marius's *Luther* (London, 1975), p.203, which itself cites P. Wiener's pamphlet "Martin Luther: Hitler's Spiritual Ancestor" (London, 1945).

[741] Fund, John, "Overused Cries of Racism Make It Harder for Us to Unite," *National Review*, Feb. 11, 2018. <https://www.nationalreview.com/2018/02/shani-davis-racist-coin-toss-accusation-shows-racism-charge-overused>.

Luther never seemed to tire of spurting scurrilous abuse at his opponents who would not embrace his new orthodoxy. The man most often praised for taking a bold stand for freedom of conscience could be ruthless and merciless toward those whose consciences disagreed with his own. His published loathing in his later years against the Jews exceeds that of any other group of dissidents or unbelievers. One can draw similarities with President Trump who, like Luther, takes hardline positions which leaves few options. For Luther, each human stands between the realities of this world and the next. One's eternal fate is in the balance; and for Luther, eternal life with God was far more significant than one's limited lifespan on earth. His primary concern was not in the confrontations of the world but rather the struggle for salvation that overarched all earthly events. Luther's early salvation-based perspective had little room for conversion by force, such as burning or banning. His concern was for real conversions which could only come from within, as a work of God. Like his twin negotiating with North Korea, Trump applied the principles in his *Art of the Deal*, acknowledging it is better to walk away with no deal than to enter what he viewed could be a bad "accommodating" deal. The concluding prayer that ended Luther's shocking anti-Jewish tract beseeched "Christ, our dear Lord, to convert them [Jews] mercifully and preserve us steadfastly and immovably in the knowledge of Him, which is eternal life. Amen!"[742]

Even the elderly Luther's perspective on the End Times held salvation to be universal and available to all, including Jews. He retained his vision of a Christian Church that included Jews and the heathen as a New Jerusalem.... His final adamant exhortation to the counts of Mansfeld [days before his death] to banish all Jews also contained a proviso: "If, however, they convert, give up usury, and receive Christ, then we will gladly regard them as our brothers,"[743] which certainly doesn't come from a racist's heart. Nevertheless, Luther should never have advocated that Jews be persecuted for their faith which he faulted for misinterpreting Scripture and thus rejecting the Messiah who had come in Jesus as the Christ. He should have continued to preach the Gospel faithfully and left the rest in God's hands. It is the sign of the power of sin that he contradicted the Gospel even as he sought to be loyal to it by being a faithful witness of Christ in desiring Jews to receive the saving grace God extends.

Luther believed he was called not only to take up the fight to cleanse the Church, but "As the prophet of God, he was to return the people to the path to salvation, including Jews, God's blood relatives. Their failure to respond to his prophetic words could be

---

[742] LW 47:306. *The Christian in Society IV*, "On the Jews and Their Lies."

[743] LW 58:458. *Sermons V*, "Admonition Against the Jews."

evidence only of obduracy."[744] While his hope for Jewish converts remained, it was being overshadowed by both his disappointments in the slim number coming to Christ and the threats Jewish evangelism was creating in drawing some Christians away from their Savior. Yet, Luther always insisted that Jews who converted should be treated as "brothers." He never recommended the extermination of Jews, nor in beating them physically, and he did not advocate mob violence against them. As noted Reformation scholar Richard Marius* puts it,

> Luther never organized any campaign against the Jews, and...despite the ferocity of his tirades against them, he never truly renounced the notion of coexistence between Jews and Christians. But the fact that Luther's hostility to Jews was not the same as modern anti-Semitism does not excuse it. It was as bad as Luther could make it...[745]

And it was that bad, but we should be cautious not to allow Hitler and his henchmen to determine our attitude of Luther on this issue. In no way should he be equated with the racial hatred which drove the Holocaust. The end was near, and Luther saw himself at the epicenter of the final battle for the Gospel on earth. Heiko Oberman frames Luther's very special concern this way:

> As Luther neared the end of his days on earth, the issue was not a Turkish crusade, or hatred of Rome or the Jews, it was upholding the Gospel against all enemies in the confusion of the Last Days.... He saw in the Jews' resistance to the Reformation, to the rediscovered Gospel, an obstinately persistent estrangement from God and thus a new formed alliance of all the forces inimical to God.[746]

It is easy to judge the harsh polemics used by both our warriors as being wrong, abusing their influence, and even especially hurtful as we witness the risk they both make. And they're both wrong in that, and we should not give them a free pass, but that isn't necessarily

---

[744] Schilling, *Upheaval*, p.488.

* Richard Marius, an acclaimed novelist and popular teacher at Gettysburg College, the University of Tennessee, became the director of Expository Writing at Harvard University, where he taught English until his death in 1999. His biography of Martin Luther was his last major work.

[745] Marius, Richard, *The Christian between God and Death* (Cambridge, MA: Belknap Press, 1999), p.380.

[746] Oberman, Devil, p.296.

being anti-Semitic or racist as those charges are so freely alleged. We need to understand both Luther and Trump in their context. It was not an ethnic motivation that prompted Luther in his concern about the Jews, nor was it so with Trump's concern about immigrants entering the country illegally, nor in the travel ban to keep "Muslim terrorists" from entering the country—actions his predecessors took, and his opponents previously endorsed and supported. For Luther, it was a theological issue and for Trump a national security issue.

However, historians, like journalists and the media, can be selective in what and how they present their accounts, quoting a portion of a statement by ignoring facts, or slanting the context to bolster and re-enforce their pre-determined narrative. We've seen this selectivity in reporting the President's comments on the illegal immigrants crossing the border, and the characterization of participants in the Charlottesville riot being the cause of mass shootings. Headlines and storylines reported Trump as saying, "Mexicans are rapists," and "Neo-Nazis are fine people." Those definitive conclusions are far from the actual words spoken and intent of the President, especially when the context is considered:

> When Mexico sends its people, they're not sending their best. They're not sending you. They're sending people that have lots of problems, and they're (those that have lots of problems) bringing those problems with them. They're bringing drugs. They're bringing crime. They're rapists, and some, I assume, are good people. But I speak to border guards, and they tell us what we're getting. [He went on to say that] they are coming from more than Mexico, from all over South and Latin America, and it's coming probably from the Middle East. But we don't know. Because we have no protection and we have no competence, we don't know what's happening. And it's got to stop, and it's got to stop fast.[747]

Leaders of both parties, including past presidents, have publicly decried the flood of illegal immigrants, unvetted persons coming across the border in pre-Trumpian days, and they never received the media's rage. Neither did we witness the outcry of the press or politicians when dealing with the situation at the border, as children were separated from their parents and placed in cages which were not the creation of the Trump administration. Jeh Johnson, former Obama Department of Homeland Security (DHS) Secretary, has been one of the few straight shooters, admitting that "chain link barriers, partitions, fences,

---

[747] Schwartz, Ian, "Mexico Not Sending Us Their Best," *RealClear Politics*, June 16, 2015.

cages, whatever you want to call them, were not invented on January 20, 2017, okay?"[748] he said in reference to POTUS Donald Trump's inauguration. The Trump administration is merely continuing Obama-era policy, including using some of the same facilities that the previous DHS authorized. As Freedom Wire correctly reported, "Thomas Homan, Obama's executive associate director of ICE revealed in a recent conference about immigration, that the 'cages' were not only built under Barack Obama, but they were *HIS* idea!"[749]

That's not exactly what the rest of the media has reported, nor do we learn of a correction or an apology for falsely (and perhaps intentionally) *mis*reporting. What we hear repeatedly is that Trump is a bigot, a racist or a xenophobe because of his stance on immigration. If this was done under Obama, then who is really the racist, bigot and xenophobe? Yet in the view of Sean Robertson, liberals don't realize

> that their chosen one, Barack Obama, was WAY tougher on immigration than Trump.... He deported more than 2.5 MILLION people from the United States. What's funny is nobody cared what ICE was doing under Obama. When he used them as a weapon against criminal illegal immigrants, no one batted an eye—but when Trump does the same, the Left's call to "abolish ICE" can be heard all over the internet and in marches everywhere.[750]

Again, to correct the misleading and distorted accounts regarding the Charlottesville confrontation, here are the unambiguous actual words of the President:

> Excuse me, they didn't put themselves down as neo-Nazis, and you had some very bad people in that group. But you also had people that were very fine people on both sides. You had people in that group—excuse me, excuse me, I saw the same pictures you did. You had people in that group that were there to protest the taking down of, to them, a very, very important statue and the renaming of a park from Robert E. Lee to another name.

---

748 Rosas, Julio, "Obama's DHS Secretary: Migrant Cages Weren't Invented When Trump Became President." <https://www.washingtonexaminer.com/news/obamas-dhs-secretary-migrant-cages-werent-invented-on-jan-20-2017>.

749 Robertson, Sean, "Trump's Wall vs Obama's Cages," *FreedomWire*, June 18, 2019. <https://freedomwire.com/trumps-wall-vs-obamas-cages>.

750 Ibid.

After taking another question at that press conference, Trump became even more explicit:

> 'I'm not talking about the neo-Nazis and white nationalists because they should be condemned totally.'...These Charlottesville statements leave little room for interpretation. For any honest person, therefore, to conclude that the President somehow praised the very people he actually derided, reveals a blatant and blinding level of bias.[751]

This bias and the untruthful accusations continue to this day in the media, and even by those who sought to replace Trump, throwing their hat into the ring running for the Democratic nomination. President Biden claims Charlottesville was the reason he stepped into the race, still claiming those dishonest accounts despite the repeated denunciations by the President, and video clips upholding what he actually said regarding the events in Charlottesville.

In Luther's day, as we have witnessed, there were over-zealous evangelical warriors, led by Andreas Bodenstein von Karlstadt, who had adopted iconoclastic* views, pushing reforms and wreaking havoc while Luther was in hiding at Wartburg Castle. These radical reformers, including Thomas Muntzer, were destroying stained glass windows, statues, altarpieces, and icons in efforts to purify the Church. They felt they were advancing the Reformation cause with their interpretation of the Commandment that one should not make graven images. As a result, "Images that had been venerated for generations were labelled as idols and smashed to pieces. Churches that had been filled with representations of sacred history were stripped bare."[752] Luther had been encouraged to come out of hiding from his Wartburg sanctuary to care for his Wittenberg people, who were cowering in fear of the iconoclasts. He wanted to provide care and instruction so his people could properly deal with images. As we have referred to previously, through these "Invocavit Sermons" preached during the week after the first Sunday in Lent (known as Invocavit Sunday), Luther taught how change should occur in the Church. It is not through violence or force, he strongly counseled, as

---

[751] Cortes, Steve, "Commentary: Trump Didn't Call Neo-Nazis 'Fine People.' Here's Proof," *RealClear Politics*, March 21, 2019. <https://www.realclearpolitics.com/articles/2019/03/21/trump_didnt_call_neo-nazis_fine_people_heres_proof_139815.html>.

* Iconoclasm is the act of rejection or destruction of religious images (icons) as heretical.

[752] Heal, Bridget, *Art History, Introduction: Art and Religious Reform in Early Modern Europe*. <https://onlinelibrary.wiley.com/doi/full/10.1111/1467-8365.12305>.

he preached against the destructive mobs and their excesses. Change in the Church, he proclaimed, comes through the working of God's Spirit in the Word.

Luther's dealings with the iconoclasts didn't end there. While Luther sought to win Karlstadt back, the former friendship suffered greater division over understandings of the Last Supper that takes Christ's words "*this is*" to mean "this signifies," and the rejection of baptizing infants, positions that Karlstadt embraced with sharp attacks on Luther's positions. When the printed tracts came to Luther's attention, he realized how widespread Karlstadt's opinions were being received, and how close they were to those of Zwingli and other antagonists. Because these contested issues were at the heart of The Reformation, Luther was compelled to refute, and refute he did, in a violent style with harsh and blunt language. The result was his authorship of "Against the Heavenly Prophets," which reaffirmed his position made in those Invocavit sermons. In this treatise, he addresses the false teachings of the "image-breakers" and "enthusiasts" (or "fanatics," to use another familiar Luther term) who he accuses of misreading and undermining the authority of the Scripture. In the process, he says, they violate freedom and practice a false sense of works' righteousness. In his typical rational thinking, he makes a definitive statement about the impossibility of an "image-less faith:"

> Of this I am certain, that God desires to have His works heard and read, especially the passion of our Lord. But it is impossible for me to hear and bear it in mind without forming mental images of it in my heart. For whether I will or not, when I hear of Christ, an image of a man hanging on a cross takes form in my heart, just as the reflection of my face naturally appears in the water when I look into it. If it is not a sin but good to have the image of Christ in my heart, why should it be a sin to have it before my eyes?[753]

Likewise, we see posturing and duplicity in charges of "nationalism." Where was the media coverage of the Black Hebrew Israelites at the Washington, D.C. "March for Life" and their confrontation with Covington, Kentucky, students?

> Organizations like the Southern Poverty Law Center have argued that some Black Hebrew Israelite groups are "hate groups" and fit into a rise of black nationalism…who openly condemn whites as evil personified, deserving

[753] LW 40:99-100. *Church and Ministry IV*, "Against the Heavenly Prophets in the Matter of Images and Sacraments (1525)."

> only death or slavery, and also have a history of sexist and anti-LGBTQ remarks.... Far from engaging in racially motivated harassment, the group of mostly white, MAGA-hat wearing male teenagers remained relatively calm and restrained despite being subjected to incessant racist, homophobic, and bigoted verbal abuse by members of the bizarre religious sect of Black Hebrew Israelites who were lurking nearby.[754]

In defiance of these details and videos of the event, "White Nationalism" becomes a new banner thrown around, and a rallying cry of many who do not understand the word's meaning, but only possess a vague reference, negative connotation, or association to Nazi Germany, which desired to exterminate a race and used Luther's diatribes on Jews to pave the way for Hitler. That is not the original meaning of the word. Study the word's etymology and one will discover what Trump advocates in his slogans "Make America Great Again" and "America First," hometown pride or the spirit behind an athletic team, with a Styrofoam hand's index finger declaring "we're number one!"

Or one can contrast the way obvious spoofs were handled by the press regarding both Trump and Clinton's comments about obtaining evidence. "Russia, if you're listening, I hope you're able to find the 30,000 [Clinton] emails that are missing," Trump said at a press conference. "I think you will probably be rewarded mightily by our press. Let's see if that happens. That'll be nice."[755] Trump was referring to the subpoenaed emails Clinton said she deleted because they were personal in nature. She was investigated for her use of a private email server while she served as Secretary of State. Trump's remarks came after Clinton's camp said that Russian hackers were likely responsible for breaching the computer networks of the Democratic National Committee and leaking emails of top officials to WikiLeaks for publication. Acknowledging the ability of Russians to access the Democrats' computer system, Trump made his comedic response, which was taken literally by the press as proof of collusion and considered to be of such importance as to be included in Special Prosecutor Robert Mueller's report as a "possible" form of attempted collusion with Russia.

In an interview with MSNBC's Rachel Maddow, Clinton was asked about the President not choosing to release his tax returns. Her response played off Trump's comments, turning the tables by suggesting a plea one of the 2020 Democratic presidential candidates could

---

[754] Lockhart, P.R., "The Black Hebrew Israelites and Their Connection to the Covington Controversy, Explained," *Vox*, Jan. 22 2019. <https://www.vox.com/identities/2019/1/22/18193352/black-hebrew-israelites-covington-catholic-phillips-maga>.

[755] <https://www.youtube.com/watch?v=3kxG8uJUsWU>.

have made: "China, if you're listening, why don't you get Trump's tax returns? I'm sure our media would richly reward you."[756] Nowhere was that comment taken seriously by anyone as "proof" of her possible collusion with China, but was clearly understood by most to be a form of satire. The contrast on the internet with accounts of Trump's comments clearly demonstrates the bias and lack of integrity in the media's coverage. For Trump it was about his breaking U.S. law, rewriting history, and Russia hacking Clinton's server as proof of Trump's collusion with the Russians. It is crucial to view not only comments in their entirety but also within their context and intent, absent any spin or deception.

Likewise, it seems to me that we must avoid viewing an individual, who was a product of the sixteenth century, only through the lens of the crimes of the twentieth century, and it is clear that anti-Semitism is a twentieth-century phenomenon. This understanding is supported by the conspiracy publication "The Protocols of the Elders of Zion" which is a fabricated anti-Semitic text purporting to describe a Jewish plan for global domination. Most agree this hoax, first published in Russia in 1903 and then translated into multiple languages, kicked off the modern practice of Aryan-style anti-Semitism as we know it. German Protestant theologian Johannes Wallmann argues that "Luther's so-called anti-Semitism of the 1540's never drew significant interest until Hitler's henchmen used it in their inhuman propaganda of the 1940's."[757] Heinz Schilling emphatically agrees: "It is wrong… misleading in attributing to Luther a historical causality that had meaning only for later generations. The dreadful words of hatred against the Jews for which Luther was responsible did not lead directly and inevitably to the Holocaust." Undoubtedly, hostility towards Jews, fostered by using Luther's words and expressions, turned easily into racial anti-Semitism in the twentieth century. Heinz Schilling thus marvels how "scholars who approach the sources critically have overlooked the historical distinction between the religiously determined anti-Jewishness of Old Europe and the racial anti-Semitism of the modern age."[758]

One cannot claim that Luther's anti-Semitism was the Aryan racism of German National Socialism. It was instead part of the cultural anti-Semitism that permeated Medieval Europe and erupted in political and economic persecution during Luther's lifetime. His treatise entitled "On the Jews and Their Lies" (1543) contained mostly exegetical discussions of disputed messianic passages in the Old Testament. Again, one cannot defend his violent language against the Jews, nor does it make his angrily advocating setting fire to their

---

756 <https://www.politico.com/story/2019/05/01/hillary-clinton-china-tax-returns-1296868>.

757 Zersen, David, "Did Luther Really Say? Contexts for Luther's Comments on the Wends." <https://www.academia.edu/36898659/>.

758 Schilling, *Upheaval*, p.471.

synagogues, destroying their houses, and confiscating their prayer books and money any less repulsive, but it does demonstrate that the bulk of Luther's opposition to the Jews was theological anti-Judaism, rather than the racially motivated anti-Semitism of our time.

Throughout his life, Luther was an evangelist who longed that Jews should be converted and join the Church. Hitler, however, never wanted Jews to join the Nazi Party. That's the difference between anti-Semitic and anti-Jewish. Hitler spread his beliefs in racial "purity" and in the superiority of the "Germanic race"—what he called an "Aryan master race." Luther wasn't opposed to the Jews because of their blood. He was opposed to the Jews because of their religion. He wanted them to join the Christian Church. If you're really anti-Semitic, you're against Jews because of their blood, and there's nothing Jews can do about that. That's not a change they can affect to make a difference.

To clarify the distinction, Mark Edwards contends that

> Luther identified a Jew by his religious belief, not by his race. (Identification of a Jew by his race is, in any case, a concept foreign to the sixteenth century.) If a Jew converted to Christianity, he became a fellow brother or sister in Christ. For racial anti-Semitism religious belief is largely irrelevant. For example, under National Socialism, a person was considered Jewish if either of his grandparents were Jewish, whatever his religious convictions. Scholars who point this out are not condoning religious anti-Semitism. They are only pointing out that the logic of religious anti-Semitism leads to attempts at conversion, not to genocide.[759]

Pelikan cautions us, rightly so, that "Neither the lame excuses offered by some Lutherans for whom their hero could do no wrong, nor the efforts both by Nazis and by anti-Nazis to make him a kind of Proto-Hitlerite represent historical justice."[760] In Eric Metaxas' judgment,

> If it hadn't been for the Nazis, almost no one would ever have heard of these writings. When Luther wrote them, he had little idea that four centuries in the future a political malevolence would rise up in his beloved Germany and that its most diabolical proponents would ferret out from the mountains of his writings those few passages of his most injudicious writings to aid their cause. Or that that diabolical cause would end with the murder of six million Jewish

---

759 Edwards, *Last Battles,* p.139.

760 Pelikan, "The Enduring Relevance of Martin Luther."

> noncombatants in as cold-blooded and calculated a manner as anything in the history of the world. That the Nazis' cynical master of propaganda would find the few vile words Luther had written against Jews and broadcast them to the world, ignoring the 110 volumes of Luther's other writings, is of course fathomlessly cynical. Even at the time, those who knew Luther's other works very well either were unaware of this pamphlet or simply ignored it, feeling that it was such a strange outlier it could hardly be understood rationally. Still the main question remains: How is it that someone so very focused on the love and grace of God for so much of his life could come to say things that seem to contradict what he said earlier in life?[761]

That is a concern or question we often hold, especially within the realm of politicians, where it is often easier to perceive their "flip-flops" as convenient for political purposes than discovering how one might have evolved as a result of new insights. Changing one's mind in view of new information can be a virtue rather than a sin. Holding oneself rigidly to a policy position based solely on ideological considerations when the facts argue otherwise is not necessarily an admirable or desirable quality in a politician, theologian or journalist.

Yet Luther, who apprehended God's expansive grace and love and preached it faithfully, failed grievously at times to apply it to all persons, especially to his Jewish neighbors. There were times when he had difficulty practicing what he proclaimed, demonstrating that Luther the man was, as Luther the theologian said, "righteous and a sinner at the same time ["*Simul Justus et Peccator*"]," as all believers are.

Luther came to know himself fully, first and always as a flawed human in the service of God, even as he disclosed and succumbed to his weaknesses and errors of judgment. Martin Luther's vision of the sweeping nature of God's love for the world, and his contradictory and painful failure to apply that vision to all people, resulted in hateful and destructive attacks against both his Jewish neighbors and the abused peasants. Like Trump, the Augustinian could be just as blunt, strident, and ill-tempered, with outbursts in defense of what he thought was right regardless of the consequences. Yet it is abundantly clear that a gracious God used Martin to change the world, and chooses to use others, not precluding their humanity and sinfulness, in extraordinary ways.

The more the Catholic Church squeezed Luther to recant, the more Luther became emboldened to criticize the Church about its practices and theology. The more opposition and resistance to Trump manifests itself through staged and coordinated outbursts, rioting

---

[761] Metaxas, *Rediscovered*, pp.416–17.

(even violence) and fabricated hate crimes, the more energized he seems to become, which invigorates his supporters.

Roland Bainton, in his classic book on Luther, *Here I Stand*, contends that

> the center about which all the petals clustered was the affirmation of the forgiveness of sins through the utterly unmerited grace of God made possible by the cross of Christ, which reconciled wrath and mercy, routed the hosts of hell, triumphed over sin and death, and by the resurrection manifested that power which enables one to die to sin and rise to newness of life. This was of course the theology of Paul, heightened, intensified, and clarified. Beyond these cardinal tenets, Luther was never to go.[762]

Luther in the 16th century was, without a doubt, the most well-known man in Europe, the most published, and the most outspoken. Trump hasn't only gained attention from being a wealthy real estate mogul and a reality TV celebrity who decided to run for president, but also from his dismissive speech and unceremonious manners. Both are famous for being plain-spoken and candid, often using caustic words that spread like wildfire to cause a response among audiences, communities, and respective countries, that have earned each of them renown as well as powerful enemies. And both have given evidence of deliberately playing on the hatreds, prejudices and emotions of their followers.

Unlike their predecessors, they display little caution for being politically correct, especially as they abandon the passive or defensive posture and instead launch into the offensive with counterattacks in the language that resonates with the common person on the street. As we have already witnessed, contemporaries of both leaders have reacted the same in their attempts to denounce rather than debate the issues in a manner that can lead to enlightenment. President Trump has discovered what Luther experienced: one cannot say a word that will not be heard, pondered, exaggerated, and slanted to support preconceived positions.

Luther, with a spine of steel, courageously took on the academicians and theologians at prestigious universities, as well as the bishops, councils, popes and emperor when he published his "Disputation Against Scholastic Theology." This critique was called the "Ninety-Seven Theses," which preceded the "Ninety-Five" (he learned to be more succinct!) that would later grab the public spotlight. The late Medieval theological method of Scholasticism revived the teachings of Aristotle, where "quid pro quo" logic became the

---

[762] Bainton, *Here I Stand*, p.68 (Abingdon); Mentor pb, p.51.

end-all and be-all when it came to thinking and learning, even in ethics, Biblical theology and Church practice—do this and you are rewarded; don't and you are punished. "The old (theological method) relies on 'therefore' (*ergo*)—if, if, therefore—which makes for nice logic, but the Bible teaches 'nevertheless' (*dennoch* in Luther's German): I am lost and dead. Period. *Nevertheless*, God loves me and saves me through Christ Jesus. That message is the product of the new method Luther was determined to usher in."[763] Luther understood and appreciated Paul's teaching of the law as not suggesting that one is capable of keeping its mandates, but rather making it crystal clear that we cannot. One is thus left to despair, as Luther often did, until God's free gift in Christ alone becomes a reality that sets one free as it did for the Reformer in his "Reformation Discovery."

---

[763] Rosin, Robert, "Luther, Learning, and the Reformation: A Look at Then with Some Thoughts for Now," *Concordia Journal*, 43:1&2, Winter/Spring 2017, p.91.

22

The Perfect Storm

There are always several contextual factors that contribute to a monumental shift in history. For the 15th and 16th centuries, one could say there was a convergence of such factors both within and outside the Church that aided the reformers: the socio-political situation in Europe, the corruption of the Roman Curia and the papacy, unfavorable balance of payments, the new insights of textual criticism emerging from the return to sources advocated by Renaissance humanism, and the impact of the groundbreaking technology of the printing press. All of these, combined with Luther's theological insights, created the "perfect storm" known as the Protestant Reformation, and coalesced to make Luther the center of one of Europe's greatest transformations.

Socio-Economic and Political Context

Luther astutely read the political scene, having a deep understanding of his times and environment. He arrived on the stage of history at a time when spiritual and nationalistic hunger met. Luther's world of war, violence, plague, and famine encountered concerns about having basic sustenance, security and health. Europe was in a state of great unrest. Resentment and occasional revolt against the feudal system led to its subsequent decline, along with social relationships in exchange for an economy in which goods and services were traded for money. The old face-to-face way of engaging with the world was being replaced with a more decentralized and impersonal economy. Early formation of what could be called the "middle class" was taking shape with the creation of guilds, or associations of craftsmen, tradesmen and merchants. Disruption was further created by the developing technology, and social divisions were deepening. People sought to assert their individual interests and power, and rivalries between cities and nationalistic sentiments emerged, with local princes in the jigsaw of hundreds of states looking for more autonomy, all creating competition within Germany and throughout Europe for hegemony. The pope, *pontifex maximus* and sovereign prince of the Church and Papal States, caused alarm and aroused great hostility. The pious could see the political authority of the Bishop of Rome as unscriptural despotism and were resentful of Italian authority. Hierarchical relations of deference had lost their mystique. A more dynamic society of burghers, guilds, and a more educated laity was taking place. The cultural fabric of Europe was shifting, and the changing economy made it more susceptible to tearing.

Though the Holy Roman Empire was also fragmented, both politically and culturally, the Catholic countries of Europe were still connected by the common tongue of Latin at both the academic level and in the Church, with its books and worship services. Surrounded by Europe's many linguistic obstacles, Latin was a universal language used not only in theology but also in law, science, international trade and politics. But with the decline of Latin and the growing preference for non-Latin languages, the bond between Western European Christians further eroded. The articulation of emerging nationalistic German sentiments was defined in terms of opposition to Rome. Ulrich von Hutten, a Franconian nobleman, was one of the most outspoken critics of papal Rome. For Hutten, to be German is to be anti-Rome: "The German nation has recovered its eyes and now recognizes how unjustly it has been led around by the nose and defrauded" by the Pope who is "a betrayer of the people."[764]

There had also been long-standing economic discontent over the flow of money into Italy, or more specifically to the Vatican, which was dominated by Renaissance princes whose artistic and architectural vision outstripped their spiritual responsibilities. Arguing from the point of view of not just a Christian, but a *German* Christian, Luther could not stand idly by while the forces of Rome pillaged his country. Dramatically he portrays a Germany that is being ruined by the Roman Church, asking the German populace in his treatise "To the Christian Nobility" "If we are right in hanging thieves and beheading robbers, why should we let Roman Avarice go free? He is the worst thief and robber that has ever been or could ever come into the world, and all in the holy name of Christ and St. Peter!"[765]

> Poor Germans that we are—we have been deceived! We were born to be masters, and we have been compelled to bow the head beneath the yoke of our tyrants, and to become slaves. Name, title, outward signs of royalty, we possess all these; force, power, right, liberty, all these have gone over to the popes, who have robbed us of them. They get the kernel, we get the husk....

---

[764] Brady, Jr. Thomas A., *German Histories in the Age of Reformation, 1400-1650* (Cambridge, UK and New York: Cambridge University Press, 2009), p.139; Ulrich von Hutten, *Opera quae reperiri potuerunt omnia,* 1:61-62, 1:112.

[765] LW 44:156. *The Christian in Society I,* "To the Christian Nobility of the German Nation Concerning the Reform of the Christian Estate; *Three Treatises,* "An Open Letter to the Christian Nobility," p.44.

> It is time the glorious Teutonic people should cease being the puppet of the Roman pontiff.[766]

This was all, of course, in reference to the Church using indulgences from 1100-1500 to raise armies and build cathedrals. The so-called "Turk Tax" brought in revenue to fight the constant threat of conquest from the East by the Muslim Turks, while other indulgences were being sold by Vatican emissaries sent into Germany to gather money to fund the reconstruction of St. Peter's in Rome. Luther tapped into this popular animosity toward the Vatican's financial enterprise of draining money from the German economy, hurting commoners and nobles. In the 86th of the Ninety-Five Theses, Luther asks pointedly, "Why does not the pope, whose wealth today is greater than the wealth of the richest Crassus,* build this one basilica of St. Peter with his own money rather than with the money of poor believers?"[767]

Even before the Emperor at the Diet of Worms, playing to the audience of German nobles, counts, princes and electors, Luther defended his writings which had fueled a national independence movement. Understanding clearly that the Germans were eager to throw off the oppressive and degrading shackles of their Italian overlords from Rome, he blatantly appealed to these nationalistic sentiments. "Property and possessions, especially in this illustrious nation of Germany, have been devoured by an unbelievable tyranny and are being devoured to this time without letup and by unworthy means.... Should I have retracted these writings...I would have opened not only windows but doors to such great godlessness."[768] Germans obviously found Luther to be their standard-bearer against the tyranny of Rome.

Donald Trump entered the political arena at a time when the people of the United States were perhaps more divided and polarized than any time since our country's Civil War. Islamic militant movements, having roots in the Ottoman Empire wars, and current jihadists motivated by versions of Osama bin Laden's global ideology, continue to wreak

---

[766] "Appeal to the German Nobility," *Documents of the Christian Church, 2nd Edition,* selected and edited by Henry Bettenson (London: Oxford University Press, 1963), pp.275-276, citing LW 44:210 whose colorful translation better reflects Luther's comment: "The pope gobbles the kernel while we are left playing with the husk!" Also, *Three Treatises,* p.104.

* Marcus Licinius Crassus (153-11 B.C.) was a Roman general and politician who played a key role in the transformation of the Roman Republic into the Roman Empire. He is often called "the richest man in Rome."

[767] LW 31:33. *Career of the Reformer I,* "Ninety-Five Theses."

[768] LW 32:110. *Career of the Reformer II,* "Luther at the Diet of Worms."

terrorism in our country as well as in Europe today. Trust in major institutions, politics, the Church, banks, big business, the media, high-tech providers, trade unions, and professional sports has fallen precipitously. Equal justice under the law has come under attack, along with Constitutional guarantees of "due process" and purported spying on Americans. As a result, people are more cynical and skeptical, disillusioned and disappointed.

Fragmentation has heightened this unrest, with groups pitted against each other, a "middle class" that has felt forgotten, and the multitude of issues arising from "identity politics" ascending to the forefront, often creating disruptions and even violence that drown out any semblance of civil discourse. We have become a people who no longer know how (nor even care) to converse with those whose views differ from our own. We are in the center of a crisis of civility that mirrors the divide Luther encountered and to which he contributed.

Dennis Peacocke* observes that the alternative world views of our twenty-first century, the "left" and the "right," with obvious nuances within them, have so "trapped us all in a stalemated conflict where conversation is increasingly impossible because neither side truly understands the 'both-and' dimension of their common concerns and are locked into a no-win, 'either-or' paradigm."[769] Undocumented or unsubstantiated hearsay, undisclosed sources, anonymity and confidentiality, distorted headlines, and edited soundbites lend support to positions that are often treated as "gospel," resulting in individuals taking hardened sides, determined to prove that power prevails. Language, diversity, immigration, refugees, borders, guns, police brutality, women's health concerns (abortion), and collusion were concerns that led to "agenda items" of partisan politics, producing intensified disunity and intolerance within the populace. And indeed, there are separatist movements finding expression in "sanctuary" cities and states, as well as proposals to divide the state of California and parcel parts of Virginia. The forest is being ignored for the sake of individual trees.

Years ago, our synod's bishop, Dr. Kenneth Sauer, on whose team I was privileged to serve, developed a "Bi-Focal Vision" theme to guide our Ohio congregations in the upcoming year. The emphasis centered on the wider, more comprehensive view of the Church's mission anchored in the Sources (the commission Christ gave to His disciples and the promise of His Spirit to guide) that should direct and enlighten how we deal with the local issues and concerns at the congregational level. Having clarity in both near and far-sighted vision is crucial, but it is tempting for humans to forego the "big picture" for

---

* Dennis Peacocke is a pastor, author, founder and president of Go Strategic, a leadership organization dedicated to demonstrating the relevance of Christianity to every area of contemporary life.

[769] Peacocke, Dennis, "The Bottom Line." <https://www.gostrategic.org/bottom-line-archive/reformation-part-two-worldview-utopianism-christ-public-square>.

the sake of those tantalizing side excursions that may benefit the locals but, in the process, detract from the central task and privilege entrusted to the Church. Majoring in minors seems to be our preferred course. Another mentor, a parishioner and psychology professor at the University of Illinois, Dr. Joseph Zaccaria, reminded me constantly at our frequent coffee get-togethers of the wisdom Stephen Covey set forth in his succinct axiom: "The main thing is to keep the main thing, the main thing!"[770]

Luther was able to refocus the Church following his encounter with the Lord through his study of Scriptures, when he discovered and experienced God giving him an inexpressible gift rather than making impossible demands upon him. As a result of this "breakthrough" which he described as "walking through the open gates of paradise. There a totally other face of the entire Scripture showed itself to me."[771] Luther was able to distill a clear message about the Gospel which he gladly and joyfully proclaimed. The Good News God gave us was the gift of His Son, the Word made flesh, who chooses to live "in and through us" because He is "with us and for us." Luther's insights were captured in short and striking slogans, easily remembered: by "Grace Alone," through "Faith Alone," in "Christ Alone," according to "Scripture Alone," for "God's Glory Alone." These became the foundational principles summarizing the Reformer's theological convictions about the essentials—the "main thing"—of our Christian faith.

Likewise, the founding documents of our country and the rule of law are claimed by the President as being essential to guide decisions for governance today. He saw respect for our flag and our national anthem being symbolic of an over-arching and prevailing demonstration of that which unites us. In other words, it is important to understand the foundational and core values that have shaped us as a nation and for which many have willingly sacrificed their lives to defend and protect us. Otherwise, we will find ourselves like *"a wave of the sea, driven and tossed by the wind"* (James 1:6 [NRSV]). Despite objections to national patriotism which he upholds, our President acknowledges that while we are not perfect as a nation, we continue to strive toward that "more perfect union." Barry Farber, the late pioneer of talk radio, is quoted as saying, "Never in the history of mankind has there been a country like the United States that has accumulated more power and abused it less than this country." Sean Hannity adds "that there's never been a country that has

---

[770] Covey, Stephen R., Merrill, A. Roger, Merrill, Rebecca R., *First Things First* (New York: Fireside, 1994), p.75.

[771] LW 34:337. *Career of the Reformer IV*, "Preface to the Latin Writings." ("I felt that I was altogether born again and had entered Paradise itself through open gates"). See also <https://whenmercyfoundme.com/2015/08>.

done more to advance the human condition than this country."[772] Think about what those proud statements say about our history and who we are as a people: Never has there been a country which has acquired more power, and accumulated more wealth to advance human conditions in the world, than the United States. President Trump salutes this country that has used its wealth, power and blood in the service and for the benefit of its citizens and others, and he views our people as the most charitable in the world.

Like Luther, however, Trump confronted the flow of money leaving the country seeking "fair" trade deals, resulting in a more favorable balance of payments, and sought to hold other countries accountable in their treaty obligations. At the G7 conference on June 9, 2018, President Trump doubled down on his tough stance on trade, telling reporters, "We're [the U.S.] like the piggy bank everyone is robbing."[773] His "America First" emphasis is an essential pillar in his promise to "Make America Great Again!"

Corruption within the Church

The people in Luther's day were indignant, perhaps even embarrassed by the Church's wealth and, in particular, by the papacy's exploitation—financial and spiritual—of the Holy Roman Empire. With his holdings and secular power, "The Pope," writes English historian Hilaire Belloc, "was becoming as much an Italian Prince as he was head of the Church."[774]

For centuries Christians had been expressing concern about the low standard of their ordained clergy and church hierarchy. They found fault with priests drinking, gambling, living with concubines, and being exempt from taxation and civil responsibilities. The clergy were so preoccupied with worldly matters, money, and warfare that many neglected their flocks. The Renaissance popes seemed to allow Christ to be forgotten, fostering and preying upon the foolish superstitions of common folk who found themselves mired in a controlled maze, attempting to seek salvation through the worship of images and relics, pilgrimages, and the buying of indulgences. The Church had in effect become a stock exchange for trading merits. It was important to Luther that the Church restore a clear message about grace that could be understood in the vernacular and received in the heart. Grace is not a commodity that can be traded but is the personal presence and experience of the Lord in His Word.

---

[772] <https://www.foxnews.com/transcript/hannity-on-democrats-bashing-america-over-july-4th-holiday>.

[773] <https://www.newsweek.com/donald-trump-g7-summit-speech-justin-trudeau-canada-967978>.

[774] <https://www.intellectualtakeout.org/article/5-causes-protestant-reformation-besides-indulgences>.

Luther's attack on the corrupt practice of selling indulgences—remissions from punishment earned by sin for a fee—demonstrated his pastoral heart, his profound empathy for and understanding of those placed under his care. He was especially concerned for the poor within the congregation, who were giving up scarce coins and their life savings in the hope of saving their loved ones from the tortures of purgatory, so they could be fast-tracked into heaven.

While being deceived by the meaningless promises made by peddlers ripping them off by intimidation, scared Christians were emptying their pockets for fear of eternal damnation as the Church grew ever richer. This led Luther to boldly call out the arrogance and self-deception of his more sophisticated theological peers. For Luther, there was nothing in the Bible that gave the Church the right to charge people for their salvation. The Church was supposed to be a spiritual sanctuary, not a marketplace where salvation was essentially being sold. In his critique, the Reformer was also assailing the Pope's claim to having authority over the souls of the dead.

There are those who contend that all the young Wittenberg professor simply wanted was to explore a question of pastoral care in that normal way academicians discussed new ideas, by posing theses for debate. Accordingly, Luther drafted his Ninety-Five Theses out of his concern for the lack of faithful pastoral care being provided by the Church. As Reformation scholar Jane Strohl suggests, "One could describe Luther's career as the mounting of a life-long pastoral malpractice suit against the Church's authority at every level of the hierarchy."[775] For Erik H. Herrmann,* Director of the Center for Reformation Research at Concordia Seminary St. Louis, Luther's concern went far beyond obscure differences to be debated in the ivory tower of the university. It created a "Copernican revolution" in theology that effected reverberations which continue to make an impact today.

> No, Luther was only interested in matters that touched on the heart of everything—the whole of theology and the salvation of all was at stake. When Luther began to change things in the university curriculum at Wittenberg where he taught, he did so because of how it would affect the weekly preaching, teaching, and pastoral care on the parish level. That was the goal of reformation for Luther.[776]

---

[775] Strohl, Jane E., "General Introduction," *Luther's Spirituality* (Paulist Press, 2007), p.xxiii.

* Erik H. Herrmann is Professor of Historical Theology and Dean of Theological Research and Publication at Concordia Seminary, St. Louis, Missouri.

[776] Hermann, Erik H., "The Relevance of Remembering the Reformation," *Concordia Journal*, 43:1&2, Winter/Spring 2017, p.20.

Prior to the Reformation, pastoral care was being extended through the sacrament of penance, the selling/buying of indulgences, private masses, and a number of false "*Geistlichkeiten*"—spiritual practices or "*spiritualities*," as Luther called them—that attempted to provide consolation and hope in relics, pilgrimages, and prayers to the saints, instead of practices that would saturate one's life with the Word of Christ. In supporting this view, Hermann claims "questions of doctrine and theological authority arose for Luther as a means to a greater end: the pastoral care that nurtures a genuine Christian life.... Only in this deep connection to Christ did Luther find freedom and strength to live in a world shaped by the contradiction of God's providence and the continual presence of sin and suffering."[777]

Professor Hermann makes a convincing argument that Luther's repeated attacks on what he believed to be false "*Geistlichkeiten*" practices were because he saw them as various ways of pushing God back up into heaven, away from the world, and thus permitting the faithful to place their security in lesser "deities." He postulates that the posting of the Ninety-Five Theses on the eve of All Saint's Day, while it may have been a coincidence, was probably intentional, with his attack on a saintly treasury of merits and the feast celebrating that pantheon of holy intercessors. Intermediators could not do what Luther acknowledged was God's saving activity in deciding to enter into the breach between goodness and sin, suffering and salvation. In Christ, God deigned to suffer for and with humankind personally because of His love for His creation.[778]

Harbingers of the Main Event

In addition, within the Church there had been a widespread acknowledgment that corruption in the Roman Curia and the office of the pope was great, and reform was needed. Over the centuries prior to the Reformation, the earlier efforts of Peter Waldo* (12th century), Francis of Assisi (13th century), John Wycliffe (14th century), John Hus (15th century), and a half-century later, Girolamo Savonarola, had failed. Not surprising, the current awareness in the sixteenth century for needed reform reflected the same concerns of these previous

---

[777] Ibid., p.21.

[778] Ibid.

* Peter Waldo's thought was introduced to the author in 1963 while I was a participant in a European Study Project for the Church and had the privilege of studying at the Waldensian Agape Retreat Center near Prali (Turin) in northwestern Italy's Alp mountains (Piedmont region), on the border with France.

groups which were labeled as heretical by the Church, notably the Waldensians, Lollards and Hussites. They were harbingers of the main event yet to come.

The Czech theologian Jan Hus had been called to Constance in 1415 to face charges of heresy. Despite the promise of safe conduct, he was imprisoned and brought to trial where he was given no chance to defend himself, only asked to recant teachings that would strongly influence Luther. Uncannily, as the official executioner was about to light the pyre at the feet of Jan Hus, whose name means "goose" in Bohemian, the reformer prophesized that "Today you will roast a lean goose, but a hundred years from now, you will hear a swan sing (which God will awaken), whom you will leave unroasted and no trap or net will catch him for you."[779] Hus was excommunicated and burned at the stake on July 6, 1415. The words of the roasting "goose" may be legend, but they are not for that reason any less prescient. The prophecy was fulfilled in Martin Luther a little more than 100 years after the death of Hus, and the swan became a symbol for Luther and his Reformation.

A Bohemian Goose and A Saxon Swan

Left: Jan Hus being burned at the stake in 1415 for believing in the authority of Scripture. Right: Luther with a swan, in a painting in the church at Strümpfelbach im Remstal, Weinstadt, Germany, by J.A. List. Center: a contemporary cartoon by Paul and Stephanie Cox.

(Images: Left and right, public domain, retrieved at Wikimedia. Center, retrieved at the website of Paul and Stephanie Cox)

[779] <https://www.thereformationroom.com/single-post/2017/01/12/The-Goose-and-the-Swan>.

John Foxe in *Acts and Monuments of the English Martyrs* writes that "although through might [the Pope] stopped the mouth of John Huss, God hath appointed the press to preach, whose voice the Pope is never able to stop with all the puissance of his triple crown."[780] A hundred years later, Martin Luther picked up his "goose quill" and penned his Ninety-Five Theses, perhaps while sitting on the toilet as some have surmised. Interesting is "The Dream" reported by the Lutheran Press:

> The evening before October 31, 1517, the Elector Frederick [III] of Saxony had a dream which was recorded by his brother, Duke John. The dream, in short, is about a monk who wrote on the church door of Wittenberg with a pen so large that it reached to Rome. The more those in authority tried to break the pen, the stronger it became. When asked how the pen got so strong, the monk replied, "The pen belonged to an old goose of Bohemia, a hundred years old." The Elector was unsure exactly what the dream meant, but believed he had an interpretation which he thought may be accurate. The very morning he shared his dream, Martin Luther was posting his theses.[781]

The Power and Strength of the Mighty Pen

To the right, Luther is portrayed studying his Bible receiving light and inspiration from above.

The woodcut produced for the 1617 Centenary Jubilee of the Reformation shows Martin Luther inscribing the first of his 95 objections on the door of a church. In the cartoon, Luther's giant quill pierces the ears of a lion, as Emperor Charles V was known, and goes on to knock off the papal tiara of Pope Leo X as a way of symbolizing the effect The Reformation had in destabilizing the State and the Roman Catholic Church. (Image: Public domain, retrieved at Ohio State University's "Origins: Current Events in Historical Perspective" website)

---

[780] Foxe, John, *Acts and Monuments of the English Martyrs, Volume III*, ed. G. Townsend (London, 1844), p.720.

[781] <https://lutheranpress.com/the-swan>.

Luther then strategically utilized the ingenuities of the printing press to capitalize upon the dissemination of his views, and the essential need to get the Bible into the hands of the laity so that the Church "at large" could see for themselves the egregious errors of the Church's high elite.

Adding to the more than four hundred years of frustrated reform efforts was the increasing role the papacy was playing in the secular rule of Europe. Then too, there was that period known as the "Great Schism" which produced several rival claimants to the papacy. It had only been a matter of a hundred years since the Church had experienced leadership by three competing popes simultaneously. The seesaw battle between popes and anti-popes weakened the idea of the pope as a central spiritual authority in the minds of many Christians.

Trump saw his mission as fighting a corrupt political system that had abandoned the needs and desires of the American people. The government and its bureaucrats (those not elected by, nor accountable to, the people), the legislative process, business practices, corruption, unemployment, stagnant wages, illegal immigrants, overly rigid business regulations, political correctness, hypocrisy, and a two-tier system of justice were all concerns within Trump's sight.

"*Ad Fontes*:" Return to the Sources

One is compelled to also note the changes in the political and ideological systems influencing The Reformation era. Technical discoveries such as the compass and the printing press revolutionized navigation and communication. Geographical discoveries, such as Columbus's voyage to the Americas in 1492, nine years after Luther's birth, literally changed the way people looked at the world. At the same time, there was a decline in the Scholastic method and a flourishing in the "New Learning" of Renaissance humanism, prompted by a re-discovery of Classical Greek and Roman civilizations. The cultural interests of Renaissance humanists were expanding to encompass ancient philosophy, literature, politics, history, and educational theory, which Luther supported in transforming the study of liberal arts. He brought the Bible into the center of theological instruction and thus changed the focus of the curriculum, away from its scholastic syllabus based on Aristotle and the use of Peter Lombard's "Sentences." He specifically set about modernizing what was taught at Elector Frederick the Wise's newly founded University at Wittenberg.

The guiding principle of this humanist movement that aided Luther's Reformation was "*Ad Fontes!*"—back to the sources—back mainly to the original Greek writings from the

Classical period. Luther wanted to study Scripture taking into consideration the advances being made among humanists in the recovery of the original Biblical languages.[782] Academic influences, most notably for the Church, included insights from textual criticism, which Luther championed in returning to the sources and the beginnings of the Christian tradition. The method of direct engagement with the original text would serve Luther well as he pursued his fevered scrutiny of Scripture. Everything in the Church was to be conducive to the hearing of the Word and the proper response of faith. The Word in all its forms needed to be placed at center stage, and that which obscured or confused it had to be eradicated. He was consistent in his conviction that right teaching would produce the necessary changes in the Church.

In early 1518, when the Ninety-Five Theses were making tabloid headlines, Luther wrote to his former teacher in Erfurt, Jodocus Trutvetter, who was greatly disturbed about the debate centering on the source and norm of Christian Truth.

> I simply believe that it is impossible to reform the Church unless the canon law, the Decretals, the Scholastic theology, the philosophy, and the logic as they are now taught are thoroughly rooted out and other studies put in their stead. With respect to this opinion, I proceed in such a way that I daily ask the Lord as far as now may be that the pure study of the Bible and the Fathers may be restored. You think I am no logician; perhaps I am not, but I know that I fear no one's logic when I defend this position.[783]

This was coupled with Luther's "hermeneutics" or methodology of Biblical interpretation, taking the words seriously by seeking the meaning behind the text, not just literally but rather viewing the text within its context and its intended purpose. In short, for our "doctor in Biblia," the most important principle of Biblical interpretation was "Scripture interprets Scripture." Luther never forgot that he had received a doctorate in the Holy Scriptures, and viewed his vocation as teaching and preaching the written Word, which points us to Christ.

---

[782] Hart, D.G. "The Printing-Press Prophet," *The Wall Street Journal,* Janurary 8, 2016; <https://www.wsj.com/articles/the-printing-press-prophet-1452290894>.

[783] Luther, *Luther: Lectures on Romans,* edited and translated by Wilhelm Pauck (Louisville, KY: Westminster Press, 1961), p. lxiv, quoting from WABr 1:170,33.

The Primacy of the Preached Word

The Reformer Preaching Christ and Him Crucified

Lucas Cranach's painting of Luther preaching from the pulpit of the Hartenfels Castle Church, the first newly constructed Lutheran Church in the world, built in Torgau, Germany. The artist captures Luther's understanding of the primacy of the Word and the foundation from which all teachings, sacraments and doctrine are rooted. This portrayal forms the predella of Cranach's masterful Altarpiece at the City Church of St. Mary's in Wittenberg. With his left hand on the Scriptures and his right arm extended, pointing to the hovering image of the crucified Christ, Luther is driving home the message of Scriptural authority – "Christ and Him crucified" — who is over traditional Church authority.

Luther knew it took time to listen to the past, to learn what the past has to offer, and to learn how to apply those learnings to the present needs in the current context, but he found it was worth the effort. The Church is always challenged to engage the present and not merely reprise the old. Know the past, yes! Live in the past, no! Our task is to discern what should be upheld and insisted upon, and what should be left alone, from that which should be discarded or changed, and to understand what is really in Luther's word just "*adiaphora*"—those matters not regarded as essential to faith, but nevertheless permissible for Christians and thus allowed in their local church. Then, like now, there could be variations in the way local church "is done," as we, like the early Church, and those that followed, continually sort through context to serve people in their varied circumstances.

Reformers adopted these humanist approaches in ferreting out the meanings of ancient Biblical texts, and so it was that Luther translated the Scripture from the original texts into the vernacular language of common people, using the revolution in printing to place the Bible into a greater number of hands. He was convinced that God's Word was for the people and should be in the language of every-day folk rather than the lofty, scholarly language of the educated and wealthy. Luther's magisterial German translation of the Bible played a major role in shaping a modern German language, as he made use of living, colloquial German in his translation. Seeking a fresh, vigorous idiom, he truly listened to the common people—"looked them on the mouth"[784] in pursuit of hearing the language of the common people which was not too lowly to be the language of God. He made forays into towns and villages, even into different regions, to pick up on the many different dialects used by the butcher, the merchant, the housewife, the people on the street, and the children. He wanted to hear how the people spoke so that his translation of the New Testament could be as close to ordinary contemporary usage as possible, without distorting or violating the source and its meaning. He loved alliteration, repetition, and forceful rhymes, making his texts easy and pleasing to read aloud, even to children.

Before Luther, there was no single German language, just numerous regional dialects. Combining the many dialects of the Germanic people, Luther's language resonated with the people far more so than the scholarly academic or religiously pious usage of Latin the people could hear but not understand. Ben Witherington III makes the claim that "the most dangerous thing Luther ever did was translating the Bible into the ordinary German and encouraging its widespread dissemination."[785] He made the Bible the people's book at church, school, and home, and that sterling translation facilitated the coalescing of the many dialects, promoting the unified German language that we know today as High German (Hoch-deutsch). It further facilitated a strong surge of nationalism, demonstrating how language and culture are intimately connected, something we today are easily ignoring. As Patrick Cox put it in his Public Radio International show "The World in Words," "While Luther is best known as the father of the Reformation, he is also the father of the German language as we know it."[786]

Those in the pews would no longer have to rely only on the word of priests and bishops, instead of the direct Word of God. Up until the Renaissance, the vast majority of Bible teaching was based on Latin translations of the Biblical text, not the original Greek and Hebrew in which it was written. Christian humanism during the Renaissance taught that "if one could discover the real sources of Western Christian civilization—the Bible, the Church Fathers, the classics—one could purify Christianity of its medieval accretions and

---

[784] Schaff, Phillip, *History of the Christian Church, Volume VII*, ch. 4 sec. 62.

[785] Witherington III, Ben, "The Most Dangerous Thing Luther Did," *Christianity Today*, October 2017. <https://www.christianitytoday.com/history/2017/october/most-dangerous-thing-luther-did.html>.

[786] Cox, Patrick, "The World in Words," *Public Radio International*; <https://www.pri.org/stories/2015-04-02/martin-luther-didnt-just-reform-church-he-reformed-german-language>.

corruptions, thus restoring it to its pristine form."[787] Renaissance humanism thus cultivated the ground for the Reformation to take root, by re-engaging with the writers of the early Church.

German historian Bernd Moeller goes so far as to say, "No humanism, no Reformation."[788] "That little says a lot" in the view of Robert Rosin, Professor Emeritus of Theology at Concordia Seminary and Luther scholar:

> Without the "New Learning," as the liberal arts revival was called, Luther's Reformation as we have come to know it, simply would not have happened. To be clear (since definition matters): Renaissance humanism is much different from Twentieth Century Secular Humanism, the Bertrand Russell sort with God absent from the picture that revolves around humankind alone. Humanists in Luther's day were Christians…[who] died within the pale and under the pall of the Church…. The *studia humanitatis*, the study of humanity, saw people as the foremost creatures of God.[789]

We have obviously strayed from the focus of liberal arts that was the impetus of Luther's curriculum reform at Wittenberg. Today the pressure is on specializing, and it is hard to convince "woke" students that a liberal arts education can really serve through a lifetime. But a broad education that teaches people how to continue to learn, how to think critically, how to question, how to assess and form judgments, and how to deal with problems as well as opportunities, can open all sorts of doors, not just to new landscapes while overlooking the backyard, but more importantly by having new eyes that provide broader and deeper insight. I remember reading French novelist Georges Bernanos's *Diary of a Country Priest*, who observed, "Nothing is so deceptive as problems wrongly stated."[790] It seems we have experienced the facing of an abundance of problems wrongly stated (perhaps even

---

787 Thompson, Bard, *Humanists and Reformers: A History of the Renaissance and Reformation* (Cambridge: William E. Eerdmans Publishing Company, 1996), p.333.

788 Moeller, Bernd, "The German Humanists and the Beginnings of the Reformation," *Imperial Cities and the Reformation: Three Essays*, trans and ed. by H.C. Erik Midelfort and Mark U. Edwards, Jr. (Philadelphia: Fortress Press, 1972), p.36.

789 Rosin, Robert, "Luther, Learning, and the Reformation: A Look at Then with Some Thoughts for Now," *Concordia Journal*, 43:1&2, Winter/Spring 2017, pp.91-92.

790 Bernanos, Georges, *The Diary of a Country Priest*, translated by Pamela Morris (Macmillan Co., 1937, 1965). <http://www2.fairmontState.edu/users/pedwards/syllabus.pdf>.

intentionally) by so-called "experts" who are often blindly followed by deceptive and clever hype instead of the Truth that guides us toward the Light.

The global scholar on Luther and the Reformation, Robert Rosin of Concordia Seminary, reminds us that

> Some years ago, Yale professor Stephen Carter argued in *A Culture of Disbelief* that not only was American society actually structured at its founding to welcome a theological/philosophical voice, but he insisted that the absence of a theological voice today has skewed how we tackle problems and leaves us with incomplete solutions. With a context that seems to increasingly dismiss theology's place in the public square, its voice grows ever more distant, even as politics—a kind of faux religion—promises its version of a new heaven and a new earth via this program or that set of regulations designed to fix, direct, and control. In contrast, theologian Reinhold Niebuhr once remarked that democracies are an attempt to find proximate solutions to insoluble problems. Don't we know it! But it is precisely because of life's ragged edges that theology ought to pull up a chair at the table and weigh in on the discussion.[791]

Assured by the Gospel and mindful of life's vocations God gives—theological insights from the Reformation—Dr. Rosin proclaims we cannot afford to sit this one out as having only some antiquarian interest. Our past, both as the Church and a nation, reminds us in broad terms how we got here. More, it stops any hiding in some mountaintop shrine, or taking at face value whatever the media promotes in their scripted biased agendas or what grandstanding politicians espouse in their frequent hypocrisy and hyperbole to score points with the public they need to maintain power. As people of God and heirs of the Reformation, it seems to me that we as churches and faith communities have a critical role to play as we encounter and are confronted with the issues of our day. From the beginning of the Church, we've had experience in convening, nurturing and motivating people as we seek to ground them in ultimate convictions and values through our proclamation and teaching ministries. Merely pontificating platitudes and serving pablum, however, no longer cuts it with those living through the complexities of life in the stormy sea of modernity. In

---

[791] Rosin, "Luther, Learning, and the Reformation," pp.102-103. Rosin references Stephen L. Carter's *The Culture of Disbelief: How American Law and Politics Trivialize Religious Devotion* (New York: Basic Books, 1993).

such changing times with fast-paced social and cultural adaptation and periods of turmoil, Father Daniel Horan* recalls how

> People throughout history have sought easy answers and simple frameworks in an effort to make sense of a changing and, at times inexplicable world… Many people look to religion to be an anchor of meaning and a source of security…The problem is that too many refashion Christianity—its doctrinal teachings and moral guidance—into an idol of their own making, in order to grasp a misguidedly simple and falsely clear message. Typically, such people unintentionally fall into a kind of heresy because they appropriate ideas, propositions, perspectives and elements of the Christian faith only in part and only insofar as it serves their worldview, in an attempt to assuage their anxiety about the complexities of life.
>
> Ironically, such unknowing heretics purport to be "traditional" or "orthodox," touting an absolutist line from their propositional worldview that in turn rejects the broad range of legitimate Christian perspectives…[792]

Sadly, this underlying predisposition of desired simplicity and black-and-white thinking is often encouraged and aided by "culture warriors"—including religious leaders who reduce the rich and nuanced moral teachings of the Church. Many are seeking to be "liked" or being advocates of empathy and compassion for the criminal but not for innocent victims and their families. They champion a discriminate justice system making an unjust or prejudicial distinction in the treatment of different categories of people, especially on the grounds of ethnicity, sex, age, or whether one is wealthy or well connected. We have viewed political orientation contributing to an arrogant attitude of unequal justice being rendered according to the practice of following "Rules for Thee but Not for Me" or asserting "Nobody is Above the Law" when applied only to the opposition instead of adhering to those four words etched above the doors to the Supreme Court: "Equal Justice Under Law" based on the Fourteenth Amendment.

---

* Daniel P. Horan is a Franciscan priest, Director of the Center for Spirituality, Professor of Philosophy, Religious Studies and Theology at Saint Mary's College in Notre Dame, Indiana, a columnist for the *National Catholic Reporter*, and the author of fourteen books.

792 Horan, Daniel P., "The Heresy of Oversimplified Christianity," *National Catholic Reporter*, Aug. 19 2020. <https://www.ncronline.org/news/opinion/faith-seeking-understanding/heresy-oversimplified-christianity>.

Scripture, as we will further examine, and Luther discovered, must be interpreted, contextualized, and understood as its original audience did in their own time to better understand how the Holy Spirit is speaking to us in our time. Scripture cannot always be reduced to propositional claims or read literally. That's the implied and crucial understanding of Christ's Great Commission to both "*make disciples*" and "*teach them*" to obey everything He has commanded (Matthew 28:19-20). The teaching ministry of the Church thus inherently includes ethics and morality as we nurture and equip individuals to return to "the plain" where they live busy lives in all the abundance our Lord promises (John 10:10) as they minister and serve their neighbors in love.

Dealing with moral dilemmas however, will not be solved by memorizing a list of rules, lifting proof texts from Scripture to justify and serve a worldview, or by reducing Christianity to a single issue lens—usually an issue of one's own personal preference or choosing – as the sole standard for judgment without any of the necessary consideration of prudential judgment or conscience. Without critical thought or fuller appreciation and deeper understanding of our faith or the significance of our country's history, we can easily, indiscriminately, and unwittingly surrender to the prevailing political ideologies and shifting cultural mores shaping our societies.

Instead, as followers of Christ gather in groups and congregations we are privileged and compelled to serve as communities of moral deliberation and ethical discourse for the common good. It is therefore incumbent that we commit ourselves to the diligent study of God's Word, the issues and circumstances of our day. We can take comfort in the assurance that the Holy Spirit is alive and active in our understanding of doctrine, the interpretation of Scripture, and the formation of our consciences. Embracing the truth that His Spirit works in and through others as He does us, we are eager to be open, to collaborate, and be enriched by the perspective others bring to the table as we face the challenges in defining the good and the right together. That "will require" concedes Dr. David Pfrimmer of Waterloo Lutheran Seminary, "a new more humble orientation taking seriously the pluralism and the multifaith realities of our world" including non-religious convictions and doing so with mutual respect and civility. "As groups and publics so engage one another they are more likely to articulate, enunciate, and enact the common good or the public purpose."[793]

---

[793] Pfrimmer, David G. A., "Martin Luther's Contribution to Public Ethics Today," *Consensus*, 38:2, 2017, Article 10. <https://scholars.wlu.ca/cgi/viewcontent.cgi?article=2358&context=consensus>.

23

"We the People" and the "Priesthood of All Believers"

Enter into the unrest of the "forgotten" middle class of the 21st century the flamboyant figure of Donald Trump. As Conrad Black put it in the *National Post*, "Trump attacked the entire political class, including all political factions of both parties, the immense corruption in American government, the bias of the national media, and the ludicrous interventions of Hollywood airheads masquerading as the political conscience of the nation."[794]

In his Inaugural Address, Trump declared that "Today we are not merely transferring power from one administration to another, or from one party to the other—but we are transferring power from Washington, D.C., and giving it back to you, the American people." The new president was stating his intent to recover the principles of the Declaration of Independence, that just government is based on the consent of the governed. His demand is more than bipartisan, it is fundamental: "What truly matters is not which party controls our government, but whether our government is controlled by the people. January 20, 2017, will be remembered as the day the people became the rulers of this nation again. The forgotten men and women of our country will be forgotten no longer."[795]

Trump was reaffirming a government for the governed, not just for itself and its administrative state clients, just as Luther envisioned a Church not serving the papacy, prelates, and clergy, but rather a Church made up of a "priesthood of all believers." At the heart of this understanding was Luther's radical assertion that the clergy do not constitute a superior spiritual class (much to the disbelief of many of my colleagues). He resisted the stark divisions between "secular" and "religious" occupations by dignifying all legitimate work.[796] With this understanding he saw that all Christians—clergy and laity—are fundamentally equal in dignity and responsibility before God. Professor of Law and Ethics at Emory

---

794 Black, Conrad, "Trump is Grating, But He's a True Leader—and America Needs Him," *National Post*, June 22, 2018; <https://nationalpost.com/opinion/conrad-black-trump-is-grating-but-hes-a-true-leader-and-america-needs-him>.

795 Trump, "Inaugural Address."

796 LW 44:130. *The Christian in Society I*, "To the Christian Nobility." Also, *Three Treatises*, p.16f.

University, John Witte, Jr., assesses this radical paradigm shift as bequeathing the laity with more influence in the Church. Luther's doctrine of the "priesthood of all believers" transferred the mantle of spiritual authority from the educated clergy to the humblest of Christians, who read the Bible for themselves or hear it read and acknowledge the free gift of their own salvation in Christ. At once, Luther "laicized the clergy and clericized the laity, treating the office of preaching and teaching as just one other vocation alongside many others that a conscientious Christian could properly and freely pursue."[797] This view resonated well with those eager to attack the privileged elite and endeared Luther to "*Herr Omnes*" ("Mr. Everyman"),[798] according to writer Michael Massing.*

It is instructive to recall that for about 300 years after Pentecost, relational ministry grew from small house gatherings to ordained "holy men" called "priests" who took over the duties of the believers. As I study and read the Scriptures which are the treasure of the Church, I find the early Apostles teaching Christ's commands to minister to one another through everyday relationships and gatherings for communal worship, praise, and thanksgiving. Luther's concept of every believer being a priest recovered the New Testament norm of everyone being a witness and minister. He sought to dismantle and redress the divide that for centuries had existed between the clergy and the laity. Luther sought to clarify that "there is no true, basic differences between laymen and priests, princes and bishops, between religious and secular, except for the sake of office and work, but not for the sake of status."[799] He believed clergy were different only in terms of their office or function and their work or responsibility. I am compelled to question whether we in the Church today have abandoned that hallmark which Luther restored in lifting all believers to the status of ministers in the Church, by our hiring and exalting "specialists" to do the ministry *for us*, the people of God? In my estimation, it is too much like a mirror image of leaving it to politicians to attend to the affairs of State, thinking "what can we do about it?" We often then fail to assume our responsibilities of good citizenship in speaking out, defending our rights and liberties, participating where we can, and upholding the values which have distinguished America,

---

797 Witte, Jr., John, "Freedom of a Christian: The Lutheran Reformation as Revolution;" *Journal of the Historical Society*, Issue 2, Summer 2001, pp.109-121.

798 Massing, Michael, "Luther vs. Erasmus: When Populism First Eclipsed the Liberal Elite, *The New York Review*, February 20, 2018; <https://www.nybooks.com/daily/2018/02/20/luther-vs-erasmus-when-populism-first-eclipsed-the-liberal-elite>.

* Michael Massing is a writer and former editor of the *Columbia Journalism Review*. He has written for *The American Prospect, The New York Times, The Nation, The New Yorker, The Guardian, Politico, and The Atlantic.* He is also the author of *Fatal Discord: Erasmus, Luther, and the Fight for the Western Mind* centering on the rivalry between these two men and the movements they represented—Christian humanism and evangelical Christianity.

799 LW 44:129. *The Christian in Society IV*, "To the Christian Nobility." Also *Three Treatises*, p.16.

which President Trump has sought to uphold and instill. Perhaps instead of investing money in mega buildings, could we as disciples be investing in people who multiply themselves?

It is time again for the Church to reclaim this foundational doctrine of the "Priesthood of Believers" through training, and equipping the saints to live out their calling by putting into practice what we say we believe. Jesus calls us fools if we hear His Words and do not act on them (Matthew 7:26). I believe our main purpose is to embrace the Truth of Whose we are, and to rejoice in the gift of being saved so that we may proclaim and serve our neighbor. After the writer of First Peter calls believers God's "*chosen race, a royal priesthood, a holy nation, God's own people...*" he emphatically affirms the purpose of "our" high calling: We are so privileged "*in order that [we] may proclaim the mighty acts of Him who has called [us] out of darkness into His marvelous light*" (1 Peter 2:9 [NRSV]). St. Paul continually reminds his hearers and readers to "*Love your neighbor as yourself. Loves does no wrong to a neighbor; therefore, love is the fulfilling of the Law*" (Romans 13:9f, Galatians 5:14 [NRSV]) and he doesn't allow us to forget that "we," to whom the ministry is entrusted, are to be "*ambassadors for Christ, since God is making His appeal through us...*" (2 Corinthians 5:19-20 [NRSV]) the people of God, not just through the "professional hired hands."

As we have acknowledged, the doctrine of the universal "Priesthood of All Believers" led to one of the most important by-products of The Reformation: the translations of the Bible into the various vernaculars of Europe, making the Holy Scriptures available to all. In addition, according to contemporary scholarly consensus, Luther's principle of individual conscience became the cornerstone for the evolution of the key tenets of secular democracy. As literacy increased, education and knowledge spread, and the Enlightenment followed with emerging liberation movements. Jane Caro* asks,

> After all, if every man could have their own relationship with God, why not every woman? Why not every slave? This democratization of the Word of God led inexorably to democracy itself; predicated on the idea that all men (even, perhaps, women) were created equal. Everyone ended up entitled to not just a relationship with God but with a vote and a say. One followed inevitably; I think from the other. As those in power understand only too well, once a few difficult questions began to be asked, a great many more would follow.[800]

---

* Jane Caro is an author, novelist, journalist, broadcaster, columnist and social commentator. Her most recent book is *Plain Speaking Jane* (Macmillan Australia, 2015).

[800] Caro, Jane, "The Virtual Reformation," *Kill Your Darlings*, January 16, 2017; <https://www.killyourdarlings.com.au/article/the-virtual-reformation>.

Many looked on the Reformer as their great emancipator, just as many have found in Trump a champion for devolving power from the high levels of government to "We the People." For Trump and Luther, these bold assertions were born out of the Sources, the very foundations upon which our nation and the Church emerged. These twins, each in their unique way, were affirming human dignity over and above hierarchy and bureaucracy.

These disruptors saw the administrative State or "Deep State" being blind to its faults and indifferent to its victims. Either way, such positions oppose the common good. Luther abhorred those holding positions of authority in the Church, who turned a blind eye to the corruption because they were too faint-hearted or mealy-mouthed to confront even the grossest ecclesiastical wrongdoing. In a letter to his friend George Spalatin, Luther wrote what Trump surely must think when he is censured for being critical: "I wonder where this new religion arose, in which anything said against an adversary is labeled abuse."[801]

Luther's dramatic "call for freedom—freedom of the Church from the tyranny of the Pope, freedom of the laity from the dominance of the clergy, and freedom of the conscience from the strictures of canon law and human traditions"[802]—launched the transformation of society with immense historical influence, in the view of Dr. Witte, who directs the Center for the Study of Law and Religion at Emory University. Trump offers instead a new birth of freedom for Americans, a celebration of patriotism and self-knowledge. He sees the contemporary embrace of identity politics, and one's passionate devotion to one's various subgroups, undermining patriotism as traditionally understood, and divisive for our country. Emphasizing differences which divide often minimizes that which unites. Furthermore, collective judgments are made by groups condemning other groups; and whether 500 years ago or today, fragmentation is heightened, and "individual differentiation becomes impossible. Individual human beings disappear behind uniforms foisted upon [them and they are labeled as part of a reprobate group]."[803]

Trump said, "At the bedrock of our politics will be a total allegiance to the United States of America, and through our loyalty to our country, we will rediscover our loyalty to each other."[804] For Luther, freedom is a gift of God, but it entails responsibility: "A Christian is a perfectly free lord of all, subject to none. A Christian is a perfectly dutiful servant of all,

---

[801] MacArthur, John, "Forward," *The Legacy of Martin Luther*, edited by R.C. Sproul and Stephen J. Nichols (Sanford, FL: Reformation Trust Publishing, 2016), p.2.

[802] Witte, Jr., John, "The Legacy of the Protestant Reformation in Modern Law." <https://politicaltheology.com/the-legacy-of-the-protestant-reformation-in-modern-law>.

[803] see Oberman, *Devil*, p.229.

[804] Trump, "Inauguration Speech."

subject to all."[805] For Luther, "religion" is spelled "Do!" (what we need to accomplish) and "Christianity" is spelled "Done!" (what Christ has accomplished for us). Having been gifted, we are privileged and free to serve our neighbor. In other words, we don't "*hast*" to, but we "*gits*" to be His heart, hands, and voice! Or "having been blessed, we are to be a blessing!" and thus a privileged partner in God's ongoing creative mission as He works in and through us. Working cooperatively with the Holy Spirit, we respond to what God is doing rather than what social forces are demanding us to think or do.

Both Luther and Trump express their aspiration, which Abraham Lincoln conveyed in his greatest speeches, as did Aristotle in his *Ethics* and *Politics*, when they spoke of the political friendship of fellow citizens united in mind and deed. Trump sees that vision inspiring a "totally unstoppable" America. In Luther's understanding, we serve God and our fellow human beings with self-conscious joy as we position ourselves before the Almighty in an openness to possibilities!

Trump thus presents a succinct defense of Constitutional duty for officeholders and citizens alike at his inauguration. While acknowledging that most would rather claim rights or assert their earned privileges than commit to service, Trump asked us to instead embrace the freedom and duties of patriotic American citizens, much as President Kennedy did in his inaugural address: "Ask not what your country can do for you—ask what you can do for your country."[806]

Nationalism and Patriotism

Not long ago, President Donald Trump proudly proclaimed, "I am a nationalist" and as occurs with most statements he makes or positions he takes, he was attacked by the media, politicians, and those who oppose him, often (as in this case) with little or no understanding of the origin of the word "nationalism." Nearly five hundred years ago, Martin Luther announced, "I am born for my Germans, whom I want to serve…"[807]

Complimenting Luther on his steadfastness in the face of controversy, Justus Jonas* referred to Luther as the "Prophet of the Germans," phraseology to which Melanchthon

[805] LW 31:334. *Career of the Reformer I*, "Freedom of a Christian," also *Three Treatises*, p.277.

[806] <https://www.jfklibrary.org/learn/education/teachers/curricular-resources/elementary-school-curricular-resources/ask-not-what-your-country-can-do-for-you>.

[807] LW 48:320. *Letters I*, "To Nicholas Gerbel, Wartburg, November 1, 1521 (100)," who Luther greets as "distinguished by education and Christian piety, a lawyer and my most faithful friend in Christ."

* Justus Jonas, friend, colleague, fellow theologian, and leader in Wittenberg, Germany.

would refer in his oration at Luther's funeral. Luther himself acknowledged this "title" in his "Warning to His Dear German People:"

> But since I am the *"Prophet of the Germans"*—for this haughty title I will henceforth have to assign to myself, to please and oblige my papists and asses—it is fitting that I, as a faithful teacher, warn my dear Germans against the harm and danger threatening them and impart Christian instruction to them regarding their conduct in the event that the emperor, at the instigation of his devils, the papists, issues a call to arms against the princes and cities on our side.[808]

Nationalism is one of those slippery concepts easily thrown around and manipulated, or in the words of Suzanne Fields, "pushed and pulled into all manner of shapes and colors like a child's Play-Doh, defined and distorted in the service of ideology."[809] It is a word fraught with an ambiguity that demands context. The debate today is more often over what adjective might go, or should go, in front of the word when it is used.

Nationhood is defined by common citizenship. A "civic" nation consists of all those who subscribe to its political creed regardless of race, religion, gender, or language. It is democratic, as it invests sovereignty in all of its citizens. "Ethnic" nationalism is defined by language, religion, customs and traditions, which contribute to a shared heritage. "Racial" nationalism advocates an identity based on blood or color, and seeks to preserve itself through policies such as banning race mixing and the immigration of other races. Race is not the same as ethnicity.

Loyalty and Devotion to a Nation

In the Western world, just about everyone is a nationalist in one way or another. More specifically, regardless of our ethnicity, economic status, or political or religious inclinations, we are civic nationalists—that is, people who define nationhood as a shared culture, much as we express "team spirit" or "hometown pride." This is correctly understanding the origin and meaning of the words Suzanne Fields illuminates in her article, "When Nationalism

---

[808] LW 47:29. *The Christian in Society IV*, "Luther's Warning to His Dear German People."

[809] Fields, Suzanne, "When Nationalism Is a Worthy Twin of Patriotism," *Creators Webpage*, July 7, 2017. <https://www.creators.com/read/suzanne-fields/07/17/when-nationalism-is-a-worthy-twin-of-patriotism>.

is a Worthy Twin of Patriotism."[810] It was within this very context that the President said in his address to the U.N. General Assembly (Sept. 19, 2017), "I will always put America first, just like you, as leaders of your countries will always, and should always, put your countries first."[811] That doesn't necessitate a hostile attitude toward everything foreign, nor signal a withdrawal from being a participant in the family of nations. Instead, it acknowledges a sense of belonging, allegiance, and gratitude which binds people together in a common culture and heritage. Honoring symbols of patriotism; singing "The Star-Spangled Banner;" standing for the presentation of the colors; and cheering the nation's heroes, whether soldiers, astronauts or athletes, are traditions worthy of preserving. "National consciousness does not necessarily confer on a nation a sense of superiority of their values and of its right to exercise authority over others."[812] Nor does patriotism discard the idea of "*e pluribus unum*"—"out of many, one." American nationality has long combined both "civic" and "ethnic" in its understanding of being a "melting pot." It is, then, that "nationalism" and "patriotism" enhance and complement each other as worthy twins. "Such patriotic pride, no matter who the president, forge a national identity that is always moving toward that more perfect union."[813] Influential journalist Irving Kristol, dubbed a father of neoconservatism, fused the two ideas more than three decades ago by saying, "Patriotism springs from love of the nation's past; nationalism arises out of hope for the nation's future, distinctive greatness."[814]

American patriotism is rather rooted in the nation's democratic values and ideals of America the Beautiful, the land of the free and the home of the brave. It's about the values of liberty and the rule of law, with the Bill of Rights and the Constitution as its foundation. This stands in stark contrast to a singular "ethno-" or more specifically "racial-nationalism," which was the ideology espoused by the Nazis in Germany, that focused on race (blood) rather than culture. It is a celebration of the civic, not the ethnic or racial in any superior or exclusionary way. To conflate the two as the National Socialists did in the 20th century, or as attempts are being made in the 21st century, ignores the context and discredits a historical understanding of "nationalism" for one's own ends.

---

810 Ibid.

811 <https://www.whitehouse.gov/briefings-Statements/remarks-president-trump-72nd-session-united-nations-general-assembly>.

812 Kistner, W., "The Reformation and the Roots of German Nationalism," *Theoria: A Journal of Social and Political Theory*, No. 46, 1976, p.62. <www.jstor.org/stable/41801600>.

813 Fields, "When Nationalism Is a Worthy Twin of Patriotism." <https://www.creators.com/read/suzanne-fields/07/17/when-nationalism-is-a-worthy-twin-of-patriotism>.

814 Kristol, Irving. *Reflections of a Neoconservative: Looking Back, Looking Ahead* (New York: Basic Books, Inc., 1983), p.xiii.

NATIONALISTIC PRIDE and PATRIOTIC SPIRIT

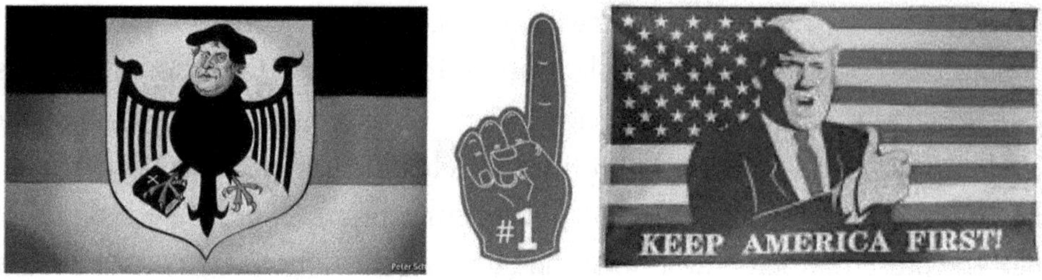

Peter Schrank Walmart.com

(Left) The caricature of Luther is superimposed on the black eagle coat of arms which is laid on the German flag, consisting of three equal horizontal bands displaying the national colors of Germany: black, red and gold.

(Center) The large foam hand with an extended index finger pointing # 1 is often worn on the hand to show support for a particular team to signify "We Are #1."

(Right) The image of Trump, overlayed on the U.S. flag with the re-election campaign logo "KEEP AMERICA FIRST" to salute and celebrate our nationhood as a shared culture, much as we express "team spirit" or "hometown pride." (Images, from left: *The Economist*; Walmart product listing)

As Oberman reminds us, "The National Socialists celebrated in Luther the national hero, but they did not create this image of him. Religious conviction and national pride had for centuries entwined themselves around his image, especially during the Bismarck era."[815] Luther's role as a symbol of national unity can be well documented by the celebrations of his 400th birthday in 1883, and the 400th anniversary of the Reformation in 1917. Yet, as Oberman admits, "there exists a national, cultural and theological exploitation of Martin Luther which consistently distorts the Reformer solely for its own purposes. In the process the man himself is lost from sight, as contemporary concerns overtake him, pass him by, and leave him far behind."[816]

Heinz Schilling underscores this intentional misrepresentation contending "Luther's pronouncement (and self-stylization as 'Prophet of the Germans') deserves our attention both for what it can tell us about the Reformer's sense of self and for the light it throws on where Luther stood within the complex events of his age; it must not be allowed to exist only as misinterpreted by nationalist perceptions of a later age...Luther's interest in Germanness was primarily cultural and not political."[817]

---

[815] Oberman, Heiko A., "The Nationalist Conscription of Martin Luther," *The Impact of the Reformation: Essays* (Grand Rapids, MI: William B. Eerdmans Publishing Company, 1994), p.71.

[816] Ibid., p.69.

[817] Schilling, *Upheaval*, p.223.

Martin Rade, prominent Marburg theologian, departed from the imperial Protestant triumphalism in 1917 by emphasizing that

> Luther's center of gravity lay not in his German manner, his German sensibility or his actions, but solely in his faith, in his Christianity. [Rade further emphatically demanded that Luther be taken for] what he intended and wanted to be; not the creator or author of a new culture—for all that he may have done for education, literature, art, science, morality, and politics. Luther was a preacher of the Word, a professor of divinity, a theologian. That is all he was—but he was that wholly and completely.[818]

For all that profundity, Oberman recognizes that "We ought not ignore the national-patriotic thrust in Luther's thought nor its influence on his conception of reform, even though these were brought into such ill repute by National Socialists."[819]

Preceding the powder keg of The Reformation, friction had been growing between the Church, the Emperor, and the German States. Grievances were mounting against the abuses of the Church and the expansion of the Emperor's power, thus creating political and fiscal complaints on both fronts. Called the "*Gravamina nationis Germanicae*" or "*Gravamina*," these growing "grievances" of the Holy Roman Empire and its Church against the Pope and Curia helped foster a sense of Germanic identity and, in the words of Joachim Whaley, "helped to generate a growing perception of crisis"[820] which Luther was quick to capitalize on to help launch his program of religious reform.

Growing awareness of people belonging together as a nation was also heightened by a younger generation of humanists at the beginning of the 16th century. As a result of insights gained in their studies of classical literature and love for antiquity, they wanted to bring about changes in Church and society. Thus, even before the publication of Luther's 95 Theses, this awareness of national identity and unity of the German people transcended their tribal differences. But the German humanists influenced primarily the intellectual classes. They had not managed to bridge the class differences and bring their message to the peasants

---

818 Rade, Martin, quoted in Heiko A. Oberman's "The Nationalist Conscription of Martin Luther," in *The Impact of the Reformation: Essays*, (each authored by Oberman), (Grand Rapids, MI: Eerdmans Publishing, 1994); p.71.
819 Ibid., p.70.
820 Whaley, Joachim, *Germany and the Holy Roman Empire, Vol. One: From Maximilian I to the Peace of Westphalia, 1493-1648* (Oxford: Oxford University Press, 2012), p.87.

and the underprivileged groups in the cities. It was at this point that the contributions of Luther to German national consciousness and to the German humanist movement took place. He used and shaped the German language, as we have witnessed, in such a way that it was understandable not only to people of different German tribal traditions and dialects but also to people of all classes and of all education levels.

Central to Luther's theological understanding was

> the role in God's plan for salvation assigned in Scripture to the people. For Luther those "people" were not Germans in a "nationalist" sense, but the people of God, and more specifically in his case those to whom he had been called to bring the unadulterated Word of God. For German people to understand the message sent to them by God, it would have to be communicated to them in a language they could understand. Here, then is the real context for the statement, "I am born for my Germans."[821]

Thus, Luther announced that the texts he had been working on at the Wartburg, where he was a "guest" after his staged kidnapping, would be printed *omnia vernacula*, "all in German," in the language of the people, not in Latin. About a month later, he had decided to translate the Bible into German, crafting a version of the language for everyday worshippers and that everyone could understand. This became the best-known fruit of Luther's concern for getting God's Word into the hands of "his Germans." Nor can we overestimate the significant effect of Luther writing for the "laity" in de-mystifying the religious, political and economic systems that controlled the people.[822]

---

[821] Schilling, *Upheaval*, pp.223-4.

[822] See Vitor Westhelle's "Communication and the Transgression of Language in Martin Luther" in *The Pastoral Luther: Essays on Martin Luther's Practical Theology*, ed. Timothy J. Wengert (Grand Rapids: Eerdmans, 2009), pp.59-81, here specifically p.64.

24

Circumventing the Gatekeepers of Information

Luther's pamphlets and illustrated broadsheets were cheaply produced in great numbers on the printing press and easy to understand. Convinced his prophetic call was to re-establish the pure Gospel, he believed he was then compelled to spread God's Word amongst humankind. To effectively proclaim such "Good News," he intuitively recognized he had to focus on the people's language they could read and understand. So, Luther took pains to make the Biblical message relevant to the people of his day, especially to simple people. According to the English historian A.G. Dickens, in his *The German Nation and Martin Luther*, Luther's criterion for correct interpretation is evident from the following statement he made:

> We do not have to inquire of the literal Latin, how we are to speak German, as these asses do. Rather we must inquire about this of the mother in the home, the children on the street, the common man in the marketplace. We must be guided by their language, the way they speak, and do our translating accordingly,[823] [or as gets translated by A. G. Dickens,] "look them in the mouth to see how they speak, and afterwards do our translating."[824]

In understanding Luther's legacy, we need to remind ourselves that The Reformation of the sixteenth century was initially and primarily a German event. Capable of relating closely to his people, Luther succeeded in channeling their bitterness of being oppressed by foreign tyranny to inspiring aspirations for their unity and betterment. While the Pope was the enemy and symbol of oppression to Germany, Luther became viewed as a symbol of German pride and a fighter for those whose voices were not being heard and "the model of a man for Germany and described with exaltation, 'every inch of you is a German man.'"[825]

---

[823] LW 35:189. *Word and Sacrament I*, "On Translating: An Open Letter to Wenceslaus Link."

[824] Dickens, A. G., *The German Nation and Martin Luther* (London: Edward Arnold, 1974), p.56.

[825] Castro, William, "Luther and German Nationalism," *Reformation 21, Alliance of Confessing Evangelicals*, November. 29, 2017, <http://www.reformation21.org/blog/2017/11/luther-and-german-nationalism.php>.

Luther had won the support of the people by presenting a laundry list of social and economic reforms that he thought Germany needed in his most direct and seminal political writing, "To the Christian Nobility of the German Nation." There he discusses many of the grievances raised in the *Gravamina*, including the infamous financial abuses and the high "taxes" paid to the Pope by the German estates. Much like President Trump refers to the U.S. being a "piggy bank" paying disproportionately for the operations and protection of NATO member nations, or bearing the cost of unfair agreements with our trade partners, Luther felt Germany was being gouged unfairly. He dramatically portrays Germany being ruined by a morally bankrupt Italy, destroyed by the pride of a corrupt Roman Church: "Now that Italy is sucked dry, they come into Germany and begin oh, so gently. But let us beware, or Germany will soon become like Italy."[826] President Trump points not only to a once-wealthy Venezuela which is now collapsing, but to Cuba and other countries as failed states, which to their ruin, pushed socialism not unlike that which several candidates desiring to succeed him were advocating. Luther further laments,

> I believe that Germany now gives much more to the Pope at Rome than it used to give to the emperors in ancient times...and people are impoverished! We should rather wonder that we still have anything to eat!....They think that those half-witted Germans will always be gullible, stupid fools, and will just keep handing over money to them to satisfy their unspeakable greed.[827]

I hear much of Luther in President Trump's "America First" theme and his concern about other nations taking advantage of America's generosity because "our leaders and officials have been stupid and incompetent and are terrible negotiators."[828] He also decries politicians willing to provide healthcare for undocumented immigrants who illegally enter the country when many of our veterans are still among our homeless citizens living in the street encampments of our cities, and when many other Americans are without or are struggling to pay their own healthcare bills.

---

[826] LW 44:141. *The Christian in Society I*, "To the Christian Nobility, or Three Theses," p.28.

[827] Ibid., LW 44:143–144 or Three Treatises, 30, 32–32.

[828] Nexon, Daniel, "Mind the Power Gap," *The Duck of Minerva* (website), January 31, 2017, quoting Donald Trump on NATO and NAFTA agreements. <https://duckofminerva.com/2017/01>.

One cannot claim lack of compassion when it comes to immigrants, as America legally admits over a million people a year according to the Migration Policy Institute.[829] Our country's foreign aid totaled $49 billion in 2016 and $50 billion in 2017, according to the Council on Foreign Relations,[830] plus Americans privately contributed $410 billion to charity in 2017.[831] This does not include the cost of services (education, healthcare, housing, Supplemental Nutrition Assistance Program ["food stamps"], Medicare, Supplemental Security Income and social and security services, etc.) provided by our cities, states and federal government to those who enter the country illegally. The FAIR* study in 2017 found illegal immigrants are a net consumer of taxpayer benefits worth more than $100 billion a year, not including the cost of enforcing the border. "The payout for the taxpayer is enormous and income to the Treasury is minuscule," according to Dan Stein, Director of the Federation for American Immigration Reform.[832] According to the American Retirement Insider, which tracks the cost of illegal immigrants, the amount to the Treasury is actually $135 billion per year and steadily rising, while the Federation for American Immigration Reform reports they paid only $19 billion in taxes[833] and contribute only an estimated $11.74 billion to state and local economies[834] because a large portion of their paychecks is sent back to Mexico for their families.

> The German estates' conflict with the Emperor was based mostly on the issues of the Emperor's right to tax and to raise an imperial army (and the discussion of whether the Reich should finance a standing army).[835] "Finding revenue to finance the war against the Turks became an increasingly futile endeavor for the Hapsburg emperors; as the Turkish threat became more dire…. The Reichstag rejected requests three different times…claiming that

---

829 <https://www.migrationpolicy.org/programs/data-hub/charts/Annual-Number-of-US-Legal-Permanent-Residents>.

830 <https://www.cfr.org/backgrounder/how-does-us-spend-its-foreign-aid>.

831 <https://givingusa.org/giving-usa-2018-americans-gave-410-02-billion-to-charity-in-2017-crossing-the-400-billion-mark-for-the-first-time>.

* Federation for American Immigration Reform (FAIR) study.

832 <https://www.foxnews.com/us/the-cost-of-illegal-immigration-migrants-cost-us-taxpayers-billions-a-year>.

833 <https://americanretirementinsider.com/the-cost-of-illegal-immigration>.

834 <https://immigrationforum.org/article/fact-sheet-immigrants-and-public-benefits>.

835 Whaley, *Germany and the Holy Roman Empire*, p.73.

> they could not provide funds for the Emperor until the grievances found in the *Gravamina* have been redressed."[836]

Shutting down a portion of the government, and finding an impasse between Congress and the President with finances and politics, may not be quite as distinct and unique as we moderns may have thought when issues divide and compromise cannot be reached.

Other concerns centered on the increase of French and Spanish in the Curia at the expense of German representatives, and the right of the Pope to rule both temporally and spiritually. This struck a chord with many secular leaders within Germany as "rulers everywhere resented papal claims to temporal power and Italian meddling in their internal affairs."[837] It is not difficult to perceive how these sentiments, particularly the portrayal of Italy and the papacy as enemies of Germany, would lay behind the strong secular and local political support given to the forces of Luther and his reforms[838] as well as a call to patriotic duty of all Germans.

Adding to the dynamics, Luther was demanding that "those who have the appropriate power, i.e. Christian authorities [princes, dukes, even the Emperor] must call to account a clergy and hierarchy which is no longer fulfilling its responsibilities and must take the reform of the Church into their own hands."[839] Arguing that "the ruling princes had a right and a Christian duty to exercise supervisory powers over the State" gave aspiring princes "the opportunity to realize fifteenth-century ambitions to assert secular power over ecclesiastical power."[840] Where ruling princes acted as the highest clerical authority in their realm, it was called "*summus episcopus*," and effectively created a form of State Church governed by secular leaders exercising the powers of an "emergency bishop," as Luther called them.[841]

Hitler and the Nazis bolstered their ethno-nationalistic ideology and assault on the Jewish race by exalting Luther as a German hero who centuries earlier expressed a national consciousness and concern for his countrymen. Many Protestants felt attracted to Hitler and

---

[836] Ibid.

[837] Ozment, *Reform*, p.205.

[838] Ibid.

[839] Brecht, Martin, *Martin Luther and His Road to Reformation*, trans. James L. Schaaf (Minneapolis: Fortress Press, 1985), p.372.

[840] Whaley, *Germany and the Holy Roman Empire*, pp.262, 268.

[841] Ibid., p.268.

the Nazis because, in their estimation, it meant the defense of Christian values that were in danger under atheistic and communist thought. After all,

> Hitler promised that the church would enjoy the "committed protection" of his nationalistic government. He even called the Church "the basis of our entirely morality." He called on Protestants and Catholics together to defend and work for the resurgence and German renaissance in an uncompromising manner, a nationalized Christianity that would stand up for Germany first.[842]

To this appeal, Eric W. Gritsch, Professor of Church History at Lutheran Theological Seminary in Gettysburg, Pennsylvania, notes how "the National Socialists used Luther to support their racist anti-Semitism, calling him a genuine German who had hated non-Nordic races."[843]

As the most pre-eminent Luther scholar and biographer, Heiko Oberman has asserted:

> Luther considered himself a German; and the German patriotic movement, which was just then beginning to move beyond mere protests against Roman influence and papal exploitation, bid with high hopes for his favor. Indeed, the sixteenth century saw the first signs of a national consciousness, [and] the connection between the Reformation and national consciousness may not be overlooked.[844]

Without the recent invention of the printing press some 40 years before his birth, Martin Luther might be remembered only as a footnote to history: an academic monk who posted scholarly critiques of the Catholic Church's indulgence push. Or maybe worse, happily consigned by the Church to a heretic's fiery death at the stake as Jan Hus and others had been.

Gutenberg devised a machine that could produce identical documents quickly and cheaply using movable metal letters and oil-based ink, creating a new information medium. Steve Jobs created a new information medium through the "smartphone," permitting direct connectivity and thereby vaporizing the traditional political protocols and gatekeepers of our information flow. Both inventions sparked a transformative communications revolution,

---

842 Castro, "Luther and German Nationalism."

843 Gritsch, Eric W., "Was Luther Anti-Semitic?" *Christian History*, Issue 39. <https://www.christianitytoday.com/history/issues/issue-39/was-luther-anti-semitic.html>.

844 Oberman, *Impact*, p.70.

resulting in a seismic change that has shaken the institutions of culture and society to the ground in both the sixteenth and twenty-first centuries.

The tremors we are experiencing with the rise of the high-tech giants reflect the upheaval Luther's use of the printing press created in exposing and threatening the powerful "Big Church" dominance in controlling information which was reinforced with its presumed divine association. Donald Trump has threatened and exposed "Big Media," propped up by "Big Tech" overlords Google, Facebook and Twitter. These high-tech companies have the ability to harvest data and control the flow of information; and by sharing "signals," present a coordinated effort in determining what their users can view while suppressing alternative, especially conservative, points of view.[845] Being adherents of a single political agenda, these Orwellian tech "overlords" label divergent views as bigotry or "misinformation," even censoring President Trump's tweets. As Matthew Schmitz put in the *New York Post*, "The tech giants further enjoy being cloaked from public view and resistant to political scrutiny."[846]

There is much romance and legend surrounding the posting of the Ninety-Five Theses, which is celebrated as igniting The Reformation. Whether Luther actually nailed the Theses on the cathedral doors, which served as the university bulletin board, has been doubted by most Luther scholars. The Theses were not a list of non-negotiable demands for Church reform in accordance with Brother Martin's standards, as is often imagined. Written in Latin, the language of scholarship, they were points intended for a university audience of theologians, to be thrashed out in public disputation within academia and the Church. Luther himself wrote in a letter to Pope Leo dated May 30, 1518, that he "published some propositions for debate, inviting only the more learned to discuss them with me, as ought to be plain to my opponents from the preface to my Theses."[847] The Theses were most probably wheat-pasted to the door by perhaps a student or "the church custodian who was typically responsible for posting important notices,"[848] rather than by an angry monk armed with a hammer. Bobbi Dykema notes that "More recently, a handwritten note by Luther's secretary, Georg Rorer, found in the university library at Jena, indicates that the Ninety-Five Theses

---

[845] <https://www.politico.com/news/2020/11/17/facebook-twitter-senate-tech-hearing-436975>; Facebook CEO Mark Zuckerberg and Twitter chief executive Jack Dorsey grilled by lawmakers 11/17/20.

[846] Schmitz, Matthew, "Big Tech's Speech-Squelching More Dangerous Than Government Censorship." <https://nypost.com/2020/10/20/big-tech-speech-squelching-more-dangerous-than-government-censorship>.

[847] <http://beggarsallreformation.blogspot.com/2011/10/95-theses-nailed-to-church-door-or.html>.

[848] Metaxas, *Rediscovered*, p.108.

may indeed have been posted on the door of the Schlosskirche."[849] Whatever the case, the posting would have been fairly routine in Luther's day. Martin Marty interestingly observes that "theses of this sort were unfinished products, designed to provoke debate. Luther asked for and scheduled an academic disputation. Not a single person showed up for it."[850]

Having greater impact were letters and copies of the Theses Luther sent to his ecclesiastical superiors, the Bishop of Brandenburg, Jerome Schulze, and Archbishop Albrecht of Magdeburg/Mainz, who in turn forwarded the Theses to the Pope in Rome. Others copied—even translated—the Theses and had them printed in major cities. What was initially intended for academic dispute instead burst onto the public square. His Theses weren't merely debated in the offices of the Church and in cloisters, they were being discussed on the streets and inside homes. According to Luther's friend, Friedrich Myconius, "hardly fourteen days had passed when these propositions were known throughout Germany and within four weeks almost all of Christendom was familiar with them."[851]

Texts That Fly

While Luther had a notoriously ambivalent attitude toward the still new technology of printing, he was so overcome with the surprising result that his propositions "are printed and circulated far beyond my expectation,"[852] that he readily embraced its ability and began blogging, or should we say "pamphleteering." Acknowledging the unexpected potential of this new medium and grasping the dynamics of how quickly this new medium carried his new anti-establishment message across Germany, he admitted that he "should have spoken far differently and more distinctly had [he] known what was going to happen."[853] The rapid

---

849 Dykema, Bobbi, "Reading Visual Rhetoric: Strategies of Piety and Propaganda in Lucas Cranach the Elder's *Passional Christi und Antichristi*," referencing Martin Treu's "Der Thesenanchlag fan wirklich statt: Ein neuer Beleg aus der Univesitatsbibliothek, Jena," *Luther*, 78:3, 2007, pp.117-118; and others, including Volker Leppin in *Luther*, 78:3, 2017, pp.145-150. <https://www.academia.edu/9540838/_Reading_Visual_Rhetoric_Strategies_of_Piety_and_Propaganda_in_Lucas_Cranach_the_Elders_Passional_Christi_und_Antichristi_>.

850 Marty, M.E., *Martin Luther: A Life* (New York: Penguin, 2008), p.33.

851 Standage, Tom, "How Luther Went Viral, Social Media in the 16th Century," *The Economist*. <www.Economist.com/node/21541719>.

852 George, Timothy, "The Typographical Reformation," *First Things*. <https://www.firstthings.com/web-exclusives/2017/02/the-typographical-reformation>.

853 *The Economist*, January 16, 2017, <https://medium.economist.com/how-the-16th-century-invented-social-media-a132128d715c>.

spread of the Ninety-Five Theses was the first-ever example of a piece of writing "going viral." It alerted Luther to what modern media theorists refer to as a "networked public," the passing of information from one person to another, in contrast to an "audience" just consuming the information.[854]

Following a stern rebuke from the Catholic establishment, Luther, in a masterstroke of resistance, published a simplified, non-academic pamphlet in the 1517 language of the people instead of the language of the Church leaders, thereby widening his readership. This pamphlet, "Sermon on Indulgences and Grace," also went "viral" and spread far more quickly and widely than the Ninety-Five Theses. Luther, who loved to preach, and was himself a professor, knew that sermons tend to be more powerful than academic papers! (Maybe that's the reason I'm getting some preachin' in with this publication!) While it would be considered slow by today's standards, the printed sermon was, nevertheless, the equivalent of a blog or tweet going viral within a few hours or less. It was the impact this proclamation had that makes some historians consider its publication to be the actual start of the Reformation, rather than the posting of the Ninety-Five Theses.

Luther and his followers used the emerging print technology to distribute flyers, broadsheets, and the new literary genre known as pamphlets or "*Flugschriften*" to quickly reach the people, spread Luther's ideas, and foment a widespread uprising against the distant, out-of-touch taskmasters of the elite establishment, thus making him an enemy of the hierarchy within the Church. "*Flugschriften*" is the German word for such pamphlets, and that word captures the new reality Luther was creating, in that "*flugschrift*" technically translates as a "text that flies."[855] His writings had accumulated a surprising amount of frequent flyer miles!

Soon the Holy Roman Empire was awash with millions of single-page tracts, flyers, posters and pamphlets. The vast bulk of these printed instruments portrayed the Church as a corrupt institution that oppressed the consciences of the laity, even as it emptied their pockets. David Bagchi, who specializes in the history and thought of The Reformation, cites as examples

---

[854] *The Economist*, December 17, 2011, <https://www.economist.com/christmas-specials/2011/12/17/how-luther-went-viral>.

[855] Martin, John Jeffries, "Why Martin Luther Was an Early Media Revolutionary," *Duke Today, University Communications*, October 30, 2017; <https://today.duke.edu/2017/10/why-martin-luther-was-early-media-revolutionary#>.

> Monks and friars [being] excoriated for their hypocrisy in professing poverty while amassing great wealth. Similarly, they portrayed the Pope, while arrogating to himself the title of Vicar of Christ, as preferring the pomp and circumstance of his court to the hard life of the first disciples and of their Master. They (the leaflets and hand bills) claimed that the straightforward message of the Gospel had been distorted and displaced by human inventions—canon law, scholastic theology, the cult of the saints, masses for the dead—and that the Italian-led Church had for too long exploited the proverbial slow-wittedness of the Teutons. But at last, they proclaimed, even the Germans were waking up to their misfortune.[856]

The First Modern Media Star and The Tweeter-in-Chief

Andrew Pettegree, author of "Brand Luther," makes the claim that the Wittenberg professor's prodigious, instinctive, and towering writing talent, along with his commercial acumen, ensured that "print and public communication would never be the same again. It was an extraordinary legacy for an extraordinary man."[857] Without what is considered one of the most ingenious inventions of all time, Luther would not have been able to effectively indulge in the fast-paced polemics of The Reformation. Publishing single-page tracts and short theater-playbill-sized pamphlets contributed immensely to the essential dissemination of his message. Not only did they take little time to produce, but they were also cheap and relatively easy to conceal from authorities, especially after the papal edict forbidding possession of "heretical" material. In the exhibition "From Luther to Twitter," Berlin's Deutsches Historisches Museum explored the connection between media and politics, from the printing press to social media. It described the Protestant Reformation as "the first major media event in European history" and Luther "as the first modern media star"[858] or celebrity whose face was the most recognized man in Europe. As he traveled, people would flock to the high road to see his cart go by, much like how people line the highway and streets when President Trump's motorcade passes by.

---

[856] Bagchi, David, "Printing, Propaganda, and Public Opinion in the Age of Martin Luther," *Oxford Research Encyclopedia*, August 31, 2016; <http://religion.oxfordre.com/view/10.1093/acrefore/9780199340378.001.0001/acrefore-9780199340378-e-269>.

[857] Pettegree, *Brand Luther*, p.338.

[858] Grenier, Elizabeth, "What Trump and Luther Have in Common," *DW*, September 10, 2020; <https://www.dw.com/en/what-donald-trump-and-reformer-martin-luther-have-in-common/a-54876691>.

These printed writings and sermons spread among the laity of Luther's day as prolifically as Trump's tweets have on the ecosystem of blogs, social networks, and discussion threads. Sending out short repartees that respond immediately to their opponents and detractors, and making commentary on developing stories, events and issues, were the pamphlets' and broadsheets' role, and served the information flow just as the 280-character messages broadcast Trump's thoughts in this digital age. Both warriors refused to let any challenge go unanswered, giving as good (and more often far better) than they got!

These pamphlets, which could be considered the precursor to the modern paperback, easily remind us in both their content and tone of the internet age. These affordable little tracts in the vernacular were eagerly torn from the hands of traveling news sellers outside churches and in the marketplace. Opponents of The Reformation lamented the potency of cheap print for propaganda and agitation among the people, and did their best to counter the evangelical writers by launching their own literary campaigns. But as Tom Standage notes, these pamphlets "posed a dilemma for the Church which was initially reluctant to respond with pamphlets of its own, because doing so would be an admission that theological matters were open to debate."[859]

By refuting what Luther wrote, the Roman propagandists had to explain what Luther wrote, thereby exposing more people to Luther's views. Catholic counterattacks in pamphlet form piqued the interests of readers, who then went on to read Luther's pamphlets. As Mark U. Edwards astutely observes, "Catholic counterattack necessarily helped propagate the very message it wished to expunge."[860]

Rome had tried many tactics to squash Luther's voice and put out the flames of open revolt against Rome's authority. For example, representatives of Rome claimed that Luther was conceived when the devil raped his mother in an outhouse.[861] Their smear campaign against the German monk reflected a crude political campaign more than a theological debate. Its classic form of "name and shame" is mimicked by Trump's opponents as they level charges of being "racist" to cower and intimidate the President's supporters.

While we are familiar with President Trump's persistent "tweets" which circumvent the press and media outlets, and bypass the political gatekeepers, Luther and his followers used

---

859 Standage, Tom, "Martin Luther and the Viral Superstars," *Foreign Policy*, November 1, 2013. <https://foreignpolicy.com/2013/11/01/martin-luther-and-the-viral-superstars>.

860 Edwards, Jr., Mark U., *Printing, Propaganda, and Martin Luther* (Berkeley: University of California Press, 1994), p.58.

861 Acocella, Joan, "How Martin Luther Changed the World," *The New Yorker Magazine*, October 30, 2017. See also <https://honorshame.com/reeformation-3-honor-shame-facts>.

the new media of their day, the printing press, to do an end run around the cultural elites who formed the previously impenetrable wall of ecclesiastical power. Knowledge had long been controlled by educated scholars, most of whom were priests of the Catholic Church, who were the sole conduit of information because they could read the Bible and religious texts written in Latin, which the vast populace did not understand. Furthermore,

> One of the tenets of the Catholic Church was that "ordinary" people should neither read the Word of God nor pray to God directly. Their only contact with their Maker had to be through [an intermediary] a man of God: a priest. Everything else was heresy. In this way the priests and the Church controlled virtually all information for centuries. And through controlling information, of course they also controlled the population.[862]

The election of 2016 was the first to be truly dominated by mobile communication and the social networking it sparks. For Trump, it was his mastery of the emerging radical new communication platforms known as social media which has drastically changed the way people communicate, helping him challenge an out-of-touch elite media that had succeeded in controlling what was to be consumed by the public. Tweets from the President of the United States spread virally, thus making it impossible to suppress. New forms of communication have a way of challenging traditional forms of intellectual authority. Both the printing press and the social media have spurred the democratization of thought, and the result in both ages has proved to be messy, often making discourse downright uncivil. David Gibson, an award-winning journalist, author, filmmaker, and national reporter for Religion News Service (RNS), claims that Luther's use of the printing press was "as big a shift as the 1,500 years before Luther from scrolls to the bound codex, and it changed the Western world religiously, politically, and culturally."[863] There is little doubt we are currently in the midst of a dramatic shift, proving to be ever as impactful upon our culture and society as the printing press proved to be more than half a millennium ago.

Not always recognized was the threat Luther's "mass communication" posed to the Catholic Church's zealous domination over the spread of information in Europe. We are still grappling with and assessing the effect of Trump's "tweets" on those who have had the

---

862 Caro, Jane, "Virtual Reformation."

863 Gibson, David, "Martin Luther as History's First Tweeter? An Ongoing legacy, 500 Years Later," *Religious News Service*; October 7, 2016. <https://religionnews.com/2016/10/07/martin-luther-as-historys-first-tweeter-an-ongoing-legacy-500-years-later>.

ability to control the flow of information, and how the President leverages his attack on "Fake News" and his claims of unfavorable coverage on his administration by the "corrupt" mainstream media. What is certain is that change is the new normal.

In our day, we marvel at the new technology which has emerged, allowing people to spread information to massive groups of people faster than ever before. While this age of "social media" is used to promote new ways of thinking and believing, it also can be used to incite fear and anger, amplify a cause, or promote false and misleading information as well as propaganda. This is an apt description of how the printing press was also used during the years of the Reformation by those who attacked as well as by those who defended the Pope. Ironically, it was on a Gutenberg press that indulgence certificates were also printed.

The popularity of Luther's ideas and his theological concepts was certainly advanced through one of the most masterful media campaigns in history, through a movement 500 years ago that changed the course of history in Europe and the world. The Reformation's utilization and dependence on published materials and their popularity also had the positive benefit of encouraging literacy, which swelled the number of Europeans who could read and write.

The Economist republished an article from the 2011 Christmas double issue for its January 16, 2017, publication to highlight how 500 years ago, social media helped bring about the Reformation by shaping and coordinating public opinion. Both Luther and Trump had quickly grasped the dynamics of a new media environment, and both were equally eager to issue "new posts" to spread their messages to their followers:

> Luther would pass the text of a new pamphlet to a friendly printer (no money changed hands and Luther did not receive a penny for his writings during his career) and then wait for it to ripple through the network of printing centers across Germany.... As with "likes" and "retweets" today, the number of reprints indicated the popularity of an item. Luther's pamphlets were the most sought after.[864]

Propagandists from both the Church and the reform movement published documents about Church doctrine to either retain their believers or influence new believers. They became effective and powerful means to educate, entertain, and sway the emotions of the readers or those who heard them read.

---

864 "How the 16th Century Invented Social Media," *The Economist*, January 16, 2017. <https://medium.economist.com/how-the-16th-century-invented-social-media-a132128d715c>.

This technological advance of the printing press, with its ability to mass-produce literature, coincided with a "perfect storm" that had been gathering, which we have noted. "The message of the Lutheran Reformation," observes David Bagchi, "with its emphasis on the proclamation of God's Word to all seemed to occur perfectly with the emergence of a new medium that could, for the first time, transmit that Word to all."[865]

Trump, like candidates before him, used the print media effectively with his *Trump: The Art of the Deal* and *Time to Get Tough* for the 2012 presidential election, and his 2015 release of *Crippled America* which outlined his 2016 political agenda to "Make America Great Again." He so effectively promoted his views on the emerging communication platforms, and so skillfully manipulated the media narrative surrounding his campaign, that mainstream news coverage negated the need for him to fund conventional advertising against his opponent. Commentators have noted that Trump's Twitter account is an incredibly successful tool, with one stating simply, "Donald Trump's Twitter feed is pure magic."[866]

His tweets became the broadsheets or flyers of the digital age, allowing him to interact directly with the voters of America. Like Luther, Trump employs colloquial language with little regard for political correctness, and at times speaks to shock and delights in the outrageous.[867] We witness the insurgent natures of Trump and Luther clearly expressed and even exacerbated through their reflexive adversarial opposition to being forever under siege.

In her biography* of her husband Frank, who revolutionized the chicken industry, Mitzi Perdue gives the descriptive tagline, "It takes a tough man to make a tender chicken." Could it be that throughout history there are those times when individuals who are disliked and who seemingly demonstrate traits viewed as unpolite, undignified, and "un-presidential," and whose impulsive, volcanic eruptions exhibit the very personality "defects" that are the cause of the achievements made? New York writer and author of *Fatal Discord: Erasmus, Luther, and the Fight for the Western Mind,* Michael Massing, seems to acknowledge that possibility by pointing to our twins having those attributes that have helped them cut through the façade of self-serving political and religious hypocrisy. "Trump's insults, invective, and mocking tweets against enemies real and perceived seem a long way from the Sermon on

---

[865] Bagchi, David, "Printing, Propaganda, and Public Opinion in the Age of Martin Luther."

[866] Becker, Kyle, "Donald Trump's Twitter Game Is Pure Magic Right Now," *Independent Journal Review,* 2016. <http://ijr.com/2016/01/524690-donald-trumps-twitter-timeline-is-pure-magic-right-now>.

[867] Pettegree, *Brand Luther,* p.4.

* Mitzi Perdue wrote *Tough Man, Tender Chicken: Business & Life Lessons* (R.J. Myers Publishing, 2015).

the Mount, but they very much mirror the pugnacity, asperity, and inflammatory language of the First Protestant."[868]

It's Not Always Nice to Be Nice

The swamp is a tough place, and as Luther discovered with Rome, Trump recognized that you can't change Washington by being Mr. Nice Guy, withholding punches, or issuing carefully constructed statements, instead of his 2:00 a.m. tweets to which the media often overreacts by casting additional light on a subject that the President has exposed. Within the two kingdoms, as we have previously noted, there are different roles and expectations assigned to civil authorities than to those directed specifically to family and Church in the spiritual realm. It's not always nice to be nice. At times, being aggressive and forceful is necessary for the common good; or in Mitzi Perdue's words, "It takes a tough man to make a tender chicken."[869]

While technology has the ability to bring forth more truth, some adopt or misuse its ability by distorting, editing, or intentionally distributing false propaganda. This has always been the promise and pitfall of technology, seen in both the printing press of Luther's time and the social media innovations of today. In Professor Robert Kolb's estimation,

> Luther recognized both the promise and the ambiguity of new technology and new modes of communication. In a world in which God's material blessings flow richly with gifts that can aid our thinking and our communicating, new modes of communicating can also be hijacked by Satan. Further complicating matters, disciplines always carry ideological baggage and need Christ critique. In such a world, Luther's ability to marshal technology as well as an array of colleagues and their teaching across the spectrum of the curriculum of the time should serve as a model for us.[870]

---

[868] Massing, Michael, "How Martin Luther Paved the Way for Donald Trump." *The Nation*, April 19, 2018. <https://www.thenation.com/article/archive/how-martin-luther-paved-the-way-for-donald-trump/>.

[869] <https://www.skipprichard.com/tough-man-tender-chicken-lessons-from-frank-perdue/>; <https://www.amazon.com/Tough-Man-Tender-Chicken-Business/dp/0990757412>.

[870] Kolb, Robert, "Luther's Truths, Then and Now," address at the International Conference on Confessional Leadership in the 21st Century, Wittenberg, Germany, 2015. <https://reformation500.csl.edu/2015/05/06/luthers-truths-then-and-now>.

The social media, including the internet and Trump's tweeting, is as revolutionary as the printing press was for Luther, and has had an enormous effect on today's information gatekeepers. While for Luther the "gatekeeper" was the Church, in our day it has been the medium called "the news," with traditional journalists at newspapers and magazines, wire services and major TV networks, which held a monopoly on what was and was not reported. With the internet, that medium has been in a precipitous decline, especially as journalists have often belied their claim of professionalism through obvious gross bias in reporting. They have increasingly violated the principles of journalism whose first obligation is to the truth, followed by allegiance and loyalty to its citizens, and then exercising the professional discipline of verification while maintaining a stance of independence from those they cover.[871]

In a 2020 Gallup poll, distrust in the media hit a new high as it continues to rapidly decline. Gallup first asked this question in 1972 when trust ranged between 68% to 72% in the 1970s.

> At a time when Americans are relying heavily on the media for information about the coronavirus pandemic, the presidential election and other momentous events, the public remains largely distrustful of the mass media. Four in 10 U.S. adults say they have "a great deal" (9%) or "a fair amount" (31%) of trust and confidence in the media to report the news "fully, accurately, and fairly," while 6 in 10 have "not very much trust" (27%) or "none at all" (33%)."...Recent Gallup/Knight Foundation polling has shown that although Americans increasingly see bias in news coverage, they nonetheless believe that an independent media is key to democracy.[872]

From his civic pulpit, Trump has continually shamed and challenged "Fake News" that doesn't report favorable news about his administration, but rather chooses to distort or withhold "The Rest of the Story" to denigrate the President while supporting and advancing their biased agenda. Jane Caro views the internet at least as revolutionary as the printing press, and we have certainly witnessed its effect on yesterday's information gatekeepers:

---

871 "Principles of Journalism," *American Press Association.* <americanpressassociation.com/principles-of-journalism>.

872 Brenan, Megan, "Americans Remain Distrustful of Mass Media," *Gallup,* September 30, 2020. <https://news.gallup.com/poll/321116/americans-remain-distrustful-mass-media.aspx>.

The mainstream media, particularly newspaper proprietors—the high priests who used to set the daily political agenda—big business, banks, retailers, and governments are all feeling the loss of control. Many are thrashing about in protest, trying to hold onto a power that they once acquired so effortlessly that they may have begun to see it as a divine right. Now that everyone with a "smart device" has access to the numerous outlets as well as the ability to create content themselves, things that used to be kept quiet are getting [leaked] out; everyone can have a direct relationship with what used to be privileged information.[873]

873 Caro, "The Virtual Reformation."

25

Assessing Criticism as a Badge of Merit

Many of Luther's public statements made from the pulpit or in his writings were under attack not only by his opponents within the Catholic Church but also by colleagues who were initially within the Reformation movement and thus allies. Like Trump who takes on his opponents on the "other side of the aisle," as well as "never-Trumpers" or "RINOs" (Republicans In Name Only) within the Republican Party, and especially the "Fake News" media, Luther was not averse to calling out those with whom he disagreed. "With evident pride in his success as an author he put in their place "'those clever clogs…who wanted to tell me how I should write'…and he would most like to stop his ears against 'those blind, ungrateful creatures who seek nothing in me but causes of offense.'"[874]

Our rebel warrior, Luther, easily acknowledged the consternation he stirred continuously, by writing,

> Oh, well, if I were not used to being judged and condemned, I might become excited; but nothing makes me prouder than when my work and teaching suffers reverses and is crucified. No one is satisfied unless he can condemn Luther. Luther is the target of opposition. Everyone has to win his spurs against him and carry off the honors of the tournament. In these matters everyone else has a higher spirit than I, and I must be altogether fleshly. Would to God that they had a higher spirit! …for I have not as yet seen them undertake very much that does not bring them to sin and shame.[875]

Could it be that our President, taking yet another page out of Luther's playbook, has fashioned his own Trumpian understanding and style of speech after his "ancestral" twin?

President Trump could not only empathize with Luther but has expressed pretty much the same opinions about the coverage he is subjected to by the media, his opponents and his

---

874 Schilling, *Upheaval*, pp.263-4, quoting WR 17:1.

875 LW 46:63-4. *The Christian in Society III*, "An Open Letter on the Harsh Book against the Peasants."

detractors, and does so in his Trumpian style that is so reflective of Luther. In an interview with George Stephanopoulos on ABC, Trump spoke of the enmity he has encountered:

> I have a very unfair press. It's fake news. I have people that are so dishonest. I mean, I had a case of it recently with the *New York Times* where they're writing things knowing it was wrong. Knowing. If I don't get the word out.... I call it social media.... I put it out, and then it goes onto your platform. It goes onto ABC. It goes onto the networks. It goes onto all over cable. It's an incredible [phenomena].... And when I'm treated badly by the press—and nobody's ever been treated as badly like me.... Abraham Lincoln was treated supposedly very badly. But nobody's been treated badly like me. And this way I can fight the dishonest media, the corrupt media, the fake news.[876]

Contrast those remarks of one who can say of himself that he has been treated worse than any president in history, with the warrior's twin in a colloquial manner and reactive response to what Luther encountered five hundred years before him:

> I believe that I alone—not to mention the ancients—have suffered more than twenty blasts and rabbles which the devil has blown up against me. First there was the papacy. Indeed, I believe that the whole world must know how many storms, bulls, and books the devil raged against me through these men, how wretchedly they tore me to pieces, devoured and destroyed me.... [There were those] whose venomous and base writings and words I had to endure.... At times, I, too, breathed on them a little, but accomplished no more with it than to enrage and incite them all the more to blow and blast me without ceasing to the present day.[877]

The hypocrisy so visible today in much of the resistance and obstruction demonstrates not "loyal opposition" offering constructive criticism but rather crass "presidential harassment." No longer bound by loyalty to fundamental interests, principles and values, double standards are established and practiced; positions adamantly triumphed in recent years are reversed; Constitutional provisions such as the presumption of innocence or due process are ignored;

---

876 <https://abcnews.go.com/Politics/transcript-abc-news-george-stephanopoulos-exclusive-interview-president/story?id=63749144>.

877 LW 47:115-116. The Christian in Society, "Against the Antinomians."

and impartiality is stripped from our judicial system as we discover it has obviously been weaponized for political bias, as well as justice not being administered equitably. Lady Justice has been stripped of her blindfold to ensure that her scales are tipped unfairly in favor of the political and media elite.

To say that the big networks haven't exactly had a love affair with Donald Trump, as they plainly did with President Obama, is an understatement. It is as if the "media" has become the opposition party, or at least complicit with it. A recent survey by the Media Research Center shows that not only is coverage of Trump overwhelmingly negative—92%—but the President's biggest accomplishment—the roaring economy—gets almost no attention."[878]

Newspapers—direct products of the printing press invention—appear to be on the brink of extinction, at least in hard copy and on weekdays. News magazines are also in decline. News stories no longer break on the evening news or in first-edition headlines, or even on radio. They break on Twitter, Instagram and Facebook.

The response of today's powerful class and the majority of the media to their loss of control mirrors that of the Catholic Church five hundred years ago. It is human nature to react to a sense of losing control by clamping down on anything you can control, even if it means "manipulation" by slanting, editing, deleting, giving misleading headlines, quoting anonymous sources, failing to report that which would be favorable, fueling misinformation, and intentionally spreading "Fake News" to advance political agendas. Opinions spread quickly and repeatedly through the "echo chambers" which only hear themselves "regurgitating" the same memo, repeating the same key descriptive words, phrases, taglines and talking points which have gone out from The Democracy Integrity Project (TDIP).

The TDIP pitches daily reports to staffers, reporters and news producers at major media outlets, and to Democratic aides on Capitol Hill, unwittingly exhibiting evidence of collusion within the mainstream media who supposedly "report" the news "objectively":

> The organization is running an elaborate media influence operation that includes driving and shaping daily coverage of the Russian collusion theory, as well as pushing stories about Trump in the national media that attempt to tie the president or his associates to the Kremlin. The group also feeds information to the FBI and congressional investigators and then tells reporters that authorities are investigating those leads. The tactic adds credibility to

---

[878] *Investor's Business Daily*, "Editorials," October 10, 2018; <https://www.investors.com/politics/editorials/media-trump-hatred-coverage>.

> TDIP's pitches…[and] mirrors the strategy federal authorities themselves deployed to secure FISA warrants to spy on the Trump campaign: citing published news reports of investigative details their informants had leaked to the media to bolster their wiretap requests.[879]

In addition, as we have noted, we are experiencing the impact of allegations that powerful tech giants—Amazon, Google, Apple, Microsoft and Facebook—are acting like censors with "filter bubbles" that selectively present material based on information about the user, such as location, past click behavior and search history. Thus, social media platforms can serve not only as content developers, but selectively determine the particular content and order in which information is presented or withheld from their users, as well as directing searches in preferred political directions. Whistleblowers have exposed Google for their political bias in "tweaking its search algorithms to promote liberal agendas that it favors and that this is intended to help 'prevent the next Trump situation' in the upcoming election."[880]

"Luther made the bold and radical decision to speak beyond an informed audience of trained theologians and credentialed elite to address the wider German public in their own language"[881] that they actually used on a day-to-day basis. Similarly, by circumventing and surmounting dishonest partisan and hostile media through his use of Twitter, Trump uses language beyond that expected of politicians and thus projects himself both as one outside the political system, and as one suitably in touch with the electorate by being "a man of the people" who can affect meaningful change.

In campaigning and continued in his presidency, Trump has held several widely attended rallies throughout the country, which corresponds to Luther traveling extensively throughout Germany in an intentional "supervisory inspection" and visitation to congregations as well as to promote his views on God's Word and his challenges to the authority of the Catholic Church. These rallies and travels were of great importance to the development of each of their public personas.

---

[879] Sperry, Paul. "Trump-Russia 2.0: Dossier-Tied Firm Pitching Journalists Daily on 'Collusion,' *The National Sentinel*, March 20, 2022. <https://thenationalsentinel.com/2019/03/20/trump-russia-2-0-dossier-tied-firm-pitching-journalists-daily-on-collusion>.

[880] *RT*, "Google Pulls Videos Accusing It of Election Manipulation from You Tube… Which It Owns," June 25, 2019, <https://www.rt.com/usa/462619-google-removes-veritas-report>.

[881] Pettegree, *Brand Luther*, p.xii.

Personas Publicly on Display

Luther Preaching to the Crowds in Mora

(Left: Evangelical Lutheran Church in America website)

Trump Rally in Toledo, OH, Sept. 20, 2020

(Right: WTVG-13 ABC)

Both warriors were avant-gardists in the adoption and masterful employment of new technology—the printing press and social media—to reach a mass audience in ways that no one had ever done before. Luther turned the new technology of print into a fast-paced medium of debate and dispute, creating a media storm, and became the most prolific and first bestselling author, just as Trump has become the most famous tweeter to an extended "networked public." Luther's pamphlets were vociferously produced and were the most sought after amongst many others being printed on both sides of the debate. It led one of his contemporaries to observe that Luther's works "were not so much sold as seized" by the people, whereas the Catholic tracts, written in dense Latin rather than German, were "desired by no one and could not even be given away."[882] Horrified churchmen, including Papal Nuncio Aleander,* said that "Every day it rains Luther books in both German and Latin.... Nothing else sells but the books of Luther, even at the Imperial court."[883]

Whereas Luther's works spread like wildfire, the pamphlets of the Pope's defenders fizzled, and censorship of Luther failed. In the prefaces to his works, Luther urged his readers to discuss his pamphlets with others and read them aloud to the illiterate. Obviously, Luther was following the pattern of the Apostle Paul whose writings were intended to go beyond

---

[882] *The Economist, Christmas Special,* "How Luther Went Viral, Dec. 17, 2011." <https://www.economist.com/christmas-specials/2011/12/17/how-luther-went-viral>.

* Girolamo Aleander, the Italian cardinal appointed by Pope Leo X to be his representative at the Diet of Worms to head the opposition to Martin Luther. A "nuncio" is a papal ambassador or emissary to a foreign court or government.

[883] Hendrix, Scott, *Martin Luther, Visionary Leader* (New Haven: Yale University Press, 2015), p.101.

the recipient, as he directed in Colossians 4:16 (NRSV): *"And when this letter has been read among you, have it read also in the church of the Laodiceans; and see that you read also the letter from Laodicea."* In the same manner, Luther's works were read in homes, discussed in shops and churches, and debated in taverns. They were "read in spinning bees in Saxony and bakeries in Tyrol," Church historian John A. Hartman writes. "In some cases, entire guilds of weavers or leather-workers in particular towns declared themselves supporters of the Reformation, indicating that Luther's ideas were being propagated in the workplace. It was said that 'better sermons could be heard in the inns of Ulm than in its churches.'"[884]

In Germany, literacy was estimated as low as five percent in rural areas and peaking at thirty percent in urban centers. A literate person, such as a doctor, lawyer or teacher, would acquire Luther's latest pamphlet and then read it to crowds or households gathered for the purpose. Those who could read, read to others.[885] In this two-stage communication exercise, influential, literate opinion-formers could advance and promote Luther's new ideas among the wider population orally.

Andrew Pettegree, an expert on the Reformation at St. Andrew's University, explains in *"Reformation and the Culture of Persuasion"*: "It was the superabundance, the cascade of titles, that created the impression of an overwhelming tide, an unstoppable movement of opinion.... Pamphlets and their purchasers had together created the impression of irresistible force."[886]

The Reformation obviously was not primarily a technological printing event, given the low rates of literacy, but it did reinforce St. Paul's understanding that *"faith comes from what is heard, and what is heard comes through the Word of Christ"* (Romans 10:17 [NRSV]). According to Robert Scribner, Luther's recovery of the Gospel facilitated the "new faith" being heard "in a range of formal and informal situations: from hedge-, street-, and saloon-bar-preaching as much as from the pulpit; from public disputations and private conversations; and from plays and popular songs."[887]

---

884 Mansch, Larry D., and Peter, Curtis H., *Martin Luther: The Life and Lessons* (Jefferson, NC: McFarland & Company, Inc. Publishers, 2016), p.147.

885 Waugh, Barry, "The Importance of the Printing Press for the Protestant Reformation, Part Two," October 2013. <http://www.reformation21.org/articles/the-importance-of-the-printing-press-for-the-protestant-reformation-part-two.php>.

886 Mansch and Peters, *Life and Lessons,* p.147, quoting Andrew Pettegree in *Reformation and the Culture of Persuasion* (Cambridge: Cambridge University Press, 2005), p.163. Also cited in Tom Standage's *Writing on the Wall, Social Media—The First 2000 Years* (New York: Bloomsbury, 2013), p.61 in his chapter, "How Luther Went Viral" which can be accessed www.economist.com/node/21541719.

887 Scribner, Robert, "Oral Culture and the Diffusion of Reformation Ideas," *History of European Ideas,* issue 5, 1984, p.238.

As important as the printed, proclaimed, and shared words were, Scribner notes that a multimedia campaign was literally taking place simultaneously. Luther drove home the Word of God through speaking and singing, rhyming and preaching, writing and reading, and paintings and drawings. Ballads, songs, and hymns were often set in lyrical form to known musical tunes, tunes learned through communal singing, or tunes the traveling minstrels sang in delivering the news.

Luther understood how powerfully music expresses faith and theology. Recognizing the edifying powers of music, he infused theology into melodies that would aid the people's memories. I don't recall President Trump turning to the playbook page of composing lyrics set to music yet, like his twin...but who knows?

Being aware of the persuasive value of illustrations, Luther did not drag his feet but became a master at having his printed words highlighted with woodcuts—many in satirical cartoon fashion, some astonishingly crude and graphic—as we have seen. Paintings were also employed to interpret for the illiterate as well as to reinforce his message by visual aids for those who could read or hear the new teachings. He even supervised the drawing of many woodcuts to make sure that the artist confined himself to illustrating the text with literal simplicity and with no "*schmieren*" of any "*unnutzige Dinge**."[888] Luther wrote that "woodcuts made the book good for laymen" and remarked that "without images we can neither think nor understand anything."[889] "For the first time in human history," A. G. Dickens, renowned for his authoritative works on The Reformation, writes in his 1966 book, *Reformation and Society in Sixteen Century Europe*, "a great reading public judged the validity of revolutionary ideas through a mass-medium which used the vernacular languages together with the arts of the journalist and the cartoonist."[890]

While the pictorial aspect of print could communicate to the illiterate with images, many would make little or no sense without some understanding of the accompanying text or some good knowledge of Scripture. Once explained, however, the image repeated the story to the observer, as in many cases, week after week viewing the art on the altarpieces as the

---

* "*Schmieren*" of any "*unnutzige Dinge*" literally means "smeared or lubricated with useless things." "*Schmieren*" was one of Luther's colorful expressions. In this context Luther is basically saying, "Keep the text pure and without adding unnecessary things [verbiage or meanings]."

888 Mayor, A. Hyatt, "Renaissance Pamphleteers Savonarola and Luther," *The Metropolitan Museum of Art Bulletin*, 6:2, 1947, pp.66–72. <https://doi.org/10.2307/3257336>.

889 *The Economist*, January 16, 2017, "How the 16th Century Invented Social Media." <https://medium.economist.com/how-the-16th-century-invented-social-media-a132128d715c>.

890 White, Svend, "Martin Luther & the Mass Media," *Religion Dispatches*, March 12, 2009. <http://religiondispatches.org/martin-luther-the-mass-media>.

people worshipped. Many of the works were produced by famed printmaker and portraitist Hans Holbein of Augsburg, gifted and versatile artist Albrecht Durer of Nuremberg, and especially Luther's neighbor and close friend, chief pictorial propagandist and image maker for the Reformation movement, Lucas Cranach, all thus proving the adage that "a picture is worth a thousand words." Works of art have the ability to convey multiple messages at once. They can evoke feelings, even personal and unique messages to each individual who views it, and in this way, art can push far beyond what mere words can communicate. Much has been written about the role image played in advancing The Reformation. Bobbi Dykema postulates from her analysis that "it may well be that the success and long-lasting resonance of the Protestant Reformation owes as much to the sheer numbers, availability, and cleverness of its negative portrayals of the Catholic hierarchy as it does to the attractiveness of its own theology."[891] At the outset, Luther astutely understood that the printed medium needed to reflect the beauty of the message being conveyed.

The Visual Sermon

Lucas Cranach the Elder and Younger's Altarpiece in Wittenberg's Stadtkirche of St. Mary's
(Image: Public domain, retrieved from Nature History Heritage)

---

[891] Dykema, Bobbi, "The Ass in the Seat of St. Peter: Defamation of the Pope in Early Lutheran *Flugschriften*, p.16. <https://www.academia.edu/9540882>.

Nowhere do I discover that adage's truth about the worth of a picture more profoundly exhibited in the art of Martin Luther's time than in the magnificent altarpiece of St. Mary's Church in Wittenberg. This crowning piece of art exhibits a perfect blending of Luther's theology with the skills of the masterful visualizer of The Reformation, Lucas Cranach with his son's assistance and completion. Its presence gives a vivid testimony as it complements what Luther preached and wrote regarding that which he held dear to his heart: salvation by grace alone, through faith alone, in Christ alone.

The altarpiece is comprised of three panels called a triptych, set upon a predella or platform at the back of the altar. Theologically, this altarpiece, which highlights the importance of the Word of God, has at its center the person and work of Christ upon whom is built the sacramental life of the Church. Each of the four panels teaches one of the four main ways in which Christ's word of forgiveness comes to us: preaching, Holy Baptism, the Office of the Keys, and Holy Communion. In the predella's panel below the triptych, Luther is painted preaching from the pulpit in Torgau Castle to signify the primacy of the Word and the foundation from which all teachings, sacraments and doctrine are rooted. In between Luther and the listening congregation (made up of prominent local Lutherans, including wife Katie with an infant in her lap and their deceased daughter Magdalena standing behind her mother, the bearded Cranach Senior near the back wall, and his godchild, Hans Luther, front and center) is Christ being crucified. With his left hand on the Scriptures, and his right arm extended and pointing to the hovering image of the crucified Christ, Luther is driving home the message of Scriptural authority—"Christ and Him crucified"—who is over traditional Church authority.

In the triptych's left wing, the Sacrament of Baptism is highlighted, with Philip Melanchthon baptizing an infant by sprinkling to emphasize that anyone may baptize, and that Baptism need not be done by immersion or an ordained person, as Melanchthon was a lay theologian, not a member of the clergy. Cranach, Sr. is pictured to Melanchthon's right, and to his left with an open Bible is Elector Frederick, emphasizing that the Word is necessary for the water to be a Baptism.

The panel on the right shows Johannes Bugenhagen, pastor of St. Mary's, in an open confessional holding keys in each hand as he "binds" the sins of the man on his left, while "loosing" those of the kneeling penitent on his right. The keys are the symbols of the role of the pastor in a congregation, as contrasted with the papacy.

At the center and focal point of the triptych is Christ and the disciples seated at a round table, with the paschal lamb in the middle of the table to depict the Last Supper. Christ is seen with John sleeping comfortably in his lap, extending two fingers of His right hand—in a gesture we would associate more closely with blessing than feeding—and giving a morsel of bread to Judas with a moneybag by his side and his foot already outside the circle (reception by the unworthy!) who is literally feeding on Christ's flesh, but shown to be breaking away from the communion. On the other side of the table, Martin Luther is shown as one of The Twelve and depicted as Junker Jorg, receiving the communion cup offered to him by another disciple who shows considerable resemblance to the Younger Cranach. A recent resurgence of interest in the Cranachs has revealed through modern research that Lucas the Younger's brush is attributed to substantial portions of the center panel and to the two side wings, thus we may have a self-portrait of the Younger Cranach communing Luther.

The altarpiece furthermore reflects a very Lutheran ecclesiology, in that it is the Wittenberg congregation hearing the Word and participating in the sacraments. Not only were artists inclined to paint themselves in the pictures but portrayed local "stand-ins" as real people. Here Christ is found in the whole Church and in the congregation where the Word is "rightly preached and the Sacraments rightly administered." Old and young, male and female, even a pregnant woman, are all present in the worshipping congregation. It is an inclusive picture of community life. All are included in God's gracious call.

The Reformation altar in Wittenberg gives visual expression to Luther's deep conviction that God, who is hidden and invisible, accommodates Himself to our finite and fallen nature by revealing His love toward us through material things: in the incarnation of His Son, in the Sacraments, and in the Good News of the Scriptures received. The altar piece is an embodied, material and visual communication of that embodied, material communique! "Above the entire work hangs a panel with the words of 1 Corinthians 3:11, '*For no one can lay a foundation other than that which is laid, which is Jesus Christ.*' Indeed, Christ crucified and risen for the life of the world is the eternal Gospel which this masterpiece proclaims to every nation and tribe and language and people."[892]

Once the "thousand words" are exhausted in explanation, the meaning of the altarpiece becomes fixed in one's mind, so that a recital of the Church's basic teachings are brought forth every time one's eyes focus upon its not so "silent" witness.

In one of the most effective and successful visual pieces of Reformation propaganda, Cranach the Elder published his *Passion of Christ and Antichrist.* As we have established, Cranach possessed a thorough understanding of Luther's theological positions, as well as Luther's views on the Church as an operating "physical organism." It was a series of 13 paired woodcuts contrasting Christ's pious behavior with that of the decadence and corruption of the Pope.

---

[892] <https://christlutheranjacksonms.org/cranach-altarpiece>.

Images for the Simple and Words for the Wise

During the Reformation, Lutheran artists in Wittenberg and Nuremberg produced dozens of broadsheets and pamphlets satirizing the Pope, clergy, and many Catholic beliefs. Their aim was to teach the common people who were illiterate about the life of Christ and Luther's teachings, in stark contrast to the teachings of the Church. Conceived by Luther, Lucas Cranach illustrated and Philip Melanchthon supplied the text for the resultant small sharp-witted pamphlet. "Passional Christi und Antichristi" was produced in Wittenberg in 1521, and was a widely circulated booklet comparing the passion of Christ with that of the Antichrist, the Pope. Using visual antithesis, thirteen pairs of woodcuts clearly distinguish their respective behavior as one reads the pictures. The *Passional* was the first great blow inflicted upon the enemies of Luther by means of the printed picture. A "*passional*" is a small devotional booklet depicting scenes of the life of Christ or the saints, meant for pious meditation by the unlearned, and here it served simultaneously as visual propaganda to vilify the Church in Luther's day.

To truly vilify something it is necessary to illustrate or exhibit it and this Cranach masterfully executes as he displays the corrupt papacy. Employing a number of artistic, visual-rhetorical strategies, he makes the case that the excesses of the office of the Supreme Pontiff are so extreme that the Pope can justly be considered the Antichrist.

As a work of both text and image, Latin and vernacular, *Passional* was designed to engage both seeing and reading in an audience with a wide spectrum of literacy. Its vivid illustrations and simple language were simultaneously aimed at literate, semi-literate, and illiterate, young and old, theologically sophisticated and piously simple with a memorable tale of the holiness of Christ contrasted with the greed and gaudiness of the papacy. The creators' hope in putting together this "tool" was to persuade the reader-viewer irrefutably that the devil was at work in the highest office of Christendom. Their strategy entailed "re-educating" Christians by leading them through a series of "meditations" on the life and ministry of Christ that contrasted with the juxtaposed depictions of papal pretense to both spiritual and temporal power.

The advent of print culture with the ability to illustrate with woodcuts shifted the reception of information from a large-scale communal experience to a more individual, personal appropriation which dovetailed nicely with the Lutheran emphasis on individual conscience, and having a personal experience and relationship with Christ and communication with God.

Visual Antithesis:
Exemplary Life of Christ and Sacrilegious Actions of the Antichrist (as the Pope)

Passinal Christi
Die Wueherer Christus *austreibt* vom Tempel sein—

und Antichristi.
Mit Bullen, Bannbriefen zwingt sie der Papst wied'r *hinein.*

Driving Money Changers from Temple

Counting the Sales of Indulgences

(Image: Public domain, retrieved from https://ghdi.ghi-dc.org/sub_image.cfm?image_id=3311)

In the twelfth set, Christ drives the money changers out of the Temple in Jerusalem, drawn from Matthew 21. The bankers and vendors recoil as Christ kicks over a table and wields his knotted scourge. Opposite, the Antichrist sits in God's Temple and displays himself as God. In exchange for money, the Pope sells dispensations, indulgences, bishoprics and other church offices, dissolves marriages, makes and breaks law, blesses and damns. While his actions are listed in the inscription, Cranach's simple image immediately distinguishes the Pope's interests from Christ's. These images helped communicate to all, one of the central aspects of Luther's theology—namely, the corrupt state of the established Church.

Luther's manifestos of 1520 also criticize the sale of indulgences. In writing "To the Christian Nobility," he warns: "The pope seduces you away from the gifts of God which you receive unpaid for, to his own 'gifts' which you must buy.... Be content with the one sure norm; what you have to buy from the Pope is neither good nor godly." [John Dillenberger, ed., *Martin Luther: Selections From His Writings. "An Appeal to the Ruling Class,"* Garden City: Doubleday, 1961, p. 460; also, LW 44:189.]

Polemical Prints:
Contrasting Images between Gospel accounts of Jesus and Pope Leo X

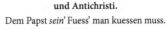

Passinal Christi
Der HErr *ihre* Fuess' den Juengern wusch—

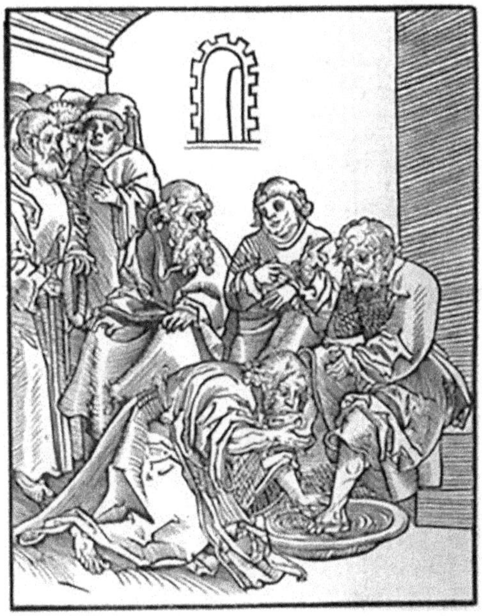

Christ Washing the Feet of His Disciples

und Antichristi.
Dem Papst *sein'* Fuess' man kuessen muss.

Kissing the Feet of the Pope

(Image: Public domain, retrieved from https://ghdi.ghi-dc.org/sub_image.cfm?image_id=3312)
Bloor, Joshua, "Lucas Cranach: A Hidden Face of the Reformation," Seedbed, November 7, 2001. <https://www.seedbed.com/lucas-cranach-a-hidden-face-of-the-reformation>

This set illustrates the contrast between Jesus' humility and service, as He washes and kisses the feet of one of His disciples (John 13) compared to the Pope on the right sitting arrogantly on a throne, proudly delighting over the line of people waiting to kiss his feet.* Cranach the Elder created multiple significant images during the Reformation, including woodcuts of which the "Passional" booklet of 26 was the most popular. These 13 pairs of woodcuts contrast Jesus's holy life with the corrupt life of the Pope, as the Lutherans saw it. The provocative images depict the Pope as the Antichrist—a devilish opponent of Jesus—indulging his selfish desire for power, pleasure and wealth. The final set depicts the ultimate end of each: Christ's glorious ascension into heaven, while the Pope, clad in all the paraphernalia of his office, is cast into hell, where tortured sinners are consumed bodily by eternal fires. Undeniably, Joshua Bloor* stresses how the talented artist "powerfully communicated the ideas of the Reformation to those who could not read about them. While we often are quick to admire the impact of the written words of The Reformation, it is worth remembering that for the vast majority of people, it was Cranach's visual creations which helped to communicate and spread the ideas of The Reformation."

---

* Luther addresses this "unchristian" kissing of the Pope's feet which was part of the "adoration" which the Pope claimed as his right in the Reformer's "Open Letter to the Christian Nobility" in LW 44:168, *The Christian in Society I* or *Three Treatises*, p.57.

* Bloor is an Adjunct Lecturer in Biblical Studies at Nazarene Theological College in Manchester, England.

In addition to tweeting on social media to exploit the 24-hour news cycle, Trump has just as effectively used his widely attended mass rallies throughout the country, as we have seen, with supporters thronging to see and hear the President. Strikingly, town clerk and hymn writer Lazarus Spengler (1479-1534), who was the prominent Protestant leader and supporter of Luther in Nuremberg, observes:

> "No teaching or preaching has seemed more straightforwardly reasonable, and I also cannot conceive of anything that would more closely match my understanding of Christian order as Luther's and his followers' teaching and instruction (based on the Holy Gospel, the prophets, and St. Paul.)" ...Spengler claimed not to be alone in this opinion. "Up to this point," he remarked, "I have also often heard from many excellent highly learned people of the spiritual and worldly estates that they were thankful to God that they lived to see the day when they could hear Doctor Luther and his teachings."[893]

Hearing Concerns and Views of Students

Left: Luther in conversation with Swiss students in the Jena Hotel Restaurant, Gasthof der Baren, in March 1522.

(Image: Public domain, retrieved at LCMS Pastors' Resources website)

Right: Trump meeting with students in the wake of the Parkland, Florida, shootings, killing 17 and injuring 17 others at the Marjory Stoneman Douglas High School on February 14, 2018.

(Image: ABC News Walt Disney; Tom Brenner/The New York Times via Redux)

---

[893] Edwards, *Printing*, p.53, quoting Lazarus Spengler's "Why Dr. Martin Luther's Teaching Should Not Be Rejected As Unchristian but Rather Be Regarded As Christian," the first German defense written by a layperson. See reference *Flugschriften der fruhen Reformationsbewegung* (1518-1524). Edited by Adolf Laube, Annerose Schneider, and Sigrid Looss. 2 vols. Berlin, 1983, 1:504-505.

Trump used numerous informal news conferences, Q&As upon boarding the helicopter or Air Force One, and roundtables with various sectors—portions of which were open to the media—to listen to the views, not only of government and business leaders, but those of the people, and to speak in their colorful street language as we experienced Luther doing through his visitations and his meeting with students and leaders from both the secular and religious realms.

Both marshaled people through their impassioned targeted "conversation" which is pedestrian, and in a "folksy plain style" easily grasped by the masses. This was in stark contrast to the way most politicians and the educated fringe spoke "from the heights" of idealism with lofty sounding rhetoric which distracts, leaving questions about what is really being said. Our populist warriors differentiated themselves as they sought to go "down and out among the people" to hear and learn from them. Today's humanists, like those in Luther's time, will profess a love for humanity, while frequently appearing isolated from and disdainful of the "barbarians" (in Erasmus' view), "deplorables" (in Clinton's view), or those who "cling to guns or religion or antipathy to people who aren't like them" (in Obama's view). All this intolerance supported with liberal pundits in the media dismissing the "retrograde lot" who deserve scorn because they don't know what's good for them.

Collaborating, Receiving Views and Input from Others

Four Reformers Translating Bible

Pierre Antoine Labouchère, 1847

(Left): Martin Luther collaborating with linguists Philip Melanchthon, Johannes Bugenhagen (Doctor Pomeranus) and Casper Cruciger to translate.

(Image: Public domain, retrieved at The Reformation Room)

Trump Hosting National Economic Session

White House Roosevelt Room, March 9, 2017

(Right): Donald Trump meeting in a "National Economic Listening Session" with independent community bankers.

(Image: Kevin Dietsch/UPI Forbes)

Not unlike Trump, who often entices his enemies to make critical, even derogatory remarks and evaluations of his presidency to purposefully expose their intent, Luther's enemies likened the spread of his ideas to a sickness. The papal bull "Exsurge Domine," threatening Luther with excommunication in 1520, said its aim was "to cut off the advance of this plague and cancerous disease so it will not spread any further…"[894] This bull of condemnation accused Luther of promoting forty-one heresies and "pestiferous (highly infectious) errors." One of the alleged errors was his view that "the burning of heretics is against the will of the Holy Spirit."[895] The papal bull excommunicating Martin Luther and his followers, "Decet Romanum Pontificem," claimed these heretics were devoted to purposes of evil by dragging multitudes along "to share their own error and ruination, contaminating them with what amounts to a contagious disease."[896] The "Edict of Worms" in 1521 warned that the spread of Luther's message had to be prevented, otherwise "the whole German nation, and later all other nations, will be infected by this same disorder."[897]

Recognizing the benefit the printing press gave to the "rapid and cheap dissemination of ideas," David Bagchi notes how significant it was that at the Diet of Worms,

> Luther was required to retract not his ideas but the books that contained them, and the resulting Edict made special mention of the unauthorized printing of books calculated to spread heresy. Far from putting an end to the propagation of Luther's cause through the press, the Diet and its Edict were followed by an even more massive output of religious publishing than had gone before.[898]

Although Luther had been declared a heretic in 1521, and owning or reading his works was banned by the Church, the extent of his popularity and local political support, especially the patronage of Luther's sympathetic prince, Frederick the Wise, the Elector of Saxony, prevented authorities from risking open rebellion. Thus, Luther escaped execution and The Reformation became established in much of Germany, where Luther was viewed as "Prophet, Hero, and Saviour."[899]

---

894 <http://www.papalencyclicals.net/leo10/l10exdom.htm>.

895 <https://news.nationalgeographic.com/2017/10/martin-luther-freedom-protestant-reformation-500>.

896 <http://www.papalencyclicals.net/leo10/l10decet.htm>.

897 <https://salemcc.instructure.com/courses/121/pages/the-edict-of-the-diet-of-worms-may-1521>.

898 Bagchi, "Propaganda."

899 Rehn, Dana K. "Exhibition Word, Image, Song," University of Adelaide Library. <https://danarehn.com/2017/10/16/exhibition-luthers-reformation>.

Many attributed Luther's success to the proliferation of his writings and to his enormous stamina, like we see in Trump. Luther would write his broadsheets and pamphlets in the common tongue with a literary style that was lucid, accessible, and to the point. Not only was he a quick student in grasping how to use the revolutionary technology of the printing press, but he took great pains to understand the printing process from the ground up, including the economics of the business, which gave him a tremendous advantage over his adversaries. He understood the significance and was proficient in his use of the new communication technology, much as Trump grasped the use of Twitter to exploit the round-the-clock platform better than anyone else thus spurring democratization of thought.

Far from his initial hesitation, Luther later famously hailed printing during one of his "Table Talks" as "God's ultimate and greatest gift. Indeed, through printing God wants the whole world, to the ends of the earth, to know the roots of true religion and wants to transmit it in every language. Printing is the last flicker of the flame that glows before the end of this world."[900] Luther's remark was the prescient observation of a man who had closely identified himself with this new "black art" as printing by moveable type came to be known, as he understood how the printed book would become one of the most important instruments lighting the way into the modern era.

Not discounting his praise, he was also fully aware of how easily the new technology and modes of communication could be misused, abused, and hijacked by Satan. We too are discovering downsides of the new gifts of social media that can aid our thinking and our communicating but is proving to have harmful effects upon the current generation.[901]

While it may seem surprising, Luther was also critical and condemned Gutenberg's invention for the unprecedented ability to mangle the printed word beyond recognition. With the ability to produce pamphlets and broadsheets quickly and in large numbers, the temptation to rush a sure-fire bestseller into print before one's publishing rivals was too strong for many to resist; yet a rushed or even a pirated print job risked distorting the very

---

[900] Carefoote, Pearce J., *Flickering of the Flame: Print and the Reformation*, "Introduction" (to exhibit by the curator Pearce Carefoote, Fisher Library, University of Toronto). <https://fisherdigitus.library.utoronto.ca/exhibits/show/reformation/introduction> also <https://fisher.library.utoronto.ca/exhibition/flickering-flame-book-and-reformation#:>.

[901] See for example *The Atlantic*'s "Have Smartphones Destroyed a Generation?" by Jean M. Twenge." <https://www.theatlantic.com/magazine/archive/2017/9/has-the-smartphone-destroyed-a-generation/534198>.

message it was supposed to carry. Luther was so outraged by these underhanded practices that he prefaced a collection of Lenten sermons with a foreword addressed to "'my dear printers, who so openly rob and steal from each other.... I could put up with their crimes [of theft and fraud],' he admitted, 'did they not ruin my books so badly in the process. But they print them so quickly that when they come back to me, I no longer recognize them.'"[902]

As we have discovered, President Trump likewise cannot often recognize the news reports he hears or reads from the media, which malign what he actually said or distort his message by ignoring the context, assigning a misleading and prejudicial headline, or not delivering the entire quote which may have qualifiers. Sadly, it appears today that the dark side of human nature is often aided more than stifled by technology.

---

[902] WA 17/II:2-3, cited in Bagchi's "Propaganda."

26

Micro-Managing Energizer Bunnies

One can understand why Luther was a hands-on and detail-oriented "supervisor" who tended to micro-manage every step of the publishing process and the editing of his pages. As Blake Adams puts it, "One can imagine him buzzing over the workers in the print shop, reviewing their work, giving orders, offering criticisms, and approving final copies."[903]

Those around Trump often speak of his "Energizer Bunny" qualities: always working, on the go, with so little sleep that it exhausts them just to observe the President in action. One has only to view the magnitude of Luther's writings, filling 122 volumes (of which twenty-two consists of his sermons) in the Weimar edition, known as the *Weimarer Ausgabe* (WA).[904] The English edition, known as *Luther's Works* (LW), is now being expanded to fill 82 volumes. In addition, Luther's career included translating the Bible, writing hymns, supervising congregations, overseeing monasteries, debating scholars, lecturing at the university, consulting with civil leaders, preaching—often multiple times each week—as well as being a husband, father, and host to students and friends staying at the "Lutherhaus." Their residence was the former "Black Cloister," an Augustinian monastery, which was given to the Luthers as a wedding gift from Frederick the Wise, and which Luther's wife Katarina von Bora administered and managed with exceptional skill as "Herr Katie."

Luther demonstrated having a master's eye for good printing, even to the look of the fonts used, the inviting use of white space between the lines of text, and margins on the sides controlling the thickness of the printed columns. He cared about the aesthetics, presentation and quality of the workmanship on his material, all of which exhibited a creative Luther who tenderly cared for his movement. He did not want the Gospel to be "sinned against" by shoddy or sloppy workmanship. A movement that articulated the primacy of the Word necessitated giving critical attention as to how such words would appear, because it would

903 Adams, Blake, "Martin Luther, a Master of Media? A Review of Andrew Pettegree's *Brand Luther.*" <https://pushpay.com/blog/brand-luther>.

904 Thomas, Derek W.H., "Spare Everything but the Word: Luther as Preacher;" *The Legacy of Luther*, ed. R.C. Sproul and Stephen J. Nichols (Orlando, FL: Reformation Trust Publishing, 2016), p.268.

proclaim something about how credible that work was understood to be in relation to the "Word." Thus, Luther would constantly be checking with his printers to ensure the high standards of professionalism he demanded.

Luther had lured a top printer, Melchior Lotter,[905] from Leipzig, to be paired with the talented illustrator, Lucas Cranach (the Elder). His neighbor had become the Reformer's graphic artist, creating visual elements to clothe Luther's works in a new and distinctive form, which would be immediately recognizable and pop out on a crowded bookstall. Luther wrote, Cranach drew, carved and painted, and Lotter did the presswork. Intuitively, Luther understood that his books needed to be as beautiful as their contents if customers were going to pick them up.

In a sense, it could be said Luther was one of the first authors to claim intellectual property rights. The resulting iconography established, in today's terminology, Luther's own "brand," and the Wittenberg editions were themselves a powerful literary stratagem advancing the movement: decorative title page frames, careful use of space, design and typography—even highlighting the author's name front and center, so it would "spring off the page catching the eye of purchasers."[906] So significant was Cranach's contribution that Pettegree claims, "It was Cranach who would be the authentic creator of Brand Luther."[907]

Not only would the pamphlet provide the buyer with a delightful and profound read, but it was also a miniature work of art. The printing press and the masterful way it was utilized by Luther played a key role in popularizing ideas associated with the new Protestant faith during the European Reformation. "The Reformation saw the first major, self-conscious attempt to use the recently invented printing press to shape and channel a mass movement,"[908] says Mark U. Edwards of Harvard Divinity School. It also had the effect of removing "control of written material from the Catholic Church and made it difficult for the Church to inhibit the spread of what it regarded as heretical ideas."[909]

---

[905] Price, David H., *In the Beginning Was the Image: Art and the Reformation Bible* (New York: Oxford University Press, 2021), pp.136-137.

[906] Pettegree, *Brand Luther,* p.162. Also in "Long Before Twitter, Luther Was a Media Pioneer." <https://www.nytimes.com/2016/10/30/arts/design/long-before-twitter-martin-luther-was-a-media-pioneer.html>.

[907] Ibid., p.157.

[908] Edwards, *Printing,* p.1.

[909] Kennedy, Rita, "What Impact Did the Invention of the Printing Press Have on the Spread of Religion?" *Classroom.* <https://classroom.synonym.com/impact-did-invention-printing-press-spread-religion-6617.html>.

"Luther was the 16th-century equivalent of a social media master," claims Mike Haynes, who taught journalism at Amarillo College from 1991 to 2016:

> Luther surely would have used Twitter had it been invented.... In fact, some of the "95 Theses" would have fit nicely into 140 characters, such as No. 27: "They preach man-made doctrines who say that so soon as the coin jingles into the money-box, the soul flies out of purgatory," and No. 54: "Injury is done to the Word of God when, in the same sermon, an equal or longer time is spent on pardons, than on the Word."[910]

(Image: Mr. Leverett's World History)

(Image: Vector Stock)

In every generation, President Barack Obama's adviser and bestselling author Van Jones observes, the

> triumphant politician is the one who first masters his era's media tools.... FDR was the first "radio" president. JFK emerged as the first "television" president (only outdone when an actual screen actor rose to the highest office in the land: Ronald Reagan. The Gipper's televised charisma helped earn him the moniker "the Great Communicator," and Donald Trump...possibly the first "social media" and "reality TV" president...every political era is shaped by the media environment of its time...[911]

and the reality show candidate did become reality as the "Social Media President."

Historian Andrew Pettegree presents Luther as the first media star of the printing age, and others claim Luther to have been the "first bestseller" of printed books and the most

---

910 Haynes, Mike, "Luther Used 'Modern' Technology to Spread the Reformation." <http://www.amarillo.com/faith/2017-01-24/haynes-luther-used-modern-technology-spread-reformation>.

911 Jones, Van, "Trump: The Social Media President." CNN *Opinion*, October 26, 2015. <https://www.cnn.com/2015/10/26/opinions/jones-trump-social-media>.

published author in Europe. He was the first writer who could sell his new books based on his name alone. Today, Luther would be at the top of Amazon's list of books for a very long time. Few individuals have written as much as Martin Luther and no one has had more books written about them in history except Jesus Christ. Some point to the library shelf space occupied by Jesus Christ and Martin Luther to justify their claim. I am confident that in the years to come, many will publish similar books about Trump's life, his rise to the presidency, and perhaps even a parallel book to Luther's "Table Talk," entitled "Trump's Twitter Feed!"

The Reformation literally took on the character of a literary enterprise—advancing through and fueled by the book, while transforming a printing industry that had been around for 70 years. Pettegree concludes his book with the assessment that "Luther could not have been a force in the German Church without his instinctive, towering talent as a writer. This was his most astonishing gift to the Reformation and to the German print industry."[912]

> Since Elizabeth Eisenstein's two-volume study of the printing press as "an agent of change" (1979), many studies have analyzed the connection between the advent of printing and the rise of the Protestant movement. That Protestants themselves saw printing as a divine gift bestowed from above to spur the work of Reformation is beyond doubt.[913]

John Foxe spoke for many others when he wrote in 1837,

> the blessed wisdom and omnipotent power of the Lord began to work for His Church; not with sword and target to subdue His exalted adversary, but with printing, writing, and reading: to convince darkness by light, error by Truth, ignorance by learning. So that by this means of printing, the secret operation of God hath heaped upon that proud kingdom a double confusion.[914]

The enduring influence of the Reformation transformed not only the Church but also the world of publishing, which in turn, by lending power to the reader, transformed how we conduct public dialogue and exchange ideas. The new and powerful technology of our 21st century is producing a similar revolution that is in all respects just as challenging, disruptive and radical as the Gutenberg press was to The Reformation of the 16th century.

---

[912] Pettegree, *Brand Luther*, p.338.

[913] George, "Typographical Reformation."

[914] *The Acts and Monuments of John Foxe: A New and Complete Edition, Volume III*, edited by The Rev. Stephen Reed Cattley, M.A. (London: R.B. Seeley and W. Burnside, 1837), p.719.

27

Images Then and Now

The world we live in today is a vast sea of images. To say that is not an understatement, especially with the technology we possess, not just with big-screen TVs and computers but also with hand-held devices that go where we go, and too often win the competition over the non-electronic images human eyes and facial expressions provide constantly and naturally in abundance. By way of illustration, ask yourself what your eyeballs were exposed to today that had anything to do with or was connected to your faith practice? In Luther's day, tangible images had the purpose of portraying Biblical scenes, individuals and saints, moral lessons, or important individuals occupying the ruling and upper class. Through the carving of woodcuts, the newly invented printing press could print multiple copies of images to enhance the printed word. Artists—painters, illustrators, wood carvers and sculptors—relied upon the Church and/or wealthy families to make a living through their talent.

But even then, the concept of images extended beyond the artistic ability to produce works or objects for viewing. There was also the language and its use, as we read and hear as well as view facial characteristics that shape our image or impression of a person.

Interesting, too, is how people view others, especially prominent individuals, whether they be celebrities in entertainment, politicians, evangelists or pastors, athletes, musicians, artists or writers. Some we like and some we dislike. Our opinions and tastes differ from others. There are also obviously many components, including our vulnerability and sensitivity to the personal evaluations other people make of us, as well as our own self-understanding and the persona we project to others.

Luther saw himself called by God to be an evangelist, inspired to write commentaries, catechisms and treatises, and translate the Bible to help people better understand God's Word; to be a preacher gladly proclaiming the Good News revealed to him through the Word he diligently studied and the Church Fathers he searched; and to do what he thought was his main job in life, to be a teacher of the Scriptures in which he was schooled as a Doctor at the University of Wittenberg, through Bible classes with friends.

How Luther Viewed Himself

Evangelist

Preacher

Teacher

(Left) "Luther as Evangelist." Woodcut, 1524, by Hans Sebald Beham (1500–1550). Cover woodcut for "Das New Testament Deütsch," Nuremberg (H. Deutsch), 1524.

(Center) Martin Luther In The Pulpit, c. 1530.

(Right) Bible class with Luther and friends. Luther sits at the table with his finger poised over a passage of the Bible. On the left is Bugenhagen, a rabbi, and Jonas. Behind him stands Philip Melanchthon and beside Melanchthon is Georg Rörer, Luther's personal secretary and an editor of Luther's "Table Talk." Another rabbi sits near the window reading. (Die Reformatoren: ein Gedenkbuch für die Evangelische Christenheit.)

(Images: Public domain, retrieved at (Left) AKG Images; (Center) the Reformissio website; (Right) University of Otago [New Zealand] Library)

Donald Trump publicly expresses no doubt about his superior qualities in being a gifted and visionary leader. In his characteristically self-admiring pronouncements, we hear such assertive convictions as, "No one is smarter than me;" "Nobody's ever been more successful than me;" "Ultimately I'm always right." The messianic implication is unmistakable, as he believes he was the "Chosen One" to deal with China and destined to restore America's greatness. He sacrificed his life of wealth and celebrity to selflessly serve the country he loves by saving "We the People" from a New World Order, or from the evils of Socialism and Marxism which aims to supplant our dependency and trust in God with big government controlling our lives. He has said, "I don't want to win for myself I only want to win for the people.... I think I've made a lot of sacrifices. I work very, very hard.... I didn't need [the presidency]. I didn't need it! I had a very nice life." He came to Washington as a public servant to drain the swamp, to slay the dragons, and to take on the world's demons and tame them with no thought of self-enrichment or the exercise of self-serving power.

How Trump Portrays Himself

(Images: [L] Daily Kos; [C] Pixels.com; [R] Fine Art America)

In our exploration of these twin warriors, we discover people viewing each as either the proverbial horned Devil incarnate or the haloed Saint personified. They both elicit intense emotions and reactions among the people, from cult-like devotion to vindictive loathing.

Haloed Saints Personified

Left: Public domain, retrieved at Stadt Museum Berlin

Right: Daily Kos

Horned Devils Incarnate

Halo and Horns Effect

Can both images be correct? What could possibly account for this incredibly polarized, and therefore divisive and antagonistic, perception of the very same person? Why do some see the negative side of an individual and others only the positive? Stephen A. Diamond, a clinical psychologist in Los Angeles and author of *Anger, Madness, and the Daimonic*, explains that this "halo and horns effect" occurs when attributes and behaviors are viewed through the lens of initial impressions:

> We form this initial impression of a person from the persona and personal narrative he or she presents, as well as the circumstances under which we first meet or see them. We then form an opinion of that person and tend to view all subsequent information regarding his or her behavior and character through the lens of that preconceived perception. *Confirmation bias* is the human tendency to seek support for such already existing perceptions by selecting and interpreting information or evidence to confirm already existing beliefs while rejecting, denying, or ignoring any and all conflicting information to the contrary.[915]

Uncivil verbal hostility toward those holding opposing views is often the result of our defense mechanisms of denial and projection kicking in to demonize the "other," psychologists claim, rather than recognizing it first in ourselves. Prominent individuals like the Reformer or the President become the object of both personal and collective projections, both positive and negative. They are revered and respected by some and despised and demonized by others, depending on their nationality, politics and point of view. It occurs naturally in many other settings in which someone is perceived to be in a position of power, leadership and authority. Many saw Luther in his day and Trump in our day as their savior. But others saw Luther as a heretic and outlaw, and Trump as one of the most evil, narcissistic, Machiavellian and dangerous men in the world today. Both are merely human beings, an amalgamation of both good and evil, positive and negative, possessing both creative and destructive traits as we have previously acknowledged. Neither is totally devoid of goodness and certainly neither are pure evil.

---

915 Diamond, Stephen A., "The Savior, the Devil, and Donald Trump," *Psychology Today*, January 10, 2021. <https://www.psychologytoday.com/us/blog/evil-deeds/202101/the-savior-the-devil-and-donald-trump>.

Demonized and Revered Twins

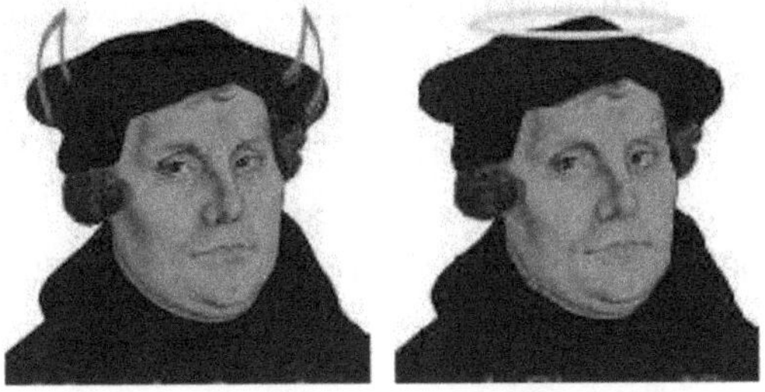

Mathew Block, Martin Luther: Saint and Sinner
(Left: The Canadian Lutheran)

Bill Dougal
(Right: CaricatureDrawing.net)

As Diamond puts it, "One way of understanding this strange and frightening phenomenon has to do with what psychologists call the 'halo effect,' known also as the 'halo and horns effect.'"[916] Another slant, expressed by Fyodor Dostoyevsky, points to the contradiction and fickleness we discover within the human species: "Men reject their prophets and slay them, but they love their martyrs and honor those they have slain."[917] Prophets are a thorn in the side of those who disagree with them, angering especially the powerful and influential. They demand change, garnering the animosity of those who are in control or content with the status quo. Martyrs, though dying for a cause they believed in enough to make the ultimate sacrifice, don't ask anyone to do anything. While they also called for change, they aren't alive to continue angering people by saying "I told you so" when time and circumstances prove they were right. Besides, as astutely put in a recent Reddit thread on the subject, through "the rose-tinted lens of memory, their irritations and flaws are swept away as they become paragons of their cause.... The good tales of their life and death are idealized, their legacies are remembered and refined, and everyone who hated them in life eventually dies."[918]

So how do we perceive our populist warriors—one living and one who lived 500 years ago? Perhaps the way they viewed themselves has shaped our impression so strongly that we do not feel the necessity to consider insights others may share that differ from our own, or that we could discover from diligent study and research. Instead of seeking to deepen or enrich our understanding of the context and circumstances surrounding an issue, we tend

---

916 Ibid.

917 <https://www.powerquotations.com/quote/men-reject-their-prophets-and>.

918 <https://www.reddit.com/r/AskReddit/comments/aolkhw/why_do_men_reject_their_prophets_and_slay_them>.

to fall into a mindset where religious or political opponents are deemed idiots or monsters. We have an abundance of picture propaganda in woodcuts and cartoons caricaturing Luther and Trump as our hero or villain. If we're fortunate enough at times to allow ourselves to be open, we may develop greater appreciation for what these movers and shakers both stood for and accomplished, as we discovered in "The Rest of the Story" with Robert E. Lee in Chapter 3.

Let's look at how they saw themselves and that which helped shaped their followers' or detractors' view of them.

Called to Follow the Leader

There are parallels Luther drew between his own biography and that of the Apostle Paul, including their conversion experiences following the "light" from heaven. It is clear both took their cue about leadership from Jesus, not from the lessons the world promotes. Jesus said,

> *You know that the rulers of the Gentiles lord it over them, and their great ones are tyrants over them. It will not be so among you; but whoever wishes to be great among you must be your servant, and whoever wishes to be first among you must be your slave; just as the Son of Man came not to be served but to serve, and to give His life as a ransom for many* (Matthew 20:25-28 NRSV).

The word "*lutherisch*" was already in extensive use, first and most particularly by Luther's enemies, but also by his friends and followers, as well as to describe his teachings. Luther wanted no part of it. He saw himself as a reformer of the Catholic Church, not as the founder of a new Church. In his "Sincere Admonition to All Christians" which he wrote upon returning to the Wartburg Castle after his attempt to quell the disturbances in Wittenberg, he adamantly asserts:

> In the first place, I ask that men make no reference to my name; let them call themselves Christians, not Lutherans. What is Luther? After all, the teaching is not mine [John 7:16]. Neither was I crucified for anyone [I Cor. 1:13]. St. Paul, in I Corinthians 3 [:22, cf. 1:12 and 3:4], would not allow the Christians to call themselves Pauline or Petrine, but Christian. How then should I—poor stinking maggot-fodder that I am—come to have men call the children of Christ by my wretched name? Not so, my dear friends; let us abolish all party names and call ourselves Christian after Him whose

> teaching we hold...the one universal teaching of Christ, who is our only master [Matt. 23:8].[919]

He was aghast that the word "Lutheran" was being used, and preferred the word "evangelical" (which means "Gospel-centered") to describe himself and his doctrine, which to this day is the word used to identify Lutheran churches in Germany. He reiterated this position a couple of months later in his "Receiving Both Kinds* in the Sacrament" with one critical caveat when disavowal of the name Lutheran is tantamount to a disavowal of Christ.

> But if you are convinced that Luther's teaching is in accord with the Gospel and that the pope's is not, then you should not discard Luther so completely, lest with him you discard also his teaching, which you nevertheless recognize as Christ's teaching. You should rather say: Whether Luther is a rascal or a saint I do not care; his teaching is not his, but Christ's.[920]

Leadership is about service, whether it be Christian or secular. The Apostle Paul "reminded his fellow leaders that he never used his position as a leader to take from others. He regarded leadership as a platform for serving others. Paul didn't want his colleagues to take advantage of the weak, nor use leadership to enrich themselves—something leaders in every culture and age are tempted to do."[921] Earlier, we singled out how many of our political leaders have become wealthy while serving in government, whereas President Trump was wealthy prior to entering the political arena as a candidate and, once being elected, served without pay, donating his salary back to the government.

Luther was passionately convinced he had been commissioned, just like St. Paul, to be an Apostle proclaiming the Gospel to the nations before the Last Judgment. In his writings about the Epistle to the Galatians, Luther in fact compares himself to the Apostle Paul in his defense of the Gospel.[922] Martin Luther loved the Epistle so much, he once said "it is

---

919 LW 45:70-71. *The Christian in Society III*, "A Sincere Admonition to all Christians."

* Both kinds refer to receiving both bread and wine in the sacrament of Holy Communion, as opposed to receiving just the bread as was practiced in the Roman Catholic Church.

920 LW 36:265. *Word and Sacrament*, "Receiving Both Kinds in the Sacrament."

921 Moore, Steve, *The Top 10 Leadership Conversations in the Bible* (Atlanta: Nexleader, 2017), p.13.

922 Johnson, George D., *What Will A Man Give in Exchange for His Soul*, "Martin Luther," (Harrisburg PA: Light of the Savior Ministries, 2011) p.30. Also see <https://www.greatsite.com/timeline-english-history/martin-luther.html>.

my Epistle. To it I am as it were in wedlock. It is my Katherine."[923] He clearly presented himself as "a faithful teacher" of the Word of God, and at times referred to himself as the prophet of the German people, but also an apostle. These images were already present during his lifetime, as his contemporaries described him as God's chosen instrument and a new Elijah.

Proclaiming and Announcing

The Triumphant Luther

Martin Luther Triumphans

(Left: The Royal Historical Society [UK])

The Aspirant Trump

Ben Garrison*

(Right: GarrisonGraphics.com)

Similar to the teacher and prophet Moses, Martin Luther holds out the open Bible to Pope Leo X sitting on a throne that is about to topple as "the books upon which he stands" disappear. Behind the Pope are torches in the hands of the Dominicans, indicating their role in the Inquisition; and below them, the Jesuits try to support the wavering papal throne. Leo's "key," the symbol of the Petrine office, is crumbling in the Pope's hand. Below Luther is a group of reformers led by Philipp Melanchthon, each holding a Bible. In the center below Leo is Friedrich Staphylus depicted as Judas Iscariot. Staphylus was a student of Melanchthon's, who rejoined the Catholic Church in 1533.

Donald Trump comes down the golden escalator at the Trump Tower in New York City with his wife, Melania, to announce his candidacy for President of the United States. Caricatured as Moses descending Mt. Sinai, Trump carries two tablets of stone chiseled with the campaign slogans and issues he promises to address with corrective measures: MAGA [Make America Great Again], Better Deals, Jobs, Wall [Southern Border], SCOTUS [Supreme Court nominees], Peace through Strength, Tax Cuts, Drain the Swamp, Lock Her [Hillary] Up, and Jerusalem. He is heckled by a donkey representing the Democrats who view him as a "joke" and an improbable candidate.

Eric Gritsch points out that "Catholic biographers employed the best scholarly methods to produce the worst image of Luther. The popular and detailed analysis by the Jesuit

---

[923] Martin Luther, *A Commentary of St. Paul's Epistle to the Galatians* (Grand Rapids: Kregel Publications, 1979 [reprint]), p.iv.

*Ben Garrison, American political cartoonist personally granted perrmission for the author's use of this cartoon and graciously suggested updating the title line in the cloud to better reflect what was going on at the time—Trump announcing his run for office. That courtesy was received by the author on September 4, 2021.

scholar Hartmann Grisar portrayed Luther as a man who was a victim of stubbornness and pride."[924] Using newly developed insights of psychology, Grisar wrote in terms which many would find just as, if not more, applicable to Donald Trump as he assessed Luther's own self-image:

> With regard to his self-image, he is under the influence of ideas which disclose various pathological symptoms, all of which together raise serious questions as to the nature of his changing state of mind. Since he feels chosen by God to do great things, since he is not only "the prophet of the Germans" but also the restorer of the Gospel for the whole Christian world, he thinks that he has been equipped by providence with faculties which hardly anyone else received. He frequently says so, even though he insists that God is behind it all. He like to compare himself not only to his papistical opponents, but also to the most famous figures in the Church of the past. In the same fashion, he likes to measure the opponents in his own camp against his own personal greatness. Thus it happens that he talks and sounds like a megalomaniac; and he likes himself so much in this role that he does not even notice how tasteless and offensive some of his exaggerations are.[925]

In analyzing the various "lives of Luther," Robert Kolb identifies a trajectory of prophet to teacher to hero in his definitive work on the subject.[926] Derek R. Nelson, a theologian who teaches at Wabash College in Crawfordsville, IN, and co-authored with Timothy F. Lull *Resilient Reformer: The Life and Thought of Martin Luther*, writes:

> The first efforts at memorializing Luther saw him as the next in line of the great prophets of the Bible and early Church with a special mandate and authority from God to challenge the powers of Christendom. [In Melanchthon's] eulogy at Luther's funeral in Wittenberg...he clearly

---

924 Gritsch, *Jester*, p.205.

925 Hartmann, Grisar, *Luther: His Life and Work, 3 Volumes in 1*, trans. E.M. Lammond, ed. Luigi Cappadelta (St. Louis: Herder, 1930; German original, Frieburg i.Br.: Herdersche Buchhandlung, 1911-12), p. 650, quoted in Gritsch's *Jester*, p.205.

926 Kolb, Robert, *Martin Luther as Prophet, Teacher, and Hero: Images of the Reformer, 1520-1620, Texts and Studies in Reformation and Post-Reformation Thought* (Grand Rapids, MI: Baker, 1999).

> identifies Luther as a prophet, as Elijah for the German Church. His speech on Luther and the "ages of the Church" of 1548 did the same thing. Isaiah, John the Baptist, Paul, Augustine...Luther...
>
> [Another] portrayal of Luther by his contemporaries comes from the pen of Cyriacus Spangenberg. Spangenberg was...one of the very last students of Luther's at Wittenberg. He was in awe of the Reformer and was furious at what he viewed as Melanchthon's later betrayals of Luther's theology. Thus. Spangenberg became the Gnesio-Lutheran* biographer of Luther. In 1561 he published a short overview of Luther and his writings, highlighting the authority they carried second only to Scripture. Luther's theology was for Spangenberg, "David's slingshot, Paul's mouth, John's finger, Peter's key, and the Holy Spirit's sword."[927]

Good prophets are brilliant and confusing, perhaps in about equal measure. But good teachers are clear. In the decades after Luther's death, theological debates raged about how his teachings ought to be systematized and written into confessions. Thus, the portrayals of Luther from this time tend to depict him as a teacher of truth, in keeping with the inheritance of the early church. Matthias Flacius Illyricus, for instance, assembled a book called *Catalogus Testium Veritatis* (Catalog of Witnesses to Truth). It consisted of quotations drawn from Luther's writings (and from some by the other Reformers) placed alongside selections from the church fathers with which they cohered. The result was to show not how Luther was a prophetic interruption in the history of Christianity but how he was an important continuer of its essence and message [as the Fifth Apostle].[928]

---

* Gnesio-Lutherans (from the Greek *γνήσιος* [*gnesios*]: genuine, authentic) is a modern name for a theological party in the Lutheran churches, in opposition to the Philippists (followers of Philip Melanchthon) after the death of Martin Luther and before the Formula of Concord in 1577.

[927] Nelson, Derek R., "Portrayals of Martin Luther in Print, Stage and Film," *Oxford Research Encyclopedia*, March 29 2017, containing the Spangenberg quote in Kolb's *Martin Luther as Prophet*, p.48. <https://doi.org/10.1093/acrefore/9780199340378.013.302>.

[928] Ibid.

The Intruders

Four Apostles - + - Martin Luther

Four Apostles

Albrecht Durer

Left: AlbrechtDurer.org

Martin Luther

Lucas Cranach the Younger

Center: LucasCranach.org

Four Presidents - + - Donald Trump

Mount Trumpmore

Titus Toons

Right: TitusToons.com

The two-panel masterpiece entitled "The Four Apostles" portrays four New Testament authors and is acclaimed as Durer's greatest achievement. The artist captures the principles and foundations of the Evangelical faith centering on the primacy and authority of the Word. The two dominate figures which take up most of the front of each canvas are Martin Luther's most admired apostles, St. John on the left and St. Paul on the right, each holding the Bible. Peter appears to be peering over John's shoulder to read from the Bible in John's hands, while he holds the "golden key" which represents the Church's power of unlocking heaven for people. Durer's painting has that Bible open to Luther's German rendering of the first verse in John's Gospel: "Am Anfang war das Wort—in the beginning was the Word." Behind the Apostle Paul, who is looking outward as if he is staring into the eye of the viewer, is Mark, holding a scroll of his Gospel. Perhaps for our purpose, Mark's startled expression could be responding to what Paul is signaling with his eye—who the heck is this Luther guy including himself as the third panel of our famous painting?

According to *USA Today*, Trump tweeted on Monday, August 10, 2020, that he thought it would be a "good idea" to have his face on Mount Rushmore, but the President denied it, tweeting, "This is Fake News never suggested it although based on all the many things accomplished during the first 3 ½ years, perhaps more than any other Presidency, sounds like a good idea to me." When Trump arrived in South Dakota for his speech at the monument on the eve of Independence Day, Governor Kristi Noem presented him with a four-foot replica of Mount Rushmore that included his face carved beside the other four presidents, saying she "'knew that was something that he would find special'.... Noem said in 2018 that Trump once told her that it was his dream to have his face carved into the monument. He later joked at a campaign rally about joining the presidents on the massive monument."[929]

Trump had, in fact, at a 2018 rally in Youngstown, Ohio, asked the crowd in his characteristic boastful humor whether they thought someday his face would be added to the iconic cliff carved by Gutzon Borglum in the Black Hills of South Dakota. Obviously, the commentators and cartoonists had a field day, portraying in word quips and illustrations the reaction of the presidents already enshrined to a new occupant. And here in the above caricature, I would imagine "the Donald" being extremely dumbfounded at the anguished expressions displayed by his predecessors at his presence and inclusion on the now "Mount Trumpmore" monument!

The Chief of Interpretation and Education at the landmark, Maureen McGee-Ballinger, informed reporters that the rock surrounding the sculpted faces is not suitable for additional carving, which could cause "potential instabilities in the existing carving..." She further added that Borglum chose those four presidents specifically "to represent the first 150 years of the history of the United States—the birth, growth, and preservation of our country" and "not to represent the individuals themselves...the memorial represents the ideals and meaning for which the nation was founded." While Mount Rushmore is not an option, Governor Noem jokingly suggested to Trump another possibility: that he "come pick out a mountain."[930]

There were indeed many in Luther's day who acknowledged the Reformer as a "holy man," obviously "set apart," and represented him as a saint. H. Laux Gemigger's *To the Praise of Luther and to the Honor of All Christendom*, is lifted up by Professor Mark U. Edwards, Jr. as a prime example.

> Published in two editions towards the end of 1520 or early in 1521, this verse treatise praised Luther as "a light of Christendom" chosen by God "to tell us Your divine Word." ...At one point, however, Gemigger suggested that Luther had taught "Christ's teaching," namely, "how we have turned from good to

---

[929] Groves, Stephen, AP. "Gov. Kristi Noem Gave President Trump Bust with Face on Mount Rushmore," *Argus Leader*, January 21, 2021. <https://www.argusleader.com/story/news/2021/01/21/go-kiristi-noem-president -trump-bust-face-mount-rushmore/6664448002>.

[930] Cummings, William, "Trump Says Adding His Face to Mount Rushmore Would Be a 'Good Idea.' It Likely be Impossible." *USA TODAY*, August 10, 2010. <https://www.usatoday.com/story/news/politics/2020/08/10/trump-likes-idea-adding-his-face-mt-rushmore-possible/3333312001>.

> evil," and had laid out the "teaching of the evangelists...without additions." Luther had also explained "God's Word and increased faith in Christ." ... The passage continues to read, "For this reason Luther was sent by God to teach us God's Word and good morals and to drive out the Antichrist here on earth, also to see to it that God's Word not be fully spoiled and that the Roman tyranny be recognized, that they should have no kingdom here on earth."[931]

Throughout the ensuing years, Luther has been celebrated and recognized for his insights that gave clarity to one's reliance on God's promise rather than human effort. For the 1817 "Centurial Jubilee" celebrated by all the Reformed Churches (the Lutheran Synods of New York, Pennsylvania, Maryland and adjoining states), "A Countryman of Martin Luther" wrote:

> No sooner had [Luther] yielded to that holy inspiration, [aka "the Tower Experience"] then behold! He found himself changed into a new man, into an Apostle, into an Ecclesiastes by way of excellence, appointed by God, into a fifth Evangelist, into a Doctor of Doctors: It is impossible to conceive, much less to express what an abundance of light and heavenly gifts were poured down from this moment, into this pure and humble soul. A cursory view of the principal particulars of the life and spirit of this ever blessed man of God, will convince the rising generation, that a man like this cannot come but from God, the author of all truth and sanctity, that the work of the Reformation cannot but be a godly work, and that Dr. M. Luther, was, if not superior, at least, by no means whatever inferior to the apostles of Christ Himself.... My intention is to prove that Martin Luther is a saint, and that the Reformation is a godly work: now this cannot be made good but from his works according to the oracle of Christ, "*from their fruits you shall know them* (Matthew 7:20)," and from the apostolical spirit and virtues which were so conspicuous in the blessed patriarch of the Reformation.[932]

---

931 Edwards, *Printing*, p.52, quoting Laux Gemigger's "Zü lob dem Luther vnd eeren der gantzen Christenhait (Strasbourg, 1520)," *Flugschriften der frühen Reformationsbewegung (1518-1524), Volume 1*, ed. Adolf Laube, Annerose Schneider and Sigrid Looss (Berlin, 1983), pp.548-557, here specifically pp.552-553.

932 Kohlmann, Anthony, *Centurial Jubilee, To Be Celebrated by All the Reformed Churches throughout the United States* (1817), p.9. <https://www.google.com/search?tbm=bks&q=Anthony+Kohlmann%3A++Centurial+Jubilee+celebrated>.

Warriors Portrayed as Saints

Luther as a Saint

By Hans Baldung-Grien

Donald J. Trump as a Saint

By Ron Irvine: The Beatification of Donald Trump

This woodcut by the artist Hans Baldung Grien (d. 1545), a supporter of The Reformation, derives from the first printing of an extended report of Luther's trial in Worms and depicts the Reformer as a saint. Dressed as an Augustinian monk, crowned with a nimbus, and with the Holy Spirit in the form of a dove above him, Luther holds the Bible from which he expounds the Christian faith. (Left Image: Public domain, retrieved at the Emory University website)

Ron Irvine satires Donald Trump with his "Beatification" of the President haloed as one who is godly and thus in a state of bliss. With a feather writing quill, Trump pens his understanding of government of the people, by the people and for the people which is good news ("*evangelium*") when adhered to by those elected to represent the people they are to serve instead of themselves, their party's agenda, or a political ideology. (Right Image: Orange Trump Monkey)

In 1520, the German artist Albrecht Durer (1471-1528) wrote in his diary, "And God help me that I may go to Dr. Martin Luther; thus, I intend to make a portrait of him with great care and engrave him on a copper plate to create a lasting memorial of the Christian man who helped me overcome so many anxieties." Unfortunately, Durer never had the opportunity to portray Luther from life. Most Europeans came to recognize Luther's features through portraits made by two of Durer's artistic contemporaries: Lucas Cranach the Elder (1472-1553), who became one of Luther's closest friends, and Hans Baldung Grien (ca1484-1545), who had trained in Durer's workshop between 1503-1507. Both artists created images of Luther which were disseminated widely in print during the early stages of the Reformer's publishing career.[933]

---

[933] *SMU Libraries: Bridwell Library Special Collections*, "Published Portraits: Martin Luther in the Age of Print." <https://www.smu.edu/Bridwell/SpecialCollectionsandArchives/Exhibitions/Luther/Portraits>.

Based on the early Cranach engraving of Luther while he was still an Augustinian canon at Erfurt, Hans Baldung Grien, who had become one of the outstanding painters and graphic artists in northern Renaissance art, produced and issued the above woodcut in 1521. Martin, wearing a monk's habit and shown with a tonsure (hair on top of the monk's head is shaved), is portrayed with saintly qualities, crowned with a nimbus illuminated by a halo, and enlightened or inspired by the Holy Spirit in the form of a dove above his head. He holds an open Bible from which he expounds the Christian faith. The constellation of these visual signs enabled the people to perceive Luther as a saint or one considered to be like a Father of the Church or both. The image became popular during the Diet of Worms, where Luther had been summoned to renounce or reaffirm his views in response to a papal bull by Pope Leo X.

Others portrayed Luther as the German Hercules, crushing his papal opponents and causing Satan to flee in shame, as we examined in Chapter 9. However, Professor Kolb writes that Luther

> did not regard himself as a Herculean hero. But he did assume the epistolary style of Saint Paul as early as 1522, and he drew parallels between the career of the apostle and his own career, moving out of works-righteousness into the proclamation of the Gospel of God's grace. Furthermore, he could call himself a prophet of the German, an apostle and evangelist in German territory, an Isaiah or Jeremiah. Yet Luther did not always possess this prophetic self-confidence. He often engaged in self-examination. He was plagued by repeated doubts about his own person. Yet he could also state, "I do not say that I am a prophet.... But if I am not a prophet, I am nevertheless certain for myself that the Word of God is with me and not with them, for I indeed have Scriptures on my side." ...For him, what mattered was God's Word.
>
> Luther had no illusions about being Enoch or Elijah returned from the grave.... What counted for Luther—and what linked him in his own mind with Elijah—was the Word of God in their mouths. He was firmly convinced that his tongue and pen proclaimed the same Word of God which Elijah proclaimed. Only because of this could he place himself in the ranks of prophets and apostles. Thus, much of the medieval notion of the prophet was not of importance for Luther. He claimed to possess no special gift beyond the Word which had been present in the mouths of the Biblical

> prophets. His estimate of himself, as constructive promoter of the Gospel or as destructive critic of false teaching, was only and only connected with the Word of God.[934]

Emboldened by that Word alone, Luther was not afraid to publish or preach what he believed and did not care if it were offensive or outlandish so long as he was convinced it was based on Scriptural truth and would enable change leading to reforming the Church. He lived at a time when truth was still indivisible, and our "Evangelist" was firmly convinced that he was specifically called to represent and proclaim that Truth, as was the Apostle Paul. Some would characterize his stubborn position epitomized in the "Here I stand!" posture as exhibiting arrogance; and it is true that, among theologians especially, he tolerated basically only listeners and disciples. In a sense, to defy Luther was to deny God. He was therefore extremely protective of the integrity of his religious vision as a prophet and could be an incredibly determined and violent hater as we have observed.

Emboldened and Adamant Combatants

"Here I Stand"
Left: Public domain, retrieved at the University of Chicago website

Trump's Pistol Hand Gesture
Right: ResearchGate.net

In a strikingly comparable manner, Trump is considered arrogant and often perceived as a loose cannon with his bluster, and what appears to be outlandish statements or claims. Yet with confidence rooted in deeply held values and convictions like Luther, he takes calculated risks. Regardless of one's viewpoint, it takes a confident person to be able to lead

[934] Kolb, *Images*, pp.31-32.

others effectively. Can you remember the last time you were influenced by someone who lacked confidence? Knowing himself well, Trump says, "Show me someone without an ego, and I'll show you a loser,"[935] and "You have to think anyway, so why not think big?"[936] Thus, he encounters "Rocket Man," Kim Jong-un of North Korea, with blatant either-or consequences, and in the Oval Office meeting with Democratic leaders on funding border security he brags, "I am proud to shut down the government for border security.... I will take the mantle. I will be the one to shut it down."[937]

Taking a stand on principles and values, he is doing what he promised for the sake of protecting the country, which he considers the most important part of his Constitutional responsibility. The President is not afraid to say what he believes, no matter how much criticism he receives, even about his efforts to "drain the swamp." How can he and Luther attempt to force their heady dreams to "Make America Great Again" or for the true Church to re-emerge from papal darkness with no regard for losses? Reformers are rarely appreciated when they are up to their waist in the swamp they are seeking to drain. Both are passionately convinced of their own rightness, and tell it like it is, sometimes in blunt and crude terms, and not so ironically to the consternation of the establishment. They are both so emboldened to think that anyone who disagreed with them was either ignorant, stupid or evil. Such overconfidence led them to frequently speak in shocking and unsavory terms that undeniably resulted in their being misunderstood and criticized. Amazingly, though, they discovered their support increasing rather than diminishing. More than surmise, both Luther and Trump are manifestly convinced many of their colleagues who disagree or take offense with them secretly know the truth but refuse to acknowledge it.

In his day, Luther had enemies as bitter as those opposing Donald Trump today. Sermons from Luther or pronouncements from Trump were not received by everyone with equal enthusiasm and support. Heinz Schilling, in his biography *Martin Luther, Rebel in an Age of Upheaval*, observes that many of Luther's "sermons...provoked open dissent, even anger—some of his audience protested by ringing bells or creating a racket in other ways, and he was also threatened physically,"[938] especially during the social unrest resulting in the Peasant's War. Trump, likewise, has experienced his share of scorn and hatred through protestors (often well-orchestrated), pundits, comedians, staged disruptions at his rallies, and even amid Congressional hearings, and has encountered threats from those who wish him harm.

---

[935] <http://www.quotationspage.com/quote/33928.html>.

[936] <https://www.brainyquote.com/quotes/donald_trump_153798>.

[937] <https://newrepublic.com/article/152614/i-proud-shut-government-border-security-says-trump>.

[938] Schilling, *Upheaval*, p.256.

It is challenging for all who are of the human species to follow St. Paul's admonition in Ephesians *"to speak the Truth in love"* (4:15 [PME]) especially when we experience negative reactions from those who do not desire to be confronted with Truth. Professor of the History of Christianity at the Divinity School of Harvard University, Mark U. Edwards, Jr., writes,

> [Laux] Gemigger explained at one point, "that accounts for the treatment of the pious Luther, who is unjustly and improperly treated because he reveals to us the Roman rascality as well as their great heresy." They even sought Luther's life. "He who now dares to tell the truth must turn himself over to death," Gemigger claimed, explaining, "If speaking kindly makes good friends, then saying the truth makes great enemies. It is because Luther has proclaimed to us the divine Truth that people are so hostile towards him." On several occasions Gemigger labled the papacy the Antichrist and suggested that the clergy needed to be reformed with *cold steel*.[939]

Gemigger's observation and assertion could apply to both our combatants. In the context of obstruction and resistance, Luther admitted that he would get angry when challenged. "I find nothing that promotes work better than angry fervor. For when I wish to compose, write, pray, and preach well, I must be angry. It refreshes my entire system, my mind is sharpened, and all unpleasant thoughts and depression fade away."[940] Obviously, the modus operandi for many Twitter users is just the opposite: no pause for thought; no walk to the mailbox to reconsider whether a letter is worth sending. Rather, react immediately in the intemperate shorthand that the now 280-character limit imposes, and click "Send." For Luther, however, "anger is sometimes necessary and proper. But [he cautions] be sure that you use it correctly. You are commanded to get angry, not on your own behalf, but on behalf of your office and of God; you must not confuse the two, your person and your office."[941] We have observed both our warriors making that distinction. In the face of threatening personal injury to body and reputation, the office held dictated their righteous indignation coming out of concern for the well-being and future of the State and Church.

---

[939] Edwards, *Printing*, p.53, quoting Gemigger's "Zü lob," (*To the Praise of Luther and to the Honor of All Christendom*, Strasbourg, 1520)," in *Flugschriften der frühen Reformationsbewegung (1518-1524), Volume 1*, ed. Adolf Laube, Annerose Schneider and Sigrid Looss (Berlin, 1983), pp.548-557, here specifically p.554..
[940] Martin Luther, "Entry No. 2410b," *Off the Record with Martin Luther: An Original Translation of the Table Talks*, trans. and ed. Charles Daudert (Kalamazoo, MI: Hansa-Hewlett, 2009), p.110.
[941] LW 21:83. *The Sermon on the Mount and The Magnificat*, "Matthew 5:27-30."

If one thinks the President is somehow intimidated by the various and powerful media, daunted by celebrities crying and throwing temper tantrums, shaken by elected officials screaming "impeach," or dismayed by special investigations into collusion with Russia, think again. He continually mystifies his critics who underestimate his resolve and commitment to Making America Great. It has been heartening to see someone as confident and impervious to criticism as Trump standing up to what seems to be an ever-present mob and winning. He has exhibited a stubborn stance, much like we view in Luther's position against the powers of the Pope and Emperor, who sought his excommunication and death. Luther did not fear those consequences; and so it is with Trump, even in facing impeachment. In Peter Stanford's assessment, Luther

> had the courage to take on a monolithic Church in the full expectation that it would cost him his life, but he did it, nonetheless, confronting the might of the first truly universal religion, in person and often alone, with an extraordinary passion, intensity and energy. And most remarkable of all, not only did Luther survive, he triumphed, and we are all better off because of him.[942]

---

942 Stanford, Peter, "Five Centuries."

28

The Epoch Trial

Luther had discovered colossal corruption within the institutional Church and its leaders, much as Trump discovered within the government, especially within agencies' upper echelons of leaders and bureaucrats. Both rebels, in attempting to "drain the swamp," discovered that corruption, then and now, is a stubborn, self-serving creature. They were striking at the heart of institutional elite power and control over the people they were neglecting. Confrontation was inevitable.

Upon receiving a copy of the Ninety-Five Theses, the Pope began to see Luther as a larger threat than he had first imagined. On August 7, 1518, Luther received a summons from Pope Leo X to appear in Rome to answer accusations of false teachings and contemptuous resistance to authority. Frederick the Wise, exercising his political clout, prevailed in having the hearing on heresy moved to Augsburg, where the Imperial Diet or Congress of rulers in the Holy Roman Empire—Emperor Maximilian, nobles, knights, counts, free cities called "The Estates," and top rulers called "the Electors"—was already taking place. This first step toward a potential trial for heresy could be compared to the House of Representatives' investigation and hearings on impeachment before submitting articles for the trial to be held in the Senate.

For three days in October (12th through 14th) Luther defended himself under the questioning by papal legate Cardinal Cajetan. The focal issue was the Pope's authority to issue indulgences and his infallibility. Luther adamantly refused to recant, asserting "His Holiness abuses Scriptures…I deny that he is above Scripture."[943] Luther stood firm in his claim that only the Scriptures were infallible, unlike popes and councils who could err. The hearings degenerated into a shouting match and Luther's confrontation with the Church cast him as an enemy of the Pope. Bainton writes that Luther "had not made the arduous journey to Augsburg to do what he could have done quite as well at Wittenberg. He would like to be instructed as to his errors."[944]

---

943 Bainton, *Here I Stand*, p.96 (Abingdon) and p. 73 (Mentor pb).

944 Ibid., p.94 (Abingdon) and p.72 (Mentor pb).

Cajetan demanded that Elector Frederick arrest and deliver Luther to Rome. Again, his protectorate argued that Luther be given the opportunity to debate his interpretation of Scripture before judges in a university setting for an unbiased decision. Frederick stated he would send Luther to Rome only if and after he has been convicted of heresy. He did not want anyone to rush to judgement condemning Luther in advance, as we have sadly witnessed with premature judgments pronounced by politicians, media, and Church leaders before all the facts were known, and as occurred with Trump where presumption of innocence was ignored, evidence of impeachable crimes was lacking, and "due process" according to House rules was ignored, regarding conduct of such investigations.

Charles V

A new emperor, Charles V*, at the tender age of 19 had ascended the throne on June 28, 1519, facing tumultuous challenges and threats from France, the Pope, and the Muslim armies advancing into Europe. It was precisely at this moment that our German Augustinian monk threatened the unity the empire needed. The "Wild Boar" was gaining tremendous fame and popularity with his key writings in 1520 (*On the Freedom of a Christian, The Babylonian Captivity of the Church,* and *Address to the Nobility of the German Nation*) which Rome could no longer ignore. Pope Leo X was compelled to issue an initial papal bull (*Exsurge Domine*) on June 15, 1520, warning the Wittenberg monk that he would be excommunicated unless he recanted 41 sentences included in his Ninety-Five Theses within sixty days. On the tenth of October, the bull reached Luther, to which he replied with a tract entitled "Against the Execrable Bull of Antichrist," in which he writes:

> Luther, who is used to *bellum,* is not afraid of *bellum* (A state of open and often prolonged conflict carried on between parties). I can distinguish between inane paper and the omnipotent Word of God...
>
> I wish to be instructed, not respectively, but absolutely and certainly. I demand that they show absolutely, not respectively, distinctly, and not confusedly, certainly and not probably, clearly and not obscurely, point by point and not in a lump, just what is heretical. Let them show where I am a heretic, or dry

---

* Holy Roman Emperor Charles V, who presided over the Diet of Worms where Luther, having been excommunicated by the Church, was tried as a heretic. The State had to ratify the papal decree to carry out the Church's decision. (Portrait by Bernard van Orley, 1519. In the public domain; retrieved at Google Arts and Culture.)

> up their spittle.... So then, you impious and insensate papists, write soberly if you want to write. Whether this bull is by Eck or by the pope, it is the sum of all impiety, blasphemy, ignorance, impudence, hypocrisy, lying—in a word, it is Satan and his Antichrist.[945]

One doesn't have to stretch the imagination to make the transference to Donald Trump responding as he did to erroneous accusations by his opponents, Fake News distorting his words and not giving proper interpretation, neglecting critical context, and refusing to present the rest of the true story, which would often contradict the biased, agenda-driven headlines. Luther concludes his tract:

> If anyone despise my fraternal warning, I am free from his blood in the last judgment. It is better that I should die a thousand times than that I should retract one syllable of the condemned articles. And as they excommunicated me for the sacrilege of heresy, so I excommunicate them in the Name of the sacred Truth of God. Christ will judge whose excommunication will stand. Amen.[946]

Tortuous negotiations continued within and between both sides, leading to strife centering on whether Luther, a heretic of the Church, should be permitted to appear before a secular tribunal to be examined over matters of faith. "Never!" was the resolve of the papal nuncio Aleander who was the inquisitor or prosecutor assigned to the Luther case by Pope Leo X. He concluded his remarks using the taunt of Luther's critics:

> The authority of the Holy See should not be prejudiced by subjection to the judgment of the laity. One who has been condemned by the Pope, the cardinals, and prelates should be heard only in prison. The laity including, the Emperor, are not in a position to review the case. The only competent judge is the Pope. How can the Church be called the ship of Peter if Peter is not at the helm? ...Has the Catholic Church been dead for a thousand years to be revived only by Martin? Has the whole world gone wrong and Martin only has the eyes to see?[947]

---

[945] Ibid., p.162 (Abingdon) and pp. 125-126 (Mentor pb).
[946] Ibid., p.163 (Abingdon) and p.126 (Mentor pb).
[947] Ibid., pp.172-173 (Abingdon) and p.134(Mentor pb).

The Emperor seemed to be impressed and on the seventeenth of December rescinded the invitation he issued to bring Luther to the Diet. With Luther's open defiance of Rome's demands and Church leaders urging the Pope to reinforce the authority of the Church, on January 3, 1521, Pope Leo issued *Decet Romanum Pontificem* ("It Befits the Roman Pontiff") to affect the excommunication threatened by his earlier papal bull, *Exsurge Domine.* Then the Emperor was pressed to ratify the Pope's decree with a civil injunction against Luther, which German law required to carry out the Church's decision. Such action would demonstrate the unity of Church and State against heretics, and would be taken up by the forthcoming Diet in Worms (pronounced "Vohrms").

Conscious of the public antagonism toward Rome, and fearing a mass uprising should Luther be found guilty of heresy and condemned by the Church without an impartial hearing, the hierarchy of the Church continued their delicate dance of politics, piety, and diplomacy. The influence of the powerful Elector Frederick and the magnitude of Luther supporters certainly had an effect in changing the course of the proceedings. Of course, Luther did not neglect his own defense. Douglas O. Linder, creator of the Famous Trials website, cites the "Appeal to Caesar" Luther sent to the new emperor, asking "the Emperor to allow his guilt or innocence on the heresy charge to be determined after a hearing by non-ecclesiastical officials. Luther had boldly asserted in his August appeal that Church officials should be answerable to the State."[948] "For three years I have sought peace in vain. I have now but one recourse. I appeal to Caesar. I have no desire to be defended if I am found to be impious or heretical. One thing I ask, that neither truth nor error be condemned unheard and unrefuted."[949]

Frederick was puzzled and now determined to get a clarification of Charles' position. The Elector astutely first inquired of Luther if he would be willing to go the Diet of Worms if the Emperor personally "re-invited" him. He was anxious to appear and answered:

> You ask me what I shall do if I am called by the emperor. I will go even if I am too sick to stand on my feet. If Caesar calls me, God calls me. If violence is used, as well it may be, I commend my cause to God. He lives and reigns who saved the three youths from the fiery furnace of the King of Babylon, and if He will not save me, my head is worth nothing compared with Christ. This

---

[948] Linder, Douglas O., "The Trial of Martin Luther: An Account," *Famous Trials.* <https://www.famous-trials.com/luther/286-home>.

[949] Bainton, *Here I Stand,* p.151 (Abingdon) and p.117 (Mentor pb).

> is no time to think of safety. I must take care that the Gospel is not brought into contempt by our fear to confess and seal our teaching with our blood.[950]

The Emperor answered Frederick, promising to assume responsibility for Luther's case, but shared that he could not act alone in executing the papal edicts without concurrence of the princes; and so the Diet was being invited not to ratify, but simply to implement the papal verdict. There was evidently no indication that Charles' promise meant Luther would have a public hearing before the Diet. Being informed of the Emperor's response, Luther replied to Frederick, "I am heartily glad that His Majesty will take to himself this affair, which is not mine but that of all Christianity and the whole German nation."[951] One could surmise that Luther's selflessly noble and elevated response had informed President Trump's commitment to reviving the hearts and protecting the livelihood of American people, whom he was serving in his drive to "Make America Great Again."

A plenary session of the Diet was summoned by Charles for the thirteenth of February, 1521. Aleander was given three hours to prepare their minds in what was deemed a much better case against Luther than the bull in asserting Luther as an obstinate heretic. With the recognized gift of eloquence and redoubled zeal, Aleander rose to the occasion to overthrow the truth. In her book *The Great Controversy*, Ellen White* reports, "Charge after charge he hurled against Luther as an enemy of the Church and State, the living and the dead, clergy and laity, councils and private Christians. 'In Luther's errors there is enough,' he declared to warrant the burning of 'a hundred thousand heretics.'"[952]

In casting aversion and contempt upon the adherents of Luther's teachings with fierce denunciations, Aleander prosecuted Rome's case before the august assembly:

> What are all these Lutherans? A crew of insolent pedagogues, corrupt priests, dissolute monks, ignorant lawyers, and degraded nobles, with the common people, who they have misled and perverted. How far superior to them is the Catholic party in number, ability, and power! A unanimous decree from this

---

[950] Ibid., p.174 (Abingdon) and 135 (Mentor pb).

[951] Ibid., p.175 (Abingdon) and 136 (Mentor pb).

* Ellen G. White, one of the founders of the Seventh-day Adventist Church and held in esteem as a prophetess or messenger, describes how the timeless "Great Controversy" theme plays out between Jesus Christ and Satan in the world of human affairs.

[952] White, Ellen G. *The Great Controversy*, "Luther Before the Diet," *The Ellen White Information Website.* <https://www.ellenwhite.info/books/ellen-g-white-book-great-controversy-gc-08.htm>.

> illustrious assembly will enlighten the simple, warn the imprudent, decide the waverers, and give strength to the weak.[953]

Prevalent today in our cancel culture and political life, we experience the all-too-familiar "put-downs" of opponents using pejorative and demeaning words to describe those who "disagree," who dare not to follow in lock-step the establishment's position, or who voice an inconvenient view. Ellen White writes, "With such weapons the advocates of truth in every age have been attacked. The same arguments are still urged against all who dare to present, in opposition to established errors, the plain and direct teachings of God's Word.... They are unlearned, few in number, and of the poorer class...ignorant and deceived."[954] As we have already called attention to this polarization being exacerbated with such condescending insults as "bigots," "deplorables," "racists," "white supremacists," and "homophobic," fear is thus enkindled by the "protected class," and individuals cower in retreat, remaining quiet rather than be diminished or cancelled should they counter, as Luther would have done were he present and as Trump has done.

The legate's speech made a deep impression upon the Diet. "No more damaging case could have been made against Luther before the Diet," claims Bainton, "which was now asked to endorse the imperial edict proclaiming Luther a Bohemian heretic and revolutionary."[955] The presentation of the edict precipitated a raucous storm, with the estates demanding a time-out. On the nineteenth they answered, offering the cautionary concern that

> Luther's teaching was already so firmly rooted among the people that a condemnation without a hearing would occasion grave danger of insurrection. He should be brought to the Diet under safe conduct, to be examined by learned men. He should be brought to answer, not to argue. If he would renounce what he had said against the faith, other points could be discussed. If he refused, then the Diet would support the edict.[956]

---

[953] D'Aubigne, Jean Henri Merle, *Book 7, The Diet of Worms – 1521 to May,* "Chapter 3." <https://bibletruthpublishers.com/chapter-3/jean-henri-merle-daubigne/book-07-the-diet-of-worms-1521-january-to-may/history-of-the-reformation/la103795>; D'Aubigne, B7, ch.3.

[954] White, *The Great Controversy,* "Luther Before the Diet."

[955] Bainton, *Here I Stand,* p.178 (Abingdon) and p. 138 (Mentor pb).

[956] Ibid.

The Emperor immediately renewed his earlier invitation for Luther to come to the Diet, the assembly of the German States, which had convened in Worms shortly after his ascension to the throne. General excitement was created as news circulated that Luther was to appear before the Diet, and of course before the new, young Emperor. On March 29th the herald sent to personally escort Luther to Worms arrived in Wittenberg. Luther and his companions set forth on the 325-mile journey on April 2nd. In some ways the journey was like a victory parade for a celebrity, through cities where he was welcomed enthusiastically, such as in Erfurt, Gotha, and Eisenach where he preached, and cheered and welcomed as he passed through Leipzig, Weimar and Frankfurt. Some among the crowds were obviously gawkers, others moved by faith and piety, some moved by patriotism and populism, and many eagerly warning him of the intention of the Romanists to burn him. Without a doubt Luther knew where his heart was grounded and understood that this could be his death march, following in the steps of reformers before him like Hus and Wycliffe who were condemned and burned. Responding to these well-intended concerns, Luther responded, "Though they should kindle a fire all the way from Worms to Wittenberg, the flames of which reached to heaven, I would walk through it in the name of the Lord...."[957] Maintaining his strong conviction of faith and trust, he wrote to his friends that he was prepared to give his life for his faith and the cause of Christ. "I will enter Worms under the banner of Christ against the gates of hell." Obviously "...he had no illusions as to the probable outcome. After an ovation at Erfurt he commented, 'I have had my Palm Sunday. I wonder whether this pomp is merely a temptation or whether it is also the sign of my impending passion.'"[958]

Many had read his writings and pamphlets, viewed the woodcuts, and saw prints and portrait drawings of the man viewed as some sort of savior or the German Hercules. With a small band of supporters, Luther entered Worms on the early evening of April 16 in a Saxon two-wheeled cart, to the sound of trumpets and the cheering throng of two thousand well-wishers. The excitement was broken by a funeral dirge being chanted to warn Luther of the fate that awaited him. "'God will be my defense,' said Luther as he alighted from his carriage."[959] Dignitaries in Worms had lined up to personally meet the defendant and give him encouragement, as many persons appeared on the balconies and others climbed to the roofs to gain a glimpse of the dauntless monk.[960] The papists who did not believe Luther would venture into Worms expressed their consternation at the excitement that far exceeded

---

[957] White, *The Great Controversy*, "Luther Before the Diet."

[958] Bainton, *Here I Stand*, p.179 (Abingdon) and p.139 (Mentor pb).

[959] White, *The Great Controversy*. "Luther Before the Diet."

[960] Linder, "The Trial of Martin Luther."

the welcome given to greet the new emperor. They told the Emperor to get rid of the heretic at once. "'We are not bound either to give or observe the safe-conduct of a heretic.' 'No,' said the Emperor, 'we must keep our promise.'"[961]

Greeted by Crowds

Luther's Entry into Worms for Diet

Trump leaving Dallas in "The Beast"

(Left) Luther arriving in the City of Worms where the Diet of Worms had convened to welcome the new emperor and where Luther had been summoned to defend his attacks on orthodox Catholic beliefs and answer for his books and teachings. He denied the power of Rome to determine right and wrong in matters of faith and the authority of the Pope over Scripture. On the basis of conscience and the Word of God, he refused to recant which would have compromised his principles. (Image: Lea Millis/Reuters)

(Right) Supporters and detractors line the road as President Donald Trump (viewed in the back window) rides in "The Beast," the Presidential limo, after leaving Gateway Church in Dallas, on Thursday, June 11, 2020. President Trump was in town for multiple events and gathers large crowds of bystanders wherever he travels. (Image: Vernon Bryant/ Dallas Morning News)

The following day, every avenue to the hall was crowded with spectators, and Luther had to be escorted through back doors and passageways because of those eager to view the monk who had resisted the authority of the Pope. Finally in the hall before the council, with the Emperor occupying the throne, Luther was asked if the pile of books on the table were his writings and whether he would recant what he had written. When the titles were read, Luther responded that the books were his, but declined to answer whether he would retract, saying it would be rash to reply without time to meditate. He was granted that time to think things over and told to come back the next day with his answer.

The next day he entered a larger hall filled to overflowing. Asked to "'Explain yourself now. Will you defend all your writings, or disavow some of them?' Luther saw an opportunity to give a speech, rather than a 'yes' or 'no' answer and he took it. He replied by drawing

---

[961] White, *The Great Controversy*, "Luther Before the Diet."

a distinction between his various writings."[962] First, there were devotional writings about faith and the Gospel even his enemies found profitable. Second were books written against the papacy, papal scheming, abuses and tyranny by the Pope, and canon law against the German people whose wealth was being devoured by unworthy means. "'Yet the papists,' Luther states, 'by their own decrees (as in dist. 9 and 25; ques. 1 and 2*) warn that the papal laws and doctrines which are contrary to the Gospel or the opinions of the Fathers are to be regarded as erroneous and reprehensible.'"[963] Luther explained, as President Trump did continuously through investigations and impeachment hearings, that if he were to revoke those books, it would only strengthen tyranny and greater godlessness, just as for Trump, ignoring the Constitution and rule of law, due process, and the established rules of the House would open the floodgates for more unlawful threats and devious erosion of our Republic's foundation.

The third category contained writings against those persons, both private and distinguished, who attacked his doctrine and teachings or were defending the abuses of the Church. Giving his sole concession, Luther confesses that "I have been more violent than my religion or profession demands. But then, I do not set myself up as a saint; neither am I disputing about my life, but about the teaching of Christ."[964]

Luther continued his defense saying that "When Christ stood before Annas, He said '*Produce witnesses*' (John 18:21). If our Lord, who could not err, made this demand, why may not a worm like me ask to be convicted of error from the prophets and the Gospels? If I am shown my error, I will be the first to throw my books into the fire."[965]

> Luther had spoken in German and was now requested to repeat the same words in Latin.... The minds of many of the princes were so blinded by error and superstition that at the first delivery they did not see the force of Luther's reasoning; but the repetition enabled them to perceive clearly the points presented. Those who stubbornly closed their eyes to the light, and

---

[962] Linder, "The Trial of Martin Luther."

* LW 32:110. *Career of the Reformer II*, "Luther at the Diet of Worms," This seems to be a reference to Decretum Magistri Gratiani, dist. IX, c.8. Migne 187, 50 according to the editors' footnote 4.

[963] Ibid.

[964] Ibid., LW 32:111.

[965] Bainton, *Here I Stand*, p.184 (Abingdon) and p.143 (Mentor pb).

> determined not to be convinced of the Truth, were enraged at the power of Luther's words.[966]

We have witnessed many occasions where Trump could empathize with his elder twin, even as critics of the President made false allegations, distorted facts, and even chose to deny truth when facts and evidence blatantly proved they were wrong in their assessment and initial judgment.

The spokesperson and prosecutor for the Empire, John Eck (not to be confused with the John Eck of the Leipzig debate), an official of the Archbishop Elector of Trier, angrily claimed that Luther was required to give a clear and precise answer. According to Luther, what was sought from him was not a "horned"* response, but a simple "yes" or "no" as to whether or not he wished to retract. Here he answered:

> Since then your serene majesty and your lordships seek a simple answer, I will give it in this manner, neither horned nor toothed: Unless I am convinced by the testimony of the Scriptures or by clear reason—for I do not trust either in the Pope or in Councils alone, since it is well known that they have often erred and contradicted themselves—I am bound by the Scriptures I have quoted and my conscience is captive to the Word of God. I cannot and I will not retract anything since it is neither safe nor right to go against conscience. I cannot do otherwise, here I stand, may God help me, Amen.[967]

It was reported that

> the whole assembly were for a time speechless with amazement.... The courage and firmness which he now displayed, as well as the power and

---

[966] White, *The Great Controversy,* "Luther Before the Diet."

* "Horned" or "*Cornutum.*" A "*horned*" syllogism is a sophisical, ambiguous reply.

[967] LW 32:112-113. *Career of the Reformer II.* "Luther at the Diet of Worms."

These words are given in the first printed German and Latin texts upon which this translation is based. However, the words "Here I stand, I cannot do otherwise," though not recorded on the spot, may nevertheless be genuine, because the listeners at the moment may have been too moved to write, suggests Bainton in *Here I Stand*, p.185. The editors of LW 32:113 state, "There is good evidence, however, that Luther actually said only: 'May God help me!'" (Cf. *Deutsche Reichstagakten, Vol.II: Deutsche Reichstagsakten* under Kaiser Karl V [Gotha, 1896, p.587]). In either case, there is no doubt about the "stand" Luther took in this epoch trial and in his life and ministry.

> clearness of his reasoning, filled all parties with surprise. The Emperor, moved to admiration, exclaimed: 'This monk speaks with an intrepid heart and unshaken courage.' …It was evident that he could not be induced, either by promises or threats to yield to the mandate of Rome.
>
> The papal leaders were chagrined that their power, which had caused kings and nobles to tremble, should be thus despised by a humble monk; they longed to make him feel their wrath by torturing his life away. But Luther, understanding his danger, had spoken to all with Christian dignity and calmness. His words had been free from pride, passion, and misrepresentation. He had lost sight of himself, and the great men surrounding him, and felt only that he was in the presence of One infinitely superior to popes, prelates, kings, and emperors. Christ had spoken through Luther's testimony with a power and grandeur that for time inspired both friends and foes with awe and wonder…
>
> The Elector Frederick…with deep emotion listened to his speech. With joy and pride, he witnessed the doctor's courage, firmness, and self-possession, and determined to stand more firmly in his defense. He contrasted the parties in contest, and saw that the wisdom of popes, kings, and prelates had been brought to naught by the power of Truth. The papacy had sustained a defeat which would be felt among all nations and in all ages.[968]

Thus, this righteous man made his "stand" upon the sure foundation of the Word of God. He threw up his arm in the gesture of a victorious knight, told his supporters, "I've come through!" and slipped out of the hall to return to his lodging, while the princes gathered to begin deliberating his fate. Roland Bainton characterized the moment that the monk stood before the monarch Charles, heir of a long line of Catholic sovereigns, and before the power and supremacy of the papacy, "a miner's son with nothing to sustain him save his own faith in the Word of God: Here the past and future were met. Some would see at this point the beginning of modern times. The contrast is real enough."[969] Luther had emerged on the stage of world history, giving rise to a pivotal chapter in the life of Christ's Church. His trial was epochal, establishing the modern fundamental principle of human rights.

---

[968] White, *The Great Controversy*, "Luther Before the Diet."

[969] Bainton, *Here I Stand*, pp.181-182 (Abingdon) and p 141 (Mentor pb).

Resentful Anger for Penetrating Sanctimonious Ranks

Excommunication – **Impeachment**

Luther Making His Stand at the Diet of Worms

Trump Responds to Impeachment Vote

Both Seemingly Acquiescing to a Higher Power

(Left) Excommunicated by the Pope in January 1521, Luther first appeared before Emperor Charles V on April 16, and the next day made his stand at the Diet of Worms, refusing to disavow his writings on which he is pictured as having placed his left hand, asserting: "Since then your imperial majesty and your lordships demand a simple answer, I will give you one without teeth and without horns. Unless I am convicted of error by the testimony of Scripture or by manifest evidence...I cannot and will not retract, for we must never act contrary to our conscience." Luther was pronounced a heretic and an outlaw or enemy of the State at the Reichstag, meaning he could be killed by anyone without threat of punishment. (Image: Public domain, retrieved at The Babylon Bee)

(Right) President Donald Trump reacts to the impeachment vote in the House during a campaign rally in Battle Creek, Michigan, December 18, 2019, saying, "They've cheapened the impeachment process. This is a sacred position. Anybody who becomes president, they could have a phone call and they could become impeached." Charged in two articles—Abuse of Power and Obstruction of Justice—the President was acquitted in the Senate and exonerated of all charges in both impeachments. (Image: Lea Millis/Reuters)

As the papal representative perceived the effect produced by Luther's speech, he feared as never before for the security of the Romish power, and resolved to employ every means at his command to affect the Reformer's overthrow. Sound familiar? Efforts made to undermine Trump's credibility by spying and fabricating false claims during the campaign and transition period, as well as efforts to thwart any success or "win" at the expense of contradicting their own position on issues that would benefit citizens, and attempting means to prevent Trump from running again in a future election? "With all the eloquence and diplomatic skill for which he was so eminently distinguished, [Eck] represented to the youthful Emperor the folly and danger of sacrificing, in the cause of an insignificant monk, the friendship and support of the powerful see of Rome."[970] Is this not the sad practice of what we so often experience in our political life today? Cronyism? To be expedient rather than right, yielding

[970] White, *The Great Controversy*, "Luther Before the Diet."

to the dictates of worldly pride to maintain power rather than trust the values inherent in serving the people?

His words obviously had impact, as Charles informed the Diet on the following day his determination to carry out the policies of his predecessors to maintain and protect the Catholic religion:

> Since Luther had refused to renounce his errors, the most vigorous measures should be employed against him and the heresies he taught. "A single monk, misled by his own folly, has risen against the faith of Christendom. To stay such impiety, I will sacrifice my kingdoms, my treasures, my friends, my blood, my soul, and my life. I am about to dismiss the Augustine Luther, forbidding him to cause the least disorder among people; I shall then proceed against him and his adherents as contumacious heretics, by excommunication, by interdict, and by every means calculated to destroy them."[971]

The Emperor, as protector of the Church, would be taking action against him, but declared Luther would have 21 days to return home safely before the promised safe conduct ended.

> On May 6, a final draft of the Edict of Worms, prepared by Aleander, was submitted to the Diet. It was finally signed by the Emperor on May 26. The Edict called Luther a "reviver of the old and condemned heresies" and an "inventor of new ones." It called for the burning of his books and for confiscation of his property. It cut him off from the Church, called for his arrest, and forbid anyone from harboring or sustaining him. Finally, it warned that anyone who dares to directly or indirectly oppose this decree… will be guilty of the crime of *lese majeste* [insulting a monarch; treason] and will incur our grave indignation as well as each of the punishments mentioned above.[972]

The popular Church historian of the 19th-century, J. H. Merle d'Aubigne, writes that Luther was denounced in this decree as "Satan himself under the form of a man and dressed

---

[971] Ibid.

[972] Linder, "The Trial of Martin Luther."

in a monk's frock."[973] Luther and two companions left Worms on April 26 to return to Wittenberg before the Edict was issued. They were traveling to visit friends near Eisenach on May 4 when ambushed by men on horseback with crossbows. Frederick of Saxony had devised a plan with the cooperation of friends to hustle Luther away to a safe place following a staged kidnapping. Separated from his attendants, Luther was secretly and hurriedly conveyed through the forest on horseback to the castle of Wartburg, an isolated mountain fortress where he would be securely hidden from friend and foe.

Accustomed to a life of activity, heightened by stern conflict, Luther obviously could not endure being idle while "imprisoned" and masqueraded as Junker Jorge on his rocky mountain Patmos "retreat." He took up his pen, writing a host of letters now known as "From the Wilderness" or "From the Isle of Patmos," tracts that were circulated throughout Germany, and lectures on Christian values. Most notably, he served his countrymen by translating the New Testament into their own tongue. For nearly a year he found ways to do what he loved best—proclaiming the Gospel—while isolated on his Patmos, a reference to the Greek island where John authored the book of Revelation while being in exile.

---

[973] d'Aubigne, J.H. Merle, *History of the Reformation of the Sixteenth Century*, b.7, ch. 11, quoted by Ellen G. White in *The Great Controversy.*

29

Protecting Citizens by Building a Wall

Though Luther distinguished the spiritual and temporal worlds and saw himself as a reformer and prophet of God, he kept a close eye on the affairs of the civic community. "Unlike the clergy of the Roman Church, who claimed a standing distinct from that of regular citizens, Luther viewed himself as a full member of his community and as responsible, like all citizens [should be], for the public good and therefore for moral order and social peace."[974]

There were a couple of troubling concerns regarding the incorrigible bailiff and town captain in charge of security in Wittenberg, Hans von Metzsch, which Luther felt obliged to bring to the personal attention of Duke John Frederick the Magnanimous, who had succeeded Frederick the Wise as Elector in Saxony. One centered on this highest local official continuing his scandalous and promiscuous lifestyle with harlotry and dealings with prostitutes. After private admonition by Luther, and failing to change his behavior, the fornicator was privately excommunicated, [975] and Luther wanted to give the Elector a "heads-up" that he might need to publicly address the scandal of the Elector's own official.

Luther also wanted to make the Elector aware of the town captain's heavy-handedness in the reconstruction of the medieval city wall, a project intended to give Wittenberg a stronger modern fortification. What had been considered an excellent system of protection for its citizens in the 14th and 15th centuries—a wide moat, a stone wall, and raised embankments encircling the city—was now falling into various stages of disrepair. With Wittenberg's growing prominence and importance as the cradle for the Reformation, protection became more necessary.[976]

It was in 1502 that Frederick the Wise, although residing in Torgau, founded Wittenberg University, in a town of about 2,000 permanent residents on the Elbe River. It quickly became famous as an educational center, doubling its population with students. "During the tenure of Martin Luther and Philipp Melanchthon, more than 20,000 students matriculated

---

[974] Schilling, *Upheaval*, p.304.

[975] LW 54:159. *Table Talk*, "A Fornicator Excluded from the Sacrament, No 1646."

[976] See E. C. Schwiebert's "The Electoral Town of Wittenberg" (*Luther and His Times: The Reformation from a New Perspective* [St. Louis: Concordia, 1950], chapter 6, pp.199 ff) for a picturesque verbal look at Luther's Wittenberg, especially the map between pages 192-193 (Plate II) showing the wall fortification, and the map on page 203.

there from all over Europe.... Wittenberg in the 16th-century was a walled city, completely surrounded by a deep moat, and well-guarded day and night. Entry to the town was by three gates from west, south, and east."[977]

In a headstrong way, Metzsch moved the re-fortification "project forward without the agreement of the town council which in Spring 1531...he had almost 100 meters of the old town wall torn down before legal details had been worked out with the people of Wittenberg and before proper building plans had been developed. With a gaping hole in the wall, it was possible to enter the town unobserved and unchecked for several months."[978] As a good citizen, Luther felt Elector John should be aware of how alarming Metzsch's actions were to the inhabitants of Wittenberg. "I know very well how concerned one has been until now with the gates of the city, so that the city would be properly locked. But now the city stands open day and night because [of a significant breach in the wall] of more than one hundred paces, so that pigs and all kinds of animals run into [town]."[979] "Pigs and all kinds of animals," or as the footnote in *Luther's Works*, Volume 50, Letters III suggests, "Literally: 'pigs and all.' Instead of 'animals' Luther could also have thought of 'undesirable' people."[980] It is noteworthy that it was in 1975 that the editors translating Luther's letters felt it significant to put forward this probable expansive meaning in a footnote, given the context of Luther's concern presented to the Elector.

Luther's Concern about the Wittenberg Wall

Walls and moat around Wittenberg, Germany, 1550

---

[977] <https://www.encyclopedia.com/places/germany-scandinavia-and-central-europe/german-political-geography/wittenberg>.

[978] Schilling, *Upheaval*, p.305, referencing WABr 6:1826.

[979] LW 50:25. *Letters III*, "To Elector John [Wittenberg], June 16, 1531, (No. 243).

[980] Ibid., fn 6.

Wittenberg, 1536

Trump's Concern about the Wall on the Southern Border

The Southern American Border Wall

View of Tecate, Mexico to the right

(Images: Unsplash, used under the terms of their Creative Commons license)

Sounding very much like President Trump expressing his concern about national security, those crossing illegally on our southern border, and his promise to "Build the Wall," Luther was not only expressing the concern of local citizens for "border security" but was also giving voice to his own personal concern for his students: "My head is full of worry because there are many children [i.e. students] of important and good people here [at the university], and times are very dangerous. God might allow something to happen which we would have to deplore belatedly and in vain."[981] Luther was expressing the fear that gripped

981 Ibid.

the parents of students who had expected their sons would be safe in a "good, peaceful, and law-abiding town"[982] like Wittenberg. How many tragic accounts we have witnessed when illegal immigrants, who had been deported for felonies, re-entered the country illegally to become horrific repeat offenders? Luther clearly understood the God-ordained role and purpose of civil authorities, such as the Immigration and Custom Enforcement (ICE) officers discharging their responsibilities to protect the border.

Seven years earlier, in 1524, Luther had shared similar concerns about the responsibilities of those in government to ensure protection to the citizens, in a sermon to the Christians in Riga:

> Why, then, does [God] urge us to labor and watch, and want us to have walls, armor, and all manner of supplies, just as He commanded the children of Israel to put on their armor and fight against the Canaanites? Are we to provide no supplies, leave our gates and windows open, make no effort to defend ourselves but allow ourselves to be pierced through and become lifeless corpses as they did in the book of Maccabees? [1 Macc. 2:34-38]. By no means! You have just heard that those in authority should be watchful and diligent, and perform all the duties of their office: bar the gates, defend the towers and walls, put on armor, and procure supplies. In general, they should proceed as if there were no God and they had to rescue themselves and manage their own affairs; just as the head of a household is supposed to work as if he were trying to sustain [and protect] his and himself by his own labors.[983]

Recognizing the realist Luther was, even when viewing the actual causes of international tensions and war, Dr. George Forell contends Luther "preferred that if wars had to be fought they be fought for the defense of a city or the preservation of a border rather than in defense of the Christian faith or of the Holy Trinity."[984] He therefore warned the Emperor against crusades, yet encouraged him to defend the borders of Germany and protect the life and property of its citizens against the Turkish attacks. From this viewpoint Luther wrote in his book *On War Against the Turks* that

---

[982] Ibid., LW 50:26.

[983] LW 45:331. *The Christian in Society II*, "Exposition of Psalm 127 for the Christians at Riga in Livonia, 1524."

[984] Forell, George, "Luther's Theology and Foreign Policy."

> the emperor is not the head of Christendom or defender of the Gospel or the faith. The Church and the faith must have a defender other than emperor and kings.... The emperor's sword has nothing to do with the faith; it belongs to physical, worldly things.... Christians have been stirred up to take the sword and fight the Turk when they ought have been fighting the devil and unbelief with the Word and with prayer. Here is what should be done. The emperor and the princes should be exhorted concerning their office and their bounded duty to give serious and constant thought to governing their subjects in peace and to protecting them against the Turk.[985]

Luther's insights and sensible reasoning are as helpful and correct today as they were in the sixteenth century:

> Temporal power is in duty bound to defend its subjects, as I have frequently said, for it bears the sword in order to keep in fear those who do not heed such divine teaching and to compel them to leave others in peace. And in this the temporal power seeks not its own but its neighbor's profit and God's honor; it would gladly remain quiet and let its sword rust if God had not ordained it to be a hindrance to evil doers. Yet this defense of its subjects should not be accompanied by still greater harm; that would be but to leap from the frying pan into the fire. It is a poor defense to expose a whole city to danger for the sake of one person, or to risk the entire country for a single village or castle, unless God enjoined this by a special command as He did in former times. If a robber knight robs a citizen of his property and you, my lord, lead your army against him to punish this injustice, and in so doing lay waste the whole land, who will have wrought the greater harm, the knight or the lord? David overlooked many things when he was unable to punish without bringing harm upon others. All rulers must do the same. On the other hand, a citizen must endure a certain measure of suffering for the sake of the community, and not demand that all other men undergo the greater injury for his sake. Christ did not want the weeds to be gathered up, lest the wheat also be rooted up with them. (Matt. 13:29). If men went to war on every provocation and passed by no insult, we should never be at peace and have nothing but destruction. Therefore, right or wrong is never

[985] LW 46:185-186. *The Christian in Society III*, "On War Against the Turk, 1529."

> a sufficient reason indiscriminately to punish or make war. It is a sufficient cause to punish within bounds and without destroying another. The lord or ruler must always look to what will profit the whole mass of his subjects rather than any one portion. That householder will never grow rich who, because someone has plucked a feather from his goose, flings the whole goose after him.[986]

In addition to this sober realism and that which could be described as political pragmatism or common sense, notice too the pastoral concern Luther offered and then the caution:

> But he must watch out that his heart does not come to rely on these deeds of his, and get arrogant when things go well or worried when things go wrong. He should regard all such preparation and equipment as being the work of our Lord God under a mask, as it were, beneath which He Himself alone effects and accomplishes what we desire.[987]

As we have observed in Luther's understanding of the Two Kingdoms, exercising our responsibilities in the civil realm is not righteous work gaining our salvation. Those who exercise the function of government, which is ordained by God, should face the complexities of statecraft and political life realistically, and exercise their responsibilities prudently and virtuously, something Luther readily acknowledged was not all that easy. But then as now, defense of its borders and protection of life and property of its citizens are the first priorities of a temporal government.

---

[986] LW 21:337-38. *The Sermon on the Mount and The Magnificat*, "The Magnificat."

[987] LW 45:331. *The Christian in Society II*, "Exposition of Psalm 127," (Riga, Livonia).

30

The Environment Under the Sun and Within the Earth

In the era of the Green New Deal, Mark Hubert Lack noted that

> the quincentenary of the promulgation of Martin Luther's Ninety-Five Theses that set in motion the Protestant Reformation, 2017 also marked the notable anniversary of another seminal document. It was 50 years prior that the historian, Lynn White, famously argued that the earth's environmental crisis stemmed in part from the attitudes and actions of Christians. In an essay published in the journal *Science*, White contended in 1967 that Christianity was the most anthropocentric religion because Christians held that the sole intent of creation was to serve humankind.[988] As a result, this attitude, coupled with humankind's distortion of the divine injunction in the book of Genesis to have dominion over the earth, had contributed to the exploitation and impairment of the natural environment. While Christianity was but one of the contributing factors in White's argument, it was the one that garnered all the attention and the one raised repeatedly ever since by environmentalists.[989]

Mark Lack of Mississauga, Ontario, is a geo-scientist and environmental consultant with a Master of Theology degree from the University of Toronto. He writes that "popular sentiment and scholarly papers contend that Christians, particularly evangelicals and "conservative Protestants," are less inclined to support causes that safeguard the environment and the planet's future" due to their fixation on "heavenly matters while forsaking earthly

---

[988] White, Jr., Lynn, "The Historical Roots of Our Ecologic Crisis." *Science*, issue 155, No. 3767, March 1967, pp.1203-7.

[989] Lack, Mark Hubert, "Cherishing the Trees, as Christ is Lord Over All and the Center of All Things: Martin Luther's Tacit Ecotheological Ethic," *Living Traditions: Half a Millennium of Re-Forming Christianity*, ed. Kimberlynn McNabb and Robert C. Fennell (Eugene, OR: Wipf and Stock Publishers, 2019) pp.1-2.

ones." However, he acknowledges that Luther "did not share such an indifference towards the earth. He certainly was no enemy of the environment.... I maintain that the Reformer's theology contains a tacit ecotheological ethic."[990]

Luther's appreciation for the natural world is scattered throughout his teachings as one reads his sermons, catechisms, and Biblical commentaries. He viewed the material world as a divine blessing over which Christ has dominion with His all-pervasive immanence. His theology therefore can and should contribute to our contemporary dialogue with environmentalists by celebrating the gift of creation, while from a grateful heart promoting and practicing responsible stewardship of its resources.

Humankind's exploitation and despoiling of the natural environment would have been witnessed by Luther, who did not have to venture far from his childhood home in Mansfeld to see the destructive effects from hundreds of years of mining. Historian Lyndal Roper notes that "from the house the effects of mining would have been visible everywhere: Slag heaps pockmarked the landscape and the large pond below the town was polluted with the slag water from the two smelters outside the town walls."[991] Destruction of agricultural lands and the harvesting of hardwood timber—to produce charcoal to fire the furnaces, to fortify deepened mine shafts, and to build the large waterwheels and waterworks that powered the machinery—resulted in extensive deforestation which would have been clearly visible on the landscape.

This is where Luther grew up and he held life-long fondness for Mansfeld and its people. His father, Hans, was a miner and smelting master who operated copper mines and an ore smelting facility around Mansfeld. It was this region in the Harz Mountains of Germany that provided Europe with a significant source of silver, copper, and lead, making that area the most industrialized region of Germany. As we will discover, Luther maintained a deep appreciation for the bounteous gifts God provides in His creation and was sure that God hid the ore in the mountains and deep within the earth to be discovered and used to benefit humankind.

The late 15th century saw an explosion in population across Europe, a period that included Luther's own birth in 1483:

> With that growth came economic expansion and increased manufacturing, trade, and resource development. The era saw the rise of the modern money-based economy and the corresponding demand for metals. Silver and copper

---

[990] Ibid., pp.2-3.

[991] Roper, Lyndal, *Martin Luther: Renegade and Prophet* (New York: Random House, 2017), p.6.

> coins were needed to fund commercial trade and everyday transactions—including the payment of papal indulgences. Copper metal was also needed for the printing presses that launched the book publishing industry of the late 1400s. Metal movable type and engraved plates also turned out the certificates of indulgence and in response, the tracts and treatises that spread the Reformation teachings.[992]

Luther recognized that in the gift of creation, God richly provided and sustains humankind with all the necessities for earthly life, and he never ceased to recognize and point out creation's splendor. He describes creation as the most beautiful book, and admired the divine handiwork in the beauty of a rose.[993] With the curiosity of a scientist he observed that "If you were to search out everything about a kernel of wheat in the field, you would be so amazed that you would die. God's works are not like our works."[994]

The Gift of God's Creation

(Image: Loralu James)

In referencing our heritage during the Independence Day weekend, Trump spoke of "our profound obligation to protect America's extraordinary blessings for the next and many generations, frankly, to come. Among the heritage we must preserve our country's

[992] Lack, "Cherishing the Trees…," pp.4-5. (We have pointed to Luther's relationship with the publishing trade and the early printing industry as described in detail by Pettegree in his book *Brand Luther.*)
[993] LW 54:355. *Table Talk*, "A Rose Suggests a Lesson About God's Gifts."
[994] LW 36:344. *Word and Sacrament II*, "The Sacrament of the Body and Blood of Christ."

incredible natural splendor—that is the shared obligation that brings us together today."[995] While extolling nature's beauty and the wonder of God's creation, Luther lamented the lack of gratitude and indeed the apathy people show toward the natural world, in part owing to its familiarity. In his lectures on Genesis he says, "We do not marvel at the wonderful light of the sun, because it is a daily phenomenon. We do not marvel at the countless other gifts of creation…it is a great miracle that a small seed is planted and that out of it grows a very tall oak. But because these are daily occurrences, they have become of little importance like the very process of our procreation."[996]

In a Table Talk meditation on Christmas Day in 1538, Luther allowed himself to reflect on

> the fact that God is in all creatures…that the power and wisdom of God [is] in even the smallest flowers! …Who can imagine how God creates, out of the parched soil, such a variety of flowers, such pretty colors, such sweet vernal grass, beyond anything that a painter or apothecary* could make! Yet God can bring out of the ground such colors as green, yellow, red, blue, brown.

The vitamin company which brands their product "Balance of Nature" boasts that color is vital to one's health as it points to the value of color in the vegetables and fruits we consume. Having viewed Luther in the "raw," it would not be preposterous to imagine Luther continuing the commercial by humorously reminding listeners that in the final "end" after consuming and benefiting from the colorful "nutrients" the "waste" returns to the color of the ground out of which they came.

He then likens our indifference and our ingratitude for the earth's splendor with the visual invective of "cattle or other beasts trampling the most beautiful blossoms and lilies underfoot."[997]

---

995 Trump, Donald, "Remarks on the Environment, July 8, 2019." <https://trumpwhitehouse.archives.gov/briefings-statements/remarks-president-trump-americas-environmental-leadership/>.

996 LW 1:126. *Lectures on Genesis Chapters 1-5*, "Chapter 2:21." (an informative and instructive *life* "wonderment" made between a seed in the ground and semen received by a woman.)

* In the sixteenth century paints were prepared and sold by apothecaries.

997 LW 54:327. *Table Talk*, "Meditation at Table on Christmas Day 1538, No.4201."

In the Large Catechism, Luther explains that we are creatures of the Creator who

> has given and constantly sustains our body, soul, and life, members great and small, all faculties of mind, reason and understanding, and so forth; my food and drink, clothing, means of support, wife and child, servants, house, and home, etc. Besides, He makes all creation help provide the comforts and necessities of life—sun, moon, and stars in the heavens, day and night, air, fire, water, the earth and all that it brings forth, birds and fish, beasts, grain and all kinds of produce. Moreover, He gives all physical and temporal blessings—good government, peace, security. Thus, we learn…that none of us has his life of himself, or anything else…nor can he by himself preserve any of them.[998]

Then he instructs in his characteristic manner, while asserting his theological premise, that

> He does all of this out of pure love and goodness without our merit, as a kind father who cares for us…. Hence, since everything we possess, and everything in heaven and on earth besides, is daily given and sustained by God, it inevitably follows that we are in duty bound to love, praise and thank Him without ceasing, and, in short, to devote all these things to His service.[999]

It may be surprising to learn that Luther in the sixteenth century advocated against the abuse of nature, whether it was greed-driven exploitation, careless misuse, abuse or malicious destruction, as we have witnessed with forest fires set by arsonists in Australia. Yet there is a major difference in perspectives. Luther respected and appreciated the provisions God has provided us, with all the riches of the earth to enjoy "in proportion to [our] need."[1000]

In favoring modest consumption of natural resources, he was also promoting nature's protection. The earth was to be respected even during warfare. "Moderation should be

---

998 Martin Luther, "The Large Catechism, The Creed – First Article," *Book of Concord*, p.412.

999 Ibid.

1000 *LW 1:39. Lectures on Genesis Chapters 1-5*, "Chapter One (vs.11)."

observed in war, namely, that they should not cut down fruit-bearing trees but use those that bear no fruit for siegeworks…and not to devastate a land which has not sinned…"[1001]

Quite differently from what one may read or view most days in the media, President Trump shared the Reformer's appreciation for creation and the need to safeguard the environment and promote appreciation for its beauty and the wonders of God's creation. U.S. Secretary of the Interior David L. Bernhardt reports:

> It was President Trump that called for Congress to deliver the single largest investment in America's national parks and conservation in history. The Great American Outdoors Act establishes the National Parks and Public Land Legacy Restoration Fund, providing $9.5 billion for national parks, wildlife refuges, campgrounds, forests and American Indian Schools over the next five years and it permanently funds the Land and Water Conservation Fund at $900 million per year…. He deeply appreciates the conservation legacy that President Teddy Roosevelt left us over a century ago…
>
> America has among the cleanest water in the world and last year (2019) had the largest absolute decline of energy-related carbon dioxide emissions of any country in the world. President Trump signed the Save Our Seas Act, protecting our oceans from waste and pollution, and this year, the Trump administration is investing more than $91 million in the Great Lakes—nearly 30% more than previous funding. [1002]

Viewed as a one-sided deal, Trump withdrew from the Paris Climate Accord after which the U.S. reduced carbon emissions to their lowest level in 25 years by cutting energy-related CO2 emissions by 12% from 2005 to 2018 while the rest of the world increased emissions by 24 percent. Between 2017 and 2019 the air became 7 percent cleaner. In the fiscal year 2019, the Environmental Protection Agency (EPA) cleaned up more major pollution sites than in any other year in nearly two decades, and recovered more endangered or threatened species than any other administration in its first term.[1003] Trump affirmed America's commitment to promoting conservation efforts by joining the World Economic Forum's One Trillion Trees

---

[1001] LW 9:204. *Lectures on Deuteronomy,* "ChapterTwenty (vs. 1)."

[1002] Bernhardt, David L. "Trump's Environmental Record Is Unprecedented," *Albuquerque Journal,* October 19, 2020. (Press Release from U.S. Department of the Interior) <https://www.doi.gov/pressreleases/icymi-trumps-environmental-record-unprecedented>.

[1003] <https://trumpwhitehouse.archives.gov/issues/energy-environment>.

initiative to plant, grow, conserve and restore trees on American soil and around the world. During his first three years, the Department of the Interior planted more than 58 million trees and was on track to plant an additional 22 million trees by the end of 2020.[1004]

Luther believed God desires human beings to participate with Him in the husbandry of His "good" creation—the ongoing procreation of His children, the cultivation and production of edible crops or of animals for food, and the tending of environmental concerns through conservation practices. Demonstrated care of the earth should therefore be a reflection of our gratitude to the Provider while exhibiting concern and providing for the needs of the neighbor to excoriate our human response of ignorance, our nonchalant attitude, and even worse, our greed, which he considered the most dangerous and corrupting force in Christendom, along with false teaching that corrupts faith.[1005] In his teaching about the role of the Creator in the First Article of the Creed, he bemoans how

> We all pass over it, hear it, and recite it, but we neither see nor consider what the words enjoin on us. For if we believed it with our whole heart, we would also act accordingly, and not swagger about and brag and boast as if we had life, riches, power, honor, and such things of ourselves, as if we ourselves were to be feared and served. This is the way the wretched, perverse world acts, drowned in its blindness, misusing all the blessings and gifts of God solely for its own pride and greed, pleasure and enjoyment and never once turning to God to thank Him or acknowledge Him as Lord and Creator.[1006]

1004 <https://trumpwhitehouse.archives.gov/articles/president-trump-signs-one-trillion-trees-executive-order-promoting-conservation-regeneration-nations-for>.

1005 LW 21:167. *The Sermon on the Mount and The Magnificat*, "Sermon, Matthew 6:19-21."

1006 "The Large Catechism—The Creed," *Book of Concord*, pp.412-13.

31

Greed—Always Being in Want

Greed for Luther could indeed express itself in the despoiling of creation as well as in our exploitation of others. However greed is demonstrated, he viewed it as the manifestation of idolatry and thus, at its core, rebellion against the Creator. Humans are profoundly turned inward by sin and thus see themselves as the primary subject in the world. He often used the phrase "*incurvatus in se*" to express how our insatiable hunger for things and our disregard for others' well-being curves our lives in on ourselves as we seek only self-gratification. To reinforce this understanding in the hearts and minds of my students, both youth and adults, I taught them to spell "sin" with a big bold capital "**I**"—"s**I**n"—the placing of me, myself and **I** at the heart and center of all things.

In his Large Catechism's explanation of the Seventh Commandment, "You shall not steal," Luther describes the multi-faceted means of stealing beyond physically "acquiring another's property by unjust means." He exposes the greed behind "taking advantage of our neighbor in any sort of dealing that results in loss to him." This includes dishonest conduct in the marketplace or "wherever business is transacted, and money is exchanged for goods or labor." The far-reaching ramifications of stealing include being less than faithful or honorable in exercising our vocation by being lazy or careless on the job, wasteful or unreliable, or cheating or overcharging. These practices did not escape Luther's notice. Neither did

> underhanded tricks and sharp practices and crafty dealings. Or again, one [who] swindles another in a trade and deliberately fleeces, skins, and torments him. Who can even describe or imagine it all? In short, thievery is the most common craft and the largest guild on earth. If we look at mankind in all its conditions, it is nothing but a vase, wide-stable full of great thieves.[1007]

[1007] Luther, "The Large Catechism, The Ten Commandments, The Seventh Commandment", *Book of Concord*, pp395-399, here specifically p,396.

To the encompassing list of "guilds" where Luther cites "greed" as the dominant driving force, Trump would no doubt strongly suggest that "professional government" is a guild rivaling those medieval guilds Luther experienced. If you haven't been indoctrinated and initiated into its ways and become one of its members and follow the prescribed protocols, you cannot serve, and Trump obviously is not in the club of the Deep State. We have witnessed for more than four years what the "pros" do when amateurs try to walk in on them: they spy, investigate, fabricate false evidence, and deny due process and equal justice under the law, as they threaten and send them to jail, even to solitary confinement. More dangerously, they weaponize the tools of power to bring them down. Is this not unlike what Luther confronted with the "guild of power" exercised by the Pope and the Emperor, and the fear he had of the growing money economy? With both twins we have witnessed their stand before trials held at the Diet of Worms, Germany and the impeachments held in Washington, D.C.

It's the Economy, Stupid!

It seems every election season we are reminded of James Carville's astute observation in the phrase, "It's the economy, stupid!"[1008] He was a strategist in Bill Clinton's successful 1992 presidential campaign. He targeted those "kitchen table" issues which seem to be most dominant in driving and influencing one's vote. Unspoken is the greed—or in Luther's understanding, the curvature of one's concern turning in on one's own self-interest.

Paul Wee,* an ELCA pastor and former International Theological Director of the Luther Center in Wittenberg, Germany, finds it astonishing that with all the opportunities provided during the ten-year lead up—known as "the Luther Decade"—to the 500th observance of the Reformation, "scant attention has been paid...to the manner in which Luther's teachings led to concrete change in the everyday life of the common people. This is unfortunate since it is precisely this dimension of the Reformation heritage—its sweeping social and economic reforms—that might spark interest in and commitment to the Church's ministry today."[1009]

[1008] Breslin, Niall, "It's the Economy Stupid," *A Lust For Life.* <https://www.alustforlife.com/the-bigger-picture/its-the-economy-stupid>.

* Paul A. Wee is an ELCA pastor who has held various leadership roles in worldwide organizations, including the Lutheran World Federation, The Luther Center in Wittenberg, Germany, and Lutheran World Ministries. He is the author of numerous articles and an editor of *The Forgotten Luther: Reclaiming the Social-Economic Dimension of the Reformation*, (Minneapolis, MN: Lutheran University Press, 2016).

[1009] Wee, Paul, "The Forgotten Luther: Reclaiming the Social Dimension of the Reformation," www.churchandlife.org/2017-02-forgotten-luther.htm

It is not as if Luther was ill-informed on the economic issues of his day that led to his sharply worded attacks on the emerging profit economy. "On the contrary!" says Carter Lindberg, an American historian, Professor Emeritus of Church History at Boston University School of Theology, and author of *The European Reformation.* "Luther was no stranger to economic issues. As his father rose in the mining industry and experienced its entrepreneurial hazards, the family was part of the early modern transition from an agricultural economy to that of early capitalism. Luther's educational contexts acquainted him with wealthy families."[1010]

We've commented on his association with one of his closest life-long friends and neighbor, Lucas Cranach, who was the premier businessman and real estate developer in Wittenberg. He owned and operated the publishing house that benefited from Luther's prolific writings and which he proudly enhanced by adding artistic value. Luther knew the ins and outs of that business, including not just the mechanics of printing but the financial aspects as well. Luther, with his wife who served as "finance minister," operated their large cloistered home as a boarding house for students and guests. And as a monk, Luther had garnered extensive economic and commercial experience while serving his Augustinian order as a district vicar over eleven cloisters plus his own.

And of course, we'd be derelict if we neglected the economic awareness that contributed to Luther's indignation with the Medieval Church—"their clever wedding the market economy to the economy of salvation and exploiting a mercantile logic for the purchase of paradise."[1011] In "Constructing the Boundaries of Community: Nationalism, Protestantism, and Economics in a Sixteenth Century Broadsheet," Pia Cuneo cites the observation of the 1530 broadsheet, "The Minter's Reply:" "The pontiff is likened to a sly merchant who exchanges tainted wares for good money; he has commodified spirituality by selling indulgences, dispensations, offices, and ultimately, salvation itself."[1012] As we have previously pointed out, the Church had become the marketplace for spiritual wares. Luther was now experiencing his fears about the potential for fraudulent practices and greed of the new money economy materialize before his very eyes within the Church!

[1010] Lindberg, Carter, "Luther on a Market Economy," *Lutheran Quarterly*, Vol. 30, No. 4, Winter 2016, pp.373-4. <https://muse.jhu.edu/article/643593/pdf>.

[1011] Ibid., p.375.

[1012] Cuneo, Pia F., "Constructing the Boundaries of Community: Nationalism, Protestantism, and Economics in a Sixteenth-Century Broadsheet," *Infinite Boundaries: Order, Disorder, and Reorder in Early Modern German Culture*, ed. Max Reinhart (Kirksville: Thomas Jefferson University Press, 1998), pp.171–185, here specifically p.176.

Demanding money be paid for holding masses and prayers of intercession drained the people of their money; and worse, reinforced a theology of works righteousness which contradicted Luther's understanding of the Gospel. The sale of indulgences to free one's deceased loved ones from the "waiting room" called purgatory where sins were purged only exacerbated an intolerable contradiction of Scripture, which he saw as also contributing to making people poor. The joyful proclamation that God announces is that His grace is freely bestowed in Christ. Lindberg reminds us that "the Latin name for Rome, 'Roma,' became an acrostic for 'avarice is the root of all evils' (*'Radix Omnium Malorum Avaritia'*)."[1013]

Helge Peukert, an economist and political scientist, views Martin Luther as "a modern economist" who critiques "the amalgamation of the Medieval Church with the spirit of capitalism, i.e., an improper mix of religious and financial or commercial affairs."[1014] For Luther, preaching that the purchase of an indulgence could remit a sin was a fundamental deception, misleading people away from the true source of salvation by faith. From his own experience, he understood that such a practice in "pursuit of righteousness is an asymptote:* You can approach it, but you'll never get there on your own."[1015] It is a gift to be received by believers.

Luther's concern was for people who were being exploited not only by the Church but by the rising class of economic entrepreneurs. In his Ninety-Five Theses, Luther proclaimed in Thesis 43 that "Christians are to be taught that he who gives to the poor or lends to the needy does a better deed than he who buys indulgences."[1016] Through several writings, including a tract entitled "Trade and Usury," Luther was vehement in his concern about the exploitative practices of the profit economy. He attacked the financial houses and trading companies whose manipulative and fraudulent practices he felt oppressed the common people and small businesses. His assault was not just against personal greed, but also against the structures and practices of the new market economy itself. These new entrepreneurs through their controlling practices caught Luther's attention with their writing the rules of trade, developing cartels, fixing prices, manipulating markets, and extracting huge interest

---

[1013] Lindberg, "Luther on a Market Economy," p. 375.

[1014] Peukert, Helge, "Martin Luther: A Modern Economist," *The Reformation as a Pre-Condition for Modern Capitalism*, ed. Jürgen Backhaus (Berlin: LIT Verlag, 2010), pp.13–63, here p.13.

* Asymptote: a line that continually approaches a given curve but does not meet it at any finite distance.

[1015] Walsh, Colleen, "Martin Luther, Fallible Reformer," interview with Michelle C. Sanchez. <https://hds.harvard.edu/news/2017/10/31/martin-luther-fallible-reformer/>.

[1016] LW 31:29. *Career of The Reformer I*, "The Ninety-Five Theses."

rates. Contemporary practices similar to the lending Luther condemned would be the exceedingly high interest rates on credit card debt, or worse, the quick-cash operations that charge exorbitant rates of interest for consumers on the so-called "payday loans." Luther wrote in his treatise "To the Christian Nobility of the German Nation:"

> We must put a bit in the mouth of the Fuggers* and similar companies. How is it possible in the lifetime of one man to accumulate such great possessions, worthy of a king, legally and according to God's will? I do not know…I leave this to men who understand the ways of the world. As a theologian I have no further reproof to make on this subject except that it has an evil and offending appearance, about which St. Paul says, *'Avoid every appearance or show of evil'* (1 Thessalonians 5:22).[1017]

One cannot avoid hearing the same concerns many have about Donald Trump's wealth, or that of Joe and Hunter Biden, the Clintons, or those millionaire/billionaire aspirants who sought the nomination to oppose Trump, as well as those wealthy contributors who fund the campaigns. Martin Luther undoubtedly would be pointing to Rupert Neate's report in November 2017 that "The three richest people in the U.S.—Bill Gates, Jeff Bezos and Warren Buffett—own as much wealth as the bottom half of the U.S. population, or 160 million people"[1018] as evidence of his life-long criticism and fear of early capitalism.

Karen Bloomquist directs attention to Luther's widespread pastoral and ethical concern for those affected negatively by economic matters, which is reflected extensively in his writings and counsel by stating,

> He called on Christians to exercise neighbor-love or charity to those in need, both through individual and governmental means (e.g., the "common chest,"

---

* The Fuggers were the greatest international bankers of the 16th century and bankers to the Roman Curia. Their control of large amounts of capital enabled them to advance large sums of money to the territorial rulers. In return they received monopolistic concessions. The spiritual lords as well as the secular lords availed themselves of the services of this accommodating firm. They were the Pope's financial representative in Germany and made the financial arrangement between the Pope and Albrecht of Mainz to purchase his ecclesiastical offices through the selling of indulgences, which led to the controversy of 1517.

1017 LW 44:213-14. *The Christian in Society I*, "To the Christian Nobility" or *Three Treatises* p.107

1018 Neate, Robert, "Bill Gates, Jeff Bezos and Warren Buffett Are Wealthier than Poorest Half of U.S.;" *The Guardian*, Nov. 8, 2017. <https://www,theguardian.com/business/2017/nov/08/bill-gates-jeff-bezos-warren-buffett-wealthier-than-poorest-half-of-us>.

> and early versions of government social welfare.) Economic matters should not remain autonomous or in a sphere apart from spiritual matters. When they threaten to become a power of domination ruling over people—as was occurring through the early capitalist practices of Luther's time—then they become a spiritual matter of idolatry (an idol being whatever we trust in instead of God).[1019]

Luther was convinced that Jesus' call to "*love thy neighbor*" (Matthew 22:39 [KJV]) placed demands on economic life.

The Aisle of GoBeDo

Accordingly, we see Luther condemning the emerging trade economy and beseeching German political leaders to place restraints on abuses. But he did even more. In *Healing a Broken World,* Cynthia Moe-Lobeda characterizes Luther's position in an interesting, significant, and meaningful way:

> He articulated norms for economic life that subverted standard economic practices and inaugurated and theologically legitimized local systems of social welfare as outgrowths and components of worship.... Social welfare for Luther was...the "*liturgy after the liturgy,*" a work of the people flowing from worship...Poor relief expressed this community solidarity.... It was, in fact, an act of worship, of divine service.[1020]

The Church's action for the neighbor is thus rooted in worship. In his "Preface to The German Mass and Order of Service," Luther acknowledges that "very few use it [worship or liturgy] for the glory of God and the good of the neighbor; most use it for their own advantage and pleasure" while failing to understand how it "may yet serve the neighbor."[1021] "In promoting the 'good of the neighbor'" Carter Lindberg positions Luther's standing "in the ancient Christian tradition of the 'common good,' but also advocates working with

---

[1019] Bloomquist, Karen L., *Seeing—Remembering—Connecting: Subversive Practices of Being Church* (Eugene, OR: Cascade Books, 2016), pp.20-21.

[1020] Moe-Lobeda, Cynthia D., *Healing a Broken World: Globalization and God* (Minneapolis: Fortress Press, 2002), p.89.

[1021] LW 53:61. *Liturgy and Hymns,* "The German Mass and Order of Service."

all persons of good will for the benefit of all. The ethos of the common good is the most profound basis for Luther's critique of capitalism."[1022]

Several years ago I proclaimed this very teaching in a sermon entitled "The Aisle of GoBeDo." The aisle of the church not only leads us to the altar, where we offer our praise and worship and where we receive the assurance of God's free gift of forgiveness, but just as importantly, the aisle launches or propels believers out from the altar into the world as a lover of neighbors. There, we "***Go***" to fulfill our joyful privilege in making disciples by sharing the Good News; "***Be***" who we are as God's chosen people—His heart, hands, and voice; and "***Do***" what we've been empowered and compelled to affect in serving our neighbor as a "little Christ," because of the indwelling Christ in our hearts. So it is that many of our worship services conclude with the dismissal: "Go in peace, Serve the Lord."

Omer Westendorf's popular hymn accents this linkage between the Lord's Supper and our life in the world. *"The supper is ended. Oh, now be extended the fruits of this service in all who believe."*[1023] Liturgy is not our cultic activity that we do, reversing the flow as Rome had done making it a sacrifice offered and a work performed rather than a gift to be received through Word and Sacrament. In Lutheran theology, God is the subject rather than the object and Christ is the donor and benefactor giving His gifts to be received by faith alone. The introduction to *Lutheran Worship* echoes this hymn's sentiment by telling us "Our Lord gives us His body to eat and His blood to drink. Finally His blessing moves us into our calling, where His gifts have their fruition."[1024] This vital linkage is lost if we want to do as a work what we may receive as a gift. Serving as the living presence of Christ's Body in the world is the logical extension of what the Eastern tradition calls "the liturgy after the liturgy."

Yet Luther was not naïve enough to believe such greed-driven profits and abuse was confined to the top one percent, nor to the nobility, the monied monopolists, nor the merchant bankers, as is a predominant claim heard today. He recognized that the emerging market economy presented opportunities for the lower classes to also engage in corrupt and exploitative business practices as well. The problem for the Reformer is not money or property. They are God's good gifts to be shared with one's neighbor. He clearly

---

[1022] Lindberg, "Luther on a Market Economy," pp.383-384

[1023] Westendorf, Omer E., "Sent Forth by God's Blessing," ELW Hymn 547; LBW Hymn 221; LSB Hymn 643; and LW Hymn 247.

[1024] *Lutheran Worship*, Concordia, p.6.

understood that economic activity is a natural necessity. The problem is the greedy misuse and the worldly striving to acquire it:

> If silver and gold are things evil in themselves, then those who keep away from them deserve to be praised. But if they are good creatures of God, which we can use both for the needs of our neighbor and for the glory of God, is not a person silly, yes, even unthankful to God, if he refrains from them as though they were evil? For they are not evil, even though they have been subjected to vanity and evil.[1025]

Citing again from Cynthia D. Moe-Lobeda's article on "Luther's Economic Ethic," the

> norm of neighbor-love pertains to every aspect of life for Christians, including economic life. According to [Luther], economic activity is intrinsically an act in relationship to neighbor. For this reason, economic practices that undermine the well-being of the neighbor (especially of the vulnerable) were to be rejected and replaced with alternatives. About this, Luther was vehement and specific.[1026]

Consequently, we discover in Luther's writings a widespread pastoral and ethical concern for those affected negatively by economic matters. He not only called on Christians to exercise neighbor-love or charity to those in need, but with his Wittenberg colleagues in 1522 worked to establish the "Common Chest" and early versions of government social welfare programs. His stance was wrapped around his understanding of Deuteronomy 15:4 (KJV)[1027]—"*...there shall be no poor among you*"—and therefore sought to develop both preemptive and restorative social assistance initiatives. He taught "...to help a man that does not need to become a beggar is just as much of a good work and a virtue and an alms as to give to a man and to help a man who has already become a beggar."[1028] In the "Ordinance of a Common Chest," he wrote for Leisnig which had already been implemented in Wittenberg, begging was outlawed.[1029] He believed that "Every city should support its own poor, and if

---

[1025] LW 2:331. *Lectures on Genesis Chapters 6-14,* Chapter 13 (vs 2).

[1026] Moe-Lobedo, Cynthia D., "Luther's Economic Ethic." <https://elca.org/JLE/Articles/1266>.

[1027] LW 9:147-8; *Lectures on Deuteronomy,* "Chapter 15 (vs. 4);" see also LW 45:161, 281-82, and 286-87.

[1028] LW 13:54. *Select Psalms II,* "Psalm 82."

[1029] LW 45:185-86. *The Christian in Society II,* "Ordinance of a Common Chest."

it was too small, the people in the surrounding villages should be urged to contribute..."[1030] and designed means by which begging would be unnecessary. Weekly contributions were to be collected to fund the Common Chest in addition to later receiving monies expropriated from ecclesiastical endowments and from the sale of vacant monasteries and convents, other gifts, wills, and an annual tax from every noble, townsman and peasant living in the parish. These revenues were to be used for education, poor orphans, loans and grants to students, the purchase of commodities for those in times of need, a form of social security for the elderly, and even a doctor to provide free care for the poor.[1031]

Loving in these forms, we become more fully who God made us to be, as we embody Christ's love on earth. I have always believed and taught that the popular Christmas maxim "Jesus is the reason for the Season" has it upside down about His coming. Jesus as the Son of God had it all (and then some!). We are the reason for the season! He came to "*dwell among us*" (John 1:14 [NEB]—literally "pitched His tent" to live among and in us) and promises to "*abide in us*" (John 15:4). Could it be that we are overly polite in not wanting to associate sexual connotations with pregnancy, or we don't want to reflect the Roman Catholic view attributed to the "Virgin" Mary? Nevertheless, there is and has been among Protestants not only a shyness but a perceived negativity associated with Mary, though Luther regarded her highly and held her in great honor.

Perhaps Luther understood what I've always appreciated about the unexpected reality Mary found herself in, and how "pregnant" the meaning and significance of "the Christ"—literally and physically—dwelling within her truly was, and how she appropriated that Truth in her life. Then when "*in the fullness of time*" (Galatians 4:4-7), God's love "for us" which Mary bore within her could no longer be contained, but had to be "borne" into physical life for *our* sake! And it is He, whom the Church teaches, that chooses to live within us and through us bestowing the honor and privilege of embodying Christ's love on earth by being His physical presence. "We are Church" indeed, and thus "pregnant" with Christ dwelling within us! We are privileged to be the very presence of Christ's love in the world today, and we can't be just partially pregnant, bearing that love that chooses to "abide" within us. That love came initially when God "*formed us in our mother's womb, and knew us before we were born*" (Jeremiah 1:5), and chose to manifest itself through us being born to be expressions of that love which we then are honored to deliver into the lives of our neighbor by our witness and service!

[1030] LW 44:189. *The Christian in Society I*, "To the Christian Nobility," or *Three Treatises*, p.81.

[1031] See Paul Wee's article "The Forgotten Luther." <www.churchandlife.org/2017-02-forgotten-luther.htm>.

Courtney Cherest expresses this Biblical perspective, which Luther championed, in her life's mission and purpose statement:

> *God's Word is my greatest love.*
> *Sharing it is my greatest privilege.*
> *Watching it grow in others is my greatest joy!*[1032]

For Luther, of course, salvation is received, not achieved. Salvation is by grace alone apart from works, no strings attached! His teaching on justification by grace alone was at the heart of his social ethics. Christian actions expressing love for one's neighbor, including care for the poor, Luther argued, were not preconditions for but consequences of faith. Faith, he insisted, was itself a free gift of God's grace.

*Faith Active in Love** is the title of George W. Forell's investigation into the principles underlying Luther's social ethics, and is reminiscent of the acronym often used by the former Lutheran Church in America (LCA), "Love Compels Action." The point here, says Ryan Cumming, Program Director of Hunger Education for ELCA World Hunger, "is that *'right faith'* begets *'right sight.'* Faith is not just a matter of believing but of perceiving. Perception is crucial to action. Faith is a lens through which the disciples see Christ and through which they—and we—see the world. To have faith that is well founded is to have clear sight,"[1033] or as one might say instead, "insight."

Carter Lindberg infers that

> Luther's attack on works-righteousness was equally an attack on the early profit economy. Both reveal the drive to secure one's existence, and as such express the counterfeit gospel that a person's worth depends upon achievement. To Luther, the Good News is that human worth is independent of success whether measured in terms of good works or acquisition of the world. The capitalist drive to acquire the world is the same "coin" as salvation by works. By striving to acquire the world, trust is placed in self-achievement rather than God. Meanwhile the neighbor is neglected.[1034]

[1032] <https://www.instagram.com/courtneycherest>.

* Forell, George Wolfgang. *Faith Active in Love* (Minneapolis: Augsburg Publishing House, 1954).

[1033] Cumming, Ryan, *BREAD and JUSTICE* newsletter of the Metropolitan New York Synod Hunger Committee, Spring 2017. <https://www.mnys.org/assets/1/6/bread_and_justice_2017.pdf>.

[1034] Lindberg, "Luther on a Market Economy," p.377. <https://muse.jhu.edu/article/643593/pdf>.

"Luther was convinced," according to Lindberg, "that the new profit economy divorced money from use for human need, necessitated an economy of acquisition, fed the mortal sin of avarice, and eroded the common good. 'After the devil there is no greater human enemy on earth than a miser and usurer for he desires to be God over everyone.'"[1035] The insatiable drive to acquire wealth for Luther was therefore perceived not just as an expression of greed but also an expression of economic idolatry and thus a violation of the First Commandment, "*You shall have no other gods…*" (Exodus 20:3 [NRSV]). In his explanation of that commandment in the Large Catechism, Luther states

> To have a god is nothing else than to trust and believe him with our whole heart…. That to which your heart clings and entrusts itself is, I say, really your God…. Many a person thinks he has God and everything he needs when he has money and property; in them he trusts and of them he boasts so stubbornly and securely that he cares for no one. Surely such a man also has a god—mammon by name, that is, money and possessions—on which he fixes his whole heart.[1036]

Luther's preference was that the economy be ruled by love of one's neighbor, not by an impersonal market and autonomous laws of economics he considered as idolatrous and socially destructive. However, "Luther made a clear distinction between his ideal Christian State as a model and capitalist reality as it unfolded during his own life and age. He wrote in his Letter to the Councilmen of Danzig in 1525, how interest was something entirely normal and permissible if certain rates and boundaries were not exceeded."[1037]

> I have often taught thus, that the world ought not and cannot be ruled according to the Gospel and Christian love, but by strict laws and with sword and force, because the world is evil. It accepts neither Gospel nor love but lives and acts according to its own will unless compelled by force. Otherwise, if only love were applied, everyone would eat, drink, and live at ease at someone else's expense, and no one would work. Indeed, everyone would

---

1035 Ibid. Lindberg, p.380 and quoting Luther from WA 51:396-97.

1036 "Large Catechism, First Commandment," *Book of Concord*, p.365.

1037 Rossner, Philipp Robinson, "Martin Luther and the Making of the Modern Economic Mind," *International Review of Economics*, 2019. <https://link.springer.com/article/10.1007/s12232-018-0307-x>.

take from another what was his and we would have such a state of affairs that no one could live because of the others.[1038]

In Luther's understanding, we have seen how thievery expresses itself in many forms. In explaining the Seventh Commandment, the transgression of stealing applied not only to individuals but to corporate bodies and institutions within society. The "lust for profit" manifested itself through many clever financial expressions in the marketplace, as well as through national and international commerce, creating an adverse effect on everyone, especially the poor. "Daily the poor are defrauded. New burdens and high prices are imposed. Everyone misuses the market in his own willful, conceited, arrogant way, as if it were his right and privilege to sell his goods [and services] as dearly as he pleases without a word of criticism."[1039]

Big Thieves Act as Judges and Hang Little Thieves

Usury, defined as the illegal action or practice of lending money at unreasonably high rates of interest, certainly had Luther's wrathful attention, and became the shorthand language he used for a broad host of practices that took advantage of the consumer, such as manipulating prices and markets by withholding or dumping goods, offering crooked deals, or simply misrepresenting shoddy merchandise. "Such usury," Luther argued, affects everyone...and "is felt in our markets and our kitchens. The userers are eating our food and drinking our drink." Even worse, however by manipulating prices, "usury lives off the bodies of the poor."[1040]

As we have pointed out, Luther, like his younger twin Trump, often used frank speech, and in his own inimitable style Luther exploded: "The world is one big whorehouse, completely submerged in greed"[1041] where the "big thieves act as judges and hang the little thieves."[1042] Have we not evidenced that as an apt description for the greed of the bureaucratic "Deep State" in their actions to protect, defend and promote their power and control? They are anxious not to be outed, so they shield themselves by projecting onto their opponents what they themselves have practiced. Throughout the Trump administration we

---

1038 LW 45:264. *The Christian in Society II*, "Trade and Usury, 1524."

1039 "The Large Catechism: Ten Commandments," *Book of Concord*, p.397.

1040 Lindberg, Carter, "Luther on a Market Economy," p.381. quoting WA: 51:417.

1041 LW 21:180. *Sermon on the Mount and The Magnificat*, "Sermon on the Mount."

1042 LW 25:172. *Lectures on Romans*, "Chapter Two (vs.1)"

have witnessed the Left's toxic addiction to such projection—the psycho-political syndrome of attributing one's own sins to one's opponent by successfully lodging those charges most familiar and applicable to themselves. So many of these promulgators have known firsthand the crimes they allege on others as their own, accusing the innocent of their own perceived guilt. For example, Victor Davis Hanson of the Hoover Institute cites that many

> "*people of color,*" who are the loudest about focusing on the evils of privilege and lack of equity, are themselves multimillionaires or multibillionaires, such as the Obamas, Oprah Winfrey, LeBron James, Jay-Z, or Meghan Markle. Accusing an entire group—white people, or conservatives, or Trump supporters—of being privileged deflects the apparent shame of elitism away from oneself on the cheap.... The elite accuser knows especially how to level such charges given his own intimacy with what wealth, power, and influence bring.[1043]

One can only imagine how Luther would describe the hypocrisy, double standards, and two-tiered system of justice we have witnessed in the accusations, investigations, convictions and exonerations, as well as the weaponization of federal agencies going after organizations, campaigns and individuals for the benefit of those who control the Deep State "guild" or "swamp." Perhaps we don't have to imagine, but only read his concerns in his commentary on the Seventh Commandment and apply it to our political arena. He says:

> Who can even describe or imagine it all? ...If we look at mankind in all its conditions, it is nothing but a vast, wide stable full of great thieves. These men are called gentlemen swindlers or big operators [armchair bandits and highway robbers (in another translation)]. Far from being picklocks and sneak-thieves who loot a cash box, they sit in office chairs and are called great lords and honorable, good citizens, and yet with a great show of legality they rob and steal.[1044]

1043 Hanson, Victor Davis, "Why the Left Always Projects American Greatness," November 14, 2021. <https://amgreatness.com/2021/11/14/why-the-left-always-projects>.

1044 "The Large Catechism, The Ten Commandments, The Seventh Commandment," *Book of Concord*, p.396.

In his commentary on the Sermon on the Mount (Matthew 6:22-23) Luther points out "How skillfully 'Sir Greed' can dress up to look like a pious man if that seems to be what the occasion requires, while he is actually a double scoundrel and liar."[1045]

There is little doubt that Luther, like Trump, would also have not only concerns, but appropriate words to direct toward the high and mighty, who as self-perceived paragons of virtue love to sit in judgment over those having committed minor offenses, when they themselves are guilty of doing the same on a much grander scale. Instead, they are absolved or given a pass by their associates within the "guild" who likewise seem to escape retribution by being vindicated.

Hear in Luther's own words the description of the way he saw his world then, and apply that same reasoning to those today who have held high positions being exonerated and those of lesser positions being indicted, even thrown into solitary confinement, for far less serious crimes, just to validate their costly and faulty investigations into bogus allegations of collusion and unconstitutional impeachment trials:

> Those who can steal and rob openly are safe and free, unmolested by anyone, even claiming honor from men. Meanwhile the little sneak-thieves who have committed one offense must bear disgrace and punishment so as to make the others look respectable and honorable. But the latter should be told that in the eyes of God they are the greatest thieves, and that He will punish them as they deserve.[1046]

While Luther condemned the emerging trade economy, especially internationally, he admitted, "It cannot be denied that buying and selling are necessary. They cannot be dispensed with, and can be practiced in a Christian manner, especially when the commodities serve a necessary and honorable purpose."[1047] For him, "foreign trade, which brings from Calcutta and India and such places wares like costly silks, articles of gold and spices*—which minister only to ostentation but serve no useful purpose, and which drain away the money of land and people—would not be permitted if we had [proper] government

---

1045 LW 21:183. The Sermon on the Mount and The Magnificat, "Sermon on Mount (Matt. 6:22-23)"

1046 "The Large Catechism, The Ten Commandments, The Seventh Commandment," *Book of Concord*, p.396.

1047 LW 45:246. The Christian in Society II, "Trade and Usury."

* In the absence of refrigeration, spices served frequently as a food preservative.

and princes."[1048] In his treatise "Trade and Usury,"[1049] written in 1524, he explains and sets forth examples of merchants' abuse, such as selling their goods for the highest possible price, thus gouging, or in Luther's understanding, stealing from one's neighbor and opening the door to all sorts of avarice. Such abuses are seen by Luther as attempts to better one's lot in life at the expense of another, and thus he beseeched German political leaders to oversee the market and fix prices when needed to ensure that justice and equity rule the economy in order to protect the consumer's interest.

Yet, he was also fully aware of the necessity of profits. "Now it is fair and right that a merchant take as much profit on his wares as will reimburse him for their cost and compensate him for his trouble, his labor, and his risk. Even a farmhand must have food and pay for his labor. Who can serve or labor for nothing? The Gospel says, '*The laborer deserves his wages*' [Luke 10:7 (RSV)]."[1050]

David H. Eaton, Professor of Economics at Murray State University, reminds us that

> In contrast to those who might wish to remake the economy in Christ's image, Luther argues that the world is sinful, and these are the practices of a sinful world. His thrust is to help Christians live in the world as it is, not to reform the practices of the world. Luther is a forceful advocate for the role of the secular authorities to keep the practices of the world in check.[1051]

We have evidenced Luther's fervent realization that since in everyone "greed is a disobedient and unbelieving scoundrel,"[1052] it is the proper role of civil authorities to limit the effects of greed, especially as it affects the impoverished, by regulating the economy. Throughout the economic revolution that was gradually transforming a peasant-dominated agricultural Germany into an emerging capitalist economy, Luther saw rising prices, growing disparity of wealth, and increasing poverty. The poor were providing a cheap labor pool, much like the flood of illegal immigrants supply today, having the effect of keeping wages depressed.

1048 Ibid.

1049 LW 45:231-310. *The Christian in Society II*, "Trade and Usury."

1050 Ibid., LW 45:249.

1051 Eaton, David H., "The Economists of the Reformation: An Overview of Reformation Teaching Concerning Work, Wealth, and Interest." <https://journals.sagepub.com/doi/full/10.1177/2158244013494864>.

1052 LW 45:170. The Christian in Society II, "Ordinance of a Common Chest."

The local social welfare systems inaugurated by Luther created jobs and provided interest-free loans and healthcare to impoverished people. All of this was being guided by norms he established for everyday economic life that prioritized meeting human needs over maximizing profit. Likewise, we will be viewing in greater detail Trump's economic actions that have created jobs, raised wages, provided relief in getting drug prices lowered, as well as providing Economic Impact Payments to help bridge the gap citizens and businesses were experiencing financially as a result of the Covid-19 shutdown of the economy, and his push for medications and vaccines to deal with treating and preventing preventing the coronavirus illness.

As I have attempted to demonstrate, Luther was a realist and a very pragmatic individual. His interest in economic issues—far from a lack of understanding its basic principles—was born primarily from a pastoral concern for one's neighbor. He viewed many of the business practices and financial attitudes as being incompatible with a faithful life. He believed that the common good was being undermined by the activities of the large financial houses and businesses that the emperor could not even hold in check or make accountable. While Luther could support what economics would describe as a competitive market, he could not support an unfettered market. Unbridled capitalism, gain for the sake of gain, or gain at the expense of others, he condemned. Luther always seemed to see the larger picture, arguing that social need—concern for our neighbor—always stood above selfish personal gain. In the assessment of Paul Wee, his

> protest against the exploitation of the weakest members of society places him directly in the line of the Biblical prophets. Yet he went beyond protest to propose structural reforms that would change the face of Wittenberg and cities throughout Saxony and Germany. In later years, the economic model Luther proposed would have a profound effect on social life throughout Europe...[such as] providing care for the elderly, basic health care and education for the citizenry.[1053]

[1053] Wee, Paul, "The Forgotten Luther," www.churchandlife.org/2017-02-forgotten-luther.htm

32

Heigh-Ho, Its Off to Work We Go!

Luther would probably have been excited to use the lyrics of "Happy Work Song" in Disney's *Snow White and the Seven Dwarfs* as his theme song for promoting his understanding on the nature of work, though I suspect he'd use a chorale to convey the words. The seven dwarves of the movie's title joyfully sing, "Heigh-ho, heigh-ho, it's off to work we go! We dig, dig, dig in a mine the whole day through! To dig, dig, dig is what we like to do!" [1054] Really? Most individuals, unfortunately, probably would better identify with the actual words they sing in the mine before they head home: "Heigh-ho, heigh-ho, it's home from work we go!"

Paul Wee also provides insight into how

> the Church, in its teaching of righteousness through works, contribute[d] to the spiritual and material impoverishment of the people; it sought to obscure the harshness of this reality by romanticizing the state of poverty itself. It claimed that poverty and godliness went hand-in hand, that to be poor was to claim a status that was pleasing to God. Luther found no Biblical justification for the teaching of St. Francis of Assisi in which poverty was seen as a virtue and begging a sign of Christian humility. He accused the professional beggars of being parasites and asked that they be expelled from the community. Luther scholar, Albrecht Steinwachs notes "Begging was at that time a lucrative business, and this tempted many to go into the comfortable life of begging rather than take a normal job."[1055]

In 1508 when Luther arrived in Wittenberg, he was immediately struck by the number of beggars on the streets who were seeking charitable contributions. Some were students, others were members of the Franciscan and Dominican mendicant orders, and others simply poor.

[1054] <https://genius.com/Walt-disney-records-heigh-ho-lyrics>.

[1055] Wee, "Forgotten Luther," <www.churchandlife.org/2017-02-forgotten-luther.htm>.

One cannot read Scripture without understanding that God does not approve of situations where some people having material possessions in abundance ignore those who go to bed hungry. As a matter of fact, in his Large Catechism, Luther offers broader interpretations in his explanations of how the Ten Commandments are violated beyond the specific and literal mandates. For example, the Fifth Commandment, *"Thou shall not kill"* (Exodus 20:13 [KJV]), is broken not only when an individual actually does the evil act of taking another's life or intentionally endangering or harming the life of one's neighbor, "but also when he fails to do good to his neighbor, or, though he has the opportunity, fails to prevent, protect, and save him from suffering bodily harm or injury."[1056] To further expound on the fullest meaning of violating this commandment, Luther provides additional examples:

> If you send a person away naked when you could clothe him, you have let him freeze to death. If you see anyone suffer hunger and do not feed him, you have let him starve. Likewise, if you see anyone condemned* to death or in similar peril and do not save him although you know ways and means to do so, you have killed him. It will do you no good to plead that you did not contribute to his death by word or deed, for you have withheld your love from him and robbed him of the service by which his life might have been saved.[1057]

We have already witnessed how expansive Luther is in explaining the Seventh Commandment, *"Thou shall not steal,"* as it applies to everything from petty theft of an item from one's place of employment to cheating on paying one's taxes or in financial dealings or misusing technological and intellectual property. These thefts of jobs, the robbing of America's "piggy bank" through trade deals, engaging in fraud to steal an election, the biased manipulation and censorship by giant tech companies and their harvesting of information from social media platforms, and the danger posed with technological and intellectual property being stolen and smuggled to potential adversaries, became heightened concerns of the Trump administration.

Also in comparison, Luther's contemporary twin, President Trump, has expressed his dismay at the increasingly disgusting conditions of the homeless in "our great American cities…that are an embarrassment…a disgrace to our country…. It's a shame the world

---

[1056] "The Large Catechism: Ten Commandments, The Fifth Commandment," *Book of Concord*, pp.390-91.
* Variant reading: innocently condemned.
[1057] Ibid., p.391.

is looking at it. Look at Los Angeles with the tents and the horrible, horrible disgusting conditions. Look at San Francisco. Look at some of your other cities."[1058] White House spokesman Judd Deere said in a statement, "In June [2019], the President took action and signed an Executive Order to confront the regulatory barriers to affordable housing development, a leading cause of homelessness. President Trump has directed his team to go further and develop a range of policy options for consideration to deal with this tragedy."[1059]

Unfortunately, one has to actively search to find any media mention of the Opportunity and Revitalization Council signed into law by an executive order of President Trump on December 12, 2018. The White House Council, headed by Urban Development Secretary Ben Carson, includes representatives from 13 federal agencies, who will develop, direct and oversee a $100 billion initiative aimed at helping economically distressed communities designated as "Opportunity Zones:"

> With the creation of today's council, the resources of the whole federal government will be leveraged to rebuild low-income and impoverished neighborhoods that have been ignored by Washington in years past, [the President said]. Our goal is to ensure that America's great new prosperity is broadly shared by all our citizens. Our country is doing better than ever, economically, and we are able to do that.[1060]

Without a doubt, the impact of illegal immigrants has resulted in forcing down wages, and through the lure of sanctuary cities offering protection and other incentives, poverty has increased dramatically in these cities, not to mention the many contributing factors at play with state and local issues. In addressing the border crisis, President Trump said, "America proudly welcomes millions of lawful immigrants who enrich our society and contribute to our nation. But all Americans are hurt by uncontrolled, illegal migration. It strains public resources and drives down jobs and wages. Among the hardest hit are African Americans and Hispanic Americans."[1061] Interesting, these very concerns were expressed by his predecessors in the Oval Office as well as prominent senators and representatives of

---

1058 <https://abcnews.go.com/Politics/trump-homelessness-problem-california-cities-clean/story?id=65538949>.

1059 Ibid.

1060 <https://www.westernjournal.com/media-blackout-trump-launches-urban-council-invest-100-billion-black-communities>.

1061 <https://whitehouse.archives.gov/briefings-Statements/president-donald-j-trumps-address-nation-crisis-border/>.

both parties, up until the time Donald Trump assumed office, and then this issue triggered a decidedly political divide.

While obviously everything isn't where it could be, one can surmise that Luther would be applauding the benefits arising from the growing "pre-Covid-19" economy in our country. He was convinced that if people were able-bodied, they should work; otherwise, they were simply a drain and should be expelled from the community. "Anyone not incapacitated by reason of age or illness shall work or, with the aid of the authorities, be expelled from the parish, the city, and the villages."[1062]

Likewise, Luther would certainly concur with Trump in reimposing work requirements for Americans on welfare, revoking an Obama-era policy that had urged states to apply for waivers exempting the poor from having to show they were either getting job training or looking for work to qualify for aid. Requiring work was a key part of the 1996 welfare reform law enacted and signed by then-President Bill Clinton. President Trump's move restored the law as originally written. "Chairman Brady believes that work requirements are essential to providing Americans with real paths out of poverty and up the economic ladder," said Shane McDonald, spokesperson for House Ways and Means Chairman Kevin Brady. "Today's action by the Trump administration ties in seamlessly to the work that he and the committee are doing to deliver policy solutions that truly improve the lives of American families nationwide."[1063]

Work is More than the Daily Grind

At the heart of The Reformation, having an impact upon both his world and our own, was the unveiling of the Gospel by Luther's articulation of the doctrine of Justification by grace through faith alone. As grateful as I am for the recovery of that fundamental truth, I also celebrate how the revolutionary ideas of his theology have undergirded multiple aspects of our life, including his insightful understanding of work being more than a "job" or "the daily grind." Luther perceived "work" or one's labor to be a vocation or divine calling:

> *Confirm in us Your Gospel Lord, Your promise of salvation.*
> *And make us keen to hear Your Word And follow our vocation.*[1064]

[1062] LW 45:186. *The Christian in Society II*, "Ordinance of a Common Chest,"

[1063] <https://www.washingtontimes.com/news/2017/aug/30/trump-moves-restore-work-requirement-welfare>.

[1064] Hubert, Konrad, "I Trust, O Christ, in You Alone," LBW Hymn 395; and LW, Hymn 357.

In their article on "Luther's Notion of Work," Dr. Chr. Lucas Zapf and Dr. Peter Seele grouped the Reformer's interpretations of work into three broad categories. First, work is a *social activity*:

> Luther describes society as a body to whose health every single member contributes with his or her work. Every man [and woman] in every job is a priest, fulfilling his work as a God-given duty. Aggregated, individual work leads to social coherence. Luther interprets work as practiced caritas [charity] based on the division of labor. Work is service for the fellow man.... As work has the nimbus of the social, not to work becomes antisocial.[1065]

Rest is needed to refresh the body and soul; however, being idle does not contribute to the community.

In his "Treatise on Good Works," Luther teaches that we should not place our confidence in gold or money and references our Lord's instruction in Matthew 6:31-32 that "*we should not be anxious as to what we eat, drink, and how we clothe ourselves since God cares for all this and knows that we need these things.*" He anticipates the disbelief of his readership who would think, "Then why work?"

> some people will say, "Well then, just rely on that, do not be concerned, and see whether a roasted chicken will fly into your mouth." I do not say that a man need not work and seek his livelihood. But I do say that he is not to be anxious, not covetous; he is not to despair that he is not going to have enough. For in Adam, we are all condemned to labor, as God says in Genesis 3 [:19], "*In the sweat of your face you shall eat your bread...*"[1066]

Secondly, Zapf and Seele point to Luther's understanding of work being part of the *natural order.* Work is "a divine assignment and material task to human's existence on

---

[1065] Zapf, Dr. Chr. Lucas and Seele, Dr. Peter, "Martin Luther's Notion of Work as an Individual Source for Meaning," *Faith & Work: Christian Perspectives, Research, and Insights into the Movement*, ed. Timothy Ewest (Charlotte, NC: Information Age Publishing Inc., 2018), p.104.

[1066] LW 44:108. Christian in Society I, "Treatise on Good Works."

earth.... Work has a naturalistic implicitness."[1067] Luther summarized his work ethic in the verse from Job 5:7:

> "*As the bird is born to fly, so man is born to work*" Job 5:7 Now birds fly without anxiety and without covetousness, and so we should work without anxiety, and without covetousness. But if you are anxious and greedy and want the roast chicken to fly into your mouth, then go on worrying and coveting and see if you will fulfil God's commandment and find salvation.[1068]

"To negate this natural state by being idle is an open affront to the structuring nature of work and considered counterproductive for social well-being."[1069] Legendary football coach Lou Holtz used to remind his players, as he reminds us all, "No one has ever drowned in sweat."[1070]

And thirdly, work is *self-realization.* We become who God meant us to be through work:

> Subsistence is only one, maybe even the lesser aspect of work. It is supposed to be meaningful, useful, and worthwhile. It reflects the worker's personality and fulfills his or her inner expectations of what is good. While Luther clearly articulates the social aspects of work, he also articulates the individualistic aspect of work. Work serves the working individual.[1071]

Our current society has focused more on the individual, which is an important aspect of work. However, Luther balanced self-realization with community. Both are important.

Finding meaning, purpose, and significance in one's work is derived from both self-actualization and love of neighbor. Meaning is destroyed when humans are unemployed or under-employed. Being idle when desiring to work, or being underemployed in a mind-numbing job, violates the natural order and does not allow workers to reach self-actualization nor support their community. It is rather those times when we have a song in our heart, like the dwarves were singing in *Snow White.*

[1067] Zapf and Seele, "Martin Luther's Notion of Work," p.105.

[1068] LW 44:108. Christian in Society I, "Treatise on Good Works."

[1069] Zapf and Seele, "Martin Luther's Notion of Work," p.105.

[1070] <https://247sports.com/Coach/3618/Quotes/No-one-has-ever-drowned-in-sweat-35966560>.

[1071] Zapf and Seele, "Martin Luther's Notion of Work," p.106.

Everyday Vocations are Divine Callings

"Indeed," writes economist David Eaton of Murray State University,

> even in Eden work was needed. It was not until the Fall that work became burdensome. Luther reformed the view of work with his teaching of the Priesthood of all Believers.... Traditionally, the Church had taught that some were "called" into a church-related vocation. For these individuals, various monastic orders were set up so they could live out their calling safe from the dangers and temptations of the world. As Bonhoeffer (1959) would later characterize this situation, this set up a two-tiered Christianity. Those who were very devout and holy would be cloistered in the monastery, while those who could not reach this level of commitment would live out their lives as best they could in the secular realm.[1072]

While the term "calling" traditionally had referred to monastic life, Luther viewed all labor as the exercise of one's vocation. His understanding of the "priesthood of all believers" was revolutionary, asserting there was no distinction between those whose vocation was in the professional ministry within the religious realm and those whose secular employment was in the world. "The Lutheran understanding of vocation," enunciated by Kathryn Kleinhans,* "...focuses on how God is already at work in one's everyday life here and now.... One does not move farther away from God or closer to God depending on the choices one makes; rather the Christian's task is to discern God's will and to try to act responsibly in each concrete role or situation."[1073] All are called to serve God in their labors—not just in churches, but in the home, the kitchen, the cellar, the workshop, the marketplace, and the fields. In the treatise "To the Christian Nobility," Luther enunciates a fundamental truth we reiterate again to enlighten our self-understanding:

> a cobbler, a smith, a peasant—each has the work and office of his trade, and yet they are all alike consecrated priests and bishops. Further, everyone must benefit and serve every other by means of his own work or office so that in

---

1072 Eaton, David H. "The Economists of the Reformation."

* Kathryn Kleinhans is the Dean of Trinity Lutheran Seminary at Capital University, Columbus, Ohio.

1073 Kleinhans, Kathryn, "The Work of a Christian: Vocation in Lutheran Perspective," *Word & World*, p. 401. <https://wordandworld.luthersem.edu/content/pdfs/25-4_Work_and_Witness/25-4_Kleinhans.pdf>.

> this way many kinds of work may be done for the bodily and spiritual welfare of the community, just as all the members of the body serve one another [1 Corinthians 12:14-26].[1074]

The everyday work of the Christian was just as pleasing to God as the priests', if one's skills, talents and energy were viewed as service to God by rendering meaningful labor through neighborly love that benefited others. David Eaton's article on "The Economists of the Reformation" concludes with the assessment: "The striking change brought about by The Reformation was the new attitudes toward work. No longer was work seen as toil and something that hindered the Christian life. Indeed, now one's work was seen as one's Divine calling and was to be carried out in service to God and for the good of the community."[1075]

For Kathryn Kleinhans, "Christian vocation is theology for living. It informs how we earn our daily bread and how we live our daily lives. It shapes our sense of identity and our relationships with others."[1076] It also transformed the workplace as well, and brought meaning and purpose to the labors of all Christians who desired to work unto the Lord by and through that work which served God's children.

> *A world in need now summons us to labor, love, and give;*
> *To make our life an offering to God, that all may live...*
> *O God, who gave Yourself to us in Jesus Christ Your Son,*
> *Teach us to give ourselves each day until life's work is done.*[1077]

Confessing God as Creator for Luther acknowledged not only God's original work but also recognized His ongoing work as He creatively sustains His creation through His partnership with His human creatures. In his lectures on Genesis, Luther says, "God wants to act through His creatures, whom He does not want to be idle."[1078] God gives food through nature assisted by human labor, rather than through miraculous appearance of manna, and He creates human beings through sexual union rather than out of dust. As Gustaf Wingren explains it, "With persons as His 'hands' or 'coworkers,' God gives His gifts through the earthly vocations (food through farmers, fishermen and hunters; external peace through

---

1074 LW 44:130. *The Christian in Society I*, "To the Christian Nobility," or *Three Treatises*, pp.16-17.

1075 Eaton, David H., "The Economists of the Reformation."

1076 Kleinhans, "The Work of a Christian," p.402.

1077 von Christierson, Frank, "As Saints of Old," LBW Hymn 404; and ELW Hymn 695.

1078 LW 3:274, *Lectures on Genesis III Chapters 15-20*, "Chapter Nineteen (vs.14)."

princes, judges, and orderly powers; knowledge and education through teachers and parents, etc.)."[1079]

Washing Diapers for God's Glory

Through the work of human beings, God's creative work goes forward, leading Philip Hefner to describe us as "created co-creators."[1080] It is therefore incumbent that the Christian seek to discern God's will and try to act responsibly in each specific task, role and situation, since all human work becomes a means to participate in God's creating and sustaining activity on earth. Into even the most menial tasks, Luther breathes fresh Gospel air:

> What then does Christian faith say to this? It opens its eyes, looks upon all these insignificant, distasteful, and despised duties in the Spirit, and is aware that they are all adorned with divine approval as with the costliest gold and jewels. It says, "O God, because I am certain that Thou hast created me as a man and hast from my body begotten this child, I also know for a certainty that it meets with Thy perfect pleasure. I confess to thee that I am not worthy to rock the little babe or wash its diapers, or to be entrusted with the care of the child and its mother. How is it that I, without any merit, have come to this distinction of being certain that I am serving Thy creature and Thy most precious will? O how gladly will I do so, though the duties should be even more insignificant and despised. Neither frost nor heat, neither drudgery nor labor, will distress or dissuade me, for I am certain that it is thus pleasing in Thy sight."
>
> ....Now you tell me, when a father goes ahead and washes diapers or performs some other mean task for his child, and someone ridicules him as an effeminate fool—though that father is acting in the spirit just described and in Christian faith—my dear fellow you tell me, which of the two is most keenly ridiculing the other? God, with all his angels and creatures is smiling—not because the father is washing diapers, but because he is doing so in Christian faith. Those who sneer at him and see only the task but not the faith are ridiculing God with all His creatures, as the biggest fools on

---

1079 Wingren, Gustaf, *Luther on Vocation*, p.27.

1080 Hefner, Philip, *The Human Factor, Evolution, Culture and Religion* (Minneapolis: Fortress Press, 1993), pp.31-32, and "The Evolution of the Created Co-Creator," *Currents in Theology and Mission*, issue 15, No. 6, December 1988, p.522.

> earth. Indeed, they are only ridiculing themselves; with all their cleverness they are nothing but devil's fool.[1081]

Changing and washing a diaper becomes more than a tedious task, knowing that God is working through you to love and care for that little image-bearer. God cares even about that work—even the most menial and basic of tasks. So allow the changing of that odious diaper to be transformed into an act of worship—a fragrant offering, pleasing to God—and let the neighbors snicker at such "unmanly labor" as they did in Luther's world. A man who washed diapers was no man at all, and the insult "diaper washer" referred to a man who did not wear the pants in his home.[1082] Luther would therefore admonish us today, as he preached then, to step outside the gender boundaries and to remove the word "*just*" from the way we describe our jobs and everyday tasks. The homemaker is not "*just* a housewife," but the one divinely called to shepherd and care for the home and family. The financial planner is not "*just* a stockbroker," but those entrusted by God with the long-term financial provision of their clients. The plumber and repair person are not "just fix-it" individuals but service personnel who render assistance in time of need. The sanitation worker is not "just a garbage man," or "just a trash man," and the custodian "*just* a janitor," but those called to care for the beautiful world God created and the facilities that house His children.

God's Work, Our Hands

Hans Schauffelein,
Diaper Washer, [1536?]

Jost Amman, 1539
Cobblers, Shoemakers

Jost Amman, 16th Century
Tailors

[1081] LW 45:39-40; 40-41. *The Christian in Society II*, "The Estate of Marriage (1522)."

[1082] The "Battle for the Pants" and Hans Schauffelein's "Diaper Washer" woodcut (above) are vividly portrayed and described in Keith Moxey's *Peasants Warriors and Wives: Popular Imagery in the Reformation* (Chicago: University of Chicago Press, 1989), pp. 101-26. In this richly illustrated study we discover the visual culture of Luther's time....even the "Battle of the Sexes" 500 years ago.

There are "delicious quotations" on the internet attributed to Luther about the maid who sweeps the kitchen and the shoemaker doing his Christian duty not by putting little crosses on the shoes, but by making good shoes, because God is interested in good craftsmanship. However, while those quotes, as well as the one about his planting an apple tree today even if he knew the world would end tomorrow, sound like Luther, the source is never attributed, because they haven't been discovered in his writings. What Luther did say about work refers to a "creaturely service of neighbor and world within a fully Christ-centered eschatological perspective."[1083] This is witnessed in what Luther did say:

> The prince should think: Christ has served me and made everything to follow him; therefore, I should also serve my neighbor, protect him and everything that belongs to him. That is why God has given me this office, and I have it that I might serve him. That would be a good prince and ruler. When a prince sees his neighbor oppressed, he should think: That concerns me! I must protect and shield my neighbor.... The same is true for shoemaker, tailor, scribe, or reader. If he is a Christian tailor, he will say: "I make these clothes because God has bidden me do so, so that I can earn a living, so that I can help and serve my neighbor." When a Christian does not serve the other, God is not present; that is not Christian living.[1084]

"Living as a faithful father or mother, an obedient worker, a responsible citizen or temporal ruler was the real religious life, more pleasing to God than all the vows and daily offices together," is how Professor Erik Herrmann interprets Luther's view. "Everyday vocations were divine callings. When coordinated with other vocations and ordinary works, the neighbor was served and loved and the community flourished. The Body of Christ had many members, each with its own function and role."[1085] Throughout an individual's life, one experiences a plurality of callings and a multiplicity of roles that need to be filled. What is determinative is not so much the nature of the work as it is the faith one has in responding to God's call to be of service. The invitation to live all of life "before the face of God" (as the Reformer would say) is an invitation to abide in relationship with Him as dearly beloved

---

1083 Gaiser, Frederick J., "What Luther Didn't Say about Vocation," *Word & World*, 25:4, Fall 2005, p.60. <https://wordandworld.luthersem.edu/content/pdfs/25-4_Work_and_Witness/25-4_Editorial.pdf>.

1084 WA 10/3:382. See also Frederick Gaiser's translation of this sermon passage, p.361.

1085 Herrmann, Erik H., "The Relevance of Remembering the Reformation," p.24.

children, walking with Him through our day-to-day labors, as He works in and through us as we joyfully sing:

> *Bless, Lord the labor we bring to serve You,*
> *that with our neighbor we may be fed.*
> *Sowing or tilling, we would work with You,*
> *harvesting, milling, for daily bread.*[1086]

And for Luther, "daily bread" in the fourth petition of the Lord's Prayer[1087] includes all that which is necessary for life, including food, clothing and shelter; physical health; family, friends and neighbors; fiscal resources; and stable government.

The Birthright Gift to Become Myself

We have often heard the architectural axiom enunciated by Louis Sullivan, "Form follows function,"[1088] meaning that the shape of a structure (or its form) is or should be dictated by its intended use (or its function). While that seems to make perfectly logical sense in erecting a building, it seems to be another instance where our ways turn God's way upside-down. In the Kingdom of God, Scripture instructs us that "function follows form" theologically. We are created in the image of God; "formed" and "known" in our mother's womb before we were born (Jeremiah 1:5); in Baptism our identity is given as His child, gifted and shaped for ministry (Romans 12:4-8; 1 Corinthians 12; Ephesians 4:8-15; 1 Corinthians 7:7). Rick Warren in his bestselling *The Purpose Driven Life* uses the acronym "SHAPE" to signify the **S**piritual gifts, **H**eart or passion, **A**bilities or talents, **P**ersonality, and **E**xperiences which one has, in a customized combination of capabilities to become who we are[1089] and let our lives speak!

Luther is generally credited with the recovery of the word "vocation," which means "calling." Prior to Luther, the use of that term typically referred to a "special calling" to religious life, which was considered to be a higher calling than working in the home or in civil life. The significance of its wider, more inclusive application led Jurgen Moltmann* to

---

1086 Bayly, Albert F., "Praise and Thanksgiving ," LBW Hymn 409; LW Hymn 403); ELW Hymn 689; and LSB Hymn 789).

1087 Martin Luther, "Large Catechism (1529)," *Book of Concord*, p.430.

1088 <https://www.thoughtco.com/form-follows-function-177237>.

1089 Warren, Rick, *The Purpose Driven Life* (Grand Rapids: Zondervan, 2002), pp.236-248, here p.236.

* Jurgen Moltmann is a German Reform theologian and Professor Emeritus of Systematic Theology at the University of Tubingen. He is the author of *Theology of Hope, The Crucified God*, and *God in Creation.*

identify Vocation as "the third great insight of the Lutheran Reformation,"[1090] after Word and Sacrament. Mirroring the more comprehensive recognition of Luther's understanding, and that contemplated by Thomas Merton, Pope Francis proclaimed that "vocations aren't the result of planning, but an encounter with God that changes your life."[1091] By helping one see the "treasure of their true self"—the discovering of who they are, who they were born to be as a child of God—they detect the presence of One who dwells within them, eagerly seeking to guide and direct their path as they "abide" in each other. Jesus teaches, "*Abide in Me as I abide in you. Just as the branch cannot bear fruit by itself, unless it abides in the vine, neither can you unless you abide in Me. I am the vine, you are the branches. Those who abide in Me and I in them bear much fruit*" (John 15:4-5 [NRSV]).

Thomas Merton, an influential Catholic author of the twentieth century, describes this strange, inspiring and meaningful birthright gift of self in his book *No Man Is an Island*:

> For each one of us, there is only one thing necessary to fulfill our own destiny according to God's will to be what God wants us to be. Discovering vocation does not mean scrambling toward some prize just beyond my reach but accepting the treasure of true self I already possess. Vocation does not come from a voice outside there calling me to be something I am not. It comes from a voice in here calling me to be the person I was born to be, to fulfill the original selfhood given me at my birth by God.[1092]

To this understanding, Merton writes, "A man knows when he has found his vocation when he stops thinking about how to live and begins to live."[1093] There are always those impulses, Luther would admit, being implanted by the Devil, demanding that we strive to become someone else instead of becoming oneself. There is a wonderful Hasidic tale told by Martin Buber* which reveals this universal tendency to want to be someone else and the ultimate importance of becoming oneself:

1090 Moltmann, Jurgen, "Reformation and Revolution," *Martin Luther and the Modern Mind*, ed. Manfred Hoffman (Lewiston, NY: Edwin Mellen, 1985), p.186; cited in D. Michael Bennethum's *Listen! God is Calling! Luther Speaks of Vocation, Faith and Work* (Minneapolis: Augsburg Fortress, 2003), p.41.

1091 <https://ignatiansolidarity.net/blog/tag/vocation>.

1092 Merton, Thomas, *No Man is an Island* (New York: Houghton Mifflin Harcourt Publishing, 1955). <https://www.azquotes.com/author/10004-Thomas_Merton/tag/vocation>.

1093 Merton, Thomas, *Thoughts in Solitude* (New York: Farrar, Strauss and Giroux, 1956), p.99.

* Martin Buber was an Austrian Jewish and Israeli philosopher best known for his philosophy of dialogue, a form of existentialism centered on the distinction between the I–Thou relationship and the I–It relationship.

> A rabbi named Zusya died and went to stand before the judgment seat of God. As he waited for God to appear, he grew nervous thinking about his life and how little he had done. He began to imagine that God was going to ask him "Why weren't you Moses or why weren't you Solomon or why weren't you David?" But when God appeared, the rabbi was surprised. God simply asked, "Why weren't you Zusya?"[1094]

Similarly, Viktor Frankl, the eminent Jewish psychiatrist and Holocaust survivor, says

> Everyone has his own specific vocation or mission in life to carry out a concrete assignment which demands fulfillment. Therein he cannot be replaced, nor can his life be repeated. Thus, everyone's task is as unique as is his specific opportunity to implement it.[1095]

That is to say, the life task or mission of each person is to be him or herself, not someone else, striving to be your own person, the best version of yourself, the very best at being you. In doing that, you will have become the person God made you to be. Our Declaration of Independence acknowledges that we are endowed by our Creator with certain unalienable rights, and yet as we struggle as individuals and as a nation, we find ourselves letting others disabuse us of the freedom to become who we are. Parker J. Palmer, founder and Senior Partner Emeritus of the Center for Courage and Renewal in Madison, Wisconsin, writes that

> We are surrounded by expectations that may have little to do with who we really are, expectations held by people who are not trying to discern our selfhood but to fit us into slots. In families, schools, workplaces, and religious communities, we are trained away from true self toward images of acceptability; under social pressures like racism and sexism our original shape is deformed beyond recognition; and we ourselves, driven by fear, too often betray true self to gain the approval of others.[1096]

Whose I am and who I am shaped to be should determine what I do and how I function. Discovering those individual characteristics God has invested in me equips and enables

---

1094 Buber, Martin, "Tales of the Hasidism." <https://chippit.tripod.com/tales1.html>.

1095 Frankl, Viktor E., *Man's Search for Meaning*, 3rd ed. (New York: Simon and Schuster, 1984), p.113.

1096 Palmer, Parker J., "Now I Become Myself," *yes! Magazine*, Spring 2001 ("Working for Life").

neighbor love to flow from my worship of my Creator and Lord into my relationships and work in unique ways. This understanding was frequently communicated by radio talk show host Rush Limbaugh's belief that he possessed "Talent on loan from God."[1097] Bestselling author of *The 5th Wave,* Rick Yancey, expresses this Biblical conviction from a little different perspective in his quotable quote: "God doesn't call the equipped, God equips the called. And you have been called!"[1098] In the Biblical understanding, we are to let our life speak in word and deed!

However, most of us harbor those insecurities Luther experienced in not being good enough in God's eyes, and therefore seek to prove our self-worth not only to our Creator but also to our neighbor. How especially true that is as we encounter our consumer culture bombarding us with messages of lack, deficiency and status. As a result, Pastor Ben McIntire of Nebraska contends

> we spend an enormous amount of treasure and energy trying to be something we are not, expecting too much from ourselves, trying to belong, and fit in with "everyone else," feeling that our lives have little value, or they are not good enough. Some people feel like they are failures who can never measure up. Others are perfectionists who keep striving long after it is necessary for things to be done just so. Still others suffer constantly from extreme guilt over the past, things done and left undone. We often place ourselves under intolerable burdens that we cannot possibly live up to. These expectations and worries produce both stress and fatigue [physically, mentally, and spiritually]. To be able to relax and be ourselves is one of the greatest benefits our faith gives us.[1099]

Like Luther, Søren Kierkegaard, the great Danish theologian (and as a former philosophy major, my favorite philosopher), suffered and wrote about his extreme bouts of melancholy, concluding "And now with God's help, I shall become myself."[1100] He too discovered the liberating truth of that freedom Luther equated with the "gates of paradise" opening before him. With God's grace, acceptance and promise of the Gospel of Jesus Christ, we can

---

[1097] <https://www.quotes.net/mquote/841869>.

[1098] <https://www.goodreads.com/quotes/814413-god-doesn-t-call-the-equipped-son-god-equips-the-called>.

[1099] McIntire, Ben, "Yokes," *PB & J* (Pastor Ben & Jesus), Blog July 2, 2014 <https://benmcintire.wordpress.com/2014/07/02/yokes>.

[1100] <https:///www.goodreads.com/quotes/423155-now-with-god-s-help-i-shall-become-myself>.

simply be ourselves and experience the true freedom of becoming ourselves—not what you think you *should* be, or what others *expect* you to be. When we realize that God has initially chosen us to be His, yoked to His Son (Matthew 11:29-30) and guided by His Spirit, we discover we no longer need to rely upon our stressful pretenses and misguided strivings toward perfectionism. Whose acceptance do we need to achieve or receive other than our Creator's and the One who gifts us with His redemption?

John Newton, the author of "Amazing Grace," once wrote, "I am not what I ought to be, I am not what I want to be, I am not what I hope to be in another world; but still I am not what I once used to be, and by the grace of God am what I am."[1101] Then too, there is John Lennon expressing the similar understanding in the Beatles' song "All You Need Is Love," when he optimistically wrote, "You can learn how to be you in time; it's easy."[1102] Following St. Paul's summary of the Biblical narrative, especially the sweeping history of salvation recounted in Romans, Luther witnessed God's promise breaking into the lives of His people as they discover their "Yes" to life in Christ (2 Corinthians 1:20) who is not only *for* us but promises to be *with* us. That's our birthright! It is the death and resurrection of Christ that promises hope and gives meaning and purpose to one's own story, including our vocation.

Luther insisted on the dignity and value of all labor, including the virtues of manual labor "in the sweat of one's brow." As we have learned, he denounced the separation of sacred and secular work by elevating everyone's lawful labor into a service for God and for the benefit of the community or "neighbor." And while Luther had grave concerns about uncontrolled capitalism fostering greed, he unwittingly contributed to its development with his exaltation of work being a blessing ordained of God from the foundation of the world; his exhortation to work not only as a means of subsistence, but as a means of serving others; and his excoriation of poverty. How we work has greatly changed since Luther's sixteenth-century world, but understanding Luther's notion of work is still vitally relevant today.

Luther would give a tip of his academic hat to salute the pre-Covid-19 economic achievements of the Trump administration registering the highest recorded number of employed persons in our country, resulting in low unemployment numbers, especially the lowest number of unemployed among minorities ever tracked. Added to these records, we also experienced the lowest poverty rate since 1959, as "low-wage workers experienced the fastest pay increases" according to the *New York Times*,[1103] and CNBC also reporting "Workers at the lower end of the pay scale finally are getting the most benefit from rising

---

[1101] <http://jodyhedlund.com/wp-content/uploads/2016/09/BCC-John-Newton-Quotes.pdf>.

[1102] Lennon, John, "All You Need Is Love." <https://www.thebeatles.com/all-you-need-love-0>.

[1103] <https://www.nytimes.com/2019/05/02/business/economy/wage-growth-economy.html>.

wages."[1104] Seeing the depressed economic zones throughout the nation, especially in our inner cities, being identified and targeted for renewal opportunities in job creation and housing for the underprivileged would certainly meet with Luther's enthusiastic praise. So too would getting drug prices lowered for consumers, along with the "warp speed" directives cutting through bureaucracy to achieve the fastest development and testing of a vaccine to temper Covid-19, and additional therapeutic medicines for those stricken with the virus that are now on the horizon. Like Luther, Trump has functioned and led with life experience from the ground up, not from the top down through the heavily bureaucratic, theoretic procedures of an elite hierarchy of Church and State.

On October 4, 2019, President Trump not only reported "the best numbers that we've had in many, many, many, decades.... We have the best economy we've ever had; we have the best jobs numbers in 51 years, the best unemployment numbers that we've had in a half a century.... People are working, they're making money."[1105]

The strong Trump economy, bolstered by measures to bring manufacturing jobs back to America, created, prior to the Covid-19 pandemic, an environment where job opportunities were abundant, and Americans were being lifted out of poverty, realizing dignity and gaining a sense of worth in their lives. "The Census Bureau says that median income rose 0.9% to an inflation-adjusted $63,179 from $62,626 in 2017. The poverty rate fell to 11.8%.... That improvement reflects increased income over the past several years for many workers in low-wage jobs."[1106] "The latest data (January 8, 2020) from the Department of Agriculture [which administers the Supplemental Nutrition Assistance Program, or SNAP] shows that 7.7 million fewer Americans were receiving food stamps now than did when Trump entered the White House."[1107] This number was before the administration's proposals for tightening eligibility, by re-instituting the Clinton "work-fare" policy, took effect.

The growth of that booming economy (now in recovery from the hit taken by the lockdown) was attributed to the tax cuts, minimum-wage increases and effects of deregulation, which has led to higher wages during a tighter, more competitive market for jobs. The later deregulation at first glance would seem to contradict his twin Martin, who

---

[1104] <https://www.cnbc.com/2019/03/13/workers-at-lower-end-of-pay-scale-getting-most-benefit-from-rising-wages.html>.

[1105] <https://www.cnbc.com/2019/10/04/black-and-hispanic-unemployment-is-at-a-record-low.html>.

[1106] <https://www.whitehouse.gov/briefings-Statements/americans-backgrounds-experiencing-economic-success-trump-economy>.

[1107] <https://www.washingtonexaminer.com/policy/economy/food-stamp-rolls-have-declined-by-7m-under-trump-even-before-reforms-take-effect>.

favored regulation 500 years ago. They are, however, more identical in these economic matters than what might appear at first glance.

Oversight Is Not Overreach

Both reformers favored oversight and accountability to restrict abuse, especially as it relates to the poor and elderly. As we have seen with Luther wanting the government to step in and regulate the market when needed to protect the consumers' interest, so too has Trump demonstrated such intervention. We saw the administration step up its scrutiny of the biggest tech companies, as regulators are divvying up antitrust oversight of the Silicon Valley giants. In this information technology (IT) world, concerns are centering on the ability to stifle competition, the spread of disinformation, privacy breaches, political bias, and cybersecurity. Trump signed into law legislation to provide the FCC (Federal Communications Commission) with the tools it needs to crack down on robo-calls which are annoying at best and predatory at worst. "These calls often originate from scam artists intent on ripping off unsuspecting consumers, particularly seniors. This is a bipartisan win…that gives the FCC the tools it needs to be the cop on the beat to go after these bad actors," says Representative Peter Welch of Vermont who proposed the legislation.[1108]

Previously, President Trump also signed into law the Elder Abuse Prevention and Prosecution Act which increases penalties for criminals who target older Americans with scams and financial exploitation.[1109] In addition, the administration is scrutinizing Big Pharma and has taken steps proposing guidelines for the importation of certain prescription drugs to further reduce prices of prescription drugs which have been decreasing.[1110]

> Today's announcement outlines two pathways for the safe importation of certain prescription drugs to help provide safe, effective, more affordable drugs to American patients, (said Health and Human Services Secretary Alex Azar). These are historic actions by HHS [Health and Human Services]

1108 <https://vtdigger.org/press_release/welch-championed-legislation-cracking-down-on-robocalls-signed-into-law>.

1109 <https://www.whitehouse.gov/presidential-actions/president-donald-j-trump-proclaims-march-4-march-10-2018-national-consumer-protection-week>.

1110 <https://www.whitehouse.gov/articles/prescription-drug-prices-falling-historic-levels-thanks-trump-administration-policies>.

> and the FDA [Food and Drug Administration], and they represent the bold nature of President Trump's agenda for lowering drug costs. The President has recognized the opportunity to lower costs for American patients through safe importation, and we at HHS and FDA are delivering on that possibility through a safe, commonsense approach.[1111]

On Friday, July 24, 2020, President Trump signed four executive orders to build on his extensive efforts to drive down prescription drug prices and ensure that Americans have access to life-saving medications. The orders will enable the HHS and FDA to enact the earlier announced plans by requiring

> federal community health centers to pass the giant discounts they receive from drug companies on insulin and EpiPens directly to their patients… second, to allow the safe and legal importation of prescription drugs from Canada and other countries where the price for the identical drug is incredibly lower…same everything, same box, same pill—and yet, it's 50, 60, 70 percent lower…[noting] We pay for all of the research and all of the development, and foreign countries absolutely nothing, and our consumer gets charged…. The third revolutionary order I'm signing today will prevent middlemen—and women, I guess…[who] are making a fortune along with pharmacy benefit managers…just bilking Medicare patients with these high drug prices while they pocket gigantic discounts…of up to 50% …Under this [fourth] transformative order, Medicare will be required to purchase drugs at the same price as other countries pay…. We pay 80% more than nations like Germany, Canada, and others for some of the most expensive medicines, identical in all respects…if somebody else pays $1 and we pay $5. We're paying $1…instead of paying the highest price, Medicare will pay the lowest price (following "Favored Nation Pricing for Drugs") and so will lots of other U.S. buyers.[1112]

President Trump is acknowledging the greed Luther identified, which led to the Reformer's apprehension with the emerging capitalistic practices and the need for the

---

1111 <https://www.fda.gov/news-events/press-announcements/trump-administration-takes-historic-steps-lower-us-prescription-drug-prices>.

1112 <https://miragenews.com/us/-president-trump-at-signing-of-executive-orders-on-lowering-drug-prices>.

government to step in with preventions. While regulations and controls are intended to protect, we have seen in our time "regulations" become part of a political spoils system by which various special interests impose their will on the public and profit from government favor, replicating the very concerns Luther had about corporate greed. The proliferation of lobbyists and special interest groups on K Street in Washington, DC, attests to how even well-intentioned regulations can get twisted into burdensome, time-consuming and costly processes, as well as demonstrating favoritism in who really benefits from such action.

One of President Trump's goals for his administration was to reduce needless red tape and regulatory costs that impede efficiency and effectiveness. Agencies are now, by Executive Order 13771, to "offset the cost of any new regulation (or guidance) with at least two deregulatory actions." The Administrator of the Office of Information and Regulatory Affairs, Neomi Rao, said, "[I]n modern times, the expansion of the administrative state has placed undue burdens on the public, impeding economic growth, technological innovation, and consumer choice.... Our reform efforts emphasize the rule of law, respect for the Constitution's separation of powers, and the limits of agency authority."[1113]

We Are "Rusty Tools"

There are certainly justifiable reasons for the government to police, regulate, monitor and inspect for the safety and protection of its citizens. As we have shown, greed and the desire for power and control have necessitated civil government's use of the "sword" to enforce law and order for the well-being of all. By maintaining order in society and preventing it from falling into chaos, the administration of God's left hand supports the work of the Gospel. On the other hand, it is the task of the Church through its teaching and preaching to radiate the Gospel into the kingdom of the world, thus encouraging believers to be model citizens in discharging their civic and social responsibilities. Neither of the two governments, both of which are under God's rule, writes Luther, "is sufficient in the world without the other."[1114] For Luther, Christians are citizens of both kingdoms, "two different persons in one,"[1115] both righteous and a sinner at the same time (*simuli justus et peccator*), and therefore need both the spiritual and the temporal rule.

[1113] <https://www.heritage.org/government-regulation/commentary/heres-how-much-red-tape-trump-has-cut>.

[1114] LW 45:92. *The Christian in Society II*, "Temporal Authority."

[1115] LW 21:23. *The Sermon on the Mount and The Magnificat*, "Sermon—Fifth Chapter St. Matthew."

In his lectures on Galatians, Luther expounds on this paradox, that "a Christian man is righteous and a sinner at the same time,* holy and profane, an enemy of God and a child of God." [1116] He later explains, "Therefore if you look at faith, the Law has been fulfilled, sins have been destroyed, and no Law is left. But if you look at the flesh, in which there is no good, you will be compelled to admit that those who are righteous in the spirit through faith are still sinners."[1117] A saint by faith in Jesus Christ still remains a sinner by nature.

Dr. Forell comes to the same conclusion:

> Of course, it is impossible for man to separate the Old Adam clearly and neatly from the new. Man cannot say, "here I am righteous, and the New Adam is active and here I am unrighteous and the Old Adam is active." Such a procedure would demand a split personality. Luther realized that and said in his commentary on Romans: "One and the same man is spiritual and carnal, righteous and sinful, good and evil."[1118] "And the just man is like a rusty tool, which God began to polish, but which, where it is rusty, does not cut until it is perfectly polished."[1119] "This process of polishing goes on as long as man lives."[1120] But it is God who does the polishing: that is the important difference between Luther's ethics and the ethics of Rome.[1121]

Luther's astounding claim that God, not human works, makes us righteous and leads to a justification that we discover, is transformative. And this I believe is key: Justified sinners gradually are changed through the indwelling presence of Christ, into people now more

* The Latin phrase "*simul justus et peccator*" is the technical term for the Reformation doctrine of being simultaneously declared righteous (saints) while acknowledging the truth that we are indeed sinners.

1116 LW 26:232. *Lectures on Galatians 1535 Chapters 1-4*, "Chapter Three (vs.6)."

1117 LW 27:231. *Lectures on Galatians 1535 Chapters 5-6* and *Lectures on Galatians 1519 Chapters 1-6*, "Chapter Two (vs.18)."

1118 WA 56, 343, 18. (Comm. Romans, 1515-16).

1119 WA 2, 413, 27.

1120 WA 36, 364, 19. (Sermon on I Tim., Nov. 24, 1532): ...if I have a clear conscience before men and show love from a pure heart, the Old Adam, the sinful flesh and blood remains within me...as the Apostle says in Gal. 5:17 "the flesh lusteth against the spirit...and in Romans that he must without ceasing fight and war against himself and cannot do the good things he would do...the flesh is present and attacks and fights... and so there is an eternal struggle and resistance within us.

1121 Forell, George W., *Faith Active in Love: An Investigation of the Principles Underlying Luther's Social Ethics* (Minneapolis: Augsburg Publishing House, 1954), p.92.

attuned to seeking the well-being of others. Good works do not and cannot cause salvation, but rather flow from the happy realization that they are saved. In Forell's words, "Faith is never unethical faith. He who has faith will be sanctified and do good works. Justification and sanctification are for Luther two aspects of the same process and therefore mutually interdependent."[1122] The startling economic implications of neighbor-love for Luther were thus inherently based on a presupposition about the nature of neighbor love as a Biblical norm, following our Lord's example ("*that you also should do as I have done to you*" [John 13:15 (NRSV)]), not primarily on emotional feelings of goodwill or affection. It was a steadfast commitment to serve the well-being of one's neighbor, and one's "neighbor" is whomever one's life impacts!

Summarizing Luther, Cynthia Moe-Lobeda writes,

> We are never—this side of death—fully freed from the human proclivity to serve self at the expense of others. We remain, in Luther's honest words, God's "*rusty tools.*" [She concludes her article acknowledging this honest reality:] In these faithful ventures and modes of living out our calling, we will be fallible, faulty, at times fearful, and encumbered by the incessant lure of self-curved in on self—as was Luther [and is Donald Trump]. However, that we are "rusty" tools makes us no less makes us no less precious tools in God's sight and in God's liberating healing work on earth.[1123]

Our former president seems to recognize the challenges inherent in being a "rusty" tool in attempting to maintain a balance between conflicting goals. We've experienced the dilemma between compassion or mercy and justice in immigration, and as we find ourselves wrestling in our care for both the environment and the economy. After citing examples of being a net exporter of clean, affordable natural gas, being number one in the world for access to clean drinking water, air pollution being six times lower in the U.S. than the global average, with carbon emissions declining more than any other country on Earth (all the signatories to the Paris Climate Accord lag behind America in overall emissions reductions) and with the tremendous future of solar energy, the President stated that the United States does not have to sacrifice our own jobs to lead the world on the environment. The so-called Green New Deal with a nearly $100 trillion estimated cost is clearly not affordable. "It'll kill millions of jobs, it'll crush the dreams of the poorest Americans, and disproportionately

---

[1122] Ibid., pp.85-86.

[1123] Moe-Lobeda, Cynthia D., "Luther's Economic Ethic of Neighbor." <https://elca.org/JLE/Articles/1266>.

harm minority communities. I will not stand for it. We will defend the environment, but we will also defend American sovereignty, American prosperity, and we will defend American jobs…"[1124]

At the American Center for Mobility in Detroit, Michigan, President Trump proclaimed on March 15, 2015 that "…no country can long lead the free world if it does not protect its industries and care for its people and protect its borders…. Our great Presidents, from Washington to Jefferson to Jackson to Lincoln, all understood that a great nation must protect its manufacturing, must protect itself from the outside."[1125]

With realism and optimism, President Trump sounds like Martin Luther, who also spoke admirably about the mining industry, obviously with some prejudice. In the museum attached to Luther's birthplace in Eisleben, I viewed a mining display with the following quote from Luther in 1536: "Then tell us, who puts the gold and silver into the mountains that we can find it? Is it the work of man? True, he finds it by working, but God must first put it there and gives it, for it to be found by hard work."

As we have noted, Luther not only appreciated the bounty and beauty of creation, but he would also have witnessed the human impact on the environment in his hometown of Mansfeld. We should not ignore, however, that he developed his doctrine of creation from his study of Genesis, and his trust in God's wondrous provision and workings of the Spirit through human beings to participate with Him in tending that creation. Such teachings, as proclaiming Christ's dominion over the natural world, can rouse Christians to engage in environmental concerns that can serve their neighbors by caring for the planet on which we live. Luther reminds us of our role in collaborating with the Creator who "does not work [in us] without us, because it is for this very thing He has re-created and preserved us, that He might work in us and we might cooperate with Him."[1126] In our ELCA denomination the slogan has been "God's Work, Our Hands" which Martin Luther would fully subscribe to and which Donald Trump is seeking to balance.

Though Luther left Mansfeld when he was fourteen, he maintained a lifelong loyalty to Mansfeld. He was the son of a rough-hewn miner whose arduous work and business deals would have provided daily lessons for the young Martin of that important industry. In all probability, he learned about the exploration for minerals and the ways in which small miners

---

1124 <https://www.whitehouse.gov/briefings-Statements/remarks-president-trump-americas-environmental-leadership>.

1125 <https://www.whitehouse.gov/briefings-Statements/remarks-president-trump-american-center-mobility-detroit-mi>.

1126 LW 33:243. *Career of the Reformer III*, "The Bondage of the Will."

and smelters were pushed around by the powerful forces of investment banking, as well as by the Church and government authorities.[1127] Yet the excavation of mines never stood in the way of his admiration and gratitude for the Creator's handiwork and the generosity of His gifts and provisions.

Perhaps his last "civic" involvement best manifests the fondness and concern for the region and its people he retained his entire life. He had been asked to represent and be an advocate for the area's miners and smelters in their dispute with the Mansfeld nobility, who wished to nationalize the mining industry. Familiar with the economics of the industry, Luther believed such action would threaten the livelihood of the locals. Trump, in campaigning, expressed concern for workers in the coal mining industry as well as those in the oil producing states. He asked for his audiences to place their faith in the American worker and the ingenuity and innovative spirit that continues to make our nation great, and with the perseverance required of us in the years to come. Sadly America is now again dependent on foreign sources (who are not our friends) for our energy, when during Trump's presidency the U.S. was net exporter. Trump, who was challenged and attacked, especially from left-wing socialists, continually warned of the impact and danger of such "take-overs" with proposed policies that would nationalize and control vital segments of the economy, such as energy and healthcare, by pointing to countries where such policies have never succeeded.

Yes, cognizant of his mining roots, and all the time exhibiting an affection for Mansfeld, Luther, one of Europe's leading thinkers, late in his life still asserted that he was *"ein Mansfeldisch Kind"*—a child of Mansfeld"[1128]—and a "Rusty Tool."

[1127] Huffman, Tim. "Luther, Forgotten, but Not Gone," *BREAD and JUSTICE*, The Newsletter of the Metropolitan New York Synod World Hunger Committee, Spring 2017, p.5. <https://www.mnys.org/assets/1/6/bread_and_justice_2017.pdf>.

[1128] Lack, Mark, "Cherishing the Trees, as Christ is Lord Over All and the Center of All Things," *Living Traditions*, ed. Kimberlynn McNabb and Robert C. Fennell (Eugene, OR: Wipf and Stock Publishers, 2019), p.4, quoting "Nr. 4157," 189.

33

Maligned House-Wives of The Black Cloister and The White House

In viewing the similarities between Martin Luther and Donald Trump, it would be unpardonable not to mention the resemblance in the verbal and abusive attacks made on their wives. "Fat Luther" was accused of yielding to the

> lascivious impulses of his blood, marrying a nun who had broken away from the cloister.... [This] persistent cliché was based on a malicious invention of Luther's opponents that some of his contemporaries were all too willing to parrot [without evidence]. The reality was very different. Averse to overhasty innovation, Luther remained celibate for a good many years after he had launched his assault on monastic life.[1129]

In autumn 1524, Luther informed his trusted friend Spalatin that he was not at all minded to marry. "It is not that I do not feel my flesh or sex, since I am neither wood nor stone, but my mind is far removed from marriage, since I daily expect death and the punishment due to a heretic."[1130]

Luther had helped engineer a daring nighttime rescue of twelve nuns from the Cistercian convent of Marienthron in Nimbschen at a time when removing a nun from a cloister was an offense punishable by death. The nuns, having encountered Luther's teachings against the celibate vows of Catholic clergy and nuns, fled their convent and arrived in Wittenberg, where the Reformer played matchmaker amongst the eligible former priests, pastors and professors who were looking for wives. Many of his supporters had repeatedly urged Luther to align his own lifestyle with his teachings. Katharina von Bora, one of the "rescued" twelve, proved to be a challenge as she turned down a number of suitors; or perhaps better stated, she was determined to use her newly won Christian freedom to determine her life for herself, and besides, she had her eyes on taking "Doctor Martinus" in marriage.

1129 Schilling, *Upheaval*, p.267.

1130 LW 49:93. *Letters II*, "To George Spalatin, November 30,1524.

While in Wittenberg, she lived at the home of Lucas Cranach, where Luther was a frequent guest. After a couple of years had passed, Luther himself resolved to marry Katie, mostly on theological grounds and out of a sense of responsibility and duty more than from affection or desire. One might even say it was an arranged marriage, born out of defiance more than love. As he later recalled, "Suddenly and when my mind was on other matters, the Lord snared me with the yoke of matrimony."[1131] Their wedding would be "a marriage of convenience for her and of inconvenience for him, or so he thought."[1132] He concluded, however, that "his marriage would please his father, rile the pope, cause the angels to laugh, and the devil to weep, and would seal his testimony"[1133] by strengthening his criticism of monastic celibacy and elevating the Bible's view of God's daughters. Such revolutionary views created a seismic cultural shift that undermined long-held societal and religious assumptions about both women and marriage.

Martin and Katharina's Marriage and Family Life

The Luther Wedding

Making Music in the Circle of His Family

<https://commons.wikimedia.org/wiki/File:131-the_wedding_of_martin_luther_to_catherine_von_bora.jpg>

Martin Luther marries Katharina von Bora on June 27, 1525, with Luther's friend, Johannes Bugenhagen, who was the parish priest at Wittenberg's St. Mary's, officiating; Dr. Justus Jonas, John Abel and painter Lucas Cranach and his wife, Barbara, with whom Katie had been living for some time, as witnesses.

Luther was a talented musician and hymn writer who played the mandolin and sang with his family. He understood how powerful hymns are because of the way they distill the influence of conviction to a compact confession or focus one's mind on the heart of the Gospel in meter and tune.

(Images: Public domain, retrieved at Wikimedia)

1131 Somervill, Barbara A., *Martin Luther, Father of the Reformation* (Minneapolis: Compass Point Books, 2006), p.82.

1132 James, Carolyn Custis, "The Pigtails that Sparked a Revolution," *Missio Alliance*, October 31, 2017. <https://www.missioalliance.org/pigtails-sparked-revolution>.

1133 Lindberg, Carter, "Martin Luther on Marriage and the Family," p.29. <http://www.emanuel.ro/wp-content/uploads/2014/06/P-2.1-2004-Carter-Lindberg-Martin-Luther-on-Marriage-and-the-Family.pdf> or <https://notjustwivesandmothers.wordpress.com/2020/10/26/katharina-von-bora-the-straight-talking-wife-of-martin-luther/>.

Surprised by Marriage

As Luther knelt at the marriage altar to become Katie's* lawfully wedded husband, he was living out his theology. The distant regard he initially held for Katie soon became marital affection, and he fell deeply in love with her, discovering her strengths an asset on which he could safely rely in their "blessed alliance." "Luther appreciated the sheer increase in his physical comfort," Joan Acocella reveals. "When he writes to a friend, soon after his marriage, [he shares] what it is like to lie in a dry bed after years of sleeping on a pile of damp, mildewed straw"[1134] from perspiration, and how he fondly loved waking up to see pigtails on the pillow next to him.[1135]

Gossip and "Fake News" surrounded the marriage of a monk and nun, both of whom had broken their chastity vows. Their marriage was viewed as a scandal that reverberated across Europe. "Predictably, Luther's enemies seized on Katharina as a weak point, hoping that by discrediting her they could undermine Luther's credibility as a man of God. [How typically we see that pattern played out in our body politic.] She was called an alcoholic, money-grubbing, and a slut."[1136] Even Melanchthon, Luther's trusted right-hand man, stated that "the nuns have used their arts against him."[1137]

"Sixteenth-century marriages in Germany were typically two-stage affairs," as Eric Metaxus enlightens his readers:

> There was first a small ceremony with a handful of witnesses and then a larger event with a church procession and guests from out of town. But the initial event was capped with the consummation of the marriage, so the marriage—actually called the *Kopulation*, which is etymologically related to the more anodyne word "couple"—was in fact consummated *before the*

---

* Katharina von Bora, wife of Martin Luther, was also known to her husband as Katherine, Catherine, Master Kate, Katy, Kathe, Kathie, Kitty my rib, as well as Katie. These variations seem to result through translation from German, by the circumstance or situation of the couple's conversation with each other, or by Luther speaking admiringly about his wife to others.

1134 Acocella, Joan, "How Martin Luther Changed the World," *The New Yorker*, October 23, 2017. <https://www.newyoker.com/magazine/2017/10/30/how-martin-luther-changed-the-world>.

1135 LW 54:191. Table Talk, "Much Adjustment Required in Marriage, No3178a," June 1522.

1136 Curry, Andrew, "How a Runaway Nun Helped an Outlaw Monk Change the World." <https://nationalgeographic.com/news/2017/10/martin-luther-wife-protestant-reformation-500>.

1137 Schilling, *Upheaval*, p.273, citing *Luther's Correspondence and Other Contemporary Letters, Vol. 2: 1521-1530*, trans. and ed. Preserved Smith and Charles M. Jacobs (Philadelphia, PA: 1918), letter 692, p.325.

> *wedding.* If the marriage was not consummated, the wedding would not happen. And if the marriage was consummated, the couple were as good as married before the wedding…
>
> Odder far than the idea that these marriages were consummated before the weddings was the idea that they must be consummated in full view of a witness. So after the small ceremony, the couple were escorted to their bedroom in the cloister, where [Justus] Jonas did the curious honors, watching the two become one flesh literally and figuratively…. There was often an observation deck above the bed, though this detail seems not to have been observed in this case…. For those in Luther's day who were not prudes about the facts of life, and who considered the marriage bed not less than holy, and who saw in the physical union of man and woman a living picture of the union between the Bridegroom, Jesus Christ, and His Bride, the Church, it was a real place and real time where heaven bowed down to kiss the earth…. And out of this came that which was impossible, the bounteous miracle of life itself."[1138]

Without paparazzi taking photographs and the ubiquitous cameras and cell phones to document the celebrities' every move, the official eyewitness account was a person in the room with Marty and Katy as they became a "couple!" That marriage would be celebrated at the wedding feast two weeks later, so that out-of-town guests could be present since the marriage itself was hastily arranged.

Many close to Luther were concerned about the expected loss to his reputation, and Luther responded to a friend's worried questioning by explaining

> that I was suddenly married to Catherine; [I did this] to silence the evil mouths which are so used to complaining about me. For I still hope to live for a little while. In addition, I also did not want to reject this unique [opportunity to obey] my father's wish for progeny, which he so often expressed. At the same time, I also wanted to confirm what I have taught by practicing it; for I find so many timid people in spite of such great light from the Gospel. God

---

[1138] Metaxas, *Rediscovered*, pp.343-44.

> has willed and brought about this step. For I feel neither passionate love nor burning for my spouse, but I cherish her.[1139]

All the makings for a bestselling romance novel! But as we have observed, Luther finds meaning—and I would say "revelation"—from the most minute to the most surprisingly huge experiences he encounters. Eric Metaxas collaborates that view by surmising,

> He knew that this act would have meaning and very real power in the spiritual realm. It was an act of worship to God as much as anything anyone could ever do, and its spiritual significance was tremendous. Luther was in his person and with his own body countering the falsely pious antipathy to the physical and specifically to the erotic. God had created the physical and sexual as good, and he had redeemed them from their broken fallenness via marriage. Thus, not only was there nothing dirty about this, but the opposite was true. Luther thought unnatural celibacy to be of the devil and natural and healthy marital sex to be something that glorified God.[1140]

In addition, Luther demonstrates the freedom to allow his orneriness to be on full display to his colleagues, and to us, by sharing how much pleasure he took in viewing his marriage to a nun as delivering "a whirling roundhouse kick to the devil's own snout!"[1141]

Nevertheless, the gossip—which was spread even by Desiderius Erasmus, once ally and now antagonist—claiming that the marriage had been blessed a few days after the wedding by the bride giving birth to a child, was naturally welcomed with open arms in the Catholic Church. Anti-Reformation pamphleteers accused her of having children with Luther out of wedlock as they broke their vows to God, broke God's law, and forsook their purity before marriage.

Katharina "was seen as self-confident, strong-willed, and independent which were all negative attributes for women at the time," says Martin Treu, historian at the Luther Society in Wittenberg and author of a von Bora biography. "Women at the time were supposed to be seen and not heard."[1142] Some of Luther's supporters were noticeably "uncomfortable

---

1139 LW 49:117. *Letters II*, "To Nicholas von Amsdorf [Wittenberg] June 21, 1525."

1140 Metaxas, *Rediscovered*, p.342.

1141 Ibid.

1142 Curry, "Runaway Nun."

with his wife's outsized presence and referred to her as *'Doctorissa'* in abusive, mean-spirited digs"[1143] while her adoring husband who admired her intellect called her *"Doctora Lutherin."*

She could be quite direct with her criticism, even of her husband, often in creative and provocative ways. Once, Luther—who for years had been used to solitude—locked himself in his study and sanctuary, The Reformation's "command central," for three days until a frustrated Katie

> tending children and taking care of the household without his help, decided it was time for Martin to emerge and take up his paternal duties. After beckoning him several times with no answer, Katie skillfully removed the heavy door from its hinges and let it fall to the floor. Seeing that his options had diminished, Martin resumed his duties as her *"willing servant."*[1144]

Another time, she sought to wrench him from one of his lengthy bouts of depression. None of Katy's counsel would help so she came to breakfast one morning in a funeral dress. Martin asked, "Who died?" Katie replied, "God died." Martin proceeded to rebuke her for such an outrageous reply. She waited until he was done and said, "Well, Martin, the way you been acting, I thought He was dead and I wanted to join you in your mourning."[1145]

Even though eight months later, Erasmus had the magnanimity to retract his false accusations, confessing to malicious gossip, the stigma of uncontrolled sexuality as the reason behind the surprising marriage was long retained and unquestioned, as is the case with many of the allegations surrounding President Trump and his wife, Melania. The widespread loathing and slut-shaming accusations against Melania, who was a successful fashion model, entrepreneur, dancer, and, yes, had posed nude for a few photos earlier in her career before she ever met her husband, sound similar to those who vilified Katharina "as a 'faithless nun' and disreputable 'dancing maid' who had thrown herself at the Wittenberg monk, and while in Spain she was allotted a career in a brothel before her marriage."[1146]

[1143] Ibid.

[1144] Costanzo, Eric, "Katherine von Bora and the Martin Luther's Family Dinner Table." <https://ericcostanzo.me/2011/08/30/katherine-von-bora-and-the-martin-luthers-family-dinner-table>.

[1145] Markwald, Rudolf K. and Markwalkd, Marilynn Morris, *Katharina Von Bora: A Reformation Life* (St. Louis: Concordia Publishing House, 2002), pp.139-140.

[1146] Schilling, *Upheaval*, p.276, quoting Siegfried Brauer's "Katharina von Bora, die Lutherin—im Urteil der Zeit;" *Monschshure und Morgenstern, 'Katharina von Bora, die Lutherin'*, ed. Peter Freybeu (Wittenberg, 1999), p.24. See also WB 4, no. 1305, supplement, p.527.

The First Ladies and Their Warrior Husbands

Martin

Katharina

Melania

Donald

Paintings of Martin and Katharina were completed in 1526, by one of the most important German Renaissance artists, Lucas Cranach, the Elder a year after they were married. Cranach was a good friend of Martin and neighbor of the Luthers. (Peter Moser, *Lucas Cranach: His Life, His World and His Art*, Bamberg: Babenber Verlag, 2005, Central ND588 C8 MW51)

(Images: Public domain, retrieved at the University of Otago website)

(Images: Britannica)

There were some theologians who even prophesized that the sacrilegious marriage would inevitably produce the Antichrist! (As Erasmus says, "It was at that time an almost universal sentiment that the Antichrist would be the son of a monk and a nun…)"[1147] Others awaited the birth of their first child with fear and trepidation, as superstition held that a two-headed monster would be the product of such a sacrilegious union. Apparently, even today, seeing a woman *au naturel* deems that woman unintelligent, amoral, and worst of all "unclassy"—qualities that many view as incompatible with the position of the First Lady. Never mind the fact that Melania speaks five languages (her native Slovenian, English, French, Serbian and German, according to CBS News, while other sources also include Italian),[1148] was a successful fashion model where early in her career she posed nude for a few photos, and an entrepreneur selling jewelry on QVC. Nevertheless, she has been excoriated as a

> slut, bimbo and a "dumb cunt"… who made her way up in the world simply by opening her legs for a guy with the right amount of $100 bills in his

---

[1147] Morris, John Gottlieb, *Catherine de Bora: Or Social and Domestic Scenes in the Home of Luther* (Philadelphia: Lindsay & Blakiston, 1856), p.37.

[1148] <https://www.elitedaily.com/p/how-many-languages-does-melania-trump-speak-more-than-her-husband-for-sure-18747276>.

> wallet. Such slut-shaming reached a fevered pitch when her husband was actually elected President, with headlines expressing utter incredulity that a mere "trophy wife" could ever hold the office of First Lady. Even relatively innocuous pieces like this *USA Today* story (Nov. 10, 2016) feel the need to point out that she will be the first First Lady whom we have all seen naked—a lurid piece of trivia, to be sure, but hardly a reflection on Melania's morals, or what kind of First Lady she will be.[1149]

New York Times writer Jacob Bernstein called Melania Trump a "hooker" in remarks made privately to model Emily Ratajkowski at a Fashion Week party. According to Leora Tanenbaum, Opinion Contributor at *U.S. News and World Report*, "Bernstein leveled his insult not at the president but at his wife. And it is never acceptable to insult a woman based on her real or presumed sexual history. Doing so is straight-up slut-shaming." Tanenbaum further reports that Ratajkowski was so disgusted by the "hooker" comment that she engaged in her own form of shaming, disclosing the comment on Twitter and writing:

> Labels like "slut," 'ho," or "hooker" say that women's primary value comes from being sexually desirable and available. But there's a paradox here because being sexually desirable and available reduces women's worth. And while there is nothing wrong with being sexually desirable or available, that is not the sum total of whom anyone is.[1150]

Melania has been continually bashed for her Christmas decorations at the White House, sneered for her fashion choices—infamous "storm stilettos," Timberland boots in visiting the troops, her "I Really Don't Care" (about media's criticism) jacket—not being "culturally American," and her Slovenian accent. Conspiracy theories from late-night comedians to mainstream news organizations were floated about her MIA status when she was being treated for a kidney condition in a hospital, even to speculating that she was a victim of

---

[1149] Dickson, E.J., "Slut-Shaming Melania Trump Is Not The Answer To Your Anger," *yahoo! News*. <https://in.news.yahoo.com/slut-shaming-melania-trump-not-204000015.html>, also <https://www.refinery29.com/en-us/2016/11/129581/slut-shaming-melania-trump-nude-photos-anti-feminist>.

[1150] Tanenbaum, Leora, "The Slut-Shaming of Melania Trump," *U.S News and World Report*, Feb. 15 2017. <https://www.usnews.com/opinion/civil-wars/articles/2017-02-15/melania-trump-slut-shaming-enabler-does-not-deserve-to-be-slut-shamed>.

domestic abuse. A promotional salacious video featuring a First Lady look-alike stripping in the White House Oval Office was used as a vulgar attack to denigrate the First Lady and to taunt the President.

The Other Lord of Martin Luther's Life

Katharina proved to be extraordinarily adept when it came to running the "Lutherhaus" or former Black Cloister, which, while only half-finished, had already fallen into disrepair. She quickly turned the derelict 30-room monastery into a home, and initiated plans for the building to also serve as a small private student hostel, known as a "*Burse*," where twenty to thirty paying students and visitors could receive lodging and boarding. She oversaw the renovations, repairs, and needed expansions to effectively transform the three-story former monastery building into the 16th-century equivalent of a dormitory, guest house, conference center and a residence for her growing family. In addition to students, the Luthers housed relatives and the numerous friends, guests and visiting professors who desired access to Luther's ideas and prestige. Her domestic skills, flair for the practical, and incredible financial management and business acumen served Luther well in what turned into a commercial enterprise for which critics assailed her as "that businesswoman!" "Scornful writings appeared from old opponents of Luther.... No reaction by Katharina is recorded. It is not clear whether she read Joachim von Heyden's German piece of invective against her at all. Luther claimed in his reply that he had used it immediately as toilet paper."[1151]

When it came to meeting the needs of the family and other members of the larger academic household, it was Luther's "*Herr Kathe*" or "My Lord Katie" who made the extensive arrangements for purchases at the market for food and drink for the table and for the maintenance of livestock. She was a force of nature wearing many hats. Not only did she manage the fishponds—netting trout, carp, pike and perch—the vineyards, and the large fields, orchards and gardens, she was also the beekeeper and the one who milked the cows, bred the farm animals, and did the slaughtering, owning more cows and pigs than anyone in Wittenberg. Brewing beer was also in her skillset, running the household

---

[1151] Treu, Martin, "Katharina von Bora, the Woman at Luther's Side," *Lutheran Quarterly*, Vol. XIII, 1999. <www.lutheranquarterly.com/uploads/7/4/0/1/7401289/timelinetreu.pdf>.

brewery which produced 8,800 pints of ale each year,[1152] along with possessing the medical competence to minister to the sick on-site, including her often sick husband, as a nurse. She administered what became a large-scale agricultural and hostel enterprise, exercising financial savvy with management skills "so expertly that the provisioning of the household and [business] generated a profit that could be invested in property."[1153] She was indeed a resourceful woman and a well-spring of encouragement for her husband. Martin could not stand the thought of losing his "rib," as he often jokingly and affectionately called "Kitty."[1154]

As the crowning conclusion to overseeing all the renovations and construction of an expanded kitchen, two regular cellars and a special wine cellar, and of course a brewhouse, Katy designed the elaborate and expensive Gothic portal doorway to their home, as a gift to Luther for his fifty-seventh birthday.[1155] She supervised up to ten employees, and fed between 35-50 people seated at one long table in the former refectory of the Augustinian monastery, which was Luther's old home as a friar.[1156] And, in addition to being mother to six children and taking care of four adopted children, the Luthers housed no less than eleven orphaned or otherwise homeless children who were treated as members of the family.[1157] She was known for her hospitality and as the Reformation movement spread, the house that Katharina ran became its epicenter. After dinner, the table she spread became an important place where Reformation ideas were shared and disseminated. It is questionable whether we'd have "Table Talks" if she hadn't provided the table at which Luther and select guests and students discussed theology and politics over a stein of her homebrew.

[1152] <https://germanculture.com.ua/famous-germans/katharina-von-bora>, also Bainton's *Here I Stand*, Abingdon (p.292) and Mentor pb (p.228).

[1153] Schilling, *Upheaval*, p.287.

[1154] In a fictionalized biography, the heartwarming story of Katharine Luther, a woman of courage and devotion, is told by E. Jane Mall in *Kitty, My Rib* (St. Louis: Concordia Publishing House, 1959).

[1155] Schilling, *Upheavall*, p.286.

[1156] Ibid., p.288.

[1157] Ella, George M., "The Morning Star of Wittenberg," *New Focus*, Dec. 28 2005. <http://go-newfocus.co.uk/articles/app/category/biography/article/katharina-luther-the-morning-star-of-wittenberg>.

The Black Cloister Becomes the Luther House

The Luther House in Wittenberg

(Image: Augnet)

Katharina's Portal

(Image: F. Stariltz)

The Lutherhaus had previously been the Augustinian friary at Wittenberg. The central tower contained Luther's study above the lower-level heated cloaca where he claimed that his theological breakthrough (his Turmerlebenis, or "tower experience") happened. On the right side of the base of the tower is the Katherinenportal (the "Katherine door') that Luther's wife designed and arranged to have inserted there as an appropriate entry way to receive the "Doctor's" many guests. The niches on each side functioned as seats. Above the two stone seats, Katy had the stonemasons carve a white rose with a red heart and the black Cross of Christ, which as a monk Luther had selected for his seal and has become known as the "Luther Rose," and a symbol of Luther's Christ-centered theology. Luther lived here in his final years as an Augustinian friar, and later took up residence in the Black Cloister with his wife in the wedding gift provided by Frederick the Wise.

Luther noted that his Katharina was "…a wise woman and doctor…[who] might also give counsel."[1158] And that she did, as she shared her counsel and opinions with Martin, which influenced him on the printing of his texts and even on theological and ecclesiastical issues. Luther even entrusted her to handle dealings with his printers. His trust and confidence in "*Mein Herr Kathe*" or "My Lord Katie" led Luther to making her his sole inheritor and naming her guardian of their children, which was unheard of at the time. To those familiar with the German language, that favorite title for his wife shows that Luther not only felt Katie's affection strongly, but also her influence. "He paid her the highest tribute," in Roland Bainton's assessment, "when he called St. Paul's Epistle to the Galatians 'my Katherine von Bora.'"[1159] As the saying goes, "behind every successful man there is a woman," and one

---

1158 LW 50:209. *Letters III*, No. 290, "To Mrs. Martin Luther, Weimar, July 2, 1540."

1159 Bainton, *Here I Stand*, Abingdon (p.293) and Mentor pb (p.228).

must wonder what Luther's impact would have been without Katie as his partner in that "Blessed Alliance." Being married to a man like Martin would certainly take a strong woman of remarkable character. She was not only able to endure Martin's good-natured ribbing but was always ready with a witty retort in their frequent repartees. "From the beginning, their marriage relationship was unique," says Eric Costanzo. "For the first time, both Martin and Katherine had met their match in will and wit."[1160]

Marriage brought many changes to their individual ways of having lived in a convent and monastery as nun and monk. "'There's a lot to get used to,' reflected Martin.... He soon discovered that a husband must take the wishes of his wife into account,"[1161] and then children brought additional dynamics. Family life is exacting, and the rearing of children is a trial for both parents. There's no room for the exercise of unbridled individualism. Early in his ministry, Luther's writings suggest that marriage was to serve as a remedy for sin by preventing sexual immorality. Insight into God's intent led him to conclude that love between a man and woman was to reflect the self-giving love God has for His children. Thus, as historian Roland Bainton says, the Reformer began to see marriage as "the School of Character"[1162] where love was not excluded. The mutual affection between Katy and Martin is unmistakable, as we witness in their heartfelt letters and in the conversations held at the table. "Of course, the Christian should love his wife, said Luther. He is bound to love his neighbor as himself. His wife is his nearest neighbor. Therefore, she should be his dearest friend"[1163] or as often gets translated, "his deepest love." Notice again Luther's priority in who the "nearest neighbor" is and how it extends to the family, to the faith community, and then to wider spheres of service. The greatest grace of God is when His love permeates a marriage and exists within the family. The marriage of Martin and Katie, their tremendous love for each other, as well as for their children in that "First Parsonage Family," reminds us today of Christ's love for His Church, and the Father's love for us as His redeemed children. That marriage displayed an intimacy and depth that any marriage would do well to aspire to in our day.

[1160] Costanzo, Eric, "Katherine von Bora and the Martin Luther Family;" Aug. 30, 2011. <https://ericcostanzo.me/2011/08/30/katherine-von-bora-and-the-martin-luthers-family-dinner-table>.

[1161] Bainton, *Here I Stand*, Abingdon (p.290) and Mentor pb (p.226).

[1162] Ibid., Abingdon (p.300) and Mentor pb (p.234). In *Here I Stand*, Bainton includes an entire chapter on "The School for Character," (Abingdon pp.286-305; Mentor pb, pp.223-237).

[1163] Bainton, *Here I Stand*, Abingdon (p.301) and Mentor pb (p.235).

Entrepreneurial Wives **First Ladies**

(Left to Right) Bronze sculpture of Katharina von Bora, the wife of the Reformer Martin Luther in the garden of the Luther House in Lutherstadt Wittenberg. (Image: Norbert Neet)

Melania Trump was a successful fashion model icon and entrepreneur, selling jewelry on QVC "long before she was the First Lady of the United States. Her classic looks and statuesque figure are breathtaking in so many ways. She knows what designs flatter her figure and understands how important selecting the perfect designer jewelry and accessories are to pull off her signature *head to toe* look." (Image: GQ)

Katharina von Bora, Martin Luther's wife and First Lady of the Reformation from a picture that hangs in the house where the Reformer died in Eisleben. (Image: Public domain)

On her husband's Inauguration Day, Melania Trump was "the country's first immigrant First Lady since Louisa Adams to pay homage to the old guard of American fashion [wearing] a powder blue casmere suit by Ralph Lauren Collection. The choice seemed to bespeak the First Lady's implicit declaration of her commitment to this new, dignified, perhaps unexpected position she now assumes—to serving a nation that is not natively hers but which it is now her charge to represent before the world."* (Image: Vice)

Not surprisingly, as time passed and people got to know Katherine, experiencing her gracious and open hospitality—and because she rose so early in the morning to begin fulfilling her numerous chores for the day—she was being complimented as Wittenberg's "Morning Star" and later, of course, as the "First Lady of the Reformation." Peggy Pedersen gives tribute to the Reformer's Wife:

> From her baptism through convent life, through her service to her husband and his ministry, raising their children, showing hospitality and faithfully fulfilling her many duties, Katharina perfectly demonstrated Christian vocation. [Her] favorite psalm was Psalm 31 which Martin urged her to commit to memory. "It will be a comfort to you." Indeed it was! Through

---

* Christensen, Lauren, "Why Melania Trump Wore Baby Blue," Harper's Bazaar, Jan. 20 2017. <https://www.harpersbazaar.com/culture/features/a20098/why-melania-trump-wore-blue-ralph-lauren-inauguration>

> adversity and need, acquainted with joys, tragedy, and grief, and at the time of her death she repeated that psalm over and over. On her deathbed she said: "I will cling to Christ, as a burr clings to a coat." She indeed clung to Him like a burr and He held her firm to Himself—just as He will hold each of us who put our faith in Him.[1164]

When we observe a statue of Luther, there really ought to be one with "Lutheress" by its side.

In his address to CPAC on February 29, 2020, President Trump shared with the audience how the First Lady gave him both a message to share and supportive spousal counsel: "Say hello to everybody." Then she reminded him, "Your first duty and your highest loyalty is to the American citizens. And you really have to let the people know." In astonishment, the President exclaimed, "Melania told me this. Can you believe this? She's giving me a history lesson. Our First Lady is giving me a history—"[1165]

[1164] Pedersen, Peggy, "Katie Luther: Reformer's Wife," The Canadian Lutheran, September/October 2014. <https://www.reformation2017.ca/saint/katie-luther> or <https://www.canadianlutheran.ca/woman-of-faith-katie-luther-reformers-wife>.

[1165] <https://trumpwhitehouse.archives.gov/briefings-Statements/remarks-president-trump-2020-conservative-political-action-conference-national-harbor-md>.

34

The Word Among Words

Luther and Trump both demonstrate that the power of words and the quality and substance of our ideas matter. Despite Luther's sometimes reprehensible writings and Trump's offensive rhetoric, both understand clearly how the use of words can convey far more than the combination of letters and sounds of syllables alone convey. Linguists refer to "performative speech" as those sentences or utterances which not only describe a given reality, but also change the social reality they are describing. Our spirited and emphatic twin orators go beyond recognizing the impact of words governed by social constructions and conventions. Luther asserts that when God speaks, new realities come into being, which like all reality flows from the dynamic, sustaining "re-creative Word." As we have earlier noted, Trump frequently speaks beyond the literal, using simple superlatives which the hearer can easily picture in his or her mind. In a world where one often experiences how words used as weapons can hurt and harm us more than "sticks and stones," and where politicians speak to please but often fail to deliver, the President claims "Promises Made, Promises Kept" much as Luther assures us and continually re-assures us that the Word of the Lord accomplishes what it promises and endures forever (Isaiah 40:8; 1 Peter 1:25).

Recall the unflinching courage and intellectual coherence of Luther's dogmatic stance when he made his defense before the Emperor in Worms: "I cannot and I will not recant anything, for to go against conscience is neither right nor safe. God help me. Amen!"[1166] There are scholars who question whether Luther actually uttered the words, "Here I stand, I cannot do otherwise" because it was not recorded on the spot and thus is not included in the earliest transcript, though its adamancy certainly reflects Luther's stance, and the earliest printed version did add those words.

Luther had met with considerably higher-ranking clerics who hoped to rein in the rebel. He seemed willing to change his mind about recanting if anyone could point out his error in Biblical interpretation or his reasoning, but no one succeeded. For too long, simply being an authority figure invested that individual with the ability to say what was right and wrong.

1166 LW 32:112f. Career of the Reformer II, "Luther at the Diet of Worms;" and Roland Bainton, *Here I Stand*, Abingdon (p.185) and Mentor pb (p.144).

Luther disagreed and stood up as staunchly as we have witnessed President Trump doing in challenging world leaders, the Washington establishment, and unelected bureaucrats who, along with much of the media, have self-determined what is right and wrong, what is to be protected and revealed, and who is to control what to say and how to say it.

While Donald Trump has exposed new meaning to the terms "hypocrisy" and "double standard," our leaders in both State and Church, along with much of the media, expect us to blindly accept their word. The 2020 election season, along with Covid-19, has dramatically demonstrated how they adhere to the same principle: people are merely serfs who should do just as their "leaders" say rather than as they do. Opponents of Trump promise unity and healing in America, when they did not give the duly elected Trump a moment's rest during his presidency—no honeymoon, no bipartisanship, nor even acceptance of his presidency—just obstruction, resistance, and harassment. He has endured a coup attempt and bogus investigation after bogus investigation—including the 40-million-dollar-plus Mueller Report, without a shred of evidence produced to show that he had colluded with Russia—yet his opponents conducted unconstitutional impeachments while simultaneously evidence had mounted on Hillary Clinton's subpoenaed email scandal, and her bought and paid for "dirty dossier" to bring her opponent down in the 2016 campaign. Ironically, the charge leveled against the President was being boastfully admitted to by Joe Biden with his "quid pro quo" of threatening to withhold 1 billion dollars of U.S. aid to Ukraine unless that government fired the prosecutor investigating the company to which Biden's son, Hunter, was financially connected.

Could not the case be made that, with all the investigations of President Trump without a shred of evidence produced, former Vice President and now President Biden should be under investigation for possible conflict of interest, with his son holding a directorship in the Ukrainian gas company Burisma, as well as the questionable circumstances of money laundering with Russia, China and Ukraine? Evidence of these transactions has now appeared, with the FBI in possession of Hunter's computer and leaked emails. Or will this too escape judicial scrutiny in a system of justice where Lady Justice is been stripped of her blindfold, as it was with Hillary Clinton and her subpoenaed e-mails and purchase (collusion?) of the "dirty dossier" along with the DNC, and with the hypocrisy of their banner call "Nobody is above the law?"

Peter Stanford, author of *Martin Luther: Catholic Dissident*, argues that Luther challenged the late medieval way of doing things and the results were strikingly modern. For Luther championed individual conscience informed by reading the Scriptures over the Dictates of Church rules and regulations. Read the Scriptures and make up your own mind. This, in its turn, opened the door in the 17th and 18th centuries to the Enlightenment notions of human liberty, free speech and even human rights, all of which today shape life in Europe"[1167] [and America].

Specifically, to the thrust of our comparisons, the results of Luther's revolution of the spirit were shattering and led eventually not only to religious but political and cultural upheavals, culminating (amid other developments) in the framing of the U.S. Declaration of Independence and the U.S. Constitution. These were documents affirming the existence of God-given rights, permitting individuals to develop for themselves their particular conceptions of the good life; or as Jefferson put it in the Declaration, "the pursuit of happiness," which Donald Trump has sought to recapture in his drive to "Make America Great Again."

Captive to the Word of God and Endowed with Inalienable Rights

Martin Luther

Holding the Word of God Close to His Heart Public domain, retrieved at Wikimedia)

Donald Trump

Upholding the Free Exercise of Religion (Brendan Smialowski/*USA Today)*

[1167] Stanford, Peter, "Five Centuries on, Martin Luther Should Be Feted as Hero of Liberty and Free Speech," *The Guardian*, March 18, 2017. <https://www.theguardian.com/world/2017/mar/19/martin-luther-relevance-anniversary>.

The number of paintings and statues portraying the *"doctor in Biblia"* holding a Bible—often opened—attests to the public recognition of his deep love and reverence for the Word of God. Endowed with Biblical knowledge, he believed it to be the source and goal of the Christian life and believed that the Church was born and is sustained solely by the Word preached, heard, read, sung and believed. Both prophet and apostle, of which he saw himself called to be, profess the same: *the Word of God endures forever.* Unwaveringly, Luther's heart clung to *"the one thing needful"* (Luke 10:42).

In response to a nation gripped by protests and violent riots resulting from the death of George Floyd, a black man who had been pinned at the neck to the ground by a white police officer's knee, President Trump made a Rose Garden speech promising a crackdown on violent protests and asserting the need for "law and order." He ended his remarks by saying, "and now I am going to pay my respects to a very, very special place." Prior to walking across the street through Lafayette Square to St. John's Episcopal Church, the "Church of Presidents," in which every one of our country's presidents have worshipped, protesters were cleared from the park. There Trump stood in front of the church, holding up a Bible. A fire had been set in the church's basement during protests the night before. Wall-to-wall coverage claimed that President Trump had ordered the Black Lives Matter protesters be cleared from Lafayette Square with Park Police using rubber bullets and tear gas for his "photo-op" in front of the church. An independent investigation by the Interior Department Inspector General Mark Greenblatt concluded that "the evidence did not support a finding that the [United States Park Police] cleared the park on June 1, 2020, so that then President Trump could enter the park." The protesters were instead removed "to allow a contractor to safely install anti-scale fencing in response to destruction of Federal property and injury to officers that occurred on May 30 and May 31"[1168] during other BLM protests.

In the words of Kayleigh McEnany, White House Press Secretary, "It was powerful and important to send a message that the rioters, the looters, the anarchists, they will not prevail—that burning churches are not what America is about."[1169] The President took the opportunity to underscore the First Amendment's connection between the "free exercise" of

---

[1168] <https://www.nbcnews.com/think/opinion/trump-photo-op-church-wasn-t-why-lafayette-square-was-ncna1270502>; see also, <https://abcnews.go.com/Politics/police-clear-lafayette-park-area-trump-hold-bible/story?id=78171712>.

[1169] <https://abcnews.go.com/Politics/police-clear-lafayette-park-area-trump-hold-bible/story?id=78171712>; see also <https://www.npr.org/2020/06/03/868779265/trump-defends-symbolism-of-photo-op-at-st-johns-church>.

religion and "the right of the people peaceably to assemble, and to petition the Government for a redress of grievances." The Law is contained and supported within the pages of the Bible as civil magistrates are entrusted with its enforcement for the peaceful existence of citizens who are to respect and honor their authorities (Romans 13).

For Joseph Loconte*, associate professor of History at The King's College in New York City, Luther's courageous claim before the emperor "laid a foundation for all subsequent demands for religious freedom in the West."[1170] Luther always elevated the individual girded with the Bible above any earthly authority. "A simple layman armed with Scripture is to be believed above a Pope or a council without it."[1171] In addition, neither prince nor pope could invade the sanctuary of one's conscience. This, Luther proclaimed, is the "inestimable power and liberty of Christians."[1172]

A Spiritual Bill of Rights

"Luther offered more than a theory of individual empowerment. He delivered a spiritual bill of rights. Generations of reformers...would praise his achievement. Half a millennium later, his message of freedom has not lost its power."[1173] Loconte supports his thesis by claiming "virtually every important defense of religious freedom in the seventeenth century—the radical thinking of William Penn, Roger Williams, and John Locke—nodded in Luther's direction."[1174]

In the eighteenth century, the United States became the first nation to enshrine in its constitution the rights of conscience. James Madison, the most important mind behind the First Amendment, understood full-well the legacy of Luther's achievement. Loconte cites a letter to F.L. Schaeffer, dated 1821, in which "Madison explained that the American model of religious liberty 'illustrates the excellence of a system which, by a due distinction, to which

---

* Joseph Laconte also serves as a senior editor at *Providence: A Journal of Christianity and American Foreign Policy.*

1170 Loconte, Joseph, "Luther's Challenge to the Conscience of the West," Religious Freedom Institute, July 19, 2016. <https://www.religiousfreedominstitute.org/cornerstone/2016/7/19/luthers-challenge-to-the-conscience-of-the-west>.

1171 Bainton, *Here I Stand*, Abingdon (p.117) and Mentor pb (p.90).

1172 LW 31:355. *Career of the Reformer I*, "The Freedom of a Christian," or *Three Treatises*, p.290.

1173 Loconte, Joseph, "How Martin Luther Advanced Freedom," *Wall Street Journal*, Oct. 26 2017. <https:/// www.wsj.com/articles/how-martin-luther-advanced-freedom-1509059066>.

1174 Loconte, "Luther's Challenge to the Conscience of the West."

the genius and courage of Luther led the way, between what is due to Caesar and what is due God, best promotes the discharge of both obligations.'"[1175]

At the end of the eighteenth century, in his letter to the Massachusetts Militia, John Adams wrote, "We have no government armed with power capable of contending with human passions unbridled by morality and religion. Avarice, ambition, revenge, or gallantry would break the strongest cords of our Constitution as a whale goes through a net. Our Constitution is designed only for a moral and religious people. It is wholly inadequate for any other."[1176]

Alan Cross, a Baptist pastor and author, doesn't

> think that Adams was talking about the Church being sanctioned by the State or pining for theocracy. He was saying that our system of government works best when religious and moral people exert influence in appropriate ways, because you cannot possibly write down enough laws to govern the affairs of men who hold themselves apart from the judgements of a Higher Power.
>
> For Christians in America, this is not only our heavenly call but our earthly right. The commands of Romans 13:1-7 which call upon Christians to be subjects to the governing authorities…mean that we should participate vigorously in our democratic republic. Our system of government is different from what the Apostle Paul addressed. In many ways, in America, the rulers in question are not the President or Congress, but rather, "We the people."
>
> The State has a role to play in the ordering of society, to be sure. But the Church also has a role to play to guide the State morally and ethically through prophetic witness. If the Church is subverted to the State in acquiescence, all manner of evil can proliferate without a check. But, when the Church upholds the good and denounces the bad and calls our leaders to repentance—that is

---

[1175] Ibid.

[1176] "John Adams to Massachusetts Militia, October 11 , 1798," *Founders Online*, National Archives. <https://founders.archives.gov/documents/Adams/99-02-02-3102>.

> for the good not just of individuals or the Church, but also for all of society. Whether our leaders like it or not.[1177]

Laconte further notes that

> When the modern human rights movement took shape after the Second World War, a committee of public intellectuals acknowledged Luther as they searched for a philosophical basis for an international bill of rights. Their 1947 UNESCO document cited The Reformation—"with its appeal to the absolute authority of the individual conscience"—as one of two historical events most responsible for the development of human rights, including the rights of conscience.[1178]

Thus, the language of The Universal Declaration of Human Rights in Article 18 pays homage to Luther's vision, proclaiming "everyone has the right to freedom of thought, conscience, and religion." Its prime author, Lebanese Ambassador Charles Malik, an Arab Christian and a student of The Reformation, said "People's minds and consciences are the most sacred and inviolable things about them, not their belonging to this or that class, this or that nation, or this or that religion."[1179]

These references reinforce the understanding of why many historians view Luther as "the last medieval man and the first modern one"[1180] or at least a prophet of modernity. But Luther's goal was never to usher in modernity, but simply to make religion religious again, and in that process many transformations were set in motion that were larger than himself. He threw off the traditionalisms and authority practiced by the Church and put the

---

[1177] Cross, Alan, "Jerry Falwell Jr.'s Trumpian Theology," *The Bulwark*, January 10, 2019. <https://thebulwark.com/jerry-falwell-jr-s-trumpian-theology>.

[1178] Loconte, "Luther's Challenge to the Conscience of the West," November 3, 2015 <https://www.josephloconte.com/commentary/georgetown-university-luthers-challenge-to-the-conscience-of-the-west/>.

[1179] Loconte, Joseph, "Martin Luther and the Long March to Freedom of Conscience," *National Geographic*, October 27, 2017. <https://nationalgeographic.com/news/2017/10/martin-luther-freedom-protestant-reformation-500>. Also in Loconte's "Luther's Challenge to the Conscience of the West," *Religious Freedom Institute*, July 19 2016. <https://www.religiousfreedominstitute.org/cornerstone/2016/7/19/luthers-challenge-to-the-conscience-of-the-west>.

[1180] Marty, Martin, "Luther's Living Legacy." <https://www.christianitytody.com/history/issues/issue-39/luther-s living-legacy.html>.

individual and one's own conscience at center stage, by redefining humankind's relationship to God anew, which is ultimately essential for modern ideas of human rights.

It could be further argued that the Catholic Church, once a fierce opponent of religious liberty, built upon Luther's foundation and has today become one of the most vigorous defenders of religious liberty on the world stage. John Courtney Murray, a powerful thinker behind the Second Vatican Council's full-throated defense of religious freedom, wrote that "no man is to be forcibly constrained to act against his conscience."[1181] Here, it seems, is an echo of Luther's conceptual approach to the nature of religious belief: "I will preach it, teach it, write it, but I will constrain no man by force, for faith must come freely without compulsion."[1182]

Regardless of one's political views, Trump's presidency compels us to address some very fundamental, consequential and existential questions which he poses regarding the divisions he has exposed and views as real threats to our cherished way of life. Both of our warriors have demonstrated the power of words—used either as derogatory epithets, intolerant assaults, or descriptive slogans—unleashed to a broad public with sheets of paper flying off the printing press or texted characters sailing effortlessly through cyberspace and political speech enthusiastically expressed at rallies. Those words have meaning and a powerful effect on the dominant social, political and religious forces of the day. Just as today's news media and new social media platforms are easily used to spread falsehoods and biased viewpoints, and to fire up popular hatreds which debase our civic discourse and our culture, they mirror the intolerance and sometimes deplorable writings unleashed during The Reformation as they play on the emotions and hatreds of readers and followers alike.

Challenges of Civil Discourse in the Internet Age

As we have noted previously and experience in our Internet Age, new forms of communication always challenge traditional forms, imposing new rules as to what can and cannot be said. John Jeffries Martin* reminds us that

[1181] Murray, John Courtney, "This Matter of Religious Freedom," Georgetown University Woodstock Theological Library. <https://www.library.georgetown.edu/woodstock/murray/1965k>.

[1182] LW 51:77. *Sermons I*, "Second Sermon, March 10,1522, Monday after Invocavit."

* John Jeffries Martin, author and chair of the History department at Duke University, where he is a historian with a particular interest in early modern Europe.

> Democratization of thought is inherently disruptive. And when the doors to public debate swing open—as they did in Luther's time and as they are again today—the conversation can quickly turn ugly.... In Luther's time, the acceleration in the spread of ideas upended social and political hierarchies. That's not unlike what the social media and other new technologies are doing today.... There was also money to be made from the new media of the time [as people are seized by a Gutenberg or a Zuckerberg]. Just as there are today, there were those in Luther's time who were willing to make a profit off fake news.... In the sixteenth century, the printing press became one of the great driving forces of history. Today, new communication technologies are already placing significant strains on our institutions. Preserving democracy in the digital age will be no small challenge.[1183]

Crucial concerns include cyber-attacks on businesses and industrial systems, like the Colonial Pipeline or our power grid, as well as the threat posed by those creative but dishonest scammers who with their ability capture personal information, and by hacking into our technological marvels steal intelligence. As we mentioned earlier, there are regulations being urged on who can control what is placed on the social platforms, and who can close an account and for what reasons. What does it mean today to have freedom of speech in the public square without being cancelled? Or where one group can fabricate and lie about another group which cannot in turn speak the truth about the other? Flipping the coin, it continues to be a source of amazement that politicians are so oblivious to the ease of retrieving contradictory positions they have espoused that is now recorded on video and easily discovered through the search engines dominating the internet.

Civil conversation seems to me to be the starting point in support of a deliberative democracy in which all citizens can freely discuss and debate the issues of the day. However, that demands listening as well as speaking, respecting different—even conflicting—points of view, speaking the truth and citing evidence while maintaining a genuine openness to changing one's mind. That is a tall and challenging order, especially in the face of critical opposition. Perhaps we need first to unlearn the practices we've witnessed and heard on radio and TV talk shows where opponents out-shout each other, to blogs where anything can be posted as truth without supporting evidence or facts, to political debates that get

---

1183 Martin, John Jeffries, "Martin Luther—Lessons and Legacy in the Age of Social Media," *The Hill*, Oct. 30, 2017. <https://thehill.com/opinion/technology/357815-martin-luther-lessons-and-legacy-in-the-age-of-social-media>.

hijacked by the angriest and loudest voices in the room, or Congressional hearings that make a mockery of persuasive rhetoric and Constitutional law. Too often so-called debate centers in putting down another's position by personal attacks and hostile rhetoric intended to incite and attack rather than to inform and persuade through constructive discovery.

New ways of speaking to one another on social media or even on the printed page has resulted in speaking past one another, resulting in increased polarization, because we do not have to see each other face-to-face. It is why Luther cherished the opportunity of mingling and speaking with folks, sometimes preaching to the people twice each day, and why Trump becomes so energized during rallies, so both can personally encounter and experience the effect their words have upon the people.

Given what we know about Luther being a well-liked preacher, it is "hard to fathom that Luther felt the need at times to chastise some [worshippers] who did not listen well, saying that some fell asleep and some even snored during the sermon, adding that they sometimes coughed whenever he preached on justification [or understanding what he was saying] only to wake up again whenever he told a story.[1184] Times do not seem to have changed. However, when we speak to each other through the printed page or on Twitter or Facebook, we do not have to see each other face-to-face. Studies show that we say things on social media and often in print that we would never say if we had to look our opponent in the eye. Tim Cooper, a professor of Church History at the University of Otago, reminds us

> there is no opportunity to register the effect our words might be having on a real person. Something of our humanity is taken away when we lose a physical presence. So, if there is any response to the current cultural climate moment it is a local one: real people, not digitally enhanced images on Facebook; physically present, not mediated by technology; speaking words that bring greater understanding and concord, not further entrenched tribal hostilities. But if history is any guide, that is not what we're in for, not for a long time yet.[1185]

Paul Chadwick, an editor at *The Guardian*, cites the impressive study of researchers at Massachusetts Institute of Technology to the serious threat "Fake News" powered by the social media is posing, not only to journalism but to democracy. The researchers have shown

---

[1184] Thomas, Derek, "Spare Everything but the Word: Luther as Preacher," in *The Legacy of Luther*, p. 270.
[1185] Cooper, Tim, "Speaking to the People," *Otago Daily Times*, July 27, 2020. <https://www.odt.co.nz/opinion/speaking-people>.

that good journalism is needed more than ever to counter rumors undermining democracy. In addition to the MIT study published in the journal *Science*, Chadwick states

> A growing bundle of studies shows that this is a qualitatively and quantitatively new problem, not just a digital manifestation of the yellow press of old.... The (MIT) study found that "falsehood diffused significantly farther, faster, deeper and more broadly than truth in all categories of information." False political news reached more people faster and went deeper into their networks than any other category of false information.[1186]

Charles Sykes and Carolyn Lukensmeyer* claim what we know as the new normal: civility is now a foreign concept in American politics, and they attempt to explain how we got here and suggest how we fix it.

> Restoring civility doesn't mean that we must agree on the issues, or that we must avoid vigorous debate. Nor does it mean quiescence or milquetoast appeasement. But personal attacks and scorched earth rhetoric, not only degrade democratic norms, they are often counterproductive, poisoning the culture without advancing the cause. Civility also means having empathy for your fellow Americans. Too many Americans refuse to entertain the possibility that an opponent might be a decent human being despite being wrong about an issue. So instead of conversations that might change minds, we reduce our debates to toxic confrontations.[1187]

We can all do better! Civility pertains especially to disagreements and the idea that our disagreements have to be somehow moderated or constrained so as to remain verbal as opposed to physical or violent. Civility is supposed to keep us in the realm of words and fend off the battle of swords.

[1186] Chadwick, Paul, "Why Fake News on Social Media Travels Faster Than the Truth," The Guardian, March 19, 2018. <https://www.theguardian.com/commentisfree/2018/mar/19/fake-news-social-media-twitter-mit-journalism>.

* Charles J. Sykes is a former talk show host, conservative commentator, and author of *How the Right Lost Its Mind.* Carolyn J. Lukensmeyer is the Executive Director of the National Institute for Civil Discourse.

[1187] Sykes, Charles J. and Carolyn J. Lukensmeyer, "Civility Is Now a Foreign Concept in American Politics," *NBC News*, May 11, 2018.
<https://www.nbcnews.com/think/opinion/civility-now-foreign-concept-americans-politics-how-did-we-get-ncna873491>.

There certainly is a recognition that there has been a death of reasoned discourse within our society, as we witness civil disagreement often escalating tragically in violence. In Mathew Block's opinion,

> Argument has given way to anger. Dialogue has given way to diatribe. And civility is considered a sign of weakness. We need not even know who precisely we are angry at or why, so long as we rage loudly enough.... How different from our own time, when to think differently is to demand censure. And more than censure: the offending party must also be punished. Wishes of ill-will are now the norm, not the exception. "We are the outrage," the masses cry. And all acquiesce, lest we perish in the wrath"[1188] [of being labeled and branded].

Civil discourse is a life skill, a foundational principle of community, and should be the engine for politics, religion, economics as well as culture. The bedrock of our country is a set of values that supports the common good while protecting and respecting the individual as we seek the truth, not obtaining a political win at the expense of the common good. How to listen is crucial in the words of Proverbs: "*Let the wise listen and add to their learning*" (1:5 NIV). We are physically reminded of that wisdom whenever we acknowledge that we are created with two ears and only one mouth. Then when opening our mouth, we owe it to others and ourselves that we state our informed opinions forcefully but with respect for others, while demonstrating a genuine openness to new insights and views. "Democracy, of necessity, relies on people willing to engage in the marketplace of ideas. But this can only happen if we can relearn how to listen to one another, work together, and use our words to persuade, rather than divide."[1189] It is incumbent for all, especially for Christians, that we should look to the merits of the policy instead of condemning one another or making sure the opposition loses. Instead of discrediting others or viewing another as somehow less Christian because we hold divergent opinions, we need to be reminded that they too were created in the image of God and as such have inherent worth and value. Have we Christ-followers forgotten there are four Gospel accounts and not just one telling in Scripture?

[1188] Block, Mathew, "The Age of Outrage," *First Things*, March 4, 2016. <https://www.firstthings.com/blogs/firstthoughts/2016/03/the-age-of-outrage>.

[1189] Skykes and Lukensmeyer, "Civility."

In their *Age of Discovery*, co-authors Ian Goldin and Chris Kutarna* "define the present day as a 'New Renaissance'—a rare moment of flourishing genius and risk that promises to reshape all our lives."[1190] While they acknowledge that there is no way to chart a precise course amidst the level of complexity of our times, they offer some hard realities and suggestions that parallel the rapid developments in technology and culture during the Renaissance which began in the late fifteenth century. Names like DaVinci, Columbus, Copernicus, Gutenberg, and our populist warrior Luther, recall

> an era in which an unprecedented rush of discovery and disruption broke through long-standing barriers and broke down the long-standing powers (of the elite establishments). That rush entangled the whole world politically, economically, (religiously), and intellectually, and reshaped society. Now the same forces that converged 500 years ago to spark genius and upend social order—great leaps in science, trade, migration, technology, education, and health—are once again present, only stronger, and more widespread.[1191]

The challenge today is to remain optimistic for what the future may hold amidst the risks in pushing the boundaries without embracing fundamental values and understanding the lessons from the past. Our world, with its increasingly short-term focus, is not only challenged but hindered in fashioning our own Golden Age in this "new Renaissance" which could have the potential of leaving an enduring legacy that the world will still celebrate half a millennium from now. Ian and Chris take the position that the winners in this new age will be those who best embrace the new while still learning from the old. They pose some formidable questions, asking humanity to give of its best just when the stakes are highest:

> How do we maintain the respectful discourse upon which democracy depends without it being drowned in unaccountable lawlessness or partisan bias which favors unintelligible communities over the interests of the nation as a whole?

---

* Ian Goldin was the founding director of the Oxford Martin School, and is currently Oxford University Professor of Globalization and Development and Director of the Oxford Martin Program on Technological and Economic Change. Chris Kutarna holds a doctorate in politics from the University of Oxford and is a Fellow of the Oxford Martin School. Having been a consultant with the Boston Consulting Group, then an entrepreneur, his research on the political thinking of China's middle class is reflected in his being a regular op-ed contributor and presenter.

1190 Goldin, Ian and Chris Kutarna, *Age of Discovery: Navigating the Risks and Rewards of Our New Renaissance* (New York: St. Martin's Press, 2016). <https://iangoldin.org/books/age-of-discovery>.

1191 Ibid.

> How do we maintain the sovereignty of our own citizens in a globally open financial, economic and media age that easily admits foreign interference?
>
> How do we pass on to each new generation the value of their democratic freedoms, if they take them for granted or ignore them as irrelevant?
>
> How do we improve inclusion for those left behind by rapid change, without impeding the positive forces driving change?[1192]

In our own transformative and disruptive Internet Age, John Jeffries Martin, Chair of the Department of History at Duke University, suggests that Luther offers a clue to how we survive the noise of our new media revolution without sacrificing the democratic traditions and institutions we most value.

It is becoming abundantly clear that if we wish to preserve democracy, the swamp of the "Deep State" will indeed need to be drained and

> we will need acts of conscience on many fronts: against those who use insults to divide, against those who exploit falsehoods [and practice hypocrisy] to consolidate power, and against those who connive to undermine [and weaponize] our democratic institutions. And Luther's story makes it clear that the quality of our ideas matter regardless of the medium. Despite [what some characterize as] Luther's authoritarian tendencies, the eventual emergence of democracy owed much to one of his central ideas: that an individual's conscience matters. In the end, that important idea survived the chaotic media revolution of Luther's time. That's a contribution worth celebrating as we confront the unsettling upheavals of our own time. And in the midst of ever-shifting media, Luther's central message—that individual conscience matters—bears repeating, five hundred years later![1193]

That takes courage, which reflects the Reformation spirit of Luther, as well as the Biblical witness of a Joshua who entered into the dangers of the Promised Land: "*Be strong and courageous. Do not be frightened or dismayed, for the Lord your God is with you wherever you go*" (Joshua 1:9 [NRSV]). Or to the storm-tossed Church, straining at the oars and in danger

---

[1192] Goldin, Ian and Chris Kutarna, "Why Donald Trump Is a Second Savonarola," *The Irish Times*, November 6, 2017. <http://www.irishtimes.com/culture/books/why-donald-trump-is-a-second-savonarola-1.3281556>.

[1193] Martin, John Jeffries, "Martin Luther—Lessons and Legacy in the Age of Social Media." <https://thehill.com/opinion/technology/357815-martin-luther-lessons-and-legacy-in-the-age-of-social-media>.

of capsizing, do we hear the new Joshua saying, "*Take heart, it is I; do not be afraid*" (Mark 6:50 [NRSV]). Courage begins with the knowledge that our Good Shepherd is present (Psalm 23:4), and we are secure in the promise that "*those who lose their life for My sake will find it*" (Matthew 10:39 [NRSV]).

In an article appearing in *First Things*, Princeton Professor Robert P. George rallies us to the cause:

> The lynch mob is now giddy with success and drunk on the misery and pain of its victims. It is urged on by a compliant and even gleeful media. It is reinforced in its sense of righteousness and moral superiority by the "beautiful people" [Hollywood]and the intellectual class [including academia]. It has been joined by the big corporations [including the tech giants] who perceive their economic interests to be in joining up with the mandarins of cultural power. It owns one political party and has intimidated the leaders of the other into supine and humiliating obeisance.
>
> And so, who if anyone will courageously stand up to the mob? Who will resist? Who will speak truth to its raw and frightening power? Who will refuse to be bullied into submission or intimidated into silence? …Are there political or religious leaders who will step forward? Are there intellectual or cultural leaders who will muster the courage to confront the mob? …If we refuse to surrender, we will certainly be demonized; but everything will depend on whether we refuse to be demoralized. Courage displayed in the cause of Truth—and of right—is powerful.[1194]

Here we find Luther helpful in affirming our rightful role as Christ-followers instead of assuming the arrogancy that "God should exist by our grace and do according to our choosing." Realistically, he quickly adds, "Well, this has been the bone of contention in the world ever since the beginning, and I suppose it will remain that until the end." He cites the example of Cain displaying a sense of superiority or self-importance, wanting God to conform to his pattern. Luther sees this as reversing our Lord's teaching in John 15:16 (NRSV)—"*You did not choose Me but I chose you*"—and firmly declares:

1194 George, Robert P., "Who Will Stand?" *First Things*, April 5, 2015. <https://www.firstthings.com/blogs/fristthoughts/2015/04/who-will-stand>.

> *"You cannot and shall not choose Me, but I must choose you. Things will not go as you plan, but as I will. I will be your Lord and Master; I refuse to be taught by you."* Throughout Scripture, therefore, God condemned and rejected all such choosing without and contrary to His commandment. St. Paul, too, is a bitter enemy of this vice. In Colossians 2:18 he says: "*Let no one disqualify you, no one disqualify you, insisting on self-abasement*"; also verse 23: "*These have indeed an appearance of wisdom in promoting rigor of devotion and self-abasement.*"[1195]

So it is with Joseph Loconte and many others who find in Luther

> a witness for Truth who defied the forces of religious oppression and reimagined the political ideals of European Christianity. In his defiance he delivered a challenge to the conscience of the West like no other since the Sermon on the Mount. If Luther was a flawed prophet of human freedom, his voice was utterly indispensable—and remains so in our day.[1196]

I am convinced future historians will reflect upon our times and Trump's presidency and conclude that though flawed in many ways, we have witnessed an unparalleled leader who defied the "prescribed orthodoxy" of politics, undeterred by severe opposition and harassment. The vitriol he attracted was certainly exacerbated by his unexpected penetration into halls of the "powers that be" which could threaten to expose the "crookedness" of those in the "swamp" who were more concerned with maintaining their power and control than in serving the people they were elected to serve. With glaring hypocrisy and dishonesty, attempts—resistance, witch-hunts and hoaxes, even impeachment without evidence of a crime—were taken to cover up corruption the perpetuators themselves had committed. Yet through it all, the President succeeded, accomplishing exceedingly more than one could ever have expected.

Here's the point: While we have examined the cultural and political influences surrounding both our populist warriors, we cannot deny the tremendous impact the new information media had on the success of their reform endeavors. They both utilized the new technology effectively, seemingly giving credence to the phrase coined by Marshall McLuhan—can you believe back in 1964?—that "the medium is the message."[1197] Yet John Tetzel and other defenders of the pope also used the printing press as we have noted,

---

1195 LW 24:260. *Sermons on the Gospel of St. John Chapters 14-16*, "Chapter Fifteen (vs.16)."

1196 Loconte, Joseph, "Luther's Challenge to the Conscience of the West."

1197 McLuhan, Marshall, *The Medium is the Message.* Retrieved at <https://medium.com/@obtaineudaimonia/the-medium-is-the-message-by-marshall-mcluhan-8b5d0a9d426b>.

and Gutenberg's own press as we have seen was used to print indulgences. Despite all the circumstances which impacted their success, both Luther and Trump brought something incredibly unique to the challenges they unabashedly confronted: themselves! It was not *just* the medium but more importantly the message that the medium transmitted. It was the content of what these twin warriors stood for, and thus why their message became so popular. For Luther it was the Gospel of salvation freely given by the grace of God through faith in Christ crucified. For Trump it was his crusade to "Make America Great Again" by refocusing and reclaiming those fundamental principles that initially made our country great and distinctive. Clearly, politicians and theologians, reformers, and revolutionaries, need more than technology.

Would that we could understand and practice the truthful insight author and Pastor Nathan Campbell* offers in his St. Eutychus blog:

> Luther was sure his words were going to be held to account by God; and in some sense his speaking was an act of attempting to hold others to account to God's Word, but also to traditions he believed the church had walked away from. We can't simply dismiss the voices of our forebears as though we moderns are more enlightened or our pressing questions more pressing.... In purely effective terms, Luther is almost without peer as a communicator and an example of someone who grasped hold of a new technology to great effect. He's also, for all his faults, a great model of harnessing the power of new mediums to promote theological reforms he believed were necessary, and grappling with the questions of institutional authority that follow...these words from the Diet of Worms (where he may or may not have said "here I stand, I can do none else") are a reasonable starting point, and perhaps ending point, in this conversation for all of us: *"I am bound by the texts of the Bible, my conscience is captive to the Word of God, I neither can nor will recant anything, since it is neither right nor safe to act against conscience."* What that looks like...well. Let's keep talking and listening.[1198]

---

* Pastor Nathan Campbell serves City South Presbyterian Church in Brisbane, Queensland, Australia, and as an author frequently publishes pieces about the intersection between Christianity and culture in a variety of publications, most frequently on his blog, "St. Eutychus." (Eutychus refers to the young man of Troas who fell asleep during a long discourse Paul was giving and fell from a three-story window to his death and was tended to by St. Paul who insisted that he was not dead. This is related in the book of the Acts of the Apostles 20:7-12.)

1198 Campbell, Nathan, "The Internet, the Reformation." <https://st-eutychus.com/2017/the-internet-the-reformation-and-the-priesthood-of-all-believers-how-a-democratised-platform-might-keep-us-reforming>.

35

Looking Back to Live Forward

Both Luther and Trump understood the perception people had that leaders in the Church and State had lost touch with the ideals and values that were supposed to guide them, and that the systems and institutions were negligent in serving the people for whom they were created, now rather abusing the people.

Both disruptors became heroes of the disenfranchised and were irascible and strong-headed pivotal leaders who turned society upside down. As a result, there were very few aspects of their lives that did not come under scrutiny and become controversial. Our twin warriors remind us both how remote and how close the sixteenth century is to our own. Controversy is a two-edged sword. It makes old insights fresh again, but it also goads one to find new insights when old ones are obviously out of date or not serving the people. The value of our controversial populists is that they do both. Two of my favorite quotes underscore the validity of this understanding, which I believe both Luther and Trump intuitively have understood.

Jaroslav Pelikan, the late great scholar and Yale Professor of Ecclesiastical History, once observed: "Tradition is the living faith of the dead; traditionalism is the dead faith of the living. And, I suppose I should add, it is traditionalism that gives tradition such a bad name."[1199] In other words, "tradition" embodies values and meanings that are just as relevant for today, whereas "traditionalism" is that which is held onto and observed without understanding why we observe doing the "same ole thing"...we just do it because we've always done it!

Both of our populist warriors urge us to look ahead by reminding us first to look back and claim our heritage and roots as a Church and Nation. As someone who challenged authority and introduced a people's Christianity, Luther was a transformative figure in modern European history. Trump, likewise, has been a transformative figure in modern American politics as well as on the stage of world leaders. Transformations—of institutions or people—are not "once and done" affairs. They are ongoing resulting in changes that are,

[1199] Pelikan, Jaroslav, *The Vindication of Tradition* (Yale University Press, 1984), p.65.

Janus*

*Janus, in Greek mythology, is the god usually depicted as having two faces, one looking backward and the other forward. The month of January is named after Januarius, or Janus.

to say the least, disruptive, but hopefully corrective and add to our collective past, wisdom that can provide insight for the future.

Søren Kierkegaard, "Life can only be understood backwards; but it must be lived forwards,"[1200] and that living, because we're on this side of eternity, reminds us of the necessity of reforming, which is always unfinished business, or as we Lutherans proclaim: "*semper reformanda*"—always reforming! These insightful quotes reawaken the admonition drummed into my head during my seminary days: "Think like a Hebrew," especially when reading and interpreting Scripture.

In our modern Western world, we view the past as behind us and the future as that which lies ahead of us. But "in the Hebrew mind," Chad Bird*, who cohosts the podcast "40 Minutes in the Old Testament," reminds us, "the future is behind you and the past is in front of you. The Hebrew word for 'in front of' *(qedem)* is the same word for 'past' because you can see it 'in front of you' as already accomplished. And the word for 'behind' *(achar)* is the basis for the word for 'future' *(acharit)* because it is unseen, behind you, at your back."[1201]

From a Biblical perspective, the past is in front or literally what is before us, and the future is literally what is behind us. We of Western civilization see time from the perspective of passing through it. As we have walked through the past, we speak of it as now behind us, and the future, which we have not yet walked in, lies yet in front of us. The Hebrews, however, wrote the Bible from the perspective of ancient Eastern philosophy, in which the past is known and therefore can be seen, but the future is not yet known and therefore cannot be seen. So it is,

> especially when it comes to Biblical interpretation, the Church always walks backwards into the future, looking at what has been as a guide to what will be.... [Thus] As Israel walked into the future, she did so facing backwards,

---

1200 <https://www.quotes.net/quote/49962>; (Journals IV A 164 (1843).

* Chad Bird is a Scholar in Residence at 1517. He has served as a pastor, professor and guest lecturer in Old Testament and Hebrew. He holds master's degrees from Concordia Theological Seminary and Hebrew Union College. He has contributed articles to *Christianity Today, Modern Reformation, The Federalist* and *Lutheran Forum*, among other journals, and is the author of several books. His newest release is *The Christ Key: Unlocking the Centrality of Christ in the Old Testament.*

1201 Bird, Chad, "Rabbis, A French Nihilist, and the Layers of Baptism," *Lutheran Forum*, Fall 2017, p.19.

> eyes locked on the early story of Abraham, to see described therein the servitude and salvation that would happen to her. Israel's past was pregnant with her future.[1202]

To discard the past is to ignore the enlightenment that can illuminate and better help us understand the present as well as guide us into the future. The ancient proverb wisely claims, "Experience [our past] is the best teacher [which guides us into the future]."[1203]

Luther's hermeneutical dictum in the Reformation phrase "Scripture interprets Scripture" follows this rabbinical understanding which he fully comprehended. Chad Bird further explains

> one of the ways in which Scripture contains within itself its own interpretation is by earlier narratives, especially those in the Torah, sowing the seeds that will blossom as the Biblical story unfolds.... When the prophets preached, they simply extracted from and built upon the revelation at Sinai. Everything post-Exodus 20 was, as it were, inspired commentary. Despite Luther's often-colorful critique of rabbinic exegesis...[1204]

Bird sees Luther echoing much the same sentiment when he speaks of the formative, foundational character of the Mosaic books by referencing two examples:

> Moses is the source from which the holy prophets and, also the apostles, inspired by the Holy Spirit, extracted divine wisdom. This being the case, we shall not live up to our calling better and in greater harmony with God's will than by leading our followers to this Source and showing them in our own way the seeds of divine wisdom which the Holy Spirit, through Moses, has sown in such a manner that neither reason nor the power of human nature, if it does not possess the Holy Spirit, can see or understand them.[1205]

1202 Ibid., p.19.

1203 The great Roman leader Julius Caesar recorded the earliest known version of this proverb "Experience is the teacher of all things," in *De Bello Civili* (c. 52 B.C.). <https://www.phrases.org.uk/bulletin_board/21/messages/1174.html>.

1204 Bird, "Rabbis," p.19.

1205 Ibid., p.20; Bird cites Luther in his commentary on "Psalm 90;" *Selected Psalms II*, LW 13:75.

Or, as Luther writes in "Reasons from Scripture for Avoiding the Doctrines of Men:"

> Nothing new has been added [in the writings after the Pentateuch], for the same thing that is found in the books of Moses is found also in the others. These other books, while using different words and narratives, do nothing more than illustrate how the word of Moses has been kept or not kept. Throughout them all there is one and the same teaching and thought. And here we can challenge them to show us one word in all the books outside Moses that is not already found in the books of Moses. For this much is beyond question, that all the Scriptures point to Christ alone. Indeed, in John 5[:46] Christ says, "*Moses wrote of Me.*" Therefore, everything in the other books is already in the books of Moses, as in a basic source.[1206]

The fitting posture for faith and civics, according to Luther and Trump, is walking "backwards [heels first] into the future, peering into the sources and 'deeds of the fathers,' to discern what is sketched in black and white and will be, by degrees, colorfully illuminated in later generations."[1207]

For Luther, (and insight for those in our "woke" culture today)

> the historians, therefore, are the most useful people and the best teachers, so that one can never honor, praise, and thank them enough. That may very well be a work of great lords, as the emperor, king, etc., who in their time deliberately had histories written and securely preserved in the libraries. Nor did they spare any cost necessary for supporting and educating such people as were qualified for writing histories. One can see especially in the books of Judges, Kings, and Chronicles that among the Jewish people such masters were appointed and retained.[1208]

[1206] Ibid., Bird cites Luther quoting Deuteronomy 4:2, "*You shall not add anything to the Word which I speak to you, nor take anything from it,*" in LW 35:132, *Word and Sacrament I.*

[1207] Bird, "Rabbis," p.20.

[1208] LW 34:276. *Career of the Reformer IV,* "Preface to Galeatius Capella's History 1538."

The Word Who Has Acted, Is Acting, and Will Act

Luther cherished the Word (capital "W") present with the Creator at the beginning of time when God "spoke" Life into being through His Primordial Word: *"Let there be…and there was!"* (Genesis 1). The phrases *"God said," "the Word of the Lord came to me," "the voice of the Lord"* and *"thus says the Lord,"* for Luther, means not only the utterance of God but also the actions and deeds of God. God's "Word" is always followed by action. The prophets speak, and in their speaking the deed of God is accomplished. "In the case of God, to speak is to do, and the Word is the deed,"[1209] says Luther. God's Word acts and accomplishes His will. This creative Word continued to sustain and *"makes all things new"* (Revelation 21:5), and *"in the fullness of time"* (Galatians 4:4) became that *"Word made flesh"* in Jesus the Christ, who chooses to dwell, to literally "pitch his tent," among His people (John 1:14), and is continually revealed and present in the Word of Holy Scriptures and the Sacraments.

Professor Herrmann demonstrates how Luther gave more intentional thought to how the Scriptures functioned as the Word of God:

> There is a saying that "there are some books that you read, and then there are some books that read you." For Luther, the Bible was that second kind of book. He does not see the Scriptures primarily as the object of our interpretation, but rather we are the object as the Scriptures interpret us. Now this is not to say that Luther thinks there is no need to try to understand the text, or that Scripture requires no study and no explanation. It's simply that for Luther the primary function of the Scriptures is to shape us, form us, to lead us into a new creation, to kill us and make us alive again. He writes, "Note well, that the power of Scripture is this: it will not be altered by the one who studies it; instead it transforms the one who loves it. It draws the individual in—into itself—and into its own powers." The Scriptures draw you in—into its world, its history, its story—so that we read our world, our history, our story against the backdrop of the Bible. The Biblical narrative becomes the key to understanding our life, the defining story that interprets our world. It's not that we find the Bible meaningful to our life, but rather our life receives its meaning from the Bible.[1210]

1209 LW 12:33. *Selected Psalms I*, Psalm 2."

1210 Herrmann, Erik H., "The Relevance of Remembering the Reformation," p.24.

> For Luther the Scriptures are not merely a deposit of divine propositional Truth. They do contain such Truth, but the Scriptures are properly more than this. They are the story of the living God of Israel who brings kings and mighty men to naught and raises up the lowly and the orphan, who brings forth springs in the desert and gardens in the desolate places, who makes patriarchs out of pagans, who cuts down the olive tree and makes the stump blossom, who chooses the things that are not, to bring to nothing the things that are. And what's more, this story confronts us with the remarkable claim that it is also our story.[1211]

As One Who Speaks for God

By the same understanding, God chooses to employ our words, the words of finite human beings, to communicate with us. Luther illustrates, "For just as a man uses the tongue as a tool with which he produces and forms words, so God uses our words, whether Gospel or prophetic books, as tools with which He Himself writes living words in our hearts."[1212] Paul Althaus, theologian and leading authority of his day, explains:

> God's Word, however, is never merely an external word, spoken by human lips and heard with human ears. On the contrary, at the same time that this Word is spoken, God speaks His Truth in our hearts so that men receive it not only externally but also internally and believe it. This is the work of the Spirit of God.... The Spirit does not speak without the Word...(but) through and in the Word.[1213]

The work of the Holy Spirit is to create faith by hearing the Word which in proclamation comes from outside us. Althaus quotes Luther saying that God "has therefore arranged that the external word should be preached and go before—so that after a man has heard the word with his ears and grasped it with his heart, the Holy Spirit, the real teacher, comes and

---

[1211] Ibid., p.25.

[1212] LW 10:212. *First Lectures on the Psalms I, Psalms 1-75*, "Psalm Forty-Five," (vs.1).

[1213] Althaus, Paul, *The Theology of Martin Luther*, trans. Robert C. Schultz (Philadelphia: Fortress Press, 1966), p.36.

gives power to the word so that it takes hold"[1214] as the Word. Luther was emphatic that faith comes only through the work of the Holy Spirit, and that is done only through the external word, as God chooses to use us as partners together with Him.

The external word thus becomes the inner Word as it works in the heart and thereby proves that it is God's Word. As we communicate God's Word, God's Spirit loves to get to work!

> Word and Spirit not only belong together but constitute an indissoluble unity. Luther illustrates this from nature and from human speech. The Word and the Spirit are closely related to each other like the heat and the light which the sun always produces together, or like the voice and breath in speaking. "One cannot separate the voice from the breath."[1215]

One cannot have the Spirit without the Word, and it is the Spirit's work to confer in our hearts the assurance that God wills to be our Father, forgive our sin, and bequeath eternal life on us.

My homiletics professor, Dr. Stanley Schneider, who shared his philosophy on preaching in the book *As One Who Speaks for God*, would concur with Dennis Ngien, Professor of Systematic Theology at Tyndale Seminary in Toronto, who states

> the uniqueness of Luther's theology of preaching lies in that preaching is not mere human speech about God, rather it is God's own speech to human beings. Preaching is indeed the minister's activity; it is also God's activity. When we hear the sermon, we do not hear the pastor. The voice is his, but the words he uses are really spoken by God. God meets human beings through the agency of human voice. Preaching is God's Word speaking to us, not a rehashing of the old stories.[1216]

With a solid Lutheran understanding and deep appreciation for the importance of proclaiming the Word, Dr. Schneider addressed "The Why of Preaching" with chapters entitled "To Reveal One Lord," "To Reveal by One Word," "To Reveal to One Person,"

[1214] Ibid., p.37.

[1215] Ibid., p.38.

[1216] Ngien, Dennis, "Theology of Preaching in Martin Luther," *Themelios* 28.2 (Spring 2003), pp.28-48. <https://biblicallstudies.org.uk/pdf/themelios/luther_ngien.pdf>.

and "To Reveal in One Church."[1217] He unmistakably stood in the tradition of St. Paul and Martin Luther on the centrality of the Word and the significance of people "hearing" that Word.

While experiencing spiritual temptations, being mentally terrorized by fears and doubts, Luther, encouraged by his abbot at the Augustinian monastery, learned that he could not find consolation by approaching the Scriptures through the traditional scholastic theology of the Medieval doctors that shaped the academic curriculum of his time. The empathetic "Father," Johann von Staupitz, seeing his protégé's formidable intellect in distress, sent him to Wittenberg to study the Holy Scriptures and theology and then assigned him the task of preparing lectures on the Psalms, Galatians and Romans. Luther soon began to discover he was dealing with something other than ancient religious documents printed on parchment. Luther later recalled in a letter to Albrecht of Mansfeld, "I was once bogged down in such thoughts and doubts. And if Dr. Staupitz—or rather God through Dr. Staupitz—had not helped me, I would have drowned in them and long been in hell."[1218] *"Hearing,"* reading, studying and writing provided "the Damascus Road" experience and became instruments of salvation for Luther. For me, the paternal Staupitz who had become one of the most formative figures in Luther's life is the unsung hero of The Reformation. He was content to be merely supportive of Luther, encouraging him in his Reformation ideas, even though he himself chose to remain within the Catholic Church throughout his lifetime.

In the canon of Scripture, Luther encountered Christ and learned the meaning of the Master's words, *"You search the Scriptures, because you think that in them you have eternal life, and it is they that testify on My behalf"* (John 5:39 [NRSV]). God was revealing Himself and could thus be encountered in the Holy Scriptures. For Luther, the Bible was the very Word of God and Christ meets us there as Savior. All of Scripture points to the Christ, who is the Word made flesh:

> Therefore, you must continually keep God's Word in your heart, on your lips, and in your ears. For where the heart stands idle and the Word is not heard, the devil breaks in and does his damage before we realize it. On the other hand, when we seriously ponder the Word, hear it, and put it to use, such is its power that it never departs without fruit. It always awakens new

---

1217 Schneider, Stanley D., *As One Who Speaks for God: The Why and How of Preaching* (Minneapolis: Augsburg Publishing House, 1965).

1218 WABr 9:627, lines 23-25; letter 3716 quoted in "Beggars All." <http://beggarsallreformation.blogspot.com/2018/04/luther-if-it-had-not-been-for-dr.html>.

> understanding, new pleasure, and a new spirit of devotion and it constantly cleanses the heart and its meditations. For these words are not idle or dead, but effective and living.[1219]

Just as Luther came to believe that Christ was "in, with, and under" the elements of bread and wine in the Lord's Supper, so he was also convinced that the Master was "in, with, and under" the words and text of sacred Scripture which gave witness to Him and His love. The Bible was for Luther God's love letter to us and the Church.

In Torgau, Germany, on October 5, 1544, dedicating the first built Protestant church, Luther declared, "It is the intention of this building that nothing else shall happen inside it except that our dear Lord shall speak to us through His Holy Word, and we in turn talk to Him through prayer and praise." Then we hear this notable singularity of purpose which marked his entire ministry in words that must be our watchword: "We can spare everything except the Word."[1220] Luther understood that whenever the Word of God recedes from people's lives and is pushed out from the center of Church life, as it had been in the Church he loved, everything in the Church goes askew. The prophets of the Old Testament frequently spoke of a "*famine of the Word of God*" (i.e. Amos 8:11), and throughout the pages of Church history we find such times of spiritual famine.

"The Mouth House" or Preaching the Word

Recovering the Gospel was only half of the battle Luther faced: how Luther preached it was just as important. He preached about a direct encounter with the Lord, and preached in a way that expected listeners to experience the Lord directly. At the heart of The Reformation's success was its bold and clear proclamation of Christ. That emphasis would certainly have been a stark contrast to the sermons Luther would have been exposed to growing up as a young man, which emphasized the horror of eternal suffering in hell because of sin. Dr. Stanley D. Schneider cites John P. Dolan, a Roman Catholic bishop and writer, who comments on the content of preaching at the threshold of The Reformation:

> Preachers were preoccupied with the theme of sin and the grim face of death waiting for the moment of merited punishment. There was an emphasis on the horrors of hell and the suffering of the damned. Their

---

1219 "The Large Catechism," The Third Commandment, *Book of Concord*, p.379.

1220 LW 53:14. *Liturgy and Hymns*, "Concerning the Order of Public Worship."

> sermons were filled with descriptions of burning trees on which hung the souls of those who did not attend church services, vultures gnawing at men's vitals, venomous serpents stinging the unholy, boiling lakes, frozen fens, heated ovens, and vile dungeons. Scripture, when quoted, was completely torn from its living, historical context. Its personalities and their sayings were distorted and mutilated into passive conveniences for moral dilation. Everywhere the emphasis was on the negative side of man's salvation, his sins and punishment.[1221]

One can better appreciate the fear young Luther experienced when, as a student at the University of Erfurt, he was nearly struck by lightning in a severe summer thunderstorm and made his "911" call to St. Anne (the mother of Mary) that changed the trajectory of his life and the course of history. According to the Church of that day, Luther was quite right to be unsure of his eternal destiny. Such storms were thought to be the devil's work and the terrified wayfarer invoked the power of St. Anne, patron saint of miners, vowing to become a monk if she spared him from this heavenly fury. Not forgetting the promise made in circumstances of mortal peril, he entered Erfurt's Augustinian monastery in July 1505. There he set about becoming the best monk possible, attempting to be a paragon of holiness. Without knowledge of the Good News of Christ's sufficient and gracious salvation, and without an understanding of what he would soon recover for the Church—"Justification by Faith Alone"—he had no hope of heaven despite all his efforts to be holy. Luther wrote,

> Tis true [that] I was [once] a pious monk, and I kept so strictly to [the rules of] my Order that I may state [that] if ever a monk got into heaven through monkery, I, too, would have gotten in. All my colleagues [brothers] in the cloister who knew me will hear me out on this. For I would have martyred myself to death with vigils, prayers, reading, and other work, etc., if I had kept on longer.[1222]

Luther discovered that searching the depths of his soul for some saving goodness was to no avail. Living the monastic life of celibacy, poverty and obedience, and striving to be the

---

[1221] Schneider, Stanley, "Luther, Preaching, and the Reformation," *Interpreting Luther's Legacy*, ed. Fred Meuser and Stanley Schneider (Minneapolis: Augsburg Publishing House, 1969), p.124.

[1222] WA 38:143, quoted in Edwards' *Luther's Last Battles*, pp.61-62. See also <https://www.christianity.com/church/church-history/timeline/1501-1600/martin-luther-monumental-reformer-11629922.html>.

most virtuous monk, was not good enough and certainly did not abate his self-loathing and severe spiritual struggle, or "*Anfechtungen*," the feeling of being forsaken by God. Honoring his monastic vows faithfully through prayer, fasting, vigils and cleaning latrines did not help. He tried to save himself and inevitably failed.

David Lose, with whom I began this treatise, reminds us that "We don't come to church to read about God or be given information about God, but rather to hear about what God is up to in our lives and world today and to have that Good News addressed to us personally."[1223] I need to hear, as Luther needed to hear, that Christ's promises are for *ME!*; *REAL* forgiveness in *REAL* time. Jesus Christ, in preaching, wants to be given as a gift, not as an example. "*Christ Jesus came into the world to save sinners*" (1 Timothy 1:15 [NRSV]) and that is the most exuberant Good News which emphatically cuts through the gloom like a glorious and utterly unexpected sunbeam. It is like a cashier's check. You don't have to wait for the check to clear. "The love of God does not find but creates that which is pleasing to it.... Rather than seeking its own good, the love of God flows forth and bestows good. Therefore, sinners are attractive because they are loved; they are not loved because they are attractive."[1224]

"The saying, 'the devil's in the details' is really quite incorrect," according to Dr. Herrmann:

> the devil is much better at general platitudes; it is God who descends into the irreducible sweat and blood of human history—as Luther says, "into the muck and work that makes His skin smoke." It is in real life, with all its contradictions and uncertainties that God speaks to us, that He draws near to us in the flesh of His Son.[1225]

Here is where Luther's theology is so important and urgent for our day, which is experiencing the tearing down of traditional values, assumptions and foundations. Herrmann identifies it as "an ever-growing cultural '*Anfechtung*' that simultaneously rejects authority but still longs for certainty."[1226] We experience the decline of trust in our institutions, leaving our society in a state of disorientation, disillusionment and anxiety. We have earlier pointed

---

1223 David Lose, "Does Luther's Preaching Still Preach?" *Living Lutheran*, April 2017. <https://www.livinglutheran.org/2017/04/luthers-preaching-still-preach>.

1224 LW 31:57. *The Career of the Reformer I*, "The Heidelberg Disputation 1518 (Proof 28)."

1225 Herrmann, "The Relevance of Remembering the Reformation," p.27.

1226 Ibid.

to researcher Hugh MacKay identifying our time as the "Age of Anxiety" and James Robbins exposing the naivete and arrogance in *The Erasing of America.* On TV interviews, Author Eric Metaxas, whom we have quoted, shared that we are experiencing "normalcy under attack" and Dr. Robert Woodson, physician, community development leader, founder and president of the Woodson Center in Washington, D.C., defined our culture as being in a "Crisis of Meaning." "We are living in a nominal Christian culture."[1227]

Throughout this uncertain climate with all its confusion and doubts, Luther's theology points us to a gift and a promise! He directs us to hear the One whose Word is synonymous with the gift of love and faithfulness, promising us hope and life:

> From the beginning of the Biblical story until the end, Luther witnessed God's promise continually breaking into the lives of His people in order to claim the last word so that everything else is penultimate—sin, death, the devil, even the law. Only by the promise does Israel live in faith, and only through faith in the promise do the Gentiles find their spiritual home, for "*all the promises of God find their Yes in Christ*" (2 Cor 1:20). And this story of promise confronts us as itself a promise—*Christus pro nobis*—Christ for us. So it is that the Scriptures, confronting us as a promise, require and produce faith. Therefore, in the midst of defeat, the fear of death, the doubts and trials that seem to contradict the power and mercy and justice of God, it is nevertheless the death and resurrection of Christ that promises hope and gives meaning and purpose to one's own story.[1228]

We Are All Beggars

Any wonder that shortly before his death, a piece of paper was found left lying on his table (or another version has it being found in his pocket), containing these words in his handwriting?

> '*Hoc est verum. Wir sind alle Pettler.*' 'This is true. We are all beggars.' The end came quickly…at 1:00 a.m. he suddenly woke up. 'Oh, dear Lord God! He shouted. 'My pain is so great!' The whole crowd rushed to Luther's bedside…

1227 <https://www.realclearpolitics.com/video/2020/03/16/bob_woodson_1776_project_reaffirms_the_values_of_1776_brings_america_together.html>.

1228 Herrmann, "Relevance of Remembering," p.26.

> to comfort him. But Luther kept repeating *"For God so loved the world that He gave His only Son"*.... Jonas knew what was happening. He broke in and asked, "Do you want to die standing firm on Christ and the doctrine you have taught?" Luther's body moved, and in a loud voice he said, *"Ja!"* It was now almost 3:00 a.m. Luther's heart burst. The Reformer died.[1229]

Very explicitly, Luther, in his sermon for the Third Sunday of Advent 1524, asserts that "Only Christ is a gift; other saints can be examples. He is above all others in that He is a Gift.... The Gospel is not the preaching of Christ as example, but, proclaiming Him as a Gift. Whether a man stands or falls he is a Christian only if he has Christ. Looking for evidence elsewhere only brings uncertainty. Cling only to the Word."[1230]

Underscoring this dynamic and distinctive quality of the Word is Rhys Bezzant, Dean of Missional Leadership at Ridley College, Melbourne, Australia:

> A sermon must address the very people listening, for it should not be conceived as a knowledgeable essay but a focused spiritual address. Like a carpenter, Luther said, the preacher must work with the very piece of wood before him, with its own unique grain, knots, and shape. The sermon is a direct Word to this very congregation from the Lord. The messenger of the Lord doesn't bring a message *about* the Lord, but a message directly *from* the Lord, as Paul teaches: *"How are they to believe in Him whom they have never heard?"* (Romans 10:14)[1231]

Luther assumed that our encounter with the Word will be primarily located within the church gathered together in community to hear Scripture preached, and to taste the Word on their tongues as they partake in the Lord's Table. In the introduction to *One Holy and Catholic Church*, editor Han-Peter Grosshans writes that for Luther

> the Church provides a space of Truth and freedom within our world, where we can be safe and reconciled with God and with one another. The Church

---

[1229] Kittelson, *Reformer*, p.297, quoting WATr 5:168 (LW 54:476) and St. L.21/2,3385, 3387.

[1230] Pless, John T., "Martin Luther: Preacher of the Cross," *Concordia Theological Quarterly*, 51:2-3, April-July 1987, p.96, quoting WA XV, 777. <http://www.ctsfw.net/media/pdfs/plesspreacherofthecross.pdf>.

[1231] Bezzant, Rhys, "Why Did the Reformation Succeed?" <https://au.thegospelcoalition.org/article/why-did-the-reformation-succeed>.

> is the social space in which faith and salvation on earth are enacted and lived out. The Church is where Christian faith is lived out and enacted. The church is the earthly enactment, the earthly abode of faith. The Church is the frame around which faith grows, the channel through which it moves; it is the Christian form of life…. The Church is there where the salvation wrought by God is enacted on earth. It is the earthly space opened up by the Truth of the Gospel, the place where the faithful live reconciled with God and one another. And this earthly space of reconciled life is intended to encompass all of humankind.[1232]

It was for this reason that in his sermon for the First Sunday of Advent 1522, Luther insisted on calling the Church a "mouth house," not a "pen house"[1233] (notice the word is "pen" as in a writing instrument, not "pent!"). While Luther wrote voluminously, he gave himself tirelessly to the priority of preaching. As we have noted, Luther was a preaching machine, preaching "five to seven times a week in either the [University] Castle Church of All Saints or the City Church of St. Mary's in Wittenberg" according to Stephen Nichols.[1234] He believed that preaching is the very Word of God and therefore never placed his written works on the same level with his proclamation of God's Word. He truly understood St. Paul's assertion clearly that "*faith comes from hearing*" (Romans 10:17 [TEV]). "It is the way of the Gospel and of the New Testament that it is to be preached and discussed orally with a living voice." Luther boldly maintained that "Christ Himself wrote nothing, nor did He give command to write, but to preach orally."[1235]

Not only was Luther a first-rate thinker whose writings can be read today with great spiritual profit, but he understood that good theology must be preached to serve the spiritual growth of the laity. For Luther, good preaching must have clear and sharp application and exhortation. Good theology must be able to take the form of direct address through proclamation so that it finds its home in the faith of the one who hears. "Those who hear a

---

1232 Grosshans, Hans-Peter, "Introduction," *One Holy, Catholic and Apostolic Church*, ed. Hans-Peter Grosshans (Minneapolis: Lutheran University Press, 2009), pp.12-13. <https://www.lutheranworld.org/sites/default/files/DTS-Studies-OneChurch-2009-full.pdf>.

1233 Martin Luther, "First Sunday in Advent," *Sermons of Martin Luther, Volume 1*, ed. John Nicholas Lenker (Grand Rapids, MI: Baker Book House, 1983), p.44.

1234 Nichols, Stephen J., "Luther and His Significance," *Tabletalk Magazine*, October 2017. <https://tabletalkmagazine.com/article/2017/10/luther-and-his-significance>.

1235 Martin Luther, *Sermons*, Lenker, p.44. See also WA 10/1:48.

creative and clear Law and Gospel sermon experience the move from death to new life and are propelled to live in the world with hope and confidence."[1236]

David Lose goes on to affirm that

> Luther's preaching was animated by the fundamental conviction: the God we encounter in Jesus Christ is consistently and completely "*for us*"…. For it is in the sermon that we hear the life-altering news that God not only knows we exists, but cares—and cares deeply—about our ups and downs, our dreams and disappointments. This makes preaching a present-tense encounter between hearers and the God who will go to any length to communicate God's profound and life-changing love. In preaching, we realize that God sees us now, accepts us now, loves and forgives us now, and sends us out in freedom and hope now. In the sermon, God is at work—here and now—choosing us as God's beloved emissaries and equipping and sending us out to care for the world God loves so much.[1237]

The unimaginable Good News of our forgiveness and redemption cannot be contained in the newly created hearts of those who believe and just cling to "*the one thing needful*" (Luke 10:42) but spills over into the lives of others as we become "little Christs" to our neighbor. Love isn't something one can horde, or earn, or save up, or stash away, or protect, or keep safe. Love can only be given and shared. Being gifted with God's inestimable riches in Christ, Luther declares,

> I will therefore give myself as a Christ to my neighbor, just as Christ offered Himself to me; I will do nothing in this life except what I see is necessary, profitable, and salutary to my neighbor, since through faith I have an abundance of all good things in Christ…from faith thus flow forth love and joy in the Lord, and from love a joyful, willing, and free mind that serves one's neighbor willingly and takes no account of gratitude or ingratitude, of praise or blame, of gain or loss.[1238]

1236 Lose, David, "Does Luther's Preaching Still Preach?" *Living Lutheran*, April 2017. <https://www.livinglutheran.org/2017/04/luthers-preaching-still-preach>.

1237 Ibid.

1238 LW 31:367. *Career of the Reformer I*, "The Freedom of a Christian."

We become our truest selves when we give ourselves in serving others as we are gifted and called to be our Lord's heart, hands and voice. Intuitively we experience the truism memorably espoused by Edwin Markham: "There is a destiny which makes us brothers; none goes his way alone. All that we send into the lives of others comes back into our own."[1239]

I have always considered it a privilege to assist others in their understanding and appreciation of this broader, more expansive, more meaningful, and indeed more compelling understanding of the Scriptures' dynamic quality through Bible study, catechumen, discipleship classes and my preaching. By lifting up and distinguishing the various "expressions" of the "Word" of God, we can experience the manifold ways in which God's grace comes to us: in the "printed Word" we know as the Bible or the Holy Scriptures; the "spoken Word" which is preached and taught; and the "visible Word" we touch and taste in the Sacraments of Baptism and Holy Communion, all of which are subordinate to the "revealed" or "incarnate Word"—The Word made flesh—Jesus Christ. The sacraments are thus not something in addition to the preached Word, but rather another form or expression of the Word through which the salvation in Christ might be brought near through the assurance that our sins are forgiven. For Luther, it is Word and Sacrament, not vice-versa. It is not the Church that creates or authorizes the Scriptures, but rather the Church which is born and sustained solely by the Word preached, heard, read, sung and believed. Scripture as a form of the Word gives birth to the Church by calling together the saints; or in Luther's understanding, the Church is a "*creatura verbi divini*," a creature of the Word.

> For the Church was born by the Word of promise through faith, and by this same Word is nourished and preserved. That is to say, it is the promises of God that make the Church, and not the Church that makes the promise of God. For the Word of God is incomparably superior to the Church, and in this Word the Church, being a creature, has nothing to decree, ordain, or make, but only to be decreed, ordained, and made. For who begets his parents? Who first brings forth his own Maker?[1240]

Essentially, the Church is not the one who births the Word, but she is born and sustained solely by the Word of God. Thus, she is a creature of the Word. The Church is the work of

---

[1239] <https://www.brainyquote.com/quotes/edwin_markham_163790>.

[1240] LW 36:107. *Word and Sacrament II*, "The Babylonian Captivity of the Church."

God (*opus Dei*) and not of humankind (*opus hominum*).[1241] Elsewhere Luther puts it like this: "For since the Church owes its birth to the Word, is nourished, aided and strengthened by it, it is obvious that it cannot be without the Word. If it is without the Word, it ceases to be a Church."[1242] This concept of the Word of God permeated Luther's entire theology.

For Luther, the Word of God is the fundamental reality from which everything else follows. As Dr. Erik Herrmann contends,

> Thus, when it came to the Bible, it too was the Word of God, but especially because it was a witness to this same [creative Word that became flesh in] Jesus. Through its recorded histories, its laws, its poetic and prophetic utterances, and its apostolic testimonies, the Bible is the Word that urges us onward toward Christ, or as Luther puts it, "*was Christum treibet*" [what Christ does in that definitive act exhibited in the death and resurrection of Jesus] …For Luther the New Testament is not so much a book…but it is first and foremost a divine promise. The New Testament is God's promise to save humankind from its own destructive path – a promise that stretches back to Eden and runs through the lives of the patriarchs, prophets and kings until its fulfillment arrives in Christ.
>
> At its heart, then the New Testament is not only a set of writings but God's faithful fulfillment of a promise, a declaration of grace, an announcement of Good News—that God has reconciled us in His Son…which must be preached and performed by word of mouth and a living voice. Christ Himself has not written anything, nor has He ordered anything to be written, but rather to be preached by word of mouth…. In the sermon, the living voice of the New Testament finds its home, that is, in the faith of the one who hears. The promise that was fulfilled in Christ spills over and is fulfilled again and again in the hearts of those that believe.[1243]

The prophet asserts that God's Word "*will accomplish what I desire and achieve the purpose for which I sent it*" (Isaiah 55:11 [KJV]). The essence of Luther's Reformation

---

[1241] Schwöbel, Christoph, "The Church as Creature of the Word," *On Being the Church: Essays on the Christian Community*, ed. Colin E. Gunton and Daniel W. Hardy (Edinburgh: T&T Clark, 1989), p.122.
[1242] LW 40:37. *Church and Ministry II*, "Concerning the Ministry 1523."
[1243] Herrmann, Erik H., "Luther: 'The Word Did Everything.'" <https://www.csl.edu/2017/03/luther-the-word-did-everything>.

discovery is the primacy of that "*efficacious*" Word. The Word doesn't only *say* things but *does* things.

One of the traits many individuals attribute to Donald Trump is that he is unlike other politicians who make promises, but after the election do not deliver, and many of those issues never seem to see the light of day. The President nor his supporters are embarrassed to extoll "Promises Made are Promises Kept!" and acclaim their love for him.

Luther insisted that it is the Word's encounter with the world that ultimately gives the latter its shape:

> These are the Scriptures which makes fools of all the wise and understanding, and are open only to the small and simple, as Christ says in Matthew 11:25. Therefore dismiss your own opinions and feelings, and think of the Scriptures as the loftiest and noblest of holy things, as the richest of mines which can never be sufficiently explored, in order that you may find divine wisdom which God here lays before you in such simple guise as to quench all pride. Here you will find the swaddling cloths and the manger in which Christ lies.[1244]

The distinctive mark of Luther's theology is the centrality of the Word which points to Jesus Christ as the unconditional Gift. Luther was convinced that Christ is truly the Word made flesh, who is present and chooses to "dwell" with us. In his treatise of 1525, Luther writes:

> If now I seek the forgiveness of sins, I do not run to the cross, for I will not find it given there. Nor must I hold to the suffering of Christ, as Dr. Karlstadt* trifles, in knowledge or remembrance, for I will not find it there either. But I will find in the Sacrament or Gospel the Word which distributes, presents, offers, and gives to me the forgiveness which was won on the cross. Therefore, Luther has rightly taught that whoever has a bad conscience from his sins should go to the sacrament to obtain comfort, not because of the bread and the wine, not because of the body and blood of Christ, but because

---

[1244] LW 35:236. *Word and Sacrament I*, "Prefaces to the Old Testament."

* Andreas Rudolph Bodenstein von Karlstadt, also known as Andreas Karlstadt, Andreas Carlstadt, Andreas Karolostadt or simply Andreas Bodenstein, was a German Protestant theologian, University of Wittenberg chancellor, and contemporary of Martin Luther, who favored more radical reform along with Muntzer.

> of the Word which in the sacraments offers, presents, and gives the body and blood of Christ given and shed for me. Is that not clear enough?[1245]

Martin Luther famously believed and asserted that God caused the Reformation of the Church. He claimed he

> simply taught, preached, and wrote God's Word; otherwise I did nothing. And while I slept [cf. Mark 4:26-29] or drank Wittenberg beer with my friends Philip (Melanchthon) and (Nicholas von) Amsdorf, the Word so greatly weakened the papacy that no prince or emperor ever inflicted such losses upon it. I did nothing; the Word did everything.[1246]

The religious core which permeated Luther's entire theology was his deep love and reverence for the unchanging Truth of God's Word, which was truly the real "hero" of The Reformation, not Luther. Amidst the cultural changes swamping and challenging the Church, the prophet assures us that *"The grass withers, the flower fades; but the Word of our God will stand forever"* (Isaiah 40:8 [NRSV]). And 1 Peter quotes Isaiah, adding, *"That Word is the Good News which was preached to you"* (1 Peter 1:24-25 [KJV]).

"Sola Scriptura" understandably became a Reformation plank, but more accurately for Luther, a Biblical one. His critics incessantly charged that Luther was throwing out fifteen hundred years of Church history, indeed the Church and its tradition along with the communion of saints through the centuries. For Luther, however, "*sola*" did not mean "solo" as in the only authority apart from or isolated from tradition, or from the Church as the body of Christ. In Stephen Nichols's* view, "It's a mistake to think Luther thought so highly of his own views that he totally disregarded the views of all others."[1247] Luther indeed found value in Church history, the Church Fathers, healthy tradition, sound doctrine and councils, but only to the extent that they support the centrality and prominence of the Word of God. "Unhealthy traditions (or 'traditionalism' in Pelikan's understanding) exalt the externals, the forms over internal realities and ultimately over Christ Himself. This happened among the Pharisees and Sadducees in the first century, and it happened in the sixteenth century.

1245 LW 40:214. *Church and Ministry II*, "Against the Heavenly Prophets 1525."

1246 LW 51:77. *Sermons I*, "The Second Sermon, March 10, 1522, Monday after Invocavit."

* Dr. Stephen J. Nichols is president of Reformation Bible College and chief academic officer for Ligonier Ministries. Author of numerous books, he co-edited *The Legacy of Luther* with R.C. Sproul.

1247 Nichols, Stephen, "Biblical Authority." <https://www.ligonier.org/learn/articles/biblical-authority>.

It happens in our day."[1248] For Luther, the Bible is the highest and final authority, and must be placed at the center of all that we do. Tradition, history, doctrine and councils can be helpful and instructive, but they do not rise to the position of final authority.

Some have also mistakenly understood "*Sola Scriptura*" as a license for a radical individualism or rejection of Church authority, which was not the reformers' intent. "Me and my Bible" may assert elevating the Bible to the position of having the last word, with the freedom to understand what that means in "my" own "libertine" way. Such a position suggests that we do not trust God's Word to have acted on any Christians other than ourselves. Instead, we end up elevating ourselves as the ultimate judge over both Scripture and the God who has shared His Word with the Church down through history.

For our theologian of the Word, while he certainly spent long hours in the study, meditating on the Scriptures and writing devotional material for others, he firmly believed that the primary location for the reading, interpretation and study of Scripture was the local congregation. He clearly understood that we cannot rightly interpret Scripture without coming to it within and through the communion of saints, which also includes the saints of the past. "The writings of all the holy Fathers should be read only for a time so that through them we may be led into the Scriptures.... Our dear Fathers wanted to lead us to the Scriptures by their writings."[1249] We read and study God's Word together with the "*great cloud of witnesses*" (Hebrews 12:1) and under its tutelage. The New Testament clearly sanctions the office of teacher to help us understand God's Word, to love His Word, and to live out His Word in our lives and through our relationships with others. The history of the Church, its creeds and confessions give witness to other Christians who have been shaped by and wrestled with the Word of God and provide their inspired and valuable insight with us.

For all of Luther's lofty language about the Word, he celebrates what I have always cherished and taken comfort in when feeling so unworthy to proclaim, announce forgiveness, or administer the sacraments—the everyday, mundane and even fragile ways and means through which God chooses to come to us in His Word:

> The "*swaddling cloths*" mentioned above are "shabby and poor, yet precious is the treasure wrapped in them for it is Christ." The preacher, too, is just one sinner among many—a clay vessel [often a "*cracked pot!*"] carrying this same treasure. God's Word takes up no uniquely divine language, but clothes itself in what seems all too human and too foolish to accomplish such great things

[1248] Ibid.

[1249] LW 44:205. *The Church in Society I*, "To the Christian Nobility" or *Three Theses*, p.98.

> [even through flawed presidents and pastors]. Nevertheless, both prophet, and apostles, [and pastors] profess the same: *"the Word of God endures forever."*[1250]

When reading the Gospels, Luther also fondly spoke about loving the "words" of Jesus more than His "works," saying, "If I had to do without one or the other—either the works or preaching of Christ—I would rather do without the works than without His preaching. For the works do not help me, but His words give life as He Himself says [John 6:63 (NRSV)]."[1251] *("It is the Spirit that gives Life.... The words that I have spoken to you are Spirit and Life.")*

Now, not unlike the time in which Luther lived, it is my judgment that we, the Church, must return to the narrative of our salvation, to be who we are in the unfolding story of a bride and groom that leads to the ultimate consummation of Christ and His Church. Our own people have been led astray not simply by the doctrines of our culture, but also by the stories our culture tells, and thus we too eagerly adopt the ways of the world so that we reflect the world in a rush to be relevant, instead of being *"the light"* we are commissioned to be that illuminates the world (Matthew 5:14-16). In such an environment, we do well to heed the words of Jesus as He offers His Supper: *"Do this in remembrance of me"* (Mark 14:22-25; Luke 22:19; 1 Corinthians 11:24). If there is anything our culture, nation and Church needs right now, it is remembrance. We unfortunately tend to be like the man in the book of James who looks in the mirror but forgets what he looks like (James 1:23–24):

> Luther formulated a way of being Christ's people in whatever society and culture God has placed His chosen. H. Richard Niebuhr* dubbed Luther's approach to the Church's place in human cultures "Christ and culture in paradox." It is more aptly described as "Christ's people and culture in two dimensions," two realms. In what seems to be becoming a more hostile world, Luther's twenty-first-century followers must resist the temptation to drift into what Niebuhr labeled a "Christ of Culture" model or into a "Christ against Culture" pattern. The household of faith needs Lutheran witness to

---

1250 Herrmann, "Luther: 'The Word Did Everything.'"

1251 LW 35:362. *Word and Sacrament I*, "Preface to the New Testament (1522)."

* H. Richard Niebuhr, legendary professor at Yale and considered one of the most important Christian theological ethicists in 20th Century America. Best known for his 1951 book *Christ and Culture*.

> Luther's manner of practicing sharp critique of society's sins while affirming God's extravagant gift of the blessings of one's culture.[1252]

It would be interesting to hear how Luther and Niebuhr would describe the "cancel culture" movement in our present reality. Without being overly simplistic about the root of our concern for the Church and for our country, I believe our very identity is at stake. For Luther, our identity as the Church is as the bride of Christ, His body and presence in the world. As men and women created in the image of God, we discover that we have been entrusted with His sacred mission of living, proclaiming, interpreting and teaching that Word which reveals God's love for all. For Trump, it is our identity as American citizens endowed with the Bill of Rights, our identity as a Democratic Republic—one nation under God, indivisible, with liberty and justice for all—which shall have a new birth of freedom, and that government of the people, by the people and for the people shall not perish from the earth. How is it possible that we have so soon forgotten?

Perhaps we have not so much forgotten our past as we do not know or understand its significance and relevance; and if this is true, we have been negligent in not passing on the story and meaning of our salvation—the drama of our gifted existence in Christ here and for eternity—and that we, as citizens, have neglected to pass on the story of our founding, the meaning of our democracy, the Truth that all are created equal, and the drama of our nation's distinctive experiment in exercising the unalienable rights of life, liberty and the pursuit of happiness. Maybe after two millennia since Jesus, half of a millennium since Luther, and a quarter of a millennium since the Founding Fathers, the past has something to teach us after all. Luther, like our forebears who founded this country, was one of those who touched off something much larger than himself, namely The Reformation. For when we tell the story of Jesus Christ, Martin Luther and Donald Trump—the story of the Church and the source of our salvation, and the story of our democracy and the source of our freedom—we are telling our own story as well. As a philosophy major in college, I recall those who attribute to Plato, writing more than 400 years before Christ, the quote that the two most important questions are "Who will teach the children?" and "What will they teach them?"[1253] He also taught that "Education is teaching our children to desire the right

---

1252 Kolb, Robert, "Luther's Truths, Then and Now." <https://reformation500.csl.edu/2015/05/06/luthers-truths-then-and-now>.

1253 <https://www.goodreads.com/quotes/148532>.

things."[1254] Could Plato's concerns be any more relevant for what we discover being taught and not being taught to our children by parents and our schools today?

"At its core," in Dennis Peacocke's view,

> The Reformation was about how one sees God, the meaning of creation, and one's place in it. It was aimed at issues far, far beyond just the reforming of practices of the Roman Catholic Church. Its theological implications laid the groundwork for changes yet to be experienced even today. It proved its true historical breadth by the affects it had on society, economics, national political identity, and the future challenges of the uneasy relationship between political activity and the role of theology in the management of nations. It literally redirected history.[1255]

It also opened the doors of social change that have impacted generations for five centuries and will continue to do so for coming generations.

What began as a squabble between a bold monk and the Catholic hierarchy soon extended beyond a religious dispute, setting off a chain reaction that literally changed the course of history. The consequences of Luther's ideas gave birth to the "modern individual" as a free actor endowed with a conscience and "God-given rights" that exist independent of government or any other institution. Stephen Cornils of Wartburg Theological Seminary ventures:

> The Protestant empowerment of the individual led to capitalism and the Enlightenment, just to name two by-products of Luther's protest. The American Revolution with its idea that individuals "endowed by their Creator with certain unalienable Rights" should be free to form their own government, was another. Of the 56 signers of the Declaration of Independence, all but one was Protestant.... No other single figure made more of an impact on the modern world than the German Monk, Martin Luther. And even he would be surprised to know that.[1256]

1254 <https://solitaryroad.com/a1250.html>.

1255 Peacocke, Dennis, "The Great Reformation (Part 1)," *International Coalition of Apostolic Leaders*, March 1, 2017. <https://www.icaleaders.com/news/2017/3/1/the-great-reformation-part-1-by-dennis-peacocke>.

1256 Cornils, Stephen. <https://namelyliberty.com/how-the-reformation-shaped-your-world>, or <https://www.limitstogrowth.org/articles/2018/12/31/prageru-how-the-protestant-reformation-led-to-modern-freedoms-and-the-united-states-of-america>.

The handprints of "Luther's revolution," in Samuel C. Baxter's* judgment, "has influence on nearly every facet of modern culture. Certainly, there are theological implications, but it also influenced law, ethics and the humanities." He then cites the report of the German public state-owned international broadcaster, *Deutsche Welle*, "'Protestantism contributed largely to the development of the American nation and its self-image,' says the [500-year Protestant anniversary] exhibition organizers in Berlin. 'It impacted the idea of America as the Promised Land and of the Americans as the Chosen People.'"[1257]

Is it possible that we are on the beginning edge of such an almost cosmic event today? I believe that we are, and my conviction is that this current time in which we are living is a God-timing bridge of history worthy of exploring in its monumental possibility. The challenge, according to Peacocke, is "...how we understand and work cooperatively with the Holy Spirit in our responses to what God is doing rather than what social forces are demanding us to think or do.... Biblical faith requires positioning ourselves before God in what might I call 'an openness to possibilities.'"[1258]

Luther's Gospel was by grace alone, through faith alone, for Christ alone, based on the Scriptures alone. For Luther, theology could not be divorced from reform nor faith from life. His insight was the connection between them. While sociological and other external factors played their part, Luther and The Reformation succeeded in renewing the life of the Church, because its leaders were grasped by and compelled to share a vision that Christians, no matter their estate, could have assured access to the Lord. People had a taste for hearing and reading God's Word and discovering the "Good News" that God saves sinners, not based on how they repent, but entirely by His grace bestowed freely upon everyone who believes. People did not and could not, as Luther discovered, become righteous in God's sight through religious ritual or ecclesiastical services like indulgences. For Rev. Dr. Timothy Wengert, professor of Church History, Lutheran Seminary, Philadelphia, "Here's what the Reformation is all about: it's about discovering quite surprisingly that our relationship to God is not based upon what we do but rather what God does for us in Jesus Christ."[1259]

In Rhys Bezzant's analysis, "...preachers demonstrated this theological confidence through sermons which preached the central message of the Scriptures with clarity.

---

* Samuel C. Baxter is the Associate Editor for *The Real Truth* magazine of the Restored Church of God.

1257 Baxter, Samuel C., "Revolution: 'How the Reformation Shaped the Modern World,'" *The Real Truth Magazine*. <https://rcg.org/realtruth/articles/170821-001.html>.

1258 Peacocke, "The Great Reformation (Part 1).

1259 Wengert, Timothy, *Christian History*, Issue 115, p.3 (quote on ad page).

This in turn provided leverage for structural and moral renewal. It may not be altogether unreasonable therefore to say with Luther that it was the Word that did everything."[1260]

Luther stated that connection lucidly in his blunt formulation in 1518: "I teach that people should trust in nothing but Jesus Christ alone, not in prayers and merits or even in their own works."[1261]

> In other words, "Justification by Faith" [God's holy act of declaring a sinner righteous by faith alone through God's divine grace] was a direct challenge to the penitential system of the Church and to the religiosity which that system encouraged. The result was the liberation of people from these wrong kinds of works and freedom for the right kind of works which could be called truly "good"; the service of others and the exercise of a responsible secular calling.[1262]

If one can be saved by faith alone, and all good works motivated by a desire to avoid purgatory and hell and to get entry into heaven are "intrinsically sinful," David Crane of *The Spectator* then states the unavoidable conclusion: "...the whole penitential edifice of the medieval Church—the sale of indulgences, the intercession to Mary and the saints, the cult of relics, the authority of the Pope, the distinct existence of a priestly caste to mediate between man and God—would be all so much rubble."[1263]

1260 Bezzant, Rhys, "Why Did the Reformation Succeed?" *The Gospel Coalition, Australia Edition,* October 10 2017. <https://au.thegospelcoalition.org/article/why-did-the-reformation-succeed>.

1261 WABr 1.160, quoted in Scott H. Hendrix's *Martin Luther: A Very Short Introduction* (New York: Oxford University Press, 2010), p.45.

1262 Hendrix, Scott H., "The Controversial Luther," *Word & World,* 1983, p.394. <https://wordandworld.luthersem.edu/issues.aspx?article_id=453>.

1263 Crane, David, "The Man Who Changed the World," *The Spectator,* Issue 11, June 2016. <https://www.spectator.co.uk/2016/06/martin-luther-one-man-who-changed-the-world>.

36

Christians Living in Plague Times

There is one other relevant similarity in our twins and that is how they responded to a crisis not of their making, which we cannot dismiss. The circumstances of major plagues and how our warriors responded to the epidemics they encountered command our attention. It was on August 2, 1527, when a case of the bubonic plague re-emerged in Luther's hometown of Wittenberg and neighboring cities. The highly virulent, contagious disease was much more deadly than the coronavirus afflicting not only America but almost every nation on earth today. It was spread by infected rats and other vermin and communicated to humans by fleas. Infections in the cuts or abrasions of the skin led to a fever and a rapid pulse. Boils quickly appeared as large as hen's eggs on the neck, legs or armpits, infecting the bloodstream and leading to death in three or four days.

Living in a time before Louis Pasteur had discovered his germ theory, and not having the benefit of the scientific development of medical research, Luther surmised that breathing the aerial spirit escaping when the sick coughed spread the contagion, as we will discover in his writing. Coming in contact with the clothing or excrement of the ill could also transmit the disease. In addition, not only were the people living with an awareness of the Black Death plague which had killed nearly half the population of Europe less than 200 years earlier, but subsequent outbreaks obviously left deep emotional scars and terror in their memories. It is understandable that the whole city panicked, just as we have witnessed in our nation with the Covid-19 coronavirus. Fear swells in the hearts of people. Hysteria develops. People in Luther's day attempted to avoid the plague, fleeing the cities for the countryside, leaving the sick and dying behind. Shops were closed, doctors refused to see patients, and priests refused to administer the last rites.

Luther's prince, Elector John the Steadfast of Saxony, had ordered the famous professor and Reformer to leave Wittenberg for Jena immediately to save his own life, but Luther's pastoral heart compelled him to stay to minister to the stricken. Unmoved by the prince's letter or by the pleas of his friends, Luther and his pregnant wife refused to leave. Instead of running for the hills, they stayed, turning the former monastery, which was their home, into a makeshift hospital for the sick. It was a devoted response, fueled by love and sustained by faith in their sovereign God. There they were surrounded by the disease and its suffering victims as they demonstrated genuine Christian hospitality, risking their own lives in the process. "The wife of the mayor, Tilo Dene, virtually died in Luther's arms as Luther boldly stood in the gap along with many others to minister hope and the Word of God in a desperate situation."[1264] Among those who also remained to minister to the sick and frightened people was Johannes Bugenhagen, Luther's father-confessor, and pastor of the city church in Wittenberg who, with his family, moved into Luther's house for mutual encouragement.

Carl J. Schindler, who writes the introduction and translates Luther's letter on "Whether One May Flee from A Deadly Plague" in *Luther's Works*, records

> eighteen deaths by August 19th. Two other women were sick in the Luther house and his little son Hans refused to eat for three days and almost died; chaplain George Rorer's wife was also pregnant and took sick, lost both her baby and her life.... Writing to Nicolaus von Amsdorf, [friend, supporter, and defender of the Reformer], Luther spoke about his own "*Anfechtungen*" and about the hospital in his house, closing his letter by saying:
>
> "So, there are battles without and terrors within, and really grim ones; Christ is punishing us. It is a comfort that we can confront Satan's fury with the Word of God, which we have, and which saves souls even if that one should devour our bodies. Commend us to the brethren and yourself to pray for us that we may endure bravely under the hand of the Lord and overcome the power and cunning of Satan, be it through dying or living. Amen."[1265]

Schindler then reports that "by the end of November the plague had definitely receded and in December Luther's wife was happily delivered of her child, Elisabeth."[1266] While one-year-old Hans recovered, infant Elisabeth died less than eight months into her life.

Notice the similarity in which both our warriors characterize their confrontation with the plague's deadly attack. President Trump refers to himself as a "wartime president" in a different kind of battle, fighting an "invisible enemy," known as the coronavirus or Covid-19.

[1264] Davis, Andrew, "When the Deadly Outbreak Comes, Counsel from Martin Luther," *The Gospel Coalition*. <https://www.thegospelcoalition.org/blogs/evangelical-history/when-the-deadly-outbreak-comes-counsel-from-martin-luther>; see also LW 43:115, *Devotional Writings II*, "Introduction to Whether One May Flee From a Deadly Plague."

[1265] LW 43:115-116. *Devotional Writings II*, "Introduction, Whether One May Flee from a Deadly Plague."

[1266] Ibid., p.116.

"One day we'll be standing up here and say, 'Well, we won.'"[1267] For both, the fight was a "war" with the "invisible enemy" over which Christ would ultimately reign victorious as Lord.

Many leaders and pastors had besieged the famous Reformer to make a statement as they sought his advice on how they should respond to the plague, asking whether it was permissible for a Christian to flee from such a deadly peril in order to save their own life. Luther did not immediately respond, due to an illness and spells of depression he had been suffering. Then Pastor Johann Hess in Breslau, who was the recognized leader of The Reformation in Silesia, wrote seeking the same advice, to which Luther took up these questions, addressing those concerns in an open letter or pamphlet entitled "Whether One May Flee From a Deadly Plague."

In Luther's conviction, anyone who stands in a relationship to another has a vocational commitment not to flee. First, those engaged in a spiritual ministry, he wrote,

> such as preachers and pastors must remain steadfast before the peril of death. We have a plain command from Christ, "*A good shepherd lays down his life for the sheep, but the hireling sees the wolf coming and flees*" [John 10:11] For when people are dying, they most need a spiritual ministry which strengthens and comforts their consciences by Word and sacrament and in faith overcomes death.[1268]

After all, Luther reasons, "*If Christ laid down His life for us, we ought to lay down our lives for the brethren*" (1 John 3:16 [RSV]).

Martin Luther Ministering to the Needs of the Plague Victims

Art work by Gustav König, 1847
Left: Public domain, retrieved at Diospi-Suyana.de

Luther, Corona, and the Pest
Right: Public domain, retrieved at MartinLuther.de

1267 <https://abcnews.go.com/Politics/trump-coronavirus-task-force-economic-public-health-steps/story?id=69646672>.

1268 LW 43:121. *Devotional Writings II*, "Whether One May Flee."

Secondly,

> those in public office such as mayors, judges, and the like are under obligation to remain. This, too, is God's Word, which institutes secular authority and commands that towns and country be ruled, protected, and preserved, as St Paul teaches in Romans 13 [:4], *"The governing authorities are God's ministers for your own good."* To abandon an entire community which one has been called to govern and to leave it without official or government, exposed to all kinds of danger such as fires, murder, riots and every imaginable disaster is a great sin. It is the kind of disaster the devil would like to instigate wherever there is no law and order.[1269]

Remembering and Honoring the Wounded and the Fallen

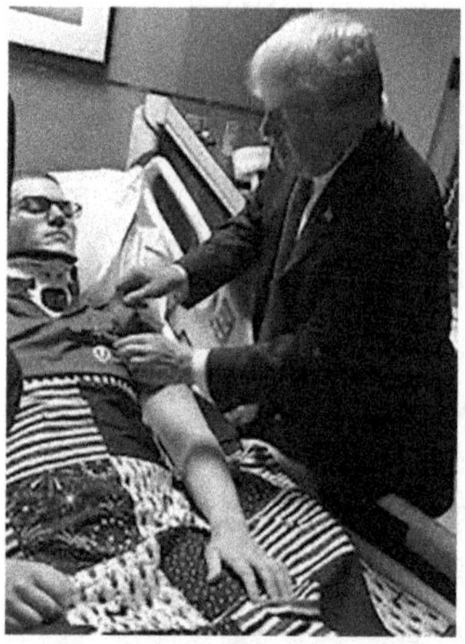

(Left) President Trump bestows a Purple Heart to First Lieutenant Victor Prato who was wounded during deployment to Afghanistan at Walter Reed National Military Medical Center, Dec 22, 2017. (Image: Dan Scavino Jr.)

(Right) President Trump looking on as members of the military transferred the remains of Scott A. Wirtz, a Defense Department contractor who was killed in Syria, at Dover Air Force Base in Delaware in January. (Image: Doug Mills/ New York Times)

[1269] Ibid.

A Tribute to First Responders

Then thirdly, we are again confronted with Luther's core understanding that out of love for God emerges the practice of love for neighbor with an understanding of his priority being directed by proximity:

> What applies to these two offices [Church and State] should also apply to persons who stand in a relationship of service or duty toward one another. A servant should not leave his master nor a maid her mistress except with the knowledge and permission of master or mistress. [Likewise] a master should not desert his servant or a lady her maid unless suitable provision for their care has been made somewhere. In all these matters it is a divine command that servants and maids should render obedience and by the same token masters and ladies should take care of their servants. (Ephesians 6:5-9). Likewise, fathers and mothers are bound by God's law to serve and help their children, and children their fathers and mothers. Likewise, paid public servants such as city physicians, city clerks and constables, or whatever their titles, should not flee unless they furnish capable substitutes who are acceptable to their employer.[1270]

[1270] Ibid., p.122.

Serving One's Neighbor

Clearly Luther did not intend to limit caring for the sick just to healthcare professionals, public officials or church leaders. Lay citizens, without any medical training, may find themselves in a position of providing care to the sick as to love of neighbor, and thus tending Christ Himself (Matthew 25:41-46). Luther doesn't ask the popular WWJD (What Would Jesus Do?) question of our day, but rather gives the insightful observation in a brilliant quotation:

> This I well know, that if it were Christ or His mother who were laid low by illness, everybody would be so solicitous and would gladly become a servant or helper. Everyone would want to be bold and fearless; nobody would flee but everyone would come running. And yet they don't hear what Christ Himself says, "*As you did to one of the least, you did it to Me*" [Matthew 25:40]. When He speaks of the greatest commandment He says, "*The other commandment is like unto it, you shall love your neighbor as yourself*" [Matthew 22:39]. There you hear that the command to love your neighbor is equal to the greatest commandment to love God and that what you do or fail to do for your neighbor means doing the same to God. If you wish to serve Christ and to wait on Him, very well, you have your sick neighbor close at hand. Go to him and serve him, and you will surely find Christ in him…whoever wants to serve Christ in person would surely serve his neighbor as well.[1271]

[1271] Ibid., pp.130-31.

For Luther, love of neighbor is the expected embodiment of his theology. Through my study, research for this book, and getting reacquainted with one who continually amazes and yes, even surprises me, I believe the slogan initials "ONM," standing for "Our Neighbors Matter," is far more significant and certainly more Biblical and theological than BLM. I am confident Luther would encourage us to remember that motto and pray each day those words on the plaque I have on the wall by the door that I cannot overlook as I leave my study: *Father God, please love your children through me today. Be in my words and in my serving.*

Luther was a realist and recognized that some believers have a stronger faith than others in the face of calamities and death. Acknowledging that there are many who are weak, he could not simply place the same expectation or burden upon everyone. As we have witnessed in the consistency in Luther's thought, he reminds his readers that salvation is not dependent on these good works. Participation in aiding the sick arises out of grace, not obligation.

Therefore, he affirms that fleeing may be a believer's faithful response provided that no emergency exists, that there is no need for additional helpers, and that provisions and substitutes have been made for those who will take care of their sick neighbors in their stead and nurse them. The caring and understanding pastor wants to trust that whether one decides to stay or flee during the plague, they will arrive at a faithful decision through prayer and meditation on the Scriptures. Furthermore, he encourages the faithful to be gentle with and pray for those who are afraid and flee their civic duties as being mutually bound together in community, even if that brings some risk—even death—to ourselves.

Yet he recognizes that

> A man who will not help or support others unless he can do so without affecting his safety or his property will never help his neighbor. He will always reckon with the possibility that doing so will bring some disadvantage and damage, danger and loss.... Anyone who does not do that for his neighbor, but forsakes him and leaves him to his misfortune, becomes a murderer in the sight of God, as St. John states in his epistles, "*Whoever does not love his brother is a murderer,*" and again, "*If anyone has the world's goods, and sees his brother in need [yet closes his heart against him], how does God's love abide in him?*" [1 John 3:15, 17][1272]

[1272] Ibid., p.126.

And then Luther offers his understanding, not to chide but to offer pastoral encouragement, to those who may be overcome by the horror and repugnance in the presence of a sick person that would prevent them from serving their neighbor, by saying:

> he should take courage and strength in the firm assurance that it is the devil who stirs up such abhorrence, fear, and loathing in his heart. He is such a bitter, knavish devil that he not only unceasingly tries to slay and kill, but also takes delight in making us deathly afraid, worried, and apprehensive so that we should regard dying as horrible and have no rest or peace all through our life. And so, the devil would excrete us out of this life as he tries to make us despair of God, become unwilling and unprepared to die, and, under the stormy and dark sky of fear and anxiety, make us forget and lose Christ, our Light and Life, and desert our neighbor in his troubles. We would sin thereby against God and man; that would be the devil's glory and delight. Because we know that it is the devil's game to induce such fear and dread, we should in turn minimize it, take such courage as to spite and annoy him, and send those terrors right back to him. And we should arm ourselves with this answer to the devil: "Get away, you devil, with your terrors! Just because you hate it, I'll spite you by going the more quickly to help my sick neighbor. I'll pay no attention to you…[for] I know that helping my neighbor is a deed well-pleasing to God and all the angels…"[1273]

To give further encouragement from God's Word, Luther reminds those who may be reluctant to minister to those in need of our Lord's own sacrifice in serving those truly in need of God's love and acceptance:

> If Christ shed His blood for me, why should I not expose myself to some small dangers for His sake…. The service we can render to the needy is indeed such a small thing in comparison with God's promises and rewards that St. Paul says to Timothy, "*Godliness is of value in every way, and it holds promise both for the present life and for the life to come.*" [1 Timothy 4:8]. Godliness is nothing else but service to God. Service to God is indeed service to our neighbor…. But whoever serves the sick for the sake of God's gracious promise…has the great assurance that he shall in turn be cared for.

[1273] Ibid., pp.127-128.

> God Himself shall be his attendant and his physician, too. What an attendant He is! What a physician! Friend, what are all the physicians, apothecaries, and attendants in comparison to God? Should that not encourage one to go and serve a sick person…?[1274]

In all of this, Luther understood clearly that seeking to save one's life was a natural God-given inclination. God gives humans a tendency toward self-protection and trusts that people will take care of their bodies (Ephesians 5:29; 1 Corinthians 12:21-26). He then cites Biblical incidents to prove that fleeing death is not wrong in itself. King David had fled from both Saul and Absalom (1 Samuel 19:20-27). Abraham had escaped death by pretending that his wife, Sarah, was his sister (Genesis 12:13). And several others, including Isaac and Jacob, "fled from death when it was possible and saved their lives, yet without depriving their neighbors of anything but first meeting their obligations toward them."[1275]

His letter constantly straddles these two competing goods: honoring the sanctity of one's own life, and honoring the sanctity of those in need. Ultimately Luther left the personal decision to flee or stay to the individual in light of God's Word, not to governmental mandates.

As we have witnessed previously, our 16th-century warrior takes the Devil seriously as the enemy of God, and he uses his most choice and vehement language to assail the opponent who works through our "flesh" and our world. In his Small Catechism's explanation to the Sixth Petition of the Lord's Prayer *("lead us not into temptation")*, Luther explains "God tempts no one to sin, but we ask in this prayer that God would watch over us and keep us so that the devil, the world, and our sinful self ['flesh' and fleshly reason] may not deceive us and draw us into false belief, despair, and other great and shameful sins."[1276]

Theologian Paul Althaus describes the Reformer's teaching, and indeed his own experience, of "Man Between God and Satan" by identifying the power to which everyone is subject in one's sinfulness. For Luther,

> each of these three powers (the devil, the world, and flesh) seduces men to sin and holds them captive in it; all three are opposed to God, to His Word, and to faith…the Devil works through our "flesh" and through "the world." He is the lord of this world, as both Luther and the Bible say. Though the three

---

1274 Ibid., pp.128-129.

1275 Ibid., p.124.

1276 Martin Luther, "Sixth Petition of Lord's Prayer," *The Small Catechism in Contemporary English* (Minneapolis: Augsburg Publishing House, and Philadelphia: Fortress Press, 1979), p.21.

> powers are still quite distinct, all three concepts represent that unified will which surround us on every side and is opposed to God. It is in us, around us, and over us. For Luther, evil is much more than a power which grasps all mankind. It is both the effect and the realm of a personal will which grasps not only the will of the individual but also the joint will of all mankind; it is a superhuman will directed against God, one that has its own existence.[1277]

Not only can one sin on the one hand by ignoring the needs of neighbors, but Luther points to others also sinning on the other hand. He warns against the over-confident underestimating the seriousness of the plague, testing God or being frivolous toward God, ignoring precautions with the cavalier assertion that God will protect them:

> They are much too rash and reckless, tempting God and disregarding everything which might counteract death and the plague. They disdain the use of medicines; they do not avoid places and persons infected by the plague, but lightheartedly make sport of it and wish to prove how independent they are. They say that it is God's punishment; if He wants to protect them, He can do so without medicines or our carefulness. This is not trusting God but tempting Him. God has created medicines and provided us with intelligence to guard and take good care of the body so that we can live in good health.
>
> If one makes no use of intelligence or medicine when he could do so without detriment to his neighbor, such a person injures his body and must beware lest he become a suicide in God's eye.... It is even more shameful for a person to pay no heed to his own body and to fail to protect it against the plague the best he is able, and then to infect and poison others who might have remained alive if he had taken care of his body as he should have. He is thus responsible before God for his neighbor's death and is a murderer many times over.[1278]

"In a nutshell," says Kevin Martin, serving Our Savior Lutheran Church (LCMS) in Raleigh, North Carolina,

> Luther found that elusive middle ground between panic and foolhardiness. Luther was aware some people were tempting God by refusing medicine or

---

[1277] Althaus, Paul, *The Theology of Martin Luther,* p.161.

[1278] LW 43:131. *Devotional Writings II,* "Whether One May Flee from a Deadly Plague."

> sensible precautions. He compares them to people who see their neighbor's house on fire and do not help put it out, saying, "God if He wills, can extinguish it without water. It's probably His judgment." Luther excoriates such senselessness as the mirror image of the hysteria that leads people to abandon their neighbors in time of grave need.[1279]

Having weighed the responsibilities of leaders and ordinary citizens during a contagion, Luther also provides advice that perhaps served the Trump administration and its Coronavirus Response Team as they guided us through the infectious disease outbreak we have experienced.

Luther did not ignore common sense, as has already been noted. He encouraged preventive measures as staying away from the sick, unless you are aiding your neighbor in need, washing hands with soap and water, and covering coughs. Is it surprising to note that 500 years ago he, who believed the source of all bad things originated from the evil instigation of the Devil, was of "the opinion that all the epidemics, like any plague, are spread among the people by evil spirits who poison the air or exhale a pestilential breath which puts a deadly poison into the flesh"?[1280]

Exercising "Neighborly" and "Patriotic" Concern for Others

Reformer Martin Luther

(Image: "He Rice Tanned!" website)

President Donald Trump

(Image: CNN)

[1279] Martin, Kevin, "Christian Life in Plague-Time," *First Things*. <https://www.firstthings.com/web-exclusives/2020/03/christian-life-in-plague-time>.

[1280] LW 43:127. *Devotional Writings II*, "Whether One May Flee from a Deadly Plague."

He thus encouraged individuals who were ill or infected to self-quarantine and stay at home until they were well, to use the gift of medicine God has inspired, and chastise (as we have observed) those who knew they were sick yet exposed others to the illness as murderers. "Yet, some are so foolish as not to take precautions but aggravate the contagion, giving the devil a heyday and many will die [which] is a grievous offense to God and to man—here it is tempting God."[1281]

> If in the Old Testament, [Luther reasons], God Himself ordered lepers to be banished from the community and compelled [them] to live outside the city to prevent contamination [Leviticus 13-14], we must do the same with this dangerous pestilence so that anyone who becomes infected will stay away from other persons, or allow himself to be taken away and given speedy help with medicine…Then the poison is stopped in time, which benefits not only the individual but also the whole community, which might be contaminated if one person is permitted to infect others.[1282]

In his response to Pastor Hess, Luther said, "I shall ask God mercifully to protect us." Then he spoke remarkably like the CDC's guidelines today of taking proactive measures, fumigating house, yard and street, and even "social distancing:"

> What else is the epidemic but a fire which instead of consuming wood and straw devours life and body…I shall fumigate, help purify the air, administer medicine, and take it. I shall avoid places persons and places where my presence is not needed in order not to become contaminated and thus perchance infect and pollute others, and so cause their death as a result of my negligence. If God should wish to take me, He will surely find me, and I have done what He has expected of me and so I am not responsible for either my own death or the death of others. If my neighbor needs me, however, I shall not avoid place or person but will go freely as stated above. See, this is such a God-fearing faith because it is neither brash nor foolhardy and does not tempt God.[1283]

[1281] Ibid., LW 43:132.

[1282] Ibid., LW 43:133.

[1283] Ibid., LW 43:132.

In addition, Luther advocated the use of certain buildings to be used as hospitals and urged cities to plan for such facilities for the future, so that the sick did not need to remain in their private homes. He also advocated that public cemeteries be placed outside the town center to the edge of town to avoid infection from the corpses.

Was Luther a trailblazer in this too, far ahead of his time, incorporating practices 500 years ago that we in the 2020s have implemented in the midst of Covid-19, as we follow CDC guidelines that are remarkably similar to Luther's advice? We have also witnessed President Trump ordering the Army Corps of Engineers to build hospitals and convert convention centers to provide beds for the sick, instituting "social distancing" and people working remoting from their homes, and closing places where large numbers would congregate, while encouraging the use of masks in public.

In the entirety of Luther's counsel given in his letter, there is no panic. He thought hysteria had gripped much of the populace, which was leading to great harm, just as we have experienced in America. One of President Trump's early goals was not to incite panic in the populace, but rather to be a daily presence during news conferences to inform and instill confidence within the citizenry that the government was doing all it could to protect and provide for them.

The best defense against the plague, Luther insists, is regular worship, hearing the Word, receiving the Sacrament and the assurance of forgiveness. The Devil loves to terrorize us with our fears, and for most people the greatest fear is death, which for Luther is God's punishment for our sins. The "*wages of sin is death*" (Romans 6:23 [NRSV]), and since we all are sinners, we will all eventually die. However, that is not the end of the story, as the Devil would have us believe. For Christians are given the Easter promise of eternal life that swallows death in victory (Isaiah 25:8; 1 Corinthians 15:54). In worship through God's Word, we learn how to live and how to die with Christ our Lord. "There we are fully fed by Christ's Word and Spirit, His Body and Blood. There we are encouraged to face the devil and his terrors with faith in God and love for our neighbor. Our safety is not guaranteed by the means of grace, but a joyful life and a good death certainly is."[1284]

Finally, Luther reminds us as he also addresses the most practical advice of all. People should prepare in time for their own death by going to Confession, listening to the sermon, receiving the Sacrament, and becoming reconciled with one's neighbor or with those one has wronged. Luther would have us as Christ's followers to display in a world gripped by fear that God is BIG! "*Greater is He who is in you than he who is in the world*" (1 John 4:4 [WEB]). Encompassed by any challenge we face, Luther prays that we find that comfort and

---

1284 Martin, "Christian Life in Plague Time."

peace which passes all understanding in our God who is big, strong, and serves as our never-failing Rock and Refuge. *"If God is for us, who can be against us?"* (Romans 8:31 [PME]).

Though God's children face earthly sufferings, those who proclaim faith in Christ share in a heavenly promise of freedom from illness and suffering:

> In an "open letter" calling for prayer from Christians around the globe, an anonymous Wuhan pastor affirms "[Christ's] peace is not to remove us from disaster and death, but rather to have peace in the midst of disaster and death, because Christ has already overcome these things." Both Luther and the Wuhan pastor express the reality of suffering but recognize that death and suffering do not have the final word.[1285]

While in plague time, be it the return of the bubonic plague in 1527 or the coronavirus of the 2020s, it's a fair question to ask how one can minimize fear. It is important amid reports and listening to the media not to be manipulated by overreactions and political tactics. With the hype given to the coronavirus by the media, supported not by facts of science but by computer models, with projections of 1.7 to 2.2 million deaths in the United States, hysteria has dominated our way of life in all its sectors, even to the shortage of toilet paper! Our country is reporting nearly one million deaths as of Spring 2022. Statistical records, however, are presently being adjusted, as distinctions are now being acknowledged between those *with* Covid who died from underlying conditions and those who died *because* of Covid. Certainly most individuals would concur it is better to error on the side of caution and better yet to have exercised superb governmental preparedness for such events as pandemics, floods, hurricanes, etc. It has been a challenge with the continuous "flip-flopping" of experts to distinguish whether it is medical science or political science being espoused. It is solid facts that inform, whereas induced fear causes panic as we have witnessed, and for Luther the latter is the devil's playground.

"Fear not!" is the most repeated command in the Bible. In fact, it's been said that there are 365 *"Fear not"* or *"Be not afraid"* directives in Scripture, one for every day of the year. Lloyd Ogilvie, in *Facing the Future Without Fear,* says there are 366, one for every day of the year including Leap Day. Actually, there are far more "fear nots" than one for every day if you include the derivatives which reference the meaning of the Biblical word "fear,"

[1285] Ko, Stephen, "Coronavirus Fears Mean We Need More Communion, Not Less." <https://www.christianitytoday.com/ct/2020/january-web-only/martin-luther-coronavirus-wuhan-chinese-new-year-christians.html>.

specifically relating to reverence for God alone and *not fearing anyone or anything else.* Expanding the search to look at verses encouraging us to receive God's peace and strength when we're worried or anxious would add many, many more "fear nots" in the Scriptures. It is with this understanding of the word "fear" that Luther begins his explanation to each of the Ten Commandments in the Small Catechism, "We are to fear and love God so that..."[1286] This usage points to the "reverence" and "awe" we are to have before Almighty God, which inspires trust and confidence so that we do not need to fear anyone or anything else. Place that thought in the context of Philip Yancey's quote: "The opposite of faith is not doubt, but fear."[1287]

I have never forgotten that conference where Leonard Sweet,* the creative wordsmith and renowned futurist, theologian, professor, pastor and author, was the presenter. He spoke about the beauty of the word "astronaut," which literally means "one who sails the stars." Then in what he does best, he informed us that being baptized with water and the Spirit, we are "pneumanauts," those who sail the "wind" of the Spirit, or Holy "Gust" [*sic*!] of discipleship. Being a "follower of Christ" involves Jesus teaching us to become pneumanauts. As we have been discovering, becoming who we are is not easy. It involves learning what to look for and learning what to ignore in the tumultuous times in which we live. It's about developing what we might call a sixth sense, one guided by love, not fear. It acknowledges not knowing the future precisely because *"the wind blows where it chooses and you hear the sound of it, but you do not know where it comes from or where it goes. So, it is with everyone who is born of the Spirit"* (John 3:8 [NRSV]).

It is ironic that as we speak of that sixth sense of love driving and guiding pneumanauts as they trustingly sail the "wind of the Spirit," President Trump launched the Space Force on December 20, 2019, as our country's sixth military branch. He sought to fulfill his oath to "protect and defend" the nation at this time from potential technological perils in the earth's orbit in addition to those threats on land, sea or air. The twenty-first-century Space Force "Guardians" will use and protect satellites that are essential to modern warfare, communication, transportation guidance and financial operations within our high-tech

---

[1286] Luther, *The Small Catechism in Contemporary English*, Augsburg/Fortress, pp.3-7.

[1287] Yancey, Philip, *Reaching for the Invisible God* (Grand Rapids: Zondervan, 2000). <https://dbsuch.wordpress.com/2018/03/07/the-opposite-of-faith> or <https://marcalanschelske.com/quote-doubt-is-not-the-opposite-of-faith>.

* Leonard Sweet, Methodist pastor and theologian working with graduate students at four institutions: Drew University where he has held the E. Stanley Jones Chair; Tabor College; George Fox University; and Evangelical Seminary, holding the Charles Wesley Senior Professorship of Doctoral Studies. Prolific writer of more than 200 articles, 1,500 published sermons, and 60 books.

economy that could be targeted by potential adversaries. The explanation Luther gives to the First Article of the Creed in his Small Catechism reveals the spiritual parallel to Trump's temporal concern in creating the Space Force. Luther clearly asserts it is the Creator's will and purpose of His Spirit to "defend [believers] against all danger and [promises] to *guard* and protect [pneumanauts] from all evil."[1288] We have seen how Luther has made the Scriptural case that God has granted governments the authority and responsibility to protect the people and defend the country in the effort to maintain peace and tranquility for His children.

Without minimizing the pain, suffering and death caused by the coronavirus, some are arguing that the economic consequences might be worse and far more costly than even the number of deaths. Could the cure be worse than the illness, especially when we're told 98+% recover and survive Covid-19? Could the shutdown resulting in the unemployment of over 40 million, causing despair, leading to increased opioid and alcohol usage, depression and other mental issues, suicides, domestic abuse, and the pain and suffering from not being able to address elective surgeries, receive needed treatments, or care for emergencies, thus be exacerbating other health issues?

Likewise, how does one calculate the cost and adverse effect on children deprived of those crucial developmental and relational social skills not so easily communicated virtually online in contrast with face-to-face classroom experiences? The shutdown and school closings has resulted in an escalating rate of suicides and suicidal behaviors among schoolchildren, creating an alarming psychosocial issue throughout the world. It is reported that a student is 10 times more likely to die from suicide than from the virus, and it has become the second leading cause of death among younger people aged 10-24. Stressful life events, mental health conditions, and family environments including economic stability are major risk factors for suicidal behavior among children.[1289] We have also witnessed other unintended consequences, for example the over-supply of oil, and farmers dumping thousands of gallons of fresh milk, smashing eggs, plowing under vegetables and euthanizing thousands of animals, because of the lack of demand due to the shutdown and closures of schools and restaurants.[1290]

1288 "The Creed, "<https://catechism.cph.org/en/creed.html>. Also see Luther, *The Small Catechism in Contemporary English*, p.11.

1289 Philip, Bibin V., "Escalating Suicide Rates Among School Children During COVID-19 Pandemic and Lockdown Period," *Indian Journal of Psychological Medicine*, January 8, 2021. <https://journals.sagepub.com/doi/full/10.1177/0253717620982514>.

1290 <https://www.nytimes.com/2020/04/11/business/coronavirus-destroying-food.html>.

It is hard to choose between competing harms, especially while we understand we are not free to harm others. And especially in a democratic republic, it is crucial to remember that fear makes us as people easier to control, as we are more likely to cede our liberties to the government, such as the right to assemble and to worship. As you might expect, I question the basis on which abortion clinics, liquor stores, tatoo parlors and lottery ticket windows are deemed "essential," but churches are not. Or that casinos and "big box stores" can open, and protesters and rioting crowds can gather, but churches are shut down or, when opened, must limit the numbers worshipping while forbidding singing. Leaders and politicians may suggest, recommend or ask people to stay home or keep their distance, but ordering the same under penalty seems to me to be over-reach and a violation of our Constitutional rights. Fear can easily be used to help politicians gain not only wealth, but power and control.

It seems logical to ask why this particular virus caused such alarm when previous annual influenzas, for which preventative inoculations were available, tallied high numbers of contractions, hospitalizations and deaths but without the hysteria associated with the present Covid-19 pandemic? For example, "In the U.S, between April 2009 and April 2010, the CDC estimates there were 60.8 million cases of swine flu [H1N1], and that 150,000 to 575,000 people died of the pandemic virus infection in the first year of the outbreak. 80% of the virus-related deaths were estimated to occur in those who were 65 years of age or older."[1291] Since we haven't heard much of anything about the numbers associated with the flu, one has to wonder whether those numbers have been co-mingled with the Covid-19 figures. Reports have also shown the numbers being inflated with "false-positive" tests being recorded along with those who completed the form, but then did not wait in line to be tested. Then too, with contradictory information being reported by the CDC, medical experts have affirmed that many in the high-risk categories for the coronavirus—especially those in nursing homes and in long term facilities—would likely have died from other underlying causes and old age than from Covid. In addition, as we have already indicated, health officials are confirming they have added those they "presume" died *with* the virus, without verification to the mortality number, in sharp contrast to those who died because *of* the coronavirus, which is a much smaller number.

Luther himself was not afraid of being God's servant and minister amongst those who were afflicted and suffering, nor afraid of standing up to the powerful Roman Catholic Church as he exposed their false doctrine for which he was under the sentence of death by

---

[1291] <https://www.cebm.net/covid-19/covid-19-deaths-compared-with-swine-flu>. See also Kimberly Hickok, "How Does the Covid-19 Pandemic Compare to the Last Pandemic," March 18, 2020. <livescience.com/covid-19-pandemic-vs-swine-flu.html>.

the Emperor and excommunication for heresy by the Pope. He was convinced that the fear of death was the Devil's work, and that no Christian should yield to it. Our journey into these days with the coronavirus is not over, and we pray it will soon dissipate into the dim memories of the medical history books. In the meanwhile, we are witnessing opportunities for many Christians to display the love of Christ to their neighbors, and to live out the fearlessness of death in the thick of a horrible disease, as well as natural disasters, and other calamities because of that which Christ has won for all His children in His resurrection... Life eternal!

37

Valiant and Fearless Warriors for Church and Country

Luther saw himself only as a theologian, a theologian in Dr. James Atkinson's* view, "called by God to bring the Church back from its secularism and materialism to the role God had intended for it in Christ, to restore its original charter and message, to offer *re-formatio* to that which had suffered *de-formatio.* So Luther understood himself: so I understand and interpret him."[1292] Atkinson argues further that

> to no man was the Gospel vouchsafed in its totality and immediacy more clearly, more poignantly than it was to Luther...He has a great deal to say for the healing of the nations and for the mending of the churches. As there is more Gospel in Paul than in the Gospels in that it is so incisively expressed, so there is more Gospel in Luther (the second Paul) than in any other Church Father or doctor. And just as Paul divided men into Judaisers and believers, and yet has the secret to unite them (Rom. 9-11), so Luther, who divided Christendom, will yet prove the ground of its unity.[1293]

Luther's concern was for the purity of the Gospel and affirmed that all the truths necessary for salvation are contained in Scripture. While he was an academic and an intellectual of considerable proportions, he nevertheless maintained the priority of faith over knowledge and intellect. His overwhelming experience of God accepting him and calling him in spite of his awareness that he was nothing but "poor stinking maggot-fodder"† or literally a "bag of worms"[1294] brought him more than peace to his foreboding mind. He

---

* James Atkinson, an English Anglican priest, Biblical scholar, and theologian specializing in Martin Luther and the Protestant Reformation. He was Professor of Biblical Studies at the University of Sheffield, England from 1967 to 1979, and then served as Canon Theologian of Sheffield Cathedral.

1292 Atkinson, James. *Martin Luther: Prophet to the Church Catholic* (Grand Rapids, MI, Eerdmans, 1983), p.43.

1293 Ibid., Atkinson in a footnote pp.44-45.

† Maggot-fodder was a favorite term of Luther for designating the perishable body, the mortal man.

1294 LW 45:70. *The Christian in Society II*, "A Sincere Admonition to all Christians," 1522.

realized a compelling purpose for living and the certainty of joyous life with God forever as His beloved child. Responding in faith to his "call" he wagered his all on God as a fearless warrior and would not be silenced unless proven wrong by Scripture. All he could do was to live gratefully in the promise and proclaim it faithfully with prophetic zeal through the gifts of spiritual insight and vision he received from God.

> Luther's significance for the twentieth century, indeed for any century, is the same now as it was in the sixteenth: to show the significance of Christ and to open up every age to a living *re-formatio* of what perpetually suffers *de-formatio*. Every church in every age needs cleansing and renewal under God. Luther is poison as much to Protestantism as he is to Catholicism. But he is that curative, beneficient, therapeutic poison that kills not the patient but the Adamic pathogen within the system of the patient that is itself lethal for both the individual and his church. To change the metaphor, we might say that Luther is the salt that alone can preserve the meat of Catholicism.[1295]
>
> Yet Catholicism in the form of the papal church rejected its God-given doctor as Israel rejected Jeremiah (and all the prophets), as Jerusalem would have none of Christ. The children put up memorials to the prophets their fathers rejected (Matt. 28:29-38). The important thing is to take heed of these errors, for the future lies with those who do. Hubert Jedin,* the great Catholic scholar of the Reformation, concedes that the rejection of Luther by the papacy was an unmitigated tragedy, a position taken up nowadays by a large and telling number of Catholic scholars throughout the world. When the papacy rejected Luther and his teachings, Catholicism then transmuted itself to *Roman* Catholicism, and has not been truly catholic since. Luther belongs to the Catholic Church even though it reject him exactly as Christ belongs to Judaism, even though Judaism reject Him.[1296]

1295 Atkinson, pp.45

* Hubert Jedin was a Catholic historian from Germany whose publications specialized on the history of ecumenical councils in general and the Council of Trent in particular. For a significant assessment of the influence of Jedin on Catholic research into the Reformation, see John O'Malley's essay "Catholic Reform" in *Reformation Europe*, ed. Steven Ozment (St. Louis, 1982), pp.297-319.

1296 Ibid., pp.45-46.

> A further consequence was that those who sought reformation were forced into confessional positions, with a grotesque situation of a church now called "Lutheran," a most lamentable matter, which Luther never wanted and continually disclaimed. [On the other hand,] Roman Catholic scholars have further conceded that the Lutheran confessional statement known as the Augsburg Confession of 1530 (written not by Luther but by Melanchthon) is, as was said at the time, "a pious and true catholic confession."
>
> When John XXIII called a council, he expressed the hope that the separated brethren of Protestantism would be brought into Catholicism. Many have taken this to mean that the Protestants would have to return to the fold…but his words and hopes were more profound than this. He envisaged a renewed and reformed Catholicism that could incorporate evangelical theology into itself and thereby allow the Luther protest finally to fulfil itself by restoring the Roman Catholic Church to the one truly holy catholic Church. It cannot become this until and unless it takes to itself the total witness of Luther for the Gospel, as well as his entire evangelical theology.[1297]

Luther's aim was never to divide or create a new Church, but only to reestablish the true original Church as it had been instituted by Christ and represented by apostolic witness found in the New Testament. Time had eroded the original design of the Founder and Luther found the Church focused upon serving itself as a secularized institution. Much had fallen away or been allowed to decay that embodied central doctrines or teachings of the Church as humanly devised innovations and heresies or foreign teachings emerged. All Luther sought was to bring the Church in its beliefs and practice to the vision and intent of Christ, it's Founder. For this reason and in the spirit of ecumenism I felt, encouraged, and supported naming the merging Lutheran denominations in 1988 the Evangelical Catholic Church (in America) which would reflect Luther's wishes that his followers not identify themselves as "Lutherans," but rather with the evangelical theology the Catholic Church was acknowledging and embracing, following the vision of Pope John XXIII.

Sinful human beings have a way of developing practices and ideas that seep into the life of the Church causing unnoticed *de-formatio* to take place. The Church and its congregations must always and continually examine their life and work to see whether it is in harmony with Christ's original intent and commission. Furthermore, they must constantly

---

[1297] Ibid., p.46.

be prepared to strengthen or rebuild essential things that have been weakened or eroded and to abolish innovations, additions, and abuses that hinder their purpose and partnering with God's mission.

How we love to major in the minors, making sure we go through the correct motions, procedures and processes that are of our making and not necessarily of the Spirit's, though thankfully the Spirit can cut through. From my experience in resourcing and supporting congregational ministry, and through conflicts arising over the color to paint ceilings in the sanctuary, patterns of carpet, and the "jot and tittle" of countless other issues that have no effect on the scales of eternity except that they detract and can usurp the purpose for being part of Christ's Body. While I understand and appreciate the value and necessity of "good order" it not only amazed but disappointed me that some members within the congregations could recite and worse, weaponize "St. Robert" of *Roberts Rules of Order* more readily than they could recall our Lord's or St. Paul's instruction in Scripture. I was led by the Spirit to share with congregations four helpful questions to consider in directing their focus on the purpose for which they were enlisted to be "The People of God – the Church:"

a). Before every meeting, every congregational decision ask the question: "Is what we're about to discuss right now worth the death of Jesus on the Cross?"
b). Before every gathering in this congregation, let's ask the question: "Is what we're doing right now, or fighting over right now, worth the shedding of Jesus' blood on the Cross?"
c). "Did Jesus die on the Cross so that we could be this kind of Church?"
d). "Isn't it time for us—the Church today—to put some points on the scoreboard of history like the first disciples did by *being* His heart, Hands and Voice?

Christ's Church must always be penitently willing to be reformed by Christ its founder. And discover the mind and will of the Founder is in the New Testament!

As Luther simply sought to reestablish the true original Church as it had been instituted and designed by Christ, so we witness a pugnacious President defending and preserving the legacy of America's founding with the immortal principles our nation's founders inscribed in the Declaration of Independence, the Constitution, and the Bill of Rights nearly two and a half centuries ago. At the first White House Conference on American History, held in the National Archives Museum, September 17, 2020, President Trump said:

> Our mission is to defend the legacy of America's founding, the virtue of America's heroes, and the nobility of the American character. We must clear away the twisted web of lies in our schools and classrooms, and teach our

> children the magnificent truth about our country. We want our sons and daughters to know that they are citizens of the most exceptional nation in the history of the world….
>
> On this very day in 1787, our Founding Fathers signed the Constitution at Independence Hall in Philadelphia. It was the fulfillment of a thousand years of Western civilization. Our Constitution was the product of centuries of tradition, wisdom, and experience. No political document has done more to advance the human condition or propel the engine of progress.[1298]

He sadly referenced "a radical movement" attempting to demolish this treasured and precious inheritance, "Left-wing mobs" tearing down statues of our founders, desecrating memorials, and carrying out a campaign of violence and anarchy—a total of 574 riots in our cities during the summer of 2020. They have chanted the words, "America was never great," and launched vicious assaults on law enforcement which is the universal symbol of the rule of law in America.

> Whether it is the mob in the street, or the cancel culture in the boardroom, the goal is the same: to silence dissent, to scare you out of speaking the truth, and to bully Americans into abandoning their values, their heritage, and their very way of life….In order to radically transform America, they must first cause Americans to lose confidence in who we are, where we came from and what we believe…The left has warped, distorted, and defiled the American story with deceptions, falsehoods, and lies. There is no better example than the *New York Times'* totally discredited 1619 Project [which] rewrites American history to teach our children that we were founded on the principle of oppression, not freedom. Nothing could be further from the truth. America's founding set in motion the unstoppable chain of events that abolished slavery, secured civil rights, defeated communism and fascism, and built the most fair, equal, and prosperous nation in human history.[1299]

1298 <https://trumpwhitehouse.archives.gov/briefings-statements/remarks-president-trump-white-house-conference-american-history/>.

1299 Ibid.

He also assailed the burning of American flags, the left-wing indoctrination in our schools and universities with the Marxist critical race theory holding that America is a wicked and racist nation. Imposed into workplace trainings, this theory alleges that concepts such as hard work, rational thinking, the nuclear family, and belief in God were not values that unite all Americans but were instead aspects of "whiteness."

> We embrace the vision of Martin Luther King, where children are not judged by the color of their skin but by the content of their character. The left is attempting to destroy that beautiful vision and divide Americans by race in the service of political power. By viewing every issue through the lens of race, they want to impose a new segregation, and we must not allow that to happen. Critical race theory, the 1619 Project, and the crusade against American history is toxic propaganda, ideological poison that, if not removed, will dissolve the civic bonds that tie us together. It will destroy our country.[1300]

Trump had just recently banned trainings in this "prejudiced ideology" from the federal government and to restore the urgent need for patriotic education in our schools, under his administration's leadership, the National Endowment for the Humanities awarded a grant to support the development of a pro-American curriculum that celebrates the truth about our nation's great history. He also announced that he would be signing an Executive Order establishing a national commission to promote patriotic education. It will be called the "1776 Commission" and will encourage educators to teach our children about the miracle of American history and make plans to honor the 250th anniversary of our founding. This follows his Executive Order establishing the National Garden of American Heroes which will be a vast park featuring statues of the greatest Americans who have ever lived and his previous order that if one demolishes a statue without permission, they immediately receive 10 years in prison.

There is no doubt that Trump loves America and he has been a refreshing break from the guilt and self-loathing that has marked our age. The America Trump wants to recover is, according to Thomas D. Klingenstein,* an America guided by relentless optimism and supported by grit and determination. An America which had done great things in the past

---

1300 Ibid.

* Thomas D. Klingenstein is a principal in the New York investment firm of Cohen, Klingenstein, LLC, the chairman of the Board of Directors of Claremont Institute, and a playwright.

and was eager to do more. An America properly confident in itself. Trump is still confident in America. In this time of national doubt this too is just what the doctor ordered."[1301]

Trump knows, as Luther knew in his era, it is time to take a stand, and for that we need strong individuals comfortable and confident in their own skin who have the backbone and stamina to "violate" the strictures of political correctness and take on the "expert" class which comprises so much of the "swamp." Weak individuals and leaders do anything to avoid admitting their errors and misplaced judgments, and they lack the resolve to do what truth demands from them, especially if it means being ridiculed, cancelled, and censored for as much as using the wrong pronoun.

Mark Bauerlein,* writes in *Political Magazine*† that

> Trump exposed how overrated the elites really are. Ordinary Americans looked at the elite zones of academia, Hollywood, Silicon Valley, Wall Street and Washington itself, and saw a bunch of self-serving, not very competent individuals sitting pretty, who had enriched themselves and let the rest of America slide…It wasn't Trump's politics that disgusted the college presidents, celebrity actors, Google VPs, D.C. operatives and the rest. It was because he pinpointed them as the problem—the reason factories and small stores had closed, unemployment was bad, and PC culture had cast them as human debris. And millions cheered. This was unforgivable to the elites. They sputtered in reply, which only confirmed that our betters aren't so smart or skilled or savvy, and not so virtuous either, though very good at self-help. The outburst was a long time coming. Trump gave it an outlet and the

---

1301 Klingenstein, Thomas D., "Trump's Virtues," *The American Mind*, March 2, 2022. <https://americanmind.org/salvo/trumps-virtues/> see also, Mathews, M.B. "I was Wrong About Trump," *American Thinker*, July 27, 2022. *<https://www.americanthinker.com/articles/2022/07/i_was_wrong_about_trump.html>*.

* Mark Bauerlein, a contributing editor at First Things and professor emeritus of English at Emory University, is the author of *The Dumbest Generation Grows Up: From Stupefied Youth to Dangerous Adults* (Regnery Gateway, Washington D.C., 2022) a sequel to his earlier *The Dumbest Generation: How the Digital Age Stupefies Young Americans and Jeopardizes Our Future (Or, Don't Trust Anyone Under 30*, (Jeremy P. Tarcher/Penquin, New York, NY, 2008).

† *Politico Magazine* asked "a group of 35 smart political and cultural observers to tell us what big, new insights this [Trumpian] era has given them about America—and what that insight means for the country's future." The cover theme reports, "What "Trump Showed Us About America." *Politico Magazine*, November 20, 2020.

> scorn for men and women at the top of our country is now widespread and frank. It's not going to pass any time soon.[1302]

Trump demonstrated just how powerful the elitists are being in control of all the cultural and economic powers in America and yet how far removed they are from so many of the "other" Americans who believe the system is not working for them. It is not only those who create the knowledge and the media content people consume which Trump has labeled "Fake News," but also those in position of political and other decision-making power. Trump revealed, not caused, the divide in this country. There are those who have trashed America's Founding and her history—literally erasing and rewriting it—to the point where some believe it is virtuous to hate America. Rather than advocating forgiveness where our country has sinned and urging our citizens to therefore strive toward a more perfect union, we are confronted by those advocating hairshirts,*...self-flagellation, and perpetual guilt.

Tom Nichols† who was also invited to respond to *Politico Magazine's* inquiry on "What Trump Showed Us About America," and a self-described Never Trump conservative wrote:

> Our system of government is almost entirely dependent on shared cultural norms and traditions about democracy and accountability. If we are not willing to hold our elected officials—and each other—responsible for guarding those traditions, then the law and even the Constitution itself might not be enough to sustain our democratic republic.

[1302] Bauerlein, Mark, "Trump Exposed How Overrated the Elites Really Are," *Politico Magazine*, Nov. 19, 2020.

* A hairshirt is a coarse garment made from rough animal hair, usually that of goats, intended to be worn against the skin, keeping the wearer in a state of discomfort and constant awareness of one's need for penance and constant reminder of faith so as to better avoid the temptation to sin. Some hairshirts even included bits of spiked metal meant to inflict pain and injury on the wearer. In Biblical times it was the Jewish custom to wear a hairshirt (sackcloth) when mourning or in a public show of repentance for sin (Genesis 37:34, 2 Samuel 3:31, Esther 4:1). In the New Testament, John the Baptist wore "a garment of camel's hair" as a means of repentance.

† Tom Nichols is a professor of strategy at the U.S. Naval War College and was named a fellow at the John F. Kennedy School of Government at Harvard as well as an adjunct faculty member. He is the author of *The Death of Expertise: The Campaign against Established Knowledge and Why It Matters*, Oxford University Press, New York, NY, 2017.

> In the past, we assumed that the existence of laws or constitutional requirements was sufficient to protect our rights and our institutions. We fell back on these codified and written statutes as insurance against our own behavior and insulation from our political choices...The "law" does not guarantee that we are protected by the rule of law; our commitment to rule of law as a basic value is what protects us and our rights. The Constitution does not automatically enforce itself. Institutions do not renew themselves like some kind of perennial garden; they require our actual care and attention.[1303]

We have to care about whether the laws are faithfully executed and equally administered, whether impartial justice is served; the press is honest and unbiased; elections are conducted fairly insuring one person one vote, whether the oaths our leaders take were spoken with sincerity. We have to care deeply about all of these things and more as active, involved participants in our representative democracy. Unfortunately we have seen these past few years how street politics and electoral politics run neck-and-neck. Our democracy is only as good as the people—all of us—participating.

Most of us have known, but never really had anyone champion like Trump has done that we, not the Swamp, know better how to manage our money, our time, our personal lives, our resources, and our families. We have seen more than just the creeping authoritarian mindsets taking over these uniquely personal functions and replace them with governmental overreach by so-called "experts" who believe they know better than the average American The autocratic experience projected has been "We're in charge. You are not! We know what's best!" We received more than a taste of that desire during the pandemic with COVID mandates to wear masks, to wash hands, distance and not gather in large numbers, not even for family reunions, get vaxxed, boostered, and in the closure of businesses, schools and churches. Perhaps the silver lining was what COVID's home zoom classes revealed about what children—even very young children—were being taught as they were sexualized, perverted, permitted to self-declare their gender, deliberately being alienated from their parents, and taught to hate America and white people.

President Trump has smoked rats out of their hiding places, calling a spade a spade, not always politely, but as always being forceful, authentic, and unmistakably clear. As a result,

---

1303 Nichols, Tom. "The Law and Even the Constitution Itself Might Not Be Enough to Sustain Our Democratic Republic," *Politico Magazine*, Nov. 19, 2020. <https://www.politico.com/news/magazine/2020/11/19/roundup-what-trump-showed-us-about-america-435762>.

we now know our intelligence agencies, especially those in the highest ranks are corrupt, have been weaponizing these agencies against Trump and the Republicans, and that the mainstream media is not just biased but colludes and provides cover being the propaganda arm of the Democratic Party. What is frightening is the under-informed, easily led minions, who faithfully absorb the bald-faced lies and propaganda they are fed without questioning nor investigation. Social media has allowed propaganda to be crowdsourced, and in the process those ill-informed servants of the "Big Brother" *Newspeak's** repeat and spread "official alternative facts" or falsification of historical events from George Orwell's and now President Biden's "Ministry of Truth."

> The Department of Homeland Security (DHS) has announced the formation of the Disinformation Governance Board charged with "countering misinformation related to homeland security, focused specifically on irregular migration and Russia." In a twist too implausible for fiction, the abbreviation is DGB, one letter off from KGB."[1304]

This "Ministry of Truth" will be under the leadership of DHS Secretary Alejandro Mayorkas who is presiding over the worst border crisis of our lifetimes, yet who publicly denies it is a crisis while privately admitting it is. And the person who is to lead this new "Committee of Public Information" is Nina Jankowicz, who calls herself "a disinformation fellow" and a "Russian disinformation expert." Before the 2020 election she claimed the Hunter Biden's "laptop from hell" was "a Trump campaign product" and has been a big fan of the now-discredited (and laughable) Steele dossier.[1305] Evidently, incorrect political opinions become a national-security threat as has been inferred about parents who speak out in opposition to their school boards' decisions regarding curriculum. The goal of combating mis- and disinformation, guided by those "experts" who will separate the informational wheat from the dis-informational chaff. But there's one small problem with empowering "truth experts": Experts are people!

---

* *Newspeak* is the fictional language of Oceania, a totalitarian superstate that is the setting of the 1949 dystopian novel, *Nineteen Eighty-Four* by George Orwell.

[1304] <https://www.wsj.com/articles/biden-establishes-a-ministry-of-truth-disinformation-governance-board-partisan-11651432312>.

[1305] <https://thehill.com/opinion/white-house/3472878-joe-bidens-ministry-of-truth/>.

While I *want to believe* that truth wins out, I sadly have to agree with Nicholas Carr* who comes to the conclusion that "the problem won't be solved by a naïve faith in truth's innate power to prevail over fabrication. Nor will it be solved by the removal from office of a mendacious president [or other leaders]. Without far-reaching institutional, educational and legal remedies, lies will continue to trump truth."[1306]

Trump plays to win and when you're right you have a moral duty not just to fight but to win for "We the People." Luther stands against the powers that are in Church and State for the people who where likewise being ignored and taken advantage of for their own majestic power and control.

Trump understands that what Americans of all races and creeds desire are stable and safe communities, and the opportunities to raise their families in a culture that values industriousness, self-reliance, patriotism, and freedom. We have witnessed the most towering political figure in living memory who has had the uncommon courage and firmness of purpose not only to speak out for the people, but by taking an active stand on their behalf in Making America Great Again. Trump has refused to join the permanent government of professional elites who have established themselves as the vital center between the people and the government. In his view, elite intellectual rule had undercut the political authority of the people as sovereign. Instead he has inspired a movement and if properly deployed might challenge the elite woke-comms with the reality that "'We the People' are more powerful than those elitists in power." We have a voice! It is our responsibility as Americans to activate our privileged status as free citizens—not enslaved subjects—of both Church and State and take our stand with the fortitude and backbone we have witnessed in our valiant and fearless warriors, Martin Luther and Donald Trump. They faced the relentless gale-force winds in the eye of the storm that we too are likely to encounter should we make a stand and reclaim this nation to be "under God" so that it in the words of Abraham Lincoln this government is "of the people, by the people, and for the people," not of unaccountable bureaucrats, by the self-styled elitists, and for only the powerful to exercise control solely for their benefit. To not do this but take the default position of cowering in the face of intimidation is to ignore the lessons of our founding, the Reformation, and of our most recent past and it will be forever to our sorrow to have ignored those lessons.

---

* Nicholas Carr is a writer covering technology, economics, and culture. His book *The Shallows: What the Internet is Doing to Our Brains* was a Pulitzer Prize finalist.

1306 Carr, Nicholas, "Unfortunately, Lies Can Trump Truth," *Political Magazine*, Nov. 19, 2020. <https://www.politico.com/news/magazine/2020/11/19/roundup-what-trump-showed-us-about-america-435762>.

That Luther and Trump are both still standing is an unrecognized tribute to their resilience, stamina, and willpower to fight it out to the bitter end, not giving up when bullied and subjected to levels of unwarranted abuse. My hope is certainly that for the generations that follow, it will not take 500 years to acknowledge what now the Catholic (Universal) Church is realizing that Luther, who had been rejected and mocked, was indeed a prophet and possessed Light in lifting high the banner of Truth that has benefited the Church and humankind. May it not take 500 years for our Country to waken from our wokeness to fully enjoy that for which Trump stood and fought: life, liberty and the pursuit of happiness for all. Unless "We the People" speak up, unless we stand up, the country won't wake up. The bigger the government the smaller and less significant is the individual which betrays Biblical and Democratic values.

In the thoughtful reflection of John Marini,[*] a Senior Fellow of the Claremont Institute and professor of political science at the University of Nevada-Reno,

> It remains to be seen if the American people understand or will come to understand themselves as political citizens of the nation-state, or as administrative subjects of a rational [chimerical[†]] global order. Much depends upon whether the American people have become so dependent upon the administrative state that the overthrow of the established order is not merely difficult, but undesirable. In that case, political self-government, and individual freedom, will cease to be important elements of the American regime.[1307]

---

[*] John Marini served in the Reagan Administration as a special assistant to the chairman of the U.S. Equal Employment Opportunity Commission. His latest book is *Unmasking the Administrative State: The Crisis of American Politics in the Twenty-First Century.*

[†] "chimerical" is defined as existing only as the product of unchecked imagination, hoped for but illusionary or impossible to achieve.

[1307] Marini, John, "After Trump: The Pollitical and Moral Legitimacy of American Government," The American Mind, October 23, 2018. <https://americanmind.org/salvo/the-political-and-moral-conditions-of-legitimacy-after-trump/>.

38

Epilogue

As we have witnessed, neither Luther nor Trump have always been very nice men. Some very conspicuous blemishes mar both our warriors' reputation. To be completely candid, their transgressions could be viewed as downright reprehensible, and both have unrivaled gifts for fighting dirty. They give unabashed evidence of taking no time or often just reacting off-the-cuff to deconstruct their opponents' arguments, and often with a dose of denigrating insults and crass epithets. Using today's language, we can be appalled at their seemingly arrogant demeanor and cutting sarcasm. And both have been given to inflammatory—even vulgar—rhetoric and behavior deemed especially inappropriate for the offices and roles to which they ascended. It would be folly to pretend that such colossal defects did not exist in these populist disruptors.

Equally true, one could question whether we have ever witnessed more malevolence than what we have observed being directed toward the Reformer 500 years ago or this President being blamed for every outlandish or hellish circumstance in this country and on Earth in general. According to countless publications and the talking heads of obvious low-information TV stations, it's all Donald's fault. He did it. It was him. He gets the blame. And in the midst of such unbridled hostility exhibited by countless opponents, media factions, and malcontent losers with their accusations, condemnation, vicious wrath, have we ever seen more resilient individuals enduring the countless ugly onslaughts inflicted by their enemies' irrational rage? Born for their times, these twin warriors have battled near impossible odds which would have hobbled or crushed most, and yet make their enduring *stands* in defense of and out of love for Church and country.

We ourselves at times can be crass and crude as can some of those individuals we tremendously respect and hold in extremely high degree, but do so in their own polite and artificial way. I find Victor Davis Hanson's* analysis more honest:

---

* Victor Davis Hanson is an American commentator, former classics professor at California State University, Fresno, and military historian. He has been a commentary on contemporary politics for the *New York Times*, *Wall Street Journal*, *National Review*, *The Washington Times* and other media outlets. Currently he is a Senior Fellow at Stanford University's Hoover Institution.

> I would prefer a supposed braggart cracking down on China, or a purported narcissist closing the border, or an alleged demagogue promising change in the Rust Belt than any more sermons from privileged gentlemen conservatives that tolerating illegal immigration "is an act of love," or silent agreement that those manufacturing "jobs are not coming back"...
>
> Crassness is not a requisite for needed change, but so often in a flawed world the two are shared, in the reverse fashion that gaseous pieties are frequently voiced by the sober and judicious. But all this is irrelevant when we consider what Trump *did* rather than what he *said.* I mean not just that action matters more than rhetoric, but rather to evaluate Trump by the general past standards of presidential comportment rather than through Platonic ideals. Trump is less randy and gross in office than were reckless and sexually cruel but now revered icons like John F. Kennedy or Bill Clinton. He has not weaponized the federal government for political advantage in the manner of Barack Obama (who may go down soon as the most corrupt president since Warren G. Harding).
>
> Trump, of "Crooked Hillary," "lock her up," and "Sleepy Joe" infamy, was more likely to react concretely to the plight of the inner city and the economic aspirations of minorities and the white working class, who were not just crushed by globalization but so often ignored by their supposed champions of both parties...That Trump withstood such illegal, unconstitutional, and unethical venom also says something about those who dished it our—and, in the end, did so viciously and yet so impotently.[1308]

From an unsuspected foreigner, former Russian Presidential Chief of Staff and a top adviser to Putin, Sergei Ivanov, comes a surprisingly positive evaluation of President Donald Trump:

> Sergei Ivanov, top adviser and former chief of staff to Russian President Vladimir Putin, said that "Former President Donald Trump embodies the authentic American spirit of self-determination, unwavering optimism and rugged resilience championed by the nation's Founding Fathers—and that's why Democrats and other globalists hate him," according to Samantha

[1308] Hanson, Victor Davis, "Trumpism—A Look Backward and Forward to November," *American Greatness*, August 16, 2020. <https://amgreatness.com/2020/08/16/trumpism-a-look-backward-and-forward-to-november/> or <https://americanmind.org/salvo/trumpism-a-look-backward-and-forward-to-november/>.

Chang of the *Western Journal*....his triumphs shined a glaring spotlight on their own failures. In a stinging *EurAsia Daily* op-ed on Feb 16, 2021, Ivanov slammed the globalists for attacking and obstructing Trump and then said "perhaps the best president in the history of the United States, is "The Modern George Washington."

If the first president of America fought to lay the foundation of the nation and state—the beginning of American freedom—then Trump fought and is fighting to preserve the legacy of the founding fathers to defend freedom." Ivanov continued: "He, like Washington, is the flesh of his people, 100 percent American, a classic self-made man, a living embodiment of the American dream. Trump is a successful entrepreneur, a man of action and a man of his word." Then he rattled off a list of Trump's accomplishments...and noted that he had achieved all of this despite around-the-clock media attacks and nonstop obstructionism from the Democratic Party... "Almost immediately after Trump came to the White House, the 'deep state' functionaries from both parties—not only politicians and 'public figures,' but also civil servants—provided unprecedented opposition to all of his endeavors, did everything to suppress America's impulse for Freedom," he wrote.

Ivanov said the deep state also hated that Trump was a populist champion for religious freedom, family values and constitutional rights such as the First and Second Amendments.... "Thanks to his historic victory, everyone who 'has eyes' can see where the 'world elite' is leading and who it is serving. See and fight for your future," he exhorted...His greatest achievement might be simply opening Americans' eyes to how deceptive the establishment media are and how sinister and corrupt the deep state truly is.[1309]

From another perspective, which should be most apparent, what if our thoughts, words and deeds were being recorded and subject to the judgment of our adversaries or a hostile jury of our contemporaries, would we fare very well? But as we began, we can be grateful we are known by the merciful One who came to call us His own beloved, *"sinners of His own*

1309 Chang, Samantha, "Putin's Former Chief of Staff Calls Trump the 'Modern George Washington,' Reveals Why Globalists Hated Him," *Western Journal*, March 13, 2021. <https://kithandkinobserver.wordpress.com/2021/03/13/putins-former-chief-of-staff-calls-trump-the-modern-george-washington-reveals-why-globalists-hated-him/> and <http://independentfilmnewsandmedia.com/putins-former-chief-of-staff-comes-forward-says-trump-is-the-modern-george-washington-terrifies-globalists/>.

redeeming"[1310] who have been gifted with an abundance of undeserved love, acceptance, and life everlasting. Rather than canonize our heroes on the one hand, or demonize them on the other, we can humanize them, accepting them as real persons who have both strengths and weaknesses. We may not always approve of the language they use, the points of view they espouse, the actions they take, or their lifestyle—but thankfully we don't have to! As fellow human beings created in the image of God, we are called upon to accept them as those whom God also loves! In our polarized society today, that is unfortunately increasingly more difficult to do. It is challenging, isn't it, especially with those you care about and love who feel very differently than you on critical issues to discard their opinions without discarding them?

It is easy to understand why people, especially those who are "Lutherans," want to ignore or seek to justify Luther's negatives. After all, he has been our hero in the faith for 500 years. Yet he was, as we have discovered, certainly not without his warts. It is hard to find unflawed heroes! Luther was not the perfect man nor our ultimate hero. There were colossal defects in the great Reformer's character which we haven't shied away from. Yet, he understood clearly that Jesus Christ who died for him—and for us—is the hero of this story and every story, because history is "His Story." Undeniably he was nevertheless used mightily by a gracious God to change Christendom and the world forever. Perhaps while acknowledging his humanity and sinfulness, which he understood better than anyone, we might ask whether his failures and struggles hinder, negate or cancel the Gospel work God affected through this man? Note again the pastoral and spiritual counsel Luther wrote to his friend Jerome Weller, whom we've met previously, living with the Luther family for eight years from 1527 to 1535 tutoring their children. Weller had turned from the study of law to theology under Luther's influence. His shyness and modesty contributed to his suffering fits of depression and spiritual despair, aggravated by a scrupulous conscience which his mentor could empathize with so easily. This letter of consolation is embedded in the core of Truth to which Luther was so deeply committed, even if it meant his death. It was sent to Jerome by Luther who was away from home in July 1530:

> When the devil throws our sins up to us and declares that we deserve death and hell, we ought to speak thus: "I admit that I deserve death and hell. What of it? Does this mean that I shall be sentenced to eternal damnation? By no means! For I know One who suffered and made satisfaction in my behalf. His name is Jesus Christ, Son of God. Where He is, there I shall be also!"[1311]

[1310] LBW, "Burial of the Dead," p.211; or *ELW*, "Funeral," p.283.

[1311] Martin Luther, *Letters of Spiritual Counsel*, trans. and ed. Theodore G. Tappert (Philadelphia: The Westminster Press, 1960, reprint Vancouver: Regent College Publishing, 2003), pp. 86–87.

I've heard and read several times, from catechism days through sermons and courses in college and seminary, that whenever Luther found himself tempted by the devil, he would write in chalk on his desk "*baptizatus sum*" (Latin for "I am baptized!"). Oberman in his biography quotes Luther: "The only way to drive away the Devil is through faith in Christ, by saying 'I have been baptized. I am a Christian.'"[1312] As a "chalk" reminder of one's baptism, I have provided for parishioners, friends and acquaintances a shower tag which reads: "Lord, as I enter the water to bathe, I remember my baptism. Wash me by Your grace. Fill me with Your Spirit. Renew my soul. I pray that I might live as Your child today, and honor You in all that I do."

Luther discovered that perfection is simply out of anyone's grasp, and thus welcomed the divine inspiration that God's gracious forgiveness and acceptance as a child of a loving Father applied to him and all who embrace the work, the death and resurrection, of His perfect Son, Jesus Christ, on their behalf.

As for Donald Trump, many have been willing or persuaded to overlook his faults and omissions, in the expectation that if it takes such stubborn brash haughtiness and pomposity to effectively deliver in the face of resistance, opposition and harassment from the establishment and Deep State's swamp, they can handle it and it's better than the alternative. An election in America should not be a personality contest any more than based on the gender, race or religion of a candidate, but rather on one's qualifications and demonstrated abilities. Golf legend Jack Nicholas argues, "It's about patriotism, policies, and the people they impact."[1313] Yet, a major theme emerged from a national survey of Americans showing "attitudes toward Trump appear to be chiefly driven by his personality and not by his policy or his ideology."[1314]

From another perspective, because we too have feet of clay and know ourselves, our preferences and biases, we sometimes feel embarrassed and obliged to gloss over or excuse that which is distasteful about our religious heroes and our political representatives because, if they are wrong, we feel diminished. Despite such recognition, we do not do justice to their legacy or history by ignoring the faults and failings of Luther and Trump; conversely, neither should those failures so prejudice us that we are blinded to their positive contributions and accomplishments.

1312 Oberman, *Devil*, p.105. The endnote references WATr 6. no.6830; 217, 26f.

1313 <https://www.cbsnews.com/news/jack-nicklaus-endorses-president-trump-for-re-election>.

1314 <https://abcnews.go.com/Politics/incompetent-strong-egotistical-words-people-describe-trump/story?id=50178088>.

Intriguingly, Martin Luther and Donald Trump both comprehend they have human foibles—neither heroes nor villains, but human beings with both merits and faults. God has proven relentlessly throughout history that He can accomplish incredibly important things through those who are not perfect. Both our populist warriors reveal that they are indeed flawed and sinful, like you and me. The difficulty is we not only want our warriors to fix things, but to be perfect doing it!

Mathew Block, Communications Manager for the International Lutheran Council, and editor of *The Canadian Lutheran* magazine, claims that

> when you think about it, that is the Good News of the Gospel. God justifies us "*despite*" our failings. He covers us with the blood of Christ and forgives our sin. The recognition that we are "*simul justus et peccator*" (at the same time righteous and a sinner) is a cornerstone of the faith rediscovered by Luther. On the one hand, we understand that we are sinners because of our evil inclinations and actions; on the other hand, we know we are saints because God has forgiven us. [Block contends that] It is Luther's sinfulness itself which illustrates why his message remains so vital today…we remember Luther not because he was always nice, not because he was always good, and certainly not because he was always right. He wasn't. Instead, we remember Luther because he directed attention always away from himself to Christ. It is to Christ we look for salvation, not our own holiness.[1315]

This is the very context of Luther's oft-quoted and much-maligned "sin boldly" comments in his letter to Philip Melanchthon on August 1, 1521:

> If you are a preacher of grace, then preach a true and not a fictitious grace. If grace is true, you must bear a true and not a fictitious sin. God does not save those who are only fictitious sinners. Be a sinner and sin boldly* but believe

[1315] Block, Matthew, "Standing with Martin Luther—Remembering a Sinful Saint, February 18, 2014, *First Things*; <https://www.firstthings.com/blogs/firstthoughts/2014/02/standing-with-martin-luther-1>.

* Passages such as this were misunderstood and used as the main arguments against Luther. He was interpreted as encouraging laxity and licentiousness instead of letting one's sins be strong so that you fully recognize your transgressions for what they are. For an excellent understanding of this statement, see W.H.T. Dau, *Luther Examined and Re-examined* (St. Louis, 1917), pp.111ff, also p.12.

> and rejoice in Christ even more boldly, for He is victorious over sin, death, and the world.... Pray boldly—you too are a mighty sinner.[1316]

It is to Christ that we look for salvation, not ourselves, as Luther discovered in the Scriptures he had been studying and which blossomed before him. Luther is calling us to be honest about our sin—coming clean about ourselves and recognizing sin's severity—so that we understand our need for Christ more fully. This leads to that freedom Luther experienced, as Kathryn Kleinhans explains:

> Since Christ died for "true" sinners rather than "fictitious sinners," Christians need not be paralyzed by the fear of making the wrong choice or doing the wrong thing. Justified by faith rather than by "getting it right," the Christian is free to act, accepting the possibility of failure while trusting in Christ's victory over sin and death. Thus, the life of Christian vocation is characterized by daily dying and rising.[1317]
>
> As long as we are here [in this world] we have to sin [We will commit sins while we are here]." Luther continues. "This life is not the dwelling place of righteousness [where justice resides], but as Peter says (2 Peter 3:13) we look for new heavens and a new earth in which righteousness dwells [where justice will reign]. It is enough that by the riches of God's glory we have come to know the Lamb that takes away the sin of the world (John 1:29).[1318]

Thus, I definitely can understand individuals who raise questions and concerns about supporting Trump when he thinks, speaks or acts as he does. Do we have to give him a pass and abandon our idealism by lowering the standards we expect from our leaders and others? Certainly not! But just as true, we need to honor the office of the President and continually remind ourselves that Luther and we should take seriously St. Paul's words in Romans 13:1 (NRSV): *"Let every person be subject to the governing authorities; for there is no authority except from God, and those authorities that exist have been instituted by God."*

1316 LW 48:281-282. *Letters I*, "To Philip Melanchthon, Wartburg, August 1, 1517."

1317 Kleinhans, Kathryn, "The Work of a Christian: Vocation in Lutheran Perspective," *Word & World*, 25:4, Fall 2005; <https://wordandworld.luthersem.edu/content/pdfs/25-4_Work_and_Witness/25-4_Kleinhans.pdf>, p.400.

1318 LW 48:282. *Letters I*, "To Philip Melanchthon, Wartburg, August 1, 1521."

Maybe we can find helpful suggestions from the funeral sermon Luther preached for one of his political leaders, Elector John of Saxony, where he attempted a bold move to unite supporters and detractors of the deceased official. "I shall not praise [Elector John] for his great virtues, but rather let him remain a sinner like all the rest of us…and praise the fact that he confessed Christ's death and resurrection before the whole world, and he stuck to it…"[1319] knowing his sins had been forgiven. Instead of highlighting virtues and lamenting one's vices, Luther demonstrated the need to unite the people in the Gospel rather than on political parties and platforms. M. Hopson Boulot points to Luther's example as a timely reminder that

> Politics are secondary, not primary…. He was first and foremost not a German citizen, but a citizen of heaven (Philippians 3:23). American Christians would do well to hold our political affiliations loosely while we cling to the Gospel with a vice grip. Yes, let's fight for truth and justice and pray for righteousness to prevail. Yes, let's labor to see the government exercise the sword in a God-honoring way that leads to human flourishing. Yes, let's vote for leaders who will *"act justly, love mercy, and walk humbly with our God"* (Micah 6:8). Yes, let's hope and pray for President Donald Trump. Let's praise him whenever he promotes what is just and good. Let's lovingly rebuke him whenever he promotes what is harmful and evil. But let us remember that our hope is not built on any presidency past, present, or future.[1320]
>
> *My hope is built on nothing less, then Jesus' blood and righteousness. No merit of my own I claim, but wholly lean on Jesus' name.*
>
> *On Christ the Solid Rock I stand all other ground is sinking sand.*[1321]

Or as Russell Moore, President of the Southern Baptist Ethics & Religious Liberty Commission says, Christians "are Americans best when we're not Americans first."[1322] *"Our*

[1319] LW 51:236-37. *Sermons I*, "Sermon at the Funeral of the Elector, Duke John of Saxony, August 18, 1552."

[1320] Boutot, Hopson, personal website, November 14 2016. <http://www.poquosonbaptist.org/blog/?p=170>.

[1321] Mote, Edward, "My Hope Is Built on Nothing Less," LBW Hymn 293; LW Hymn 368; ELW Hymn 596; LSB Hymn 575.

[1322] Moore, Russell, *Onward: Engaging the Culture without Losing the Gospel* (Nashville: B&H Publishing Group, 2015), p.160.

citizenship is in heaven" (Philippians 3:20 [NRSV]). Hence it is helpful for believers to be reminded that we do not elect a Messiah-in-chief to occupy the White House, but rather recognize that whoever is elected will thus not be the ideal leader but a sinner, and like all of his or her predecessors make some appalling mistakes. It is, however, imperative that we acknowledge the One who occupies heaven's throne is sovereign over heaven and earth, and the One whom we, and hopefully our leaders, will look to for guidance and wisdom as we worship and follow Him who is Lord overall.

Again, let Luther remind us that "Scripture declares that God established the states of masters and subjects, and that temporal government is His…[citing] Daniel 4:17 and 5:21: '*The most high God rules over the kingdom of men and sets over it whom He will*,' not whom we will or think. Daniel is simply saying that temporal government is purely and solely a gift and grace of God, which no man can establish or maintain by his own wisdom or strength."[1323]

Donald Trump is unique and seems to many to lack spiritual roots, at least not very deep roots. Like most people, his religious journey began with his parents. "His father was the descendant of German Lutherans," reveals Wesley Baines,* and his mother hailed from an especially religious part of Scotland, and was a devoted Presbyterian, raising her children in the same tradition."[1324]

When Donald was 28, his family transferred from First Presbyterian Church in Jamaica, Queens, to Marble Collegiate, where Donald developed a close relationship with Pastor Norman Vincent Peale. The renowned pastor became a significant figure in his life and presided at the wedding of Trump and his first wife Ivana in 1977. Peale of course is the author of *The Power of Positive Thinking*, which asserts that living a faithful life can translate into the blessings of material success, a central tenet of prosperity theology. The President certainly prides himself on being "successful," "rich" and "a winner," while being "a loser" is one of his weapons of choice in his demeaning verbal arsenal. In Wesley Baines's assessment of Donald Trump's worldview, "success is everything. To put it simply, winning is equated with good, and losers are equated with bad. This is strikingly similar to the attitude of some Evangelicals, wherein those who experience grave misfortune must have sinned or

---

[1323] LW 14:53-54. *Selected Psalms III*, "Psalm 118.

* Wesley Baines is a graduate student at Regent University's School of Divinity, and a freelance writer working in the fields of spirituality, self-help and religion.

[1324] Baines, Wesley, "The Strange Faith of Donald Trump: The Odd Religious Journey," *Beliefnet Newsletter*. <https://www.beliefnet.com/news/politics/the-strange-faith-of-donald-trump.aspx>.

suffered from a lack of faith to deserve that misfortune,"[1325] which is a complete distortion of Biblical orthodoxy that The Reformation reclaimed. I'm reminded of the line given by Adlai Stevenson, a Unitarian, running unsuccessfully for the presidency a second time in 1956, to a religious convention that Norman Vincent Peale had already addressed. Stevenson quipped, "Speaking as a Christian, I find the Apostle Paul appealing and the Apostle Peale appalling."[1326]

More recently, Barbara Walters caught candidate Trump off-guard, asking in her characteristically blunt manner, "If you lose the Republican nomination, are you a loser?" Stunned and momentarily deflated, Trump paused before reluctantly replying. "In a certain way, yeah. Hate to say it. If I lost the nomination, yeah, I guess I'd call myself a loser. I never said that about myself before."[1327]

We certainly do not have the vast autobiographical material on Trump's faith journey as Luther has provided, but he has shared significant views and understandings that have become guiding lights into decisions he has made and actions he has taken. In proclaiming January 16, 2018, as Religious Freedom Day, President Trump acknowledged that "Faith is embedded in the history, spirit, and soul of our Nation.... Our forefathers, seeking refuge from religious persecution, believed in the eternal Truth that freedom is not a gift from government, but a sacred right from Almighty God."[1328]

In his Freedom Rally address at the Kennedy Center in Washington, July 1, 2017, Trump cited the Declaration of Independence—our national birth certificate—affirming that our

> liberty comes from Our Creator.... Our rights are given to us by God and no earthly force can ever take those rights away. That is why my administration is transferring power out of Washington and returning that power back to where it belongs: to the people.... For too long, politicians have tried...to centralize authority among the hands of a small few in our nation's capital.... Bureaucrats think they can run over your lives, overrule your values, meddle in your faith and tell you how to live, what to say and where to pray. But we know," he continued, "that parents, not bureaucrats know best how to

---

1325 Ibid.

1326 <https://www.catholic.com/magazine/online-edition/appealing-and-appalling>.

1327 Walters, Barbara, interview with Donald Trump. <https://www.missioalliance.org/donald-trump-good-evangelicals>.

1328 <https://www.whitehouse.gov/presidential-actions/president-donald-j-trump-proclaims-january-16-2018-religious-freedom-day>.

> raise their children and create a thriving society. And we know that families and churches, not government officials, know best how to create a strong, loving community.... Above all else, we know this: in America we don't worship government, we worship God.... We understand that a country is more than just its geography. A nation is the sum of its citizens, their hopes, their dreams, their aspirations. As long as our country remains true to its values, loyal to its heroism and devoted to its Creator, then our best days are yet to come.[1329]

President Trump's remarks reflect a sentiment that President Reagan used in a Q&A with state and local officials during a White House briefing, May 28, 1981. He brought a quote from Cal Coolidge in 1926 which he read:

> No method of procedure has ever been devised by which liberty could be divorced from local self-government. No plan of centralization has ever been adopted which did not result in bureaucracy, tyranny, inflexibility, reaction, and decline. Of all forms of government, those administered by bureaus are about the least satisfactory to an enlightened and progressive people. Being irresponsible, they become autocratic. And being autocratic, they resist all development. Unless bureaucracy is constantly resisted, it breaks down representative government and overwhelms democracy. It is the one element in our institutions that sets up the pretense of having authority over everybody and being responsible to nobody.[1330]

Launching action to promote religious freedom at the National Day of Prayer, May 3, 2018, President Trump said

> The faith initiative will help design new policies that recognize the vital role of faith in our families, our communities, and our great country. This office will also help ensure that faith-based organizations have equal access to government funding and the equal right to exercise their deeply held beliefs. We take this step because we know that, in solving the many, many problems and our great challenges, faith is more powerful than government, and

---

1329 <https://factba.se/transcript/donald-trump-speech-celebrate-freedom-rally-july-1-2017>.

1330 <https://www.reaganlibrary.gov/research/speeches/52881a>.

nothing is more powerful than God.... Faith has shaped our families and it's shaped our communities, [he said]. It's inspired our commitment to charity and our defense of liberty, and faith has forged the identity and the destiny of this great nation that we all love. [In addition, Trump affirmed that]...prayer changes hearts and transforms lives. It uplifts the soul, inspires action, and unites us all as one nation under God.... Our country was founded on prayer. Our communities are sustained by prayer. And our nation will be renewed by hard work, a lot of intelligence, and prayer.[1331]

Faith Shapes and Prayer Sustains Families, Communities and Nation

Reforming Prayer: Martin Luther and the Heart of the Reformation

The Reformer Prays with His Family
Left: Public domain, retrieved at the Reformisso website

President Calls on Country to Pray as the Coronavirus Spreads

The President Prays with His Cabinet
Right: Doug Mills/New York Times

Love him or hate him, you cannot ignore him. Donald Trump stunned the political world in 2016 when he became the first person without government or military experience ever to be elected President of the United States. His credentials have been his successes in business and real estate, and as the centerpiece and driving force of *The Apprentice* TV franchise. His self-assurance, which some consider to be cocky or arrogant, is a determining characteristic of his success, and a necessary trait for any leader attempting to influence

[1331] Trump, Donald, "National Day of Prayer Address." <https://www.whitehouse.gov/briefings-Statements/remarks-president-trump-national-day-prayer>.

others. He is familiar with taking calculated risks and having high expectations for himself and those around him. He is extremely confident and able to dream big, even to believe he has what it takes to "Make America Great Again" by giving corrective attention to the fissures he saw being revealed in American society. While some may find his rhetoric and "in your face" style off-putting, others find it refreshing. It is this self-assuredness that has been responsible for helping him succeed in turning his undertakings into gold. He isn't afraid to stand out and go after what he wants, and definitely doesn't believe in hiding his light under the proverbial bushel basket. He has shown that he is not a follower or a "brown-noser." He isn't afraid to go against the grain, even if it means ruffling a few feathers or being unpopular with the majority. He doesn't allow the status quo or other people's opinion of him to influence his thoughts or dictate his actions, and certainly isn't afraid to voice or tweet his views. He leaves little doubt that he is a figure.

As we have previously noted about his stubbornness, he has the tenacity of a bull who doesn't back down. Many people resonate not only with his message, but also with his style of rhetoric, his comedic instinct, and the boldness they wish they had the courage to exhibit and express. Encountering individuals who embrace their individuality, dance to the beat of their own drum, and not silence their voices or guard their speech with political correctness is often *refreshing*. He has single-handedly changed the face of politics with his campaign style, straying away from sounding like a typical politician with vague, complicated or convoluted phrases to lull or impress his listeners, preserve their options, and avoid criticism. He makes no effort to hedge his statements or phrase them so that they are at least defensible. He speaks in a way that conveys competence and assures listeners that the speaker thinks coherent thoughts and holds reasonable positions regarding what he believes is the right direction to take, regardless of who it may offend. He leaves little doubt that he is a figure unlike any other in the nation's history, and that his approach to governing is equally unconventional.

We know that labels, perceptions and characterizations are not always accurate, and individuals often demonstrate that our initial assessment wasn't quite correct. Politicians, like anyone, can claim they have a faith, whether or not they've thought through the substance of those beliefs, not to say anything about how they practice those "professed" beliefs. To judge one's "effectiveness as a 'temporal' leader based solely on this marker [of one faith's assertion] is as futile as voting based on fashion sense, or musical tastes [or any single issue or factor]. When we vote, we must take the whole person into account—we must vote holistically, so to speak,"[1332] says Wesley Baines. We never have perfect candidates with whom to replace

[1332] Baines, Wesley, "The Strange Faith."

imperfect ones. They, like we, are flawed and fallible, but that does not relieve us from exercising critical thought in making our selections.

Luther, then, did not excuse sin. Nor should we today ignore Luther's, Trump's, or most of all our own negatives or sins. But with Luther, we not only recognize that the sacrifice of Christ is greater than our sin, but we are privileged to appropriate "that happy certainty" gratefully by living free as Luther experienced. We confess with him that the Lamb of God has taken away the sin of the world—*our* sin—through the free gift of grace. We don't have to go through life pulling a wagon load of sin to drag us down. Michael Reeves concludes his article on "Why The Reformation Still Matters" with these words:

> Now is not a time to be shy about justification or the supreme authority of the Scriptures that proclaim it. Justification by faith alone is no relic of the history books; it remains today as the only message of ultimate liberation, the message with the deepest power to make humans unfurl and flourish. It gives assurance before our holy God and turns sinners who attempt to buy God off into saints who love and fear Him.... Both the needs and the opportunities are as great as they were five hundred years ago—in fact, they are greater. Let us then take courage from the faithfulness of the Reformers and hold the same wonderful Gospel high, for it has lost none of its glory or its power to dispel our darkness.[1333]

None of the goodness or relevance of the Reformer's insights have faded over the last 500 years. We see his fingerprints everywhere in our modern world. He has certainly left an indelible mark. Far more than a bit of history reacting to some problem of the day, The Reformation recovered the dynamic quality of the Gospel's Truth for today as for then, and it cannot be over. As Luther declares:

> This life, therefore, is not godliness but the process of becoming godly, not health but getting well, not being but becoming, not rest but exercise. We are not now what we shall be, but we are on the way. The process is not yet finished, but it is actively going on. This is not the goal, but it is the right

---

[1333] Reeves, Michael, "Why the Reformation Still Matters," *Tabletalk*, October 2017. <https://tabletalkmagazine.com/article/2017/10/reformation-still-matters>.

road. At present, everything does not gleam and sparkle, but everything is being cleansed.[1334]

Luther references 2 Corinthians 3:18 immediately following these words. In the expanded paraphrase of Dr. Murray J. Harris* that verse reads:

> All Christians have a glory like that of the unveiled Moses: Without a veil on our faces, we all gaze at the glory of God in the person of Christ as in a mirror, and so we are progressively transformed into that selfsame image of Christ in ever-increasing degrees of glory, and so we reflect His glory. This work of transformation comes from the Lord, that is, the Spirit.[1335]

The Reflection in the Mirror

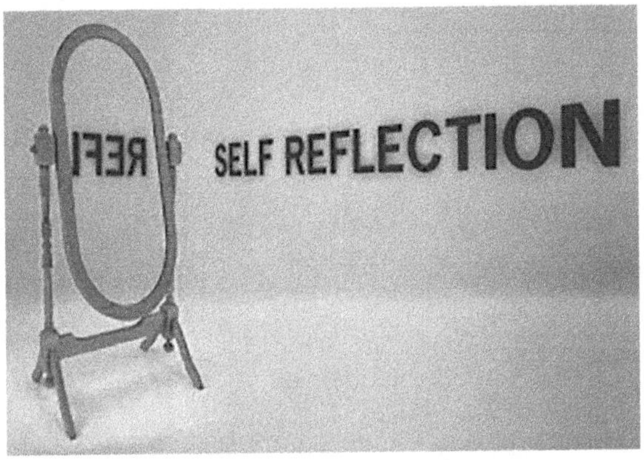

Image: Loralu James

Octogenarian Loralu James posts some significantly interesting and insightful reflections on her "The Final Chapters" blog, including "The Reflection in the Mirror." After having stopped to pause in front of a mirror, she writes,

---

[1334] LW 32:24. *Career of the Reformer II*, "Defense and Explanation of All the Articles."

* Murray J. Harris, emeritus professor of New Testament exegesis and theology at Trinity Evangelical Divinity School in Deerfield, Illinois.

[1335] Harris, Murray J., *The New International Greek Testament Commentary: The Second Epistle to the Corinthians* (Grand Rapids: Wm. B. Eerdmans Publishing Company, 2005), p.947.

> I thought about the reflection that was peering back at me. Squinting my eyes—studying the image—reflecting not only on what I saw—but who the person is that is staring back at me. As I paused and pondered, I began to see not the superficial outside—but more—much more. I peered into my eyes—deep within them—to the very core of me and who I am.... As I looked in that mirror—I tried to look with the eyes of Christ—not the eyes of the world...I see reflected love—love I have learned from His example. I see compassion for those in pain—in struggles—in need—in grief—in illness—Deep compassion that draws me to tears when I hear or see the burdens You must bear.
>
> Most important—when I gaze in that mirror through the eyes of Christ—I see His good glory reflected. His creation which He loves dearly—His Holy presence living in the very depth of my being. A reflection of the aura of His protection and provision and the beauty of His sacrificial love. I see the true reflection of me and who I am—His beloved![1336]

In the view of Dr. Timothy George, Dean and Professor of Divinity at Beeson Divinity School (Samford University), "The triumph of Grace in Luther's theology was, and still is, in the service of the whole Body of Christ."[1337] Luther always points us back to the eternal Word of God and the Gospel of Christ. He tells us to seek salvation not in our own selves and works but rather in the person and works of God's Son, the one who has defeated sin, death and the devil on our behalf. Melanchthon writes in the Augsburg Confession:

> we receive forgiveness of sin and become righteous before God by grace, for Christ's sake, through faith, when we believe that Christ suffered for us and that for His sake our sin is forgiven, and righteousness and eternal life are given to us. For God will regard and reckon this faith as righteousness, as Paul says in Romans 3:21-26 and 4:5.[1338]

1336 James, Loralu, "The Reflection in the Mirror," *The Final Chapters* blog, November 27, 2013; <http://www.loralujames.com/2013/11/the-reflection-in-mirror.html>.

1337 George, Timothy, "Reformation Day," *First Things*, October 31, 2014. <https://www.firstthings.com/web-exclusives/2014/10/reformation-day>.

1338 "The Augsburg Confession, Article IV "Justification," *Book of Concord*, p.30.

As we have observed, Luther faced his own sins honestly, first enslaved painfully, and then as one freed to live abundantly and vocationally in loving and serving his neighbor. He sought and found grace and full forgiveness in Christ alone. John MacArthur observes that

> No one ever seriously accused Luther of unchastity, dishonesty, greed or any other manifestation of the wanton lasciviousness Scripture points to as the key identifying mark of false teachers (2 Peter 2:17-22). Impartial readers of the firsthand historical data will discover that Luther was a humble, generous, hospitable, respectable man of high principles, profound compassion, a tender conscience, unflinching truthfulness and (above all) a passion for God. He was deeply beloved by those close to him, universally admired by his countrymen, and well respected (though perhaps reluctantly) even by many of his theological adversaries. Erasmus stated emphatically in a letter to Cardinal Thomas Wolsey that Luther's personal life and conduct were above reproach.[1339]

"Despite all the publicity given to his flaws," MacArthur concludes that

> Luther's indelible legacy will always be the example of his faith. His heroic courage, deep passion, steadfast integrity, infectious zeal, and all his other virtues are the fruit of his faith. This one man made an impact on the Church and on the world that still influences all Bible-believing Christians today. Luther would not have sought any honor for himself. By his own testimony, he owed everything to Christ. The story of his life confirms that testimony. Conversion utterly transformed Luther from an anxious, faint-hearted monk into a paragon of confident, contagious faith. The more he faced opposition from Rome, the more his Biblical convictions deepened. Everything positive in Luther's life points back to his life-changing encounter with the righteousness of God and the glory of Christ in the Gospel.[1340]

[1339] MacArthur, John, "Forward," *The Legacy of Luther,* ed. R.C. Sproul and Stephen J. Nichols (Sanford, FL: Reformation Trust Publishing, 2016), p.3.

[1340] Ibid., p.4.

Anglican priest, James Atkinson, who surveys the Catholic devaluation of Luther and the more recent revaluation and significance of Luther considers the Reformer to be a "prophet to the Church Catholic" writing:

> It may not be too much to claim that to no man since St. Paul had God revealed with such clarity the terrifying and stark otherness of the Gospel in its warm and vital totality; and with that revelation came God's loving and unresting care to win lost man to Himself and thereby redeem and restore His Church as the people of God. Here indeed in Luther was the totality of Biblical theology given again, opened up once more for the common man to see. He was all that God intended for mankind. God's Word addressed to man—nothing added, nothing removed; catholicism, pure and complete.[1341]

Gratefully, Roman Catholic attitudes toward Luther have and continue to change from traditional contempt for the German Reformer to having a genuinely positive opinion of one who was inviting the Church to heed his call to hear again the Gospel and allow it to be given free course. Likewise, as one who remembers well the suspicion of a Catholic occupying the White House, parental discouragement from dating a Catholic, and hearing anti-Catholic sermons on Reformation Sunday, my heart is filled with exceeding joy that Lutherans and Protestants too have changed and those religious wars of antagonism and division are being superseded by an optimistic common hope of unity. I cherish the fortuitous occurrence that my "higher" education experienced those years of promise Vatican II was bringing to the Church.

I was thrilled following my ordination in 1968 to develop a close relationship with Father Fred Anzivino who was serving St. Ann's Catholic Church in Sebring, Ohio. He was like a caring senior father with wisdom and counsel who shared the vision of hope Vatican II was instilling for future healthy and mutually enriching "sibling" relations within God's family. We weren't going to passively just dream about such possibilities but felt compelled to foster and exhibit that sentiment among and between our parishes by first swapping pulpits on Reformation Sunday, 1970. He had been Betty's and my frequent dinner guest in our home and he, recognizing our lack of facilities due to the sale of the church and parsonage, on behalf of St. Ann's opened their Parish Hall to our congregation for fellowship events which were often mutually shared experiences. I was blown away when Father Fred invited me to participate and share in their Sacrament of Confirmation at which the Bishop of the Youngstown Diocese, James Malone, would be the presiding officiant.

[1341] Atkinson, *Prophet to the Church Catholic*, p.44.

Following the service and fellowship amongst the worshippers, Father Fred hosted a reception for the Bishop and visiting clergy in the Rectory. I was privileged to be seated next to the Bishop and though we had never met before that evening we engaged in lively conversation. With a great deal of exuberance I asked him if Father Fred had shared our exchange of pulpits on Reformation Sunday when I quickly realized I had possibly stuck my foot in my mouth while at the same time perhaps causing my friend to be reprimanded. He responded, "No, Father Fred never said anything to me about that." I immediately surmised I was now in trouble having spilled the beans. But then he continued, "I'm glad he didn't because I would have had to say, 'No, you can't do it.' Now I can congratulate him for his bold decision to act on not only our Lord's prayer, but the Holy Father's and my prayer that the Church may be one." (Relief is spelled how?!)

That was my first encounter with Bishop James Malone, not knowing our paths would frequently intersect in the future. Within two years, he called me upon the death of Father Fred, and knowing of our personal relationship, invited me to participate in the funeral mass for my friend and colleague. Bishop Malone was a strong advocate of interfaith communication and cooperation and became the first Catholic leader of the Ohio Council of Churches and then served as the President of the National Conference of Catholic Bishops. In my role as an assistant to the Bishop of the Ohio Synod Lutheran Church in America deployed to Northeast Ohio, there were subsequent interactions and ecumenical services through which our partnership grew and was strengthened. It was thus a privilege in my role and connection with Wittenberg University (Springfield, Ohio) to encourage and support the nomination of Bishop Malone as the recipient of the honorary Doctor of Divinity degree.

In his address upon being awarded that honorary degree at our Lutheran Wittenberg University in 1986, he pronounced, "Luther belongs to both of us, to you and to me. The force of his personality and his teaching has impacted us all."[1342] Dr. Timothy George underscored Malone's assessment: "Martin Luther belongs to the entire Church, not only to Lutherans and Protestants."[1343] Karl Barth* had rhetorically asked back in 1933, "What else was Luther than a teacher of the Christian Church whom one can hardly celebrate in any other way but to listen to him?"[1344]

[1342] Malone, The Most Reverend James W., "Luther Belongs to Both of Us," Wittenberg University's Office of University Advancement, publication of Address, June 1, 1986.

[1343] George, Timothy, "Reformation Day."

* Karl Barth, Swiss Reformed theologian, known for his landmark commentary on the Epistle to the Romans, his involvement in the Confessing Church, and authorship of the Barmen Declaration.

[1344] Ibid.

Many of the differences between Luther and Catholicism have dissipated in light of the Second Vatican Council. Because the Catholic church has been able to eliminate many of those defects which drove Luther to the Reformation, the ensuing ecumenical movement has prompted a resurgence of Protestant scholarship along side Catholic research and theological reassessment of Luther. Gregory Sobolewski,* Professor of Theology at St. Mary's University of Minnesota traces the "fundamental shift in Roman Catholic opinion of Luther from the mid-sixteenth to the mid-twentieth century, now portraying Luther as a prophetic reformer rather than a misguided renegade." To illustrate this claim he gives "an overview of how the vast majority of Roman Catholic scholars today have abandoned the polemical assessments of their predecessors in order to establish a generally positive appraisal of Luther."[1345] This evolution of respect for Luther, particularly in the later half of the twentieth century "has emerged from serious attention to the principles of historical craftsmanship which demanded fidelity to textual sources and contextual factors."[1346]

The late Johannes P. Hessen who had been Professor of Religious Philosophy at the University of Cologne, also considered Luther to be a prophet who assailed the intellectualism, moralism, sacramentalism, and institutionalism of the sixteenth-century Church. "More than a religious man, Luther-as-prophet represents a Biblical-historical type whose genius must be appreciated together with that of the Old Testament's prophets."[1347]

This reassessment of Luther comes as a result of understanding and appreciation of the Reformer's critical primary principle of *sola fide* and his insistence on the primacy and proclamation of the Word of God over the facts of salvation. In John J. Mulloy's editorial, "The Pope, Luther and Ecumenism," which appeared in the *Wanderer* shortly after Pope John Paul II's trip to Scandinavia in 1989, he writes that the Pope referred to "the need for a new evaluation of Luther and his teaching" and "praising Luther for his profound faith."[1348]

---

*Dr. Greg Sobolewski is Professor of Theology at Saint Mary's University of Minnesota having taught in the university's Institute of Pastoral Ministries since 1994 and became its director in 1996. He was an invited participant in the U. S. bishops' national consultations on Co-Workers in the Vineyard of the Lord (2005) and served two terms as Chair of the Theology Department at Saint Mary's.

1345 Sobolewski, Gregory. *Martin Luther Roman Catholic Prophet*, (Milwaukee: Marquette University Press, 2001) p.8.

1346 Ibid., p.44.

1347 Stauffer, Richard. *Luther as Seen by Catholics, Vol. 7 of Ecumenical Study Series.* (Richmond: John Knox 1967), pp.44-46; quoting from Hessen's booklet, *Luther in katholisher Sicht: Grundlegung eines okumenischen Gespraches* (1947).

1348 Mulloy, John J. "The Pope, Luther, and Ecumenism." *The Wanderer*, July 20, 1989, p.4.

It is not surprising that the doctrine of justification, the article of faith by which Luther claimed the Church stands or falls, was the first to emerge in the ecumenically appreciative theological dialogues between Lutherans and Catholics. In anticipation of higher expectations of Christian unity, Pope John Paul II stated to Dr. Gottfried Brakemeier, President of the Lutheran World Federation in June 1997, anticipating the historic Lutheran and Roman Catholic Declaration consensus on justification:

> Because it is the will of Christ that we should seek unity, there can be no turning back on the path of ecumenism. The Lord of history invites all Christians to celebrate with joy the forthcoming Third Millennium of Redemption. We are called to respond to this special Kairos of God with generosity and an unshakable trust in the surpassing power of grace. Nor can we be satisfied simply with tolerance or mutual understanding. Jesus Christ, He who is and who is to come, asks of us a visible sign of unity, a joint witness to the liberating truth of the Gospel. (1997)[1349]

The official affirmation was signed by Lutherans and Catholics on October 31, 1999, in Augsburg, Germany, enabling subscribing Lutheran churches and the Roman Catholic church to articulate a common understanding of our justification by God's grace through faith in Jesus Christ which produces new creatures who through love want to be active in works. In 2006 the Methodist/Wesleyan family members added their signature to the Joint Declaration on the Doctrine of Justification (JDDJ).* In 2016 the Anglican Consultative Council "welcomed and affirmed the substance of the JDDJ" and the World Communion of Reformed Churches accepted "the invitation to associate with the JDDJ."[1350]

In our time, Sobolewski, concludes that

> Martin Luther can be best described to Catholics as an authentic prophet whose fundamental work was highlighting the Gospel that had become eclipsed by the Church authorized to proclaim it. Like men described in the Old Testament, Luther was eccentric yet brilliant, banal yet prayerful, unsystematic yet focused. As earlier prophets had urged the recovery of

---

1349 Sobolewski, p.153.

* Joint Declaration on the Doctrine of Justification (JDDJ). 1998. *Origins* 28:120-127. The full text of the Declaration can be found on the website of the Evangelical Lutheran Church in America: <www.elca.org>.

1350 World Communion of Reformed Churches, "JDDJ Association," <http://wcrc.ch/jddj>.

> Mosaic traditions within events that encapsulated their lives, so Luther's life provided novel expressions of faith that purified Catholic tradition even as it promoted disruption among Christians."[1351]

Once Again, the Time is Ripe

The parallels between our warriors, Trump and Luther, are undeniable, and intriguing to say the least! For me, it is not out of the realm of possibility that as Martin Luther is attributed to have been the initiator of the 1517 Reformation or at least its major catalyst, history will look back on the 2016 election and the inauguration of Donald Trump as the beginning of a reformation in American politics that values our heritage. Understanding and appreciating the foundation on which the values of our democratic republic are based and centered is critical. I sense a resurgence is now well underway, encountering the same resistance and obstruction as Luther experienced in righting the course of the Church. As with Luther re-discovering the Gospel, reshaping the world's most influential religion, and giving birth to the most successful populist movement in the history of Western Civilization, future generations are likely to look back at this political moment and Trumpian movement rendering potentially cataclysmic change as the beginning of our own reformation and restoration of tradition and the fundamental values that undergird our democracy.

In addressing the 73rd Session of the United Nations General Assembly on September 25, 2018, President Trump affirmed:

> [America's belief] in the majesty of freedom and the dignity of the individual. We believe in self-government and the rule of law. And we prize the culture that sustains our liberty—a culture built on strong families, deep faith, and fierce independence. We celebrate our heroes, we treasure our traditions, and above all, we love our country.[1352]

In President Trump's Farewell Address to the Nation he observed:

> Four years ago, we launched a great national effort to rebuild our country, to renew its spirit, and to restore the allegiance of this government to its

---

[1351] Sobolewski, p.151.

[1352] <https://usoas.usmission.gov/remarks-by-president-trump-to-the-73rd-session-of-the-united-nations-general-assembly-new-york-ny/>.

> citizens. In short, we embarked on a mission to make America great again—for all Americans...We have reasserted the sacred idea that, in America, the government answers to the people...We are, and must always be, a land of hope, of light, and of glory to all the world. This is the precious inheritance that we must safeguard at every turn.[1353]

Trump's words and stewardship on behalf of the country he loves and the people he felt privileged to serve are reminiscent of the words of former President Ronald Reagan in his inaugural address as Governor of California on January 5, 1957:

> Freedom is a fragile thing and it's never more than one generation away from extinction. It is not ours by way of inheritance; it must be fought for and defended constantly by each generation, for it comes only once to a people. And those in world history who have known freedom and then lost it have never known it again.[1354]

Trump like Reagan understood the wisdom of French philosopher Baron de Montesquieu, the principal source of the theory of Separation of Powers, pronounced in 1748 that "The deterioration of every government begins with the decay of the principles on which it was founded."[1355] It has been my intent to make the case that Montesquieu's postulation is even more accurate and acute for the Church.

No one can deny this last comparison between our twin populist reform warriors' endeavors in righting a derailed train. It has proven to be as rough sledding for President Trump as it was 500 years ago for Reformer Luther!

Within the Church today, I believe we desperately need someone like Luther to lift the banner of the Gospel and mission of the Church high above the rhetoric of identity politics, the biased Marxist socialism leaning toward a false understanding of social justice, substituting government for God, and confusing equity with equality. Like Trump and Luther, that individual would need to withstand the attacks and intimidation by those who misuse the Scriptures to advance heretical views that reflect society's secular humanistic

---

1353 <https://trumpwhitehouse.archives.gov/briefings-statements/remarks-president-trump-farewell-address-nation/>.

1354 <https://www.reaganlibrary.gov/archives/speech/january-5-1967-inaugural-address-public-ceremony>.

1355 <https://quotefancy.com/quote/1331274/Baron-de-Montesquieu-The-deterioration-of-every-government-begins-with-the-decay-of-the>.

posturing rather than Biblical Truth, and thus give religious weight by aiding and abetting those favoring a false and dangerous path for both the Church's and State's futures. We need an audacious reformer like Luther who out of love for the Truth and the Church, and the desire to bring it to light, sets the world ablaze as did Luther.

Harvard Divinity School Assistant Professor Michelle C. Sanchez offers an insightful take on the legacy that Luther leaves, and which in many respects could be as applicable to and as reflective on Trump.

> I find that Luther's ongoing impact is most felt in the challenge his life poses to us; the way in which it's both frustrating and inspiring, both embarrassing and revealing. Luther is a helpful conversation partner not because he's some kind of reforming hero, but because he's a mirror for our contradictions and struggles, for all the ways our society and our religious establishments [as well as our political establishments] continue to try and fail.
>
> And yet, in some strange way, Luther remains important because he was wise to this very dynamic. He deeply got both the joy and the tragedy of the human condition. He didn't try to explain away human flaws. He knew he was full of them. Instead, he called for us to learn to think of life in this world as a constant practice of critique, a constant practice of meeting the limitations of our own thinking. And he called on us to look for insight outside of ourselves, and especially in those places that seem most unlikely, most humble, because that's where Jesus went. For Luther we cannot forget that the highest form of divinity is revealed in the body of a criminal who was condemned by the State to death on a cross.[1356]

Jaroslav Pelikan makes the observation that

> Luther was many things—an orator, a scholar, a public figure. But, above all, he was a man of faith and a theologian, and if we are to understand his continuing appeal it must be with his theology that we begin and end. Luther's stand was so momentous an event in our history because, even to his

[1356] Sanchez, Michelle, "Martin Luther, Fallible Reformer," *The Harvard Gazette*, October 30, 2017; <https://news.harvard.edu/gazette/story/2017/10/harvard-scholar-on-the-legacy-of-martin-luther/>.

detractors, he represented the fusion of theology and individual personality in the heroism of one courageous soul defying the world.[1357]

And in the words of Mathew Block, "We therefore stand where Luther himself took his stand—indeed, where all the saints throughout the long history of the Church have always stood [or knelt]: at the foot of the cross."

"Luther was a sinner who sought salvation at the feet of the Son of God, bleeding and dying for him at Calvary. We must do likewise."[1358]

The Vatican marked the 500th anniversary of the Protestant Reformation with a postage stamp released on November 23, 2017, featuring the Crucifix before which Martin Luther and Philip Melanchthon are kneeling. Melanchthon is considered the first systematic theologian of the Protestant Reformation, principal author of the Augsburg Confession, a friend and colleague of Luther and thus one of the founders of Lutheranism. In the picture Luther holds a Bible and Melanchthon holds a copy of the Augsburg Confession, the primary confession of faith for the Lutheran Church. In the background is "a golden and timeless view of the City of Wittenberg," where Luther "supposedly" posted his 95 Theses to the doors of the Castle Church in 1517, launching the Protestant Reformation. Above the doors, which were replaced with bronze doors that bear the Latin text of the Theses in 1858, is the tympanum mosaic of the crucifixion which is depicted on the Vatican stamp.

(Reprinted with permission of Ufficio Filatelico e Numissatico, and the International Relations Office of the Vatican.)

1357 Pelikan, Jaroslav, "Enduring Relevance of Martin Luther."

1358 Block, Mathew, "Standing with Martin Luther." <https://www.firstthings.com/blogs/firstthoughts/2014/02/standing-with-martin-luther-1>.

"All of us are well aware," Pope Francis affirmed, "that the past cannot be changed. Yet today…it is possible to engage in a purification of memory, without resentment that distorts." In 2016 Pope Francis, on the occasion of his journey to Sweden for the Joint Catholic-Lutheran Commemoration of the Reformation, expressed his gratitude to God for the opportunity to remember such an important event "with a renewed spirit and in the recognition that Christian unity is a priority, because we realize that much more unites us than separates us!"[1359]

Pope Francis

Life Site News

Pope Francis' Apostolic Visit to Sweden to Commemorate the 500th Anniversary of the Reformation

L'Osservatore Romano

(Left) Pope Francis next to a statue of Martin Luther placed in the Vatican's Paul VI Hall prior to his October 2016 trip to Sweden.

(Right) In this Oct. 31, 2016, photo, Pope Francis embraces Bishop Dr. Munib A. Younan, President of the Lutheran World Federation, during a joint prayer service at the cathedral in Lund for the pope's apostolic visit to commemorate the 500th anniversary of The Reformation.

I hope that we will be able to reimagine fresh expressions of being the Church in our neighborhoods and communities to embody the Word in our contexts by being the "*heart, hands, and voice of Christ.*" My prayer is that the Church be reshaped in character to live out Gospel unity to replace the division which has characterized us for too many centuries, and in so doing, reclaim our witness to one Lord, one faith, and one baptism. We might

[1359] <https://archbishopcranmer.com/reformation-500-vatican-stamp-commemorate-luther-melanchthon>.

even consider the question asked by Pope Francis when he visited the Lutheran Church in Rome in 2015. In a brief homily, he asked, "if we have the same baptism, shouldn't we be walking together?"[1360]

The Church Always Being Reformed

"*Ecclesia semper reformanda est*." The Church is reformed and always in need of being reformed, according to the Word of God! "...always being reformed by the Spirit of God through the Word!" Often this phrase gets translated merely as "always reforming" instead of "always *being* reformed." If the Church is merely "always reforming" then grammatically, as Michael Horton* correctly points out, "the Church is the active party, determining its own doctrine, worship, and discipline in light of ever-changing cultural contexts. Progressivism becomes an end in itself, and church becomes a mirror of the world."[1361] Luther clearly made the point that doctrinal standards are subordinate to the Word of God. We have witnessed Luther's acknowledgment that "[he] did nothing" but "the Word did everything"[1362] in bringing the Church back to God's Word, and the fruit of that great work of the Spirit continues to guide us today.

The Church is always in need of being reformed, especially in our post-Christian world which demands that the Church adapt and change based on the culture surrounding it. The Reformers had no interest in "change" as an end in itself, but rather in a radical sense of returning to the "root" ("*sola Scriptura*") or to "*the faith which was once for all delivered to the saints*" (Jude 3 [WEB]). That's the reason why the second clause of the phrase is so crucial: "*according to the Word of God.*"

> One of Luther's biggest fears was that the Church would forget the Gospel. Even in his final sermon at Wittenberg, he exhorted the people to remain true to it and to never distort it. He was rightly convinced that each and

---

1360 From Martin Bashir's "The Young Man Who Shook the Catholic Church to Its Core," <https://www.bbc.com/news/world-europe-41742857>.

* Michael Horton, Professor of Theology and Apologetics at Westminster Seminary California, and Editor in Chief of *Modern Reformation* magazine.

1361 Horton, Michael, "Semper Reformanda," *Tabletalk*. <https://www.ligonier.org/learn/articles/semper-reformanda>.

1362 LW 51:77. *Sermons I*, "The Second Sermon, March 10, 1522."

> every generation would need a reformation.... [Courtney Cherest then quotes Dr. R. C. Sproul† who warns] "The Gospel is always at risk of being distorted. It has to be maintained with clarity and urgency in every generation."[1363]

"In fact," Michael Horton reminds us, "it was the medieval church's innovative distortions of Christian faith and worship that required a recovery of apostolic Christianity. Rome pretended to be 'always the same,' but it had accumulated a host of doctrines and practices that were unknown to the ancient Church, much less to the New Testament."[1364]

As we have previously affirmed, it is the Church that comes into being and is kept alive by hearing the Gospel, and thus is always on the receiving end of God's good gifts, as well as His correction in renewing it. The Spirit never leads us apart from the Word but always directs us back to Christ as He is revealed in Scripture. We always need to return to the voice of our Shepherd, and especially in times of trial and peril: *"My sheep hear My voice, and I know them, and they follow Me. I give them eternal life, and they will never perish. No one will snatch them out of My hand"* (John 10:27-28 [NRSV]).

One of the prayers in the Matins (Morning Prayer) liturgy expresses this confidence and has been a comforting assurance throughout my ministry: "Lord, God, You have called Your servants to ventures of which we cannot see the ending, by paths as yet untrodden, through perils unknown. Give us faith to go out with good courage, not knowing where we go, but only that Your hand is leading us and Your love supporting us; through Jesus Christ our Lord."[1365]

For Luther in 1527, this understanding was a particular source of comfort. Timothy Lull* and Derek Nelson†† in *Resilient Reformer—The Life and Thought of Martin Luther* report that "There were frightfully many afflicted that year, for in July a terrible plague

---

[1363] Cherest, Courtney, "The Fire Still Burns." <https://wearepatrol.com/blog/lutherpart4>.

† Dr Robert. C. Sproul was an American Reformed theologian and ordained pastor In the Presbyterian Church in America. He was the founder and chairman of Ligonier Ministries who could be heard daily on the Renewing Your Mind radio broadcast.

[1364] Horton, Michael. <https://www.ligonier.org/learn/articles/semper-reformanda>.

[1365] "Morning Prayer, Matins," LBW p.137; and ELW p.304.

* Timothy R. Lull was president of Pacific Lutheran Theological Seminary, Berkeley, and professor of Systematic Theology there before his death in 2003.

†† Derek R. Nelson is Associate Professor of Religion at Wabash College in Crawfordsville, Indiana, and author and co-author of several books.

swept through Wittenberg. Nearly all who could flee, did so, however, Luther and Johannes Bugenhagen [Luther's pastor at the City Church of St. Mary's] stayed to care for the sick, even though the Elector and others encouraged Luther to escape. Luther felt duty bound by his office as a pastor to care for the sick." The authors remind us of what we have previously learned about Luther's pastoral heart: "Concern for the poor and afflicted was one of Luther's most cherished commitments."[1366]

> Bugenhagen's pregnant sister Hanna was among the thousands who died. A post-mortem caesarian section did not save her baby. Luther was desperately sad about this, not the least because his own wife, Katy, was suffering a difficult pregnancy. In grief Luther wrote to his friend, Justus Jonas, "May my Christ whom I have purely taught and confessed, be my rock and fortress." That little word, "*fortress*," often evokes a supposed militaristic, triumphalist, or hyper-masculine note in Luther's theology.[1367]

For many, perhaps, the image of the Wartburg Castle comes to mind, where Luther, after being "marked" as a heretic by the Church and targeted as an enemy of the State, was "kidnapped" into friendly protective custody by a posse of knights sent by his protector, Frederick the Wise. Yet it was that very month he wrote his most familiar hymn, "A Mighty Fortress Is Our God." As singers or those who hear the words sung learn "that the pain of loss, of childbirth, stillbirth, and disease were decisively on Luther's mind, [they] may find his lyrics refreshingly unfamiliar, after all. It was no cataclysm of empires, but love for a dead mother and child, [those suffering from the plague] that led him [to recall Psalm 46 and] to sing:

> *God's Word forever shall abide, No thanks to foes who fear it;*
> *For God Himself fights by our side, With weapons of the Spirit.*
> *Were they to take our house, Goods, honor, child, or spouse,*
> *Though life be wrenched away, They cannot win the day.*
> *The Kingdom's ours forever!*[1368]

1366 Lull, Timothy R. and Nelson, Derek R., *Resilient Reformer: The Life and Thought of Martin Luther* (Minneapolis: Fortress Press, 2015), p.279.

1367 Ibid., p.280.

1368 Martin Luther, "A Mighty Fortress Is Our God," LBW Hymn 229; ELW Hymn 504; LW Hymn 297; LSB Hymn 657.

Luther emphatically understood that the same Gospel which created the Church sustains and renews it with our Lord's ever abiding presence. With that assurance, we can assert with Michael Horton that

> This perspective keeps us from making tradition infallible but equally from imbibing the radical Protestant obsession with starting from scratch in every generation. When God's Word is the Source of our life, our ultimate loyalty is not to the past as such, or to the present and the future, but to *"That Word above all earthly pow'rs,"* to borrow from Luther's famous hymn [in a slightly different version]. Neither behind us or ahead of us, but above us, reigns our sovereign Lord over His Body in all times and places. When we invoke the whole phrase—"the Church Reformed and always being reformed according to the Word of God"—we confess that we belong to the Church and not simply to ourselves and that this Church is always created and renewed by the Word God rather than by the spirit of the age.[1369]

In a sermon to the Lutheran World Federation, held not in Wittenberg but in Namibia in southwestern Africa, to celebrate the 500th remembrance of The Reformation, Pastor Zephania Kameeta* concludes:

> Dear sisters and brothers who are commemorating 500 years of the Reformation, let us go out from here with this liberating TRUTH, our Lord Jesus CHRIST, to be reformed and reformers, renewed and renewing, liberated, and liberating, and to live lives in which people see and experience grace, love, justice, unity, and peace.[1370]

1369 Horton, Michael, "Semper Reformanda," Ligonier Ministries. <https://www.ligonier.org/learn/articles/semper-reformanda>.

* Zephania Kameeta, a Lutheran pastor and currently the Namibian minister of Poverty Eradication and Social Welfare.

1370 Kameeta, Dr. Zephani, on the occasion of the global commemoration of the 500th anniversary of the Reformation, May 17, 2017. Quoted by Bruce Gordon in "From Wittenberg to Global Church." <https://reflections.yale.edu.article/reformation-writing-next-chapterwittenberg-global-church-reformation-belongs-world>.

In citing the reference to Namibia hosting the Lutheran World Federation, Bruce Gordon* extends Roman Catholic Bishop Malone's assessment and importance of Luther and the Reformation belonging to the whole Church, to belonging to the world! It is easy to think of the Reformation as our story in the West, but

> the 500th anniversary comes at a moment when the place of religion in the contemporary world is an urgent topic. The Reformation cannot remain in the past, the preserve of a few in academia and churches. Its principles of a radical challenge to authorities, the constant questioning of established doctrines, and adherence to the Word are vibrantly evident in the exponential growth of Protestantism in Africa, Asia, and South America. As in the 16th century, new models of churches, faith, and worship are emerging with head-spinning speed. Serious problems and controversies abound, just as for centuries disputes, rivalries, and growth pains beset The Reformation. Nevertheless, as we reflect on the 500th anniversary it should be in the humble recognition of our small place in what is now a global story. The Reformation, we can now see clearly, belongs to the world.[1371]

Martin Luther certainly was not perfect. He had his flaws, said some very stupid things, and experienced difficult periods of depression and anxiety. And yet by the grace of God and for His Name's sake, his faith and legacy flourished and has enriched the world. Several sources assessing the top 100 individuals who were the most influential in shaping the past millennium in 2000 ranked Luther as number three or within the top ten.[1372] Diving into his life, teachings and understanding of Scripture for this unusual comparative appraisal has been a wonderful way to grow in my understanding and adoration of who God is and

---

* Bruce Gordon is the Titus Street Professor of Ecclesiastical History at Yale Divinity School. His books include *John Calvin's Institutes of the Christian Religion* and *The Swiss Reformation*. He has written widely on early modern history, Biblical culture, Reformation devotion and spirituality.

1371 Gordon, Bruce, "From Wittenberg to Global Church: The Reformation Belongs to the World,." <https://reflections.yale.edu/article/reformation-writing-next-chapter/wittenberg-global-church-reformation-belongs-world>.

1372 Gottlieb, Agnes Hooper, Henry Gottlieb, Barbara Bowers, *1000 Years, 1000 People: Ranking the Men and Women Who Shaped the Millennium* (1998), Kodansha International, Bunkyo, Tokyo, Japan, <https://www.wisdomportal.com/Books/1000Years1000People.html>; A & E Biography's 100 Most Influential People of the Millennium, <https://wmich.edu/mus-gened/mus150/biography100.html>; <https://www.mcall.com/news/mc-xpm-1999-10-21-3280156-story.html>.

how He chooses to use those who, at times, are all too human, yet gifted and skilled in ways of serving their neighbor in love and contributing to humanity and the world in which we live today.

Day by Day We Magnify Thee is the title of the classic devotional book containing daily meditations for the year, drawn from Luther's sermons and other works. Subsequent volumes of devotional readings from Luther are entitled "Day by Day" which I have used in my quiet time with God. That title is also used for the folk-rock ballad from the 1971 Stephen Schwartz and John-Michael Tebelak musical *Godspell*. The words follow a prayer ascribed to the 13th-century English Bishop Saint Richard of Chichester, which appears in the 1940 Hymnal of the Protestant Episcopal Church:

> *Day by day,*
> *Dear Lord, of Thee three things I pray:*
> *To see Thee more clearly,*
> *Love Thee more dearly*
> *Follow Thee more nearly,*
> *Day by day.*[1373]

Perhaps Betty Catherine in her blog "Bit O' Betty" had this song running through her mind when she posted the following words which captures my sentiments as I conclude this manuscript:

> I appreciate [Luther's] life so much, not simply because it is a fascinating story, but **because it stirs my heart to want to know the Word more deeply, treasure its authority more passionately, share its power more consistently, and delight in the grace it teaches more steadfastly. I want to pray more– and see its effect and power. I want my heart to overflow in gratitude for the cross more….** His life motivates and encourages my heart. That is why I love His story. I hope what I shared did the same for you too![1374] [Emphasis added]

[1373] Richard of Chichester, St., "Day by Day (Hymn 429)," *The Hymnal of the Protestant Episcopal Church of the United States of America*, 1940.

[1374] Catherine, Betty, "Why I Sorta-Kinda-Actually Love Martin Luther." <https://bettycatherine.wordpress.com/2016/10/19/why-i-sorta-kinda-actually-love-martin-luther>.

I have never particularly liked the term, nor used it as a title. As a matter of fact, I actually cringe whenever I am addressed as "Reverend" or "The Reverend." I have failed and messed up so many times, it's a wonder I haven't been kicked out of school yet! But I truly appreciate and can live with the challenging descriptive prefix and vocational title Leonard Sweet has conferred upon me: "Pneumanaut!" Becoming one is not easy, given our human inclinations and the times in which we live, but I rejoice in the amazing adventures to which my "sailing on the wind of the Spirit" has led me. Like Luther, I haven't arrived, but I am still maxing out sailing in my "Re-Firement," and am grateful that the Spirit of God still moves in me and around me through others, throughout the whole Church, and the world God loves!

Abiding in that *EUPHORIC CERTAINTY!* I have been and am privileged to serve and soar!

Pneumanaut Paul F. Swartz

NOT AN ADDENDUM BUT A CONTINUUM...

OP-ED ON PRESIDENT TRUMP

President Donald Trump Departs the White House for Travel to New Jersey.

(Image: Bloomberg/Getty Images. Used with permission)

Take a moment and look at this photo.

This is NOT a political post or ad by any means. This is simply something that everyone should stop and think about.

Can you imagine the weight this man (or any person serving as President) is feeling in that office? Many of us have children who depend on us daily, yet on some days we can discover our anxiety is through the roof and feel like the weight of the world is all on us. When Trump signed up for this role (without pay) he did it for us Americans. He didn't do it for the fame or glory; he had all that. He was willing to take on whatever, but the magnitude of what we have experienced currently has to be paralyzing. And to some, NOTHING he does is ever right or good enough.

Have you ever wondered how he must be dealing with it all? When his head finally hits the pillow at night after press conferences and meetings, constantly trying to defend himself and protect our country: Does he break down and cry from all the pressure? Is he scared and confused? Is he even able to sleep? Can he shut his mind off at all? Or does he lay there and talk to God all night praying for strength and answers?

Whether he made you proud or not, look at this photo and ask God to soften your heart just a little bit and lift the individual in this office—whoever that may be—in prayer. Our leaders need our prayers right now more than ever. They carry the weight of *our* country on their shoulders, and I don't think many could have done a better job in the midst of the strong headwinds encountered than we have experienced with one who was not bred within the political system than President Trump.

Can we remind everyone to be kind and to pray for the President, and all our leaders for our country, for our Church, and for the entire world God so loves?

Printed in the USA
CPSIA information can be obtained
at www.ICGtesting.com
LVHW080813151123
763327LV00003B/3

9 781662 923821